IBM® MICROCOMPUTER
ASSEMBLY LANGUAGE

IBM® MICROCOMPUTER ASSEMBLY LANGUAGE

Beginning to Advanced

J. TERRY GODFREY

The MITRE Corporation
McLean, Virginia

PRENTICE HALL
Englewood Cliffs, New Jersey   07632

Library of Congress Cataloging-in-Publication Data

Godfrey, J. Terry,
    IBM microcomputer assembly language: beginning to advanced / J.
Terry Godfrey.
        p. cm.
    Includes index.
    ISBN 0-13-449505-5
    1. IBM microcomputers—Programming.   2. Assembler language
(Computer program language)   I. Title.
QA76.8.I1015G63   1989   88-4240
005.265—dc 19   CIP

Editorial/production supervision and
    interior design: Gertrude Szyferblatt
Cover design: 20/20 Services, Inc.
Manufacturing buyer: Mary Noonan

 © 1989 by Prentice-Hall, Inc.
A Division of Simon & Schuster
Englewood Cliffs, New Jersey 07632

Printed in the United States of America

10 9 8 7 6 5 4 3 2 1

ISBN 0-13-449505-5

PRENTICE-HALL INTERNATIONAL (UK) LIMITED, London
PRENTICE-HALL OF AUSTRALIA PTY. LIMITED, Sydney
PRENTICE-HALL CANADA INC., Toronto
PRENTICE-HALL HISPANOAMERICANA, S.A., Mexico
PRENTICE-HALL OF INDIA PRIVATE LIMITED, New Delhi
PRENTICE-HALL OF JAPAN, INC., Tokyo
SIMON & SCHUSTER ASIA PTE. LTD., Singapore
EDITORA PRENTICE-HALL DO BRASIL, LTDA., Rio de Janeiro

Trademark Information

IBM Personal Computer, DOS, XT, AT, XT286,
PC, Personal System/2 Model 30, Personal
System/2 Model 50, Personal System/2 Model 60,
Personal System/2 Model 80, PS/2, Operating
System/2, OS/2 are trademarks and IBM is a
registered trademark of International Business
Machines Corporation.
Intel is a registered trademark of the Intel
Corporation.
VEDIT is a trademark of Compuview Products,
Inc.
Microsoft is a registered trademark of Microsoft
Corporation.
Lattice is a registered trademark of Lattice, Inc.

To my wife, Judy

CONTENTS

PREFACE

This text is intended to serve as a tutorial for teaching the Macro Assembler language on IBM® microcomputers. The distinction must be made between a reference book and a book that attempts to provide the reader with the ability to practice Macro Assembler programming. Hopefully, this book is of the latter category and serves to complement reference-type books. The methodology for conveying how to program in assembler is to use complete examples which are of general interest. The material through Chapter 8 is suitable for a one-semester introductory course to the IBM Macro Assembler. Chapters 9 and 10 (Part 3) deal with the hardware/software interface and are considered as supplementary material. This book is also structured so that it is self-contained to facilitate individual learning programs. It is for people who enjoy programming. The emphasis is on developing a good programming environment with modern tools.

The evolution of late twentieth century computer technology is impressive. In the mid-to-late 1980s CPU chips such as the Intel 8088 and 8086 typically had fewer than 100,000 transistor gates, with instruction sets of roughly 100 mnemonics. By the year 2000, chips with 1,000,000,000 transistor gates (the *billion-transistor* chip) will be under development. If one linearly extended the computational power of such a chip, for example, an increase of roughly 10,000 in throughput capability would result. With the advent of new programming techniques, radically different chip architectures seem probable and even greater increases in capability could become possible.

Obviously, the spread between high-level language development and assembly language will become greater. The efficient use of these chips coupled with system software, like drivers, compilers, and operating systems, will require the use of assembler or at least a good understanding of the assembler environment.

Why Learn Assembly Language?

This question is the subject of some debate among practicing programmers. The basic division of thinking appears to revolve around the applications involved. High-level language programmers whose applications are not time-critical or who can use standard input/output devices usually do not need to call routines that are normally unavailable in their compiler library. These programmers have minimal direct need for assembly language programming.

Remember, however, someone must write the library routines these programmers employ to achieve standard interfaces. This is the non-portable portion of the language being used. These routines are written in assembly language. Also, if a portion of the high-level code is very time-intensive, the programmer usually is better off to call a special-purpose assembly language routine to accomplish the function in question. Experienced programmers can usually remember that loop that ran forever in one of their earlier programs or some similar artifact. Assembly language can be used to eliminate difficulties of this sort, or at least greatly minimize them, by optimizing the generated code.

The serious student of programming will certainly want to answer the question of how hardware is interfaced to the software. This interface is readily grasped in the microcomputer context and involves the manner in which bits are set in registers by software commands. These registers are then manipulated by the processors based on assembly language instructions. Also, if the need arises for installing a special-purpose device, the programmer must write the driver for this device. It is by far easier to write and debug such a driver in assembly language than in some high-level language which calls an interface routine written in assembler.

Once one assembly language has been learned, it becomes a very simple matter to understand alternative assembly languages. Assembly language programming is at the core of any professional appraisal of programming. A recommended procedure is to learn one assembler in depth and then extend this knowledge to other assemblers as needed. The experience of concentrating on a single language initially will generate a comprehensive understanding of the particular assembler in question and make the transition to other assembly languages a much easier process.

We have not mentioned system software which is a combination of I/O driver programming and applications programming. Clearly, such software is intermediate between high-level applications programs and assembly language hardware driver programming. Operating systems, consequently, are written in both high-level languages and assembly languages. Certainly, portions of most operating systems contain routines written in assembly language.

Future software development is tending towards compilers that have concurrency and that take advantage of parallelism in executing tasks. The development of data-flow machines, array and vector processors, parallelizing compilers, and tree or hypercube computers point toward the need for a greater knowledge of machine capabilities. While artificial intelligence (AI) techniques can reduce the actual hardware-intensive programming requirements, the ideal world of totally portable parallel code is still in the future. The challenge of developing programs for billion transistor chips will require totally new methods for systematically looking at software. A major emphasis for much of this programming will be toward creating structured architectures in the hardware and system-level code. All these developments will require programmers with a knowledge of assembly languages and the hardware/software interface.

In summary, a brief list of advantages to be gleaned from learning assembly language is as follows:

1. Ability to control hardware

2. Ability to develop program elements with fast execution capability

3. Ability to efficiently and optimally access the coprocessor

4. Understanding of methods used in implementing high-level language syntax

5. A very good understanding of microcomputer systems and the hardware-software interface

6. Discipline in programming and the basis for structured concepts

7. Understanding how data structures are handled at a low level

This is a book about programming assembler in the **IBM** microcomputer system environment. *Why choose this assembler for an introductory course?* Some of the reasons are as follows:

1. Well-defined description of hardware interfaces in BIOS such as interrupts, service routines, schematics

2. Clearly delineated system architecture

3. Good screen presentation for program development

4. Extensive software support

5. Code development facilitated by
   a. Emphasis on keyboard for syntactical I/O
   b. 80-character line
   c. Text-oriented I/O
   d. Well-developed editors
   e. Well-developed debuggers
   f. Well-developed linkers and assemblers, and
   g. BIOS being well documented

6. Finally, the IBM environment is substantial, and upward compatibility has always existed (programs running on PCs can run on XTs and ATs); hence, the user can develop programming skills that he or she can continuously build upon.

What Hardware/Software Is Discussed in This Book?

Table 1 summarizes the hardware (microcomputers) and software considered in this text. We indicate the Protected Mode architecture only. The book does not consider programming in the Protected Mode environment. All added Protected Mode instructions are applicable to operating system software only and the omission of Protected Mode programming has a minimal impact on understanding the IBM assembly language.

Goals of the Text

It is intended that the reader rapidly develop the ability to program in assembly language using this book. A programming style is suggested that emphasizes structured modular assembly language code. Tools are provided for generating programs which are upwardly expandable. This includes the ability to access disks or diskettes, the ability to implement screen graphics, the ability to employ keyboard input/output (I/O), the ability to program the coprocessor, a general emphasis on peripheral I/O handling (Chapter 9), and the use of structured concepts. The text also delineates the hardware-software interface by illustrating how software is used to control various

TABLE 1 TOPICS ADDRESSED AND USED IN THIS BOOK*

Topic	Hardware or Software	80286/80386 Only Real Address Mode Programming	80286/80386 Only Protected Mode Architecture	Conventional Assembler Programming
PC XT	H	—	—	X
XT286 or AT	H	X	—	—
PS/2 Model 30	H	—	—	X
PS/2 Model 50 or 60	H	X	X	—
PS/2 Model 80	H	X	X	—
Coprocessor				
8087	H	X	—	X
80287	H	X	X	X
80387	H	X	X	—
DOS 2.00 (1982)	S	—	—	X
DOS 2.10 (1983)	S	—	—	X
DOS 3.00 (1984)	S	X	—	X
DOS 3.10 (1985)	S	X	—	X
DOS 3.20 (1985)	S	X	—	X
DOS 3.30 (1987)	S	X	—	X
Macro Assembler				
Version 1.00	S	X	—	X
Version 2.00	S	X	—	X

* OS/2 is not addressed. However, only Protected Mode Memory Management Features (systems programs) are functionally impacted. Macro Assembler version 12 is not addressed, but this only impacts essentially 80386 instructions for the application programmer.

chips. This is accomplished using BIOS as an example in Chapter 9. Finally, the distinction among applications, hardware driver, and systems programming is made. The topic of interfacing assembly language procedures to high-level language programs (in this case, the C language is used as an example) is discussed.

Finally, some word is required concerning the assembler program used in this text. We use the IBM version of the assembler. This version has two models: a small memory model (the ASM) and a large memory model (the MASM). In addition to the IBM Macro Assembler, there are a number of alternative assemblers for the IBM family of microcomputers. Typically, Microsoft makes an assembler as do Lattice and others. These packages are all very similar and can be selected at the option of the user.

Chapter references are indicated at appropriate points in the text by enclosing the reference numbers in square brackets.

ACKNOWLEDGMENTS

A special note of thanks is due the people who contributed to the development of this textbook. The drawings appearing throughout the book, most heavily concentrated in Chapters 9 and 10, were prepared by Nancy Bernhard. All typing and a significant amount of editing was performed by my wife, Judy. Marcia Horton, senior editor from Prentice Hall, focused the evolution of this text. Of course, the varied anonymous reviewers generated much of the needed feedback which helped shape the final product. Finally, a note of thanks is to be extended Jane Matsinger, the copy editor, and Gertrude Szyferblatt (and her staff) for final design and production.

PART 1

Introductory Macro Assembler

1

Introduction

Assembly languages are specific to the form of the computer architecture used in a particular machine configuration. The component of the architecture which has the greatest impact on the associated assembler is the central processor unit (CPU). For the IBM family of microcomputers the CPU is an integrated circuit manufactured by the Intel Corporation. Specifically, for the IBM PC and XT this chip is an 8088. For the PS/2 Model 30 the CPU is an 8086. For the IBM AT, XT286, and PS/2 Models 50 and 60 this chip is the more advanced 80286. Finally, the 80386 is the CPU for the PS/2 Model 80. Each CPU chip must eventually be programmed in machine language (a series of 1s and 0s); however, suitable mnemonics are usually generated by the manufacturer to represent the hardwired instruction patterns associated with a given chip [1]. It is these mnemonics that serve as the basis for the assembler language that must be developed for a particular architecture. Clearly, the instruction set developed for the 8088 must serve as the core for the IBM PC and XT Macro Assembler and the 8086 instruction set is identical; hence, this Macro Assembler also applies to the PS/2 Model 30. Similarly, the instruction set developed for the 80286 must serve as the core for the IBM AT, XT286, and PS/2 Models 50 and 60. The 80386 instruction set is the basis for the Model 80 assembly language. The sets overlap and are upwardly compatible. 8088 programs, for example, can usually be run on 80286- and 80386-based machines. The eventual translation of the mnemonics to machine language must be accomplished by a program called the assembler, and the assembly language is the associated syntax structure based on these mnemonics.

The purpose of this book is to describe the IBM Macro Assembler in a fashion that lends itself readily to learning the assembly language and facilitates rapid program development during this learning period. A portion of the book is devoted to discussing the IBM microcomputer hardware, with particular emphasis on the IBM PC as an example [2]. This is because assembly language is used to program the various integrated circuits associated with the CPU. Hence, programming these chips is a good example of how to use the assembler. There are three basic categories of assembly language programming: applications programming, hardware driver programming, and systems programming. The latter two categories sometimes overlap. In this chapter we consider the IBM computers, associated software, and assorted preliminary topics. This discussion is introductory.

1.1 INTRODUCTION TO THE IBM MICROCOMPUTER FAMILY

The International Business Machines Corporation has developed a set of microcomputers based on the Intel Corporation 8088, 8086, 80286, and 80386 microprocessor integrated circuits [3–8], as discussed above. The 8088, 8086, and 80286 are 16-bit microprocessors (have 16-bit internal registers) and the 80386 is a 32-bit microprocessor. Associated with these microprocessors are coprocessor chips which provide a high-speed floating point capability: The 8087 is associated with the 8088 and 8086; the 80287, with the 80286; and the 80387 is associated with the 80386.

The 8088 and 8086 are programmed with a core set (equivalent) of instructions which comprise the basic Macro Assembler version 1.0. The 80286 is programmed in one of two modes: Real Address Mode or Protected Virtual Address Mode (Protected Mode, for short). In the Real Address Mode all source code developed for the 8088 and 8086 will execute. Similarly, all source code developed for the 80286 is downwardly compatible with the 8088 and 8086 when developed for Real Address Mode applications, except for a handful of instructions. The Macro Assembler version 2.0 includes these latter instructions as well as instructions for the 8087 and 80287. Until version 2.0, the coprocessor was programmed using the Escape (ESC) instruction.

In Protected Mode the 80286 quickly differentiates itself from the 8088 and 8086. System-oriented instructions exist for the 80286 which are not available under version 1.0 or 2.0 of the Macro Assembler. These instructions are not intended for use by the applications programmer. They provide for memory management, ordered protection and multitasking. The 80386 has many of the same instructions as the 80286 in both Real Address Mode and Protected Mode. Also a Virtual 8086 mode exists for running 8086 programs in a multitasking fashion. We now briefly consider each of the microcomputers in the IBM family.

1.1.1 The PC and XT (8088)

These microcomputers were the first developed by IBM. The IBM PC and XT system boards are similar. Each contains an 8088 CPU and a socket for the 8087 coprocessor near the back. Also near the back left-hand corner are five expansion board slots (eight on the XT). Adjacent to the 8088 is an Intel 8259A Programmable Interrupt Controller, which is used to acknowledge and process interrupt signals from associated peripherals. Toward the middle of the board are three chips used for intelligent support: The Intel 8255A Programmable Peripheral Interface, which transfers data to and from peripherals, the Intel 8237A Direct Memory Access Controller, which affects block input/output of data, and the Intel 8253 timer-counter, used as an event counter. The system board also has five Read Only Memory (ROM) chips located near its center. These chips contain the interpreter BASIC and the resident portions of the Disk Operating System (DOS) and Basic Input Output System (BIOS). Finally, near the front of the system board all the on-board Random Access Memory (RAM) is located. For PCs produced earlier than May 1983 this consisted of a maximum of 64K of RAM. Later versions can contain up to 256K of RAM. (Here K = 1024 bytes.)

The display capability for the PC and XT is based on a Motorola 6845 Cathode Ray Tube (CRT) Controller. This configuration employs one of three resolutions: a monochrome alpha mode with 80×25 character lines, a graphics mode with 320×200 raster lines, and a second graphics mode with 640×200 raster lines. The raster modes can be used with color monitors. Several standards have evolved for handling the raster modes: the color graphics adapter (CGA) mode and the enhanced graphics adapter (EGA) mode.

1.1.2 The XT286 and AT (80286)

The IBM AT system board uses some up-graded chips (as well as some found in the PC and XT) for intelligent support. The real-time clock is an Intel 88284. Similarly, the coprocessor is an Intel 80287, to complement the Intel 80286 CPU. A bus controller (Intel 82288) is used and two 8259As are employed to expand the number of hardware interrupts the AT can process. The timer-counter is the 8253 and two DMA controllers (8237As) are cascaded together. On-board ROM is expanded to a 128K capability. The "glue logic," including buffers and latches, consists primarily of chips used in a similar capacity in the PC and XT. The XT286 is a cross between the XT (8088) and the AT (80286).

1.1.3 The Personal System/2 Model 30 (8086)

The Model 30 is an upgrade over the 8088-based computers. It has become IBM's low-end microcomputer replacing the PC and XT. The Model 30 has a 16-bit data bus and comes with 640K bytes of memory. (We will discuss bytes shortly.) A limited expansion capability exists: three slots instead of the five on the PC and the eight on the XT. The system runs under DOS 3.3 and supports three graphics modes: a text mode, with 80×25 characters (each character is in an 8×16 character box instead of the 7×14 box in the PC, XT and AT), a graphics mode with 320×200 pixels, and a graphics mode with 640×480 pixels. An integrated graphics controller, the Multi-Color Graphics Array (MCGA), is used to provide screen control. This computer will run object code developed with the Macro Assembler versions 1.0 and 2.0. There is only one mode of operation. All PS/2 computers can use the IBM 8512, 8513, and 8514 color displays and the 8503 monochrome display.

1.1.4 The Personal System/2 Model 50 and Model 60 (80286)

The Model 50 is intended to support multitasking in a network environment, as well as stand-alone applications. It uses the 80286 and has one megabyte of memory. (Again, memory sizing will be discussed later.) The graphics controller is a new IBM standard, the Video Graphics Array (VGA), which provides a 320×200 pixel raster mode, a 640×480 pixel mode, and an 80×25 text mode on a 9×16 character box. The Model 50 has three expansion slots and is configured for table-top implementation. The system supports DOS 3.3 as well as the Protected Mode Operating System/2. A high-end System 36/38 Workstation Emulation Adapter is available as one option.

The Model 60 is a floor-mounted computer system that significantly increases the networking capability of IBM computers. Both the Model 50 and 60 use the IBM Micro Channel architecture which provides enhanced address, control, and data bus structures compatible with the 80286. The VGA controller also supports CGA, EGA, and MCGA and text. The Model 60 has a significantly increased disk storage capability: 44 megabyte, 70 megabyte, and 115 megabyte optional fixed disks can be used with the system. Again, the Model 60 can be used with DOS 3.3 or OS/2.

1.1.5 The Personal System/2 Model 80 (80386)

The Model 80 is the most powerful IBM microcomputer and it employs the Intel 80386 microprocessor for its CPU. The computer is floor-mounted in a chassis similar to the Model 60. The Model 80 source code differs in syntax from that used by other IBM microcomputers because of the 32-bit properties of the CPU. While source code developed using the Macro Assembler versions 1.0 and 2.0 will run on the Model 80, it clearly does so in a 16-bit mode. Hence, the full efficiency of the 80386 can only be realized with version 2.0. The Model 80 will also run with both DOS 3.3 and OS/2; thus, it accepts upwardly compatible software from the 8088, 8086, and 80286. The operating system instructions for the 80386 have the same syntax as those for the 80286 but are not useful for applications.

1.2 THE IBM SOFTWARE FRAMEWORK

Several programs are needed to develop assembly language software. These are treated in section 2.2, but it is useful, at this time, to examine both the operating system environment and the Macro Assembler itself.

1.2.1 The Disk Operating System

IBM microcomputers run under a high-level program that is loaded when the computer bootstraps itself after being turned on. There have been a number of editions of the IBM Disk Operating System (DOS); the most recent version commonly used in this country is 3.3 [9]. With the advent of the Personal System/2 computers a new operating system called Operating System/2 (OS/2) was developed. The DOS programs assumed a direct mapping of program or memory address to physical address location in the hardware. This physical or Real Address Mode mapping was used with the 8088, 8086 and 80286 (Real Address Mode) CPUs. A more powerful virtual address or Protected Mode is possible with the 80286 and 80386 and this can be implemented with OS/2. In Protected Mode, virtual memory addressing to one gigabyte is possible. During the development of this text only DOS was available. We do, however, discuss many of the aspects of OS/2 programming from a systems viewpoint.

The versions of DOS used during the writing of this textbook were DOS 2.0, 2.1, 3.0, 3.1, 3.2, and 3.3. One of the features of DOS is that it is possible to access the hardware capability of the microcomputer, for some peripherals such as disk drives, by using "DOS function calls." The functions involved are related to memory management and file manipulation rather than hardware input/output (I/O). To exercise these functions, the user must call a DOS interrupt, interrupt 21 (hexadecimal). (Clearly, disk I/O involves hardware device interfacing. The INT 21H functions that perform disk I/O also call drivers in the BIOS to service the needed hardware.)

IBM has defined an interrupt, function 44 (hexadecimal), that is supported by DOS in the later versions, 3.1, 3.2, and 3.3. This function, when executed, calls a service routine that can be used for device I/O of an arbitrary nature. Hence, the user can define I/O for a class of installable devices with this function. This function *does not* eliminate the need to generate a service routine; function 44 (hexadecimal) provides a method for calling a hardware device service routine. The user must develop a device driver for use with this interrupt and this driver must be written in assembly language if efficiency is needed or the device operation is time-critical.

1.2.2 Macro Assembler

We have seen that an assembler is a computer program that translates assembly language into machine instructions. The assembler is very specific to the hardware architecture associated with the computer in question. For example, in the IBM CPUs, general purpose electronic circuits capable of storage are connected together to form registers. These registers have names like AX and BX in assembly language syntax. When the assembler encounters a statement like

SUB AX,BX

it acts to insure that the contents of the BX register are subtracted from the contents of the AX register and the result stored in AX. We must remember that these registers are simply storage devices (circuits) internal to the microprocessor, and the effect of assembly is to translate instructions into a series of ones and zeros that cause the contents of these registers to be acted upon in the correct fashion. The important point to recognize is that the assembly language actually references hardware entities (in this case the AX and BX registers). Consequently, it tends to be machine or chip specific. Unlike FORTRAN or BASIC, which are high level and abstract, the assembly language is not very portable and must be applied to the class of computers that use the integrated circuits with instruction sets that determine the assembly language syntax.

Of course, an assembly language must contain syntax other than that used to instruct the processor. Typically some form of organization must be imposed on the source code and this structure is frequently interpreted by the assembler, based on non-executable statements. In IBM's Macro Assembler, non-executable statements used for structuring the source code take the form of pseudo-operations (pseudo-ops for short). The Macro Assembler divides storage in memory, for example, into segments and these segments are referenced using pseudo-ops. The assembler allows four types of segments in the 8088, 8086, and 80286 at any given point in execution: a code segment, a data segment, a stack segment, and a second data segment or extra segment. (The 80386 has two additional data segments.) As will become clear in Chapter 2, this segmentation of memory is easily described in the framework of the Macro Assembler and facilitates the placement of special memory areas (such as the stack) during program execution.

Instructions frequently reference memory locations or addresses. Associated with each memory address is a value representing the contents of this address. (We can think of a location as specified by two quantities: address and value.) Generally the assembler language has a number of ways of referencing the address of a location. For example, if BAM1 is an array of numbers, the following statements are two equivalent references to the fifth element of this array:

```
1. MOV  AX,BAM1[4]
2. LEA  BX,BAM1
   MOV  SI,4
   MOV  AX,[BX + SI]
```

In the above constructs, item 1 simply specifies that location 5 (index = 0, 1, 2, ...) of BAM1 be loaded into AX using the MOV instruction. In item 2 a more circuitous route is taken. First the address of BAM1 (BAM1[0]) is loaded into the BX register. Next an index counter is set equal to 4. Finally, the address of BX plus the index counter, SI, is computed and the memory contents at this address are loaded into AX. Here SI represents another microprocessor register.

By now the reader probably suspects, correctly, that the IBM Macro Assembler makes heavy usage of the microprocessor's internal registers. There are essentially 14 application registers in the 8088, 8086, and 80286: 12 general purpose, an instruction pointer (IP), and a flags register. The following illustrates these registers, which are discussed in more detail in subsequent chapters:

AX (AH,AL)	Accumulator Register
BX (BH,BL)	Base Register
CX (CH,CL)	Count Register
DX (DH,DL)	Data Register
SP	Stack Pointer Register
BP	Base Pointer Register
SI	Source Index Register
DI	Destination Index Register
CS	Code Segment Register
DS	Data Segment Register
SS	Stack Segment Register
ES	Extra Segment Register
IP	Instruction Pointer
SF	Status Flags Register

These registers all have 16-bits of significance. The data registers (AX, BX, CX, and DX) can be addresssed as two halves (AH, AL, . . .). This allows 8-bit computation within the confines of 16-bit registers.

1.3 PRELIMINARY TOPICS

This text assumes a minimal familiarity with microcomputer nomenclature. It is, however, necessary to understand a few simple concepts and this subsection briefly addresses these ideas: binary and hexadecimal arithmetic, which is appropriate to microcomputers, and hardware entities.

1.3.1 Number Systems

Part of any introduction to assembler programming is a description of the various number systems the reader is likely to encounter. A bit represents a single digit (either a 1 or a 0). Thus, a given digit represents one of two states and defines binary or base-2 arithmetic when coupled with other rules. By combining bits, larger numbers can be represented. Typically, N bits can be represented in the following form, where significance is from left to right:

$$2^{N-1} \quad 2^{N-2} \qquad 2^7 \quad 2^6 \quad 2^5 \quad 2^4 \quad 2^3 \quad 2^2 \quad 2^1 \quad 2^0$$

The integer 3, for example, would appear as

2^{N-1}	2^{N-2}		2^7	2^6	2^5	2^4	2^3	2^2	2^1	2^0
0	0	•••	0	0	0	0	0	0	1	1

Here $2^1 = 2$, $2^0 = 1$, and $2 + 1 = 3$. Similarly, the integer 128 would appear as

2^{N-1}	2^{N-2}		2^7	2^6	2^5	2^4	2^3	2^2	2^1	2^0
0	0	•••	1	0	0	0	0	0	0	0

Note that each box in the above numbering scheme can assume only two values. Thus, these boxes are ideally represented by switches which are either on or off. Since the circuits in computers are either on or off, they can be used to emulate these switches and, consequently, the boxes.

Now consider the decimal system (base-10) which we use every day. We must consider digits in this system (not bits) because each digit can assume more than two values. In the decimal system, N digits takes the form

10^{N-1}	10^{N-2}		10^7	10^6	10^5	10^4	10^3	10^2	10^1	10^0
		•••								

The integer 3, however, appears as

10^{N-1}	10^{N-2}		10^7	10^6	10^5	10^4	10^3	10^2	10^1	10^0
0	0	•••	0	0	0	0	0	0	0	3

Similarly, the integer 128 would appear as

10^{N-1}	10^{N-2}		10^7	10^6	10^5	10^4	10^3	10^2	10^1	10^0
0	0	•••	0	0	0	0	0	1	2	8

While this may seem obvious, it is useful to note that each digit in the decimal system cannot be represented by a simple switch with two positions, on or off. How would one represent 8 with a switch?

As a consequence of this arithmetic, base-2 or binary numbers are used by computers and decimal numbers seem to be conveniently used by programmers. Clearly, there are many other possible number systems. The only other system which we will consider is the base-16 or hexadecimal system.

How do we represent base-16 numbers? We add a few letters from the alphabet to the numbers 0, 1, 2, ..., 9. These added letters are

Decimal	Hexadecimal
10	A
11	B
12	C
13	D
14	E
15	F

Of course, 0, 1, 2, ..., 9 continue to represent the same decimal number in both systems. N digits in the hexadecimal system become

16^{N-1} 16^{N-2} 16^7 16^6 16^5 16^4 16^3 16^2 16^1 16^0

| | | ··· | | | | | | | | |

The integer 3 is given by

16^{N-1} 16^{N-2} 16^7 16^6 16^5 16^4 16^3 16^2 16^1 16^0

| 0 | 0 | ··· | 0 | 0 | 0 | 0 | 0 | 0 | 0 | 3 |

Similarly, the integer 128 would appear as

16^{N-1} 16^{N-2} 16^7 16^6 16^5 16^4 16^3 16^2 16^1 16^0

| 0 | 0 | ··· | 0 | 0 | 0 | 0 | 0 | 0 | 8 | 0 |

The integer 255 would appear as

16^{N-1} 16^{N-2} 16^7 16^6 16^5 16^4 16^3 16^2 16^1 16^0

| 0 | 0 | ··· | 0 | 0 | 0 | 0 | 0 | 0 | F | F |

There will be occasions for performing arithmetic operations with binary and hexadecimal numbers. For example, when using DEBUG, all register values and memory locations (as well as values) are specified in hexadecimal. If two values are added, subtracted, multiplied, or divided the result will be hexadecimal. Since we are familiar with decimal operations, conversion to decimal followed by the operation and conversion back to hexadecimal will yield the result of the operation in DEBUG format. Alternatively, there are a number of calculators on the market that aid in the conversion of decimal to hexadecimal. We do not recommend that the reader learn a new set of multiplication tables, although as proficiency develops this will occur to a limited extent.

Binary numbers are somewhat easier to grasp. Also, since the computer must operate in binary it is useful to consider the addition and subtraction of these numbers. (Multiplication and division can be achieved using the addition and subtraction operations.) Consider 64 subtracted from 255 in 8-bit arithmetic.

$$
\begin{array}{llll}
& 1\ 1\ 1\ 1\ 1\ 1\ 1\ 1 & (= 255) \\
- & 0\ 1\ 0\ 0\ 0\ 0\ 0\ 0 & -(=\ \ 64) \\
\hline
& 1\ 0\ 1\ 1\ 1\ 1\ 1\ 1 & (= 191)
\end{array}
$$

It is clear in this operation that a simple binary subtraction suffices with a borrow as needed. Addition is similar, and the following illustrates the addition of 143 and 79.

$$
\begin{array}{llll}
& 1\ 0\ 0\ 0\ 1\ 1\ 1\ 1 & (= 143) \\
+ & 0\ 1\ 0\ 0\ 1\ 1\ 1\ 1 & +(=\ \ 79) \\
\hline
& 1\ 1\ 0\ 1\ 1\ 1\ 1\ 0 & (= 222)
\end{array}
$$

Finally the question of negative numbers and overflow must be addressed. In the computer, binary numbers are represented as unsigned integers. Typically a 16-bit word can assume values between 0 and 65,535 or $2^{16} - 1$. If the 16th bit, for example, is used to keep track of the sign of a number, the remaining 15 bits can be used to specify a quantity with maximum value of 32,767. Thus, numbers in the range $-32,767$ to 32,767 can be represented. For the programmer, this specification of sign is somewhat arbitrary. The way the computer keeps track of signs, however, is fixed and must always be taken into consideration.

The computer uses two's-complement arithmetic. In two's-complement arithmetic positive numbers are represented in normal fashion but negative numbers are represented in complement form. The following method illustrates how this complement is calculated for the 8-bit value -79.

Procedure

$$
\begin{array}{lll}
& 0\ 1\ 0\ 0\ 1\ 1\ 1\ 1 & \text{1. Assume positive representation} \\
& 1\ 0\ 1\ 1\ 0\ 0\ 0\ 0 & \text{2. Reverse all bits} \\
+ & \hspace{4.2em} 1 & \text{3. Add 1} \\
\hline
& 1\ 0\ 1\ 1\ 0\ 0\ 0\ 1 & \text{4. Obtain two's-complement}
\end{array}
$$

What is so useful about this form? Consider the subtraction of 79 from itself.

$$79 - 79 = 0$$

Rewriting this as

$$79 + (-79) = 0$$

where the quantity in parenthesis is the two's-complement of 79, we see that the subtraction can now be converted to an addition (this is actually how the 8088 or 80286 accomplishes subtraction). In binary form this is

$$
\begin{array}{lll}
& 0\ 1\ 0\ 0\ 1\ 1\ 1\ 1 & (\ \ 79) \\
+ & 1\ 0\ 1\ 1\ 0\ 0\ 0\ 1 & +(-79) \\
\hline
(1) & 0\ 0\ 0\ 0\ 0\ 0\ 0\ 0 & (\ \ \ 0)
\end{array}
$$

Here we see that zero is the result with a carry indicated to the ninth bit position. The 8088 would interpret the result of this subtraction operation as zero.

Now we return to the question of why it is important to be aware of the computer's methodology for calculating negative numbers. In the above operation the programmer would never be aware of the use of two's-complement values. The positive quantity 79 is simply specified as being subtracted from itself with result 0. Suppose, however, that 80 were to be subtracted from 79. The two's-complement of 80 is

```
  0 1 0 1 0 0 0 0     1. 80
  1 0 1 0 1 1 1 1     2. Reverse all bits
+               1     3. Add 1
  ─────────────────
  1 0 1 1 0 0 0 0     4. Obtain two's-complement
```

Now add this to 79

```
   0 1 0 0 1 1 1 1     (  79)
 +1 0 1 1 0 0 0 0     (−80)
  ─────────────────
   1 1 1 1 1 1 1 1     ( −1)
```

In hexadecimal this is FFH. Clearly, this result must be interpreted in two's-complement fashion. The programmer who develops an arithmetic that sets the sign bit for negative numbers and keeps the remaining 15 bits in equivalent unsigned form must consider the outcome of subtractions with two's-complement results. In such an arithmetic, for example, −1 would appear as

$$1\ 0\ 0\ 0 \quad 0\ 0\ 0\ 0 \quad 0\ 0\ 0\ 0 \quad 0\ 0\ 0\ 1$$

not

$$1\ 1\ 1\ 1 \quad 1\ 1\ 1\ 1 \quad 1\ 1\ 1\ 1 \quad 1\ 1\ 1\ 1$$

Keeping track of signed numbers will be the responsibility of the programmer, and maintaining an awareness of when the computer returns a two's complement value is essential.

In the above discussion, overflow was mentioned. Consider eight-bit quantities where the maximum value specified can be 255. If the AL (lower AX) register half contained 255 and the BL (lower BX register half) contents were added to AL, an overflow would occur for all BL values but 0. This is catastrophic because AL is then meaningless. Hence, care must be exercised to insure that the results of arithmetic operations do not overflow or exceed the value that can be stored in the resulting (destination) memory or register location.

1.3.2 Registers, Buses, and Bytes

There are some conceptual entities that the user must begin to recognize. One of these, the notion of a register, has its basis in actual hardware. We have seen the 16-bit registers described earlier, and it seems plausible that other intelligent chips might also contain registers, as in fact they do.

The next entity to consider is a bus. Basically in the IBM microcomputer systems a bus consists of interconnecting wires which pass bits in parallel fashion. For example, the IBM PC, XT, and AT systems have an address bus, a control bus, and a data bus. The address bus contains provision for 20 parallel lines (one for each bit in the address), and the data bus, 8 parallel lines in the IBM PC and XT. The control bus is more fragmented. Each chip can use selected groups of wires from each bus as needed. The AT has a slightly larger bus architecture with 24 lines in its address bus and an 18 line data bus.

Finally, the reader should be aware of the standard nomenclature for describing groups of bits used to form numbers. The term byte is used to designate a group of 8 bits. Many support chips are configured to accept byte input; hence, IBM structured the PC and XT for 8-bit data traffic. Memory size is usually specified in bytes. One-half byte (4 bits) is defined as a nibble and 2-byte quantities (16 bits) are referred to as word quantities. The 8088 and 8086 are referred to as 16-bit microprocessors because the CPU internal registers are all of word length. The 80286 CPU has a similar basis and is also referred to as a 16-bit computer. In the mid-1980s a trend toward 32-bit chips started, and these bit orders are referred to as double word quantities. The 80386 is such a microprocessor.

1.4 HARDWARE DRIVER, APPLICATIONS, AND SYSTEMS PROGRAMMING

We have already alluded to the differences between assembler programming, which is used to control peripheral chips and subsystems, and that programming which acts to perform a more abstract application. An example of the latter would be programming that calculates the square root of a number or inverts a matrix. Application programming requires no specific knowledge of the hardware other than that intrinsic to the assembly language itself. Hardware driver programming, on the other hand, is intimately tied to the computer hardware architecture. Peripheral addressing, for example, is determined by the hardware configurations. Chapter 9 illustrates this aspect of driver programming by examples from the BIOS code. In addition, each intelligent support chip must be initialized and accessed using control words. The structure and timing of these words are specified by the manufacturer, and the driver programmer must properly input them to the chip. In some cases these service routines must act in a dynamic fashion such as handshaking between the CPU and a printer during output. Fortunately, IBM has provided many of these routines in the BIOS programming, and they are easily accessed using software interrupts that are called by the INT instruction. In some cases, however, it might be desirable to develop a routine (such as adding an analog-to-digital converter board) or modify an existing routine (to clear rapidly and repaint the screen, for example). A knowledge of how to program the chips in the system then becomes essential.

The third major area that involves assembly language programming is systems programming. Systems programming is the programming used to provide the framework for the executive to keep the computer active and waiting to perform tasks requested by the user, for file and memory management, and for special-purpose user instructions or commands to be executed from terminal input (such as the directory command or COPY command). As indicated, this class of programming frequently involves a mix of assembly language and high-level language coding. In Chapter 10 we discuss systems programming for the Intel family of microprocessors used in the IBM microcomputers. Many special purpose instructions for the 80286 and 80386 apply only to systems programming (for example, memory management and task protection).

1.5 IBM MACHINE DEPENDENCIES AND ASSEMBLER PORTABILITY

The purpose of this brief section is to address the portability of assembly language software written for the IBM family of microcomputers. We are specifically interested in the capability for transporting software from one IBM machine to another. Intrinsic to this process is the assembler (we use the IBM Macro Assembler version 1.0 and 2.0 in this book), and the operating system (we use DOS 2.0, 2.1, 3.0, 3.1, 3.2, and 3.3 in this book).

Assembly language has instructions that are specific to the processor involved. The Intel family used by IBM includes the 8088, 8086, 80286, and 80386 microprocessors. All but the 80386 are 16-bit processors and source code is readily transferred among these processors except for code involving a small number of 80286 application instructions (the 15 instructions that appear in Table 4.22). All programs developed in this textbook will run on all three processors. Hence, the software we consider in this text can be used on the IBM PC, XT, AT, XT286, PS/2 Model 30, PS/2 Model 50, and PS/2 Model 60. It is assumed that such software will be assembled using version 2.0 (to include the coprocessor instructions) of the Macro Assembler and will be run under an appropriate version of DOS.

The question of object code compatibility is slightly more complex. Some of the instructions in Table 4.22 have the same name when used with an 8088 or 8086. These instructions must be reassembled to insure portability. Basically, however, the bulk of object code is also portable across these processors. Again, we are talking about applications software.

The 8088 and 8086 only operate in a single mode; hence, mode is not in question when considering software portability. The 80286, however, has two modes as previously alluded to: the Real Address Mode and the Protected Mode. Applications software developed for the 80286 with version 2.0 *will not* contain instructions that are mode dependent. Therefore both source code and object code can be transported to the 8088 and 8086 (subject to the restrictions already mentioned). Linked or executable code (.EXE extension), however, will depend on the mode the linker was set up to employ.

The 80386 (PS/2 Model 80 microcomputer) is distinctly different from the 16-bit processors. It has new register definitions but the older 16-bit register names are treated as a subset. Hence software developed for the 8088, 8086, and 80286 is upwardly compatible with the 80386 at the source or object code level. Again, linked code is dependent on the mode used (Real Address Mode for DOS and Protected

Mode for OS/2). Downward compatibility, however, does not exist owing to the new register names and additional instructions.

1.6 STRUCTURE AND GOALS FOR THE BOOK

So far we have been briefly exposed to what the IBM Macro Assembler is and does. That is the subject of this book and, hence, it is appropriate to discuss the structure and objectives of the text. The following section delineates the topics by chapter. First and foremost, it is hoped that the reader will find this text an easy vehicle to Macro Assembler.

Chapter 2 begins the actual subject of Macro Assembler programming. The 16-bit registers are discussed in detail, as well as various features of the language. Several examples are presented which serve as the basis for beginning programming. Initially, a very simple program is developed and we execute this program with the IBM utility, DEBUG. DEBUG is an excellent tool for examining assembler code and determining how it functions. IBM's Program Segment Prefix (PSP) area is introduced and a method for returning to the PSP area is presented. This allows the user to achieve a normal return to DOS following the completion of program execution. Various features of IBM microcomputer software architecture (based on the 8088, 8086, 80286, and 80386) are discussed with regard to their programming in assembly language.

Chapter 3 addresses the topic of software design. The basic concerns of this chapter are top-down design, modular code, and structured programming applied to assembly language. Top-down design techniques, using Structure Charts, program flow charts and natural language constructs, are explored. Modular code, based on assembly language procedures, is developed. Finally, techniques for structuring assembly language programs are presented. These are similar in nature to the assembly language code generated by the IBM utility SALUT (Structured Assembly Language Utility) which is discussed in Appendix B.

Chapter 4 considers the Macro Assembler instructions. Both tabular data and program examples are presented. The topic of object libraries is introduced. Object libraries are part of the version 2.0 enhancements. We then consider the various IBM interrupt service calls which yield a method for executing tedious hardware functions without actually having to write the code for these functions. IBM has written this code and we access it through standardized interrupts. This code comprises Chapter 5. Several program examples are presented.

Chapter 6 continues the development of basic Macro Assembler features. Pseudo-ops are covered in depth with particular emphasis on macros. The acceptable operators are presented. At this point, no reference to the 8087 (or 80287) instructions has been made and the coverage is essentially that for the Macro Assembler version 1.0.

Chapter 7 addresses the topic of disk and diskette input/output using sequentially accessed files (extended file management). Two approaches for achieving disk I/O are developed. Chapter 8 discusses coprocessor programming. The version 2.0 has included a complete set of coprocessor instructions, which begin with the letter "F." This feature greatly simplifies programming the 8087 (or 80287). In the text several examples of coprocessor programming are illustrated with an emphasis on setting up integer and floating point variables in the IBM microcomputer environment so that full advantage of the coprocessor's capabilities can be achieved. The addition of a suitable coprocessor instruction set makes the Macro Assembler version 2.0 truly competitive with other languages for "number crunching" applications.

The material presented in Part 3 (Chapters 9 and 10) is intended to serve as an illustration of hardware driver and system programming. Much of this discussion is based on assembly language routines used for the interrupt service routine processing in the PC, XT, and AT. The service routines for the PS/2 Models 30, 50, and 60 are also considered. As part of this discussion, those portions of the hardware implementation needed to understand BIOS and DOS are described. This is primarily oriented towards definition of the port and register addresses needed by each chip, the chip selection process, and the definition of chip parameters. These items are board specific and the IBM design shows how, in practice, such implementations are created. Also, this discussion of hardware removes ambiguities associated with addressing hardware.

In summary, the coverage of the book is intended to provide the reader, as quickly as possible, with the means for achieving interactive programs. Since all input/output is controlled through interrupts, it is necessary to present these early. The reader who, for instance, is used to implementing READ and PRINT instructions in FORTRAN will find that in assembler a more elaborate procedure based on interrupts is necessary if keyboard and display input/output is to take place. In keeping with this goal, extended file management serves as the vehicle for achieving on-line storage and retrieval of data. This can then be used for the generation and access of databases.

Throughout the text, examples that employ graphic material have been illustrated. This reflects the philosophy that data is best presented in graphic fashion. The use of interrupt 10H serves as the basis for developing graphs on the display, and GRAPHICS.COM is used to obtain a hard copy of these displays. For the reader who is interested in developing presentation quality graphics, assembler and INT 10H are especially useful. The examples reflect a modular programming style. The procedure pseudo-op is used extensively to generate small compact routines that are easily combined to yield larger programs and have the added feature that they can be debugged individually. The compact modular nature of procedures facilitates debugging because only a limited amount of code and testing is involved.

REFERENCES

1. *Macro Assembler Version 2.00*. IBM Personal Computer: Computer Language Series. IBM Corp. P.O. Box 1328. Boca Raton, FL 33432 (1981).
2. *Technical Reference: Personal Computer*. Personal Computer Hardware Reference Library. IBM Corp. P.O. Box 1328. Boca Raton, FL 33432 (1981).
3. *iAPX 86/88, 186/188 User's Manual—Hardware Reference*. Intel Corp., Literature Sales. P.O. Box 58130. Santa Clara, CA 95052-8130 (1985). (210912-001)

4. *iAPX 86/88, 186, 188 User's Manual—Programmer's Reference.* Intel Corp., Literature Sales. P.O. Box 58130. Santa Clara, CA 95052-8130 (1986). (210911-003)

5. *iAPX 286 Hardware Reference Manual.* Intel Corp., Literature Sales. P.O. Box 58130. Santa Clara, 95052-8130 (1983). (210760-001)

6. *iAPX 286 Programmer's Reference Manual.* Intel Corp., Literature Sales. P.O. Box 58130. Santa Clara, CA 95052-8130 (1985). (210498-003)

7. *80386 Hardware Reference Manual.* Intel Corp., Literature Sales. P.O. Box 58130. Santa Clara, CA 95052-8130 (1986). (231732-001)

8. *80386 Programmer's Reference Manual.* Intel Corp., Literature Sales. P.O. Box 58130. Santa Clara, CA 95052-8130 (1986). (230985-001)

9. *Microsoft Corp. Disk Operating System Version 3.30.* IBM Personal Computer: Computer Language Series. IBM Corp. P.O. Box 1328. Boca Raton, FL 33432 (1987).

PROBLEMS

1.1. Many higher level languages produce assembler when source code is compiled. Would you expect this assembler to be efficient? Explain.

1.2. If the IBM PC or XT has a 20-bit address bus and the AT, a 24-bit address bus, what would you calculate as the maximum addressable memory for each?

1.3. If the 8259A generates interrupts to the CPU when a peripheral sets one of its interrupt lines LOW, what would a software interrupt using the INT instruction accomplish?

1.4. The IBM microcomputers (PC, XT and AT in Real Address Mode) are set up to use segments and offsets for generating 20-bit addresses. Each quantity is a 16-bit word and the segment is shifted left 4 bits prior to addition yielding the address.

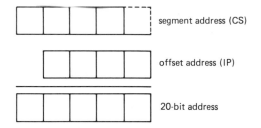

If the CS register is 07F8H and the instruction pointer is 274AH, what is the 20-bit address associated with the next instruction?

1.5. If the subtraction instruction functions as described, what is wrong with the statement

SUB AL,BX   ?

1.6. How do 8087 (or 80287) instructions differ from 8088 (or 80286) instructions?

1.7. What are the following decimal quantities in binary (use 16 bits)? In hexadecimal? (a) 5387, (b) 254, (c) 1024, (d) 512, (e) 32768.

1.8. Using an arithmetic which sets bit 16 for sign and maintains the remaining 15 bits in normal binary representation, how would you specify (a) -3086, (b) -7968, (c) 7968, (d) 513, (e) -32766?

1.9. Using an arithmetic that employs two's-complement notation, how would you specify the values appearing in problem 1.8?

1.10. In two's-complement notation what is the difference (subtraction) between (a) 62573 and 62684, (b) 512 and 7968, (c) 7968 and 512, (d) 10 and 20, (e) 32767 and 1024?

1.11. What value will cause a 32-bit register to overflow if the arithmetic is signed? Unsigned?

1.12. Why is the 8088 not a "full" 16-bit CPU like the 80286?

1.13. How many hexadecimal digits are needed to describe a byte? A word?

2

Introductory Assembler Programming

The goal of this chapter is to acquaint the beginning programmer with the fundamentals of the IBM microcomputer Macro Assembler language [1, 2] and provide him with sufficient proficiency that he can start running assembler programs. In order to accomplish this task, the method of presenting the material will be to provide a minimum language subset and follow this with several specific application programs. These application programs will be used to illustrate various features of the Macro Assembler. They constitute complete entities that can be programmed immediately and executed.

As anyone who has programmed knows, beginning a new language begs the question which comes first, the chicken or the egg? The new programmer must first become familiar with terminology that can only be fully understood by actually using ideas behind the terminology. For example, in order to implement and execute a program in Macro Assembler, various specific uses of the SEGMENT pseudo-op must be employed. These uses only become clear upon reflecting back about the nature of the program in which they appear. Therefore, the approach taken in this chapter is to build a little at a time on the language structure, and then to apply these ideas, rather than present all pseudo-ops at one time.

2.1 INTRODUCTION

All computers execute commands that reside in memory in the form of machine instructions. The purpose of a compiler or assembler is to translate these commands written in another higher language, into machine instructions. Users of FORTRAN and COBOL are familiar with compiling and linking programs prior to execution. These languages are considered high level and can be understood in an abstract sense; they make no reference to the internal architecture of the computer. They are transportable and machine independent, with minor exceptions. Assemblers, however, use instructions that are closer to actual manipulation of the computer's hardware. Consequently, they usually apply to a specific hardware implementation such as the Intel 8088 microprocessor used in the IBM PC and XT. In general, assemblers are much more efficient in the use of instructions than are high level abstract languages such as FORTRAN or COBOL. With assemblers it is possible to appear to accomplish two or more tasks concurrently. By calculating the time it takes to execute instructions for each task and then interleaving the instructions, the microprocessor seems to process the tasks simultaneously. An example of this would be the tasks of reading real-time data into the computer and simultaneously writing this data to a disk file so that no data is lost. As long as the data samples are spaced far enough apart in time so that the disk write can be executed between samples, the real-time processing can be accomplished. The general nature of higher-level languages would require too much time between instructions to accomplish such processing.

The IBM PC employs the Intel 8088 microprocessor as the basic central processor unit (CPU) in its hardware architecture [3]. IBM's Macro Assembler language is based on 8088 instructions [4]. The 8088 evolved from the Intel 8086 microprocessor which is a full 16-bit processor, unlike the earlier microprocessors that operated with only 8 bits at one time [5]. Reference to an 8-bit microprocessor indicates that the data and address buses accommodate 8 bits of information at a given time (there are some exceptions where additional bits are included in an 8-bit architecture). For 16-bit processing, each data and address bus is expanded to handle 16 bits of information in hardware. Hence, this architecture provides a capability for manipulating 16 bits with a single instruction cycle. This leads to greater precision when defining arithmetic and more address space when accessing memory. Although software can be written to accomplish 16-bit operations in an 8-bit microprocessor environment, it is usually cumbersome and slow because the hardware is not structured for such behavior. The 8086 uses 20-bit physical addresses for addressing memory. This provides up to 1,048,576 locations that may be accessed (the number 2 raised to the power 20). In the 8088 there still exist 20-bit physical addresses (and buses). Hence, the 8088 can also access approximately one million bytes of data (one megabyte). However, the 8088 employs only 8-bit data buses. The rationale behind this choice for the 8088 architecture is that many data handling peripheral chips can only operate on 8 bits (one byte) at a time. The 8088 structure allows these peripheral chips to be used with a 16-bit arithmetic logical unit (ALU).

The next section discusses the IBM microcomputer environment, with an emphasis on 8088 features that impact the way software must be programmed. Unlike higher level languages, which have many methods for inputting and outputting information to the screen and printer, assembler languages do not easily lend themselves to data input/output. In FORTRAN, the PRINT instruction allows variable values, strings, and other alphanumeric quantities to be directly output at any intermediate point. This usually helps in debugging during program execution. The assembler programmer must rely on examining memory locations and calling interrupts to alter the screen presentations. Both of these techniques require some explanation.

Because of the need to access some program variables in order to see the results of calculations, our initial emphasis will be on using tools that are available with the IBM PC software. To access memory locations, IBM has provided a debugging program called DEBUG. The reader is referred to the *IBM Disk Operating System* (DOS) manual for a description of this program [6]. DEBUG will be introduced in Subsection 2.2.4 below. Eventually, the video I/O interrupt (10H) will be introduced to further enable the beginner to affect the screen presentation. This will take place in a later chapter. There are, of course, other techniques which will be discussed as we progress through the text.

2.2 THE IBM 8088-BASED MICROCOMPUTER SOFTWARE ENVIRONMENT

The Intel 8088 microprocessor is the heart of the IBM PC. When this integrated circuit is coupled with read only memory (ROM), random access memory (RAM), a clock generator (8284A), an interrupt controller (8259A), some direct memory access chips, multiplexers, I/O peripheral drivers, and other assorted chips, a complete Personal Computer is configured. While these chips are wired together in a fixed configuration, it is the software that integrates everything and controls the movement of data among the various components.

When the PC is turned on the system boots from ROM and DOS is loaded from either the floppy or hard disk. (In this book cassette-based systems will not be addressed.) DOS is at the top of the software hierarchy and constitutes the operating system that controls the handling of all applications software. Also loaded are portions of the BIOS program, which is listed in the *IBM Technical Reference* [7]. The process by which this occurs is as follows: the bootstrap loader is read from diskette drive A (or drive C for most XT and AT systems); the two hidden files, IBMBIO.COM and IBMDOS.COM, are loaded by the bootstrap loader; COM-MAND.COM is loaded; and finally, external command files such as FORMAT are brought into memory as needed.

The two hidden files and COMMAND.COM comprise the bulk of the PC's operating system architecture. IBMBIO.COM and the ROM-BIOS (resident portion of BIOS in the ROM chips located on the system board) constitute the device-handling capability of the IBM PC software. These routines are device specific and control the I/O tasks associated with peripherals. IBMDOS.COM contains DOS service routines which are called by interrupts. These interrupt service routines will be discussed later; however, with a few exceptions they are of limited interest to the assembler programmer (exceptions are the very valuable INT 21H DOS function calls). The DOS interrupts currently implemented are listed in Appendix D of the *IBM Disk Operating System* manual. Interrupts associated with I/O device handling (BIOS interrupts) are listed in the *IBM Technical Reference* and are of much more use. We have already mentioned one BIOS interrupt, 10H, that invokes user control of the video monitor. COMMAND.COM performs a number of functions. Its major role is to handle the interpretation of user commands entered at the keyboard.

Once the interrupt service routines provided by DOS and BIOS are understood, the assembler programmer has the ability to implement external controls in programs easily. This includes interfacing with the outside world (the peripherals) as well as the operating system. It is unlikely that the user will want to tamper with these routines since they provide a framework for accomplishing very tedious programming tasks, such as moving the screen cursor or writing to diskette.

With these thoughts in mind, let us consider the basic structure of the IBM PC's software. All programs and data are loaded in memory at specific locations determined by their addresses. Since the IBM PC's and XT's 8088 has a 20-bit address word and bus, up to 1,048,576 locations may be specified. The next few sections discuss how these memory locations are subdivided in the IBM PC software architecture.

2.2.1 Segments and Offsets

The IBM PC and XT use 20 bits for addressing memory; however, they process 16-bit words in their address registers. How can this be accomplished in real-time? The answer is that the address is divided into segments and offsets. A segment is an area of memory that is continuous and can be up to 64K-bytes long. It must start on a 16-byte boundary (paragraph) and can overlap other segments by interleaving memory locations. The beginning of a segment is used to define its location. This address is contained in one of the four segment registers: code segment, data segment, stack segment, or extra segment. The code segment register contains the beginning address of the segment where the program being executed resides. The data segment register holds (points to) the beginning address of the segment where variables are defined. The stack segment register points to the segment where the stack exists. A stack is a memory structure where bytes or words can be pushed, one on top of another, and then recalled successively. The last word or byte in is the first out (LIFO). This memory structure is established by the programmer and accessed using the instructions PUSH and POP. An example of its use appears in section 2.3.1. Finally, the extra segment register points to a segment that is user definable and usually contains additional data.

The IBM PC Macro Assembler uses 16-bit address words to define segment locations. These locations are fixed by the LINK program prior to execution. Since segments can be defined up to 64K-bytes long, another parameter must be specified to establish memory locations within the segment. This parameter is the memory location offset. It requires a 16-bit word in order to define all possible locations within a maximum-size 64K-byte segment.

The full address in one megabyte memory is obtained by combining the segment and offset address. The segment address is first shifted left by 4-bit positions (with zeros appended to the right, the least significant bit positions) and then added to the offset to yield the 20-bit address. Consider the following calculation for a 20-bit address expressed in binary (recall the discussion in Chapter 1).

```
      0001 0000 1010 1111 (0000)    SEGMENT ADDRESS
           1111 0000 1111  1111     OFFSET ADDRESS
  + _____
      0001 1111 1011 1110  1111     20-BIT ADDRESS
```

In hexadecimal this addition would be

$$\begin{array}{ll} 1\,0AF(0) & \text{SEGMENT ADDRESS} \\ F0F\ F & \text{OFFSET ADDRESS} \\ + \hspace{1cm} & \\ \hline 1FBE\ F & \text{20-BIT ADDRESS} \end{array}$$

It is important to recognize that the linker defines segment addresses. Not all possible combinations of these addresses are allowed. For example, the following combination would not be permitted.

$$\begin{array}{ll} FFFF(0) & \text{SEGMENT ADDRESS} \\ 001\ 0 & \text{OFFSET ADDRESS} \\ + \hspace{1cm} & \\ \hline \text{Undefined} & \text{20-BIT ADDRESS} \end{array}$$

In this example, the one megabyte range would be exceeded for a 20-bit address. The usual notation for specifying the segment and offset address pair is to separate their hexadecimal values by a colon. The segment address is specified first. In the case of the example above, conventional notation would specify the address as

                    10AF:F0FF

The reader should become familiar with this notation because it is used extensively in the literature. Also, programs like DEBUG use this format to refer to memory locations. Four segment types have been mentioned. It should be recognized, however, that within a given type (such as the code segment) multiple segments can be dclineated.

Programmers familiar with other languages, where subroutines are used to create modular programs, will appreciate the concept of procedures in Macro Assembler. It is through the implementation of separately assembled and linked procedures that defining multiple segments becomes particularly useful. Procedures are defined by the PROC and ENDP pseudo-ops. These pseudo-ops provide an approach to programming that facilitates clarity, modularity, and ease of understanding. Also, it reduces repetition of program code. The use of procedures greatly eases the Macro Assembler programmer's tasks but makes it necessary in many cases to define multiple code segments.

2.2.2 Allocation of the One-Megabyte Memory (IBM PC and XT)

Table 2.1 illustrates a coarse picture of the memory allocation for the PC. Indicated are the start and end addresses for boundaries differentiating each major section. Also indicated in the column containing the end address for each boundary is the total memory occupied up to the boundary (given in parenthesis). Here 64K bytes denotes 2 raised to the 16th power (65,536 bytes).

The initial 64K contains random access memory (RAM). Some of this memory is used by DOS and BIOS to hold interrupts (discussed in a subsequent chapter) and

TABLE 2.1 MEMORY MAP FOR THE ONE-MEGABYTE ADDRESS RANGE

20-bit address		Description
Start	End	
00000	0FFFF (64K)	This area contains the first 64K of random access memory (RAM). Early systems can only install this amount on the system board.
10000	3FFFF (256K)	Additional 192K of memory can occupy this region of memory. On newer PC versions this can also be installed on the system board.
40000	9FFFF (640K)	This is the location for an additional 384K of user RAM bringing the total user RAM to a maximum of 640K, for the PC version.
A0000	A3FFF (656K)	These 16K locations are reserved by IBM.
A4000	BFFFF (768K)	This region contains 112K that represents the graphics and display video buffer.
C0000	C7FFF (800K)	This area of 32K bytes is intended to be a read only memory (ROM) expansion area.
C8000	C9FFF (808K)	This 8K of memory is allocated for controlling the hard disk. The memory is in ROM.
CA000	F3FFF (976K)	This area of memory is 168K and is reserved for ROM located on various adapter cards to support applications.
F4000	F5FFF (984K)	This 8K of memory is intended for user ROM and corresponds to the spare ROM socket.
F6000	FDFFF (1016K)	These 32K locations are for cassette BASIC.
FE000	FFFFF (1024K)	This 8K is reserved for the BASIC Input/Output (I/O) system.

data. The BASIC interpreter occupies the rest with a major portion (62.5K) allocated to user memory. The next 192K bytes are reserved for additional user application. This total of 256K bytes of RAM can reside on the system board in newer PC versions. The earlier models, however, can only accommodate 64K on the system board, with the remaining 192K installed in one of the expansion slots. Following the 256K boundary is an additional area of 384K for additional user memory expansion.

All user RAM is located in lower memory. The next block of space is 16K which has been reserved by IBM for future use. A block of 112K memory from A4000 to BFFFF is allocated to the video display. Finally, the remaining 256K of memory holds all read only memory (ROM).

The importance of understanding or being aware of memory allocation becomes clear when using tools such as DEBUG. The DEBUG program allows the assembler programmer to step through the software and observe what happens in memory. Calling the video display, for example, will access locations in the high BIOS ROM area. The user will understand why DEBUG addresses this area and how BIOS is loaded in his or her particular system. All words in memory are stored with the least significant byte first. It is important to recognize that when a word is accessed in memory, the first byte encountered corresponds to bits 0 through 7 of the word. The second contiguous byte corresponds to bits 8 through 15 of the word. This reverse sequence must be considered when using byte instructions to manipulate parts of memory.

2.2.3 The Intel 8088 Registers

We have seen in Chapter 1 that the 8088 has 12 internal registers, an instruction pointer (IP), and a flags register. The registers are where the work gets done in the Macro Assembler. Unlike higher-level languages where instructions tend to be symbolic (for example, where one variable equals a functional combination of others) in Macro Assembler special attention is paid to the internal registers and how they appear in instructions. Instructions frequently require that operands address registers. During assembly, the definition of what an instruction means depends on the usage of register (or other) operands appearing in the program. The MOV instruction, for example, can be interpreted by the assembler in seven general ways. Each depends on how register or data operands appear. All register definitions constitute reserved words. The four data register mnemonics are AX (Accumulator), BX (Base register), CX (Count register), and DX (Data register). Table 2.2 describes each of these registers. Unlike the remaining internal registers, these four can be subdivided

TABLE 2.2 INTEL 8088 INTERNAL REGISTERS

Register	Description
Data	
AX	The Accumulator: This register can be used for general programming storage; however, it also is used in specific instructions involving multiplication and division, I/O, and string manipulation.
BX	The Base: This register is frequently used to hold address values when accessing memory. With the interrupt service routines it must be set in some cases to select options.
CX	The Count Register: During loop operations this register holds the count index.
DX	The Data Register: This register is used for general storage, as well as multiplication and division.
Segment	
CS	The Code Segment Register: This register points to the beginning of the segment where the program is located that is being executed.
DS	The Data Segment Register: This register points to the beginning of the data segment.
SS	The Stack Segment Register: This register points to the beginning of the stack segment.
ES	The Extra Segment Register: This register points to the beginning of the extra segment.
Pointer	
SP	The Stack Pointer: This register holds offset values for the stack in some instructions.
BP	The Base Pointer: This register is similar to SP. Some instructions require it to hold an offset.
Index	
SI	The Source Index: This register holds the source address for some instructions. Frequently these instructions have no operands.
DI	The Destination Index: This register is the counterpart to SI and holds the destination address for some instructions.

into higher and lower bytes. The higher and lower bytes of each data register are designated by reserved words. AH and AL designate the higher and lower bytes of AX; BH and BL, the higher and lower bytes of BX; CH and CL, the higher and lower bytes of CX; and DH and DL, the higher and lower bytes of DX. When the assembler encounters a register byte operand, such as AH, it treats the results of all operations associated with that operand as 8-bit quantities.

The next set of internal registers are the segment registers CS (Code Segment register), DS (Data Segment register), SS (Stack Segment register), and ES (Extra Segment register). These registers point to the beginning of segments. The segment registers require a full 16-bit word in all applications. The two pointer registers frequently are used to hold 16-bit offset values with SP (Stack Pointer) usually containing offsets in the stack segment. Similarly BP (Base Pointer) typically identifies the base address of the current stack frame (the stack established for the executing module).

Finally, the two index registers, SI (Source Index) and DI (Destination Index), generally hold the addresses for source and destination operands. Several string instructions require no operands because the source and destination are inferred from the address loaded in SI and DI. Typical of these instructions are MOVSB, MOVSW, STOSB, and STOSW which are move-string (byte or word) and store-string (byte or word) instructions. These instructions will be discussed later.

It is important to recognize that the internal registers are actual hardware entities. The assembler instructions act directly on these registers when they are referenced. This aspect of the assembler language is partially responsible for the speed with which instructions are executed. The assembler programmer interacts directly with the hardware. This is different from the higher-level language programmer who is never exposed to the effect his instructions have on the actual computer architecture.

The remaining two registers are the Instruction Pointer (IP) and the Flags register (sometimes referred to as the Status Flags register). The IP points to the location where the next instruction resides that is to be executed. The 8088 architecture contains two processors that handle instructions, a bus interface unit (BIU) that fetches instructions from memory and places them sequentially into a pipeline, and an execution unit (EU) that processes the instruction in the pipeline. The IP contains the address of the fetched instruction that is to be executed next by the EU. This instruction address is an offset and must be combined with the segment address in CS. In many respects, the IP is similar to the familiar Program Counter (PC) used in other assemblers. Usually, however, the PC is a register that points to an instruction to be fetched and executed. In the case of 8088, the IP contains the address of the next instruction that has already been fetched and is ready to be executed.

Table 2.3 illustrates the occupancy for the Flags register. There are nine flags. Eight are returned by DEBUG (the Trap Flag is not considered by the DEBUG program). DEBUG will be discussed in the next section and an example given for the first assembler illustration in subsection 2.3.1. The flags are very important because they provide information about operations, such as the result was zero. The Carry Flag (CF) is set when word addition or subtraction results in a carry or borrow. In the case of a subtraction, CF would be set if a borrow from the 16th bit

TABLE 2.3 THE INTEL 8088 FLAGS REGISTER

Flag			Debug	
Bit number	Designation	Description	S	O
0	CF	The Carry Flag: This flag is 1 if addition or subtraction results in a carry or borrow. It is also set with compares.	CY	NC
1	Not used	- -	—	—
2	PF	The Parity Flag: This flag is set if the result of a data operation has an even number of bits equal to 1.	PE	PO
3	Not used	- -	—	—
4	AF	The Auxiliary Carry Flag: This flag indicates a carry or borrow from the fourth bit in a byte. It is used with packed Binary Coded Decimal (BCD) arithmetic.	AC	NA
5	Not used	- -	—	—
6	ZF	The Zero Flag: This bit is set if the result of an operation is 0.	ZR	NZ
7	SF	The Sign Flag: This bit is set if the result of an operation on signed numbers is negative.	NG	PL
8	TF	The Trap Flag: When this bit is set the 8088 processes one instruction at a time.	—	—
9	IF	The Interrupt Enable Flag: When set this flag causes the 8088 to process interrupts.	EI	DI
10	DF	The Direction Flag: This flag, when set, causes decrement of the index registers following a string operation.	DN	UP
11	OF	The Overflow Flag: This flag is set when the result of an operation exceeds the available bit length of the destination operand.	OV	NV
12–15	Not used	- -	—	—

position occurred. Parity is one when the number of bits set to 1 in the result is even and zero when the number is odd. This flag is important to check for errors in data transfers. The Auxiliary Carry Flag (AF) indicates a carry or borrow has occurred from the fourth bit. Binary Coded Decimal (BCD) numbers pack two decimal integers, 0 through 9, into each nibble (4 bits) of a byte. When BCD arithmetic is used, AF must be monitored during addition and subtraction. The Zero Flag (ZF) is set when the result of an operation is zero. SF, the Sign Flag, is set when operations involving signed numbers result in a negative number. The Trap Flag (TF) allows single-step execution of a program. Interrupt Enable (IF) is a flag that indicates to the 8088 ALU that it should stop processing the current instructions, preserve existing accessed variables, the IP, and flags on the stack, and process an interrupt. The Direction Flag (DF) indicates movement forward (increment) or backward (decrement) of the index register during string processing. Finally, the Overflow Flag (OF) is set when the result of an operation exceeds the available word size.

   If these flags seem a little unclear at the present time, their usefulness will become clearer as we proceed. The advantage of observing flags and acting based on their

TABLE 2.4 ROUTINES USED WITH THE MACRO ASSEMBLER

Program	Description
Editor	The editor is a program that is used to create source code. IBM supplies EDLIN, a line editor, with DOS. More versatile screen editors are available commercially, and VEDIT (see text) is such an editor. Screen editors move a cursor inside a line of text and allow changes within a line. Line editors require that the entire line of text be replaced.
MASM (ASM)	MASM is the IBM Macro Assembler program. It requires 96K of RAM to load. The Small Assembler (ASM) has less capability than MASM (does not handle macros, for example) but loads in 64K. MASM is used to assemble the source code and produce an object code file as output. During normal operation, MASM will prompt the user to supply file names for the source file (extension .ASM), the object file to be generated (.OBJ), a list filename (with extension .LST), and a cross-reference filename (with extension .CRF).
LINK	The LINK program is used to link together various object modules that have been generated by MASM or other compilers. This routine assigns absolute memory locations to the relocatable object code. The linker provides for the development of modular code by allowing individual modules to be combined to yield a complete program. Each module can be separately debugged and then integrated.
DEBUG	The DEBUG program is useful during program development. This routine has features that, for example, allow the user to single-step through the program, dynamically examine how memory changes, observe the flags, execute the entire program from breakpoints, and monitor how registers change.

outcome during operation will begin to manifest itself when we note that certain instructions use the flag status to determine what action should be executed. For example, the jump-not-zero (JNZ) instruction makes use of the Zero Flag. If an earlier test of two numbers indicates that they are not equal, the zero flag is *not* set and the JNZ instruction will then execute, when encountered.

2.2.4 Routines Needed for Programming

The introductory assembler programmer will find that several programs are essential in addition to DOS. Table 2.4 lists these programs with brief descriptions. In the case of Editor, the user has a wide option. EDLIN constitutes the simple line editor that comes with DOS. While this is adequate, a more versatile screen editor like VEDIT [8] is generally preferred.

2.3 THE IBM MACRO ASSEMBLER LANGUAGE

No section of the book will be more useful for the introductory programmer than this one. Here we develop a beginning understanding of the principles behind Macro Assembler instructions. Very rapidly the reader will begin programming in assembler. In this section, an assembly program will be presented and observed using DEBUG to note the way in which registers and memory change during program execution.

The 8088 has 92 instruction types. In addition the Macro Assembler has over 48 pseudo-ops. IBM provides for a minimum of 256 interrupt types (many, of course, are not used). The DOS and BIOS have many entry points that provide the user with service routines to enhance his programs. This avoids the need to write elaborate code for accomplishing such tasks as moving the screen cursor or inputting data from the keyboard. These features are an indication of the flexibility available to the Macro Assembler programmer. As with learning any computer language, introductory assembler programmers must define subsets of the available language tools appropriate for their individual needs. This knowledge base will gradually broaden to include additional features. That is the approach taken in this book and particularly this section. We begin with some of the most basic and useful assembler components.

2.3.1 Program Structure

In subsection 2.2.1 we noted that the Macro Assembler can process up to four segment types. Each type, in turn, can consist of a number of defined segments. The minimum program complement requires one code segment and a stack segment. The assembler always looks for a stack segment and will respond with an error if the user forgets to include one. How does one indicate to the assembler that a segment is being defined? The SEGMENT pseudo-op must be employed.

Pseudo-ops provide the programmer with a means of telling the assembler what it must do to set up and structure the machine language code. This machine code is based on instructions and data included in the source program. Pseudo-ops do not result in machine instructions. There are four operational types of pseudo-ops: data (SEGMENT is included in this type), conditional branches, macros, and listings. The SEGMENT pseudo-op has the following format:

segname SEGMENT align-type combine-type 'class'

Table 2.5 defines each of the parameters appearing in the segment definition above. Each segment must end with the following statement:

segname ENDS

Figure 2.1 illustrates a program with two segments defined, a stack segment and a code segment (with segment names STACK and CSEG, respectively). Both are of align-type PARA. The stack segment has combine-type STACK and the code segment is of combine-type PUBLIC. These are of 'class': 'STACK' and 'CODE', respectively, for the stack and code segments. Six other pseudo-ops appear in this program, PAGE (listing pseudo-op), TITLE (listing pseudo-op), COMMENT (data pseudo-op), DB (data pseudo-op), ASSUME (data pseudo-op), and END (data pseudo-op). Only END, DB, and ASSUME are required. The form of the END pseudo-op is

END   expression

TABLE 2.5 SEGMENT PSEUDO-OP PARAMETERS

Parameter	Description
segname	This is the name of the SEGMENT.
align-type	This parameter indicates to the assembler how the segment begins in memory. There are four types. 1. PARA This align-type is the default value and indicates that the segment begins on a paragraph boundary (address divisible by 16). 2. BYTE The segment can begin at any memory location. 3. WORD The segment must begin on a word boundary (an even address). 4. PAGE The segment must begin on a page boundary (the last eight bits of the address are zero).
combine-type	This parameter indicates how the segment is to be combined or loaded when linked. There are five types. 1. PUBLIC All segments with the same name that are public will be chained together. 2. COMMON All segments with the same name will begin at the same address and overlap. 3. AT(exp) This type is used to allow variables to be defined at fixed offsets in memory. The segment is located at the paragraph number evaluated from "exp." 4. STACK This type specifies that the segment is part of the stack. 5. MEMORY All segments of this type will be located at higher addresses than any other segments.
'class'	The class parameter is used to refer to a collection of segments. Segments with the same class name are located sequentially in memory based on the order the linker encounters them.

Here the expression is optional and must identify the starting address of the source program. If several modules are linked together, only the main module can specify this address. The PAGE pseudo-op sets the length and width of the page. This operation affects the listing file generated during assembly. The pseudo-op has the form

PAGE   operand1,operand2

The entry in operand1 indicates the number of vertical lines per page in the assembler listing (one of the output files from the assembly process). For the example in Figure 2.1 this has been selected as 50 (the default value is 66). Operand2 is the number of characters per line in the listing. The default number of characters per line is 80, and in the example, 132 has been selected.

The TITLE pseudo-op specifies the title on the first line of each assembler listing page. Spaced throughout the program are semicolons. These allow comments to be inserted. Another technique for commenting in the program is the COMMENT pseudo-op. The first non-blank character (in Figure 2.1 this is an asterisk) following the COMMENT is used as a delimiter. All characters between these delimiters will be

```
PAGE 50,132
TITLE FIRASM - FIRST ASSEMBLER PROGRAM (FIRASM.ASM)
COMMENT *

                DESCRIPTION: This module clears AX to 0
                and moves 18 into AX.  Next it subtracts
                18 from AX.  All operations are to be
                observed using DEBUG. *
;
;
STACK   SEGMENT PARA STACK 'STACK'                          ────── STACK SEGMENT
;                                                                  DEFINED
;       The stack segment will be cleared and loaded with
;       a string: 64 values of 'stack    '.
;
        DB      64 DUP ('STACK   ')
STACK   ENDS
CSEG    SEGMENT PARA PUBLIC 'CODE'                          ────── CODE SEGMENT
        ASSUME CS:CSEG,SS:STACK                                    DEFINED
;
        SUB AX,AX
        MOV AX,18D
        SUB AX,18D
;
CSEG    ENDS
        END
```

Figure 2.1　The representative program, FIRASM.ASM, which is designed to be run with DEBUG .

treated as comment text and will be ignored during assembly. Another pseudo-op appearing in Figure 2.1 is the data pseudo-op, DB, which has the form

[variable-name]   DB   expression

This pseudo-op defines a variable or initializes storage. The expression

DB 64 DUP('STACK   ')

generates the first 64 repetitions of the character string 'STACK   '. The pseudo-op DB stands for define byte. The expression "[variable-name]" is optional depending on whether or not "expression" is assigned a symbolic value.

We have also used the ASSUME pseudo-op in the program for Figure 2.1. This pseudo-op has the form

ASSUME segment register:segment name, ...

In Figure 2.1 the Code Segment register, CS, is associated with the segment name CSEG. Similarly, the Stack Segment register is associated with the segment name STACK. This statement effectively tells the assembler which segment register a given segment belongs to.

There are three Macro Assembler instructions appearing in the program illustrated in Figure 2.1. Before discussing these instructions, let us consider the general instruction format.

[label]   Instruction Mnemonic   [Operand]   [; Comment]

This format has four fields. All but the instruction mnemonic are optional depending on the instruction type. The label field is frequently used as an entry or return point. Its address represents an identity that may be referenced by other instructions. This symbolic name is the starting location for the instruction and may be up to 31 characters long. Any upper or lower case alphabetic letter, numeric digit (0 through 9) or character in the set ?.@_$ can be used in a label. However, the label must begin with a character other than a digit.

During our discussion of segments we did not address the distance attributes associated with a segment. There are two attributes, NEAR, which corresponds to a label or procedure reference within the same segment, and FAR, which corresponds to a label or procedure reference outside the current segment. With NEAR references only the IP changes, whereas, for FAR references both the IP and Code Segment register (CS) change. The label appearing in the instruction should be followed by a colon if it is referenced only from within the present Code segment (NEAR attribute). For FAR references, the label is used without a colon suffix. The programmer must keep track of references to the label or procedure and determine whether these references are NEAR or FAR. If a procedure is defined with a new code segment and called from another code segment it is FAR. Labels called from outside the existing code segment, as a FAR procedure is, should be treated as FAR.

The comment field is optional and any text must be preceded by a semicolon. This field is similar to the COMMENT pseudo-op except it occurs on the instruction line. In Figure 2.1 comments have been included and they occur as line extensions. The program appearing in Figure 2.1 was ordered to demonstrate the clear demarcation between pseudo-ops and instructions.

The Instruction Mnemonic field must contain one of the 92 instructions. Two instruction types occur in Figure 2.1, the move instruction, MOV, and the subtraction instruction, SUB. These instructions are

SUB AX,AX
MOV AX,18D
SUB AX,18D

The form of the subtraction instruction is

SUB destination, source

In the program, the content of AX (the source) is subtracted from itself (the destination) and the result (zero) stored in the destination (AX).

The assembler uses register addressing when the subtraction instruction is executed. That is, the assembler fetches the operand from the AX register directly and performs the subtraction. In the case of the second instruction,

MOV AX,18D

the assembler uses immediate addressing to move the decimal constant 18 into AX. (The D in 18D denotes decimal value and is optional.) This is a form of the To Register FROM Immediate-Data MOV instruction encoding. The last instruction merely subtracts 18 from the contents of AX and stores the resultant zero in AX. In subsection 2.3.2, forms of addressing will be considered and examples given. The two methods used above, register and immediate addressing, are among the simplest.

The order of the program appearing in Figure 2.1 was spaced to make it readable. All fields in instructions must be separated by at least one blank character. Figure 2.2 presents the sequence of commands and responses needed to assemble and link the program appearing in Figure 2.1. The source file in Figure 2.2 is FIRASM.ASM, the program in Figure 2.1. Since this program does not return to DOS, it must be run with DEBUG. Once the notion of how to run an assembler program has been demonstrated, a few additional instructions will be included to insure the normal return to DOS.

Figure 2.3 shows the output for the assembler list file, FIRASM.LST. Compressed print is used to illustrate the output for a full 132 character line. Page

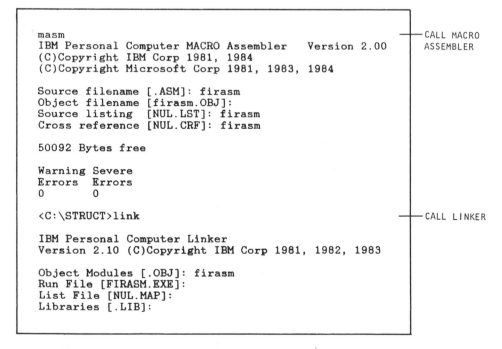

```
masm                                                        CALL MACRO
IBM Personal Computer MACRO Assembler     Version 2.00      ASSEMBLER
(C)Copyright IBM Corp 1981, 1984
(C)Copyright Microsoft Corp 1981, 1983, 1984

Source filename [.ASM]: firasm
Object filename [firasm.OBJ]:
Source listing  [NUL.LST]: firasm
Cross reference [NUL.CRF]: firasm

50092 Bytes free

Warning Severe
Errors  Errors
0       0

<C:\STRUCT>link                                             CALL LINKER

IBM Personal Computer Linker
Version 2.10 (C)Copyright IBM Corp 1981, 1982, 1983

Object Modules [.OBJ]: firasm
Run File [FIRASM.EXE]:
List File [NUL.MAP]:
Libraries [.LIB]:
```

Figure 2.2   A sample session with the Macro Assembler (MASM) and the linker (LINK).

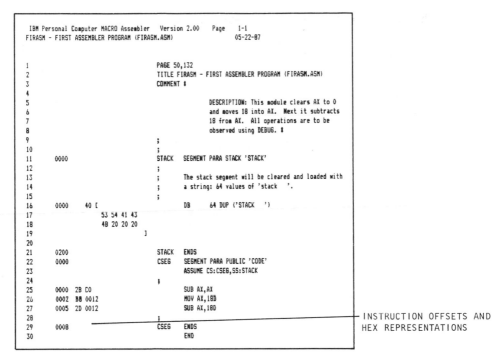

```
IBM Personal Computer MACRO Assembler    Version 2.00    Page    1-1
FIRASM - FIRST ASSEMBLER PROGRAM (FIRASM.ASM)                    05-22-87


  1                                    PAGE 50,132
  2                                    TITLE FIRASM - FIRST ASSEMBLER PROGRAM (FIRASM.ASM)
  3                                    COMMENT #
  4
  5                                              DESCRIPTION: This module clears AX to 0
  6                                              and moves 18 into AX.  Next it subtracts
  7                                              18 from AX.  All operations are to be
  8                                              observed using DEBUG. #
  9                                    ;
 10                                    ;
 11    0000                   STACK    SEGMENT PARA STACK 'STACK'
 12                                    ;
 13                                    ;   The stack segment will be cleared and loaded with
 14                                    ;   a string: 64 values of 'stack   '.
 15                                    ;
 16    0000   40 [                     DB      64 DUP ('STACK   ')
 17           53 54 41 43
 18           4B 20 20 20
 19                     ]
 20
 21    0200                   STACK    ENDS
 22    0000                   CSEG     SEGMENT PARA PUBLIC 'CODE'
 23                                    ASSUME CS:CSEG,SS:STACK
 24                                    #
 25    0000  2B C0                     SUB AX,AX
 26    0002  B8 0012                   MOV AX,18D
 27    0005  2D 0012                   SUB AX,18D
 28                                    ;
 29    0008                   CSEG     ENDS
 30                                    END
```

INSTRUCTION OFFSETS AND
HEX REPRESENTATIONS

Figure 2.3 The assembler list file output for FIRASM.ASM. This listing uses compressed print to encompass the full 132 character line.

numbering and titling are present and allowance for 132 characters per line is made. The far left-hand side simply lists output line numbers for reference. The next column of numbers contains the hexadecimal offset (from zero) for each parameter or instruction appearing in the listing. We start with the definition of the stack segment beginning at 0000H. Since pseudo-ops are not assembled, this segment actually begins with the first byte(s) of the define byte pseudo-op. The character string STACK followed by three blanks has been duplicated 64 times in the stack segment for a total of 512 bytes (200H). These characters are indicated by their ASCII equivalence: S = 53H, T = 54H.... The offset for the last byte is 01FFH. This offset is followed by 0200H, the offset for the end of the segment. Next we have the offset for the beginning of the code segment, 0000H. Each instruction occupies one or more bytes. At offset 0000H in the code segment the instruction SUB AX,AX appears. The next offset, for the MOV AX,18D instruction, is 0002H indicating that the subtraction instruction in the previous line is two bytes long (bytes 0000H and 0001H). The last two instructions are three bytes each.

The third column of the list file contains machine representations for the assembled code. Returning to the three assembler instructions, the first (SUB AX,AX) has the machine code

2B C0

What does this representation mean? The reader must refer to IBM's Macro Assembler manual under the subtract instruction encoding in order to understand this representation. The encoding indicated for "register operand and register operand" is

001010dw modregr/m

Since the destination is a register, d = 1. Similarly, the instruction involves word operands; so w = 1. Thus, the first machine code byte is

00101011 = 2BH

The second machine code byte is given by the expression "modregr/m" (see the Macro Assembler manual for a discussion of these parameters). In our case

1. mod = 11, because the register/memory field (r/m) is a register field (AX).
2. reg = 000, because the 16-bit AX register is used in both operands.
3. r/m = 000, because the effective address is equal to zero and so are BX, SI, and the displacement.

Thus,

modregr/m = 11000000 = COH

The remaining instructions may be similarly decoded.

In general, these machine codes are tedious and working with them is unnecessary. This brief discussion is intended only to demonstrate the structure of the list file.

The next region in the print-out illustrates what has been put in memory. In this case the stack region has 64 (40H) repetitions of the bytes:

53 54 41 43 4B 20 20 20

A look at the ASCII equivalence in hexadecimal shows that these bytes spell the word STACK followed by three blanks (see Chapter 6). The rest of the figure contains a source code listing and segment table, which is self-explanatory.

Figure 2.4 is a typical DEBUG session using the assembled and linked program, FIRASM.EXE. In this session only three DEBUG commands are used.

1. Trace (T)—Executes one or more instructions beginning at the current instruction pointer address (CS:IP).
2. Dump (D)—Displays memory beginning at the specified (segment:offset).
3. Quit (Q)—Terminates DEBUG.

The form of the Trace command lists all registers, the instruction pointer contents, the 8 flags mentioned earlier, and the current segment and offset address, as well as the next instruction. The first use of Trace executes the instruction at CS:0000, which, in

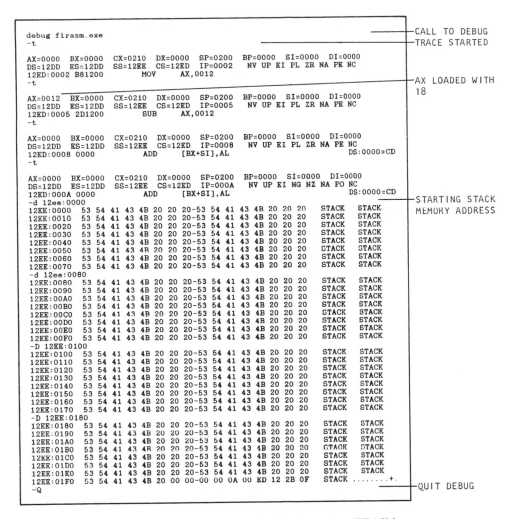

Figure 2.4 A representative DEBUG session for the program FIRASM.

this program, insures that AX is cleared. From the figure it is evident that the code segment begins at 12ED:0000. The code segment address, 12ED, will vary with the system being used. All DEBUG addresses are specific to the author's computer; however, indicated offsets should be similar to other users' computers. The MOV AX,18D instruction is at 12ED:0002 and when executed puts 18(0012H) in the AX register (note how the IP changes). Finally, the SUB AX,18D instruction is executed to once again clear AX. The remaining Trace printout is meaningless because we have not allowed the program to terminate properly. Finally, we have used the Dump command to examine stack memory beginning at SS:0000. The far right-hand side shows the contents of these locations in ASCII. Note that the last six bytes of stack memory have been altered by the program.

In summary, this subsection introduced several pseudo-ops and instructions that provided the basis for a simple Macro Assembler program. This program

(Figure 2.1) was assembled and run using DEBUG. While the program, in itself, only manipulated the AX register it is functional, simple, and illustrates the main features of how to set up and execute an assembly language program. It is assumed that the reader is familiar with the DOS command structure. In Figure 2.2 both MASM and LINK are executed from drive A. These commands are indicated in the figures so that the reader can see how the routines were actually executed.

2.3.2 Addressing

This subsection will introduce the addressing modes available with the IBM PC Macro Assembler. The terminology will seem familiar for those users of other assemblers. For the beginning assembler programmer, the methods of addressing used in instructions may at first appear numerous, but each has a specific utility.

The program illustrated in Figure 2.5 is intended to demonstrate additional features of the language. Earlier we discussed the need for providing a normal return to DOS. The sample program illustrates how to accomplish this. The concept of procedures is introduced and provides a convenient mechanism for achieving a FAR return to DOS. DOS routines exist in a segment outside the user's code segment; hence, this FAR return is required.

The program in Figure 2.5 presents five of the seven basic addressing modes. Register and immediate addressing have already been discussed. In this program a data segment is included to provide a basis for presenting the addressing techniques. The Define Word (DW) pseudo-op is used to initialize variables. Table 2.6 describes the Intel 8088 addressing techniques and uses instruction sequences from the program. In order to see how this addressing takes place, consider Figures 2.6 and 2.7. Figure 2.6 is the assembler listing and it is apparent that the offsets for variables DDDD through DDDU occupy addresses 0000H through 0013H, respectively.

When discussing the normal return to DOS, it should be pointed out that the Data Segment register (DS) is loaded with the Program Segment Prefix (PSP) address during the interrupt from DOS to the user program [9]. To access the data segment, DS must be reloaded with the address of the beginning of the data segment. The code segment instructions

```
MOV AX,SEG DATA
MOV DS,AX
```

accomplish this operation. The operator SEG determines the segment address for DATA (the data segment start address). Thus, the first instruction loads the data segment address into AX. The second instruction places this address in DS. If these instructions are not performed, DS will continue to contain the PSP address and calls to data segment variables will go to the wrong address. We must, however, save the PSP address (segment and offset) on the stack so that when the FAR return from the procedure START takes place, with execution of RET, this return can access the stack for the PSP address.

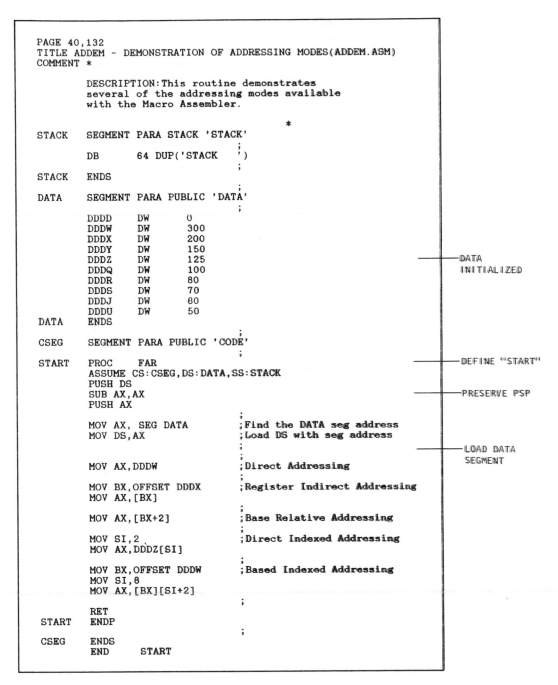

```
PAGE 40,132
TITLE ADDEM - DEMONSTRATION OF ADDRESSING MODES(ADDEM.ASM)
COMMENT *

        DESCRIPTION:This routine demonstrates
        several of the addressing modes available
        with the Macro Assembler.
                                              *
STACK   SEGMENT PARA STACK 'STACK'
                            ;
        DB      64 DUP('STACK   ')
                            ;
STACK   ENDS
                            ;
DATA    SEGMENT PARA PUBLIC 'DATA'
                            ;
        DDDD    DW      0
        DDDW    DW      300
        DDDX    DW      200
        DDDY    DW      150
        DDDZ    DW      125                              ────DATA
        DDDQ    DW      100                                  INITIALIZED
        DDDR    DW      80
        DDDS    DW      70
        DDDJ    DW      60
        DDDU    DW      50
DATA    ENDS
                            ;
CSEG    SEGMENT PARA PUBLIC 'CODE'
                            ;
START   PROC    FAR                                  ────DEFINE "START"
        ASSUME CS:CSEG,DS:DATA,SS:STACK
        PUSH DS
        SUB AX,AX                                    ────PRESERVE PSP
        PUSH AX
                            ;
        MOV AX, SEG DATA    ;Find the DATA seg address
        MOV DS,AX           ;Load DS with seg address
                            ;
                            ;                            ────LOAD DATA
        MOV AX,DDDW         ;Direct Addressing               SEGMENT
                            ;
        MOV BX,OFFSET DDDX  ;Register Indirect Addressing
        MOV AX,[BX]
                            ;
        MOV AX,[BX+2]       ;Base Relative Addressing
                            ;
        MOV SI,2            ;Direct Indexed Addressing
        MOV AX,DDDZ[SI]
                            ;
        MOV BX,OFFSET DDDW  ;Based Indexed Addressing
        MOV SI,8
        MOV AX,[BX][SI+2]
                            ;
        RET
START   ENDP
                            ;
CSEG    ENDS
        END     START
```

Figure 2.5   The program ADDEM.ASM, which illustrates five of the seven addressing modes.

TABLE 2.6 INTEL 8088 ADDRESSING MODES

Address mode	Comments
Immediate	The user specifies a byte or word constant for the source operand. This constant is assembled as part of the instruction. For example <div align="center">MOV AX,18D</div>loads 18 into the AX register.
Register	In this form of addressing, the operand is fetched from or loaded into a register. The instruction <div align="center">SUB AX,AX</div>is an example of register addressing where the Execution Unit (EU) fetches the operand from AX, fetches the destination from AX, and the ALU performs the subtract.
Direct	With this addressing, the Effective Address (EA) that the EU calculates for a memory location is contained in the instruction. This offset is added to the DS register to obtain the 20-bit address. An example would be <div align="center">MOV AX,DDDW .</div>
Register Indirect	In this case the EA is contained in BX, BP, SI, or DI. Since these are registers they must be placed in square brackets to avoid confusion with the normal register addressing mode. The EA denotes an address, not the contents of a memory location. Hence, the above registers must contain an address at the time they are used. A technique for achieving this is to use the OFFSET operator <div align="center">MOV BX, OFFSET DDDX .</div>Register indirect addressing can then be used to load the contents of the location addressed by BX into, say, AX: <div align="center">MOV AX, [BX] .</div>
Base Relative	Using base relative addressing, the EA for the operand is obtained by adding a displacement to either the BX or BP register. These registers are assumed to contain an offset address. Typically the base relative addressing scheme could be used as follows: <div align="center">MOV AX, [BX+2] .</div>
Direct Indexed	Here the EA is the sum of an index register (SI or DI) and an offset. A typical sequence of instructions would be to load the index register with an address and then combine this with a memory location. <div align="center">MOV SI,2 MOV AX,DDDZ [SI] .</div>In this example the contents of the location whose address is that of DDDZ plus 2 is loaded into AX.
Base Indexed	The EA is the sum of a base register (BX), an index register (SI or DI), and an offset (optional). A typical sequence might be <div align="center">MOV BX, OFFSET DDDW MOV SI, 8 MOV AX, [BX] [SI+2] .</div>

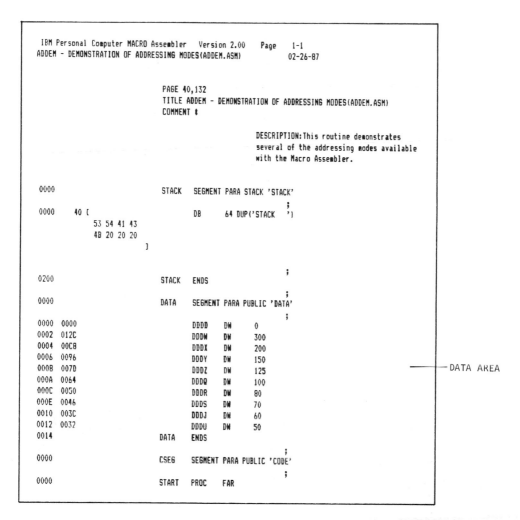

```
IBM Personal Computer MACRO Assembler   Version 2.00    Page   1-1
ADDEM - DEMONSTRATION OF ADDRESSING MODES(ADDEM.ASM)          02-26-87


                              PAGE 40,132
                              TITLE ADDEM - DEMONSTRATION OF ADDRESSING MODES(ADDEM.ASM)
                              COMMENT 8

                                        DESCRIPTION:This routine demonstrates
                                        several of the addressing modes available
                                        with the Macro Assembler.


0000                   STACK   SEGMENT PARA STACK 'STACK'
                                                          ;
0000    40 [              DB      64 DUP('STACK   ')
        53 54 41 43
        4B 20 20 20
                   ]

                                                          ;
0200                   STACK   ENDS
                                                          ;
0000                   DATA    SEGMENT PARA PUBLIC 'DATA'
                                                          ;
0000 0000                      DDDD    DW      0
0002 012C                      DDDW    DW      300
0004 00C8                      DDDX    DW      200
0006 0096                      DDDY    DW      150
000B 007D                      DDDZ    DW      125
000A 0064                      DDDQ    DW      100
000C 0050                      DDDR    DW      80
000E 0046                      DDDS    DW      70
0010 003C                      DDDJ    DW      60
0012 0032                      DDDU    DW      50
0014                   DATA    ENDS
                                                          ;
0000                   CSEG    SEGMENT PARA PUBLIC 'CODE'
                                                          ;
0000                   START   PROC    FAR
```

DATA AREA

Figure 2.6 The assembler listing file for ADDEM.ASM. This listing uses compressed print for the 132-character line.

```
        IBM Personal Computer MACRO Assembler   Version 2.00    Page   1-2
        ADDEM - DEMONSTRATION OF ADDRESSING MODES(ADDEM.ASM)         02-26-87


                                    ASSUME CS:CSEG,DS:DATA,SS:STACK
        0000  1E                    PUSH DS
        0001  2B C0                 SUB AX,AX
        0003  50                    PUSH AX
                                                           ;
        0004  BB ---- R             MOV AX, SEG DATA       ;Find the DATA seg address
        0007  8E D8                 MOV DS,AX              ;Load DS with seg address
                                                           ;
                                                           ;
        0009  A1 0002 R             MOV AX,DDDW            ;Direct Addressing
                                                           ;
        000C  BB 0004 R             MOV BX,OFFSET DDDX     ;Register Indirect Addressing
        000F  8B 07                 MOV AX,[BX]
                                                           ;
        0011  8B 47 02              MOV AX,[BX+2]          ;Base Relative Addressing
                                                           ;
        0014  BE 0002               MOV SI,2              ;Direct Indexed Addressing
        0017  8B 84 0008 R          MOV AX,DDDZ[SI]
                                                           ;
        001B  BB 0002 R             MOV BX,OFFSET DDDW     ;Based Indexed Addressing
        001E  BE 000B               MOV SI,8
        0021  8B 40 02              MOV AX,[BX][SI+2]
                                                           ;
        0024  CB                    RET
        0025          START         ENDP
                                                           ;
        0025          CSEG          ENDS
                                    END      START
```

Figure 2.6 (*Continued*)

Figure 2.7 is a sample session using DEBUG. The program ADDEM (Figure 2.5) has been assembled and linked. The run file, ADDEM.EXE, is input to the DEBUG routine. Using the Trace command, we execute the first three instructions. The reader should note that the DS register contains the PSP address 12DDH. The

MOV AX,SEG DATA

instruction assembles as

MOV AX,12F0

The quantity 12F0H is the address of the data segment (offset 0000H). Using the Dump command (D), we list the first 128 bytes starting with 12DD:0000. This contains the Program Segment Prefix. Next we list the first 128 bytes of the data segment. The reader can verify that addresses 12F0:0000 through 12F0:00013 contain the initialized data variable values for DDDD through DDDU.

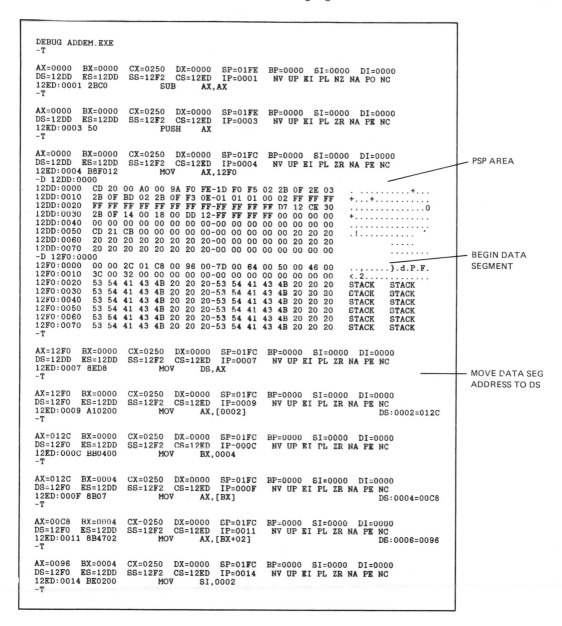

```
DEBUG ADDEM.EXE
-T

AX=0000  BX=0000  CX=0250  DX=0000  SP=01FE  BP=0000  SI=0000  DI=0000
DS=12DD  ES=12DD  SS=12F2  CS=12ED  IP=0001  NV UP EI PL NZ NA PO NC
12ED:0001 2BC0           SUB     AX,AX
-T

AX=0000  BX=0000  CX=0250  DX=0000  SP=01FE  BP=0000  SI=0000  DI=0000
DS=12DD  ES=12DD  SS=12F2  CS=12ED  IP=0003  NV UP EI PL ZR NA PE NC
12ED:0003 50             PUSH    AX
-T

AX=0000  BX=0000  CX=0250  DX=0000  SP=01FC  BP=0000  SI=0000  DI=0000
DS=12DD  ES=12DD  SS=12F2  CS=12ED  IP=0004  NV UP EI PL ZR NA PE NC
12ED:0004 B8F012         MOV     AX,12F0
-D 12DD:0000
12DD:0000  CD 20 00 A0 00 9A F0 FE-1D F0 F5 02 2B 0F 2E 03   . . . . . . . . . . +. . .
12DD:0010  2B 0F BD 02 2B 0F F3 0E-01 01 01 00 02 FF FF FF   +. . .+. . . . . . . . . .
12DD:0020  FF FF FF FF FF FF FF FF-FF FF FF FF D7 12 CE 30   . . . . . . . . . . . . . . . 0
12DD:0030  2B 0F 14 00 18 00 DD 12-FF FF FF FF 00 00 00 00   +. . . . . . . . . . . . . . .
12DD:0040  00 00 00 00 00 00 00 00-00 00 00 00 00 00 00 00   . . . . . . . . . . . . . . . .
12DD:0050  CD 21 CB 00 00 00 00 00-00 00 00 00 00 20 20 20   .!. . . . . . . . . . . .
12DD:0060  20 20 20 20 20 20 20 20-00 00 00 00 00 20 20 20       . . . . .
12DD:0070  20 20 20 20 20 20 20 20-00 00 00 00 00 00 00 00       . . . . . . . .
-D 12F0:0000
12F0:0000  00 00 2C 01 C8 00 96 00-7D 00 64 00 50 00 46 00   . . ,. . . . . }. d. P. F.
12F0:0010  3C 00 32 00 00 00 00 00-00 00 00 00 00 00 00 00   <. 2. . . . . . . . . .
12F0:0020  53 54 41 43 4B 20 20 20-53 54 41 43 4B 20 20 20   STACK    STACK
12F0:0030  53 54 41 43 4B 20 20 20-53 54 41 43 4B 20 20 20   STACK    STACK
12F0:0040  53 54 41 43 4B 20 20 20-53 54 41 43 4B 20 20 20   STACK    STACK
12F0:0050  53 54 41 43 4B 20 20 20-53 54 41 43 4B 20 20 20   STACK    STACK
12F0:0060  53 54 41 43 4B 20 20 20-53 54 41 43 4B 20 20 20   STACK    STACK
12F0:0070  53 54 41 43 4B 20 20 20-53 54 41 43 4B 20 20 20   STACK    STACK
-T

AX=12F0  BX=0000  CX=0250  DX=0000  SP=01FC  BP=0000  SI=0000  DI=0000
DS=12DD  ES=12DD  SS=12F2  CS=12ED  IP=0007  NV UP EI PL ZR NA PE NC
12ED:0007 8ED8           MOV     DS,AX
-T

AX=12F0  BX=0000  CX=0250  DX=0000  SP=01FC  BP=0000  SI=0000  DI=0000
DS=12F0  ES=12DD  SS=12F2  CS=12ED  IP=0009  NV UP EI PL ZR NA PE NC
12ED:0009 A10200         MOV     AX,[0002]                         DS:0002=012C
-T

AX=012C  BX=0000  CX=0250  DX=0000  SP=01FC  BP=0000  SI=0000  DI=0000
DS=12F0  ES=12DD  SS=12F2  CS=12ED  IP=000C  NV UP EI PL ZR NA PE NC
12ED:000C BB0400         MOV     BX,0004
-T

AX=012C  BX=0004  CX=0250  DX=0000  SP=01FC  BP=0000  SI=0000  DI=0000
DS=12F0  ES=12DD  SS=12F2  CS=12ED  IP=000F  NV UP EI PL ZR NA PE NC
12ED:000F 8B07           MOV     AX,[BX]                           DS:0004=00C8
-T

AX=00C8  BX=0004  CX=0250  DX=0000  SP=01FC  BP=0000  SI=0000  DI=0000
DS=12F0  ES=12DD  SS=12F2  CS=12ED  IP=0011  NV UP EI PL ZR NA PE NC
12ED:0011 8B4702         MOV     AX,[BX+02]                        DS:0006=0096
-T

AX=0096  BX=0004  CX=0250  DX=0000  SP=01FC  BP=0000  SI=0000  DI=0000
DS=12F0  ES=12DD  SS=12F2  CS=12ED  IP=0014  NV UP EI PL ZR NA PE NC
12ED:0014 BE0200         MOV     SI,0002
-T
```

PSP AREA

BEGIN DATA SEGMENT

MOVE DATA SEG ADDRESS TO DS

Figure 2.7   A typical DEBUG session with the program ADDEM.

```
AX=0096  BX=0004  CX=0250  DX=0000  SP=01FC  BP=0000  SI=0002  DI=0000
DS=12F0  ES=12DD  SS=12F2  CS=12ED  IP=0017     NV UP EI PL ZR NA PE NC
12ED:0017 8B840800       MOV     AX,[SI+0008]                     DS:000A=0064
-T

AX=0064  BX=0004  CX=0250  DX=0000  SP=01FC  BP=0000  SI=0002  DI=0000
DS=12F0  ES=12DD  SS=12F2  CS=12ED  IP=001B     NV UP EI PL ZR NA PE NC
12ED:001B BB0200         MOV     BX,0002
-T

AX=0064  BX=0002  CX=0250  DX=0000  SP=01FC  BP=0000  SI=0002  DI=0000
DS=12F0  ES=12DD  SS=12F2  CS=12ED  IP=001E     NV UP EI PL ZR NA PE NC
12ED:001E BE0800         MOV     SI,0008
-T

AX=0064  BX=0002  CX=0250  DX=0000  SP=01FC  BP=0000  SI=0008  DI=0000
DS=12F0  ES=12DD  SS=12F2  CS=12ED  IP=0021     NV UP EI PL ZR NA PE NC
12ED:0021 8B4002         MOV     AX,[BX+SI+02]                    DS:000C=0050
-T

AX=0050  BX=0002  CX=0250  DX=0000  SP=01FC  BP=0000  SI=0008  DI=0000
DS=12F0  ES=12DD  SS=12F2  CS=12ED  IP=0024     NV UP EI PL ZR NA PE NC
12ED:0024 CB            RETF                                      ⟵── FAR RETURN TO
-T                                                                     DOS

AX=0050  BX=0002  CX=0250  DX=0000  SP=0200  BP=0000  SI=0008  DI=0000
DS=12F0  ES=12DD  SS=12F2  CS=12DD  IP=0000     NV UP EI PL ZR NA PE NC
12DD:0000 CD20          INT     20
-Q
```

Figure 2.7 *(Continued)*

The instruction

MOV AX,DDDW

uses direct addressing and assembles as

MOV AX,[0002]

To the right of this instruction is the symbol DS:0002 = 012C. This means that address DS:0002 contains 012C hexadecimal or 300 decimal. The next execution of Trace loads AX with 012CH. This instruction implicitly assumes that the DDDW variable has segment address DS. If DS is loaded with an incorrect segment address, the AX register will receive whatever is at that address with offset 0002.

The reader can examine the DEBUG printout to see how registers and memory are affected for each of the remaining address examples. Let us consider based indexed addressing from Figure 2.7 as an illustration. The instruction sequence is

MOV BX,OFFSET DDDW
MOV SI,8
MOV AX,[BX][SI+2]

The offset for DDDW is 0002H and the first instruction above is assembled as

MOV BX,0002

Note that the BX register changes from 0004H to 0002H when this instruction is executed. The instruction

MOV SI,8

assembles as

MOV SI,0008

When executed using Trace, this instruction loads SI. Finally, the instruction

MOV AX,[BX][SI+2]

assembles as

MOV AX,[BX+SI+02]

which is an alternate form. The total offset above is

$$0002H \ (BX) + 0008D(SI) + 2D = 000CH$$

This address contains DDDR which is equal to 0050H. When this instruction is executed, 0050H is loaded into AX.

We have discussed the need for a normal return to DOS. The program in Figure 2.1 fails to accomplish this and will hang the system. The program in Figure 2.5 returns to DOS at the end of its execution. Once the user has initialized DOS and the disk drive prompt is returned, the program can be run by merely typing the run file name. At this point the program takes over and executes. Table 2.7 illustrates the status for important registers at entry and exit from the user's program.

The user must insure that, at exit, the CS register contains the Program Segment Prefix address and IP = 0000. The Program Segment Prefix area contains a number of DOS parameters, addresses and the DOS interrupt 20H. This interrupt is serviced when the user causes DOS to stop executing. The location of this interrupt has an offset of 0000H. From the table it is evident that upon entry to a user routine, DOS

TABLE 2.7 PARTIAL REGISTER STATUS ENTERING AND LEAVING USER PROGRAM

Register	Status
At Entry	
CS	This register contains the address of the user program entry point.
IP	This register equals 0000, the entry point offset.
SP	This register equals 200H, the top of the stack offset.
SS	This register contains the segment address for the stack segment.
DS	This register contains the segment address for the Program Segment Prefix area.
ES	This register is initialized the same as DS.
At Exit	
CS	This register must contain the segment address for the Program Segment Prefix area.
SS	This register value must be the same as at entry.

loads the segment address of the Program Segment Prefix into DS. This must be preserved so that at exit DOS can be resumed. There are several ways in which this address can be saved and recalled. The approach taken in this book is to use the automatic features of the return, RET, instruction to reset the Program Segment Prefix address. The procedure pseudo-op is needed to do this.

Procedures are very useful for organizing and minimizing program code. The procedure pseudo-op, PROC, is a data type and has the following form:

```
            procedure name PROC NEAR

(or

            procedure name PROC FAR)



                    . . .


                    RET


                    . . .


                    RET


            procedure name ENDP
```

The NEAR attribute is optional. Return instructions must be included for each exit point. The procedure must end with ENDP. Figure 2.5 illustrated the use of a procedure named START. This procedure contained all executable statements in the program. It is a FAR procedure because it will eventually return to DOS.

When the procedure is called, the address contained in DS is placed on the stack using the PUSH instruction. This is the PSP segment address. Next the AX register is set equal to 0000H and pushed onto the stack.

```
                    PUSH DS
                    SUB AX,AX
                    PUSH AX
```

This instruction sequence loads the stack with the needed address to define the Program Segment Prefix area start address. Upon returning from the procedure, the RET instruction will restore this address by automatically loading the first stack word (0000H) into the IP and the second stack word (DS address) into CS. For NEAR returns, only the offset is loaded. In Figure 2.7 the return restores CS:offset to 12DD:0000. This produces the normal DOS return, which is INT 20H. The first memory dump in Figure 2.7 begins at 12DD:0000 and indicates what is in this PSP area (see *DOS Technical Reference*). Attempting to write over this area will cause the return to fail.

2.4 THE IBM 8086-BASED MICROCOMPUTER SOFTWARE ENVIRONMENT

Section 2.2 introduced the IBM 8088-based software environment for the IBM PC and XT. Section 2.3, discussed the actual Macro Assembler language implementation in an introductory fashion intended to quickly provide the reader with the capability of executing assembler programs. We now return to the remaining microprocessors that are used in the IBM microcomputer family. This section briefly delineates the 8086-based microcomputer software environment, which represents an enhancement over the 8088 systems. Then the 80286 and 80386 systems are discussed.

The Personal System/2 Model 30 employs the Intel 8086 microprocessor as its CPU. The 8086 has several distinct advantages over the 8088. First, it usually obtains two bytes per Bus Interface Unit (BIU) operation (fetch). (The BIU is the element in the 8086 that loads instructions and operands for processing.) Second, the 8086 has a 16-bit data bus. The basic 16-bit registers, however, are identical for both machines. All 8088 software can run on the 8086 and vice versa.

The Model 30 will run DOS version 3.3. It will not run the OS/2 Protected Virtual Address Mode operating system designed to run on the 80286 and 80386-based machines. Since an 8086 is the CPU, the Model 30 is restricted to *equivalent* Real Address Mode operation. All programs written for the 8088 and 8086 will run on 80286-based computers in Real Address Mode.

From the perspective of a software environment, the programmer can accept that all the discussion applied to 8088 assembly language will apply to the 8086. The Macro Assembler version 2.00 will yield object code that is compatible with the 8086 and the syntax is identical to that used for the 8088. This means that software developed in assembly language for the IBM PC and XT will also assemble and run on the Model 30. The environments can be considered very similar from a programming viewpoint.

2.5 THE IBM 80286-BASED MICROCOMPUTER SOFTWARE ENVIRONMENT

Essentially all software developed for the AT and XT286 prior to 1988 was designed with the Real Address Mode as the operating environment. This is simply because many of the additional Protected Virtual Address Mode (Protected Mode, for short) instructions available to the 80286 programmer are intended for use as operating system (memory management and protection) instructions. Further, as has been indicated, the DOS 3.3 is IBM's last DOS release prior to OS/2. DOS 3.3 still executes Real Address Mode software and does not have a Protected Model capability. Hence, it is with the release of OS/2 that the first Protected Mode operating system is available for use with the IBM microcomputers. Two PS/2 computers, the Models 50 and 60, employ the 80286 microprocessor as a CPU.

The 80286 is a 16-bit microprocessor and has 19 registers, 14 of which are of interest to the general applications programmer. These 14 registers consist of AX, BX, CX, DX, BP, SP, DI, SI, CS, DS, SS, ES, IP, and the flags register, which is clearly the set of registers available for 8088 and 8086 programming. Further, these registers behave in identical fashion to their counterparts in the 8088 and 8086. The remaining five registers, used with the Protected Mode and multitasking, are

1. Global Descriptor Table Register (GDTR)
2. Interrupt Descriptor Table Register (IDTR)
3. Local Descriptor Table Register (LDTR)
4. Task Register (TR)
5. Machine Status Word Register (MSW)

These Protected Mode registers are used by the operating system to differentiate Real Address Mode from Protected Mode operation (the MSW register), to specify the segment address for the task or program currently executing (the TR register), and to specify the location and size of the table defining a local task (LDTR), interrupt routines (IDTR), and the overall system programs (GDTR). In the following subsections we consider both the Real Address Mode and Protected Mode environments.

2.5.1 Real Address Mode

Real Address Mode is Intel's 80286 operating environment which allows downward compatibility with the 8088-based machines (and 8086 machines). All addressing is accomplished using physical address locations and multitasking is not available. The IBM Macro Assembler version 2.00 supports this 80286 mode and allows the inclusion of several additional 80286 instructions that run under Real Address Mode. In subsection 4.5.1 we will examine these additional Real Address Mode 80286 instructions in detail. The important point to recognize concerning this mode of operation is that all PC and XT Macro Assembler source code will run on the 80286 machines without any modifications (in the Real Address Mode). Further, excluding the use of a few 80286-specific instructions (such as ENTER, LEAVE, BOUND) all Real Address Mode 80286 Macro Assembler source code will run on the PC and XT computers. Thus, Intel has made software compatibility complete across the three chips 8088, 8086, and 80286. That is not to say that the 80286 is not significantly advanced over the 8088 and 8086. As we have indicated earlier, aside from speed advantages, the 80286 has important new capabilities, but we must turn to the Protected Mode in order to explore these features.

Basically, the 80286 *calculates* addresses in a manner identical to the 8088 (and 8086), using segment selectors and offsets when in the Real Address Mode. Further, these addresses correspond to actual physical addresses in the system. By physical address, we mean an actual memory or port location in the microcomputer system that corresponds to a hardware entity. Clearly, when assigning such addresses, the linker must consider the overall amount of physical memory in the user's system. For a 20-bit address (segment plus offset), the 80286 can specify up to 1 megabyte of address space in Real Address Mode. This also agrees with the addressing capability of the PC and XT. We used the term segment selector when talking about the 80286 because this is the key to the 80286 memory management function. In the case of the 80286 the reader should assume that this segment selector acts similarly to a segment address when in Real Address Mode. Fortunately, the segment registers always have the correct segment address and hence, DEBUG and the system will always correctly define the absolute physical memory location of a variable or of port locations for input/output.

As a prelude to future discussion about addressing and memory allocation, it is important to point out that the AT machines use a 24-bit address bus. It is not until the Protected Virtual Address Mode is used that full advantage of this 24-bit addressing capability can be assumed. The 24-bit addressing capability of the 80286 (an actual 24 line address bus in the AT) means that 16 megabytes of physical address space can be used (2^{24}). Further, with the 80286 memory management in the Protected Virtual Address Mode, this can be extended to a virtual address space of 1 gigabyte (2^{30}). The 80286 performs the mapping between this virtual space and the actual physical locations.

2.5.2 Protected Mode

With 24 address lines, the 80286 can access up to 16 megabytes of physical address space as discussed above. Using memory management the 80286 can access up to one gigabyte. How is this accomplished? The 80286 memory management instructions must be used to set up virtual addressing. In normal 8088 or 8086 addressing, a 16-bit offset is added to a shifted 16-bit segment address to get a 20-bit physical address. In the Protected Mode the segment selector has the form

The table indicator bit (TI) defines two separate address spaces,

$$0 = \text{global addresses}$$

$$1 = \text{local addresses}$$

The global addresses are used by all tasks in a multitasking environment. Local addresses are only accessible within a single task. Since the INDEX is 13 bits, each address space may subdivide into 2^{13} segments at most. This 13-bit quantity effectively indexes a memory-resident table called a descriptor table. This descriptor table contains the mapping between a segment address and the physical locations. There is a single global descriptor table (GDT) and one or more local descriptor tables (LDT). Each descriptor table entry consists of an 8-byte value. The values are as follows:

Byte	Function
0,1	LIMIT: specifies the size of the segment up to 64K.
2,3,4	BASE: specifies a 24-bit physical base address for the start of the segment.
5	ACCESS RIGHTS BYTE:
	bit 7: Protection Present.
	bits 5–6: Descriptor Privilege Level
	0 is most trusted, 3 is least trusted.
	bit 4: Segment Descriptor
	1: Applications
	0: System
	bit 3: 1: code
	0: data
	bit 0–2: Protection access
6,7	These bytes are set equal to 0 to insure compatibility with 80386-based systems.

To generate the physical address from a 32-bit virtual address, the processor selects the GDT or one of the LDT's based on the TI-bit and multiplies the INDEX field by 8 to get the descriptor table location. The 24-bit segment base (bytes 2, 3, and 4) is then summed with the 16-bit offset to yield the 24-bit physical address. Clearly, the operating system software (the link and locate function) must insure that addressing is properly set up in order to take advantage of a 24-bit segment base and 16-bit offset.

It is important to recognize that segments are still restricted to 64K size maximums, but movement across 64K boundaries is easily possible using independent modules. Hence, as will become clear for all Macro Assembler programming, a 64K size limitation on code segments is essentially no program development handicap.

The 80286 has protection features using bits 0 through 2 of byte 5 in the descriptor tables, as well as bits 0 and 1 in the segment selector. This protection is necessary in a multitasking environment and insures isolation of system software from users, isolation of users from each other, and data access by privilege level.

Finally, the Protected Mode provides for intersegment calls and a class of control descriptors (8-byte) that facilitate transfer of program execution from one segment to another. The Protected Mode features discussed here are essentially transparent to the user and merely demonstrate the 80286 Protected Mode environment as found, for example, in OS/2.

The major reason that Protected Virtual Address Mode has met resistance by system designers is that the segment selector cannot be easily manipulated like the 8086 and 8088 addressing. Basically, the placement of the table indicator bit and protection bits requires register manipulation of the INDEX before a conversion of virtual address to physical address can be accomplished. This conflicts with the 8086- and 8088-based machines and requires a significant adjustment of their software (the segment addresses) in order to run this software in 80286 Protected Virtual Address Mode. While the 80286 can execute object code developed for the 8088 and 8086 (in Real Address Mode), this code is significantly slower in Protected Mode.

2.6 THE IBM 80386-BASED MICROCOMPUTER SOFTWARE ENVIRONMENT

The PS/2 Model 80 uses the Intel 80386 microprocessor as its CPU. This microprocessor is distinctly different from the 16-bit processors (8088, 8086, and 80286) because the 80386 is a full 32-bit microprocessor. That is, the 80386 has separate 32-bit address and data buses and registers. The 80386 also incorporates the memory management function as part of its internal architecture. As the previous subsection indicates, a substantial amount of 80286 memory management (in Protected Mode) must be accomplished in the operating system software (or with associated integrated circuits). The segment address calculation is performed, for example, using on-chip address-translation buffer memory (or caches) in the 80386.

Whereas the 16-bit CPUs employ word arithmetic, the 80386 uses double-word arithmetic. There are 8 general registers, EAX, EBX, ECX, EDX, ESI, EDI, ESP, and EBP. Here the prefix E indicates that the familiar 16-bit general registers (AX, BX, ...) have simply been extended to 32 bits. In fact, the low-order word of each of these 8 registers can be treated as the equivalent 16-bit register with all the reserved name definitions applied to these 16-bit quantities. (They further subdivide, for example, into 8-bit halves, AH, AL, BH, BL. ...) Clearly, this implies a downward compatibility for running 16-bit microprocessor (8088, 8086, and 80286) code, assuming a reassembly and link is executed.

The instruction pointer (EIP) and flags register (EFLAGS) have similar downward compatibility features. Finally, there are six segment registers, CS, DS, SS, ES, FS, and GS. The last two are new and provide for additional independent data segment access using overrides. These segment registers are each of word length. As with the 80286, many of the architectural features of the 80386 are only used by systems programmers and the intention of certain 80386 instructions was that these instructions apply only to operating system software. In addition to the registers specified above, the 80386 has the following registers:

- Memory-Management Registers (4): GDTR, LDTR, IDTR, TR (also found in the 80286)
- Control Registers (4): CR0, CR1, CR2, CR3
- Debug and Test Registers (8): DR0, DR1, DR2, DR3, DR4, DR5, DR6, DR7

Of course, aside from additional system functions using new instructions, the 80386 has a significantly improved applications capability over the 80286 and other 16-bit processors. This improved capability is due to the presence of the 32-bit architecture, which doubles the significance with which computations can be performed. As will become clear when manipulating quantities in 16-bit registers, a substantial performance loss is incurred due to round-off errors for applications that require scaling. With 32-bit register arithmetic, this source of errors is minimized.

2.6.1 Running 80286-Based Programs

The topic of this book is IBM microcomputer assembly language and the development of this subject is presented so that all programs used in the text will run on all

IBM 8088-, 8086-, 80286-, and 80386-based machines. This is easily achieved using DOS, versions 2.10 through 3.30, on an IBM PC, XT, AT, or XT286 with Macro Assembler version 2.00. The PS/2 Models 30, 50, and 60 will also run these programs using DOS 3.3 and Macro Assembler version 2.00. Finally, these programs will run on the PS/2 Model 80 using Macro Assembler version 2.00 and OS/2 (as well as the Model 50 and 60). Both the 80286 and 80386 assume Real Address Mode.

Clearly, the programs developed in the text do not require additional instructions beyond the basic 8086-core instruction set. Since many of these additional instructions (for the 80286 and 80386) are to be used by systems programmers for such activities as memory-management and protection in a multitasking environment, the impact on applications is minimal when these instructions are omitted. The major problem with running 16-bit assembly language programs on a 32-bit machine (Intel family) is the assembler program itself. The actual operation codes generated by the assembler must translate into the correct machine code for the 32-bit machine. The assembly language source code (the topic of this book) will be acceptable to an assembler designed for 32-bit processors (80386) even though it was written for a 16-bit processor (80286 or downward to the 8088). This source code simply will not take advantage of any additional application-oriented instructions added by Intel for the new processor. Clearly, only the lower half of the general registers in the 80386 is used to run the 16-bit software, characteristic of the 8088, 8086 and 80286. Since this software uses reserved names (AX, BX . . .) which are recognized by the 80386 assembler (IBM Macro Assembler version 2.00, for example), there is a one-to-one correspondence between the 16-bit programs and their execution on the 80386.

The 80386 has two methods for halting execution of the processor, exceptions and interrupts. Exceptions are events that stop the execution of the processor in synchronous fashion. By this we mean that they occur as part of the "pipelined" execution of instructions by the processor. Interrupts occur as asynchronous events either from external signals (such as from an Intel 8259A) or error conditions that abort program execution. The 80286 also has essentially equivalent exception and interrupt handling.

In Chapter 5 the topic of interrupts is discussed in detail. The interrupt service routines are pointed to by an interrupt vector number: 0, 1, 2, . . . 255. In the early systems, PC and XT, the vector table contained addresses of service routines usually found in ROM. Intel used some of these vector locations for additional Intel-defined exceptions or interrupts in the 80386 and 80286. Hence, a special vector table mapping is loaded as part of the initialization for these processors. We will not devote discussion to this topic because the reader can grasp the essentials of interrupt vector processing by examining the PC and XT interrupts indicated in Chapter 5. The 80286 and 80386 processors simply remap these vectors so that downward compatibility exists.

2.6.2 80386 Real Address Mode

The Real Address Mode of the 80386 executes object code designed for execution on the 8088, 8086, or 80286. To a programmer, the 80386 microprocessor emulates an

8086, 8088, or 80286 in Real Address Mode. The 80386 simply appears as a higher-speed processor in this mode with a few additional instructions and 32-bit registers.

The 80386 has slightly more than one megabyte of address capability in Real Address Mode because the linear address, resulting from the addition of a segment and offset, may have as many as 21 significant bits. The linear address is equivalent to the physical address in Real Address Mode. We will consider an alternate description in the Protected Mode or Virtual 8086 Mode, where *paging* is used to describe the allocation of memory. In Real Address Mode the 80386 programmer has access to additional registers beyond those found with the 80286, FS, GS, debug registers, control registers and test registers. There exist new instructions that operate on FS and GS, and these registers can be explicitly referenced using segment overrides.

In the previous subsection we briefly discussed some aspects of running 80286-based software on the 80386. In Real Address Mode there are some minor differences between 8086 program execution on the 80386 and the same software running on an 8086. The following list delineates some of these differences:

1. Instruction clock counts are different.
2. The 80386 has some operation codes not defined for the 8086 (small number).
3. The 80386 pushes SP before it is incremented (when using PUSH SP) and the 8086 pushes SP after it is incremented.
4. The 80386 limits all shifts and rotates to 32 bits or less.
5. The 80386 traps out-of-range segment references (outside 64K).
6. The 80386 avoids single-stepping of external interrupts in DEBUG. This facilitates debugging real-time code.
7. The 80386 uses a different coprocessor error vector than the 8086.
8. The 80386 adds six new interrupt vectors. These are Intel vectors that do not conflict with the basic 8086 vectors.
9. The 80386 does not wrap around addresses. Any out-of-range addresses cause an error condition.

The few differences that exist between 80286-based computers and 80386-based machines are not likely to impact software development or execution in Real Address Mode, as discussed earlier.

2.6.3 80386 Protected Mode

The 80386 Protected Mode is conceptually similar to the 80286 Protected Mode: Both perform memory management, enforce protection mechanisms, and provide for multitasking. These are all basically systems programming functions and the programmer should not expect to use instructions related to the application of these concepts. In defining the 80386 Protected Mode environment, however, we briefly consider these functions from an architectural viewpoint.

80386 memory management has perhaps the most striking Protected Mode modifications from the earlier 80286 architecture. In the 80386 the notion of linear address and paging are introduced. Paging occurs during the second phase of address transformation when a linear address is changed into a physical address (remember the descriptor tables in the 80286). The linear address is obtained in the usual fashion from a segment selector and segment offset. A 16-bit segment selector is used to obtain a 32-bit segment base from a descriptor table. When this 32-bit segment base is added to an offset in an allowed way, the 32-bit linear address is created. A linear address has the form

31	22	12	0
DIRECTORY	PAGE	OFFSET	
(10)	(10)	(12)	(BITS)

Here OFFSET specifies an offset within a page frame, which is pointed to by PAGE. The page table is, in turn, pointed to by DIRECTORY. Clearly, since each OFFSET is 12 bits long, pages can have at most 4K-byte entries (2^{12}). Offsets generally reference byte locations since they have associated values. The page table, however, references an entry which is uniquely specified over a 32-bit field. This entry includes a page frame address, a read-write bit, and other system-oriented bits. Since the PAGE entry consists of a 10-bit field, 1K entries can be specified (2^{10}) but these entries correspond to 32-bit elements. Hence, the page table is also a page frame. Finally, the DIRECTORY field can specify up to 1K page table locations (2^{10}). In Real Address Mode the 80386 has a 21-bit address, not the full 32-bit mapping illustrated here for the Protected Mode.

Protection and multitasking also involve bits set in the descriptor table. These functions must be determined by the system programmer and will not be discussed further in this chapter. We have spent considerable discussion on the Real Address Mode and Protected Mode for the 80286 and 80386. This was to emphasize the upward compatibility for software developed on the earlier machines (the 8088-based machines). There is a final 80386 mode to be considered and this is the subject of the next subsection.

2.6.4 Virtual 8086 Mode

The 80386 supports execution of one or more 8088 or 8086 programs in a multitasking environment (Protected Mode). This is the Virtual 8086 Mode and the tasks are known as V86 tasks. To get to V86 Mode, the VM bit in the EFLAGS register must be set by the system software. When set, the processor loads segment registers in the 8086-style of address formation and decodes instructions checking for input/output privilege level (IOPL) violations. Other than these two facets of V86 Mode, the system operates as if it were in normal Protected Mode. Again, the operating system must support this mode in order to allow for its configuration at run-time.

2.7 SUMMARY

In this chapter we have introduced the mechanics of creating, assembling, linking, and executing Macro Assembler programs. Two simple examples were illustrated, a

TABLE 2.8 SOFTWARE ENVIRONMENT FOR IBM MICROCOMPUTERS

Computer	Processor	Operating mode	
		Real address equivalent	Protected
PC	8088	DOS 1.00–3.10	—
XT	8088	DOS 2.00–3.30	—
XT286	80286	DOS 2.00–3.30	—
AT	80286	DOS 2.00–3.30	OS/2
System 2/Model 30	8086	DOS 3.30	—
System 2/Model 50	80286	DOS 3.30	OS/2
System 2/Model 60	80286	DOS 3.30	OS/2
System 2/Model 80	80386	DOS 3.30	OS/2

basic program that demonstrates the structure of assembler code (FIRASM.ASM) and a program that illustrates five of the seven Macro Assembler address modes (ADDEM.ASM). Each of these programs was executed using the IBM utility DEBUG. DEBUG allows the programmer to step through a program and observe the manner in which registers change. Also, memory locations can be monitored. These programs are introductory in nature and contain rather simple examples of the Macro Assembler instruction set.

The allocation of memory was discussed. Portions of the overall absolute memory areas allocated by IBM are delegated by the linker during the execution of this utility. The IBM linker actually performs two functions: It connects all needed modules (the link function) and it assigns absolute locations in memory to each module (the locate function).

Table 2.8 illustrates the software environments under which the IBM microcomputers can operate. Basically, all Protected Mode operation requires the capability to run OS/2 (80286 or 80386 systems) and DOS 3.3 will run on the 8088 and 8086 systems.

A number of instructions and pseudo-ops were delineated for the program examples. The move, subtraction, and addition instructions were illustrated. The following pseudo-ops were presented: SEGMENT, DB, ASSUME, TITLE, COMMENT, and PAGE.

Before beginning the chapter on software design techniques, it is useful to briefly reiterate the approach taken in this book. Many texts approach the subject of assembler programming by employing code fragments to delineate instruction operation. We have attempted to make minimal use of fragments and concentrate on complete program examples. These approaches illustrate a basic dichotomy in books on assembler: Some assembler books are tutorial while others tend to be reference-oriented [10–16].

REFERENCES

1. *Macro Assembler Version 1.00*. IBM Personal Computer: Computer Language Series. IBM Corp. P.O. Box 1328. Boca Raton, FL 33432 (1981).

2. *Macro Assembler Version 2.00*. IBM Personal Computer: Computer Language Series. IBM Corp. P.O. Box 1328. Boca Raton, FL 33432 (1984).

3. *iAPX 86/88, 186/188 User's Manual—Hardware Reference*. Intel Corp., Literature Sales. P.O. Box 58130. Santa Clara, CA 95052-8130 (1985). (210912-001)

4. *iAPX 86/88, 186/188 User's Manual—Programmer's Reference*. Intel Corp., Literature Sales. P.O. Box 58130. Santa Clara, CA 95052-8130 (1986). (210911-003)

5. Triebel, W. A., and Singh, A. *16-Bit Microprocessors, Architecture, Software, and Interface Techniques*. Prentice-Hall, Inc. Englewood Cliffs, NJ 07632 (1984), p. 14.

6. *Disk Operating System Version 2.10 by Microsoft Corporation*. IBM Personal Computer: Computer Language Series, IBM Corp. P.O. Box 1328. Boca Raton, FL 33432 (1983).

7. *Technical Reference Personal Computer*. Personal Computer Hardware Reference Library. IBM Corp. P.O. Box 1328. Boca Raton, FL 33432 (1981).

8. *VEDIT PLUS: Multiple File Editor/Word Processor*, CompuView Products, Inc. 1955 Pauline Blvd. Ann Arbor, MI 48103 (1986).

9. *Disk Operating System Technical Reference*, IBM Personal Computer Software. IBM Corp. P.O. Box 1328. Boca Raton, FL 33432 (1984).

10. Schneider, A. *Fundamentals of IBM PC Assembly Language*. Tab Books, Inc. Blue Ridge Summit, PA 17214 (1984).

11. Scanlon, L. J. *IBM PC Assembly Language—A Guide for Programmers*. Brady Communications Corp. New York, NY 10020 (1983).

12. Scanlon, L. J. *IBM PC and XT Assembly Language—A Guide for Programmers*. Brady Communications Corp. New York, NY 10020 (1985).

13. Abel, P. *Assembler for the IBM PC and PC-XT*. Reston Publishing Company, Inc., Reston, VA 22090 (1983).

14. Startz, R. *8087 Applications and Programming for the PC, XT, and AT*. Brady Communications Corp. New York, NY 10020 (1985).

15. Scanlon, L. J. *Assembly Language Subroutines for MS-DOS Computers*. Tab Books, Inc. Blue Ridge Summit, PA 17214 (1986).

16. Norton, P., and Socha, J., *Peter Norton's Assembly Language Book for the IBM PC*. Brady Communications Corp., New York, NY 10020 (1986).

PROBLEMS

2.1. In general, why would the following sequence of instructions not be allowed for 8088-based systems such as the IBM PC and XT?

```
      . . .
MOV DX,ADDRESS_IO
      . . .
OUT DX,AX
      . . .
```

2.2. Would the instruction sequence appearing in Problem 2.1 be allowed in the IBM AT system? Explain.

2.3. Which of the following are allowed address combinations for the IBM PC and XT? (a) F111:E111, (b) F111:F111, (c) FEEE:2220, (d) FEEE:0220, (e) EFFF:F000.

2.4. What general program information would be expected to occur at the addresses (a) F000:F000, (b) F000:E000, (c) 0000:0000, (d) B000:40AF?

2.5. When AX = 00AAH and BX = 00ABH and the instruction

SUB AX,BX

is executed, which of the following would be possible Flags register values (a) 0211H, (b) F221H, (c) 0221H?

2.6. In the assembler list file appearing in Figure 2.3, what is the meaning of hex 20? Why is the stack segment ending offset 0200H? What is the length of the MOV instruction and the SUB instruction?

2.7. What is contained in the destination operand for the instruction

SUB BX,AX

where (a) BX = 1111H and AX = 2111H, (b) BX = ABDEH and AX = 1234H, (c) BX = F000H and AX = FE00H?

2.8. What would need to be done to FIRASM.ASM to cause it to have a normal return to DOS?

2.9. What is wrong with the following instructions?

(a) MOV 18D,AX
(b) SUB BX,AL
(c) MOV CX,BH
(d) SUB 21D,17D
(e) MOV AX,70000D

2.10. Create an arithmetic that uses normal number convention in the first 15 bits (bits 0 through 14) and sets the sign bit for bit 16 as needed. Assume the programmer will check bit 16 for sign and perform normal arithmetic on the first 15 bits. How would the following numbers be represented in hexadecimal? (a) −847, (b) −65600, (c) 30000, (d) −30000, (e) 10000, (f) −10000, (g) 37000, (h) −40000, (i) 1840, (j) −2280.

2.11. When using DEBUG, the register contents will display. During program execution the segment registers will remain the same unless specifically changed by the programmer. The code segment register (CS), however, will change twice outside user control. When does this occur? What determines the assigned values for the segment registers as displayed by DEBUG?

2.12. In Figure 2.4, how many locations separate the beginning of the code segment from the beginning of the stack segment? Which is lower in memory?

2.13. Given the following data segment

```
. . .
DATA SEGMENT PARA PUBLIC 'DATA'
        DDDD1  DW 1500
        DDDD2  DW 3200
        DDDD3  DW 1200
        DDDD4  DW 3600
        DDDD5  DW 6400
        DDDD6  DW 7200
        DDDD7  DW 1200
        DDDD8  DW 5400
        DDDD9  DW  800
        DDDD10 DW 1600
DATA ENDS
```

What is the value in AX after each of the following operations:

```
         . . .
        MOV AX,SEG DATA
        MOV DS,AX
                                    ;
        MOV BX,2
        MOV AX,[BX]
        MOV CX,DDDD6
(a)     SUB AX,CX
                                    ;
        MOV SI,6
        MOV AX,[BX][SI]
(b)     ADD AX,DDDD9
                                    ;
        MOV AX,[BX][SI+8]
(c)     SUB AX,DDDD9
                                    ;
        MOV AX,7200
        MOV BX,4
        MOV CX,[BX][SI+6]
(d)     SUB AX,CX
         . . .
```

2.14. What is wrong with the following code segment instructions?

```
         . . .
START   PROC FAR
        ASSUME DS:DATA, CS:CSEG, SS:STACK
        PUSH DS
        SUB AX,AX
        PUSH AX
                                    ;
        MOV DS,SEG DATA
                                    ;
        MOV AX,18D
        SUB AX,18D
                                    ;
        RET
START   ENDP
         . . .
```

2.15. Give an example of how a move instruction would be used to access the variable D1D in the Extra Segment and load the contents of D1D into the AX register. Assume representative names for labels and variables.

3

Software Design

Modern software design applies several techniques in order to achieve program code that is logically correct, efficient, and easy to understand and maintain. These techniques include top-down design, modular programming, and structured code. Other approaches, such as bottom-up design, while technically sound for some applications, are not as useful in the assembly language environment. Consequently, in this book we will restrict the discussion to two of these techniques, top-down design and modular programming, with some mention of structured code.

The purpose of this chapter is to introduce these techniques in a way that allows them to be easily applied to the development of code using the IBM assembly language. It is worthwhile noting that assembly language does not lend itself readily to structured programming for example, and IBM has developed a utility called the Structured Assembly Language Utility (SALUT) that provides a framework that can be used for structuring this code. SALUT, which comes with the IBM Macro Assembler version 2.0, is addressed in depth in Appendix B. Modular design implies subdividing the programming task into smaller pieces that are essentially testable on an individual basis and can be integrated to perform the overall task. Finally, top-down design is an approach to programming that proceeds from a very high-level abstract statement of the problem to be solved to a detailed algorithm which can be implemented.

In addition to the above mentioned techniques for optimizing program development, two other issues are important: style and form. Style implies the actual program layout and conventions. The use of capital or lower case letters, for example, would be a simple example of style. Form, on the other hand, is more elusive and pertains to the question of what constitutes a better algorithm. When writing assembly language programs a very important trade-off is clarity versus efficiency. For applications that do not require efficiency, it is usually desirable to make programs easily maintainable. In this case form has a subtle distinction and the programmer must rely on his own judgment for deciding what constitutes the optimum approach. Fortunately, experience greatly enhances this decision process.

The techniques to be discussed in this chapter fall under the category of theoretical programming considerations. Basically, these concepts represent ideas and approaches that are language independent. These techniques relate to considerations about how programs should be designed and consequently, do not rely on the mechanics of a particular language to be understood. During the discussion of this chapter we will initially approach software design from such an abstract viewpoint; however, the focus of this book is assembly language and every effort will be made to apply these concepts in the assembly language environment. We begin the discussion with consideration of instructions that allow branching or jumps within a program. These instructions are the control instructions.

3.1 CONTROL INSTRUCTIONS

In Chapter 2 we used several pseudo-ops and instructions to write, assemble, link, and execute programs. Chapter 4 provides an in-depth discussion of the remaining Macro Assembler instructions; however, in order to understand the methodology for regulating program execution and flow with the assembler language, it is useful to consider briefly the Macro Assembler control instructions. These instructions are embodied in the jump instruction group mentioned earlier.

Table 3.1 illustrates the jump instructions. Most of these instructions are used in conjunction with an instruction that changes the flags. The CMP instruction, discussed with Table 3.2, is very useful for this purpose. For example, the JA instruction causes a jump to occur if $CF = ZF = 0$ following a compare. In this case the destination operand is greater (above) than the source operand. For the remaining jump instructions (except for the unconditional jump, JMP) execution is based on the status of various registers or flags. Some jump instructions apply to unsigned quantities where the terminology used is *above* or *below*, while others apply to signed operands where the terminology used is *greater* or *less*. All jump instructions except

TABLE 3.1   THE JUMP INSTRUCTION GROUP

Instruction	Purpose	Comments
JA short-label (JNBE)	Jump If Above/If Not Below or Equal	This jump is used in conjunction with the Carry and Zero Flags. If either or both are set, no jump occurs. Suppose two operands are compared; then if the destination is greater than the source (above), $CF = ZF = 0$ and the jump occurs. The jump is within -128 to $+127$ bytes (short-label) and unsigned operands are used.

JAE short-label (JNB)	Jump If Above or Equal/If Not Below	This jump is similar to JA, except only the Carry Flag is examined. If a previous compare, for example, is performed and the destination is greater than or equal to the source (above or equal), CF = 0 and the jump occurs. This is a short-label instruction with unsigned operands.
JB short-label (JNAE) (JC)	Jump If Below/If Not Above nor Equal/If Carry	This jump is the opposite of JAE. If the Carry Flag is set the jump will occur. Suppose a previous compare is performed and the destination is less than the source (below), CF = 1 and the jump occurs. This is a short-label instruction with unsigned operands.
JBE short-label (JNA)	Jump If Below or Equal/If Not Above	This jump is the same as JB, except it also takes place if the Zero Flag is set (below or equal). It is short-label with unsigned operands.
JCXZ short-label	Jump If CX Is Zero	Suppose an instruction sequence causes the count register (CX) to decrement. When CX reaches 0 control transfers to the short-label after execution of JCXZ. This is a short-label jump.
JE short-label (JZ)	Jump If Equal/If Zero	If the last operation to change ZF set this flag (gave a result of 1), JE will cause a jump to occur. This is a short-label jump.
JG short-label (JNLE)	Jump If Greater/If Not Less nor Equal	If ZF = 0 and SF = OF the JG instruction will cause a jump to short-label. This instruction is used with signed operands.
JGE short-label (JNL)	Jump If Greater or Equal/If Not Less	This instruction is the same as JG, except ZF is not considered. If SF = OF the jump occurs. This is a short-label instruction with signed operands.
JL short-label (JNGE)	Jump If Less/If Not Greater nor Equal	If SF ≠ OF the JL instruction will result in a jump. This instruction is short-label with signed operands.
JLE short-label (JNG)	Jump If Less or Equal/If Not Greater	If ZF = 1 or SF ≠ OF the JLE instruction yields a short-label jump. The instruction is used with signed operands.
JMP target	Jump	This is a direct and unconditional jump.
JNC short-label	Jump If No Carry	If CF = 0 this instruction yields a short-label jump.
JNE short-label (JNZ)	Jump If Not Equal/If Not Zero	If ZF = 0 this short-label jump will occur.
JNO short-label	Jump If No Overflow	If OF = 0 this short-label jump will occur.
JNP short-label (JPO)	Jump If No Parity/If Parity Odd	If PF = 0 this short-label jump will occur.
JNS short-label	Jump If No Sign/ If Positive	If SF = 0 this short-label jump will occur.
JO short-label	Jump On Overflow	If OF = 1 this short-label jump will occur.
JP short-label (JPE)	Jump On Parity/If Parity Even	If PF = 1 this short-label jump will occur.
JS short-label	Jump On Sign	If SF = 1 this short-label jump will occur.

JMP transfer control to a target label referred to as a *short-label*. This means the transfer must lie within the range -128 to $+127$ bytes of the instruction.

In the sequence

CMP AH,AL

JAE CONT1

the value of AL is subtracted from AH and the Carry Flag is set if AH is less than AL. The jump, JAE (Jump if Above or Equal), to label CONT1 takes place if the Carry Flag is not set or if $ZF = 1$. In general, all these instructions are similar and the reader should become familiar with them in order to have an understanding of how to transfer control. One particularly useful sequence is equivalent to the FORTRAN IF statement. It transfers control by creating a three-way branch depending on whether the destination is greater than, equal to, or less than the source.

```
        . . .
        CMP AH,AL        ; Compare AH and AL
        JBE CONT1        ; Jump CONT1 if AH less than or equal to AL
                         ; Instructions for AH greater than AL

        . . .
        JMP CONT3
CONT1:  JB CONT2         ; Jump CONT2 if AH less than AL
                         ; Instructions if AH is equal to AL

        . . .
        JMP CONT3
CONT2:                   ; Instructions if AH less than AL
        . . .
CONT3:
```

A second example of the jump instructions is the following sequence:

```
        . . .
        CMP AH,DDDV      ; Compare contents AH and DDDV
        JNE CONT1        ; Jump CONT1 if not equal

        . . .
        JMP CONT2        ; Go to CONT2 (Unconditional)
CONT1:  . . .

        . . .
CONT2:  . . .
```

This sequence has the IF...ELSE construction. To see this consider the control: First, the AH register is tested against DDDV and *if* these quantities are not equal a branch to CONT1 occurs; *else* the code following the JNE instruction executes. Observe that an unconditional jump was needed to bypass the CONT1 code following execution of the else code. Both paths end up at the CONT2 label.

The jump sequences discussed here are good examples of how logic is implemented and how branching occurs in the assembler syntax. These instructions are the entities that control program flow. We have used the compare instruction to provide

TABLE 3.2 THE COMPARE INSTRUCTION GROUP

Instruction	Purpose	Comments
CMP destination, source	Compare Two Operands	This instruction causes the source to be subtracted from the destination; however, only the flags are affected. The destination remains unchanged.
CMPS destination-str source-str (CMPSB) (CMPSW)	Compare Byte or Word String	The source-string (with DI as an index for the extra segment) is subtracted from the destination-string (which uses SI as index). Only the flags are affected and both DI and SI are incremented. A typical sequence of instructions could be MOV SI, OFFSET AAA MOV DI, OFFSET BBB CMPS AAA, BBB

the test that sets the flags prior to executing the conditional jumps. Consequently, it is useful to consider this latter instruction group. Table 3.2 presents the Compare Group. The CMP instruction takes the form

CMP destination, source

If the destination equals the source, $ZF = 1$ (the Zero Flag is set) and $CF = 0$. If the source is greater than the destination, $ZF = 0$ and $CF = 1$ (the Carry Flag is set). If the source is less than the destination, $ZF = 0$ and $CF = 0$. These flags can then be used by the jump instructions, for example, to determine conditions under which branching occurs. It should be pointed out that the compare instructions also affect the Overflow Flag (OF) and Sign Flag (SF). Following a test with CMP, if the destination is greater than the source, both SF and OF will be 0 (not set). If the source is greater than the destination, $SF = 1$ and $OF = 0$; hence SF does not equal OF.

We have already seen several uses of the compare instruction when testing to set flags for conditional jump instructions. This is the major function of the compare instruction: When CMP is executed, the flags are changed. The CMP instruction can be used to compare memory-register operands with a register operand, immediate operands with the accumulator, and immediate operands with a memory-register operand.

Before concluding this chapter it will be instructive to consider an additional introductory program example. Figure 3.1a is the flow chart for a program that calculates the maximum and minimum of a list. Figure 3.1b is the program. It calculates the minimum and maximum value of 20 byte-variables stored in the data segment. These data values constitute the area called TABLE1. Space is reserved for the minimum value, MIN, the maximum value, MAX, and an assignment of 20 to NUMB, the variable designating the size of TABLE1. In the program, the PSP address is preserved on the stack and DS loaded with the data segment address. Next, the minimum and maximum are calculated. First the offset of TABLE1 is stored in BX and the index set to 1. CX is loaded with the table size, 20, and decremented by

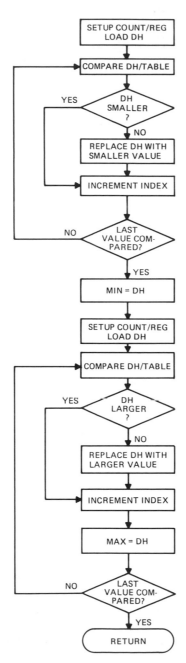

Figure 3.1a The functional flow chart for the program that calculates the maximum and minimum of a list.

```
PAGE 40,132
TITLE MINMAX - MAX/MIN OF A LIST(MINMAX.ASM)
COMMENT *

                    DESCRIPTION:This routine calculates
                    the minimum and maximum values of a
                    list of byte quantities.
                                                          *
STACK     SEGMENT PARA STACK 'STACK'
                                                   ;
          DB      64 DUP('STACK   ')
                                                   ;
STACK     ENDS
                                                   ;
DATA      SEGMENT PARA PUBLIC 'DATA'
                                                   ;
TABLE1    DB      254,223,187,54,135,23,77,44,218,199
          DB      162,209,85,24,107,233,151,36,92,100
MIN       DB      0
MAX       DB      0
NUMB      DW      20
                                                   ;
DATA      ENDS
                                                   ;
CSEG      SEGMENT PARA PUBLIC 'CODE'
                                                   ;
MINMAX    PROC    FAR
          ASSUME CS:CSEG,DS:DATA,SS:STACK
          PUSH DS
          SUB AX,AX
          PUSH AX

          MOV AX, SEG DATA      ;Load AX with DATA segment address
          MOV DS,AX             ;Load DS with DATA address
                                ;
          MOV BX, OFFSET TABLE1 ;Load TABLE1 Offset into BX
          MOV SI,1              ;Set index next word in table
          MOV CX,NUMB           ;Load counter with table size
          SUB CX,1              ;Decrement counter
          MOV DH,TABLE1[BX]
                                ;
MMIN:     CLC                   ;Clear carry flag
          CMP DH,TABLE1[BX][SI] ;Compare table entries
          JBE CONT1             ;Jump if DH smaller
          MOV DH,TABLE1[BX][SI] ;Replace DH with small value
CONT1:    ADD SI,1              ;
          LOOP MMIN             ;Loop until CX=0
                                ;
          MOV MIN,DH
                                ;
          MOV BX, OFFSET TABLE1 ;Start again
          MOV SI,1
          MOV CX,NUMB
          SUB CX,1
          MOV DH,TABLE1[BX]
                                ;
MMAX:     CLC
          CMP DH,TABLE1[BX][SI]
          JAE CONT2             ;Jump if DH larger
          MOV DH,TABLE1[BX][SI]
CONT2:    ADD SI,1
                                ;
          MOV MAX,DH
          LOOP MMAX
                                ;
          RET
MINMAX    ENDP
CSEG      ENDS
          END MINMAX
```

Figure 3.1b The program MINMAX.ASM, which calculates the minimum and maximum of a list.

1. DH is loaded with the first table value and the loop that calculates the minimum is entered. In this loop the carry flag is first cleared. Then, DH is compared with the next table value. If DH is smaller, no replacement is needed and we jump over the instruction that would move the smaller value into DH. The index, SI, is incremented by 1 and we loop back to the labeled instruction MMIN. The increment of SI will cause the instructions

CMP DH,TABLE1[BX][SI]

and

MOV DH,TABLE1[BX][SI]

to point to the next value in TABLE1. When the LOOP instruction is executed, CX is decremented by 1 until 0 is reached; then the loop is stopped.

Following the instructions for calculating the minimum are the instructions for calculating the maximum. They are very similar except JBE becomes JAE. The minimum and maximum values are moved into MIN and MAX, respectively. The code segment contains the FAR procedure MINMAX, which has all the code executed and provides a normal return to DOS.

The LOOP instruction causes the program control to return to the specified label, decrementing CX each time. When CX = 0, the program flow drops through the loop and continues execution. Consider the following instructions.

```
            MOV CX,10
LABEL1:   ...
            ...
            LOOP LABEL1
            MOV DX,10
            ...
```

```
                                              ;
0000                         DATA   SEGMENT PARA PUBLIC 'DATA'
                                              ;
0000  FE DF BB 36 87 17      TABLE1  DB      254,223,187,54,135,23,77,44,218,199  ─── DATA VALUES IN
      4D 2C DA C7                                                                     DATA SEGMENT
000A  A2 D1 55 18 6B E9              DB      162,209,85,24,107,233,151,36,92,100
      97 24 5C 64
0014  00                    MIN     DB      0                                    ─── MIN LOCATION
0015  00                    MAX     DB      0                                    ─── MAX LOCATION
0016  0014                  NUMB    DW      20
                                              ;
001B                         DATA   ENDS
```

Figure 3.2   The portion of the assembler list file that illustrates the data segment values.

Here the loop count (CX) is set to 10. The intervening code between LABEL1: and
LOOP LABEL1 executes 10 times, decrementing CX each time. When CX = 0, the
processing falls through the loop and the MOV DX,10 instruction executes.

Figure 3.2 contains a copy of part of the assembler listing for MINMAX.-
ASM. The portion illustrated is the data segment which will be needed to locate the
TABLE1 variables in memory. We see that TABLE1 is located at offsets 0000H
through 0013H. Also, MIN is located at DS:0014 and MAX at DS:0015. In Figure
3.3 the data segment start address is observed to be 12F3:0000. The TABLE1
variables are initialized and zero is loaded into MIN and MAX. These variables are
observed to contain the correct values at completion.

In the program MINMAX.ASM an additional instruction is used, the addition
instruction. This instruction has the form

ADD destination, source

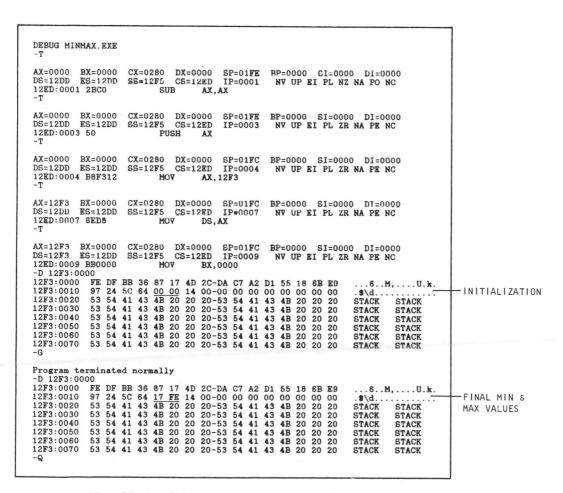

Figure 3.3 A typical DEBUG session with program MINMAX.

where the source value is added to the destination and the result returned in the destination. The type of the operands must be consistent (byte added to byte or word added to word).

3.2 DESIGN OPTIMIZATION

The optimization of assembly language programs can be achieved using top-down design, modular programming, and structured code. In presenting these topics we will illustrate the use of each technique and then employ it throughout the rest of the book, highlighting each as is appropriate. Logically, the concept of modular programming should be introduced first, since top-down design extends this idea by placing the resulting program modules in an hierarchical framework. Once modular programming and top-down design have been developed, structured code becomes a natural extension for these ideas and provides a suitable method for achieving additional clarity and efficiency in program design. We will consider a technique for approaching structured assembler, and the reader is referred to the appendix on SALUT for an actual utility that allows the development of structured concepts.

3.2.1 Modular Programming

The notion of modular programming has come to the forefront many times during the development of theoretical methods for designing programs [1, 2]. Basically, modular programming calls for the subdivision of a program task into smaller units that are independently testable and can be integrated to accomplish the overall program objective. This definition does nothing to describe how small the modules should be or what criteria should be applied to define module size, either abstractly or in terms of actual code length. Fortunately, considerable effort has been directed toward answering these questions. Each module should perform a single independent task and be self-contained, with one exit and entry point. Modular programming is implemented using procedures in assembler. These were illustrated in the previous chapter and, in many cases, roughly approximate small tasks or major portions of a task. (For those readers familiar with higher-level language subroutines, a procedure is essentially the assembler equivalent of a subroutine.) We have not explicitly defined what a procedure must do, however, and the idea of complexity should be briefly mentioned. Complexity is a measure of the degree of difficulty of a module. From a quantitative viewpoint, complexity can be assessed based on one of several metrics. Guidelines have been developed using these metrics, and a general set of empirical relations have evolved from these guidelines (the following relations have assumed that assembler code expands by a factor of 2 to 3 over similar higher-level language code).

1. Module size should lie between 20 and 200 lines of code.
2. Modules with less than 20 lines can reduce program efficiency.
3. Modules with more than 200 lines are difficult to test and maintain.
4. A module should perform one self-contained task.

Clearly, the description of modularization presented above is understood to constitute only a suggested technique for general program design. There will always be exceptional situations where these relations cannot be readily applied and the programmer must rely on his experience and judgment. In stating the limitations on size which were indicated for these relations, several implicit assumptions were made about the assembler code to be developed. First, it has been assumed that a module may contain an associated data segment that defines variables used by the module. This can greatly expand the module size for assembler routines. Second, a testable assembler module may consist of several procedures, a procedure being the basic building block of modular code. It must be remembered that a testable module should be structured to accomplish a complete task, and this may require several procedures.

A requirement for achieving modular code is the existence of a mechanism that allows data values to be passed between modules [3]. In assembler this is accomplished by several techniques. The easiest approach is to place the data value in one of the general purpose registers that remain unchanged by calls to other procedures in other modules. This works quite well when the number of parameters to be passed is small. For larger sets of parameter values it is useful to keep the same data or extra segment address and access the parameters through these segments. The programmer should exercise considerable care when planning how and what parameters are to be passed between modules. A third approach is to use the stack to pass parameters. Since the stack contains return information for procedure calls, this approach must be used with care.

3.2.2 Top-Down Design

In top-down programming the main program module is first defined and then the remaining called modules specified. It is logical to think in terms of some sort of hierarchy when developing a top-down design and the resulting planning frequently culminates with a *structure chart*. A structure chart is distinctly different from the usual program flow chart. Specifically, the structure chart is more general and conveys the sense of order, responsibility, and control that exists in the program code. Each module is represented by a rectangle with a number that represents the module's position in the overall program hierarchy. At level zero only the main program module exists. Next can be up to 3 level-1 modules. These modules reflect input/output and the actual processing accomplished by the program. There can, of course, be processing associated with I/O and this would be contained with the appropriate level-1 module.

Following the definition of the level-1 modules comes the level-2 module description (and successive levels). At level two each level-1 module should subdivide into two or more modules. If a module does not divide into at least two modules at this level, it should not be subdivided at all. There should be no single level-2 modules. Figure 3.4 illustrates a representative structure chart for a program that calculates a Gaussian random number. This program is developed in the next chapter and is presented here because it clearly demonstrates the use of modular techniques.

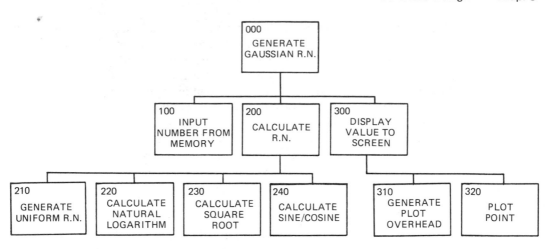

Figure 3.4 A representative structure chart for a program that calculates Gaussian random numbers.

Basically, the following definitions are used to define a Gaussian random number pair:

$$y_1 = \text{SQRT}(-2\ln(x_1))\cos(2\pi x_2)$$

$$y_2 = \text{SQRT}(-2\ln(x_1))\sin(2\pi x_2)$$

Here x_1 and x_2 are random numbers between 0 and 1. Examination of these equations indicates that a routine to generate a random number is needed. Routines to calculate square roots, take natural logarithms, and obtain sines and cosines are also needed. These are candidates for individual modules that would then be combined with an overall main calling program. That is the approach which is used in Chapter 4. The output module is actually used to plot the Gaussian random variables and, consequently, is slightly more complex than a simple print to the screen.

We have indicated that top-down design calls for the use of a structure chart in order to delineate the program. This chart is intended to demonstrate the layout of the various modules with respect to each other. Each module, in turn, can be defined from an architecture viewpoint by using one of two devices, a flow chart, which has already been alluded to, or pseudocode [4], which is a natural language description of what the program is intended to do. In the remaining sections of this chapter both approaches will be illustrated. Throughout the remainder of the book there will be a general tendency to resort to the flow chart for planning purposes because this device allows a compact representation of the algorithm to be used.

3.2.3 Structured Code Considerations

It was recognized very early in the development of theoretical program design techniques that branching or GO TO instructions frequently lead to confusion about what a particular program does when it executes. A rather general structure theorem has been developed which says that any program, however complex, that has one entry and one exit point, can be coded without the explicit use of GO TOs, provided that the language in question allows the construction of loops and CASE-type statements [5]. Unfortunately, in assembler the loop or CASE-type structure must be developed from branching instructions. Clearly these statements violate the spirit of structured programming because they explicitly transfer control within a program. It is difficult to develop a microprocessor that does not employ such control statements and the dilemma becomes one of what can be done with the microprocessor's branching instructions so that structured code is possible at the assembler level. Hence, the elegance afforded by a higher-level language is not available at this primitive stage. This is not to say, however, that some semblance of an approach to structured code cannot be achieved. In Appendix B, for example, the IBM Structured Assembly Language Utility (SALUT) version 2.00 is introduced [6]. This utility is written in BASIC and allows the assembler language programmer to introduce special-purpose structures into assembler code. These structures must be interpreted by a preprocessor, which converts the code to equivalent assembler instructions using labeling and conditional or unconditional jumps. The preprocessor output can, then, be assembled using MASM or another assembler.

    The approach taken in this book will be to identify several basic structures (the majority of special-purpose structures will be reserved for Appendix B, where SALUT is presented) which can be applied to assembler code. Coincidentally, these structures are also considered by SALUT. The nomenclature defining these structures will remain constant throughout the book. By way of example, the simple IF ... THEN ... ELSE construct, which is one of the most familiar structured programming concepts, would take the form

```
              . . .
              CMP  M              ; if M
              JNM  ELSE1          ; then
              ... (A1  Process)
              JMP  IF1
     ELSE1:   ...                 ; else1
              ... (A2  Process)
     IF1:     ...
              . . .
```

Let us briefly consider this code. The initial compare (CMP M) is needed to set up the conditional branching. IF M is true THEN the A1 process executes; ELSE the A2 process executes.

3.3 FLOWCHARTS AND PSEUDOCODE

As was indicated earlier, flowcharts and pseudocode represent two alternate techniques for delineating the content of an algorithm which is to be coded eventually in a particular programming language. Consider the development of a program to determine in which of five brackets or ranges individual numbers from a group of twenty numbers lie. Further, assume that the initial pseudocode will not be able to

take advantage of any structures intrinsic to the assembly language. The following
pseudocode might serve as a starting point for such a program.

```
BEGIN
        OBTAIN NUMBER TO BE BOUNDED
        DETERMINE LOWER BOUND
        DETERMINE CORRESPONDING UPPER BOUND
        INCREMENT INDEX
END
```

We see that this applies to a single number. Hence, it is necessary to compare all
twenty values with all five bracket ranges. This may be accomplished one of two
ways: Compare all twenty values against each of the five brackets, one bracket at a
time, or compare each value against all five brackets, consecutively. It is not initially
clear which approach will yield the better algorithm so we select the first. Also, the
concept of a loop must be introduced in order to accomplish this processing. Now we
expand the pseudocode.

```
BEGIN
      LOOP ON BRACKET RANGES
            LOOP ON NUMBERS TO BE BOUNDED
                  OBTAIN NUMBER TO BE BOUNDED
                  DETERMINE LOWER BOUND (BOUND SATISFIED?)
                  DETERMINE CORRESPONDING UPPER BOUND
                  INCREMENT INDEX (IF APPROPRIATE)
            ;NEXT NUMBER
            ENDLOOP
      ;NEXT BRACKET RANGE
      ENDLOOP
END
```

Here the statements within the construct, LOOP...ENDLOOP, are iteratively
calculated until the loop counter is set to zero.

This pseudocode begins to illustrate the nature that the structures will take for
normal programming. At this stage some control logic is needed to expand the
pseudocode.

```
BEGIN
      LOOP ON BRACKET RANGES
            LOOP ON NUMBERS TO BE BOUNDED
                  OBTAIN NUMBER TO BE BOUNDED
                  (IF) NUMBER > LOWER BRACKET
                    ;DETERMINE LOWER BOUND(BOUND SATISFIED?)
                      (IF) NUMBER < UPPER BRACKET
                        ;DETERMINE CORRESPONDING UPPER BOUND
                        INCREMENT INDEX(IF APPROPRIATE)
                      ENDIF
                  ENDIF
                  ;NEXT NUMBER
            ENDLOOP
            ;NEXT BRACKET RANGE
      ENDLOOP
END
```

The pseudocode that is illustrated in this example can now be translated to the procedure BRACKET that appears in Figure 3.5a. Note that the outer loop structure is accomplished using the conditional instruction as follows:

```
        . . .

RANGE:   MOV BX,OFFSET TABLE1

        . . .

         CMP DI,NUMR
         JB RANGE
```

The BRACKET program determines the number of data values in TABLE1 that lie in the five brackets (0,50), (51,100), (101,150), (151,200), and (201,255). These numbers are 4, 5, 2, 4, and 5, respectively. The reader should observe that all values in TABLE1 have been selected to lie in the range that can be specified by one byte (0 to 255). This program uses the index registers SI and DI to keep track of the table positions. SI is the index for TABLE1, the list values. DI is the index for the bracket values (RANGEL, for lower range, and RANGEU, for upper range).

The program has a nested loop structure; however, only one LOOP command has been used because this instruction uses and decrements CX. This loop goes from LL: to LOOP LL. CX serves as the loop counter with SI, the loop index. Within this loop, the bracket range is compared with all the list values, and NUMTAB is incremented for each list value that falls within the bracket range. The outer loop structure is the iteration on DI. The iteration begins at RANGE:, where DI is zero, and ends with the conditional jump

```
         JB RANGE
```

Prior to this jump, DI is incremented and compared with NUMR, the number of range values.

We know by now that the 20 TABLE1 values load into the data segment starting with offset 0000H. Since RANGEL is next, it must load with offsets 0014H through 0018H. Similarly, RANGEU must load with offsets 0019H through 001DH and the word entries, NUMB and NUMR, load into 001EH through 0021H, respectively. The bracket count, NUMTAB, loads 0022H through 0026H. This simple bookkeeping obviates the need to include an assembler listing for the program because all we are interested in seeing with DEBUG is how NUMTAB changes.

Executing this program, BRACKET.EXE, with DEBUG yields the result in Figure 3.5b. We know that the data segment address is acquired in the fourth instruction. Executing this instruction gives the data segment address, 12F1H. Performing a dump starting at DS:0000 demonstrates that all data segment variables have been initialized properly and the entries for NUMTAB are zero (see the figure). Next, the program is executed with the GO command and a dump performed for the data values. NUMTAB now contains the correct bracket totals, as evidenced by the figure.

Figure 3.6 illustrates the corresponding flow chart for this program. (The flow chart, of course, can be used as an alternative to pseudocode in generating the program appearing in Figure 3.5a.) Pseudocode does not translate directly into IF . . . THEN . . . ELSE type constructions, for example, and it is necessary to explicitly

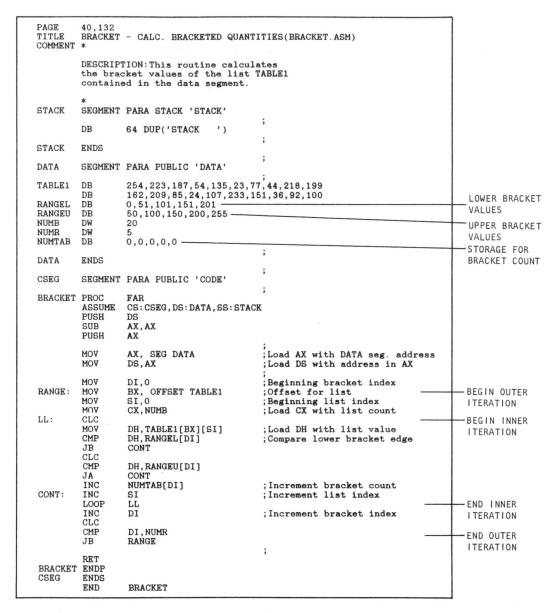

```
PAGE      40,132
TITLE     BRACKET - CALC. BRACKETED QUANTITIES(BRACKET.ASM)
COMMENT   *

          DESCRIPTION:This routine calculates
          the bracket values of the list TABLE1
          contained in the data segment.

          *
STACK     SEGMENT PARA STACK 'STACK'
                                                 ;
          DB      64 DUP('STACK    ')
                                                 ;
STACK     ENDS
                                                 ;
DATA      SEGMENT PARA PUBLIC 'DATA'
                                                 ;
TABLE1    DB      254,223,187,54,135,23,77,44,218,199
          DB      162,209,85,24,107,233,151,36,92,100
RANGEL    DB      0,51,101,151,201 ───────────────────────── LOWER BRACKET
RANGEU    DB      50,100,150,200,255 ──────────────────────  VALUES
NUMB      DW      20
NUMR      DW      5                                          UPPER BRACKET
NUMTAB    DB      0,0,0,0,0 ────────────────────────────────  VALUES
                                                 ;            STORAGE FOR
DATA      ENDS                                                BRACKET COUNT
                                                 ;
CSEG      SEGMENT PARA PUBLIC 'CODE'
                                                 ;
BRACKET   PROC    FAR
          ASSUME  CS:CSEG,DS:DATA,SS:STACK
          PUSH    DS
          SUB     AX,AX
          PUSH    AX

          MOV     AX, SEG DATA          ;Load AX with DATA seg. address
          MOV     DS,AX                 ;Load DS with address in AX

          MOV     DI,0                  ;Beginning bracket index
RANGE:    MOV     BX, OFFSET TABLE1     ;Offset for list              ─────── BEGIN OUTER
          MOV     SI,0                  ;Beginning list index                 ITERATION
          MOV     CX,NUMB               ;Load CX with list count
LL:       CLC                                                        ─────── BEGIN INNER
          MOV     DH,TABLE1[BX][SI]     ;Load DH with list value              ITERATION
          CMP     DH,RANGEL[DI]         ;Compare lower bracket edge
          JB      CONT
          CLC
          CMP     DH,RANGEU[DI]
          JA      CONT
          INC     NUMTAB[DI]            ;Increment bracket count
CONT:     INC     SI                    ;Increment list index
          LOOP    LL                                                 ─────── END INNER
          INC     DI                    ;Increment bracket index              ITERATION
          CLC
          CMP     DI,NUMR                                            ─────── END OUTER
          JB      RANGE                                                      ITERATION
                                                 ;
          RET
BRACKET   ENDP
CSEG      ENDS
          END     BRACKET
```

Figure 3.5a   The program BRACKET.ASM, which calculates the number of items in each bracketed range.

state the equivalent jump instructions at this point in the development of the Macro Assembler. The use of pseudocode versus flow charts becomes one of convenience. For purposes of exposition in this book the flow chart is preferred because, as indicated above, it is somewhat abbreviated compared to the pseudocode expansion. We have mentioned earlier that assembly language does not lend itself readily to structuring [7]. One last topic that should be mentioned is the use of CASE structures. These structures have already been mentioned in the context of the

```
DEBUG BRACKET.EXE
-T

AX=0000  BX=0000  CX=0270  DX=0000  SP=01FE  BP=0000  SI=0000  DI=0000
DS=12DD  ES=12DD  SS=12F4  CS=12ED  IP=0001    NV UP EI PL NZ NA PO NC
12ED:0001 2BC0            SUB     AX,AX
-T

AX=0000  BX=0000  CX=0270  DX=0000  SP=01FE  BP=0000  SI=0000  DI=0000
DS=12DD  ES=12DD  SS=12F4  CS=12ED  IP=0003    NV UP EI PL ZR NA PE NC
12ED:0003 50             PUSH    AX
-T

AX=0000  BX=0000  CX=0270  DX=0000  SP=01FC  BP=0000  SI=0000  DI=0000
DS=12DD  ES=12DD  SS=12F4  CS=12ED  IP=0004    NV UP EI PL ZR NA PE NC
12ED:0004 B8F112         MOV     AX,12F1
-T

AX=12F1  BX=0000  CX=0270  DX=0000  SP=01FC  BP=0000  SI=0000  DI=0000
DS=12DD  ES=12DD  SS=12F4  CS=12ED  IP=0007    NV UP EI PL ZR NA PE NC
12ED:0007 8ED8           MOV     DS,AX
-T

AX=12F1  BX=0000  CX=0270  DX=0000  SP=01FC  BP=0000  SI=0000  DI=0000
DS=12F1  ES=12DD  SS=12F4  CS=12ED  IP=0009    NV UP EI PL ZR NA PE NC
12ED:0009 BF0000         MOV     DI,0000
-D 12F1:0000
12F1:0000  FE DF BB 36 87 17 4D 2C-DA C7 A2 D1 55 18 6B E9   ...6..M,....U.k.
12F1:0010  97 24 5C 64 00 33 65 97-C9 32 64 96 C8 FF 14 00   .$\d.3e..2d.....
12F1:0020  05 00 00 00 00 00 00 00-00 00 00 00 00 00 00 00   ................
12F1:0030  53 54 41 43 4B 20 20 20-53 54 41 43 4B 20 20 20   STACK   STACK
12F1:0040  53 54 41 43 4B 20 20 20-53 54 41 43 4B 20 20 20   STACK   STACK
12F1:0050  53 54 41 43 4B 20 20 20-53 54 41 43 4B 20 20 20   STACK   STACK
12F1:0060  53 54 41 43 4B 20 20 20-53 54 41 43 4B 20 20 20   STACK   STACK
12F1:0070  53 54 41 43 4B 20 20 20-53 54 41 43 4B 20 20 20   STACK   STACK
-G

Program terminated normally
-D 12F1:0000
12F1:0000  FE DF BB 36 87 17 4D 2C-DA C7 A2 D1 55 18 6B E9   ...6..M,....U.k.
12F1:0010  97 24 5C 64 00 33 65 97-C9 32 64 98 C8 FF 14 00   .$\d.3e..2d.....
12F1:0020  05 00 04 05 02 04 05 00-00 00 00 00 00 00 00 00   ................
12F1:0030  53 54 41 43 4B 20 20 20-53 54 41 43 4B 20 20 20   STACK   STACK
12F1:0040  53 54 41 43 4B 20 20 20-53 54 41 43 4B 20 20 20   STACK   STACK
12F1:0050  53 54 41 43 4B 20 20 20-53 54 41 43 4B 20 20 20   STACK   STACK
12F1:0060  53 54 41 43 4B 20 20 20-53 54 41 43 4B 20 20 20   STACK   STACK
12F1:0070  53 54 41 43 4B 20 20 20-53 54 41 43 4B 20 20 20   STACK   STACK
-Q
```

INITIALIZATION (arrow pointing to line 12F1:0020 of first dump)

NUMBER OF ITEMS IN EACH BRACKET (arrow pointing to line 12F1:0020 of second dump)

Figure 3.5b A typical DEBUG session with the program BRACKET.

structure theorem and follow as a natural consequence of the IF ... THEN ... ELSE structure. Basically the CASE structure allows the selection of one among many alternatives [8, 9]. It is usually implemented in the following form:

```
IF ...
  (THEN ...)
    IF ...
      (THEN ...)
        IF ...
          (THEN ...)


            ...


          (ELSE ...)
        ENDIF
      (ELSE ...)
    ENDIF
  (ELSE ...)
ENDIF
```

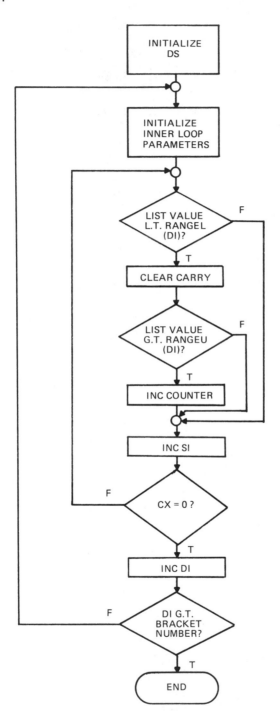

Figure 3.6 The functional flow chart for
the program BRACKET.ASM.

3.4 AN APPROACH TO STRUCTURED PROGRAMMING

In order to develop structured techniques, it is necessary to introduce several more structure constructs. Essentially, we will consider four of the basic SALUT structures described in Appendix B. Figures 3.7a through 3.7d define the syntax and structure for these constructs.

1. Simple IF (Figure 3.7a)
2. IF ... THEN ... ELSE (Figure 3.7b)
3. DO WHILE leading test (Figure 3.7c)
4. DO WHILE trailing test (Figure 3.7d)

The BRACKET.ASM program in Figure 3.5a is a good candidate for modification to reflect a structured format. This program has two loop structures and two conditional structures, with the outer loop structure implemented as a conditional branch. Since the loop structure has the form

```
            . . .
            MOV CX,NUMBER
            . . .
    LABEL:
            . . .
            LOOP LABEL
            . . .
```

it follows that only one loop can be nested using the LOOP instruction without PUSHing and POPing the CX register. Hence, the use of a conditional branch in the BRACKET program avoided the need for a PUSH and POP of CX for the outer loop. (A PUSH CX simply saves CX on the stack and the corresponding POP CX recalls CX and shifts the stack top out.)

Figure 3.8 presents the modified BRACKET.ASM program. The reader will note that the two loop structures and the two conditional branches are clearly delineated. The nomenclature is to use DOn ($n = 1, 2, \ldots$) for the associated loop labeling and IFn ($n = 1, 2, \ldots$) for the corresponding conditional branch labeling.

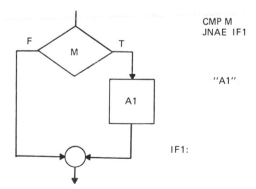

```
CMP M
JNAE IF1


    "A1"


IF1:
```

Figure 3.7a The simple IF structure.

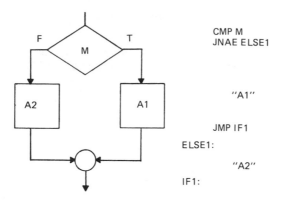

```
CMP M
JNAE ELSE1


          "A1"

JMP IF1
ELSE1:
          "A2"
IF1:
```

Figure 3.7b   The IF...THEN...ELSE structure.

```
          MOV CX,"COUNT"
DO1:

          CMP M
          JAE EXIT1

            "A1"

          LOOP DO1
EXIT1:

            or

          MOV CX,O
DO1:

          CMP M
          JAE EXIT1

            "A1"

          CMP CX,"COUNT"
          JBE DO1
EXIT1:
```

Figure 3.7c   The DO WHILE structure with leading test.

```
          MOV CX,"COUNT"
DO1:

            "A1"

          CMP M
          JAE EXIT1
          LOOP DO1
EXIT1:

            or

DO1:

            "A1"

          CMP M
          JBE DO1
```

Figure 3.7d   The DO WHILE structure with trailing test.

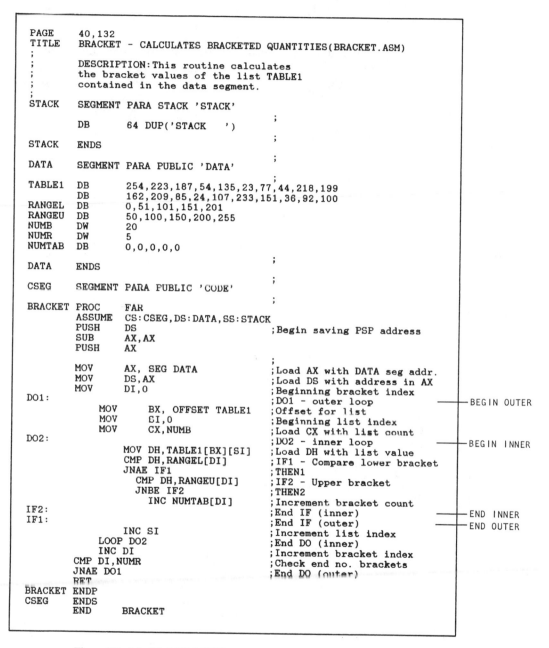

```
PAGE       40,132
TITLE      BRACKET - CALCULATES BRACKETED QUANTITIES(BRACKET.ASM)
;
;          DESCRIPTION:This routine calculates
;          the bracket values of the list TABLE1
;          contained in the data segment.
;
STACK      SEGMENT PARA STACK 'STACK'
                                                              ;
           DB        64 DUP('STACK    ')                      ;
                                                              ;
STACK      ENDS                                               ;
                                                              ;
DATA       SEGMENT PARA PUBLIC 'DATA'                         ;
                                                              ;
TABLE1     DB        254,223,187,54,135,23,77,44,218,199
           DB        162,209,85,24,107,233,151,36,92,100
RANGEL     DB        0,51,101,151,201
RANGEU     DB        50,100,150,200,255
NUMB       DW        20
NUMR       DW        5
NUMTAB     DB        0,0,0,0,0
                                                              ;
DATA       ENDS                                               ;
                                                              ;
CSEG       SEGMENT PARA PUBLIC 'CODE'                         ;
                                                              ;
BRACKET PROC      FAR
           ASSUME    CS:CSEG,DS:DATA,SS:STACK
           PUSH      DS
           SUB       AX,AX                    ;Begin saving PSP address
           PUSH      AX
                                              ;
           MOV       AX, SEG DATA             ;Load AX with DATA seg addr.
           MOV       DS,AX                    ;Load DS with address in AX
           MOV       DI,0                     ;Beginning bracket index
DO1:                                          ;DO1 - outer loop          ──── BEGIN OUTER
              MOV       BX, OFFSET TABLE1      ;Offset for list
              MOV       SI,0                   ;Beginning list index
              MOV       CX,NUMB                ;Load CX with list count
DO2:                                          ;DO2 - inner loop          ──── BEGIN INNER
                 MOV DH,TABLE1[BX][SI]         ;Load DH with list value
                 CMP DH,RANGEL[DI]             ;IF1 - Compare lower bracket
                 JNAE IF1                      ;THEN1
                    CMP DH,RANGEU[DI]          ;IF2 - Upper bracket
                    JNBE IF2                   ;THEN2
                       INC NUMTAB[DI]          ;Increment bracket count
IF2:                                          ;End IF (inner)            ──── END INNER
IF1:                                          ;End IF (outer)            ──── END OUTER
                 INC SI                        ;Increment list index
              LOOP DO2                         ;End DO (inner)
              INC DI                           ;Increment bracket index
           CMP DI,NUMR                         ;Check end no. brackets
           JNAE DO1                            ;End DO (outer)
           RET
BRACKET ENDP
CSEG       ENDS
           END       BRACKET
```

Figure 3.8 Modified BRACKET.ASM program, reflecting the use of conditional and loop structures.

3.5 STYLE AND FORM

Before concluding this chapter it is instructive to consider style and form. The
BRACKET program, and most other assembler programs in this book, use upper-
case characters to define the actual source instructions. Lower-case letters are used

```
PAGE      40,132
TITLE     BRACKET - CALCULATES BRACKETED QUANTITIES(BRACKET.ASM)
COMMENT *

          DESCRIPTION:This routine calculates
          the       bracket values of the list TABLE1
          contained in the data segment.

          *
STACK     SEGMENT PARA STACK 'STACK'
                                                     ;
          DB       64 DUP('STACK    ')
                                                     ;
STACK     ENDS
                                                     ;
DATA      SEGMENT PARA PUBLIC 'DATA'
                                                     ;
TABLE1    DB       254,223,187,54,135,23,77,44,218,199
          DB       162,209,85,24,107,233,151,36,92,100
RANGEL    DB       0,51,101,151,201
RANGEU    DB       50,100,150,200,255
NUMB      DW       20
NUMR      DW       5
NUMTAB    DB       0,0,0,0,0
                                                     ;
DATA      ENDS
                                                     ;
CSEG      SEGMENT PARA PUBLIC 'CODE'
                                                     ;
BRACKET PROC      FAR
        ASSUME  CS:CSEG,DS:DATA,SS:STACK
        PUSH    DS
        SUB     AX,AX
        PUSH    AX
                                                     ;
        MOV     AX, SEG DATA                 ;Load AX with DATA seg. address
        MOV     DS,AX                        ;Load DS with address in AX
                                                     ;
        MOV     SI,0                         ;Beginning list index
        MOV     BX,OFFSET TABLE1             ;Offset for list
DO1:                                         ;DO1 - outer loop
            MOV     DI,0                     ;Beginning bracket index
            MOV     CX,NUMR                  ;Load CX with bracket count
            MOV     DH,TABLE1[BX][SI]        ;Load DH with list value
DO2:                                         ;DO2 - inner loop
                CMP DH,RANGEL[DI]            ;IF1 - compare lower bracket
                JNAE IF1                     ;THEN1
                  CMP DH,RANGEU[DI]          ;IF2 - Upper bracket
                  JNBE IF2                   ;THEN2
                    INC NUMTAB[DI]           ;Increment bracket count
IF2:                                         ;End IF (inner)
IF1:                                         ;End IF (outer)
                INC DI                       ;Increment bracket index
            LOOP DO2                         ;End DO (inner)
            INC SI                           ;Increment list index
        CMP SI,NUMB                          ;Check end no. brackets
        JNAE DO1                             ;End DO (outer)
                                                     ;
        RET
BRACKET ENDP
CSEG      ENDS
          END       BRACKET
```

OUTSIDE INNER LOOP — points to DO2 inner loop region

NOTE INDEX — points to INC DI

NOTE INDEX — points to INC SI

Figure 3.9   The modified BRACKET.ASM program, which illustrates improved form.

for descriptive information. This is decidedly a preference of the author, and the reader should feel free to develop alternatives as desired. Also, the organization of the programs always places the data and extra segments after the stack segment and before the code segment. This is a normal convention. Again, the user should exercise judgment in the placement of these features and feel free to use some discretion in organization, while recognizing that a precedence does exist.

A more serious aspect of the program BRACKET relates to form. Remember that the program could have been implemented one of two ways: looping on all list values for each bracket range or looping on all bracket ranges for each list value. We selected the former and arrived at the program contained in Figure 3.8. A slightly more efficient program would have resulted if the second approach had been chosen. Figure 3.9 illustrates this case. Note that the instruction

```
MOV   DH,TABLE1[BX][SI]     ;Load DH with list value
```

moves from the inner loop to the outer loop. This simple change means that the instruction executes 20 times instead of 100 times, a considerable savings in execution time.

3.6 SUMMARY

This chapter has addressed the application of theoretical programming considerations to the IBM Macro Assembler. Modular programming techniques were introduced and guidelines provided for the development of appropriately sized modules in the assembler context. Generally, these assembler modules are larger than corresponding higher-level language modules because of the detailed nature of assembly code. The general rule-of-thumb is that assembler modules should lie between 20 and 200 lines of source code.

Top-down design was then developed and an example of a structure chart presented. The top-down approach to program design is intended to clarify the module linkages and the tasks to be accomplished within each module. At the conclusion of the top-down design process, a given task should be clearly understood with regard to what small tasks are needed to accomplish the task (the modules) and how these small tasks go together (the linkages). The differences between conventional functional flow charts and structure charts were explored and the use of pseudocode was contrasted with flow charts. Essentially, the programmer can use flow charts or pseudocode to develop a detailed description of the program, prior to actual coding, at the module level. The structure chart is intended to provide an overview of the actual program architecture.

Structured programming techniques were explored. The use of structured code was illustrated with the BRACKET program and the implications of style and form discussed.

The reader should recognize that the techniques presented in this chapter provide a firm framework from which to begin a study of the IBM Macro Assembler. The guidelines for developing modules should minimize the length of source code associated with a given task in the program environment. Generally, procedures will be considerably shorter than modules when developed in the assembler context. In some cases, however, a module will consist of one procedure and associated overhead (such as a corresponding data segment to define variables). The effort to reduce module source code further helps to insure that the program will be easily understood.

This book uses the IBM Macro Assembler input source format to develop programs. In Appendix B the utility SALUT is introduced. This utility comes with the IBM version of assembler and readers with an alternative assembler edition cannot be expected to have access to SALUT. Clearly we would like these users also to be able to use the book as a tool for learning the assembler language. The solution to this dilemma has been to generate normal structured assembler, keeping in mind some of the basic constructs relevant to structured programming. The reader is referred to the appendix for a more detailed use of structured programming in the assembler context using SALUT. Obviously SALUT comes highly recommended. Any utility that allows the simplification of assembler into a structured architecture, where normally the programmer is able only to structure higher level language programs, provides a mechanism for greatly enhancing the ease of understanding assembler.

REFERENCES

1. Martin, J., and McClure, C. *Structured Techniques for Computing.* Prentice-Hall, Inc., Englewood Cliffs, NJ (1985), p. 67.
2. LaBudde, K. *Structured Programming Concepts.* McGraw-Hill Book Co., New York, NY (1987), p. 26.
3. Parnas, D. "Information Distribution Aspects of Design Methodology." Carnegie-Mellon University Technical Report. Carnegie-Mellon University. Pittsburgh, PA (1971).
4. Cohen, A. *Structure Logic and Program Design,* John Wiley and Sons, Inc., New York, NY (1983), p. 6.
5. Alagic, S., and Arbib, M. A. *The Design of Well-Structured and Correct Programs.* Springer-Verlag, New York, NY (1978).
6. *Macro Assembler Version 2.00.* IBM Personal Computer-Computer Language Series. IBM Corp. P.O. Box 1328. Boca Raton, FL 33432 (1984).
7. Hordeski, M. F. *Design of Microprocessor Sensor and Control Systems.* Reston Publishing Co., Inc., Reston, VA (1985), p. 74.
8. Benton, S., and Weekes, L. *Program It Right: Structured Methods in BASIC.* Yourdan Press. New York, NY (1985), p. 120.
9. Kernighan, B. W., and Plauger, P. J. *The Elements of Programming Style.* McGraw-Hill Book Co. New York, NY (1978), p. 37.

PROBLEMS

3.1. What would the recommended minimum module size be for most higher-level languages?

3.2. Using the return instruction, RET, it is possible to achieve more than one exit point from a module, depending on the underlying logic. How can this be avoided?

3.3. Under what conditions can a module be expected to have its own associated data segment or extra segment? If a change in data segment is to occur upon entry into a module, what happens to variables that are defined in an alternate data segment? Why can the extra segment be so useful under these conditions?

3.4. Passing data parameter values among modules can be accomplished using the data or extra segments. Why is this method less desirable than using the general purpose registers, when possible?

3.5. If the user intends that the stack will hold parameters to be passed between modules, what must be done with the first (several) bytes on the stack upon entry to a procedure? When must the user pay attention to only the first byte? When must the user pay attention to the first two bytes?

3.6. Why is it logical to allow only three modules at the level-1 point in a structure chart?

3.7. While there are no general rules for designing structure charts, one guideline is that a properly subdivided module will have at least two modules at the next lower level. An exception to this rule is the situation where a single module can be subordinated to two higher-level modules. What would be a possible solution to this case?

3.8. In bottom-up program design, each module is delineated first, and then an overall task is built from the bottom up. Discuss, in general, why top-down design might be preferred. How would libraries be useful for bottom-up design?

3.9. Discuss the pitfalls that might be encountered when unrestricted use of the GO TO construct exists. Without the usage of GO TO instructions why, in general, is it necessary to provide for loop and CASE-type statements? (Consider the movement of execution processing in the program structure.)

3.10. What basic modifications to the program BRACKET.ASM (Figure 3.2a) are needed if a single list value from TABLE1 is to be compared to all five bracket ranges, consecutively, for the entire list?

3.11. Define a set of guidelines for writing pseudocode along the style of the pseudocode presented in the example for this chapter.

3.12. In the BRACKET.ASM program appearing in Figure 3.2a, where and how would the stack need to be pushed and popped in order to use a second loop instruction for the outer iteration?

3.13. Illustrate a general flowchart for the CASE-type construct.

3.14. In general, either DO WHILE structure can be applied to a given loop situation. Which one is usually preferred and why?

4

The Macro Assembler
Instructions

The previous chapter outlined techniques for achieving optimum development of assembler code. These techniques included top-down design, modular programming, and a discussion of structured code. This chapter presents the remaining 8088 instructions that form the core of the Macro Assembler. In addition to indicating the function of the 8088 instructions, we will consider several additional program examples. These examples will reflect the software design approaches presented in Chapter 3. Finally, the development of object libraries is discussed. Libraries provide an excellent means of generating modular code, and it is only through the Macro Assembler version 2.0 that the library utility has been established.

4.1 THE MORE COMMONLY USED INSTRUCTIONS

Table 4.1 contains a partial set of the 8088 instructions grouped according to functional type. Many instructions, within a group, behave in similar fashion. Program code can be structured for alternate instructions, with little or no additional effort. For example, jump instructions can be programmed from a number of options. The loop instructions can be replaced by jump instruction sequences under proper conditions. The instructions contained in Table 4.1 are commonly found in programs that execute applications that order data or perform arithmetic operations. Any instruction contained in parenthesis is equivalent to the preceding instruction.

TABLE 4.1 PARTIAL 8088 INSTRUCTION SET

Type	8088 Instruction	Comments
Arithmetic	ADC, ADD, DIV, IDIV, IMUL, MUL, SBB, SUB	These instructions are used for arithmetic operations on the source and destination operands.
Logical	AND, NEG, NOT, OR, TEST, XOR	These instructions are used for logical operations on the operands.
Move	MOV, MOVS (MOVSB) (MOVSW)	Movement of the contents of operands is accomplished with these instructions. Each instruction can be addressed in a number of ways.
Load	LODS (LODSB) (LODSW), LAHF, LDS, LEA, LES	These instructions are used to load various registers with bytes or strings and are register specific.
Jump	JA (JNBE), JAE (JNB) (JNC), JB (JNAE) (JC), JBE (JNA), JCXZ, JE (JZ), JG (JNLE), JGE (JNL), JL (JNGE), JLE (JNG), JMP, JNE (JNZ), JNO, JNP (JPO), JNS, JO, JP (JPE), JS	The jump instructions transfer processing to the target operand. The transfer can be unconditional or depend on certain conditions existing at the time the jump is executed.
Loop	LOOP, LOOPE (LOOPZ), LOOPNE (LOOPNZ)	The loop instructions allow unconditional or conditional transfer to a target until a loop counter has been decremented to zero.
Stack	POP, POPF, PUSH, PUSHF	These instructions provide the means for placing operand values and addresses on the stack and removing them.
Count	DEC, INC	These instructions are used to increment and decrement counters.
Compare	CMP, CMPS (CMPSB) (CMPSW)	These instructions compare the contents of the operands and affect flags.
Flag	CLC, CLD, CLI, CMC, STC, STD, STI	These instructions affect the flags.

The structure of this subsection is to first present a more detailed examination of each of the instruction groups appearing in Table 4.1. One of the major difficulties in writing meaningful programs at this stage is the I/O problem mentioned earlier. Until methods of inputting data are provided for the user, the programmer must rely on data being initialized in the source code, as in the data segment. This is not very flexible. The next chapter will describe BIOS interrupts and tools will be discussed that allow the programmer to use the keyboard and screen for I/O purposes. This will greatly facilitate the user's ability to generate general purpose code.

Table 4.2 illustrates the 8088 instructions for arithmetic-type operations [1]. These instructions serve as the basis for the Macro Assembler instruction set. The first two instructions, ADC and ADD, are addition operations. This addition corresponds to binary addition. Assume that AL contains the quantity FFH and BL, the quantity 02H. The instruction

ADD AL,BL

TABLE 4.2   THE ARITHMETIC INSTRUCTION GROUP

Instruction	Purpose	Comments
ADC destination, source	Addition with Carry	Performs an addition of the two operands and adds one to the result if CF is set.
ADD destination, source	Addition	Adds the two operands
DIV source	Unsigned Division	Performs unsigned division of the numerand by the divisor which is contained in the source. The numerand is contained in AL and AH for byte operation and in AX and DX for word operation. These double-length quantities return a single length quotient (in AL or AX) and remainder (AH or DX).
IDIV source	Signed Integer Division	Performs signed division using the same registers as DIV.
IMUL source	Signed Integer Multiplication	Multiples AL or AX times the source and returns a double-length product to AL and AH (byte) or AX and DX (word).
MUL source	Unsigned multiplication	Multiples AL or AX times the source and returns a double-length product to AL and AH (byte) or AX and DX (word).
SBB destination, source	Subtraction with Borrow	Subtracts the two operands and subtracts one from the difference if CF is set. The source is subtracted from the destination.
SUB destination, source	Subtraction	Subtracts the source from the destination.

will generate AL = 01H with the carry flag set. If AX = 00FFH and BX = 0002H in this example, the high order byte can be corrected with

```
                                ADC AH,BH
```

The AX register will then contain the correct result, 0101H. It is necessary to provide for a 16-bit result when doing 8-bit additions (and a 32-bit result when doing 16-bit addition). A typical sequence for 16-bit addition might look like

```
        ADD AX,MEM1     ; Add 16-bit memory to AX
        ADC BX,MEM2     ; Add high order 16-bit memory to BX
```

The important aspect of ADC is that it adds 1 to the result of the high-order 16-bit addition when the carry flag is set.

The DIV instruction performs unsigned division with the numerator contained in AL and AH (byte operation) or AX and DX (word operation). The divisor is specified by the source. A single-length quotient is returned to the accumulator (AL or AX) and a single-length remainder is contained in the extension (AH for byte operation or DX for word operation). There are four major cases: word divided by a byte, byte divided by a byte, double word divided by a word, and word divided by a word. The following examples indicate how one might accomplish these divisions.

1. Word divided by a byte

       MOV AX,AAA   ; AAA is an unsigned word quantity
       DIV BBB   ; BBB is an unsigned byte quantity
                           ; Quotient = AL, Remainder = AH

2. Byte divided by a byte

       MOV AL,AAA   ; AAA is an unsigned byte quantity
       CBW   ; Converts AL quantity to a word
       DIV BBB   ; BBB is an unsigned byte quantity
                           ; Quotient = AL, Remainder = AH

3. Double word divided by a word

       MOV CX,AAA1   ; AAA1 is high-order numerator word
       MOV AX,AAA2   ; AAA2 is low-order numerator word
       DIV BBB   ; BBB is an unsigned word quantity
                           ; Quotient = AX, Remainder = DX

4. Word divided by a word

       MOV AX,AAA   ; AAA is an unsigned word quantity
       CWD   ; Convert word to double word
       DIV BBB   ; BBB is a word quantity
                           ; Quotient = AX, Remainder = DX

IDIV works in similar fashion except all numbers are treated as two's complement signed numbers.

The multiplication instruction, MUL, performs unsigned multiplication of AL(byte) or AX(word) and the source operand. A double-length result is returned to AX(byte) or AX and DX(word). Consider

1. Multiply byte by a byte

       MOV AL,AAA   ; AAA is a byte quantity
       MUL BBB   ; BBB is a byte quantity
                           ; Product = AX

2. Multiply word by a word

       MOV AX,AAA   ; AAA is a word quantity
       MUL BBB   ; BBB is a word quantity
                           ; Product high = DX, product low = AX

3. Multiply byte by a word

       MOV AL,AAA   ; AAA is a byte quantity
       CBW   ; Convert AL to word AX
       MUL BBB   ; BBB is a word quantity
                           ; Product high = DX, product low = AX

The instruction IMUL behaves identically to MUL, except it operates on signed numbers.

The SUB and SBB instructions perform two's complement subtraction. The two instructions are similar to the ADD and ADC instructions, except a borrow sets the carry flag. A convenient example is AX = 0102H and BX = 0003H. Using

SUB AL,BL

the subtraction is given by

$$
\begin{array}{rl}
0000\ 0010 & \textit{2's complement} \\
-0000\ 0011 & \\
\hline
\end{array}
\qquad
\begin{array}{r}
0000\ 0010 \\
+(1)\ 1111\ 1101 \\
\hline
(1)\ 1111\ 1111
\end{array}
$$

Here the (1) corresponds to a borrow. Then

SBB AH,BH

yields

$$
\begin{array}{rl}
0000\ 0001 & \textit{2's complement} \\
-0000\ 0001 & \\
\hline
\end{array}
\qquad
\begin{array}{r}
0000\ 0001 \\
+\quad 1111\ 1111 \\
\hline
(1)\ 0000\ 0000
\end{array}
$$

Here the (1) corresponds to a carry, which cancels the borrow. Thus

$$AX = 0000\ 0000\ 1111\ 1111 = 255$$

which is the difference between 258 and 3.

Table 4.3 contains the logical instructions used with the Intel 8088. The AND instruction performs the bit-by-bit conjunction of the source and destination. If AX = FFFFH, then

AND AX,1111H

leaves AX = 1111H. The NEG instruction produces the two's complement of the destination. If AX = 1234H, then

NEG AX

yields AX = EDCCH.

The OR instruction produces an inclusive OR result between the source and destination. If AX = 1234H, then

OR AX,1111H

yields AX = 1335H. The TEST instruction is the same as the AND instruction except that only the flags are affected. Finally, the XOR instruction yields the exclusive disjunction of the two operands. If AX = 1234H then

XOR AX,1111H

yields AX = 0325H.

TABLE 4.3 THE LOGICAL INSTRUCTION GROUP

Instruction	Purpose	Comments
AND destination, source	Logical AND	Performs the bit conjunction of the two operands:
NEG destination	Form Two's Complement	This instruction forms the two's complement of the destination.
NOT destination	Logical NOT	Inverts the operand bit-by-bit.
OR destination, source	Logical Inclusive OR	Performs the bit logical inclusive disjunction of the two operands:
TEST destination, source	Logical Compare	Performs the bit conjunction of the two operands, causing the flags to be affected, but does not return the result.
XOR destination, source	Exclusive OR	Performs the bit logical exclusive disjunction of the two operands:

AND truth table:

S	D	D
1	1	1
1	0	0
0	1	0
0	0	0

OR truth table:

S	D	D
1	1	1
1	0	1
0	1	1
0	0	0

XOR truth table:

S	D	D
1	1	0
1	0	1
0	1	1
0	0	0

The logical group of instructions is used to generate masks that can serve as a basis for data checking. The character capital A, for example, has an ASCII value of 41H. If this byte quantity is read from the keyboard it could result in a jump to a routine as follows:

```
        MOV AL,INPUT_BYTE    ; Look for A in input
        XOR AL,41H           ; Generate zero for A
        JZ CAPA              ; Jump to CAPA
        . . .
CAPA:   . . .
```

We have already seen numerous examples of the MOV instruction. Table 4.4 briefly indicates the seven different move formats. These move instructions each generate different machine code; however, we are not too concerned with this. The reader should continue to explore this command. It is perhaps the most widely used instruction. The MOVSB command is illustrated with an example in the table. The REP instruction will simply repeat the MOVS, decrementing CX until 0 is reached; and each execution of MOVS will increment DI and SI.

TABLE 4.4 THE MOVE INSTRUCTION GROUP

Instruction	Purpose	Comments
MOV destination, source	Move	There are seven separate types of move instruction.
		1. TO Memory FROM Accumulator
		2. TO Accumulator FROM Memory
		3. TO Segment Register FROM Memory/Register
		4. TO Memory/Register FROM Segment Register
		5. TO Register FROM Register
		TO Register FROM Memory
		TO Memory FROM Register
		6. TO Register FROM Immediate Data
		7. TO Memory FROM Immediate Data
MOVS destination-string, source-string (MOVSB) (MOVSW)	Move Byte or Word String	Transfers a byte or word string from the source, addressed by SI, to the destination, addressed by DI. A typical sequence would be
		MOV SI, OFFSET AAA
		MOV DI, OFFSET BBB
		MOV CX, LENGTH AAA
		REP MOVS BBB,AAA

Table 4.5 presents the 8088 load instructions. The LODS instruction is used to load successive bytes (or words) into AL (or AX). Suppose a table, TABLE1, is to be read into AL sequentially and the largest value saved in BH. The following program code accomplishes this.

```
      . . .
      MOV CX,NUMB          ; Load CX with TABLE1 size
      DEC CX               ; Subtract 1 from CX
      CLD                  ; Clear DF to increment SI
      MOV SI,OFFSET TABLE1 ; Loads TABLE1 offset
      MOV AH,TABLE1        ; Loads first TABLE1 in AH
      ADD SI,1             ; Increments SI
DO1:  LODS TABLE1[SI]      ; Loads TABLE1 (+N) in AL
      CMP AH,AL            ; Compare AH and AL
      JAE IF1              ; Jump if AH larger
      MOV AH,AL            ; Move AL into AH if AH smaller
IF1:  LOOP DO1             ; Loop until CX = 0
      MOV BH,AH            ; Move AH into BH
      . . .
```

This code uses a number of instructions defined in Chapter 2. The main intent was to demonstrate an example of LODS. The usage

```
      LODS TABLE1[SI]
```

could have been replaced with

```
      MOV AL,TABLE1[SI]
      ADD SI,1
```

TABLE 4.5 THE LOAD INSTRUCTION GROUP

Instruction	Purpose	Comments
LODS source-string (LODSB) (LODSW)	Load Byte or Word String	Transfers a byte (or word) operand from the source, addressed by SI, to AL (or AX) and adjusts SI by 1 (up or down depending on DF) for bytes or 2 for words.
LAHF	Load AH from Flags	Transfers the flags SF, ZF, AF, PF, and CF into AH as follows:

SF	ZF	X	AF	X	PF	X	CF

The quantity X is indeterminate.

Instruction	Purpose	Comments
LDS destination, source	Load Data Segment Register	The source must be a double-word memory operand (32 bits). The higher-addressed word is treated as a segment address which transfers to DS. The lower-addressed word is an offset address which is transferred to the register specified as destination.
LEA destination, source	Load Effective Address	Transfers the offset address of the source to the destination. The source must be a memory operand and the destination can be a 16-bit general, pointer, or index register.
LES destination, source	Load Extra Segment Register	The source must be a double-word memory operand (32 bits). The higher-addressed word is treated as the segment address which transfers to ES. The lower-addressed word is an offset address which is transferred to the register specified as destination.

The instruction LAHF loads the flags into AH as indicated in the table. Both LDS and LES load segment registers. The source must be a double-word memory operand. Earlier we saw that the instructions

```
MOV AX,SEG DATA
MOV DS,AX
```

loaded the data segment register with a segment address for DATA. If the first memory location in the data segment was defined as a double word, such as

```
DDDDW DD 0
```

the sequence

```
LDS AX,DDDDW
```

would load DS with the segment address. AX above would be loaded with the second word in DDDDW (the offset address). LES behaves in a similar fashion.

TABLE 4.6 THE LOOP INSTRUCTION GROUP

Instruction	Purpose	Comments
LOOP short-label	Loop until count complete	This instruction decrements CX by 1 and transfers control to the short-label if CX ≠ 0.
LOOPE short-label (LOOPZ)	Loop if equal and if zero	This instruction decrements CX by 1 and transfers control to the short-label if CX ≠ 0 and ZF = 1.
LOOPNE short-label (LOOPNZ)	Loop if not equal and if not zero	This instruction is the opposite of LOOPE. It decrements CX by 1 and transfers control to the short-label if CX ≠ 0 and ZF = 0.

LEA is used to transfer the offset address of a memory operand into a 16-bit general, pointer, or index register. The sequence of instructions

```
MOV BX,OFFSET TABLE1
MOV SI,13
MOV AX,[BX][SI]
```

can be replaced with

```
MOV SI,13
LEA AX,TABLE1[SI]
```

The loop instructions are illustrated in Table 4.6. (We have seen the jump instructions in Chapter 3.) All three loop instructions use the count register, CX. Prior to execution of the loop instruction, the CX register must be initialized to the number of iterations to be executed. The instruction sequence

```
       . . .
       MOV CX,10     ; Initialize CX = 10
DO1:   . . .         ; Instructions to be looped
       . . .             . . .
       LOOP DO1      ; Loop jump to DO1
       . . .             . . .
```

causes the instructions between the label DO1 and the loop instruction LOOP DO1 to be executed ten times. The LOOPE instruction transfers control if a previous comparison or instruction that sets the zero flag makes ZF = 1. Consider the following sequence.

```
       . . .
       MOV CX,10      ; Initialize CX = 10
DO1:   . . .          ; Instructions
       . . .              . . .
       CMP AH,AL      ; If AH = AL and ZF = 1
       LOOPE DO1      ; Loop to DO1, CX = 0 and ZF = 1
       . . .              . . .
```

The instruction LOOPNE is the inverse of LOOPE.

TABLE 4.7 THE STACK INSTRUCTION GROUP

Instruction	Purpose	Comments
POP destination	POP word off stack to destination	This instruction transfers a word operand from the stack location addressed by SP to the destination. Then the SP register is incremented by 2.
POPF	POP flags off stack	This instruction transfers bits from the word on top of the stack to the flags register. These flags are transferred as follows:

7   0

SF	ZF		AF		PF		CF

15   8

			OF	DF	IF	TF

The SP register is incremented by 2.

Instruction	Purpose	Comments
PUSH source	PUSH word onto stack	This instruction decrements SP by 2 and then transfers a word from the source to the stack, at the position addressed by SP.
PUSHF	PUSH flags onto stack	This instruction decrements SP by 2 and transfers the flag registers (into the bits indicated for the POPF instruction) to the word addressed by SP.

The stack instructions in Table 4.7 affect the placement or removal of words on the stack. Also, two special instructions preserve the nine flags in the stack. We have already used the PUSH instruction to preserve DS and a zero offset for the FAR return to DOS. The RET instruction caused these two quantities to be popped off the stack and put in DS and IP. The POP instruction removes from the stack a word operand addressed by the stack pointer (SP). These instructions are basically self-explanatory.

The count instructions simply decrement or increment the destination operand. In the earlier example the instructions

```
...
MOV CX,NUMB      : Load CX TABLE1 size specified by NUMB
DEC CX           ; Subtract 1 from CX
...
```

caused CX to be loaded first with the size of TABLE1 and then to be reduced by 1 because intervals were needed $(n-1)$ not the total number (n). Basically, two quantities were always compared, and out of n items, $n-1$ comparisons are possible. Table 4.8 describes these instructions.

Finally, the last instructions to be discussed in this subsection are the flag instructions. These instructions are presented in Table 4.9. The flag instructions are self-explanatory, operating on the Status Flags register. They have no operands because they simply clear or set flags. The CMC flag, for example, complements CF; that is, it changes its value to the opposite value (changes to 1 if 0 or to 0 if 1).

TABLE 4.8 THE COUNT INSTRUCTION GROUP

Instruction	Purpose	Comments
DEC destination	Decrement destination by one	This instruction subtracts 1 from the destination and returns the result to that operand.
INC destination	Increment destination by one	This instruction adds 1 to the destination and returns the result to that operand.

TABLE 4.9 THE FLAG INSTRUCTION GROUP

Instruction	Purpose	Comments
CLC	Clear Carry Flag	This instruction sets the carry flag to zero.
CLD	Clear Direction Flag	This instruction sets the direction flag to zero.
CLI	Clear Interrupt Flag (Disable)	This instruction clears the IF flag and, consequently, disables interrupts which are maskable. Maskable interrupts are interrupts which are inhibited when IF = 0.
CMC	Complement Carry Flag	Complements CF: if CF = 0 it is set to 1 and if CF = 1 it is set to 0
STC	Set Carry Flag	Sets CF to 1
STD	Set Direction Flag	Sets DF to 1
STI	Set Interrupt Flag (Enable)	This instruction sets IF which enables maskable external interrupts after the next instruction.

4.2 REMAINING 8088 INSTRUCTIONS

In section 4.1 we presented many of the more commonly used 8088 instructions. Table 4.10 illustrates the grouping of the remaining 8088 instructions. Again these instructions have been grouped according to functional type with similar instructions appearing within the same grouping. These instructions tend to be more specialized and, consequently, less used. The reader should familiarize himself with them because, when needed, they can substantially improve the efficiency of program code.

Table 4.11 presents the shift instruction group. The sequence

```
    . . .
    MOV CL,15
    SHR AAA,CL
    SHL AAA,CL
    . . .
```

clears all bits except the sign bit in the variable AAA. The byte register, CL, must be used to specify shifts greater than one bit. The SAL and SAR instructions are the same as SHL and SHR except the carry flag is involved in the shift operation.

TABLE 4.10   REMAINING 8088 INSTRUCTION SET

Type	8088 Instruction	Comments
Shift	SAL, SHL, SAR, SHR	These instructions shift the destination operand left (SAL, SHL) or right (SAR, SHR) the specified number of bits.
Rotate	RCL, RCR, ROL, ROR	These instructions shift the destination operand (RCL, ROL) left or right (RCR, ROR) and wrap the outgoing bits around.
Store	STOS (STOSB) (STOSW), SAHF	These instructions are for storing arrays. The destination string identifies the storage variable and DI points to the location.
String	REP (REPE) (REPZ), REPNE (REPNZ), SCAS (SCASB) (SCASW)	The repeat instructions are continued until CX = 0. The scan instructions subtract the destination addressed by DI from AL (or AX).
Convert	CWD, CBW	These instructions convert bytes to words or word to double word.
Procedure & Control	CALL, RET, ESC, LOCK, NOP, WAIT	These instructions handle procedure calling and return, and put the system in given states.
ASCII	AAA, AAD, AAM, AAS	These instructions are used for packed decimal adjustment after arithmetic operations.
Decimal	DAA, DAS	These instructions are used for packed decimal adjustment after arithmetic operations.
I/O	IN, OUT	The contents of the accumulator are replaced by the port (IN) or vice versa.
Misc.	XCHG, XLAT	These instructions are used for exchanging operands (XCHG) or translating a table value into AL (XLAT).

Table 4.12 illustrates the rotate instructions. These instructions act in exactly the same fashion as the shift instructions, except the bits are wrapped around back into the word. For example, the sequence

```
      . . .
      MOV CL,15
      ROR AAA,CL
      ROL AAA,CL
      . . .
```

leaves AAA unchanged. For the shift instructions, the sequence cleared all bits in AAA except the highest.

TABLE 4.11 THE SHIFT INSTRUCTION GROUP

Instruction	Purpose	Comments
SAL destination, count	Shift Arithmetic Left	Shifts the destination left the number of bits specified by count (1 or CL, where CL contains a bit count). The vacated bits are filled with zeros.
SHL destination, count	Shift Logical Left	(same as SAL)
SAR destination, count	Shift Arithmetic Right	Shifts the destination right the number of bits specified by count (1 or CL, where CL contains a bit count). The vacated bits are filled with zeros. The low-order bit replaces the carry flag whose original value is lost.
SHR destination, count	Shift Logical Right	(same as SAR)

Table 4.13 presents the store instruction group. The sequence

```
        . . .
        MOV AL,AAA
        MOV DI,OFFSET DATAVL
        STOSB
        . . .
```

loads the value of AAA in AL, obtains the address of DATAVL in the data segment and stores AAA at that address. DI automatically points to an offset in the current data segment, specified by DS. The instruction SAHF simply stores the five indicated flags in the appropriate registers by transferring these bits from AH to the flag registers.

Table 4.14 contains the string instruction group. The REP and REPNE instructions cause a sequence of instructions following the instruction to be repeated

TABLE 4.12 THE ROTATE INSTRUCTION GROUP

Instruction	Purpose	Comments
RCL destination, count	Rotate Left through Carry	This instruction rotates left in wrap-around fashion the destination by count bits (1 or CL, where CL contains a bit count). The carry flag is included in this wrap-around rotation.
RCR destination, count	Rotate Right through Carry	This instruction is identical to RCL except the rotate is to the right.
ROL destination, count	Rotate Left	This instruction is similar to RCL except the high-order bit rotates into the carry flag and the low order bit. The old carry flag is lost. All other bits shift left in wrap-around fashion.
ROR destination, count	Rotate Right	This instruction is identical but inverse (shift right) to ROL. The low-order bit rotates into the carry flag and the high-order bit. The old carry flag is lost. All other bits shift right in wrap-around fashion.

TABLE 4.13 THE STORE INSTRUCTION GROUP

Instruction	Purpose	Comments
STOS destination-string (STOSB) (STOSW)	Store Byte or Word String	This instruction transfers a byte (or word) from AL (or AX) to the location pointed to by DI. DI is then incremented (decremented if DF = 1) by 1 (byte) or 2 (word).
SAHF	Store AH in Flags	This instruction transfers the specified bits of the AH register to the flags register. The bits are SF, ZF, AF, PF, and CF. They appear as follows:

7	6	5	4	3	2	1	0
SF	ZF	XX	AF	XX	PF	XX	CF

.

until CX = 0 or a jump from the sequence occurs. These instructions are used with string instructions such as SCAS or move instructions such as MOVSB. The SCAS instruction compares the byte (or word) addressed by DI with AL (or AX) and affects the flags but does not return a result. Suppose one desired to scan a string and look for a question mark and upon finding a question mark jump to the label IF2. The following sequence accomplishes this task.

```
        . . .
        MOV DI,OFFSET AAA
        MOV AL,3FH
        MOV CX,20
        REPE SCASB
        JE IF2
        . . .
IF2:    . . .
```

Here the string starts with AAA and is repeated 20 times. Note that the ASCII value for ? is 3FH.

TABLE 4.14 THE STRING INSTRUCTION GROUP

Instruction	Purpose	Comments
REP (REPE) (REPZ)	Repeat String Operation	This instruction causes the string operation that follows to be continued until CX becomes 0. When the repeat is initiated, the ZF flag is noted and if it differs after a CMPS or SCAS in the subsequent code the repeat is terminated. For these instructions ZF = 1.
REPNE (REPNZ)	Repeat String Operation	This instruction is the same as above except ZF = 0.
SCAS destination-string (SCASB) (SCASW)	Scan Byte or Word String	This instruction subtracts the destination byte (or word) addressed by DI from AL (or AX) and affects the flags but does not return the result.

TABLE 4.15 THE CONVERT INSTRUCTION GROUP

Instruction	Purpose	Comments
CWD	Convert Word to Doubleword	This instruction does a sign extension of AX into DX.
CBW	Convert Byte to Word	This instruction does a sign extension of AL into AH.

Table 4.15 represents the two conversion instructions and is fairly self-explanatory. The byte or word extension occurs from AL (or AX) to AH (or DX) and is a simple sign extension. Table 4.16 contains the procedure and control instructions, some of which we have already seen. The CALL and RET instructions apply to calling and returning from procedures and are by now quite familiar. The NOP instruction should be used as infrequently as possible because it uses machine cycles without actually accomplishing anything, thereby reducing the efficiency of the code. The ESC instruction is principally used to address other processors. Before the Macro Assembler version 2.0 this was the only way to access the 8087 coprocessor chip. LOCK and WAIT are more useful as system instructions and are only mentioned for completeness.

TABLE 4.16 THE PROCEDURE AND CONTROL INSTRUCTION GROUP

Instruction	Purpose	Comments
CALL target	Call Procedure	This instruction calls a procedure (target), and the instruction pointer is saved on the stack. If the call is inter-segment, the CS register is saved first.
RET	Return from Procedure	This instruction returns control to the address pushed by a previous CALL.
ESC external-opcode, source	Escape	This instruction accesses a memory operand (source) and places it on the bus. The external-opcode usually represents the information to be placed on the bus and can be an instruction for another processor.
LOCK	Lock Bus	This one-byte instruction effectively locks the bus for the duration of the operation caused by the instruction.
NOP	No operation	This instruction causes no operation. It can be used when delay is desired (since it occupies an instruction cycle). Also, it can be used as a termination label in MACROs where the following code in the next portion of the program is undefined when the MACRO is written.
WAIT	Wait	This instruction allows the processor to synchronize itself. All processing is terminated until an external interrupt occurs.

TABLE 4.17 THE ASCII INSTRUCTION GROUP

Instruction	Purpose	Comments
AAA	ASCII Adjust for Addition	If the first nibble of AL is greater than 9 or if AF = 1 following an addition, 6 is added to AL and 1 is added to AH. Both AF and CF are set.
AAD	ASCII Adjust for Division	AH is multiplied by 10 and added to AL. The result is stored in AL and AH is set equal to 0.
AAM	ASCII Adjust for Multiplication	AH is replaced by the result of dividing AL by 10. AL is replaced by the remainder of that division.
AAS	ASCII Adjust for Subtraction	If the first nibble of AL is greater than 9 or if AF = 1 following a subtraction, 6 is subtracted from AL and 1 from AH. Both AF and CF are set.

Table 4.17 represents the ASCII instruction group. These four instructions are used to adjust nibbles after an arithmetic operation that affects unpacked numbers. Table 4.18 represents similar instructions for packed numbers. The ASCII instructions arise when ASCII arithmetic occurs. Consider the addition of two ASCII numbers (1 and 2).

$$
\begin{array}{r}
31 \\
\underline{32} \\
63
\end{array}
$$

Clearly, the answer is 3 (contained in the first byte) and the 6 contained in the second byte should be ignored. Now consider 8 plus 3.

$$
\begin{array}{r}
38 \\
\underline{33} \\
6B
\end{array}
$$

Following with an AAA instruction, the value of hex B is added to hex 6 to yield hex 11. This is the correct answer in terms of decimal numbers. The packed decimal (binary coded decimal) instructions work the same way.

TABLE 4.18 THE DECIMAL INSTRUCTION GROUP

Instruction	Purpose	Comments
DAA	Decimal Adjust for Addition	If the first nibble of AL is greater than 9 or AF = 1 following an addition, 6 is added to AL and AF = 1. If AL is greater than 9FH or CF = 1, 60H is added to AL and CF = 1.
DAS	Decimal Adjust for Subtraction	If the first nibble of AL is greater than 9 or AF = 1 following a subtraction, 60H is subtracted from AL and CF = 1.

TABLE 4.19 THE I/O INSTRUCTION GROUP

Instruction	Purpose	Comments
IN accumulator, port	Input byte or word	This instruction moves the contents of the designated port into the accumulator. The port is specified either with a data byte (0-255) or with a port number in the DX register.
OUT port, accumulator	Output byte or word	This instruction moves the contents of the accumulator register AL (or AX) to the designated port. The port is specified either with a data byte (0-255) or with a port number in the DX register.

Table 4.19 contains the two input/output instructions. These instructions are used to move (words) bytes from and to the accumulator in reciprocal fashion with an associated port. The port assignments are contained in the hardware driver routines (BIOS assignments, for example) or in special drivers written to access external peripherals. The BIOS interrupt 10H, for example, calls a driver that accesses ports 300-30F for high resolution graphics. Finally, Table 4.20 contains instructions that fall into a miscellaneous category. These instructions are very useful for exchanging data in tables. The XCHG instruction simply swaps the destination and source operands. The XLAT instruction loads AL with a byte from the table whose start address is specified by the source-table operand. The number contained in AL at execution of the instruction represents the number of bytes past the start address at which the exchange occurs.

At this point we have considered each of the Macro Assembler instructions. The reader should examine the tabular descriptions of each instruction and refer to the *IBM Macro Assembler Reference* [2] for a more detailed discussion. We do not plan to dwell on each instruction and illustrate its function with many code fragment examples. Rather, the intent is to use the instructions (where possible) in actual working programs. This provides the reader with a mechanism for observing the execution of the instruction (as with DEBUG, for example).

TABLE 4.20 THE MISCELLANEOUS INSTRUCTION GROUP

Instruction	Purpose	Comments
XCHG destination, source	Exchange	This instruction exchanges the byte or word source operand with the destination operand. There are two forms: switching the accumulator with another register and for switching a memory/register operand with another register operand.
XLAT source table	Translate	BX is loaded with the start address of a memory location, usually a table. AL contains the number of bytes past this start address. The contents of AL are replaced by the byte from memory (table).

4.3 PROGRAM EXAMPLES

This section contains programming examples that we hope provide a further basis for understanding how Macro Assembler programs are structured as well as how the Macro Assembler instructions are employed.

4.3.1 Square Root

A useful mathematical routine to assist in the generation of geometrical shapes is the square root. Figure 4.1 presents a structure chart for a simple program that loads a set of values from memory, calculates the square root of each, and returns the values to a different array in memory. Figure 4.2 illustrates a program that calls a square root routine, WORDSR (word square root). This is an example of calling a procedure from within a code segment (CSEG), where the procedure lies in another code segment (SQRSEG). In the program, WORDSR has been declared external (EXTRN pseudo-op) with distance attribute FAR. TABLE1 contains word values whose square root is to be determined. The loop bounded by DO1: and JNE DO1 is where the call to WORDSR takes place. All general registers except AX, which contains the TABLE1 value for which the square root is being calculated, are placed on the stack prior to the procedure call. CX, particularly, must be preserved because both the loop and the procedure WORDSR use it.

    The flowchart for the square root procedure, WORDSR, is illustrated in Figure 4.3a and the procedure listing is presented in Figure 4.3b. The main program (Figure 4.2) is called ROOTPG. These are combined at link time with the command

LINK ROOTPG + WORDSR

Clearly, this code has modular form (with a module calling a single module). The procedure WORDSR constitutes a subordinate stand-alone module. Figure 4.3b

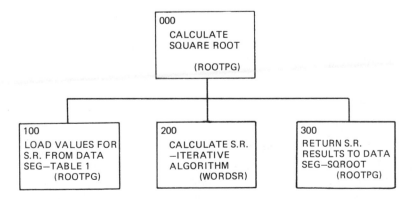

Figure 4.1   Structure chart for program that calculates the square root of a table of numbers.

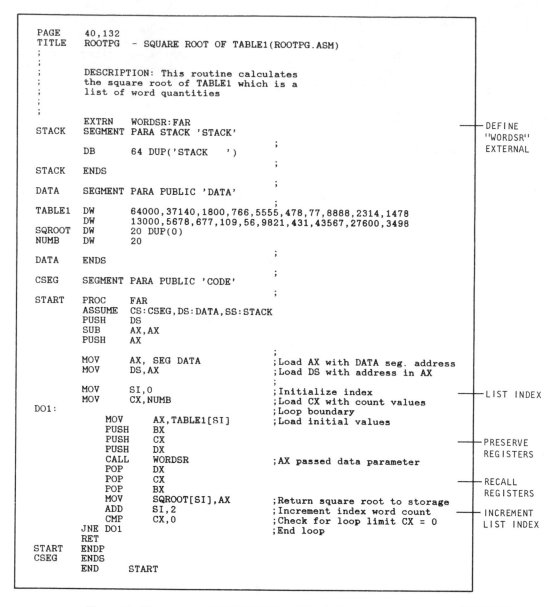

```
PAGE      40,132
TITLE     ROOTPG  - SQUARE ROOT OF TABLE1(ROOTPG.ASM)
;
;
;         DESCRIPTION: This routine calculates
;         the square root of TABLE1 which is a
;         list of word quantities
;
;
          EXTRN    WORDSR:FAR
STACK     SEGMENT PARA STACK 'STACK'                                    DEFINE
                                                                       "WORDSR"
          DB       64 DUP('STACK    ')        ;                        EXTERNAL

STACK     ENDS                                ;

DATA      SEGMENT PARA PUBLIC 'DATA'          ;
                                              ;
TABLE1    DW       64000,37140,1800,766,5555,478,77,8888,2314,1478
          DW       13000,5678,677,109,56,9821,431,43567,27600,3498
SQROOT    DW       20 DUP(0)
NUMB      DW       20

DATA      ENDS                                ;

CSEG      SEGMENT PARA PUBLIC 'CODE'          ;
                                              ;
START     PROC     FAR
          ASSUME   CS:CSEG,DS:DATA,SS:STACK
          PUSH     DS
          SUB      AX,AX
          PUSH     AX
                                              ;
          MOV      AX, SEG DATA               ;Load AX with DATA seg. address
          MOV      DS,AX                      ;Load DS with address in AX
                                              ;
          MOV      SI,0                       ;Initialize index
          MOV      CX,NUMB                     ;Load CX with count values     LIST INDEX
DO1:                                          ;Loop boundary
               MOV      AX,TABLE1[SI]         ;Load initial values
               PUSH     BX
               PUSH     CX                                               PRESERVE
               PUSH     DX                                               REGISTERS
               CALL     WORDSR                ;AX passed data parameter
               POP      DX
               POP      CX                                               RECALL
               POP      BX                                               REGISTERS
               MOV      SQROOT[SI],AX         ;Return square root to storage
               ADD      SI,2                  ;Increment index word count    INCREMENT
               CMP      CX,0                  ;Check for loop limit CX = 0   LIST INDEX
          JNE DO1                             ;End loop
          RET
START     ENDP
CSEG      ENDS
          END      START
```

Figure 4.2   The program ROOTPG.ASM, which calls the square root procedure WORDSR.

contains a code sequence that calculates the square root based on the Newton-Raphson method of successive approximations. Given a positive number N, successive estimates of the square root follow from

$$x_n = 0.5\left(\frac{N}{x_{n-1}} + x_{n-1}\right)$$

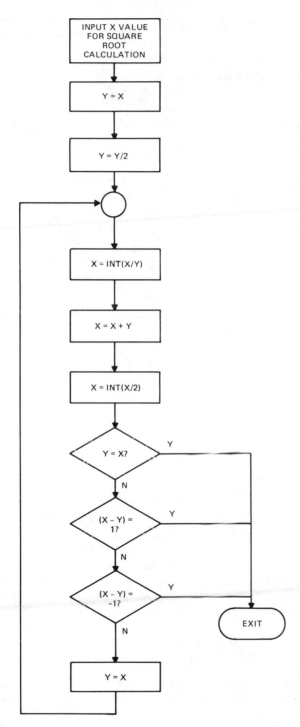

Figure 4.3a   The functional flow chart
for the square root procedure WORDSR.

```
PAGE      40,132
TITLE     WORDSR  -     CALCULATE WORD SR (WORDSR.ASM)
;
;                   DESCRIPTION:This routine receives AX
;                   as the value to be square root. It
;                   returns the square root in AX. The
;                   maximum input size is one word.
;
SQRSEG    SEGMENT PARA PUBLIC 'CODE'
          PUBLIC  WORDSR
WORDSR    PROC    FAR
          ASSUME  CS:SQRSEG
                                              ;
          MOV     CX,AX                       ;Load AX extension
          MOV     BX,AX
          SHR     BX,1                        ;Divide AX by 2
DO1:                                          ;Begin loop
              MOV     DX,0                     ;Initialize dividend extension
              DIV     BX                       ;Divide AX by BX
              ADD     AX,BX                    ;Add root estimate
              SHR     AX,1                     ;Divide by 2
              CMP     AX,BX                    ;IF1 - compare roots
              JE IF1                           ;THEN1
                  SUB     BX,AX                ;Difference of roots
                  CMP     BX,1                 ;IF2 - Check for 1
                  JE IF2                       ;THEN2
                      CMP     BX,-1            ;IF3 - Check for -1
                      JE IF3                   ;THEN3
                          MOV     BX,AX
                          MOV     AX,CX
IF3:                                          ;End IF
IF2:                                          ;End IF
IF1:                                          ;End IF
          JNE DO1                             ;End loop
          RET
WORDSR    ENDP
SQRSEG    ENDS
          END
```

Figure 4.3b   The procedure WORDSR.ASM.

See, for example, *A Guide to PL/M Programming for Microcomputer Applications*, by D. D. McCracken [3]. In this formula, x_n is the latest square root estimate (the nth estimate) and x_{n-1} is the preceding estimate (the $(n-1)$th estimate).

All the general registers are used in this procedure and the reader begins to see one of the limitations of assembler languages. These languages have a small number of registers for holding variables during computations. Initially, the quantity for which the square root is taken (N in the above formula) is put in CX where it will remain for recall at each iteration. The instructions

MOV BX,AX

SHR BX,1

provide an initial estimate for the square root ($N/2$) and load this into BX. BX will serve as the x_{n-1} estimate in the above formula. Next DX is loaded with zero. This must always be done prior to the

DIV BX

(divide by BX) instruction because DX is an extension of AX and will be treated as part of the numerator if it is non-zero. The division calculates N/x_{n-1}. Next BX is added to the result and that value is divided by 2.

At this point x_n (AX) and x_{n-1} (BX) are compared, and if the difference is 0 or 1, the calculation is stopped. If the difference is larger than the above range, the procedure continues to iterate. The error that is intrinsic to this method depends on the size of the number whose square root is to be taken. Figure 4.4 contains the results of the square root for the values in TABLE1. Again, we use DEBUG to examine memory and locate these values. Table 4.21 presents the error associated with the estimated square root for each number. Predictably, the smaller numbers have a greater percentage error because being off with either sign by 1 in the square root can lead to a significant difference for the squared value.

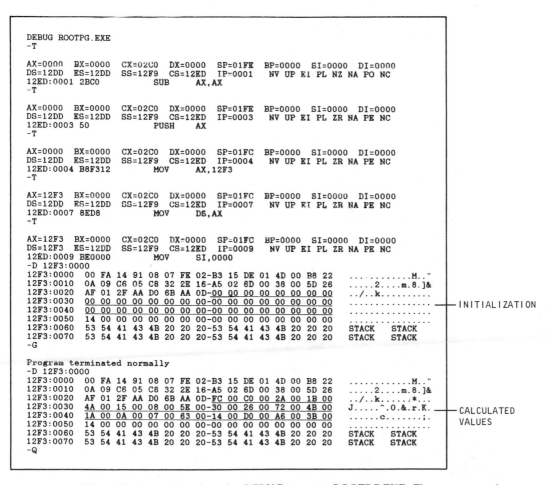

Figure 4.4   A sample session using DEBUG to execute ROOTPG.EXE. The square root values are illustrated after execution.

TABLE 4.21 THE ERROR IN THE SQUARE ROOT ESTIMATES

| | Estimated Square Root | | |
Number	Hex	Decimal	% Error
64000	FC	252	0.8
37140	CO	192	0.7
1800	2A	42	2.0
766	1B	27	4.8
5555	4A	74	1.4
478	15	21	7.7
77	8	8	16.9
8888	5E	94	0.6
2314	30	48	0.4
1478	26	38	2.3
13000	72	114	0.1
5678	4B	75	0.9
677	1A	26	0.1
109	A	10	8.3
56	7	7	12.5
9821	63	99	0.2
431	14	20	7.2
43567	DO	208	0.7
27600	A6	165	0.8
3498	3B	59	0.5

The assembler code in Figures 4.2 and 4.3b used two new pseudo-ops, EXTRN and PUBLIC. Both are data type pseudo-ops and have the following format.

1. EXTRN name:type ... where type can be BYTE, WORD, DWORD, NEAR, FAR, ABS, or a name defined by the EQU pseudo-op. This pseudo-op is used to specify symbols in the given module whose attributes are defined in another assembly module.

2. PUBLIC symbol ... where symbol can be a number, a variable, or a label. This pseudo-op makes the defined symbol available for use by other modules that will be linked to this module.

Pseudo-ops will be discussed in greater detail in Chapter 6.

4.3.2 Sorting

Figure 4.5a illustrates the flowchart for a program that sorts a table of byte quantities and orders them from smallest to largest. Figure 4.5b presents the program. Sorting techniques have been investigated thoroughly and many approaches are possible. A rather simple method is known as exchange sorting and we use this technique in the program illustrated. In exchange sorting the first value is compared to the second; if

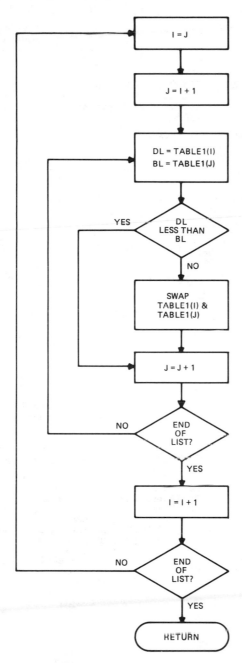

Figure 4.5a The functional flow chart for the routine SORT.ASM.

the first is larger, they are exchanged. Next, the first value (now this may be the original second value) is compared to the third, and so on. At the completion of the first pass, the first position will contain the smallest value in the table. The second pass starts with the second value and proceeds in an identical manner. Each pass ends with the smallest remaining number located in the start position for that pass. If I

```
PAGE      40,132
TITLE     SORT    - AN EXCHANGE SORT(SORT.ASM)
;
;         DESCRIPTION:This program performs an
;         exchange sort on TABLE1.
;
STACK     SEGMENT PARA STACK 'STACK'
                                                        ;
          DB      64 DUP('STACK    ')
                                                        ;
STACK     ENDS
                                                        ;
DATA      SEGMENT PARA PUBLIC 'DATA'
TABLE1    DB      20,19,18,17,16,15,14,13,12,11
          DB      10,9,8,7,6,5,4,3,2,1
                                                        ;
TOTAL     DW      20
                                                        ;
DATA      ENDS
                                                        ;
CSEG      SEGMENT PARA PUBLIC 'CODE'
                                                        ;
SSORT     PROC    FAR
          ASSUME  CS:CSEG,DS:DATA,SS:STACK
                                                        ;
          PUSH    DS
          SUB     AX,AX
          PUSH    AX
                                                        ;
          MOV     AX,SEG DATA
          MOV     DS,AX
                                                        ;
          MOV     SI,OFFSET TABLE1        ;Initialize I index
          MOV     CX,TOTAL                ;Set I index count:
          SUB     CX,1
                                                        ;
DO1:                                      ;Begin loop (outer)
          MOV      DI,SI                   ;Initialize J index
          INC      DI                      ;I+1
DO2:                                       ;Begin loop (inner)
              MOV     DL,TABLE1[SI]        ;Move I into DL
              MOV     BL,TABLE1[DI]        ;Move J into BL
              CMP     DL,BL                ;IF1 - compare I with J
              JNAE IF1                     ;THEN1
                  MOV    TABLE1[SI],BL ;Begin exchange
                  MOV    TABLE1[DI],DL
IF1:                                       ;End IF
              INC     DI                   ;Increment J index
              CMP     DI,TOTAL             ;Compare inner loop index
          JNAE DO2                         ;End loop (inner)
          INC     SI
          CMP     SI,CX                    ;Compare outer index
      JNA DO1                              ;End loop (outer)
      RET
SSORT     ENDP
CSEG      ENDS
          END     SSORT
```

Figure 4.5b   The program SORT.ASM, which sorts the list TABLE1 using exchange sort techniques.

denotes the pass number, the Ith value will be the smallest number out of all the remaining values (indexed by J).

In the program SORT, the table of values to be sorted is called TABLE1 and consists of the numbers 1 through 20, in reverse order. Initially, the first value, TABLE1[0], is compared to the remaining 19 values ($CX = 19$). The smallest number, 1, is replaced in TABLE1[0]. The exchange sort then systematically orders each number from smallest to largest. Figure 4.6 shows the values of TABLE1 in memory before and after the sort has executed. Here DEBUG has been used to execute SORT.EXE. Note that the numbers completely reverse themselves. The data segment address is 12F1 for this linkage.

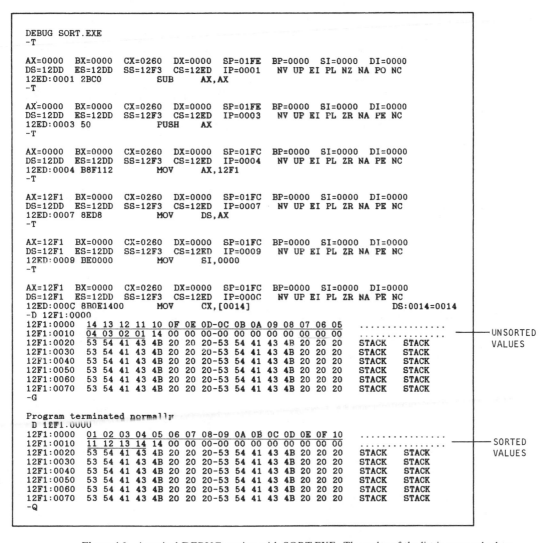

```
DEBUG SORT.EXE
-T

AX=0000  BX=0000  CX=0260  DX=0000  SP=01FE  BP=0000  SI=0000  DI=0000
DS=12DD  ES=12DD  SS=12F3  CS=12ED  IP=0001    NV UP EI PL NZ NA PO NC
12ED:0001 2BC0          SUB     AX,AX
-T

AX=0000  BX=0000  CX=0260  DX=0000  SP=01FE  BP=0000  SI=0000  DI=0000
DS=12DD  ES=12DD  SS=12F3  CS=12ED  IP=0003    NV UP EI PL ZR NA PE NC
12ED:0003 50            PUSH    AX
-T

AX=0000  BX=0000  CX=0260  DX=0000  SP=01FC  BP=0000  SI=0000  DI=0000
DS=12DD  ES=12DD  SS=12F3  CS=12ED  IP=0004    NV UP EI PL ZR NA PE NC
12ED:0004 B8F112        MOV     AX,12F1
-T

AX=12F1  BX=0000  CX=0260  DX=0000  SP=01FC  BP=0000  SI=0000  DI=0000
DS=12DD  ES=12DD  SS=12F3  CS=12ED  IP=0007    NV UP EI PL ZR NA PE NC
12ED:0007 8ED8          MOV     DS,AX
-T

AX=12F1  BX=0000  CX=0260  DX=0000  SP=01FC  BP=0000  SI=0000  DI=0000
DS=12F1  ES=12DD  SS=12F3  CS=12ED  IP=0009    NV UP EI PL ZR NA PE NC
12ED:0009 BE0000        MOV     SI,0000
-T

AX=12F1  BX=0000  CX=0260  DX=0000  SP=01FC  BP=0000  SI=0000  DI=0000
DS=12F1  ES=12DD  SS=12F3  CS=12ED  IP=000C    NV UP EI PL ZR NA PE NC
12ED:000C 8B0E1400      MOV     CX,[0014]                     DS:0014=0014
-D 12F1:0000
12F1:0000   14 13 12 11 10 0F 0E 0D-0C 0B 0A 09 08 07 06 05   ...............
12F1:0010   04 03 02 01 14 00 00 00-00 00 00 00 00 00 00 00   ...............
12F1:0020   53 54 41 43 4B 20 20 20-53 54 41 43 4B 20 20 20   STACK   STACK
12F1:0030   53 54 41 43 4B 20 20 20-53 54 41 43 4B 20 20 20   STACK   STACK
12F1:0040   53 54 41 43 4B 20 20 20-53 54 41 43 4B 20 20 20   STACK   STACK
12F1:0050   53 54 41 43 4B 20 20 20-53 54 41 43 4B 20 20 20   STACK   STACK
12F1:0060   53 54 41 43 4B 20 20 20-53 54 41 43 4B 20 20 20   STACK   STACK
12F1:0070   53 54 41 43 4B 20 20 20-53 54 41 43 4B 20 20 20   STACK   STACK
-G

Program terminated normally
 D 12F1:0000
12F1:0000   01 02 03 04 05 06 07 08-09 0A 0B 0C 0D 0E 0F 10   ...............
12F1:0010   11 12 13 14 14 00 00 00-00 00 00 00 00 00 00 00   ...............
12F1:0020   53 54 41 43 4B 20 20 20-53 54 41 43 4B 20 20 20   STACK   STACK
12F1:0030   53 54 41 43 4B 20 20 20-53 54 41 43 4B 20 20 20   STACK   STACK
12F1:0040   53 54 41 43 4B 20 20 20-53 54 41 43 4B 20 20 20   STACK   STACK
12F1:0050   53 54 41 43 4B 20 20 20-53 54 41 43 4B 20 20 20   STACK   STACK
12F1:0060   53 54 41 43 4B 20 20 20-53 54 41 43 4B 20 20 20   STACK   STACK
12F1:0070   53 54 41 43 4B 20 20 20-53 54 41 43 4B 20 20 20   STACK   STACK
-Q
```

UNSORTED VALUES

SORTED VALUES

Figure 4.6   A typical DEBUG session with SORT.EXE. The order of the list is reversed when sorted.

4.3.3 Natural Logarithm

It is possible to generate functions using the Macro Assembler with an appropriate algorithm; however, an approach which executes in a shorter period of time is the look-up table. The next two examples illustrate the use of look-up tables for the natural logarithm and the sine and cosine of an angle. Figure 4.7 presents a program that calls the procedure LNLOG and returns the natural logarithm in AX. The logarithm is calculated for the value in BX. This value is scaled by 100 over the actual value to be calculated. In this case the logarithm desired is 0.5 and the input BX value becomes 50. Figure 4.8 represents the procedure LNLOG which uses the look-up table LN, contained in the data segment DATALN, to obtain the natural logarithm value. In Figure 4.8 the existing data segment address contained in DS is preserved on the stack prior to moving the segment address for DATALN into DS. All the tabulated values are scaled by 1000 and only the input range 0 to 1 is allowed, based on the table values.

       Figure 4.9 presents a DEBUG session for the program CKLN.EXE, the linked version of the natural logarithm program. This routine was generated from the following link.

LINK CKLN + LNLOG

In the program containing LNLOG, this procedure has been declared FAR within the code segment LNCS. LNLOG was declared PUBLIC and was called from the code segment CSEG using the EXTRN pseudo-op. In the DEBUG listing, the code

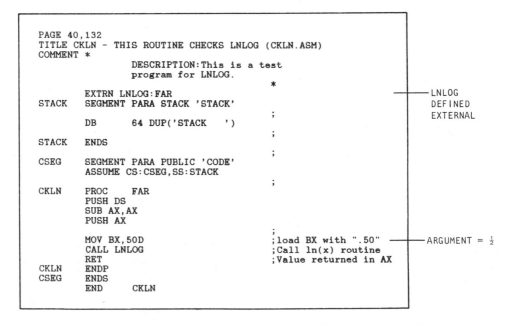

```
PAGE 40,132
TITLE CKLN - THIS ROUTINE CHECKS LNLOG (CKLN.ASM)
COMMENT *
                DESCRIPTION:This is a test
                program for LNLOG.
                                      *
        EXTRN LNLOG:FAR                                    ──── LNLOG
STACK   SEGMENT PARA STACK 'STACK'                              DEFINED
                                      ;                        EXTERNAL
        DB      64 DUP('STACK    ')
                                      ;
STACK   ENDS
                                      ;
CSEG    SEGMENT PARA PUBLIC 'CODE'
        ASSUME CS:CSEG,SS:STACK
                                      ;
CKLN    PROC    FAR
        PUSH DS
        SUB AX,AX
        PUSH AX
                                      ;
        MOV BX,50D            ;load BX with ".50" ──── ARGUMENT = ½
        CALL LNLOG            ;Call ln(x) routine
        RET                  ;Value returned in AX
CKLN    ENDP
CSEG    ENDS
        END     CKLN
```

Figure 4.7 The program that calls the procedure LNLOG, which is used to calculate a natural logarithm.

```
PAGE 40,132
TITLE LNLOG - CALCULATES A LIMITED LN(X) (LNLOG.ASM)
COMMENT *
                         DESCRIPTION:This routine calculates
                         a limited logarithm (natural) for
                         values(BX) between 0 and 1.0.  The
                         log is returned in AX and must be
                         divided by 1000.  The input values
                         are scaled (0,1) - (0,100)where the
                         multiplying scaler is 100.    *
                         ;
DATALN   SEGMENT PARA PUBLIC 'DATA'
         PUBLIC LN
                         ;
LN       DW       0000,5395,6088,6493,6781,7004,7187,7341,7474,7592
         DW       7697,7793,7880,7960,8034,8103,8167,8228,8285,8339
         DW       8391,8439,8486,8530,8573,8614,8653,8691,8727,8762
         DW       8796,8829,8861,8891,8921,8950,8978,9006,9032,9058
         DW       9084,9108,9132,9156,9179,9201,9223,9245,9266,9287
         DW       9307,9327,9346,9365,9384,9402,9420,9438,9455,9472
         DW       9489,9506,9522,9538,9554,9569,9584,9600,9614,9629
         DW       9643,9658,9671,9685,9699,9712,9726,9739,9752,9764
         DW       9777,9789,9802,9814,9826,9837,9849,9861,9872,9883
         DW       9895,9906,9917,9927,9938,9949,9959,9970,9980,9990
                         ;
DATALN   ENDS
                         ;
LNCS     SEGMENT PARA PUBLIC 'CODE'
         PUBLIC LNLOG
LNLOG    PROC     FAR
         ASSUME CS:LNCS,DS:DATALN
                         ;
         PUSH DS          ;Preserve DS
                         ;
         MOV AX,SEG DATALN
         MOV DS,AX
         SHL BX,1         ;Multiply by 2 for word index
         MOV AX,LN[BX]    ;Get Log pointer value
         SUB AX,10000     ;Calculate log value          ──── SUBTRACT
                         ;                                    10000 TO
         POP DS           ;Recall DS                          GET LNLOG
         RET
LNLOG    ENDP
LNCS     ENDS
         END      LNLOG
```

Figure 4.8   The procedure for using a look-up table to obtain natural logarithms.

segment CSEG was loaded at 12ED:0000, and the code segment LNCS was loaded at 12EE:0000. The calling routine, CKLN, has its data segment at segment address 12DDH while the routine LNLOG has its data segment address at 1310H.

The input value of DX was 50, however, this must be multiplied by 2 to specify a word location in the table LN; hence the index value 0064H in the DEBUG program. The result of the look-up operation is to load AX with 9307 (245BH). The quantity 10000 must be subtracted from this to yield the two's complement value −693 (FD4BH).

4.3.4 Sine and Cosine

A more complex example of a look-up table is illustrated in the next program which yields the sine and cosine of an angle between 0 and 360 degrees. Figure 4.10 contains

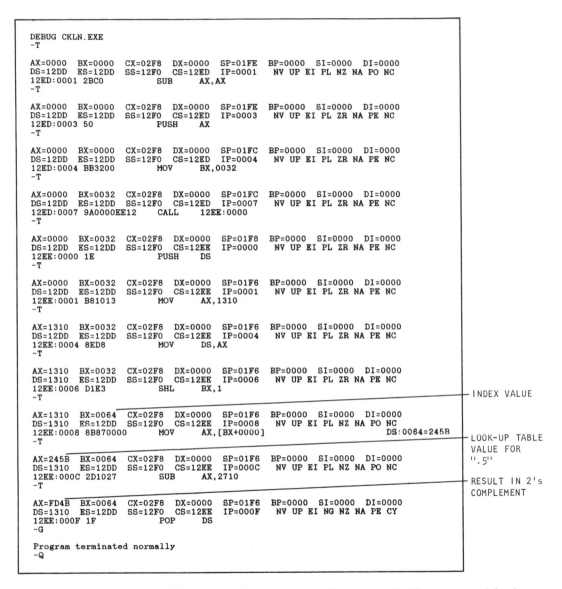

```
DEBUG CKLN.EXE
-T

AX=0000  BX=0000  CX=02F8  DX=0000  SP=01FE  BP=0000  SI=0000  DI=0000
DS=12DD  ES=12DD  SS=12F0  CS=12ED  IP=0001  NV UP EI PL NZ NA PO NC
12ED:0001 2BC0          SUB     AX,AX
-T

AX=0000  BX=0000  CX=02F8  DX=0000  SP=01FE  BP=0000  SI=0000  DI=0000
DS=12DD  ES=12DD  SS=12F0  CS=12ED  IP=0003  NV UP EI PL ZR NA PE NC
12ED:0003 50            PUSH    AX
-T

AX=0000  BX=0000  CX=02F8  DX=0000  SP=01FC  BP=0000  SI=0000  DI=0000
DS=12DD  ES=12DD  SS=12F0  CS=12ED  IP=0004  NV UP EI PL ZR NA PE NC
12ED:0004 BB3200        MOV     BX,0032
-T

AX=0000  BX=0032  CX=02F8  DX=0000  SP=01FC  BP=0000  SI=0000  DI=0000
DS=12DD  ES=12DD  SS=12F0  CS=12ED  IP=0007  NV UP EI PL ZR NA PE NC
12ED:0007 9A0000EE12    CALL    12EE:0000
-T

AX=0000  BX=0032  CX=02F8  DX=0000  SP=01F8  BP=0000  SI=0000  DI=0000
DS=12DD  ES=12DD  SS=12F0  CS=12EE  IP=0000  NV UP EI PL ZR NA PE NC
12EE:0000 1E            PUSH    DS
-T

AX=0000  BX=0032  CX=02F8  DX=0000  SP=01F6  BP=0000  SI=0000  DI=0000
DS=12DD  ES=12DD  SS=12F0  CS=12EE  IP=0001  NV UP EI PL ZR NA PE NC
12EE:0001 B81013        MOV     AX,1310
-T

AX=1310  BX=0032  CX=02F8  DX=0000  SP=01F6  BP=0000  SI=0000  DI=0000
DS=12DD  ES=12DD  SS=12F0  CS=12EE  IP=0004  NV UP EI PL ZR NA PE NC
12EE:0004 8ED8          MOV     DS,AX
-T

AX=1310  BX=0032  CX=02F8  DX=0000  SP=01F6  BP=0000  SI=0000  DI=0000
DS=1310  ES=12DD  SS=12F0  CS=12EE  IP=0006  NV UP EI PL ZR NA PE NC
12EE:0006 D1E3          SHL     BX,1
-T

AX=1310  BX=0064  CX=02F8  DX=0000  SP=01F6  BP=0000  SI=0000  DI=0000
DS=1310  ES=12DD  SS=12F0  CS=12EE  IP=0008  NV UP EI PL NZ NA PO NC
12EE:0008 8B870000      MOV     AX,[BX+0000]                    DS:0064=245B
-T

AX=245B  BX=0064  CX=02F8  DX=0000  SP=01F6  BP=0000  SI=0000  DI=0000
DS=1310  ES=12DD  SS=12F0  CS=12EE  IP=000C  NV UP EI PL NZ NA PO NC
12EE:000C 2D1027        SUB     AX,2710
-T

AX=FD4B  BX=0064  CX=02F8  DX=0000  SP=01F6  BP=0000  SI=0000  DI=0000
DS=1310  ES=12DD  SS=12F0  CS=12EE  IP=000F  NV UP EI NG NZ NA PE CY
12EE:000F 1F            POP     DS
-G

Program terminated normally
-Q
```

INDEX VALUE

LOOK-UP TABLE VALUE FOR ".5"

RESULT IN 2's COMPLEMENT

Figure 4.9 A DEBUG session with the natural logarithm program that illustrates a result for .5.

the main calling program, CSCK.ASM, for generating the sine and cosine. Both values are stored in the data segment variables NSIN and NCOS. The statements

```
MOV AX,SEG DATA
MOV DS,AX
```

load the segment address of DATA into DS. Prior to calling the sine and cosine generation procedure, 5 degrees is loaded into AX, the register that this procedure will use for input.

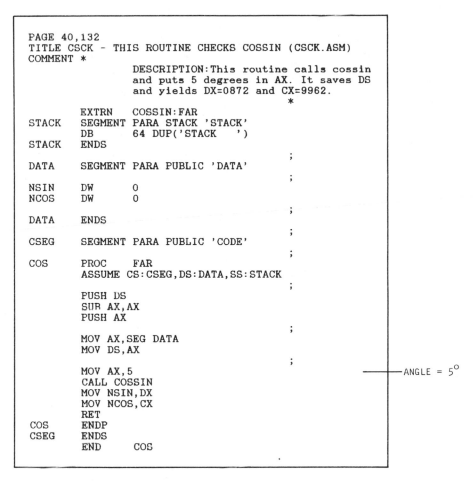

```
PAGE 40,132
TITLE CSCK - THIS ROUTINE CHECKS COSSIN (CSCK.ASM)
COMMENT *
                  DESCRIPTION:This routine calls cossin
                  and puts 5 degrees in AX. It saves DS
                  and yields DX=0872 and CX=9962.
                                             *
          EXTRN   COSSIN:FAR
STACK     SEGMENT PARA STACK 'STACK'
          DB      64 DUP('STACK   ')
STACK     ENDS
                                             ;
DATA      SEGMENT PARA PUBLIC 'DATA'
                                             ;
NSIN      DW      0
NCOS      DW      0
                                             ;
DATA      ENDS
                                             ;
CSEG      SEGMENT PARA PUBLIC 'CODE'
                                             ;
COS       PROC    FAR
          ASSUME CS:CSEG,DS:DATA,SS:STACK
                                             ;
          PUSH DS
          SUB AX,AX
          PUSH AX
                                             ;
          MOV AX,SEG DATA
          MOV DS,AX
                                             ;
          MOV AX,5                                        ———————ANGLE = 5°
          CALL COSSIN
          MOV NSIN,DX
          MOV NCOS,CX
          RET
COS       ENDP
CSEG      ENDS
          END     COS
```

Figure 4.10 The main calling program CSCK.ASM, which checks the procedure for calculating sines and cosines.

Figure 4.11a illustrates the flow chart for the procedure used to generate the sine and cosine (COSSIN). Figure 4.11b is the program listing. The look-up table, CSTBL, contains all the cosine values between 0 and 90 degrees in one degree increments. The value for the sine of the input angle is simply given by

$$\text{sine}(x) = \text{cosine}(90 - x)$$

The procedure COSSIN is somewhat longer than might be expected because both sine and cosine are returned. Hence, it is necessary to implement a dual form of bookkeeping for each of the four possible quadrants (0-90, 91-180, 181-270, 271-360 degrees). Initially, the input angle in AX is checked to see which quadrant it falls in. This is done using the compare instruction, CMP, and an IF statement in CASE format. Once the branch to the proper block of code occurs, the angle is translated back to the first quadrant and loaded into BX where it becomes a word index using the SHL instruction. The modifier SHORT indicates the jumps are within 128

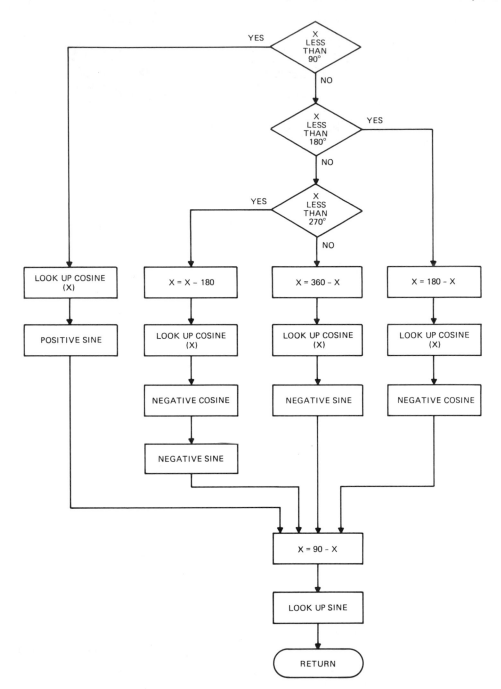

Figure 4.11a   The functional flow chart for the module containing the procedure COSSIN.

```
PAGE     40,132
TITLE    COSSIN   - CALCULATES THE SINE AND COSINE(COSSIN.ASM)
;
;                 DESCRIPTION: This routine calculates the sine
;                 and cosine of the degree value in AX. It
;                 returns sine (DX) and cosine (CX). The values
;                 are specified to word accuracy - 4 decimal
;                 digits and must be divided by 10,000.
;                 Negative values have the sign bit set. Positive
;                 values have this bit reset.
;
DATA1    SEGMENT PARA PUBLIC 'DATA'
         PUBLIC  CSTBL,SSINE
CSTBL    DW      10000,9999,9994,9986,9976,9962,9945,9926,9903,9877
         DW      9848,9816,9782,9744,9703,9659,9613,9563,9511,9455
         DW      9397,9336,9272,9205,9136,9063,8988,8910,8830,8746
         DW      8660,8572,8481,8387,8290,8192,8090,7986,7880,7772
         DW      7660,7547,7431,7314,7193,7071,6947,6820,6691,6561
         DW      6428,6293,6157,6018,5878,5736,5592,5446,5299,5150
         DW      5000,4848,4695,4540,4388,4226,4067,3907,3746,3584
         DW      3420,3256,3090,2924,2756,2588,2419,2250,2079,1908
         DW      1737,1564,1392,1219,1045,0872,0698,0523,0349,0175
         DW      0
                                         ;
SSINE    DW      0
                                         ;
DATA1    ENDS
                                         ;
ANGCS    SEGMENT PARA PUBLIC 'CODE'
         PUBLIC  COSSIN
COSSIN   PROC    FAR
         ASSUME  CS:ANGCS,DS:DATA1
                                         ;
         PUSH    DS                      ;Preserve DS
                                         ;
         MOV     BX, SEG DATA1
         MOV     DS,BX
                                         ;
                                         ;
         CMP     AX,90                   ;IF1 - check < 90
         JNA ELSE1                       ;THEN1
             CMP     AX,180              ;IF2 - check 90 < x < 180 ──┐  CASE
             JNA ELSE2                   ;THEN2                      │  STRUCTURE
                 CMP     AX,270          ;IF3 - check 180 < x < 270
                 JNA ELSE3               ;THEN3
                     MOV     BX,360      ;  270 < x < 360
                     SUB     BX,AX
                     MOV     AX,BX
                     SHL     BX,1
                     MOV     CX,CSTBL[BX] ;Angle in 4th quadrant
                     MOV     SSINE,8000H ;Negative sine
                 JMP SHORT IF3
ELSE3:                                   ;else
                     SUB     AX,180      ;Angle in third quadrant
                     MOV     BX,AX
                     SHL     BX,1
                     MOV     CX,CSTBL[BX] ;Angle in 1st quadrant
                     OR      CX,8000H    ;Negative cosine
                     MOV     SSINE,8000H ;Negative sine
IF3:                                     ;End IF
```

Figure 4.11b   The module COSSIN which calculates sines and cosines.

```
            JMP   SHORT IF2
ELSE2:                                    ;else
                  MOV   BX,180            ;Angle in 2nd quadrant
                  SUB   BX,AX             ;Angle 180 - x
                  MOV   AX,BX
                  SHL   BX,1
                  MOV   CX,CSTBL[BX]      ;Angle in 2nd quadrant
                  OR    CX,8000H          ;Negative cosine
                  MOV   SSINE,0           ;Positive sine
IF2:                                      ;End IF
            JMP   SHORT IF1
ELSE1:                                    ;else
                  MOV   BX,AX             ;Angle in 1st quadrant
                  SHL   BX,1
                  MOV   CX,CSTBL[BX]
                  MOV   SSINE,0           ;Positive sine
IF1:                                      ;End IF
            MOV   BX,90                   ;Calculate sine
            SUB   BX,AX
            SHL   BX,1
            MOV   DX,CSTBL[BX]
            OR    DX,SSINE
                                          ;
            POP   DS
            RET
                                          ;
COSSIN      ENDP
ANGCS       ENDS
                                          ;
            END
```

Figure 4.11b *(Continued)*

bytes. After calling the proper cosine value from the table, the correct sign must be applied and saved for the sine value to be calculated.

The fact that we are using word values to return a number between 0 and 10,000 means that bits 15, 14, and 13 will never be needed. Thus it becomes convenient to treat bit 15 as a sign bit rather than use full two's-complement arithmetic. Whenever a sine or cosine is negative, we simply take its value in the first 13 bits (0 through 12) and set bit 15 by using the OR instruction with 8000H. A similar approach is used to handle the sign of the sine function. The variable SSINE is either set to 0 for positive sine or 8000H for negative sine. Then, once the sine is calculated, it is OR'd with SSINE.

Figure 4.12 illustrates a DEBUG session with CSCK.EXE, the linked program for generating sine and cosine output for a 5 degree input value. The memory dumps contain the NSIN and NCOS values before and after execution. Observe that NSIN = 872(0368H) and NCOS = 9962(26EAH) as expected. Of course these values must be scaled by 10000.

4.3.5 Random Numbers

Random numbers are very useful for many applications. Although there are a number of approaches to generating random numbers, it is desirable to generate a

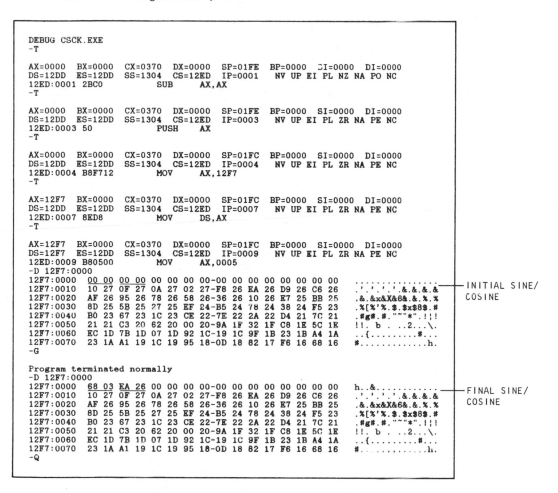

```
DEBUG CSCK.EXE
-T

AX=0000  BX=0000  CX=0370  DX=0000  SP=01FE  BP=0000  SI=0000  DI=0000
DS=12DD  ES=12DD  SS=1304  CS=12ED  IP=0001  NV UP EI PL NZ NA PO NC
12ED:0001 2BC0        SUB     AX,AX
-T

AX=0000  BX=0000  CX=0370  DX=0000  SP=01FE  BP=0000  SI=0000  DI=0000
DS=12DD  ES=12DD  SS=1304  CS=12ED  IP=0003  NV UP EI PL ZR NA PE NC
12ED:0003 50          PUSH    AX
-T

AX=0000  BX=0000  CX=0370  DX=0000  SP=01FC  BP=0000  SI=0000  DI=0000
DS=12DD  ES=12DD  SS=1304  CS=12ED  IP=0004  NV UP EI PL ZR NA PE NC
12ED:0004 B8F712      MOV     AX,12F7
-T

AX=12F7  BX=0000  CX=0370  DX=0000  SP=01FC  BP=0000  SI=0000  DI=0000
DS=12DD  ES=12DD  SS=1304  CS=12ED  IP=0007  NV UP EI PL ZR NA PE NC
12ED:0007 8ED8        MOV     DS,AX
-T

AX=12F7  BX=0000  CX=0370  DX=0000  SP=01FC  BP=0000  SI=0000  DI=0000
DS=12F7  ES=12DD  SS=1304  CS=12ED  IP=0009  NV UP EI PL ZR NA PE NC
12ED:0009 B80500      MOV     AX,0005
-D 12F7:0000
12F7:0000  00 00 00 00 00 00 00 00-00 00 00 00 00 00 00 00   ................
12F7:0010  10 27 0F 27 0A 27 02 27-F8 26 EA 26 D9 26 C6 26   .'.'.'.'.&.&.&.&
12F7:0020  AF 26 95 26 78 26 58 26-36 26 10 26 E7 25 BB 25   .&.&x&X&8&.&.%.%
12F7:0030  8D 25 5B 25 27 25 EF 24-B5 24 78 24 38 24 F5 23   .%[%'%.$.$x$8$.#
12F7:0040  B0 23 67 23 1C 23 CE 22-7E 22 2A 22 D4 21 7C 21   .#g#.#."~"*".!!!
12F7:0050  21 21 C3 20 62 20 00 20-9A 1F 32 1F C8 1E 5C 1E   !!. b  ..2...\.
12F7:0060  EC 1D 7B 1D 07 1D 92 1C-19 1C 9F 1B 23 1B A4 1A   ..{.........#...
12F7:0070  23 1A A1 19 1C 19 95 18-0D 18 82 17 F6 16 68 16   #............h.
-G

Program terminated normally
-D 12F7:0000
12F7:0000  68 03 EA 26 00 00 00 00-00 00 00 00 00 00 00 00   h..&............
12F7:0010  10 27 0F 27 0A 27 02 27-F8 26 EA 26 D9 26 C6 26   .'.'.'.'.&.&.&.&
12F7:0020  AF 26 95 26 78 26 58 26-36 26 10 26 E7 25 BB 25   .&.&x&X6&.&.%.%
12F7:0030  8D 25 5B 25 27 25 EF 24-B5 24 78 24 38 24 F5 23   .%[%'%.$.$x$8$.#
12F7:0040  B0 23 67 23 1C 23 CE 22-7E 22 2A 22 D4 21 7C 21   .#g#.#."~"*".!!!
12F7:0050  21 21 C3 20 62 20 00 20-9A 1F 32 1F C8 1E 5C 1E   !!. b  ..2...\.
12F7:0060  EC 1D 7B 1D 07 1D 92 1C-19 1C 9F 1B 23 1B A4 1A   ..{.........#...
12F7:0070  23 1A A1 19 1C 19 95 18-0D 18 82 17 F6 16 68 16   #............h.
-Q
```

← INITIAL SINE/COSINE

← FINAL SINE/COSINE

Figure 4.12   A typical DEBUG session with the program used to calculate sines and cosines.

sequence of numbers that are maximum length before repeating (really a pseudo-random sequence). For 16-bit numbers it is evident that such a sequence would be 2 raised to the 16th power or 65,536 numbers. McCracken, in *A Guide to PL/M Programming*, describes such an algorithm ([3], p. 113) and it has the following form.[2]

$$x_{n+1} = (2053x_n + 13849) \bmod 2^{16}$$

Here x_n is an input random number and x_{n+1} is the output. The modulo operation indicated simply means that $(2053x_n + 13849)$ is divided by 2^{16} and the remainder saved. In Figure 4.13a the flow chart for a procedure which calculates this random number is illustrated. Figure 4.13b illustrates the procedure listing. The remainder, following the division, is in DX, but this quantity is moved into AX before returning to the calling program.

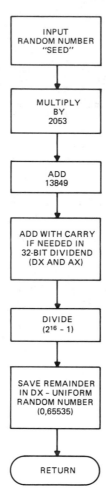

Figure 4.13a The functional flow chart for the procedure RAND1.

4.3.6 Gaussian Random Numbers

Many applications of random numbers call for normally distributed or Gaussian random numbers. The familiar Bell curve is an example of a normal distribution. In this section we present a procedure for generating Gaussian random numbers. This procedure is based on the following formulas.

$$y_1 = \text{SQRT}(-2\ln(x_1))\cos(2\pi x_2)$$

$$y_2 = \text{SQRT}(-2\ln(x_1))\sin(2\pi x_2)$$

Here x_1 and x_2 are uniformly distributed random numbers between 0 and 1, such as the normalized return from RAND1 appearing in the program of Figure 4.13b. The quantities y_1 and y_2 are independent Gaussian random numbers. We have, prior to

```
PAGE 40,132
TITLE RAND1 - PROCEDURE TO CALCULATE R.N. (RAND1.ASM)
COMMENT *
                              DESCRIPTION:This procedure calculates a
                              random number based on a previous
                              random number or seed.  The input is in CX
                              and the output is in AX.  The r.n. is 16 bits.
                                                                      *
RND         SEGMENT PARA PUBLIC 'CODE'
            PUBLIC RAND1
RAND1       PROC    FAR
            ASSUME CS:RND
                                              ;
            MOV DX,0                          ;Load upper multiplicand zero
            MOV AX,CX                         ;Load previous r.n. into AX
            MOV BX,2053                       ;Multiplier
            MUL BX
            MOV BX,13849                      ;Load additative constant
            CLC
            ADD AX,BX                         ;Add low order result
            ADC DX,0                          ;Add carry if needed
            MOV BX,0FFFFH                     ;Load 2(16) - 1
            DIV BX                            ;Calculate modulo
            MOV AX,DX                         ;Move remainder into AX
            RET
                                              ;
RAND1       ENDP
RND         ENDS
            END     RAND1
```

Figure 4.13b   The procedure RAND1.

now, generated procedures for all of the functions appearing in these expressions (square root, natural logarithm, sine, and cosine). Thus we need to simply combine these procedures in modular fashion to generate the results, y_1 and y_2. Figure 4.14 illustrates the structure chart for the program that generates Gaussian random numbers. We have included the module names. (An earlier chart, in Chapter 3, listed only the functions.)

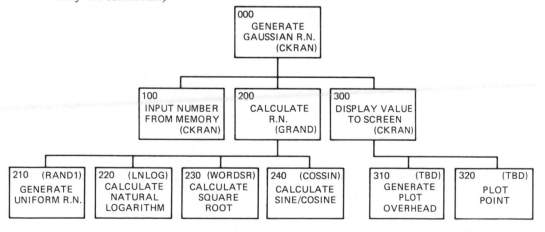

Figure 4.14   The Structure Chart for the program that generates a Gaussian random number. Each individual module is illustrated (TBD = To be Determined).

Figure 4.15 presents a calling program for the routine GRAND, which generates the Gaussian random numbers. In the program, an index, SI, is used to keep track of the random numbers as they are generated, and DI counts the number of iterations up to a total of 25. Figure 4.16a illustrates the flow chart for the procedure that actually calls RAND1, WORDSR, COSSIN, and LNLOG. Figure 4.16b is the procedure listing. All these procedures are declared FAR in the EXTRN statement. Initially the two random numbers are generated using RAND1. These numbers, NUM1 and NUM2, lie between 0 and 65535 and must be normalized to fall in the ranges required by LNLOG and COSSIN. Also, one value must be reserved to act as a seed for the next call to RAND1.

The quantity SQRT($-2\ln($NUM1$)$) is generated once the RAND1 output is scaled. Similarly, the sine and cosine output is generated using NUM2. Prior to

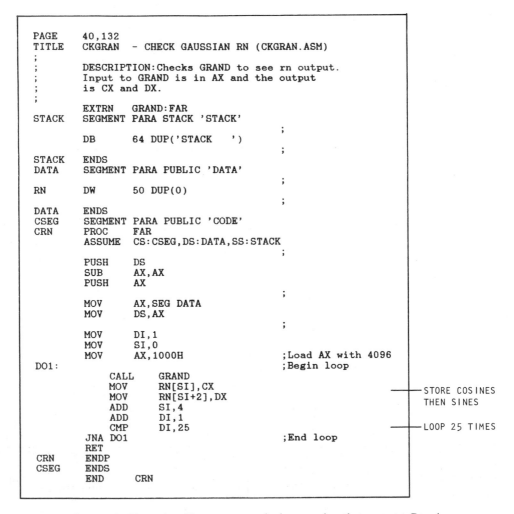

```
PAGE     40,132
TITLE    CKGRAN  - CHECK GAUSSIAN RN (CKGRAN.ASM)
;
;        DESCRIPTION:Checks GRAND to see rn output.
;        Input to GRAND is in AX and the output
;        is CX and DX.
;
         EXTRN   GRAND:FAR
STACK    SEGMENT PARA STACK 'STACK'
                                              ;
         DB      64 DUP('STACK    ')
                                              ;
STACK    ENDS
DATA     SEGMENT PARA PUBLIC 'DATA'
                                              ;
RN       DW      50 DUP(0)
                                              ;
DATA     ENDS
CSEG     SEGMENT PARA PUBLIC 'CODE'
CRN      PROC    FAR
         ASSUME  CS:CSEG,DS:DATA,SS:STACK
                                              ;
         PUSH    DS
         SUB     AX,AX
         PUSH    AX
                                              ;
         MOV     AX,SEG DATA
         MOV     DS,AX
                                              ;
         MOV     DI,1
         MOV     SI,0
         MOV     AX,1000H             ;Load AX with 4096
DO1:                                  ;Begin loop
             CALL    GRAND
             MOV     RN[SI],CX                        ── STORE COSINES
             MOV     RN[SI+2],DX                         THEN SINES
             ADD     SI,4
             ADD     DI,1
             CMP     DI,25                           ── LOOP 25 TIMES
         JNA DO1                      ;End loop
         RET
CRN      ENDP
CSEG     ENDS
         END     CRN
```

Figure 4.15 The main calling program to check a procedure that generates Gaussian random numbers.

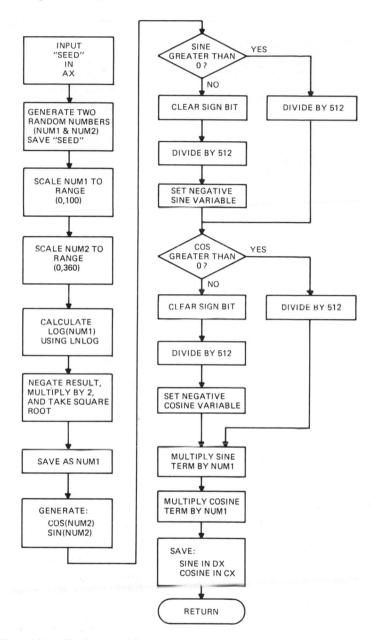

Figure 4.16a The functional flow chart for the procedure GRAND.

multiplication it is necessary to further scale these intermediate values to prevent overflow while insuring as much precision as possible. The resulting Gaussian random numbers are between −2752 and 2752 and are scaled by 617. This actually makes the range of Gaussian numbers −4.46 to 4.46. Based on probability curves, this means the numbers are Gaussian to less than 1% error. In principal, any value for a Gaussian number may be assumed; however, the distribution used in the above

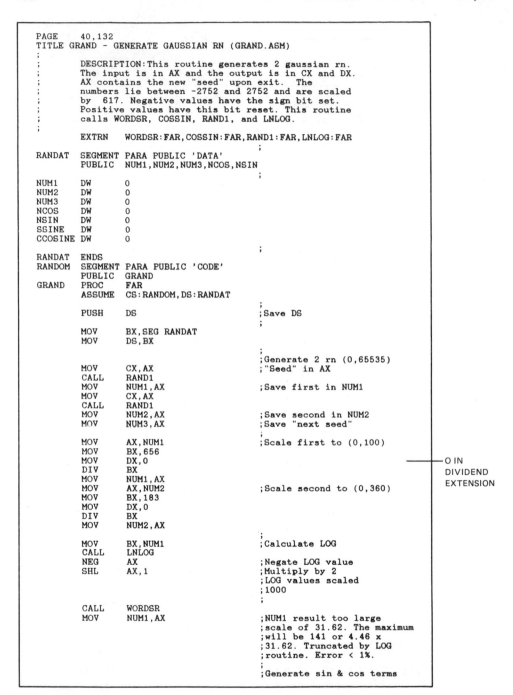

```
PAGE     40,132
TITLE GRAND - GENERATE GAUSSIAN RN (GRAND.ASM)
;
;          DESCRIPTION:This routine generates 2 gaussian rn.
;          The input is in AX and the output is in CX and DX.
;          AX contains the new "seed" upon exit.  The
;          numbers lie between -2752 and 2752 and are scaled
;          by  617. Negative values have the sign bit set.
;          Positive values have this bit reset. This routine
;          calls WORDSR, COSSIN, RAND1, and LNLOG.
;
           EXTRN    WORDSR:FAR,COSSIN:FAR,RAND1:FAR,LNLOG:FAR
                                              ;
RANDAT  SEGMENT PARA PUBLIC 'DATA'
        PUBLIC   NUM1,NUM2,NUM3,NCOS,NSIN
                                              ;
NUM1    DW       0
NUM2    DW       0
NUM3    DW       0
NCOS    DW       0
NSIN    DW       0
SSINE   DW       0
CCOSINE DW       0
                                              ;
RANDAT  ENDS
RANDOM  SEGMENT PARA PUBLIC 'CODE'
        PUBLIC   GRAND
GRAND   PROC     FAR
        ASSUME   CS:RANDOM,DS:RANDAT
                                              ;
        PUSH     DS                           ;Save DS
                                              ;
        MOV      BX,SEG RANDAT
        MOV      DS,BX
                                              ;
                                              ;Generate 2 rn (0,65535)
        MOV      CX,AX                         ;"Seed" in AX
        CALL     RAND1
        MOV      NUM1,AX                       ;Save first in NUM1
        MOV      CX,AX
        CALL     RAND1
        MOV      NUM2,AX                       ;Save second in NUM2
        MOV      NUM3,AX                       ;Save "next seed"
                                              ;
        MOV      AX,NUM1                       ;Scale first to (0,100)
        MOV      BX,656
        MOV      DX,0
        DIV      BX
        MOV      NUM1,AX
        MOV      AX,NUM2                       ;Scale second to (0,360)
        MOV      BX,183
        MOV      DX,0
        DIV      BX
        MOV      NUM2,AX
                                              ;
        MOV      BX,NUM1                       ;Calculate LOG
        CALL     LNLOG
        NEG      AX                            ;Negate LOG value
        SHL      AX,1                          ;Multiply by 2
                                              ;LOG values scaled
                                              ;1000
                                              ;
        CALL     WORDSR
        MOV      NUM1,AX                       ;NUM1 result too large
                                              ;scale of 31.62. The maximum
                                              ;will be 141 or 4.46 x
                                              ;31.62. Truncated by LOG
                                              ;routine. Error < 1%.
                                              ;
                                              ;Generate sin & cos terms
```

O IN
DIVIDEND
EXTENSION

Figure 4.16b   The module GRAND.ASM which generates a Gaussian random number pair.

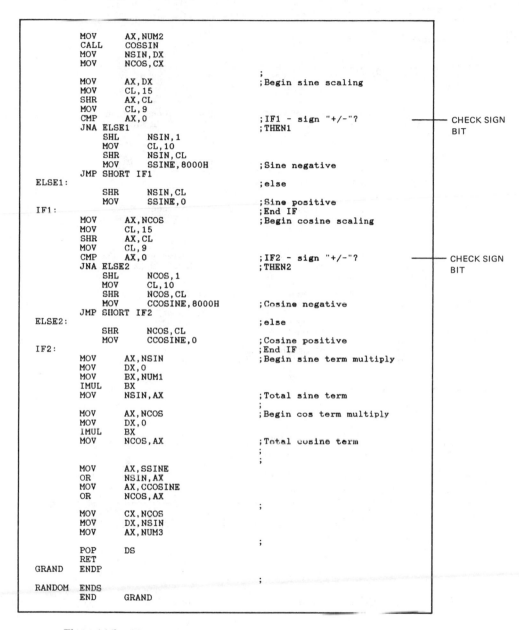

```
                MOV     AX,NUM2
                CALL    COSSIN
                MOV     NSIN,DX
                MOV     NCOS,CX

                MOV     AX,DX                    ;
                MOV     CL,15                    ;Begin sine scaling
                SHR     AX,CL
                MOV     CL,9
                CMP     AX,0                     ;IF1 - sign "+/-"?        ——— CHECK SIGN
                JNA     ELSE1                    ;THEN1                           BIT
                SHL     NSIN,1
                MOV     CL,10
                SHR     NSIN,CL
                MOV     SSINE,8000H              ;Sine negative
                JMP SHORT IF1
        ELSE1:                                   ;else
                SHR     NSIN,CL
                MOV     SSINE,0                  ;Sine positive
        IF1:                                     ;End IF
                MOV     AX,NCOS                  ;Begin cosine scaling
                MOV     CL,15
                SHR     AX,CL
                MOV     CL,9
                CMP     AX,0                     ;IF2 - sign "+/-"?        ——— CHECK SIGN
                JNA     ELSE2                    ;THEN2                           BIT
                SHL     NCOS,1
                MOV     CL,10
                SHR     NCOS,CL
                MOV     CCOSINE,8000H            ;Cosine negative
                JMP SHORT IF2
        ELSE2:                                   ;else
                SHR     NCOS,CL
                MOV     CCOSINE,0                ;Cosine positive
        IF2:                                     ;End IF
                MOV     AX,NSIN                  ;Begin sine term multiply
                MOV     DX,0
                MOV     BX,NUM1
                IMUL    BX
                MOV     NSIN,AX                  ;Total sine term
                                                 ;
                MOV     AX,NCOS                  ;Begin cos term multiply
                MOV     DX,0
                IMUL    BX
                MOV     NCOS,AX                  ;Total cosine term
                                                 ;
                                                 ;
                MOV     AX,SSINE
                OR      NSIN,AX
                MOV     AX,CCOSINE
                OR      NCOS,AX
                                                 ;
                MOV     CX,NCOS
                MOV     DX,NSIN
                MOV     AX,NUM3
                                                 ;
                POP     DS
                RET
        GRAND   ENDP
                                                 ;
        RANDOM  ENDS
                END     GRAND
```

Figure 4.16b   (*Continued*)

example has roughly 68 % of the random numbers lying between +1 and −1 (the one sigma points). At three sigma, 98 % of the random numbers lie between +3 and −3. Hence, our range of +4.46 to −4.46 excludes a very small percentage of the random values.

Figure 4.17 illustrates a DEBUG session with the program CKGRAN.EXE. The fifty Gaussian random numbers are indicated (after executing the program)

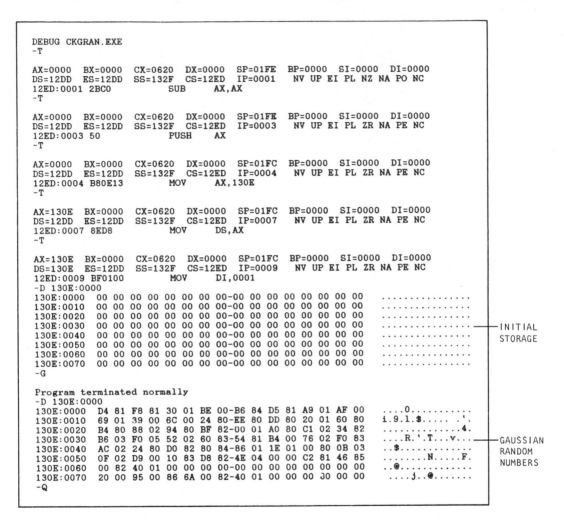

```
DEBUG CKGRAN.EXE
-T

AX=0000  BX=0000  CX=0620  DX=0000  SP=01FE  BP=0000  SI=0000  DI=0000
DS=12DD  ES=12DD  SS=132F  CS=12ED  IP=0001   NV UP EI PL NZ NA PO NC
12ED:0001 2BC0          SUB    AX,AX
-T

AX=0000  BX=0000  CX=0620  DX=0000  SP=01FE  BP=0000  SI=0000  DI=0000
DS=12DD  ES=12DD  SS=132F  CS=12ED  IP=0003   NV UP EI PL ZR NA PE NC
12ED:0003 50            PUSH   AX
-T

AX=0000  BX=0000  CX=0620  DX=0000  SP=01FC  BP=0000  SI=0000  DI=0000
DS=12DD  ES=12DD  SS=132F  CS=12ED  IP=0004   NV UP EI PL ZR NA PE NC
12ED:0004 B80E13        MOV    AX,130E
-T

AX=130E  BX=0000  CX=0620  DX=0000  SP=01FC  BP=0000  SI=0000  DI=0000
DS=12DD  ES=12DD  SS=132F  CS=12ED  IP=0007   NV UP EI PL ZR NA PE NC
12ED:0007 8ED8          MOV    DS,AX
-T

AX=130E  BX=0000  CX=0620  DX=0000  SP=01FC  BP=0000  SI=0000  DI=0000
DS=130E  ES=12DD  SS=132F  CS=12ED  IP=0009   NV UP EI PL ZR NA PE NC
12ED:0009 BF0100        MOV    DI,0001
-D 130E:0000
130E:0000  00 00 00 00 00 00 00 00-00 00 00 00 00 00 00 00   ................
130E:0010  00 00 00 00 00 00 00 00-00 00 00 00 00 00 00 00   ................
130E:0020  00 00 00 00 00 00 00 00-00 00 00 00 00 00 00 00   ................
130E:0030  00 00 00 00 00 00 00 00-00 00 00 00 00 00 00 00   ................  ── INITIAL
130E:0040  00 00 00 00 00 00 00 00-00 00 00 00 00 00 00 00   ................     STORAGE
130E:0050  00 00 00 00 00 00 00 00-00 00 00 00 00 00 00 00   ................
130E:0060  00 00 00 00 00 00 00 00-00 00 00 00 00 00 00 00   ................
130E:0070  00 00 00 00 00 00 00 00-00 00 00 00 00 00 00 00   ................
-G

Program terminated normally
-D 130E:0000
130E:0000  D4 81 F8 81 30 01 BE 00-B6 84 D5 81 A9 01 AF 00   ....0..........
130E:0010  69 01 39 00 6C 00 24 80-EE 80 DD 80 20 01 60 80   i.9.l.$..... .'.
130E:0020  B4 80 88 02 94 80 BF 82-00 01 A0 80 C1 02 34 82   ..............4.
130E:0030  B6 03 F0 05 52 02 60 83-54 81 B4 00 76 02 F0 83   ....R.'.T...v...  ── GAUSSIAN
130E:0040  AC 02 24 80 D0 82 80 84-86 01 1E 01 00 80 0B 03   ..$.............     RANDOM
130E:0050  0F 02 D9 00 10 83 D8 82-4E 04 00 00 C2 81 46 85   ........N.....F.    NUMBERS
130E:0060  00 82 40 01 00 00 00 00-00 00 00 00 00 00 00 00   ..@.............
130E:0070  20 00 95 00 86 6A 00 82-40 01 00 00 00 30 00 00    ....j..@.......
-Q
```

Figure 4.17 A sample DEBUG session illustrating the generation of 25 pairs of Gaussian random numbers.

starting at 130E:0000. This program was generated two ways. First, the link statement

LINK CKGRAN + GRAND + WORDSR + COSSIN + RAND1 + LNLOG

was used. Second, an object library in which many routines can be collected and recalled with a single link module specification was used. The creation and use of object libraries is the next topic.

4.4 OBJECT LIBRARIES

The above link statement illustrates the cumbersome manner that linking programs with many external modules can take. Ideally, we strive to develop large programs in modular fashion. To avoid confusion, it is possible to create libraries of object modules that can then be linked with a single reference.

An object library can be created using LIB.EXE on the version 2.0 diskette. To create a library named MATHLIB, which has GRAND.OBJ in it, the programmer simply specifies

LIB MATHLIB + GRAND

The response will be to indicate the IBM Personal Computer Library Manager Version 1.00, ask for a list file that contains the contents of the library, and ask for an

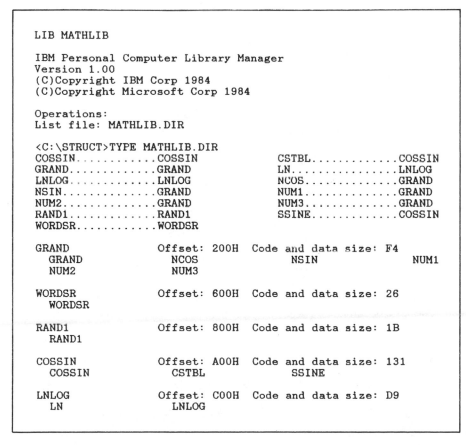

Figure 4.18 A listing of the contents of MATHLIB.LIB, based on the file MATHLIB.DIR.

```
LINK

IBM Personal Computer Linker
Version 2.10 (C)Copyright IBM Corp 1981, 1982, 1983

Object Modules [.OBJ]: CKGRAN
Run File [CKGRAN.EXE]:
List File [NUL.MAP]:
Libraries [.LIB]: MATHLIB
```

Figure 4.19   An illustration of the link procedure using libraries.

output library name if a change from MATHLIB is desired. Once created, additional modules can be added using

LIB MATHLIB + object module

Modules can be removed using

LIB MATHLIB − object module

Other possibilities exist, such as making a copy of an object module that exists in the library for external usage. The reader should consult his version 2.0 Macro Assembler manual.

Figure 4.18 illustrates a typical library consisting of the procedures that are called by CKGRAN.ASM. The library was created as described above, and a directory file was generated using

LIB MATHLIB, MATHLIB.DIR

The file was then listed. As indicated, it contains the five external modules called by CKGRAN.ASM. To generate the linked version of CKGRAN, it is necessary to specify MATHLIB as the library file when prompted by the linker. Figure 4.19 illustrates the link procedure. This is a much simpler procedure than that described above and demonstrates the power of using object libraries.

4.5 ADDED 80286 AND 80386 INSTRUCTIONS

IBM has added several instruction types for the 80286 and 80386 microprocessors [4,5]. The 80286 instructions are enabled in the Macro Assembler version 2.0 using the pseudo-op

".286C"

TABLE 4.22 ADDITIONAL 80286 APPLICATION INSTRUCTIONS

Instruction	Purpose	Comments
BOUND destination, source	Check Array Index against Bounds	This instruction insures that an index (destination) is above or equal to the first word in the memory location defined by source. Similarly it must be below or equal to source + 2.
ENTER Immediate word, Immediate byte	Make Stack Frame for Procedure Parameters	Immediate-word specifies how many bytes of storage to be allocated on the stack for the routine being entered. Immediate-byte specifies the nesting level of the routine within the high level source code being entered.
IMUL destination, Immediate	Integer Immediate Multiply	This does a signed multiplication of the destination by an immediate value.
INS/INSB/INSW destination-string, port	Input from Port to String	This transfers a byte or word string from the port numbered by DX to ES:DI. The operand destination-string determines the type of move: byte or word.
LEAVE	High Level Procedure Exit	This executes a procedure return for a high-level language.
OUTS/OUTSB/OUTSW port, source-string	Output String to Port	This transfers a byte or word string from memory at DS:DI to the port numbered by DX.
POPA	Pop All General Registers	This restores the 8 general purpose registers saved on the stack by PUSHA.
PUSH Immediate	Push Immediate onto Stack	This instruction pushes the immediate data onto the stack.
RCL destination, CL	Rotate Left through Carry	Same as RCL for 8088 except count can be 31.
RCR destination, CL	Rotate Right through Carry	Same as RCR for 8088 except count can be 31.
ROL destination, CL	Rotate Left	Same as ROL for 8088 except count can be 31.
ROR destination, CL	Rotate Right	Same as ROR for 8088 except count can be 31.
SAL/SHL destination, CL	Shift Arithmetic Left/Shift Logical Left	Same as 8088 instructions except count can be 31.
SAR destination, CL	Shift Arithmetic Right	Same as 8088 instructions except count can be 31.
SHR destination, CL	Shift Logical Right	Same as 8088 instructions except count can be 31.

TABLE 4.23 ADDITIONAL 80386 APPLICATION INSTRUCTIONS

Instruction	Purpose	Comments
BSF destination, source	Bit Scan Forward	The source word (doubleword) is scanned for a set bit and the index value of this bit loaded in destination. Scanning is from right to left.
BSR destination, source	Bit Scan Reverse	This scans as in BSF but reverse order.
BT base, offset	Bit Test	This instruction loads the bit value from base at offset in the base, into the CF register.
BTC base, offset	Bit Test and Complement	This instruction loads the bit value from base at offset in the base, into the CF register, and complements the bit in base.
BTR base, offset	Bit Test and Reset	This instruction loads the bit value from base at offset in the base, into the CF register, and resets the bit to 0.
BTS base, offset	Bit Test and Set	This instruction is identical to BTR but the resulting bit is set to 1.
CWDE, CWD	Convert Word to Doubleword	This instruction converts the signed word in AX to a doubleword in EAX.
CMPSD	Compare Doublewords	This instruction compares ES:[EDI] with DS:[ESI].
CDQ	Convert Doubleword to Quadword	This converts the signed doubleword in EAX to a signed 64-bit integer in the register pair EDX:EAX by extending the sign into EDX.
INSD	Input	Input from port DX to ES:[EDI] (doubleword).
LODSD	Load String Operand	This loads a doubleword DS:[ESI] into EAX.
MOVSD	Move Data from String to String	This moves a doubleword DS:[ESI] to ES:[EDI].
MOVSX	Move with Sign-Extend	This moves byte-to-word, byte-to-doubleword, and word-to-doubleword with sign-extend.
MOVZX	Move with Zero-Extend	This moves byte-to-word, byte-to-doubleword, and word-to-doubleword with 0 extend.
OUTSD	Output	This outputs doubleword DS:[ESI] to port in DX.
POPAD	Pop all General Registers	This pops the 8 32-bit general registers.
POPFD	Pop Stack into EFLAGS	This pops the 32-bit stack top into EFLAGS.
PUSHAD	Push all General Registers	This pushes the 8 32-bit general registers onto the stack.
PUSHFD	Push EFLAGS onto Stack	This pushes the EFLAGS register onto the stack.
SCASD	Compare String Data	This compares doublewords EAX and ES:[EDI] and updates EDI.
SETcc destination	Byte Set on Condition	This stores a byte (equal to 1), if cc, the condition, is met (following a comparison, for example). Otherwise a value of 0 is stored at the destination.
SHLD destination, Count	Double Precision Shift Left	The destination is shifted left by count.
SHRD destination, Count	Double Precision Shift Right	Same as SHLD but shift is to the right.
STOSD	Store String Data	This stores EAX in doubleword ES:[EDI] and update EDI.

TABLE 4.24 SYSTEMS-ORIENTED 80286 AND 80386 INSTRUCTIONS

Instruction	Purpose	Comments
ARPL destination, source	Adjust RPL Field of Selector	If the RPL field of the selector (protection bits) in destination is less than the RPL field of source, ZF = 1, and the RDL field of destination is set to match source.
CLTS	Clear Task Switched Flag	The Task Switch flag is in the Machine Status Word and is set each time a task change occurs. This instruction clears that flag.
LAR destination, source	Load Access Rights Byte	Destination contains a selector. If the associated descriptor is visible at the called protection level the access rights byte of the descriptor is loaded into the high byte of source (low byte = 0).
LGDT/LIDT m	Load Global/Interrupt Descriptor Table Register	m points to 6 bytes of memory used to provide Descriptor Table values (global and interrupt). This instruction loads these tables into the appropriate 80286 registers.
LLDT source	Load Local Descriptor Table Register	Source is a selector pointing to the Global Descriptor Table. The GDT should, in turn, be a Local Descriptor Table. The LDT register is then loaded with source.
LMSW Source	Load Machine Status Word	The Machine Status Word is loaded from source.
LSL destination, source	Load Segment Limit	If the Descriptor Table value pointed to by the selector in destination is visible at the current protection level, a limit value specified by source is loaded into this descriptor.
LTR source	Load Task Register	The Task Register is loaded from source.
SGDT/SIDT m	Store Global/Interrupt Descriptor Table Register	The contents of the specified Descriptor Table register are copied to 6 bytes of memory pointed to by m.
SLDT destination	Store Local Descriptor Table Register	The Local Descriptor Table register is stored in the word register or memory location specified by destination.
SMSW destination	Store Machine Status Word	The Machine Status Word is stored in the word register or memory location specified by destination.
VERR/VERW source	Verify a Segment for Reading or Writing	Source is a selector. These instructions determine whether the segment corresponding to this selector is reachable under the current protection level.
STR destination	Store Task Register	The contents of the Task Register are stored in destination.

This version does not support 80386; however, it will be useful to consider 80386 instructions available in version 2.0. To disable the 80286 mode and return to normal operation, the pseudo-op

".8086"

should be used.

4.5.1 Real Address Instructions

Table 4.22 illustrates Real Address Mode instructions that have been added for the 80286 processor. These instructions are supported by the Macro Assembler version 2.0. The ENTER, LEAVE, and BOUND instructions are used when calling a high-level procedure or function, and stack frames must be created for holding local variables and returning them when no longer needed. This concept is briefly discussed in Appendix C. The remaining instructions appearing in Table 4.22 are self-explanatory. Table 4.23 illustrates new 80386 application instructions used in Real Address Mode as well as Protected Mode. By new we mean that these instructions have no equivalents for the 8088, 8086, or 80286. It is recognized, of course, that many of the older referenced instructions now operate on 32-bit quantities when used in the 80386 context. These 80386 instructions are supported in later versions of the Macro Assembler (after version 2.0).

4.5.2 Protected Mode Instructions

In Chapter 2 we briefly considered the Protected Mode architecture for the 80286 and 80386. This mode is supported by OS/2. Systems programmers desiring to implement this mode may use the special-purpose instructions delineated in Table 4.24. These instructions are not supported for the development of normal applications and will not be considered for the bulk of this text.

4.6 SUMMARY

This chapter addressed the IBM PC Macro Assembler instruction set. We have seen how to run programs with the Macro Assembler. All output has been processed using DEBUG where memory locations contain the program variables. After execution, these program variables may change and the user can see the effect of running the program. In the next chapter we will discuss the DOS and BIOS interrupts. These useful routines will permit us to enter input at the keyboard and to print as well as display output. This will greatly increase our flexibility in designing programs.

  The impact of structuring Macro Assembler code is readily apparent in the programs presented in this chapter and produces a distinct improvement in the clarity and maintainability of such code. By now users should understand how to write small programs in structured assembler. The examples, in conjunction with the simple structures appearing in Chapter 3, have provided the groundwork for this approach.

From a purely theoretical viewpoint, structured assembler becomes very desirable because of the difficulty in programming this language. By this we mean to infer that structured programming techniques help clarify the intent of the code and ease the programmer's job of developing the algorithms. We have also emphasized modular techniques in this chapter by isolating small tasks, such as calculating a logarithm or returning a sine or cosine value to individual modules. Then we combined these tasks using top-down design techniques to accomplish larger tasks such as the calculation of a Gaussian random number.

REFERENCES

1. *iAPX 86/88, 186/188 User's Manual—Programmer's Reference.* Intel Corp., Literature Sales. P.O. Box 58130. Santa Clara, CA 95052-8130 (1986). (210911-003)
2. *Macro Assembler Reference Version 2.00.* IBM Personal Computer-Computer Language Series. IBM Corp. P.O. Box 1328. Boca Raton, FL 33432 (1984).
3. McCracken, D. D. *A Guide to PL/M Programming for Microcomputer Applications.* Addison-Wesley Publishing Co., Reading, MA (1978), p. 43.
4. *iAPX 286 Programmer's Reference Manual.* Intel Corp., Literature Sales. P.O. Box 58130 Santa Clara, CA 95052-8130 (1985). (210498-003)
5. *80386 Programmer's Reference Manual.* Intel Corp., Literature Sales. P.O. Box 58130 Santa Clara, CA 95052-8130 (1986). (230985-001)

PROBLEMS

4.1. Given AX = 1234H and BX = FFFFH, determine
    (a) AND AX,BX
    (b) NEG AX
        NEG BX
    (c) OR AX,BX
    (d) XOR AX,BX

4.2. Suppose an input value is read from the keyboard. How would you test to see if it is a Y (for YES) or N (for NO)?

4.3. Suppose an input string is read into a buffer and is of length ALEN characters. How would you test this string for the character F (use MOVS).

4.4. Use LEA to load the offset of ARRAY into AX. Contrast this with the MOV instruction.

4.5. How would two nested loops make use of the LOOP instruction? (Outline the CX register logic.)

4.6. If the sign bit of AAA is to be checked, what is wrong with the following sequence?

```
      . . .
      MOV AX,AAA     ; AAA = word variable
      SHR AX,15
      XOR AX,1       ; IF1 = compare with 1
      JZ SET
      . . .
```

4.7.   Given the sequence

```
                          . . .
                       MOV CX,NUM1
              DO1:
                          . . .
                       CALL PROC1
                          . . .
                       LOOP DO1
                          . . .
```

what should be done to insure the loop terminates properly?

4.8.   In the sequence

```
                          . . .
                       XOR  BX,F1FFH
                       JZ AAA
                          . . .
```

why would the following be preferred for some applications?

```
                          . . .
                       CMP BX,F1FFH
                       JZ AAA
                          . . .
```

4.9.   Given two modules

Module 1:

```
                          . . .
              EXTERN   CHECK
              DATA1    SEGMENT PARA PUBLIC 'DATA'
                       PUBLIC AA1
                       AAA1 DW 100
              DATA1    ENDS
              CSEG1    SEGMENT PARA PUBLIC 'CODE'
              START    PROC FAR
                       ASSUME CS:CSEG1, DS:DATA1, SS:STACK
                          . . .
                       MOV AX,SEG DATA1
                       MOV DS,AX
                          . . .
                       CALL CHECK
                          . . .
                       RET
              START    ENDP
              CSEG1    ENDS
                       END START
```

Module 2:

```
                      . . .
        EXTERN   AA1
        DATA2    SEGMENT PARA PUBLIC 'DATA'
                 AA2 DW 101
        DATA2    ENDS
        CSEG2    SEGMENT PARA PUBLIC 'CODE'
        CHECK    PROC FAR
                 ASSUME CS:CSEG2, DS:DATA2, SS:STACK
                 . . .
                 MOV AX,SEG DATA2
                 MOV DS,AX
                 . . .
                 MOV AX,AA1
                 MOV BX,AA2
                 MUL BX
                 . . .
                 RET
        CHECK    ENDP
        CSEG2    ENDS
```

What are the consequences for AA1 and AA2 when these programs are executed?

4.10. Modify the code for SORT.ASM to provide for sorting a list of word quantities.

4.11. The code in the program LNLOG, which adjusts the logarithm value, is as follows.

```
                 . . .
        MOV AX,LN[BX]
        SUB AX,10000
                 . . .
```

Rewrite this code so that it returns the actual negative log value (times 10000) with bit 15 treated as a sign bit. (Do not use two's complement arithmetic.)

4.12. Define a general procedure for calculating the sine and cosine of an angle between -32765 and 32765 degrees.

4.13. Write a procedure that calculates the logarithm to base 10 of a positive number less than or equal to 100. Use scaling. Why can't you use LNLOG?

4.14. Define a code section that calculates the modulo of a number base 3.

5

Interrupts

This chapter presents the final 8088 instruction group—interrupts. Some additional Macro Assembler version 2.0 instructions will be discussed in Chapter 8; however, these instructions are for the 8087 or 80287 coprocessor. We consider several applications with particular emphasis on the video I/O interrupt 10H, which has been mentioned in earlier chapters.

5.1 INTRODUCTION TO INTERRUPTS

Interrupts are instructions that stop program execution and transfer the instruction pointer to a specific location in memory where processing is resumed. Table 5.1 illustrates the four types of interrupt instructions in this group. The most useful member of this group is the interrupt instruction, itself:

INT   interrupt-type

When this instruction is encountered, control is transferred to the address contained in the location specified by interrupt-type times 4. For example, the interrupt 10H would transfer control to the address contained in location 0000:0040. The interrupt address table, or interrupt vector table, is contained in low memory and, hence, has segment address 0000. Figure 5.1 presents this vector table for the IBM PC. Note

TABLE 5.1   THE INTERRUPT INSTRUCTION GROUP

Instruction	Purpose	Comments
HLT	Halt	This instruction causes the processor to enter its halt state.
INT interrupt type	Interrupt	This instruction causes SP to decrement by 2 and all flags are pushed onto the stack. IF and TF are reset. SP is again decremented by 2 and CS is pushed onto the stack. CS is then filled with the high-order segment address appearing in the doubleword interrupt vector table. Next, SP is decremented by 2 and IP pushed onto the stack to save the offset. IP is filled with the offset appearing in the low-order doubleword interrupt vector. The pointer to this interrupt vector table is the interrupt-type $\times$ 4.
INTO	Interrupt If Overflow	This interrupt only executes if OF = 1. It executes in the same fashion as INT except DOS makes it point directly to an IRET instruction.
IRET	Interrupt Return	This instruction returns control to the point where the interrupt occurred. Both CS and IP are loaded from the stack.

that interrupt 10H has a vector F000 : F065 (underlined). This address is contained in the BIOS ROM area. A listing of this program content appears in Appendix A of the *IBM Technical Reference* manual for the IBM PC [1]. This particular vector points to the video I/O interrupt which we will discuss shortly. In the IBM AT an intermediate call to DOS exists; hence, the vector tables are redefined for some interrupts.

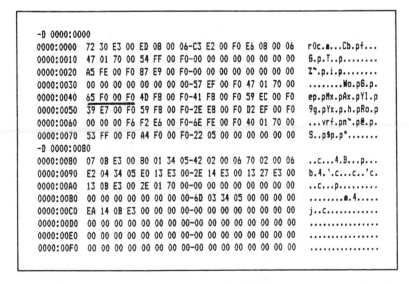

Figure 5.1   The interrupt vector table for the IBM PC.

TABLE 5.2 INTEL, DOS AND BIOS INTERRUPTS

Int.	Address SEG:OFF	20-bit	Type	Purpose	Description
0	00E3:3072	03EA2	Intel	Divide Overflow	This interrupt occurs when a divide overflow takes place. The interrupt vector varies with the DOS version.
1	0600:08ED	068ED	Intel	Single-step	This interrupt simulates single-step execution. IBM uses the Trace command in DEBUG to accomplish this task.
2	F000:E2C3 (F000:F85F – XT)	FE2C3	BIOS	Non-Maskable Interrupt	This interrupt cannot be prevented. It calls the BIOS NEAR procedure NMI_INT and results from memory errors on the system board (PARITY CHECK 1) or add-on boards (PARITY CHECK 2).
3	0600:08E6	068E6	Intel	Set Breakpoint	This interrupt stops the processing at a particular address.
4	0070:0147	00847	Intel	Interrupt If Overflow	This interrupt activates an INTO instruction return (IRET).
5	F000:FF54	FFF54	BIOS	Print Screen	This interrupt prints the screen under program control. The FAR procedure called is PRINT_SCREEN and the address 0050:0000 contains the status.
6	—	—	—	—	Not used.
7	—	—	—	—	Not used.
8	F000:FEA5	FFEA5	BIOS	Timer Interrupt	This routine handles the timer interrupt from channel 0 of the 8253 timer. There are approximately 18.2 interrupts/second. This handler maintains a count of the number of times it was called since power up. The FAR procedure is TIMER_INT and it calls an interrupt 1C H, in turn, which can contain a user routine.
9	F000:E987	FE987	BIOS	Keyboard Interrupt	This routine is FAR procedure KB_INT. It continues to address F000:EC32 and constitutes the keyboard interrupt. INT 16H is the keyboard I/O routine and is much more flexible.
A	—	—	—	—	Not used.
B	—	—	—	—	Not used.
C	—	—	—	—	Not used.
D	—	—	—	—	Not used.
E	F000:EF57	FEF57	BIOS	Floppy Diskette	This FAR procedure, DISK_INT, handles the diskette interrupt.
F	0070:0147	00847	DOS	INTO	This interrupt activates the same call as TYPE 4.

10	F000:F065	FF065	BIOS	Video Interface	This set of routines contained in the NEAR procedure VIDEO_IO provides the CRT interface. The use of this interrupt involves many options which are discussed in a subsequent table.
11	F000:F84D	FF84D	BIOS	Equipment	This procedure looks for the number of printers, any game I/O, the number of RS-232C cards, number of diskette drives, video mode, and RAM size.
12	F000:F841	FF841	BIOS	Memory Size	Determines the memory size from data.
13	F000:EC59 (C800:0256 – XT)	FEC59	BIOS	Diskette I/0	This procedure calls a series of routines that accomplish diskette I/O. Since a number of parameters are involved, this routine will be discussed separately.
14	F000:E739	FE739	BIOS	Communications Adapter	This procedure lets the user input/output data from the RS-232C communications port.
15	F000:F859	FF859	BIOS	Cassette I/O	This interrupt is used to control cassette I/O.
16	F000:E82E	FE82E	BIOS	Keyboard I/O	This interrupt manipulates AX to read the keyboard. It will be discussed separately
17	F000:FEFD2	FEFD2	BIOS	Printer I/O	This routine provides communication with the printer. It uses the AX and DX registers to setup parameters. We will discuss it later.
18	F600:000	F6000	BIOS	Cassette BASIC	This interrupt calls cassette BASIC.
19	F000:E6F2	FE6F2	BIOS	Bootstrap	Track 0 sector 1 of Drive A is read into the boot location. Control is transferred there.
1A	F000:FE6E	FFE6E	BIOS	Time-Of-Day	This routine allows the clock to be set/read. CX contains the high portion of the count and DX the low portion.
1B	0070:0140	00840	DOS	Ctrl-Break	This interrupt results when a keyboard interrupt is used.
1C	F000:FF53	FFF53	BIOS	Dummy Return	This interrupt simply calls an IRET instruction.
1D	F000:F0A4	FF0A4	BIOS	Video Parameters	This is simply a table of byte values and routines for setting up various graphics parameters.
1E	0000:0522	00522	DOS	Floppy Table	
1F	00E3:0B07	01937	DOS	Graphics Table	Used with DOS 3.0
20	PSP:0000	—	DOS	Program Terminate	This interrupt is issued by DOS to exit from a program. It is the first address in the Program Segment Prefix area.
21	relocatable	—	DOS	Function Request	This interrupt has many options and will be discussed later.
22	PSP:000A	—	DOS	Terminate Address	Control transfers to the address specified at this interrupt location when the program terminates. Do not issue this address directly.
23	PSP:000E	—	DOS	Ctrl-Break Exit Address	This interrupt is issued in response to a Ctrl-Break from the standard input.

(Continued)

135

TABLE 5.2 *(Continued)*

Int.	Address SEG:OFF	Address 20-bit	Type	Purpose	Description
24	PSP:0012	—	DOS	Critical Error Handler Vector	This interrupt is called when a critical error occurs within DOS such as a disk error.
25	relocatable	—	DOS	Absolute Disk Read	This interrupt transfers control to the device driver for a read.
26	relocatable	—	DOS	Absolute Disk Write	This interrupt transfers control to the device driver for a write.
27	relocatable	—	DOS	Terminate But Stay Resident	This vector is used by programs to remain resident after DOS regains control.
28–2E	RESERVED FOR DOS				
2F	relocatable	—	DOS	Multiplex Interrupt	This interrupt defines a general interface between 2 processes. Each handler is assigned a specific number in AH and the function of the handler in AL.
30–3F	RESERVED FOR DOS				

136

Table 5.2 is rather extensive and contains most of the interrupt vectors for the IBM PC and XT [2]. Most of these interrupts will not be useful from a programming viewpoint; however, the interrupts indicated in the description as affecting such things as I/O can make the programmer's job much simpler. Three types of interrupts are discussed: Intel, BIOS, and DOS. The Intel interrupts are common to most Intel processors in the 8086 family. The BIOS interrupts are specific to the IBM Basic Input Output System and the DOS interrupts are, of course, specific to the IBM Disk Operating System [3]. The BIOS interrupts are explained in the BIOS program listing discussed above, and the DOS interrupts are described in the *DOS Technical Reference* manual [4].

5.1.1 Interrupts 0–0FH

Interrupts 0–4 are not particularly useful to the assembler programmer because they tend to call system oriented functions. INT 5 can be used to print the contents of the screen Cathode Ray Tube (CRT) under program control. If, for example, a program generates output to the screen, it might be desirable to automatically save this output and INT 5 is useful for this purpose. INT 8 is the Timer Interrupt and returns a time count in locations 0040:006C and 0040:006E where these are the low and high count, respectively. This 32-bit time count can be used to time events in the program. INT 9 activates when keys are pressed or released and simply stops the processing. This interrupt is more of a system interrupt. The INT 16H keyboard I/O interrupt will be discussed in detail rather than focusing on INT 9. Both address the keyboard operation; however, INT 16H has considerable flexibility over INT 9. Interrupts 0AH to 0FH tend to be either unused at present or system oriented and will not be discussed further. INT 10H, however, is the video I/O routine already mentioned. This interrupt has many options as discussed in the program listing in the *IBM Technical Reference* manual. Essentially all screen I/O under program control can be implemented using this interrupt. The following discussion addresses this interrupt in some depth.

5.1.2 Interrupt 10H: Video I/O

The type 10H interrupt has 16 basic options controlled by the AH register at the time the interrupt is called. Table 5.3 describes these options and the registers that must be set to control output. The mode option (AH = 0) determines the screen resolution and what graphics are available. To handle the increased memory requirements for the graphics modes, additional video memory must be provided and is usually supplied with the graphics card purchased. The following discussion illustrates the use of this video interrupt and how to achieve screen graphics.

All standard screen modes involve the use of a raster scan which simply means the electron beam moves vertically downward after scanning across for each line from left to right. The resolution of a dot in one of the graphics modes is determined by the number of lines vertically down the screen and by the number of columns horizontally across the screen. In the 640 × 200 graphics mode, for example, the height of the screen can be thought of as 200 dots high. Similarly, the screen width would be 640

TABLE 5.3 INT 10H OPTIONS (VIDEO I/O)

AH	Purpose	Description
0	Mode	The AL register contains the mode value: $0 - 40 \times 25$ pixel black/white, $1 - 40 \times 25$ pixel color, $2 - 80 \times 25$ pixel black/white, $3 - 80 \times 25$ pixel color, $4 - 320 \times 200$ pixel color, $5 - 320 \times 200$ pixel black/white, and $6 - 640 \times 200$ pixel black/white.
1	Set Cursor Type	This option uses CH and CL: CH — (Bits 4-0) start line for cursor, CL — (Bits 4-0) end line for cursor. All other bits should be set to zero to avoid erratic behavior.
2	Set Cursor Position	(DH,DL) = (row,column) cursor. Upper left is (0,0). BH = page number (0 for graphics).
3	Read Cursor Position	(DH,DL) = (row,column) cursor on exit. (CH,CL) = cursor mode.
4	Read Light Pen Position	See the *IBM Technical Reference Manual*.
5	Select Active Display Page	This allows the user to scroll pages in video memory for the 40×25 and 80×25 displays, where more than one page can be stored. AL = 0-7 for 40×25 and AL = 0-3 for 80×25.
6	Scroll Active Page Up	AL = number of lines. Lines are blanked at the bottom and 0 blanks the entire screen. (CH,CL) = (row,column) upper left corner, (DH,DL) = (row,column) lower right corner, and BH = attribute used on blank line.
7	Scroll Active Page Down	Same as 6 except lines blanked from top down.
8	Read Attribute and Character at Cursor	BH = display page, AL = character, and AH = attribute. 40×25 and 80×25 displays only.
9	Write Attribute and Character at Cursor	BH = display page, CX = character count, AL = character to write, and BL = attribute of character.
10	Write Character at Cursor	Same as 9 with no attribute.
11	Set Color Palette	Sets the color palette. User should experiment with this option. See the *IBM Technical Reference Manual* for register settings.
12	Write Dot	DX = row number, CX = column number, AL = color value (for high resolution displays this varies the intensity).
13	Read Dot	DX = row number, CX = column number, and AL = dot read.
14	Graphics and Alpha Character Write	AL = character, BL = foreground color in graphics mode, BH = display page in alpha mode.
15	Current Video State	AL = mode, AH = number columns on screen, and BH = active display page.

dots wide. The size or intensity of a dot depends on the attribute assigned to it, usually specified with the BL register. If a monochrome monitor is used it is not possible to implement the graphics options appearing in Table 5.3; however, screen graphics can still be accomplished within the constraints of the IBM character set. This simplified graphics lends itself to bar charts and regular structures. We will not address these alpha modes because of the flexibility achievable in the graphics modes. Also, once the graphics mode is understood it will be relatively straightforward to apply these ideas to the alpha modes and the associated character set. An added reason for concentrating on the graphics mode is that it is possible to get a hard copy of the screen by simply calling GRAPHICS.COM (version 2.1 of DOS or higher) prior to execution of the program which generates the screen graphics.

   All this discussion about graphics is important because the user needs to understand what limitations are imposed by various system configurations. Also, it is presumed that once a figure is created on the screen, a hard copy will be desired. Particular attention should be paid to the printer options available when using a monochrome system, that is, how the printer handles the IBM graphic character subset. For the discussion presented here, the dot character will be used to create figures.

   What are the limitations of raster screen graphics? First, it is necessary to understand how the screen is addressed. Above, we described the screen as a matrix of locations 640 across by 200 down. Each location or pixel has a coordinate associated with it, much like an X–Y axis graph. The position (0,0) is the upper left-hand corner. The position (640,200) (or [320,200] for medium resolution graphics) is the lower right-hand corner. Here we have used the convention (column, row) in order to correspond to the familiar (x,y) description for points on a two-dimensional graph. When specifying the location of a point, it must fall within the row-column matrix of the resolution mode being used. For example, (554,199) would be allowed in 640×200 resolution but not in 320×200 resolution. Hence, frequently the data to be plotted must be scaled. The basic limitation of the raster approach then becomes one of resolution. Suppose we have two points (100,50) and (600,120), and try to draw a straight line between them using the IBM raster graphics in 640×200 resolution. In this case Figure 5.2 results, where we have included a box and tick marks. The slanted line in Figure 5.2 has a series of small steps that reflect the resolution achievable. The slope of this line is 70/500 or 0.14. The general equation for a line, which will be used shortly, is given by

$$y = y_0 + m(x - x_0)$$

where y_0 is the starting y-value, x_0 is the starting x-value, and m is the slope. In the above example, y_0 is initially 50, x_0 is initially 100, and m is 0.14. As x increases the

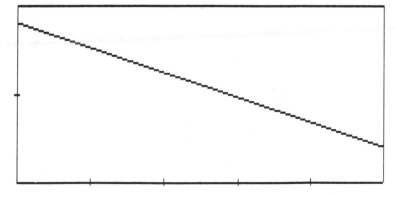

Figure 5.2   Plot of straight line using 640×200.

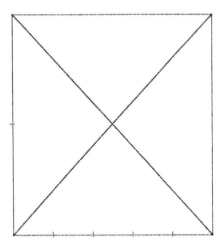

Figure 5.3 Plot of crossed lines using 320 × 200.

term $m(x - x_0)$ must increment by 1 for y to increase by 1. Since $m = 0.14$ this requires an increase in x of slightly more than 7. For an increase of 7 or less, the y value will not increase by 1. Since the raster cannot scan between lines, it simply truncates y to its earlier value. Once x increases by a factor of more than 7.14, however, the y-value increases beyond 1 and the raster jumps to the next line.

Figure 5.3 illustrates a second graphic figure that consists of a box with tick marks and two crossed lines. The lines are drawn from the following screen locations: (75,175) to (225,25) and (75,25) to (225,175). Notice that the magnitude of the slope is unity (one positive and the other negative) and the line appears straight with no steps. This graph was made using medium resolution (320 × 200).

How were these plots generated? Figure 5.4 presents procedures for generating a box and tick marks on the screen using medium resolution. (Figure 5.2 uses 640 × 200 graphics but has a similar procedure.) The routine BOX1 produces a box on that screen. This general purpose procedure uses a data area in which the column and row limits for the box, referred to as the x and y limits, are specified and can be easily changed. The tick marks are also indicated in segment DATABOX as well as the x and y limits on the ticks. XMAX and XMIN refer to a line to be drawn parallel to the x-axis or horizontal, and YMAX and YMIN similarly refer to vertical ticks.

The first call to INT 10H has AH = 6, the scroll active page up option, and clears the screen. All other registers indicated are set according to Table 5.3. Next we set AH = 0 and place the screen mode in 320 × 200 graphics (AL = 5). Two small procedures, LINEH and LINEV, generate horizontal and vertical lines, respectively. The box generator procedure (BOX1) calls LINEH to generate a line from CX = XBEG to CX = XEND at the y-position YBEG. We proceed to generate all four box lines in this fashion and return to the calling program.

The tick marks can be generated with a call to TICK1. TICK1 is a procedure which uses the data area, DATABOX, and calls LINEH for y-axis ticks and LINEV for x-axis ticks. This procedure is slightly less general in that only one tick is generated on the y-axis while any number, fixed by COUNT, may be along the x-axis. (The aesthetics of selecting number and placement of such things as tick marks,

```
PAGE 40,132
TITLE BOX320 - GENERATES A BOX 150 X 150(BOX320.ASM)
COMMENT *
                            DESCRIPTION:This routine plots a
                            box and tick marks 150 x 150.
                                                          *
                                  ;
DATBOX  SEGMENT PARA PUBLIC 'DATA'
        PUBLIC XBEG,XEND,YBEG,YEND,XT,YT,XMAX,XMIN,YMAX
        PUBLIC YMIN,X,Y,COUNT
                                  ;
XBEG    DW      75              ;Corners of box
XEND    DW      225
YBEG    DW      25
YEND    DW      175
XT      DW      105,135,165,195 ;Tick mark X-axis
YT      DW      100             ;Tick mark Y-axis
XMAX    DW      77              ;Tick vector lengths
XMIN    DW      73
YMAX    DW      177
YMIN    DW      173
Y       DW      0               ;Dummy variables
X       DW      0
COUNT   DW      6               ;No.horizontal ticks + 1
                                  ;
DATBOX  ENDS
                                  ;
CBOX    SEGMENT PARA PUBLIC 'CODE'
        PUBLIC BOX1,TICK1
BOX1    PROC    FAR
        ASSUME CS:CBOX,DS:DATBOX
        PUSH DS
                                  ;
        MOV AX,SEG DATBOX
        MOV DS,AX
                                ;This procedure draws a box
                                ;Clear screen
        MOV AH,6                ;Scroll page
        MOV AL,0                ;Blank entire window
        MOV CX,0                ;Start upper left corner
        MOV DH,23               ;Lower right corner
        MOV DL,79
        MOV BH,7                ;Attribute white on black
        INT 10H
                                  ;
        MOV AH,0                ;Set mode
        MOV AL,5                ;320 x 200 graphics
        INT 10H
                                  ;
        MOV AX,YBEG             ;Start Y-axis point horizontal line
        MOV Y,AX
        CALL LINEH              ;Draw line
        MOV AX,YEND             ;Start Y-axis point 2nd line
        MOV Y,AX
        CALL LINEH              ;Draw horizontal line
                                  ;
        MOV AX,XBEG             ;Start X-axis point vertical line
        MOV X,AX
        CALL LINEV              ;Draw vertical line
        MOV AX,XEND             ;Start X-axis point 2nd line
        MOV X,AX
        CALL LINEV              ;Draw 2nd vertical line
                                  ;
        POP DS
        RET
BOX1    ENDP
                                  ;
TICK1   PROC    FAR
        PUSH DS
                                  ;
        MOV AX,SEG DATBOX
        MOV DS,AX
                                  ;
```

BOX PARMETER AREA

Figure 5.4   Routines for generating a box and tick marks in 320 × 200 resolution.

```
            MOV AX,YT               ;Y position Y-axis tick
            MOV Y,AX                ;Draw Y-axis tick
            MOV AX,XMIN             ;Load min X-axis tick in XBEG
            MOV XBEG,AX
            MOV AX,XMAX             ;Load max X-axis tick in XEND
            MOV XEND,AX
            CALL LINEH              ;Draw Y-axis tick
                                    ;
            MOV AX,YMIN             ;Load min X-axis tick in YBEG
            MOV YBEG,AX             ;Draw X-axis ticks
            MOV AX,YMAX             ;Load max X-axis ticks in YEND
            MOV YEND,AX
            MOV SI,0                ;Set counter - X-axis
    DO1:
                MOV AX,XT[SI]       ;Load current X-axis tick pos.
                MOV X,AX
                CALL LINEV          ;Draw vertical tick
                ADD SI,2
                CMP SI,COUNT        ;Compare tick with COUNT
                JBE DO1             ;End loop
                                    ;
            POP DS                                            ───── RECALL CALLING
            RET                                                     PROGRAM DATA
    TICK1   ENDP                                                    SEGMENT
    LINEH   PROC    NEAR
                                    ;Generates horizontal line
            MOV DX,Y
            MOV CX,XBEG             ;Load begin X-value
    DO2:
                MOV AH,12           ;Write dot
                MOV AL,1            ;Attribute 1
                INT 10H
                ADD CX,1            ;Increment X-value
                CMP CX,XEND         ;Check X-value end point
                JNE DO2             ;Loop end
            RET
    LINEH   ENDP
                                    ;
    LINEV   PROC    NEAR
                                    ;Generates vertical line
            MOV CX,X
            MOV DX,YBEG             ;Load begin Y-value
    DO3:
                MOV AH,12           ;Write dot
                MOV AL,1            ;Attribute 1
                INT 10H
                ADD DX,1            ;Increment Y-value
                CMP DX,YEND
                JNE DO3             ;Loop end
            RET
    LINEV   ENDP
                                    ;
    CBOX    ENDS
            END     BOX1
```

Figure 5.4 (*Continued*)

of course, are left to the user.) Note that the lines are all drawn with AH = 12, the dot mode.

Figure 5.5a contains the flow chart for the procedure that draws lines. The sloped lines in Figure 5.3 were generated with the procedure CONNL1, shown in Figure 5.5b. Since the *y*-axis points are all less than or equal to 200 they can be treated as byte quantities. Thus we load YSTART in DH and YEND in DL. It is assumed that XSTART is less than XEND and these values must be loaded in BX and CX respectively. Also, the procedure assumes the medium resolution mode. Initially the number of points along the *x*-axis, between XSTART and XEND, is determined and loaded into NCOUNT. These are the connecting points in our plot which lie between the actual points specified at the call to CONNL1. The purpose of CONNL1 is to then draw a straight line between the actual points specified, using these

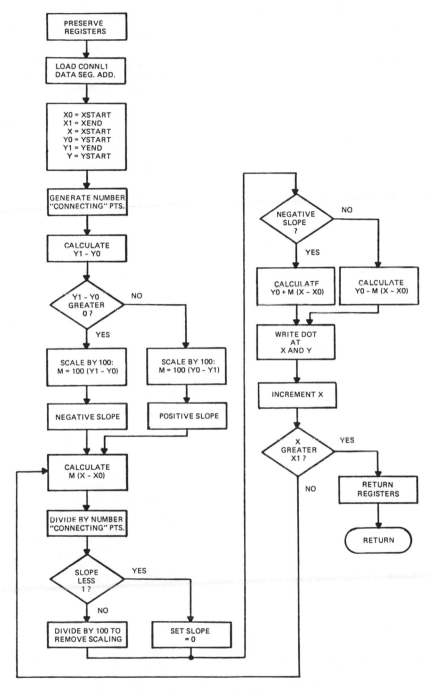

Figure 5.5a Functional flow chart for CONNL1.ASM.

```
PAGE 40,132
TITLE CONNL1- CONNECT LINE AND PLOT (CONNL1.ASM)
COMMENT *
                        DESCRIPTION:This routine reads DX =
                        (YSTART,YEND), BX = XSTART, and CX = XEND.
                        It generates a connecting line between the
                        points (XSTART,YSTART) and (XEND,YEND) and
                        plots the points.
                                                        *
DLINE     SEGMENT PARA PUBLIC 'DATA'
Y0        DW      0                   ;Y start
Y         DW      0                   ;Y-value (dynamic)
Y1        DW      0                   ;Y end
X0        DW      0                   ;X start
X         DW      0                   ;X-value (dynamic)
X1        DW      0                   ;X end
NCOUNT    DW      0                   ;Number points in line
SIGN      DW      0                   ;Sign slope
M         DW      0                   ;Scaled partial slope
                                      ;
DLINE     ENDS
                                      ;
CLINE     SEGMENT PARA PUBLIC 'CODE'
          PUBLIC CONNL1
CONNL1    PROC    FAR
          ASSUME CS:CLINE,DS:DLINE
                                      ;
          PUSH DS
          PUSH AX
          PUSH BX
          PUSH CX
          PUSH DX
          PUSH DI
          PUSH SI
                                      ;
          MOV AX,SEG DLINE
          MOV DS,AX
                                      ;Load screen coordinates
          MOV AL,DH                   ;DH contains YSTART
          MOV AH,0                    ;Clear top half AX
          MOV Y0,AX                   ;Start Y-point
          MOV Y,AX                    ;Also save YSTART in y
          MOV AL,DL                   ;DL contains YEND
          MOV AH,0                    ;Clear top half AX
          MOV Y1,AX                   ;End Y-point
          MOV X0,BX                   ;Start X-point
          MOV X,BX                    ;Save XSTART in x also
          MOV X1,CX                   ;End X-point
                                      ;
                                      ;Generate count index
                                      ;
          MOV AX,X1                   ;Larger X-value in increment
          SUB AX,X0                   ;Calculate X-increment
          MOV NCOUNT,AX               ;Number of X-points to connect
                                      ;Generate slope
          MOV DX,0                    ;Clear upper numerator register
          MOV AX,Y1
          SUB AX,Y0                   ;Begin calculation Y1 - Y0 for slope
          JB ELSE1
                    MOV CX,100        ;Scale slope by 100
                    MOV DX,0          ;Clear upper multiplicand register
                    MUL CX
                    MOV M,AX          ;Slope in M
```

Figure 5.5b   The routine CONNL1.ASM which is a general purpose PUBLIC
procedure for plotting connecting lines in a graph.

```
                    MOV AX,1        ;Sign negative for slope
                    MOV SIGN,AX     ;Sign increment Y-axis points
                    JMP IF1
        ELSE1:
                    MOV AX,Y0       ;Positive slope
                    SUB AX,Y1       ;Calculate (Y1 - Y0)
                    MOV CX,100      ;Scale by 100
                    MOV DX,0        ;Clear upper register
                    MUL CX
                    MOV M,AX        ;Slope in M
                    MOV AX,0        ;Positive slope
                    MOV SIGN,AX     ;Sign deecision Y-axis points
        IF1:
        DO1:
                    MOV AX,X
                    SUB AX,X0       ;(X - X0)
                    MOV DX,0        ;Clear upper multiplicand register
                    MUL M           ;Multiply by slope numerator
                    DIV NCOUNT      ;Begin completion slope calculation
                    MOV CX,100      ;Value corresponding to slope 1
                    CMP AX,CX       ;Check for slope less 1
                    JB ELSE2        ;Jump slope less/= 1
                            MOV DX,0        ;Clear upper register
                            DIV CX          ;Remove scaling
                            JMP IF2
        ELSE2:
                            MOV AX,0        ;0 slope
        IF2:
                    MOV BX,SIGN
                    CMP BX,1        ;Jump positive slope
                    JB ELSE3
                            MOV BX,Y0       ;Load Y-start value
                            ADD AX,BX       ;Add Mx(X-X0)
                            JMP IF3
        ELSE3:
                            MOV BX,Y0       ;Positive slope
                            SUB BX,AX       ;Generate Y0 - M x (X - X0)
                            MOV AX,BX       ;Save in AX
                                            ;
        IF3:
                    MOV CX,X        ;X-position
                    MOV DX,AX       ;Y-position
                    MOV AH,12       ;Write dot
                    MOV AL,2        ;Dot attribute
                    INT 10H
                                    ;
                    INC X           ;Next point
                    MOV BX,X
                    CMP BX,X1       ;Ck X<= X1
                    JBE DO1
                                    ;
        POP SI
        POP DI
        POP DX
        POP CX
        POP BX
        POP AX
        POP DS
        RET
CONNL1  ENDP
                                    ;
CLINE   ENDS
        END     CONNL1
```

Figure 5.5b   (*Continued*)

connecting points. This is accomplished using the equation for the straight line indicated earlier.

First the slope of the straight line is calculated using

$$m = \frac{(y_1 - y_0)}{(x_1 - x_0)}$$

where y_1 is the ending y-value (Y1), y_0 is the starting y-value (Y0), x_1 is the ending x-value (X1), x_0 is the starting x-value (X0), and m is the slope. The statements

```
MOV AX,Y1        ;
SUB AX,YO        ;Begin calculation Y1–Y0 for slope
...
MOV  CX,100      ;Scale slope by 100
MOV DX,0         ;Clear upper multiplicand register
...
```

generate $y_1 - y_0$ and scale it by 100. We will remove this scaling later. This value is stored in a variable appropriately called M. Note that the $(x_1 - x_0)$ division has not been performed at this time. Next the slope is checked to see if it is positive or negative because for positive slope we will need to decrease the y-value and for negative slope this value must increase. The m-value is multiplied $(x - x_0)$, the result divided by NCOUNT, and the scaling removed. The result is either added to y_0 (negative slope) or subtracted from y_0 (positive slope) and plotted. The process then repeats until all connecting points are plotted.

Figure 5.6 illustrates the program that used CONNL1, BOX1, and TICK1 to produce the plot in Figure 5.3. Note that INT 16H is used with AH = 0. We will talk about this interrupt shortly but, as used here, it simply halts the program and freezes the screen. Without this interrupt the program would continue to execute, process the return to 80 × 25 mode, which clears the screen of the figure, and return to DOS. The INT 16H allows the user to observe the figure on the screen and obtain a hard copy, if desired, by simultaneously pressing the Ctrl and PrtSc keys. Of course, it was necessary to load GRAPHICS.COM before CLINE1.EXE in order to get the hard copy.

A Structure Chart for a modular program that plots 25 Gaussian random numbers was illustrated in Chapter 4. Figure 5.7 presents a plot of the 25 Gaussian random numbers (sine terms) generated using GRAND. This plot is contained in the box previously generated. The effect of raster screen graphics can readily be seen, however, the plot is quite clear in communicating the variation intrinsic to these random numbers. It was necessary to scale these numbers, which lie between -2752 and 2752 (as output from GRAND), in order to have them fall within the graph limits of y (25 to 175 as indicated in BOX320.ASM). In actuality the numbers are between -4.46 and 4.46 when all scaling is removed.

Figure 5.8 contains the plot routine needed to generate the graph in Figure 5.7. The random numbers are first generated with a call to GRAND. The DI register is used as a counter and SI is the pointer to the data segment variable RN, which

```
PAGE 40,132
TITLE CLINE1 - CHECK LINE PLOT (CLINE1.ASM)
COMMENT *
                        DESCRIPTION:This routine calls BOX320.ASM
                        and CONNL1.ASM and checks their operation.
                                                             *
            EXTRN BOX1:FAR,TICK1:FAR,CONNL1:FAR
STACK       SEGMENT PARA STACK 'STACK'
            DB       64 DUP('STACK    ')
STACK       ENDS
                                              ;
CSEG        SEGMENT PARA PUBLIC 'CODE'
CCLIN       PROC    FAR
            ASSUME CS:CSEG,SS:STACK
                                              ;
            PUSH DS
            SUB AX,AX
            PUSH AX

                                              ;
                                              ;
            CALL BOX1                         ;Draw box
            CALL TICK1                        ;Draw ticks
            MOV DH,175                        ;YSTART
            MOV DL,25                         ;YEND
            MOV CX,225                        ;XEND
            MOV BX,75                         ;XSTART
            CALL CONNL1
                                              ;
            MOV CX,225
            MOV BX,75
            MOV DH,25
            MOV DL,175
            CALL CONNL1

                                              ;
            MOV AH,0                          ;Keyboard interrupt to halt screen
            INT 16H                           ;Wait for key-stroke to proceed
                                              ;
            MOV AH,0
            MOV AL,3                          ;Return to 80 x 25 mode
            INT 10H
            RET
CCLIN       ENDP
CSEG        ENDS
            END     CCLIN
```

Figure 5.6   The main program, CLINE1, which calls CONNL1, BOX1, and TICK1 to generate the graphics in Figure 5.3.

contains the pairs of independent Gaussian random numbers. CX is the output register from GRAND which contains the cosine term and DX, the sine term. Both BOX1 and TICK1 are called, and a procedure LLABEL is called for the purpose of labeling the graph. In generating Figure 5.7, LLABEL was a dummy routine; however, we will shortly demonstrate its use for labeling figures in the graphics mode. Prior to the first call to GRAND in PLOTRN the AX register was loaded with 4096 (1000H) to be used as a seed.

Following definition of the random numbers to be used, the x-axis is divided into intervals at which each point will be plotted. (CONNL1 will be called to generate the connecting points.) Next the number is scaled by a parameter appearing in the data segment SY. The value 37 is chosen to scale the points and only those

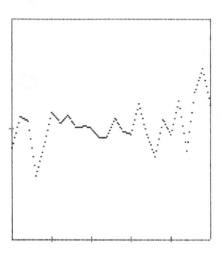

Figure 5.7   Plot of 25 Gaussian random numbers.

values between -3.0 and 3.0 are intended to be plotted (only the sine-type Gaussian random numbers are plotted). Scaling is simply a matter of bookkeeping. The user needs to translate the range of values output from GRAND to graph limits on the screen. The MINMAX procedure can be used to write a general purpose routine for scaling.

In Figure 5.8, once the scaling is accomplished and it is determined whether or not the value is positive or negative, the points to be input to CONNL1 are generated. For purposes of handling negative numbers the graph was divided into an upper half and lower half at the y-axis point 100 in absolute screen coordinates. All negative numbers, when properly scaled, were added to 100 and all positive numbers, when properly scaled, were subtracted from 100. In GRAND the negative values had the sign bit set so it was necessary to check this bit, observe that the number is negative when set, clear the bit, and branch to appropriate code for handling the negative numbers.

In the instructions

```
MOV DH,BYTE PTR Y0
MOV DL,BYTE PTR Y1
```

the pointer (PTR) operator is used. This operator is used to change the attribute of an expression and has the form

```
type PTR expression
```

PTR overrides the type (BYTE, WORD, or DOUBLEWORD) of a register or variable operand contained in the expression. It can also override the distance (NEAR or FAR) of a label contained in the expression. In the program PLOTRN we use it to change Y0 and Y1 from a word to a byte operand. The value contained in these variables is less than 256 and must load DH and DL, respectively, in order to satisfy the INT 10H call for plotting. In Figure 5.8 one JMP is LONG. This use of an out-of-range jump should only occur sparingly.

```
PAGE 40,132
TITLE PLOTRN - PLOT GAUSSIAN RN 200 X 200 (PLOTRN.ASM)
COMMENT *
                     DESCRIPTION:This routine generates 25
                     gaussian r.n. and plots them.
                                                          *
                ;
        EXTRN   GRAND:FAR,BOX1:FAR,TICK1:FAR,CONNL1:FAR
        EXTRN LLABEL:FAR
STACK   SEGMENT PARA STACK 'STACK'
        DB      64 DUP('STACK   ')
STACK   ENDS
                ;
DATA    SEGMENT PARA PUBLIC 'DATA'
                ;
RN      DW      50 DUP(0)
NUM     DW      24              ;Number of plot points
XSTART  DW      75              ;Variable depending on BOX1
XEND    DW      225             ;Variable depending on BOX1
SY      DW      37              ;Variable depending on scale
DDX     DW      0               ;X-axis increment
YO      DW      0               ;YSTART
Y1      DW      0               ;YEND
XO      DW      0               ;XSTART
X1      DW      0               ;XEND
                ;
DATA    ENDS
                ;
CSEG    SEGMENT PARA PUBLIC 'CODE'
PLOTRN  PROC    FAR
        ASSUME  CS:CSEG,DS:DATA,SS:STACK
                ;
        PUSH DS
        SUB AX,AX
        PUSH AX
                ;
        MOV AX,SEG DATA
        MOV DS,AX
                ;
        MOV DI,1                ;Load random numbers
        MOV SI,0                ;Data point index initialization
        MOV AX,1000H            ;Mask for negative number
DO1:
        CALL GRAND
        MOV RN[SI],CX           ;Cosine term
        MOV RN[SI+2],DX         ;Sine term
        ADD SI,4                ;Increment word index by 4
        ADD DI,1                ;Increment counter
        CMP DI,25               ;Compare loop limit
        JBE DO1
                ;
        CALL BOX1               ;Set 320 x 200 mode/draw box
        CALL TICK1              ;Draw tick marks
        CALL LLABEL             ;Write graph labels
                               ;Set up graph points
                               ;Use only sine array
        MOV SI,0                ;Initialize number index
        MOV DI,1                ;Initialize X-axis index counter
                ;
        MOV AX,XEND             ;Set up X increment
        SUB AX,XSTART           ;AX = XEND - XSTART
        MOV DX,0                ;Clear upper numerator register
        DIV NUM
        MOV DDX,AX              ;Save X-axis increment
                ;
DO2:
        MOV AX,RN[SI+2]         ;Load number
        MOV CL,15               ;Check negative
        SHR AX,CL               ;Shift sign to bit 0
        CMP AX,1                ;Compare sign
        JE ELSE1
        MOV AX,RN[SI+2]         ;Number was positive
        MOV DX,0                ;Clear upper numerator register
        DIV SY                  ;Scale number
        MOV BX,100              ;100 is middle of graph
        SUB BX,AX               ;Plot in upper half
        JMP IF1
```

⎯ SPECIAL
PURPOSE LABEL
PROCEDURE

Figure 5.8 Main calling program, PLOTRN.ASM, used to generate Gaussian
random number plot.

```
ELSE1:
                MOV AX,RN[SI+2] ;Number was negative
                SHL AX,1        ;Remove sign bit
                SHR AX,1        ;Shift cleared bit back
                MOV DX,0        ;Clear upper numerator register
                DIV SY          ;Scale number
                MOV BX,100      ;100 is middle graph
                ADD BX,AX       ;Plot in lower half
IF1:
            MOV Y0,BX               ;Save new Y-axis start
            MOV AX,DDX              ;Start finding new X-position
            MOV DX,0               ;Clear upper multiplicand
            MOV CX,DI              ;Get multiplier for X-axis
            SUB CX,1              ;Decrement count by 1
            MUL CX
            ADD AX,XSTART          ;Add starting X-value
            MOV X0,AX              ;Save new start X-value
                                   ;Do second point
            MOV AX,RN[SI+4]        ;Second sine point
            MOV CL,15             ;Load shift value
            SHR AX,CL            ;Shift sign to bit 0
            CMP AX,1             ;Check negative number
            JE ELSE2
                MOV AX,RN[SI+4] ;Load AX with new sine
                MOV DX,0        ;Clear upper numerator register
                DIV SY          ;Scale number
                MOV BX,100      ;100 is middle graph
                SUB BX,AX       ;Plot upper half
                JMP IF2
ELSE2:
                MOV AX,RN[SI+4] ;Load sine value
                SHL AX,1        ;Remove sign bit
                SHR AX,1        ;Shift back with cleared bit
                MOV DX,0        ;Clear upper numerator reg.
                DIV SY          ;Scale number
                MOV BX,100      ;100 is middle graph
                ADD BX,AX       ;Plot lower half graph
IF2:
            MOV Y1,BX               ;Save end Y-value
            MOV AX,X0              ;AX = new X-start position
            ADD AX,DDX             ;Add X-axis increment
            MOV X1,AX              ;Save end X-value
                                   ;Set up plot
            MOV DH,BYTE PTR Y0     ;Column value in DH
            MOV DL,BYTE PTR Y1     ;Second column value in DL
            MOV BX,X0              ;Start X-value in BX
            MOV CX,X1              ;End X-value in CX
            CALL CONNL1            ;Plot points-connected
                                   ;Check index
            ADD SI,2              ;Increment by word length
            INC DI               ;Increment counter
            MOV AX,NUM
            ADD AX,1
            CMP DI,AX             ;Compare counter with NUM + 1
            JA  LOUT             ;Jump out if greater
            JMP DO2              ;Outside short-label range
                                 ;
                                 ;Keyboard interrupt to halt screen
LOUT:       MOV AH,0
            INT 16H
                                 ;
            MOV AH,0
            MOV AL,2
            INT 10H
            RET
PLOTRN      ENDP
CSEG        ENDS
            END     PLOTRN
```

Figure 5.8   (*Continued*)

The linking procedure for generating the EXE file used to plot Figure 5.7 is as follows:

```
LINK

IBM Personal Computer Linker
Version 2.10 (C) Copyright IBM Corp. 1981, 1982, 1983

Object Modules (.OBJ): PLOTRN + CONNL1 + BOX320 + LLABEL
Run File (PLOTRN.EXE):
List File (NUL.MAP):
Libraries (.LIB): MATHLIB
```

In the case of Figure 5.7, LLABEL was a dummy routine; however, Figure 5.9 illustrates this plot with labels added. To effect labeling, it is necessary to call INT 10H, with AH = 10 character output. AH = 9 could also be used for color monitors where the attribute allows changing the color of the letters. The use of labels is somewhat aesthetic and their size is fixed by the special graphic character table contained in BIOS. The reader will need to experiment with the output and decide if it is not better to type labels on graphics that, for example, might be used to illustrate presentations.

Figure 5.10 presents the routine LLABEL used to label Figure 5.9. This is a special purpose routine that prints the ASCII characters appearing in TABLE1 and TABLE2. Recall that the Structure Chart for the Gaussian random numbers included provision for plotting the result. In Figure 4.14, for example, the "plot overhead" could be generated using PLOTRN (plus BOX1 and TICK1) and CONNL1 could be

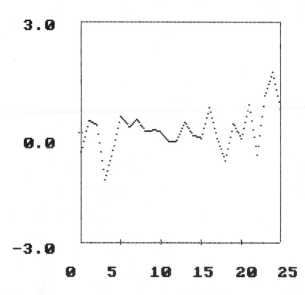

Figure 5.9 Plot of Gaussian random numbers with labels.

```
PAGE 40,132
TITLE LLABEL - PRINT LABEL ON GAUSSIAN RN PLOT(LLABEL.ASM)
COMMENT *
                      DESCRIPTION:This routine labels the gaussian
                      random number plot.  All labels and cursor
                      start positions are contained in the data
                      segment.
                                                        *
DATAL    SEGMENT PARA PUBLIC 'DATA'
                                                    ;
TABLE1   DB        'G','A','U','S','S','I','A','N',' ',' '
         DB        'R','A','N','D','O','M',' ',' '
         DB        'N','U','M','B','E','R','S'
COUNT1   DW        25
STARTX   DW        6
STARTY   DW        0
XPOS     DB        3,3,3,8,12,16,20,24,28
YPOS     DB        3,13,22,24,24,24,24,24,24
TABLE2   DB        ' ','3','.','0',' ','0','.','0','-','3','.','0'
         DB        '0',' ',' ',' ',' '
         DB        '5',' ',' ',' ',' '
         DB        '1','0',' ',' ',' '
         DB        '1','5',' ',' ',' '
         DB        '2','0',' ',' ',' '
         DB        '2','5',' ',' ',' '
COUNT2   DW        4
COUNT3   DW        8
                                                    ;
DATAL    ENDS
                                                    ;
CLABEL   SEGMENT PARA PUBLIC 'CODE'
         PUBLIC LLABEL
LLABEL   PROC      FAR
         ASSUME    CS:CLABEL,DS:DATAL
                                                    ;
         PUSH DS
                                                    ;
         MOV AX,SEG DATAL                           ;Load DS value for DATAL
         MOV DS,AX
                                                    ;
                                                    ;
         MOV DH,BYTE PTR STARTY                     ;Load row value-start
         MOV DL,BYTE PTR STARTX                     ;Load col value-start
         MOV BH,0
                                                    ;
         MOV DI,1                                   ;Initalize counters & indexes
         MOV SI,0
         MOV CX,1
                                                    ;
DO1:
              MOV AH,2                              ;Position cursor
              INT 10H
              MOV AH,10                             ;Write character
              MOV AL,TABLE1[SI]                     ;Load character from TABLE1
              MOV BL,1                              ;Attribute
              INT 10H
              ADD DL,1                              ;Increment X-space
              INC SI                                ;Increment TABLE1 value
              INC DI                                ;Increment index
              CMP DI,COUNT1                         ;Compare TABLE1 limit
              JBE DO1
```

Figure 5.10 The special purpose label routine LLABEL.ASM, used to label the
Gaussian random number plot.

```
                                      ;Write numerical labels
         MOV CX,1                     ;Initialize counters & indexes
         MOV BP,0
         MOV SI,0
DO3:
              MOV DH,YPOS[BP]         ;Outer loop-load Y-position
              MOV DL,XPOS[BP]         ;Load X-start position
              MOV DI,1               ;Reinitialize inner loop index
DO2:
                 MOV AH,2             ;Inner loop cursor control
                 INT 10H
                 MOV AH,10            ;Character write
                 MOV AL,TABLE2[SI]    ;Character from TABLE2
                 MOV BL,2             ;Attribute
                 INT 10H
                 ADD DL,1             ;Increment X-position
                 INC SI               ;Increment TABLE2 index
                 INC DI               ;Increment inner loop
                 CMP DI,COUNT2        ;Compare inner loop
                 JBE DO2
              INC BP                  ;Increment outer loop index
              CMP BP,COUNT3           ;Compare outer loop limit
              JBE DO3
         POP DS

                                      ;
         RET
LLABEL   ENDP
CLABEL   ENDS
         END       LLABEL
```

Figure 5.10   *(Continued)*

used for plotting points. INT 10H is used to move the cursor to the correct spot on the screen (AH = 2) and print the character desired (AH = 10). In general, every graphic output that contains labeling must rely on a special purpose routine for this. The parameters in DATAL, however, can be easily changed to accommodate new labeling.

5.1.3 Interrupts 11H–15H

Interrupt 11H returns a summary of what options are attached to the basic system unit. This summary is returned in AX as specified in the BIOS listing (Appendix A of the *IBM Technical Reference* manual). Interrupt 12H, when called, returns the amount of random access memory installed (in blocks of 1024 bytes). This value is returned in AX. Interrupt 13H will be discussed in a subsequent chapter on extended file management. INT 14H is used with the communications adapter. Basically, this interrupt is only used when input/output is to occur using the RS-232C interface. INT 15H is the cassette I/O routine, but since we do not discuss cassette based systems this will not be treated.

5.1.4 Interrupt 16H: Keyboard I/O

This interrupt type has already been used in the calling programs CLINE1.ASM and PLOTRN.ASM. When used with AH = 0 the program stops and waits to read the next keyboard character. We used it to halt the processing, freezing the screen so that the graphics could be observed and a hard copy generated. When this mode is used with AH = 0, BIOS reads the keyboard character and returns it in AL. It is in ASCII format. Associated with this character is a scan code which is read into AH. There is one scan code for each key on the keyboard (83 scan codes in all). Normal ASCII has 128 standard characters. The IBM PC allows 256 characters in its Extended ASCII character set. (Remember the graphics characters used in the alpha screen modes, for example.) To generate all these characters IBM introduced the scan code notion because some keys have no ASCII equivalent (function keys, scroll lock, and others). By using one or more keys members of the Extended ASCII character set can be obtained. In the next chapter we will address in detail binary to ASCII conversion (and vice versa) and at that time we will consider the representation of the first 128 ASCII characters. The reader is referred to the *IBM Technical Reference* for the remaining 128 characters.

When a character from the keyboard is input, the keyboard stores it in its own buffer area which can contain up to 20 bytes of information. After each press or release of a key one byte is stored in the buffer. This byte contains a 1 or 0 in bit seven, corresponding to a press or release, respectively, and the remaining seven bits contain the scan code. It was necessary to load the buffer after each press and release (separately) because some inputs require that two keys be pressed before any are released. The scan code is translated into an Extended ASCII character once the keyboard buffer is loaded into memory.

If INT 16H is used with AH = 1, the Zero Flag contains the buffer status. ZF = 1 indicates that the buffer is empty and ZF = 0 means input is available from the buffer and the first available character is in AX. When used with AH = 2, a keyboard status byte is returned in AL. The information contained in this byte is described in the BIOS listing (KEYBOARD_10) presented in the *IBM Technical Reference* manual.

The major limitation of INT 16H is that it is character oriented. It would be more desirable to be able to input an entire string at once. Fortunately, there exists such an interrupt: INT 21H. Since the DOS interrupt 21H has considerable flexibility for handling keyboard I/O, we will postpone a detailed discussion of the topic until this interrupt is discussed. Use of INT 21H is recommended, in turn, over INT 16H for keyboard I/O.

5.1.5 Interrupt 17H: Printer I/O

INT 17H can be used to communicate with the printer attached to the system. As for most of the interrupt routines, the value contained in AH determines which interrupt option is selected. When AH = 0 the interrupt service prints the ASCII character contained in AL. Some printers do not respond properly to the IBM ASCII Extended character set and only print the first 128 standard ASCII characters. The reader should check the printer manual to see what the printer does with with non-standard characters. Since it is necessary to create line feeds, carriage returns, and other print head action, a minimal subset of special printer control characters would be as follows:

ASCII Character	Function
08H	Backspace
0AH	Line Feed
0CH	Form Feed
0DH	Carriage Return

When AH = 1, a call to INT 17H initializes the printer, and when AH = 2, the interrupt returns a printer status byte in AH. The functions of each bit in the status byte are indicated in the BIOS listing (the routine PRINTER_10) contained in the *IBM Technical Reference* manual. The default printer assignment is 0 and should be supplied for all calls to INT 17H in register DX. BIOS supports up to 3 printers at one time (designated 0–2).

5.1.6 Interrupts 18H–20H

Interrupt 18H is used to load cassette BASIC. Interrupt 19H causes the computer to reinitialize DOS from disk. The time-of-day interrupt, 1AH, allows the programmer to set the time with AH = 1. This count is incremented approximately 18.2 times per second. The count is contained in CX (high portion) and DX (low portion). AL is non-zero if 24 hours have elapsed since the last INT 1AH. When AH = 0 the clock is read and the count returned in CX and DX. This interrupt can be used to obtain crude estimates on execution times because it changes roughly every 50 milliseconds.

INT 1BH activates when a Ctrl-Break occurs. The type 1CH interrupt points to an IRET instruction. This interrupt vector can be changed to point to a user routine that functions off periodic interrupts. INT 1CH also interrupts roughly 18.2 times a second. The 1EH interrupt points to a table of parameters needed for diskette operation. In Chapter 7 we consider extended file management and this table will be discussed at that time. INT 1FH points to table of characters used to define an extended character set only in DOS 3.00 and 3.10. INT 20H points to the beginning of the Program Segment Prefix area and causes a program termination.

5.1.7 Interrupt 21H: DOS Function Calls

Interrupt 21H has many options, depending on the value contained in AH. Table 5.4 lists these functions. It is based on the *DOS Technical Reference* manual and provides a brief description of each. Functions 5E00, 5E02, 5E03, 5F02, 5F03, and 5F04 are selected by specifying the option in the full AX register word. Users will need, at most, a subset of these functions. In this subsection we only consider the functions associated with keyboard, printer, and display I/O (functions with AH = 5, 2, 9, or 10). In Chapter 7 we consider functions associated with file control and disk I/O.

TABLE 5.4 INT 21H OPTIONS (DOS FUNCTION CALLS)

AH	Purpose	Type	Description
0	Program Terminate	Control	Terminates the execution of a program.
1	Keyboard Input	Keyboard	Waits for keyboard input, displays it, and returns it in AL.
2	Display Output	Display	Displays the character in DL.
3	Auxiliary Input	Misc.	Waits for a character from the COM port and puts it in AL.
4	Auxiliary Output	Misc.	Outputs the character in DL to the COM port.
5	Printer Output	Printer	Outputs the character in DL to the printer.
6	Direct Console I/O	Keyboard	Waits for a character from the keyboard (no Ctrl-Break check).
7	Direct Console Input with No Echo	Keyboard	Waits for a character from the keyboard and puts it in AL.
8	Console Input without Echo	Keyboard	Waits for a character from the keyboard, returns it in AL, and executes an interrupt for Ctrl-Break.
9	Print String	Display	Outputs the string to the display. String must end with $.
A	Buffered Keyboard Input	Keyboard	Reads characters from the keyboard into a buffer. DS:DX points to buffer, 1st byte = max characters, and 2nd byte = number characters read.
B	Check Standard Input Status	Keyboard	Checks to see if a character is available from the keyboard.
C	Clear Keyboard Buffer and Invoke Keyboard Function	Keyboard	Clears the keyboard buffer and executes the function call in AL (only 01H, 06H, 07H, 08H, or 0AH).
D	Disk Reset	Disk	All files not closed are lost.
E	Select Disk	Disk	Selects the drive in DL as default (0 = A, 1 = B, etc.).
F	Open File	File	Searches the directory for the file pointed to in DS:DX. AL = FFH (not found) or 00H (found). If found the FCB is filled.
10	Close File	File	Closes the file after a write. DS:DX points to FCB.
11	Search for First Entry	Disk	Searches the directory for the first matching filename. AL = FFH if none found.
12	Search for Next Entry	Disk	After a filename has been found, this call searches for the next occurrence.
13	Delete File	File	Deletes all directory entries that match DS:DX pointer.
14	Sequential Read	Disk	Loads the record addressed by the current block and record at the DTA and increments the record address.
15	Sequential Write	Disk	Opposite 14H.
16	Create File	File	Searches the directory for a matching entry, if found it is reused, if not found opens a file.
17	Rename File	File	Changes the filename at DS:DX to the filename at DS:DX + 11.

19	Current Disk	Disk	Determines the default drive and returns it in AL.
1A	Set Disk DTA	Disk	Sets the disk transfer address to DS:DX.
1B	Allocation Table Information	Disk	Returns DS:BX = pointer to media descriptor byte, DX = number allocation units, AL = numbersectors/allocation unit, and CX = size physical sector.
1C	Allocation Table Info for Drive	Disk	DL = drive number; this function returns the same parameters as 1CH.
21	Random Read	Disk	Reads the record addressed by the current block and record fields into memory at the DTA.
22	Random Write	Disk	Opposite 21H.
23	File Size	File	Searches the directory for entry matching DS:DX and sets the FCB random record field equal to the number records in file.
24	Set Relative Record Field	File	Sets the random record field to the same address as the current block and record fields.
25	Set Interrupt Vector	Misc.	The interrupt vector in AL is set to address DS:DX.
26	Create New Program Segment	Misc.	This call should not be used.
27	Random Block Read	Disk	Reads the number of records in CX from DS:DX into DTA.
28	Random Block Write	Disk	Opposite 27H.
29	Parse Filename	File	See *DOS Technical Reference* manual.
2A	Get Date	Misc.	Returns: AL = day of week, CX = year, DH = month, and DL = day of month.
2B	Set Date	Misc.	Reverse 2AH.
2C	Get Time	Misc.	Returns: CH = hour, CL = minutes, DH = seconds, and DL = hundredths of a second.
2D	Set Time	Misc.	Reverse 2CH.
2E	Set/Reset Verify Switch	Misc.	When set, DOS performs a verify operation for each disk write. AL = 0 (off) and AL = 1 (on).
2F	Get DTA	Disk	Returns the disk transfer address in ES:BX.
30	Get DOS Version No.	Misc.	Returns: DOS major version number (AL) and minor version (AH).
31	Terminate Process/Remain Resident	Control	See *DOS Technical Reference* manual.
33	Ctrl-Break Check	Control	Requests/sets BREAK, AL = 0(request) or 1(set) and DL = 0 (off) or 1 (on).
35	Get Vector	Misc.	For interrupt number in AL, it returns the pointer in ES:BX.
36	Get Disk Free Space	Disk	Returns for DL (drive) the available clusters (BX), clusters/drive (DX), bytes/sector (CX), and sectors/cluster (AX).
38	Country Dependent Information	Misc.	See *DOS Technical Reference* manual.
39	Create Subdirectory	Disk	Generates the MKDIR function with DS:DX pointing to an ASCIIZ string containing drive and directory path names.

(Continued)

TABLE 5.4   *(Continued)*

AH	Purpose	Type	Description
3A	Remove Subdirectory	Disk	RMDIR function; DS:DX points to string containing drive and path names.
3B	Change Current Directory	Disk	CHDIR function; DS:DX points to string containing drive and path names.
3C	Create File	File	CREATE function; if file pointed to in DS:DX does not exist the file is opened.
3D	Open File	File	DS:DX points to file; AL = 0 (read only), 1 (write only), or 2 (read/write). (See *DOS Technical Reference* manual).
3E	Close File Handle	File	BX contains file handle; file closed, directory updated, and internal file buffers removed.
3F	Read from File/Device	File	BX = file handle, CX = number bytes to read, DS:DX = buffer to be loaded. After call, AX = number bytes read.
40	Write to File/Device	File	Inverse of 3F.
41	Delete File from Directory	File	Removes a directory entry associated with the filename pointed to in DS:DX.
42	Move File Read/Write Pointer	File	See *DOS Technical Reference* manual.
43	Change File Mode	File	See *DOS Technical Reference* manual.
44	I/O Control for Devices	I/O	See *DOS Technical Reference* manual.
45	Duplicate File Handle	File	On entry BX = file handle, on exit AX = duplicate.
46	Force Duplicate File Handle	File	Forces the handle in CX to refer to the same file at the same position as the handle in BX.
47	Get Current Directory	Disk	DL = drive number; DS:SI = pointer to 64 byte user area to contain directory; and AX returns error codes.
48	Allocate Memory	Memory	BX = number paragraphs and AXL0000 points to the allocated blocks.
49	Free Allocated Memory	Memory	Frees the memory allocated with 48H.
4A	Modify Allocated Memory Blocks	Memory	Modifies blocks to contain new block size. ES = block segment and BX = new block size in paragraphs.
4B	Load/Execute Program	Control	Provides for overlaying. DS:DX points to program and ES:BX points to parameter block for load.
4C	Terminate Process	Control	Exits to invoking process.
4D	Get Return Code	Misc.	See *DOS Technical Reference* manual.
4E	Find First Matching File	File	Finds the first filename that matches the file pointed to in DS:DX. CX = attribute used in search.
4F	Find Next Matching File	File	Same as 4E except finds second match. The DTA contains information from 4EH or previous 4FH.
54	Get Verify Setting	Misc.	Returns the value of verify set with 2EH, in AL.
56	Rename File	File	Renames the file in DS:DX with ES:DI.

57	Get/Set File Date and Time	Misc.	On entry: AL = 0 (get) or 1 (set), BX = file handle, CX = time, and DX = date.
59	Get Extended Error (DOS 3.00 & 3.10)	Error	Returns additional error information (see *DOS Technical Reference* manual).
5A	Create Unique File (DOS 3.00 & 3.10)	File	Generates file pointed to by DS:DX (path ends with/) and CX = attribute.
5B	Create New File (DOS 3.00 & 3.10)	File	Creates new file pointed to by DS:DX with attribute in CX.
5C	Lock/Unlock File Access (DOS 3.00/3.10)	File	AL = 0 (lock) or 1 (unlock), BX = file handle, CX = byte offset high, DX = byte offset low, SI = length high and DI = length low.
5E00	Get Machine Name (DOS 3.10)	Misc.	DS:DX points to location where computer name returned.
5E02	Set Printer Setup (DOS 3.10)	Network	BX = redirection list index, CX = length string, and DS:SI points to string to be put in front of all print files.
5E03	Get Printer Setup	Network	Reverse 5E02.
5F02	Get Redirection List Entry (DOS 3.10)	Network	Returns nonlocal network assignments.
5F03	Redirect Device (DOS 3.10)	Network	Principally for networking.
5F04	Cancel Redirection	Network	Principally for networking.
62	Get PSP (DOS 3.00 & 3.10)	Misc.	Returns the Program Segment Prefix in BX.

One goal of this subsection was to provide the reader with an introduction to techniques for communicating with the various peripherals attached to the system. INT 10H served to provide graphics communication. Now, INT 21H provides the remaining I/O needed to write flexible modular, general-purpose programs. No longer will it be necessary to use DEBUG as the only source of input and output to assembled programs.

Figure 5.11 illustrates a program that uses INT 21H for keyboard, printer, and display communication. The program first clears the screen. Next it writes the message

input characters (terminate with ENTER)

to the screen using function 9. This function outputs an entire string that is pointed to by the starting address in DX. The string, in this case, is defined in the data segment starting at MESOUT. In order to delimit the string, DOS looks for a $ as the last character. Once the string has been passed to the display, function 2 is called for control. Next the keyboard is read using function OAH and loaded into CHAR in the data segment. CHAR is preceded by two bytes in the data segment: BUFFMX, which is initialized to the maximum character count allowed in the input string, and BUFFLN, a byte that will contain the number of characters read from the keyboard. After more screen control instructions, the program modifies the string for output to the screen. The last character input in the string was a carriage return and

```
PAGE 40,132
TITLE CPRINT - CHECKS INT 21H (CPRINT.ASM)
COMMENT *
                    DESCRIPTION:This program reads characters from
                    the keyboard using INT 21H (AH = 10) and writes
                    them to the screen display (AH = 9) and prints
                    them (AH = 5).
                                                          *
STACK    SEGMENT PARA STACK 'STACK'
         DB      64 DUP('STACK    ')
STACK    ENDS
                                        ;
DATA     SEGMENT PARA PUBLIC 'DATA'
                                        ;
MESOUT   DB      'input characters(terminate with ENTER)  '
         DB      '$'
BUFFMX   DB      80
BUFFLN   DB      ?                      ;Length of input buffer
CHAR     DB      80 DUP(' ')
         DB      '$'                    ;DOS INT 21H required terminator
BLANK    DB      ' '
NPRINT   DW      26                     ;Printer output line limit + 1
                                        ;
DATA     ENDS
                                        ;
CSEG     SEGMENT PARA PUBLIC 'CODE'
CPRINT   PROC    FAR
         ASSUME  CS:CSEG,DS:DATA,SS:STACK
                                        ;
         PUSH DS
         SUB AX,AX
         PUSH AX
                                        ;
         MOV AX,SEG DATA
         MOV DS,AX
                                        ;Clear screen
         MOV AH,6                       ;Scroll page
         MOV AL,0                       ;Blank entire window
         MOV CX,0                       ;Start upper left corner
         MOV DH,23                      ;Lower right corner
         MOV DL,79
         MOV BH,7                       ;Attribute white on black
         INT 10H
                                        ;
         MOV AH,2                       ;Line feed to screen
         MOV DL,0AH                     ; 0A  line feed character
         INT 21H
                                        ;
         MOV AH,2                       ;Carriage return
         MOV DL,0DH                     ; 0D  carriage return character
         INT 21H
                                        ;
         LEA DX,MESOUT                  ;Write prompt
         MOV AH,9                       ;Function 9
         INT 21H
                                        ;
         MOV AH,2                       ;Line feed to screen
         MOV DL,0AH                     ; 0A  line feed character       ASCII
         INT 21H                                                        CHARACTER
                                        ;
         MOV AH,2                       ;Carriage return
         MOV DL,0DH                     ; 0D  carriage return character
         INT 21H
```

Figure 5.11 The program CPRINT.ASM which employs interrupt 21H to read the keyboard and write to the display and printer. Interrupt 17H is used to initialize the printer.

```
                                        ;
                                        ;Read keyboard input
            LEA DX,BUFFMX               ;Location of keyboard input
            MOV AH,10                   ;Function 10
            INT 21H
                                        ;
                                        ;
            MOV CX,100                  ;Write character to display (100 times)
            MOV BH,0                    ;Load upper BH with 0
            MOV BL,BUFFLN               ;Load lower with character count
            MOV SI,BX
            LEA BX,CHAR                 ;Pointer to character string
            MOV AH,BLANK                ;Load blank in AH
                                        ;
            MOV BYTE PTR [BX+SI],AH ;Load blank in place carriage return
                                        ;
DO1:
                MOV AH,9                ;Function 9
                LEA DX,CHAR            ;Load DX character start position
                INT 21H
                LOOP DO1              ;Loop 100 times
                                        ;
            MOV DX,0                   ;Printer 0
            MOV AH,1                   ;Initialize printer
            INT 17H
                                        ;
            MOV SI,1                   ;Count index on print line
                                        ;
DO3:
                LEA BX,CHAR           ;Start character loop
                MOV DI,0              ;Index on character
                MOV AH,0              ;Reuse register for data manipulation
                MOV AL,BUFFLN         ;AX now has character count
                MOV CX,AX             ;Loop counter
DO2:
                    MOV AH,5         ;Character loop
                    MOV DL,BYTE PTR [BX+DI]   ;Print character
                    INC DI           ;Increment character
                    INT 21H
                    LOOP DO2
                MOV AH,5              ;Line feed
                MOV DL,0AH            ;Line feed character
                INT 21H
                MOV AH,5             ;Carriage return
                MOV DL,0DH           ;Carriage return character
                INT 21H
                INC SI
                CMP SI,NPRINT        ;Check line limit
                JB DO3               ;Jump if less than 26
                                        ;
            RET
CPRINT      ENDP
CSEG        ENDS
            END     CPRINT
```

Figure 5.11   (*Continued*)

this is changed to a blank. The string that was read from the keyboard is now output 100 times using function 9.

In order to use the printer, each character must be individually output. To do this a loop is established with the instructions

```
DO2:
        MOV AH,5
        MOV DL,BYTE PTR [BX+DX]
        INC DI
        INT 21H
        LOOP DO2
```

After execution of this loop the string has been printed and a line feed and carriage return take place. The outer loop causes the string to be printed 25 times.

5.1.8 Remaining DOS Interrupts

The remaining DOS interrupts are principally system interrupts and will not, in general, be called by the programmer. The capabilities of each are as indicated in Table 5.2 and the interested reader is referred to the *DOS Technical Reference* manual for a complete discussion.

5.2 AN ADDITIONAL PROGRAM EXAMPLE: PASSWORD CHECKING

The use of structured code, with its conditional nature, lends itself readily to the development of interactive programs. These are programs which call interrupts, solicit input from the user and then branch according to the reply received (performing a subsequent function that is appropriate for the user's response). The program discussed in this section presents a simply interactive example which asks for a password and accepts or rejects the input depending on whether or not it agrees with the stored version. The module is intended to constitute a simplified case and it has the advantage that it readily lends itself to illustrating the use of interrupts and the necessary setup code for processing these interrupts.

Figure 5.12a presents the flow chart for the program. Figure 5.12b illustrates the .ASM file for the password program. The name of the program is STRU1.ASM. The use of natural language syntax for program design is illustrated in a similar program contained on the Macro Assembler version 2.0 diskette that comes with the IBM software for version 2.0.

The program, STRU1.ASM, appearing in Figure 5.12b makes use of a new entity, the macro. In this figure the macro SCDEL appears at the beginning of the program. We discuss this program feature in detail in Chapter 6; however, it is useful to expose the reader to it at this point in the book. Basically, macros are so useful to assembler programming that an early introduction is valuable.

The macro structure is as follows:

```
macro-name   MACRO  [parameters]
             [LOCAL  label-list]
             ...
             ENDM
```

Here the parameter list is optional and the code, represented by the ellipsis, is actual code that will be inserted in the program wherever the macro call (using the macro-name) appears in the program. This expansion of code takes place during pass one of the assembler. Obviously, labels that might appear in a macro can potentially conflict with labels already appearing in the expanded program. Hence, the LOCAL pseudo-op is used to avoid this problem. LOCAL is followed by a label-list that contains all labels unique to the macro. Upon assembly, these are all assigned unique names that

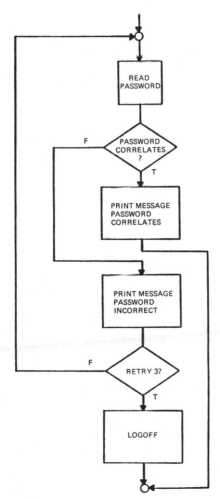

Figure 5.12a The functional flow chart for the structured program STRU1.ASM which accepts an input password.

```
PAGE      55,132
TITLE     STRU1    - PASSWORD PROGRAM(STRU1.ASM)
;
;         DESCRIPTION: This program asks for a password and
;         upon receiving it prints out a message - password
;         successful.  If after 3 tries the password is
;         unsuccessful - error message.
;
EXTRN     MESSAGE:FAR,KEYBD:FAR,CLSCREN:FAR
;
SCDEL     MACRO
;
;         MACRO to delay screen.
;
          MOV       AH,0                      ;Keyboard interrupt
          INT       16H
          ENDM
;
STACK     SEGMENT PARA STACK 'STACK'
          DB        64 DUP('STACK    ')
STACK     ENDS
;
DATA      SEGMENT PARA PUBLIC 'DATA'
          PUBLIC    BLANK,BUFFMX,BUFFLN,CHAR
;
MESO1     DB        'Input password (6 characters). ','$'
MESO2     DB        'Password successfully received. ','$'
MESO3     DB        'Password unsuccessful (Strike key to continue).','$'
MESO4     DB        'LOGOFF ','$'
;
BUFFMX    DB        80                        ;Max buffer size
BUFFLN    DB        ?                         ;Length input string
CHAR      DB        80 DUP(' '),'$'
;
PASS      DB        'A','B','C','1','2','3,'  ;Password
COUNT     DW        0                         ;Retry count
BLANK     DB        ' '
;
DATA      ENDS
;
CSEG      SEGMENT PARA PUBLIC 'CODE'
          ASSUME    CS:CSEG,DS:DATA,SS:STACK,ES:DATA
;
PPASS     PROC      FAR
          PUSH      DS
          SUB       AX,AX
          PUSH      AX
                                              ;
          MOV       AX,SEG DATA
          MOV       DS,AX
          MOV       ES,AX                     ;Load ES segment address
                                              ;
```

Figure 5.12b The program STRU1.ASM which reads and validates a password.

do not conflict with other labels. This is done regardless of the number of times the macro is expanded or how many other macros appear. The LOCAL definition is, of course, optional depending on the need to make labels local.

Figures 5.13, 5.14 and 5.15 illustrate the procedures called from STRU1.ASM. The code between the label DO1 and JNE ELSE1 clears the screen, asks for the password, reads the password, and compares this input with "ABC123" from the data segment. The comparison is accomplished using the byte-string compare instruction

```
DO1:
                                        ;
        CALL    CLSCREN                 ;Clear screen
                                        ;
        MOV     DX,OFFSET MESO1         ;Address of message 1
                                        ;
        CALL    MESSAGE                 ;Ask for password.
        CALL    KEYBD                   ;Read from keyboard
        MOV     SI,OFFSET PASS          ;Load password index
        MOV     DI,OFFSET CHAR          ;Load input parameter index
        MOV     CX,6                    ;Length password
        REPE    CMPSB                   ;Compare string
                                        ;
    JNE ELSE1
                                        ;
        MOV     DX,OFFSET MESO2         ;Address message 2
                                        ;
        CALL    MESSAGE                 ;Successful password
                                        ;
    JMP SHORT OUT1
ELSE1:
                                        ;
        MOV     DX,OFFSET MESO3         ;Address message 3
                                        ;
        CALL    MESSAGE                 ;Password in error.
        SCDEL                           ;Screen delay. MACRO
        MOV     AX,COUNT                ;Increment COUNT
        INC     AX
        MOV     COUNT,AX
        CMP     AX,3                    ;Check for 3 tries
                                        ;
    JNE DO1
                                        ;
        MOV     DX,OFFSET MESO4         ;Address message 4
                                        ;
        CALL    MESSAGE                 ;Error - LOGOFF
                                        ;
OUT1:
                                        ;
        RET
PPASS   ENDP
CSEG    ENDS
        END     PPASS
```

Figure 5.12b   *(Continued)*

CMPSB. This comparison is repeated 6 times ($CX = 6$) using the REPE instruction. In order to accomplish this comparison, the string to be compared is specified by offset SI in the data segment. The string to be compared with it is specified by offset DI in the extra segment. Three procedures are called in this code: CLSCREN, which clears the screen; MESSAGE, which provides a message to the screen asking for the password; and KEYBD, which reads the keyboard input. Since the messages to be output are contained in the data segment of the calling program, the desired message address offset is passed via DX and must be specified prior to calling MESSAGE.

If the passwords are not equal following the string comparison, the zero flag is set, the JNE ELSE1 jump takes place, and a message is output indicating an unsuccessful attempt. This is followed by a retry opportunity until the fourth retry. If the passwords agree a message is output indicating a success, and the assembler code

```
PAGE 55,132
TITLE CLSCREN - CLEAR SCREEN PROCEDURE (CLSCREN.ASM)
;
;          DESCRIPTION: This procedure clears the screen.
;
CSEG      SEGMENT PARA PUBLIC 'CODE'
          PUBLIC CLSCREN
CLSCREN PROC     FAR
          ASSUME CS:CSEG
;
          MOV AH,6
          MOV AL,0
          MOV CX,0
          MOV DH,23
          MOV DL,79
          MOV BH,7
          INT 10H
                                    ;
          RET
                                    ;
CLSCREN ENDP
CSEG      ENDS
          END
```

Figure 5.13   The external procedure CLSCREN.ASM which clears the screen.

JMP SHORT OUT1 is executed. This jump is to the exit label OUT1. Note that this unconditional jump has purposely been made short, forcing the programmer to restrict the amount of intervening code. When the passwords do not compare and the unsuccessful attempt message results, a screen delay occurs to make reading the screen messages easier. Also, the retry count is incremented and checked. The comparison,

CMP AX,3

results in the setting of the zero flag if AX = 3. The conditional branch back to DO1 executes if the retry count be less than 3 and the zero flag not be set. If AX = 3, the LOGOFF message is output and the program terminates. The exit afforded by OUT1 is a new structure concept, SEARCH with middle exit.

Figure 5.13 illustrates the screen-clear procedure. Figure 5.14 presents the message output procedure. Since this procedure is part of the calling program code segment CSEG, it can access the data segment DATA, defined in the calling program ASSUME statement. Finally, the last procedure accessed by PPASS, the calling program FAR procedure, is KEYBD and is illustrated in Figure 5.15.

Figure 5.16 demonstrates the assembly and linking for STRU1. Note the object modules that must be specified at link time. Finally, Figure 5.17 constitutes a sample interactive session. In response to "Input password (6 characters)," a carriage return was input and the unsuccessful attempt indicated. For the second query, an incorrect password, AAAAAA, was input and was also rejected. The third attempt results in a successful comparison when the input is ABC123. Had another incorrect input been made, the unsuccessful password message would have displayed followed by the message LOGOFF.

```
PAGE 55,132
TITLE MESSAGE - PROCEDURE TO PRINT MESSAGE (MESSAGE.ASM)
;
;
;         DESCRIPTION: This procedure prints a message to the screen.
;
CSEG    SEGMENT PARA PUBLIC 'CODE'
        PUBLIC MESSAGE
MESSAGE PROC    FAR
        ASSUME CS:CSEG
                                        ;
        PUSH DS
                                ;
;                       This is the message output procedure.
;
        PUSH DX                     ;Preserve message address
                                    ;
        MOV AH,6                    ;Setup for display output
        MOV DL,0AH                  ;Load line feed character
        INT 21H
        MOV AH,6                    ;Setup for display output
        MOV DL,0DH                  ;Load carriage return character
        INT 21H
                                    ;
        POP DX                      ;Recall message address
        MOV AH,9                    ;Setup to output characters
        INT 21H
                                    ;;
        MOV AH,6                    ;Setup to display character
        MOV DL,0AH                  ;Line feed
        INT 21H
                                    ;;
        MOV AH,6                    ;Setup to display character
        MOV DL,0DH                  ;Carriage return
        INT 21H
                                    ;
        MOV AH,6                    ;Setup to display character
        MOV DL,0AH                  ;Load line feed character
        INT 21H
        MOV AH,6                    ;Setup to display character
        MOV DL,0DH                  ;Load carriage return character
        INT 21H
                                    ;
        POP DS
        RET
                                ;
MESSAGE ENDP
CSEG    ENDS
        END
```

Figure 5.14   The procedure MESSAGE.ASM which accepts an output message from the screen buffer and displays it.

```
PAGE 55,132
TITLE KEYBD - PROCEDURE TO READ KEYBOARD (KEYBD.ASM)
;
;          DESCRIPTION: This procedure reads the keyboard.
;          It has the same name as the associated MACRO.
;
EXTRN      BUFFMX:BYTE,BUFFLN:BYTE,CHAR:BYTE,BLANK:BYTE
CSEG       SEGMENT PARA PUBLIC 'CODE'
           PUBLIC KEYBD
KEYBD      PROC    FAR
           ASSUME CS:CSEG
                                        ;
           PUSH DS
;                              This is the keyboard read procedure
;
                                        ;
           LEA DX,BUFFMX                ;Load input buffer start address
           MOV AH,10                    ;Read input string
           INT 21H
                                        ;;Remove carriage return string
           MOV BH,0                     ;Clear upper BX
           MOV BL,BUFFLN                ;Load input character length
           MOV SI,BX                    ;Store length in SI
           LEA BX,CHAR                  ;Load address of characters in buffer
           MOV AH,BLANK                 ;Load blank character in AH
           MOV BYTE PTR [BX+SI],AH ;Replace carriage return with blank
                                        ;
           POP DS
           RET
                                        ;
KEYBD      ENDP
CSEG       ENDS
           END
```

Figure 5.15   The external procedure KEYBD.ASM which reads the keyboard buffer.

```
LINK

IBM Personal Computer Linker
Version 2.10 (C)Copyright IBM Corp 1981, 1982, 1983

Object Modules [.OBJ]: STRU1+KEYBD+MESSAGE+CLSCREN
Run File [STRU1.EXE]:
List File [NUL.MAP]:
Libraries [.LIB]:
```

Figure 5.16   Assembly and linking of STRU1 illustrating the object modules used.

```
Input password (6 characters).


Password unsuccessful (Strike key to continue).


Input password (6 characters).

AAAAAA
Password unsuccessful (Strike key to continue).


Input password (6 characters).

ABC123
Password successfully received.
```

Figure 5.17 Representative interactive session with the linked program STRU1.EXE.

5.3 PS/2 FIRMWARE AND OS/2 SOFTWARE INTERRUPTS

This chapter deals with interrupts generated from the operating system software and the BIOS firmware (firmware is the term used to denote software "burned" into PROM). Most of the input/output services for handling peripherals are called using software interrupts based on the BIOS code which is delineated in the technical reference manuals. Similarly the system software, used to setup many functions, supports INT 21H (and the associated functions). The purpose of this section is to briefly address such software and firmware for the PS/2 microcomputers Models 30, 50, and 60.

5.3.1 Model 30 BIOS Service

The Model 30 BIOS is almost completely entry-point compatible with the BIOS for the earlier PC, XT, XT286, and AT [5]. The only differences will exist for software that is time-critical during execution. This software will not run the same on the Model 30 and the earlier machines because the Model 30 is faster (8 MHz clock versus 4.77 MHz on the PC). Table 5.5 illustrates many of the changes and additions for the Model 30 BIOS interrupt structure [6]. In the PS/2 computers, IBM has added significant new capabilities for graphics presentation and alpha mode screen display. While these video calls are still accessed via INT 10H, the meaning of the register options (specified by AH, AL, CH, CL, BH, BL, DH, and DL) reflects the MCGA format. The MCGA graphics modes, for example, are 320×200 (AL = 4, 5, or 13), 640×200 (AL = 6), and 640×480 (AL = 11). Here AH = 00H.

In Table 5.5 there are several new meanings attached to video processing such as masking to achieve gray shading. Also, the option of obtaining functionality and video state information from a table pointed to by DI is possible using AH = 1BH. These are but a few of the different options needed and available with the improved graphics. We will not dwell on the PS/2 interrupts because the interested user should obtain a copy of the appropriate technical reference. While the code is not provided by IBM for the PS/2 BIOS, it is to be inferred that much of the technique

TABLE 5.5 PS/2 MODEL 30 DIOS FUNCTIONS (DIFFERENCES)

INT	Purpose	Comment
0	Divide Overflow	Same
1	Single Step	Same
2	NMI	Same
3	Breakpoint	Same
4	Overflow	Same
5	Print Screen	Same
6	Reserved	—
7	Reserved	—
8	Timer	Same
9	Keyboard	Same
A	Reserved	—
B	Communications	Added from PC, XT
C	Communications	Added from PC, XT
D	Fixed Disk	Added from PC
E	Floppy Diskette	Same
F	Printer	Added in place of INTO
10	Video BIOS	Same (modified service)
11	Equipment	Same
12	Memory Site	Same
13	Diskette/Disk I/O	Same
14	Communications	Same
15	System Services	Added in place of cassette I/O
16	Keyboard	Same
17	Printer	Same
18	Resident BASIC	Same function
19	Bootstrap	Same
1A	Time-of-day	Same
1B	Keyboard break	Same
1C	Timer Tick	New
1D	Video	Same
1E	Diskette Parameter	Same
1F	Video Graphics Character	Same
40	DTA Fixed Disk	New
41	Fixed Disk Parameter	New
42	Video	New
43	Character Graphics Table	New
46	Extended Disk Parameter	New
4A	Real-Time Clock Alarm	New
60–67	Reserved for User Programs	New

illustrated in Chapter 9 and applied to the old BIOS will carry over to the PS/2 machines. By this statement we mean that the methodology for programming chips, which is presented in Chapter 9, will be representative of that used to program the BIOS associated with the PS/2 models. Of course, the interrupt calls for the PS/2 computers will be almost identical to those presented in this chapter. This allows the portability of code that exists across the IBM family.

As might be expected, these are called from the PS/2 BIOS. Unlike the earlier technical reference descriptions (see Chapter 9), the PS/2 technical references do not contain code listings; hence, we cannot consider the interrupt structure in as much detail and we must be satisfied with the entry-point description presented in Table 5.5.

5.3.2 Model 50/60 BIOS Service

As mentioned above, the PS/2 BIOS routines are almost completely compatible with the BIOS interrupt calls from the earlier IBM microcomputers. The advanced 16-bit BIOS comes in two versions: a compatibility BIOS, CBIOS, and an advanced BIOS, ABIOS. The former is intended for stand-alone applications while the latter is used for multitasking applications [7].

5.3.3 OS/2 Functions

This subsection is intended to briefly discuss the system software implications for the new operating system (OS/2) function calls [8]. The discussion is based on the release of information about the Microsoft version of OS/2. First and foremost, OS/2 takes advantage of the 80286 Protected Mode capabilities. It runs as a subset of the 80386 system instructions. The system will run on the XT286, AT, PS/2 Models 50/60, and the PS/2 Model 80. In this subsection we are concerned with the equivalent of the DOS interrupts, mainly INT 21H and the associated function calls. The OS/2 designers were faced with the problem that, if multitasking is used, software interrupts can stack up if called by multiple users. Under the new system, many of the interrupt services are stored on disk and can be loaded in multiple spaces, with different linkages, by different users. These service routines are called as procedures, not as interrupt handlers. Microsoft has applied the term *dyna-linking* (for dynamic linkages) to this approach, and the linkages are set up during execution, not during the link process. This is only realistically possible as a consequence of the much greater speed of the PS/2 machines (one example of where the speed advantage is critical).

Clearly, the dyna-link approach to system interrupt service is advantageous from the viewpoint of flexibility. It will be a simple matter to add service functions as the demand for specialized handlers increases. We return to the subject of OS/2 from a more general perspective in Chapter 10. From the viewpoint of interrupts, however, the reader should think of all the old interrupts as applicable but procedure-based rather than interrupt-based. Since the PS/2 computers all can run DOS 3.3, the normal interrupt service associated with DOS is applicable across the entire IBM family.

5.4 SUMMARY

The purpose of this chapter was to introduce the reader to some of the power of the language using interrupts. The programming approach has been to develop modular entities that can be assembled and tested separately, and then combined to yield larger tasks. Many of the routines presented are general purpose and can be used in a variety of applications.

The input/output processing for the keyboard, display, and printer has been presented. In the next chapter we will begin to see the advantages of this I/O. It has become clear that Macro Assembler is not ideal for "number crunching" applications. To address problems of this nature a considerable effort must be expended in manipulating registers and avoiding underflow or overflow. This was illustrated in

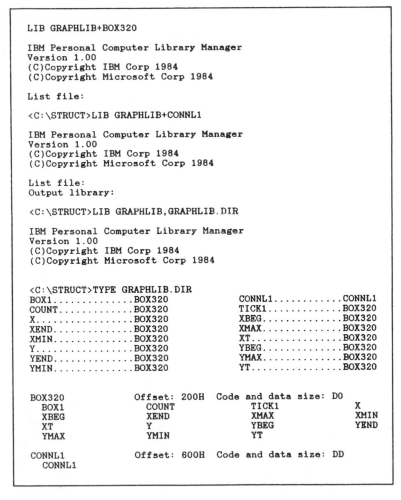

```
LIB GRAPHLIB+BOX320

IBM Personal Computer Library Manager
Version 1.00
(C)Copyright IBM Corp 1984
(C)Copyright Microsoft Corp 1984

List file:

<C:\STRUCT>LIB GRAPHLIB+CONNL1

IBM Personal Computer Library Manager
Version 1.00
(C)Copyright IBM Corp 1984
(C)Copyright Microsoft Corp 1984

List file:
Output library:

<C:\STRUCT>LIB GRAPHLIB,GRAPHLIB.DIR

IBM Personal Computer Library Manager
Version 1.00
(C)Copyright IBM Corp 1984
(C)Copyright Microsoft Corp 1984


<C:\STRUCT>TYPE GRAPHLIB.DIR
BOX1.............BOX320              CONNL1...........CONNL1
COUNT............BOX320              TICK1............BOX320
X................BOX320              XBEG.............BOX320
XEND.............BOX320              XMAX.............BOX320
XMIN.............BOX320              XT...............BOX320
Y................BOX320              YBEG.............BOX320
YEND.............BOX320              YMAX.............BOX320
YMIN.............BOX320              YT...............BOX320


BOX320              Offset: 200H  Code and data size: D0
  BOX1                COUNT             TICK1           X
  XBEG                XEND              XMAX            XMIN
  XT                  Y                 YBEG            YEND
  YMAX                YMIN              YT

CONNL1              Offset: 600H  Code and data size: DD
  CONNL1
```

Figure 5.18   The procedure for creating the object library GRAPHLIB.LIB. Also, a listing of the library's contents using GRAPHLIB.DIR.

the procedure GRAND. The principal advantages offered by the Macro Assembler are speed and access to the internal system routines (BIOS and DOS) which control peripherals and perform tedious system tasks, that are necessary for program execution. Also, the ability to write additional driver routines is perhaps best performed with assembler.

The Macro Assembler executes most instructions using one or two of the 8088 registers and the language allows direct access to these registers. Most higher-level languages do not allow access to the registers; C is an exception but in a somewhat cumbersome fashion. Programs that call these entities are best implemented in assembler. The usefulness of program modularity was reinforced with the introduction of object libraries. Figure 5.18 illustrates the procedure used to create a library that contains two graphics routines. The importance of the BIOS listing contained in Appendix A of the *IBM Technical Reference* manual becomes clear when paging through BIOS using DEBUG (after an interrupt call).

Chapter 6 is a continuation of our introduction to the Macro Assembler. The Macro Assembler pseudo-ops are discussed. Ideally the programmer would like to have access to databases in order to extract information about their contents. This requires an interface to such databases, and currently there are only a small number available in the commercial market. In Chapter 7, we present extended file management which allows the user to create his or her own permanent databases. The techniques required draw directly on the function calls associated with INT 21H, which has been introduced in this chapter. Some of the difficulties associated with "number crunching" will disappear when floating-point arithmetic is introduced in Chapter 8 where the Intel 8087 coprocessor is discussed.

REFERENCES

1. *IBM Technical Reference Personal Computer*. Personal Computer Hardware Reference Library. IBM Corp., P.O. Box 1328. Boca Raton, FL 33432 (1981).
2. Bradley, D. J. *Assembly Language Programming for the IBM Personal Computer*. Prentice-Hall, Inc., Englewood Cliffs, NJ 07632 (1984).
3. Microsoft Corp. *Disk Operating System Version 2.10*, IBM Personal Computer-Computer Language Series. IBM Corp., P.O. Box 1328, Boca Raton, FL 33432 (1983).
4. *Disk Operating System Technical Reference*. IBM Personal Computer Software. IBM Corp., P.O. Box 1328, Boca Raton, FL 33432 (1985).
5. *BYTE* Editorial Staff. "First Impressions: The IBM PS/2 Computers." *BYTE Magazine*. 12, 6 (1987):100 (Peterborough, NH).
6. *Personal System/2 Model 30 Technical Reference*. IBM Corp., P.O. Box 1328, Boca Raton, FL 33432 (1987). (S68X-2201-00)
7. *IBM Personal System/2 and Personal Computer BIOS Interface Technical Reference*. IBM Corp., P.O. Box 1328, Boca Raton, FL 33432 (1987). (9068X-2224-0001)
8. White, E., and Grehan, R. "Product Description: Microsoft's New DOS," *BYTE Magazine*, 12, 6 (1987):146 (Peterborough, NH).

PROBLEMS

5.1. Write a general purpose routine that generates a bar starting at the X-coordinate given in AX, of width given by DX, and height specified in BX. Assume the bar is drawn from the lower box axis given by BOX1 (refer to Figure 5.4).

5.2. The clear screen code in Figure 5.4 requires seven instructions. Modify this to use only five instructions.

5.3. Write a procedure that accepts one character from the keyboard and checks for Y or N. All other characters are to be ignored and the procedure continues to execute until receiving one of these two characters.

5.4. Write the sequence of instructions needed to read the time using the DOS function calls.

5.5. Write the sequence of instructions needed to set the time using the DOS function calls.

5.6. Write the sequence of instructions needed to output a character to the printer; to output a string to the printer.

5.7. Write the sequence of instructions needed to get the date.

5.8. Write the sequence of instructions needed to set the date.

5.9. Write the sequence of instructions needed to send a character out over the asynchronous communications line. Do this two different ways.

5.10. Write the sequence of instructions needed to input a character from the asynchronous communications line. Do this two different ways.

5.11. Write the sequence of instructions that loads a character from the keyboard to a variable CHAR. Do this two different ways.

5.12. Write the sequence of code necessary to return the vector pointer corresponding to a given interrupt number.

6

Operators and Pseudo-ops

This chapter completes the introductory study of the IBM Macro Assembler. We address two general topics, operators and pseudo-ops, with particular emphasis on macros. Again, the focus of the discussion is to provide programming concepts that lend themselves to the development of modular, stand-alone, portable programs. As we have seen, an out-growth of this approach is the ability to write programs capable of executing large-scale tasks by simply combining smaller general purpose routines that have already been debugged. The programmer is faced with the responsibility of insuring that the procedures used are as general as possible for this approach to work. Now that techniques for keyboard display I/O have been presented, it becomes possible to input parameter values such as the title of graphic figures.

6.1 OPERATORS

The IBM Macro Assembler language provides six types of operators to be used in manipulating data variables and operands [1–3].

1. Attribute
2. Value-returning
3. Record-specific
4. Arithmetic
5. Relational
6. Logical

We have already used some of these operators in the programs appearing in earlier chapters. Table 6.1 lists the operators and presents a brief description of their functions. The pointer operator, PTR, has been demonstrated in some of the programs of Chapter 5. Segment override operators are used to change the segment address of arguments. For example consider the following sequence:

```
        ...
DATA    SEGMENT PARA PUBLIC 'DATA'
TABLE   DB 10 DUP(?)
DATA    ENDS
        ...
        MOV AX,SEG DATA
        MOV DS,AX
        ...
        MOV AX,TABLE [BX+SI]
        ...
        MOV CX,ES:[BX+SI]
```

Here the segment override is ES:[BX+SI] which changes the location referenced by [BX+SI].

TABLE 6.1   IBM MACRO ASSEMBLER OPERATORS

Operator	Type	Description
PTR	Attribute	This operator has the form: type PTR expression. It is used to override the type attribute (BYTE, WORD, DWORD, QWORD, or TBYTE) of a variable or the attribute of a label (NEAR or FAR). The expression field is the variable or label which is to be overridden.
Seg-reg, Seg-name Group-name	Attribute	The segment override operator changes the segment attribute of a label, variable, or address expression. It has three forms: seg-reg:addr-expression seg-name:addr-expression group-name:addr-expression.
SHORT	Attribute	This operator is used when a label follows a JMP instruction and is within 127 bytes of the JMP. It has the form JMP SHORT label and changes the NEAR attribute. A pass 2 NOP instruction is avoided.
THIS	Attribute	The form of this operator is THIS type. The operator produces an operand whose segment attribute is equal to the defining segment, whose offset equals IP, and a type attribute defined by "type". For example, "AAA EQU THIS WORD" yields an AAA with attribute WORD instead of NEAR if used in the same code segment.
HIGH	Attribute	This operator accepts a number and address argument and returns the high order byte.
LOW	Attribute	This operator accepts a number and address argument and returns the low order byte.
SEG	Value-Returning	This operator returns the segment value of the variable or label.

OFFSET	Value-Returning	This operator returns the offset value of the variable or label.
TYPE	Value-Returning	For operand arguments this operator returns a value equal to the number of bytes of the operand. If a structure name, it returns the number of bytes declared by STRUC. If the operand is a label, it returns 65534 (FAR) and 65535 (NEAR).
SIZE	Value-Returning	This operator returns the value LENGTH × TYPE.
LENGTH	Value-Returning	For a DUP entry, LENGTH returns the number of units allocated for the variable. For all others it returns a 1.
SHIFT COUNT	Record-Specific	This operator is used with the RECORD pseudo-op and is the name of the record field. The format of RECORD is recordname RECORD fieldname:width. The value of fieldname, when used in an expression is the shift count to move the field to the far right within the byte or word.
MASK	Record-Specific	The format of this operator is MASK recfield. It returns a bit mask for the field. The mask has bits set for positions included in the field and 0 for bits not included in the field.
WIDTH	Record-Specific	The format of this operator is WIDTH recfield. It evaluates to a constant in the range 1 to 16 and returns the width of a record or record field.
+	Arithmetic	Form is term1 + term2. It returns the sum of 2 terms.
−	Arithmetic	Form is term1 − term2. It returns the difference of 2 terms.
*	Arithmetic	Form is term1 * term2. It returns the product of 2 terms.
MOD	Arithmetic	Form is term1 MOD term2. It returns the remainder obtained by dividing term1 by term2.
SHL	Arithmetic	Form is term1 SHL term2. It shifts the bits of term1 left by the amount contained in term2. Zeros are filled in the new bits.
SHR	Arithmetic	Same as SHL except the shift is to the right.
EQ	Relational	Form is term1 EQ term2. Returns a value −1 (TRUE) if term1 equals term2, or 0 (FALSE) otherwise.
NE	Relational	Form is term1 NE term2. Returns a value −1 (TRUE) if term1 does not equal term2, or 0 (FALSE) otherwise.
LT	Relational	Form is term1 LT term2. Retruns a value −1 (TRUE) if term1 is less than term2, or 0 (FALSE) otherwise.
LE	Relational	Form is term1 LE term2. Returns a value −1 (TRUE) if term1 is less than or equal to term2, or 0 (FALSE) otherwise.
GT	Relational	Form is term1 GT term2. Returns a value −1 (TRUE) if term1 is greater than term2, or 0 (FALSE) otherwise.
GE	Relational	Form is term1 GE term2. Returns a value −1 (TRUE) if term1 is greater than or equal to term2, or 0 (FALSE) otherwise.
AND, OR, and XOR	Logical	These operators have the form term1 (operator) term2 and return each bit position as follows:

term1 bit	term2 bit	AND	OR	XOR
1	1	1	1	0
1	0	0	1	1
0	1	0	1	1
0	0	0	0	0

| NOT | Logical | This operator complements each bit of term. Form is NOT term. |

The SHORT operator is used to increase efficiency in performing the unconditional jump instruction. This operator essentially requires one less machine instruction. THIS is used to produce a change in segment attribute with offset equal to IP. One could, for example, use it to change the attribute of blocks of code within a segment to FAR, thereby allowing transfers or entries from outside the existing segment. Both HIGH and LOW are self-explanatory as indicated in Table 6.1. The value-returning operators, SEG and OFFSET, have been illustrated earlier and are very useful for accessing variables in other segments. The reader should contrast the use of the LEA instruction with OFFSET. The remaining value-returning operators (TYPE, SIZE, and LENGTH) all return measures of the number of bytes in the argument.

The three record-specific operators apply only to version 2.0 or greater. These operators are to be used in conjunction with the RECORD pseudo-op. As indicated, this pseudo-op has the form

recordname RECORD fieldname: width [=exp], [···]

where the optional expressions have been indicated with brackets. This pseudo-op is used to format a byte or word for special bit configurations. Recordname and fieldname identify the record and field(s) within the record. Width is associated with each fieldname and may be up to 16 bits. The total width for a given record may not exceed 16 bits. If the fieldname is 7 or fewer bits, RECORD generates a byte, and if the number of bits is 8 or greater, a word is generated, not to exceed 16 bits. Consider the following example of a RECORD (called REC1).

REC1 RECORD F1:8='A', F2:3, F3:3, F4:2

The first field is 8 bits long and has been initialized to the ASCII character A. The remaining three fields are unspecified and contain 3, 3, and 2 bits, respectively. You can initialize a field to an ASCII character if it is 8 or more bits wide. The most significant fields are defined first and stored in reverse byte order, least significant byte first. Undefined bits are set at 0. Using A = 41H = 01000001B, REC1 is defined as

0100 0001 0000 0000 B

and stored as

0041 (hexadecimal)

We can initialize a record using a statement of the form

name   recordname ⟨exp,···⟩

or

name   recordname exp DUP (⟨exp⟩)

Using this statement, REC1 could be defined as

$$\text{STORE1 REC1 } \langle 8,1,1,1 \rangle$$

This is stored as

$$0010\ 0101\ 0000\ 1000\ \text{(binary)}$$

or

$$25\ 08\ \text{(hexadecimal)}$$

The following sequence of instructions illustrates the use of the record-specific operators for REC1.

```
    ...
    MOV AX,STORE1
    AND AX,MASK F2        ; Mask = 0000000011100000B
    MOV CH,F2             ; Get shift count for F2
    SHR AX,CH             ; F2 now in low order bits of AX
    MOV CL,WIDTH F2       ; CL now contains the width of F2
```

The arithmetic operators function in a fairly obvious manner, as discussed in Table 6.1. We have seen the + operator used in locating variables with instructions such as

$$\text{MOV AX,TABLE1 [BX + SI]}$$

In our routine for calculating random numbers, RAND1, we could have obtained the modulo calculation using the statement

$$\text{MOV CX,AX MOD BX}$$

where CX is loaded with the remainder of AX divided by BX. The operators SHL and SHR are intended to operate within operands and should not be confused with the instructions having the same name. For example, it is possible to have in instruction sequence such as

```
    MOV CL,AX SHL 10
    SHL BX,CL
```

Relational operators are also clear as to their function (see Table 6.1). Finally, the logical operators are designed to act on arguments in exactly the same fashion as their instruction counterpart. In our discussion of the RECORD pseudo-op the AND operator was illustrated.

6.2 PSEUDO-OPS

There are five general categories of pseudo-ops available in the IBM Macro Assembler, conditional, data, listing, macro, and mode. We have already discussed a number of the data pseudo-ops. In this section all five categories are examined and the macro pseudo-ops are presented with special emphasis because of the flexibility they lend to assembler programming.

Pseudo-ops are instructions that appear in the assembler source code but do not themselves result in machine instructions. Instead, pseudo-ops provide directives to the assembler concerning how various data items, conditional branches, listings, and macros must be implemented during the assembly process. In the following subsections, each category of pseudo-op is discussed.

6.2.1 Conditional Pseudo-ops

Table 6.2 lists the conditional pseudo-ops and provides a brief description of their functions. The normal processing structure for some of these pseudo-ops is as follows.

```
IFxxx (expression)
...
ELSE
...
ENDIF
```

They may be nested any number of times within each other. A two-level nesting, for example, would look like the following.

```
IFxxx (expression)
    ...
    IFxxx (expression)
    ...
    ENDIF
    ...
ENDIF
```

In the first example, the ELSE pseudo-op was used to provide an alternate branch in the event the expression in the conditional proved to be false.

These conditionals must have their arguments defined at assembly time. They cannot be used as if they are under program control. For example, the conditional

```
IF MI
...
ELSE
...
ENDIF
```

TABLE 6.2 CONDITIONAL PSEUDO-OPS

Pseudo-op	Description
ELSE	This pseudo-op must be used in conjunction with a conditional pseudo-op and serves to provide an alternate path.
ENDIF	This pseudo-op ends the corresponding IFxxx conditional.
IF	Form: IF expression. When the expression is true the code following this pseudo-op is executed, otherwise it branches to an ELSE entry point or an ENDIF. IF pseudo-ops can be nested.
IFB	Form: IFB <operand>. This is the if-blank pseudo-op and it is true if the operand has not been specified, as in a MACRO call, for example. The code following the IFB is executed when operand is blank. Otherwise the IP jumps to ENDIF.
IFDEF	Form: IFDEF symbol. If symbol has been defined via the EXTRN pseudo-op, this is true and the code following the pseudo-op is executed.
IFDIF	Form: IFDIF <operand1>, <operand2>. The code following this pseudo-op is executed if the string operand1 is different from the string operand2.
IFE	Form: IFE expression. The code following this pseudo-op is executed if expression = 0.
IFIDN	Form: IFIDN <operand1>, <operand2>. The code following this pseudo-op is executed if the string operand1 is identical to the string operand2.
IFNB	Form: IFNB <operand>. The code following this pseudo-op is executed if the operand is not blank.
IFNDEF	Form: IFNDEF symbol. The code following this pseudo-op is executed if symbol has not been defined using the EXTRN pseudo-op.
IF1	This pseudo-op is true if the assembler is in pass 1. It is used to load macros from a macro library (as an example).
IF2	This pseudo-op is true if the assembler is in pass 2. It can be used to inform the programmer what version of the program is being used (when coupled with appropriate logic and a %OUT).

requires that MI be known at assembly time and not during program execution. When discussing macro definitions it will be appropriate to create several macro libraries. These libraries are collections of MACRO pseudo-ops, each containing assembler instructions to be inserted into the program file during pass 1 of the assembly. Suppose a macro library called MAC1LIB.LIB contains macros to be inserted into a program. The first instruction sequence should be

```
IF1
    INCLUDE MAC1LIB.LIB
ENDIF
```

This will cause the assembler, during pass 1, to substitute those macros used in the program into the appropriate points of the code. Hence, the macros expand the program. The form of the above IF statement only provides a conditional response during pass 1.

TABLE 6.3 LISTING PSEUDO-OPS

Pseudo-op	Description
.CREF and .XCREF	This listing pseudo-op provides cross-reference information when a filespec is indicated in response to the assembler prompt (CREF). It is the normal default condition. .XCREF results in no output for cross-reference when in force.
.LALL, .SALL, and .XALL	.LALL lists the complete macro text for all expansions. .SALL suppresses listing of all text and object code produced by macros. .XALL produces a source line listing only if object code results.
.LFCOND	This pseudo-op causes the listing of conditional blocks that evaluate as false.
.LIST and .XLIST	.LIST causes a listing of source and object code in the output assembler list file. .XLIST turns this listing off. These pseudo-ops can be used to selectively list code during the assembly of programs, especially long sequences of instructions.
%OUT	Form is %OUT text. This pseudo-op is used to monitor progress through a long assembly. The argument text is displayed, when encountered, during the assembly process.
PAGE	Form is PAGE operand1, operand2. Controls the length (operand1) in lines and the width (operand2) in characters of the assembler list file.
.SFCOND	This pseudo-op suppresses the listing of conditional blocks that evaluate as false.
SUBTTL	Form is SUBTTL text. Generates a subtitle to be listed after each listing of title.
.TFCOND	This pseudo-op changes the listing setting (and default) for false conditionals to the opposite state.
TITLE	Form is TITLE text. This pseudo-op specifies a title to be listed on each page of the assembler listing. It may be used only once.

6.2.2 Listing Pseudo-ops

The listing pseudo-ops control the format, style, and parameters generated when an assembly listing is called for. Table 6.3 presents a brief description of these pseudo-ops. PAGE and TITLE have already been used in the assembler programs presented in Chapter 2. The pseudo-ops .LIST and .XLIST can be used to turn the listing process on and off during assembly. For example, if a macro has been debugged it might be undesirable to keep expanding it in the listing. By having the first line of the macro set to .XLIST and the last line set to .LIST, the code would not be expanded in any assembler listing. The %OUT pseudo-op could be used to indicate the beginning of pass 2 by placing it near the beginning of the program in the form

```
IF2
%OUT PASS2
ENDIF
```

TABLE 6.4 MODE PSEUDO-OPS

Pseudo-op	Description
.286C	This pseudo-op tells the assembler to recognize and assemble 80286 instructions used by the IBM AT.
.8086	This pseudo-op tells the assembler not to recognize and assemble 80286 instructions.
.8087	This pseudo-op tells the assembler to recognize and assemble 8087 coprocessor instructions and data formats.

The remaining listing pseudo-ops are left to the reader to use as needed and are self-explanatory.

6.2.3 Mode Pseudo-ops

This special class of pseudo-ops tells the assembler to recognize various processor options. On the IBM AT, the 80286 processor processes 80286 instructions when turned on with the .286C pseudo-op. This pseudo-op should be located near the beginning of the program. In the event an AT program is being run on an IBM PC or XT, the pseudo-op .8086 tells the assembler to ignore 80286 instructions: Provision must be made to avoid these instructions in this case. Finally, the pseudo-op .8087 informs the assembler that the coprocessor is resident and 8087 instructions are to be assembled. Table 6.4 lists these pseudo-ops.

6.2.4 Data Pseudo-ops

Many of the data pseudo-ops have already been presented. Without reiterating those previously discussed, it is useful to briefly touch on the remaining data pseudo-ops. Table 6.5 presents the data pseudo-ops and a description of their function. The EVEN pseudo-op simply insures that the code following it starts on an even (word) boundary. The GROUP pseudo-op collects all named segments within a 64K boundary. The INCLUDE pseudo-op is used to insert assembler source code from an alternate source file, such as a macro library, into the program during assembly. LABEL is used to assign an attribute to a label and can be used to define an entry point. ORG is used to change the location counter and this counter is set to the value of the expression following ORG.

   If, for some reason, the programmer desires to change the default numerical base (normally base 10 for decimal), the .RADIX pseudo-op allows this change. The RECORD pseudo-op has already been addressed. Finally, the structure pseudo-op, STRUC, can be used to allocate and initiate multi-byte variables. It must end with ENDS.

6.2.5 Macro Pseudo-ops

These pseudo-ops center around the MACRO pseudo-op, which must end with ENDM. We have already seen an example of a macro in Chapter 5, SCDEL. The

TABLE 6.5 DATA PSEUDO-OPS

Pseudo-op	Description
ASSUME	Form is ASSUME seg-reg:seg-name. ... This pseudo-op tells the assembler which segment register segments belong to.
COMMENT	Form is COMMENT delimiter text delimiter. COMMENT allows the programmer to enter comments without semicolons. It is not recognized by the SALUT program.
DB	Form is [variable] DB [expression]. It is used to initialize byte storage.
DD	DD has the same form as DB except it applies to double word quantities.
DQ	DQ has the same form as DB except it applies to four word quantities.
DT	DT has the same form as DB except it applies to ten byte packed decimal.
DW	DW has the same form as DB except it applies to word quantities.
END	Form is END [expression]. END identifies the end of the source program and the optional expression identifies the name of the entry point.
ENDP	Form is procedure name ENDP. Designates the end of a procedure.
ENDS	Form is structure name ENDS or seg-name ENDS. Designates the end of a structure or segment.
EQU	Form is name EQU expression. Assigns the value of expression to name. This value may not be reassigned.
=	Form is label = expression. Assigns the value of expression to label. May be reassigned.
EVEN	EVEN insures that the code following starts on an even boundary.
EXTRN	Form is EXTRN name:type. ... EXTRN is used to indicate that symbols used in this assembly module are defined in another module.
GROUP	Form is name GROUP seg-name. ... GROUP collects all segments named and places them within a 64K physical segment.
INCLUDE	Form is INCLUDE [drive] [path] filename.ext. INCLUDE assembles source statements from an alternate source file into the current source file.
LABEL	Form is name LABEL type. LABEL defines the attributes of name to be type.
NAME	Form is NAME module-name. NAME gives a module a name. It may be used only once per assembly.
ORG	Form is ORG expression. The location counter is set to the value of expression.
PROC	Form is procedure name PROC [attribute]. PROC identifies a block of code as a procedure and must end with RET/ENDP. The attribute is NEAR or FAR.
PUBLIC	Form is PUBLIC symbol. ... PUBLIC makes symbols externally available to other linked modules.
.RADIX	Form is .RADIX expression. .RADIX allows the default base (decimal) to be changed to a value between 2 and 16.
RECORD	Form is recordname RECORD fieldname:width [=exp]. ... RECORD defines a bit pattern to format bytes and words for bit-packing (see text).
SEGMENT	Form is segname SEGMENT [align-type] [combine-type] ['class']. (See text chapter 3 for a discussion of this pseudo-op.)
STRUC	Form is structure name STRUC. STRUC is used to allocate and initialize multibyte variables using DB, DD, DQ, DT, and DW. It must end with ENDS.

TABLE 6.6 MACRO PSEUDO-OPS

Pseudo-op	Description
ENDM	ENDM is the terminator for MACRO, REPT, IRP, and IRPC.
EXITM	EXITM provides an exit to an expansion (REPT, IRP, IRPC, or MACRO) when a test proves that the remaining expansion is not needed.
IRP	Form is IRP dummy, <operandlist>. The number of operands (separated by commas) in operandlist determines the number of times the following code (terminated by ENDM) is repeated. At each repetition the next item in operandlist is substituted for all occurrences of dummy.
IRPC	Form is IRPC dummy, string. This is the same as IRP except at each repetition the next character in string is substituted for all occurrences of dummy.
LOCAL	Form is LOCAL dummylist. LOCAL is used inside a MACRO structure. The assembler creates a unique symbol for each entry in dummylist during each expansion of the macro. This avoids the problem of multiple defined labels, for example, when multiple expansions of the same macro take place in a program.
MACRO	Form is name MACRO dummylist. The statements following the MACRO definition, before ENDM, are the macro. Dummylist contains the parameters to be replaced when calling the macro during assembly. The form of this call is name parmlist. Parmlist consists of the actual parameters (separated by commas) used in the expansion.
PURGE	Form is PURGE macro-name. ... PURGE deletes the definition of a specified MACRO and allows the space to be used. This is beneficial when including a macro library during assembly but desiring to remove those macros not used during the assembly.

MACRO pseudo-op is used to expand assembler code during assembly by replacing the macro call with the code contained in the macro. Table 6.6 illustrates this class of pseudo-ops. The macro statements can be contained in the program using them or kept separately in a macro library, which is loaded as described in subsection 6.2.1. Macros allow multiple use of a code sequence with a change each time as, for example, when using a parameter list. The PURGE pseudo-op allows the removal of a macro that is unused from a library after the library has been loaded. An alternative to the use of the PURGE pseudo-op would be to tailor macro libraries to a class of applications such as graphics, disk I/O, and so forth. The LOCAL pseudo-op is used to make labels unique to a given macro call. If, for example, several calls to the same macro occur within a given program, the labels must somehow be redefined after each call. The LOCAL pseudo-op accomplishes this task, thereby preventing multiple defined labels.

Table 6.7 presents four operators that can be used with MACROS. The programmer must remember that these operators are fixed during assembly and should not be treated as linking variables but as defining statements.

TABLE 6.7 SPECIAL PURPOSE MACRO OPERATORS

Operator	Description
&	From is text&text. This operator concatenates text or symbols. An example is

	<pre>TC1 MACRO X
	      LEA DX, CHAR&X
	      MOV AH, 9
	      INT 21H
	      ENDM</pre>

	Here a call, TC1 A would load DX with a character start position CHARA.
;;	Form is ;;text. A comment preceeded by two semicolons is not produced as part of the expansion when a MACRO or REPT is defined in an assembly.
!	Form is !character. Causes the character to be interpreted as a literal value not a symbol.
%	Form is %expression. Converts expression to a number. During expansion the number is substituted for expression. Consider

	<pre>MAC1 MACRO X
	L1 = X * 1000
	       MAC2 %L1,X
	       ENDM</pre> ;

	<pre>MAC2 MACRO Y,X
	PROD&X DB 'Production No. &X = &Y'
	       ENDM</pre>

	This yields "PROD5 DB 'Production No. 5 = 5000'," when called with MAC1 5.

6.3 FURTHER PROGRAMMING EXAMPLES

The purpose of this section is to provide additional program examples which illustrate the use of pseudo-ops, particularly the macro pseudo-ops, in the assembler context. We consider four programs: a stock market graphics program, ASCII to decimal conversion, a timer program that uses INT 1AH, and a waveform analysis program. The reader should pay particular attention to the manner in which macros are used in the programs. In general, these entities are given names related to their function and are used to reduce the complexity of code in a given module, much like procedures. Also, macros have the advantage that they can be placed in libraries for repetitive or specialized use. By this we mean that the macro may be of general utility; hence, its occurrence in a library facilitates loading it into many programs which have a like need. Alternatively, the programmer may wish to develop a set of specialized routines that are specific to a small class of programs; yet the code for these routines is programmed separately from the actual calling modules. In this latter case either procedures or macro expansions are suitable.

6.3.1 Stock Market Graphics

This subsection on stock market graphics is intended to give the reader an understanding of how to implement MACRO pseudo-ops. The focal point for the discussion is a program that accepts an input designator (in this case a stock or index code) and a title, and then plots the corresponding stock or index performance on the display. Figure 6.1a presents the flow chart for this program. Figure 6.1b illustrates the program called STKPLT1. Figure 6.2 illustrates a typical interactive session used to set up the plot for the Dow Jones index and Figure 6.3 presents the output for the six stock-index performance histories tabulated in the program. The macro library MAC1LIB.LIB, used with this program, is presented later.

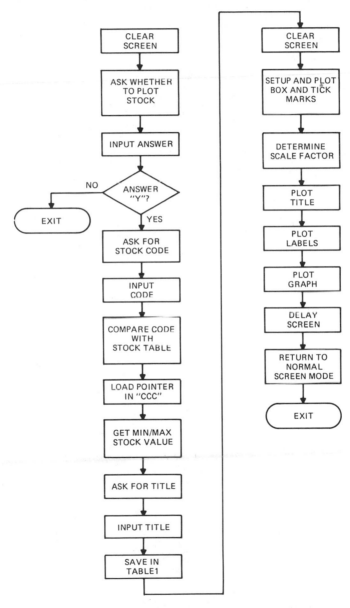

Figure 6.1a   The functional flow chart for the program STKPLT1.ASM.

```
PAGE     55,132
TITLE    STKPLT1 - PLOTS STOCK PERFORMANCE (STKPLT1.ASM)
COMMENT  *
         DESCRIPTION:Reads stock/index code, gets limits
         on      Y-axis plot, asks for title, sets tick marks,
         and     numerical labels, and plots result.
         *
IF1
         INCLUDE MAC1LIB.LIB
ENDIF
         EXTRN   BOX11:FAR,TICK11:FAR,LABEL1:FAR,CONNL1:FAR
                 ;
                 ;
STACK    SEGMENT PARA STACK 'STACK'
         DB      64 DUP('STACK   ')
STACK    ENDS
                                         ;
;        DATA TABLE OF STOCKS
;
;   STOCK1:     DJA - Dow Jones Average (Index)
;               IBM - International Business Machines
;               DEC - Digital Equipment Corp.
;               HPC - Hewlett-Packard Corp.
;               SPC - Sperry Corp.
;               STC - Storage Technology Corp.
;
;
;        These stock and index values are estimated from
;        Value Line curves.  The high has been selected.
;        Indicated values are for 1983,1984, & 1985 (monthly).
;
;
STOCK1   SEGMENT PARA PUBLIC 'DATA'
;
                                         ;Dow Jones Average(index)
TBLDJA   DW      1105,1135,1160,1225,1230,1265,1260,1210,1270,1290
         DW      1300,1270,1290,1200,1185,1190,1190,1130,1130,1215
         DW      1220,1215,1240,1205,1285,1295,1300,1280,1305,1310
         DW      1350,1340,1325,1385,1480,1480
                                         ;
                                         ;Int'l Business Machines
TBLIBM   DW      100,100,101,115,115,120,121,120,122,127,122,120
         DW      120,110,110,110,114,105,105,120,122,121,121,120
         DW      130,140,135,130,130,130,131,130,130,131,131,131
                                         ;
                                         ;Digital Equipment Corp.
TBLDEC   DW      122,127,128,127,120,121,120,110,113,109,75,76
         DW      96,91,98,99,100,94,87,100,103,106,111,120
         DW      120,122,117,107,104,104,104,105,117,119,119,119
                                         ;
                                         ;Hewlett-Packard Corp.
TBLHPC   DW      42,44,44,41,44,48,47,44,47,46,42,44
         DW      47,42,40,39,40,40,40,46,41,41,40,38
         DW      40,40,40,37,37,36,37,38,37,34,30,30
                                         ;
                                         ;Sperry Corp.
TBLSPC   DW      40,40,39,39,41,42,47,48,49,50,48,50
         DW      50,50,44,43,43,40,40,46,42,39,40,43
         DW      52,54,55,52,56,58,55,54,54,53,47,47
                                         ;
                                         ;Storage Technology Corp.
TBLSTC   DW      24,24,24,22,25,22,21,21,21,19,17,15
         DW      14,14,13,11,11,11,9,11,12,11,4,3
         DW      4,4,3,3,3,3,3,2,2,2,2,2
;
STOCK1   ENDS                            ;END EXTRA SEGMENT
                                         ;
                                         ;
```

Figure 6.1b The program STKPLT1.ASM which graphs stock performance for selected stock histories. The program is intended to illustrate the use of macro pseudo-ops.

```
DATA       SEGMENT PARA PUBLIC 'DATA'
           PUBLIC  XBEG,XEND,YBEG,YEND,XT,YT,XMAX,XMIN,YMAX,YMIN,X,Y,COUNT
           PUBLIC  TABLE1,TABLE2,TABLE3,COUNT1,COUNT2,COUNT3,STARTX,STARTY
           PUBLIC  XPOS,YPOS,SSMUL
           PUBLIC  XB,XE,YB,YE
CCC        DW      0                       ;Multiplier for pointer to stock table.
VVV        DB      'DJA','IBM','DEC','HPC','SPC','STC'
                                           ;
                                           ;
MESO       DB      ' ','$'
MESO1      DB      'Do you wish to plot stock(Y/N)?   ','$'
MESO2      DB      'Input 3 character stock code.   ','$'
MESO3      DB      'Input title(max 30 characters).   ','$'
                                           ;
BUFFMX     DB      31                      ;Start keyboard buffer
BUFFLN     DB      ?
CHAR       DB      31 DUP(' '),'$'         ;End keyboard buffer
BLANK      DB      ' '
CHAR1      DB      ?,?,?                   ;Stock-index code
                                           ;
MIN        DW      ?                       ;Minimum value
MAX        DW      ?                       ;Maximum value
BINV       DW      ?                       ;Dummy parameter
                                           ;
                                           ;Begin box & tick parameters
XBEG       DW      75                      ;Corners box
XEND       DW      215
YBEG       DW      25
YEND       DW      175
XB         DW      ?                       ;XBEG Parameter for box & ticks
XE         DW      ?                       ;XEND Parameter for box & ticks
YB         DW      ?                       ;YBEG Parameter for box & ticks
YE         DW      ?                       ;YEND Parameter for box & ticks
XT         DW      121,166                 ;X-axis tick points
YT         DW      100                     ;Y-axis tick point
XMAX       DW      77                      ;Y-axis tick limit(max)
XMIN       DW      73                      ;Y-axis tick limit(min)
YMAX       DW      177                     ;X-axis tick limit(max)
YMIN       DW      173                     ;X-axis tick limit(min)
X          DW      0                       ;Dummy
Y          DW      0                       ;Dummy
COUNT      DW      2                       ;Count number X-axis ticks
                                           ;
TABLE1     DB      31 DUP(' ')             ;This table contains title
COUNT1     DW      ?                       ;Count title characters
STARTX     DW      ?                       ;Start X-axis title
STARTY     DW      0
XPOS       DB      3,3,3,8,13,18,23
YPOS       DB      3,13,22,24,24,24,24
TABLE2     DB      11 DUP(' '),'0'
           DB      ' ',' ',' ','8','3'
           DB      ' ',' ',' ','8','4'
           DB      ' ',' ',' ','8','5'
           DB      ' ',' ',' ','8','6'
                                           ;
TABLE3     DB      ' ',' ','1','0','0'
           DB      ' ',' ','2','0','0'
           DB      '1','0','0','0'
           DB      '1','5','0','0'
COUNT2     DW      4                       ;Count characters in each number & plot
COUNT3     DW      6                       ;Count numbers in plot
SSMUL      DW      ?                       ;Scale factor for graph
XINC       DW      ?                       ;Dummy containing X-axis increment & plo
t
Y00        DB      0
Y11        DB      0
COUNT4     DW      0                       ;Index for plot points
                                           ;
```

Figure 6.1b (*Continued*)

```
DATA      ENDS
                                              ;
CSEG      SEGMENT PARA PUBLIC 'CODE'
CSTOCK    PROC    FAR
          ASSUME  CS:CSEG,DS:DATA,SS:STACK,ES:STOCK1
                                              ;
          PUSH    DS
          SUB     AX,AX
          PUSH    AX
                                              ;
          MOV     AX,SEG DATA                 ;Load start DS segment
          MOV     DS,AX
          MOV     AX,SEG STOCK1               ;Load start ES segment
          MOV     ES,AX
                                              ;
          CLS                                 ;Clear screen (MACRO)
                                              ;
          MESSG   1                           ;Plot stock? (MACRO)
          KEYBD                               ;Read answer (MACRO)
          MOV     AL,59H                      ;Compare with "Y"
          CMP     AL,CHAR
          JE IF1
             RET
IF1:
          MESSG   2                           ;stock-index code (MACRO)
          KEYBD                               ;Read answer  (MACRO)
          MOV     SI,0                        ;Index initialized
          MOV     CX,3                        ;Total characters to be read
DO1:
             MOV     AL,CHAR[SI]              ;Start save input
             MOV     CHAR1[SI],AL
             INC     SI                       ;Increment index
          LOOP DO1
                                              ;
          MOV     CX,6                        ;Outer loop count
          MOV     SI,0                        ;Load table index
          MOV     DI,0                        ;Initialize table pointer
DO2:
             PUSH    CX                       ;Save outer loop count
             MOV     CX,3                     ;Set inner loop count
             MOV     BX,0                     ;Clear parameter
             MOV     BP,0                     ;Clear input character pointer
DO3:
                MOV     AL,VVV[SI]            ;Load stock
                CMP     AL,CHAR[BP]           ;Compare stock with input
                JE IF2
                   MOV     BX,1              ;Doesn't compare
                   JMP     OUT2
IF2:
                   MOV     BX,0
                   INC     SI                ;Increment table index
                   INC     BP                ;Increment input pointer
             LOOP DO3
OUT2:
             POP     CX
             CMP     BX,0
          JE OUT1
             INC     DI
             MOV     AX,3
             MUL     DI
             MOV     SI,AX
          LOOP DO2
OUT1:
          CMP     DI,5                        ;6 = limit of stocks
          JNA IF3
             RET
IF3:
          MOV     CCC,DI
```

Figure 6.1b (*Continued*)

```
        MXMN    CCC                             ;Get max & min stock-index (MACRO)
                                                ;
                                                ;
        MESSG   3                               ;MACRO
        KEYBD                                   ;Read title  (MACRO)
        MOV     AX,WORD PTR BUFFLN              ;Save title length
        MOV     AH,0
        MOV     COUNT1,AX                       ;Save length in COUNT1
        MOV     DL,BUFFLN                       ;Load character count in title
        MOV     DH,0
        SUB     DX,1                            ;Subtract 1 eliminate carriage return
        MOV     SI,0                            ;Index initialization
DO4:
            MOV     AL,CHAR[SI]
            MOV     TABLE1[SI],AL               ;Save title
            INC     SI                          ;Increment character index
            CMP     SI,DX                       ;Compare with total characters in title
        JNA DO4
                                                ;
        CLS                                     ;Clear screen  (MACRO)
                                                ;
        MOV     AX,XBEG                         ;Load box corner parameters
        MOV     XB,AX
        MOV     AX,XEND
        MOV     XE,AX
        MOV     AX,YBEG
        MOV     YB,AX
        MOV     AX,YEND
        MOV     YE,AX
                                                ;
        CALL    BOX11                           ;Call box procedure
                                                ;
        MOV     AX,XBEG                         ;Reload box corner parameters
        MOV     XB,AX
        MOV     AX,XEND
        MOV     XE,AX
        MOV     AX,YBEG
        MOV     YB,AX
        MOV     AX,YEND
        MOV     YE,AX
                                                ;
        CALL    TICK11                          ;Tick marks.
                                                ;
        SCALE   MIN,MAX                         ;Scale stock-index data-plot (MACRO)
        TITLEL  COUNT1                          ;Put title on graph (MACRO)
        CALL    LABEL1                          ;Procedure to label graph
        PLOTGR  CCC                             ;Plot stock-index graph (MACRO)
        SCDEL                                   ;MACRO to delay screen
        RT80M                                   ;MACRO return to 80 x 25
EEND:   RET
CSTOCK  ENDP
CSEG    ENDS
        END     CSTOCK
```

Figure 6.1b (*Continued*)

The program appearing in Figure 6.1b starts by loading the macro library associated with the MACRO statements appearing in the subsequent code. This loading is effected using the IF1...ENDIF sequence of pseudo-ops. Next the stack segment is defined in the usual fashion. All stock performance history is included in the data segment STOCK1 and will eventually comprise the extra segment and be callable using a segment override operator. The stock and index data represents the monthly high, as estimated from Value Line curves [4], and spans the period 1983–1986.

A few comments are needed with regard to this format for presenting tabular data. It is cumbersome. Every program needing access to stock data must have a data table inserted. While it is clear that new programs can be created using an editor for duplication and the need for retyping all this data avoided, it is still a less than desirable method for handling data. This problem will be solved in the next chapter, when extended file management is introduced and it becomes possible to input and output data to and from disk or diskette. While the data segment contained in this program is very short (only six stock-index histories) a more complete version might contain several hundred histories and extended file management becomes an over-riding concern.

The EXTRN pseudo-op was used to define four graph related routines (BOX11, TICK11, LABEL1, and CONNL1) as FAR. These called routines reside in GRAPH-LIB.LIB and will be discussed later (except CONNL1 which was presented in Chapter 5). The actual data segment is DATA and contains all the graph parameter values as well as the message I/O and buffers for keyboard I/O. It should be noted that the graphics parameter values are loaded in the data segment defined in the calling program and are not associated with the appropriate called module (BOX11, TICK11, CONNL1, and LABEL1) as has been previously done. This vehicle for passing parameters makes them easy to change, either under program control via the keyboard or using EDLIN. It requires, however, that all called modules have the same data segment assignment, which allows the parameters to be passed by PUBLIC and EXTRN statements. To simplify this process, all called modules (except CONNL1) were structured as part of CSEG; hence there is no need to redefine the data segment address.

In the code segment, CSEG, the first procedure defined (the only one in the module STK PLT1) is CSTOCK and it initializes all the segment registers and loads the starting addresses for DS and ES. The CLS macro is called to clear the screen and message number 1 is output to the display using the MESSG X macro. This macro simply asks whether a graph is to be made. KEYBD is a macro used to read the keyboard input. Next the comparison with the ASCII character Y is made and if Y was input, subsequent processing continues. The I/O sequence repeats with message number 2 and the three-character stock-index code is saved in CHAR1 (from CHAR).

At this point it is necessary to initialize a pointer to point to the stock or index table in the extra segment which contains the appropriate history. The strings for these codes are contained in VVV and a comparison is made between this variable and CHAR, the input buffer character string. Both the stock tables and the order of the three-character codes appearing in VVV are the same, i.e., DJA and the Dow Jones table is first, IBM and the IBM table are second, and so forth.

Having obtained a pointer to the correct stock or index table, the minimum and maximum for the table entries are obtained using the macro MXMN CCC. Here CCC contains the table pointer and MIN and MAX are saved in the data segment. It is necessary to obtain the MAX because the upper Y-axis graph limit must be set in accordance with this maximum value. The macro that calculates the maximum and minimum is identical to the procedure in MINMAX.ASM appearing in Chapter 2 except it has been written in macro form.

The last step prior to plotting the graph is to accept an appropriate title for the graph. Again the macros MESSG X and KEYBD are used, with message number

3. This title is saved in TABLE1 to be used by LABEL1 for displaying the title above the plot as in Chapter 5. The procedure LABEL1 is similar to LLABEL except it calls the data segment DATA for parameters. After saving the title, the screen is again cleared prior to the plot and BOX11 and TICK11 are called to set the box and tick marks. These routines are also similar to the BOX320 procedures used in Chapter 5, except that they are slightly more general and have their parameter areas located in the data segment. One of the generalizations for these procedures has been to put the box (graph) limits into the variables XB(XBEG), XE(XEND), YB(YBEG), and YE(YEND) because TICK11 redefines these variables and they are needed later (their original values) in the macro SCALE.

To set up appropriate scaling for the x-axis and y-axis, it is necessary to define a scaling factor. This is accomplished using MAX in the macro SCALE. SCALE also defines the TABLE2 value associated with the maximum limit printed on the graph. This is accomplished by loading the correct maximum limit value from TABLE3. The title and labels are plotted next using a macro, TITLEL, and the procedure LABEL1. Finally, we are ready to plot the stock or index points.

The stock or index history points are graphed with the macro PLOTGR. Since this macro uses a pointer to the stock table, it is specialized to this program. The procedure CONNL1 is used as it appears in Chapter 5. PLOTGR sets up the data points for plotting and calls CONNL1 to generate the connecting lines. The macro SCDEL (screen delay) freezes the screen for a hardcopy and RT80M (the return to 80×25 macro) returns the display to the normal mode.

Figure 6.2, as indicated earlier, contains a typical interactive session in which the Dow Jones average is displayed. Figure 6.3 illustrates the plots obtained using STKPLT1. When access to a stock-index table database becomes possible on disk or diskette, the programmer will be able to greatly expand the capabilities of this routine. Also, the graphics facilitates an interpretation of stock performance. Later in this chapter a technique for taking moving-average performance will be introduced which allows the user to see how well a given stock performs averaged across several monthly intervals. This enhancement must await further introduction to the Macro Assembler features for disk I/O.

During assembly, the assembler loads the macro library MAC1LIB.LIB as part of pass 1. This completes the generation of expanded code for STKPLT1. At link time, however, the other routines must be included. These have been placed in GRAPHLIB.LIB as indicated in Figure 6.4. Figure 6.5 illustrates MAC1LIB.LIB. Most of these macros are simple extensions of code described in Chapter 5. The scale factor used in SCALE, for example, is calculated using

$$SSMUL = 150/MAX$$

```
Do you wish to plot stock(Y/N)?

Y
Input 3 character stock code.

DJA
Input title(max 30 characters).

Dow Jones Performance
```

Figure 6.2 A typical interactive session using the program STKPLT1.ASM, prior to graphics output.

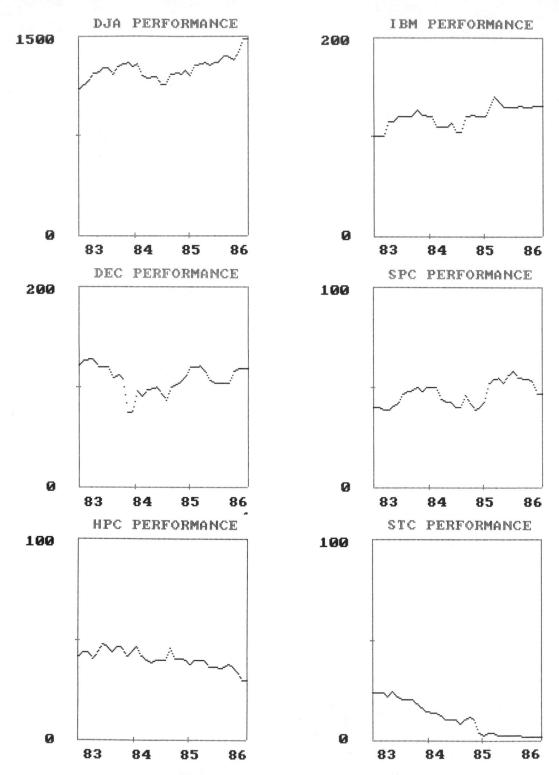

Figure 6.3 These plots illustrate the graphic output from the program STKPLT1.ASM. In each case, the 36-month history for the stock or index is plotted.

```
TYPE GRAPHLIB.DIR
BOX1.............BOX320          BOX11............BOX11
CONNL1...........CONNL1          COUNT............BOX320
LABEL1...........LABEL11         TICK1............BOX320
TICK11...........BOX11           X................BOX320
XBEG.............BOX320          XEND.............BOX320
XMAX.............BOX320          XMIN.............BOX320
XT...............BOX320          Y................BOX320
YBEG.............BOX320          YEND.............BOX320
YMAX.............BOX320          YMIN.............BOX320
YT...............BOX320


BOX320            Offset: 200H  Code and data size: D0
   BOX1              COUNT            TICK1            X
   XBEG              XEND             XMAX             XMIN
   XT                Y                YBEG             YEND
   YMAX              YMIN             YT


CONNL1            Offset: 600H  Code and data size: DD
   CONNL1


LABEL11          Offset: A00H  Code and data size: 64
   LABEL1


BOX11            Offset: C00H  Code and data size: AA
   BOX11             TICK11
```

Figure 6.4   The library GRAPHLIB.LIB which contains the new routines BOX11 and TICK11.

where there are 150 Y-axis points, and zero (for the graph) is assumed to be the lowest value on the plot. Hence, for a MAX = 100, SSMUL = 1.5. In PLOTGR, a multiplier of 100 which was used earlier is removed. This is designated as the scale divisor and was needed to prevent underflow during earlier division.

Figure 6.6 illustrates the new procedures BOX11 and TICK11. These procedures differ from BOX1 and TICK1 of Chapter 5 in that they are general purpose and have limits defined as external variables. Also, both procedures are now contained as part of the calling program code segment, CSEG. Figure 6.7 contains the graph label routine which is quite general. It uses the variable areas TABLE1 and TABLE2 which contain the title (TABLE1) and any other labeling (TABLE2). These routines are very similar to procedures appearing in Chapter 5. There are, however, significant differences in the way data is passed to them. The revised routines are presented as an illustration of the setup required when external modules use variables defined in the calling program data segment.

6.3.2 ASCII-Decimal Conversion

The next segment of programs is intended to demonstrate the features of handling ASCII to decimal and decimal to ASCII conversion. These routines employ macros for the keyboard and display I/O (based on MAC1LIB.LIB). Also, a second macro library is included which contains the actual conversion macros. One of the advantages of putting these functions in macro form is that when parameters are passed to and from the conversion routines they do not need to reside in registers but can be directly accessed in the data segment and through formal macro parameters.

```
;         MAC1LIB - MACRO LIBRARY NO. 1 (MAC1LIB.LIB)
;
;                         This MACRO library has included stock macros.
;
MESSG   MACRO   X
;
;                         This is the message output macro.
;
        MOV AH,6                ;Setup for display output
        MOV DL,OAH              ;Load line feed character
        INT 21H
        MOV AH,6                ;Setup for display output
        MOV DL,ODH              ;Load carriage return character
        INT 21H

        LEA DX,MESO&X           ;
        MOV AH,9                ;Load address message
        INT 21H                 ;Setup to output characters

        MOV AH,6                ;;
        MOV DL,OAH              ;Setup to display character
        INT 21H                 ;Line feed

        MOV AH,6                ;;
        MOV DL,ODH              ;Setup to display character
        INT 21H                 ;Carriage return

        MOV AH,6                ;
        MOV DL,OAH              ;Setup to display character
        INT 21H                 ;Load line feed character
        MOV AH,6                ;Setup to display character
        MOV DL,ODH              ;Load carriage return character
        INT 21H

        ENDM                    ;

KEYBD   MACRO                   ;

        LEA DX,BUFFMX           ;
        MOV AH,10               ;Load input buffer start address
        INT 21H                 ;Read input string

        MOV BH,0                ;;Remove carriage return string
        MOV BL,BUFFLN           ;Clear upper BX
        MOV SI,BX               ;Load input character length
        LEA BX,CHAR             ;Store length in SI
        MOV AH,BLANK            ;Load address of characters in buffer
        MOV BYTE PTR [BX+SI],AH ;Load blank character in AH
ENDM                            ;Replace c.r. with blank

CLS     MACRO                   ;
;
;                   This macro clears the screen.
;
        MOV AH,6
        MOV AL,0
        MOV CX,0
        MOV DH,23
        MOV DL,79
        MOV BH,7
        INT 10H
        ENDM
                                ;
```

Figure 6.5 The contents of the macro library MAC1LIB.LIB. These macros are primarily associated with input/output and plotting.

```
MXMN        MACRO   X
            LOCAL  DO1,DO2,IF1,IF2
        ;
        ;                   This macro calculates the min/max for
        ;                   a table: TBL&CODE in the extra segment.
        ;
            MOV AX,72               ;Load length stock/index tables
            MUL X                   ;Multiply by pointer to table
            MOV BX,AX               ;Points to stock location
            MOV SI,2                ;Variable index points to 2nd word
            MOV CX,36               ;Total words in table
            SUB CX,1                ;Now CX = total increments in table
            MOV DX,ES:[BX]          ;Load first word from table
DO1:
            CLC
            CMP DX,ES:[BX][SI]      ;Compare with indexed word
            JBE IF1                 ;Jump if still smallest
               MOV DX,ES:[BX][SI]   ;Replace with smaller value
IF1:
            ADD SI,2                ;Increment to next word
            LOOP DO1                ;Loop until all words checked
                                    ;;
            MOV MIN,DX              ;Save minimum
                                    ;;
            MOV AX,72               ;Reload bytes in each table
            MUL X                   ;Multiply by table pointer
            MOV BX,AX               ;Pointer to stock location
            MOV SI,2                ;Index points to 2nd word in table
            MOV CX,36               ;Total words in table
            SUB CX,1                ;Now total increments in table
            MOV DX,ES:[BX]          ;Load first table word
                                    ;;
DO2:
            CLC
            CMP DX,ES:[BX][SI]      ;Compare with indexed word
            JAE IF2                 ;Jump if still larger
               MOV DX,ES:[BX][SI]   ;Replace with larger value
IF2:
            ADD SI,2                ;Increment table pointer
            LOOP DO2                ;Loop through all table values
                                    ;;
            MOV MAX,DX              ;Save maximum
            ENDM
                                    ;
SCALE       MACRO   MIN,MAX
            LOCAL   ELSE3,ELSE4,ELSE5,OUT1,DO4
        ;
        ;   This MACRO scales the plot for stocks
        ;
            MOV AX,100
            CMP MAX,AX
            JBE ELSE3               Jump if MAX <= 100
            MOV AX,200
            CMP MAX,AX
            JBE ELSE4               ;Jump if MAX <= 200
            MOV AX,1000
            CMP MAX,AX
            JBE ELSE5               ;Jump if MAX <= 1000
            MOV AX,3                ;Scale on 0-1500
            MOV SSMUL,10            ;Load scale factor = 0.10
            JMP OUT1
```

Figure 6.5 (*Continued*)

```
       ELSE3:
              MOV AX,0                      ;Scale on 0-100
              MOV SSMUL,150                 ;Load scale factor = 1.50
              JMP OUT1
       ELSE4:
              MOV AX,1                      ;Scale 0-200
              MOV SSMUL,75                  ;Load scale factor = 0.75
              JMP OUT1
       ELSE5:
              MOV AX,2                      ;Scale on 0-1000
              MOV SSMUL,15                  ;Load scale factor = 0.15
                                            ;
       OUT1:
              MOV SI,0                      ;Load TABLE2 index
              MOV BX,4
              MUL BX                        ;Find TABLE3 pointer
              MOV CX,4                      ;Loop count
              MOV DI,AX                     ;Load TABLE3 pointer
       DO4:
              MOV AL,TABLE3[DI]             ;Move TABLE3 value to AX
              MOV TABLE2[SI],AL             ;Load TABLE2
              INC SI
              INC DI
              LOOP DO4                      ;Loop to load Y-axis label
                                            ;
              ENDM
                                            ;
       TITLEL MACRO    BUFLN
                                            ;MACRO to position title
              MOV AX,60                     ;Load length chararcter blanking
              SUB AX,BUFLN                  ;Subtract title characters
              MOV CL,2
              SHR AX,CL                     ;Divide by 2
              MOV STARTX,AX                 ;Load title start X-value
              ENDM
                                            ;
       SCDEL  MACRO
       ;
       ;                              This macro delays the screen erasure.
       ;
              MOV AH,0                          ;Keyboard interrupt
              INT 16H
              ENDM
                                             ;
       RT80M  MACRO
       ;
       ;                              This macro returns to 80 x 25 mode
       ;
              MOV AH,0
              MOV AL,2
              INT 10H
              ENDM
       PLOTGR MACRO    CCC
              LOCAL    DO3
       ;
       ;                              This MACRO plots the stock/index values
       ;                              using CONNL1.
       ;
```

Figure 6.5 (*Continued*)

```
            MOV AX,XEND              ;Load end X-point
            SUB AX,XBEG              ;Calculate X-axis difference
            MOV DX,0                 ;Clear upper register
            MOV BX,34                ;Load X-interval number
            DIV BX                   ;Calculate X-increments
            MOV XINC,AX              ;Store X-increment
                            ;
            MOV AX,72                ;Determine pointer to stock/index
            MUL CCC                  ;Multiply by table pointer
            MOV SI,AX                ;Load index
            MOV COUNT4,34            ;Load graph increment (0 - 34) limit
            MOV DI,0                 ;Load counter
                            ;
    DO3:
            MOV CX,100               ;Load scale divisor
            MOV AX,ES:[SI]
            MUL SSMUL                ;Multiply by scale
            MOV DX,0                 ;Clear upper register
            DIV CX                   ;Remove scaling factor of 100
            MOV BX,AX                ;Invert points on graph
            MOV AX,175               ;Maximum graph point
            SUB AX,BX                ;Inverted point
            MOV Y00,AL               ;Save first point
                                     ;
            MOV AX,ES:[SI+2]         ;Second Y-value point
            MUL SSMUL
            MOV DX,0
            DIV CX
            MOV BX,AX
            MOV AX,175
            SUB AX,BX
            MOV Y11,AL               ;Save second point
                                     ;End loading Y-values
                                     ;
            MOV AX,XINC              ;Calculate XSTART
            MOV DX,0
            MUL DI                   ;Multiply XINC by connection point no.
            ADD AX,XBEG              ;Add starting value
            MOV BX,AX                ;Save XSTART parameter
            ADD AX,XINC              ;Increment next plot point by XINC
            MOV CX,AX                ;Save XEND parameter
            MOV DH,Y00
            MOV DL,Y11
                                     ;
            CALL CONNL1              ;Plot points
            ADD SI,2
            INC DI
            CMP DI,COUNT4            ;Check for plot limit
            JBE DO3
                                     ;
            ENDM
```

Figure 6.5 (*Continued*)

Figure 6.8a presents the flow chart for a program that accomplishes ASCII to decimal conversion from the keyboard. Figure 6.8b illustrates this program, DECASC, which reads a number ($-32,765$ to $32,765$) from the keyboard, converts this number to internal decimal, clears the input buffer area, converts the number back to ASCII, and writes it to the display. The display messages are contained in MESO1, MESO2, and MESO3 in the data segment and are terminated with the $

```
PAGE      55,132
TITLE     BOX     - DRAWS BOX & TICK MARKS 200 X 200 (BOX1.ASM)
                                                ;
                                                ;Uses data segment DATA
                                                ;
          EXTRN   XBEG:WORD,XEND:WORD,YBEG:WORD,YEND:WORD,XT:WORD,YT:WORD
          EXTRN   XMAX:WORD,XMIN:WORD,YMAX:WORD,YMIN:WORD,X:WORD,Y:WORD
          EXTRN   COUNT:WORD
          EXTRN   XB:WORD,XE:WORD,YB:WORD,YE:WORD
                                                ;
CSEG      SEGMENT PARA PUBLIC 'CODE'
          PUBLIC  BOX11,TICK11
BOX11     PROC    FAR
          ASSUME  CS:CSEG
          PUSH    DS
                                                ;
                                                ;
                                                ;This procedure draws a box
                                                ;Clear screen
          MOV     AH,6                          ;Scroll page
          MOV     AL,0                          ;Blank entire window
          MOV     CX,0                          ;Start upper left corner
          MOV     DH,23                         ;Lower right corner
          MOV     DL,79
          MOV     BH,7                          ;Attribute white on black
          INT     10H
                                                ;
          MOV     AH,0                          ;Set mode
          MOV     AL,5                          ;320 x 200 graphics
          INT     10H
                                                ;
          MOV     AX,YB                         ;Start Y point horizontal line
          MOV     Y,AX
          CALL    LINEH                         ;Draw line
          MOV     AX,YE                         ;Start Y-axis point for 2nd line
          MOV     Y,AX
          CALL    LINEH                         ;Draw horizontal line
                                                ;
          MOV     AX,XB                         ;Start X point vertical line
          MOV     X,AX
          CALL    LINEV                         ;Draw vertical line
          MOV     AX,XE                         ;Start X-axis point 2nd line
          MOV     X,AX
          CALL    LINEV                         ;Draw 2nd vertical line
                                                ;
          POP     DS
          RET
BOX11     ENDP
```

Figure 6.6 This figure illustrates the new box and tick mark procedures BOX11 and TICK11.

delimiter. The keyboard buffer starts with BUFFMX. Following output of MESO1, the keyboard input provides a number in the above range. This input string consists of ASCII characters between 30 and 39 plus a possible minus sign, 2DH. These are stored in the variable string ASC. Next the string is converted from ASCII to decimal using the macro ASCDEC. The variable string ASC is set to zero to clear it so it can be reloaded and the correct values noted. The variable BINV contains the decimal number. Next the macro DECASC converts the number back to ASCII and loads this in ASC. The display indicates the number is to follow with the macro MESSG outputting MESO2. Finally, the ASCII string in ASC, which has been transferred to MESO3, is output. Table 6.8 presents the first 128 ASCII characters.

```
TICK11   PROC     FAR                              ;
         PUSH     DS
                                                   ;
                                                   ;
         MOV      AX,YT                            ;Y position Y-axis tick
         MOV      Y,AX                             ;Draw Y-axis tick
         MOV      AX,XMIN                          ;Load minimum X tick in XBEG
         MOV      XB,AX
         MOV      AX,XMAX                          ;Load maximum X tick in XEND
         MOV      XE,AX
         CALL     LINEH                            ;Draw Y-axis tick
                                                   ;
         MOV      SI,0                             ;Set tick counter - X-axis
         MOV      AX,YMIN                          ;Load minimum Y tick in YBEG
         MOV      YB,AX                            ;Draw X-axis ticks
         MOV      AX,YMAX                          ;Load maximum Y tick in YEND
         MOV      YE,AX
DO1:
             MOV      AX,XT[SI]                     ;Load current X tick position
             MOV      X,AX
             CALL     LINEV                         ;Draw vertical tick
             ADD      SI,2
             CMP      SI,COUNT                      ;Compare tick number with COUNT
         JNA DO1
                                                   ;
         POP      DS
         RET
TICK11   ENDP
LINEH    PROC     NEAR
                                                   ;Procedure for horizontal line
         MOV      DX,Y
         MOV      CX,XB                            ;Load begin X-value
DO3:
             MOV      AH,12                         ;Write dot
             MOV      AL,1                          ;Attribute 1
             INT      10H
             ADD      CX,1                          ;Increment X-value
             MOV      BX,CX
             SUB      BX,XE                         ;Check X-value end point
         JNE DO3
         RET
LINEH    ENDP
                                                   ;
LINEV    PROC     NEAR
                                                   ;Procedure for vertical line
         MOV      CX,X
         MOV      DX,YB                            ;Load begin Y-value
DO5:
             MOV      AH,12                         ;Write dot
             MOV      AL,1                          ;Attribute 1
             INT      10H
             ADD      DX,1                          ;Increment Y-value
             MOV      BX,DX
             SUB      BX,YE                         ;Check Y-value end point
         JNE DO5
         RET
LINEV    ENDP
                                                   ;
CSEG     ENDS
         END      BOX11
```

Figure 6.6 (*Continued*)

```
PAGE      40,132
TITLE     LABEL1    - GENERAL PURPOSE LABEL ROUTINE (LABEL1.ASM)
                                              ;
          EXTRN     TABLE1:BYTE,TABLE2:BYTE,COUNT1:WORD
          EXTRN     COUNT2:WORD,COUNT3:WORD,STARTX:WORD,STARTY:WORD
          EXTRN     XPOS:BYTE,YPOS:BYTE
                                              ;
CSEG      SEGMENT   PARA PUBLIC 'CODE'
          PUBLIC    LABEL1
LABEL1    PROC      FAR
          ASSUME    CS:CSEG
                                              ;
          PUSH      DS
                                              ;
                                              ;
                                              ;
          MOV       DH,BYTE PTR STARTY        ;Load row value-start
          MOV       DL,BYTE PTR STARTX        ;Load col value-start
          MOV       BH,0
                                              ;
          MOV       DI,1                      ;Initalize counters/indexes
          MOV       SI,0
          MOV       CX,1
                                              ;
DO1:
          MOV       AH,2                      ;Position cursor
          INT       10H
          MOV       AH,10                     ;Write character
          MOV       AL,TABLE1[SI]             ;Load character from TABLE1
          MOV       BL,1                      ;Attribute
          INT       10H
          ADD       DL,1                      ;Increment X-space
          INC       SI                        ;Increment TABLE1 value
          INC       DI                        ;Increment index
          CMP       DI,COUNT1                 ;Compare TABLE1 limit
          JNA DO1
                                              ;Write numerical labels
          MOV       DI,0                      ;Initialize counters/indexes
          MOV       SI,0
DO3:
          MOV       DH,YPOS[DI]               ;Outer loop-load Y-position
          MOV       DL,XPOS[DI]               ;Load X-start position
          MOV       AX,1                      ;Reinitialize inner loop index
          PUSH      AX
DO4:
          MOV       AH,2                      ;Inner loop-cursor control
          INT       10H
          MOV       AH,10                     ;Character write
          MOV       AL,TABLE2[SI]             ;Character from TABLE2
          MOV       BL,2                      ;Attribute
          INT       10H
          ADD       DL,1                      ;Increment X-position
          INC       SI                        ;Increment TABLE2 index
                                              ;
          POP       AX                        ;Recall inner loop count
          INC       AX                        ;Increment inner loop count
          PUSH      AX                        ;Save inner loop count
          CMP       AX,COUNT2
                                              ;
          JNA DO4
          POP       AX                        ;Recall inner loop index
          INC       DI                        ;Increment outer loop index
          CMP       DI,COUNT3                 ;Compare outer loop limit
          JNA DO3
          POP       DS
                                              ;
          RET
LABEL1    ENDP
CSEG      ENDS
          END       LABEL1
```

Figure 6.7   General purpose graph label routine which uses the calling program data segment DATA.

Figure 6.9a contains the flow chart for the macro, ASCDEC and Figure 6.9b presents the flow chart for DECASC. These comprise the macro library MAC2LIB.-LIB that appears in Figure 6.9c. The decimal to ASCII macro is DECASC. Similarly, the ASCII to decimal macro is ASCDEC. Figure 6.10 illustrates the display output during 4 interactive sessions, where a number is asked for, read in, and output. Figure 6.11 presents a representative DEBUG session with the program. The data segment, DATA, is loaded with segment address 134C. The variable BINV is located at 134C:0064. The ASCII string, ASC, is located at 134C:0066. In this session the string "23456" has been input and stored in ASC. After conversion BINV equals 5BAOH. The second memory dump demonstrates that ASC has been set to

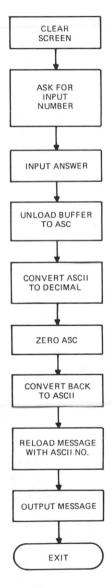

Figure 6.8a The functional flow chart for the program DECASC.ASM.

```
PAGE       55,132
TITLE      DECASC  - THIS PROGRAM CONVERTS ASC/DEC NUMBERS (DA.ASM)
;
;                  DESCRIPTION:The program reads a number from the
;                  keyboard, converts it to internal decimal,converts
;                  it back to ASCII format, and outputs the number.
;
IF1
           INCLUDE MAC1LIB.LIB
           INCLUDE MAC2LIB.LIB
           PURGE   MXMN,PLOTGR,RT80M,SCALE,SCDEL,TITLEL
ENDIF
                                              ;
STACK      SEGMENT PARA STACK 'STACK'
           DB      100 DUP ('STACK    ')
STACK      ENDS
                                              ;
DATA       SEGMENT PARA PUBLIC 'DATA'
                                              ;
MESO1      DB      'Input number (-32765,32765).   ','$'
MESO2      DB      'The number is equal to:   ','$'
MESO3      DB      6 DUP(' '),'$'             ;ASCII max character length = 6
                                              ;
BUFFMX     DB      31                         ;Start keyboard buffer
BUFFLN     DB      ?
CHAR       DB      31 DUP(' '),'$'            ;End keyboard buffer
                                              ;
BINV       DW      ?                          ;Dummy parameter
ASC        DB      31 DUP (' '),'$'
BLANK      DB      ' '
BASE       DW      ?                          ;Base value called to convert A to D
CCOUNT     DW      ?                          ;This is the output ASCII char. count
DATA       ENDS
                                              ;
CSEG       SEGMENT PARA PUBLIC 'CODE'
CDA        PROC    FAR
           ASSUME  CS:CSEG,DS:DATA,SS:STACK
                                              ;
           PUSH    DS
           SUB     AX,AX
           PUSH    AX
                                              ;
           MOV     AX,SEG DATA
           MOV     DS,AX
                                              ;
           CLS                                ;Clear screen.  MACRO
                                              ;
           MESSG   1                          ;Output message MACRO
           KEYBD                              ;Read number (ASCII).   MACRO
           MOV     AL,BUFFLN                  ;Load buffer length
           MOV     AH,0                       ;Clear upper register
           MOV     DI,AX                      ;Set DI to buffer length
           MOV     SI,0                       ;Initialize index
DO1:
           MOV     AL,CHAR[SI]                ;Begin transfer input to ASC
           MOV     ASC[SI],AL
           INC     SI                         ;Increment index
           CMP     SI,DI                      ;Check to see if end
JNA DO1

           ASCDEC  BINV,ASC                   ;Convert ASCII MACRO
                                              ;
           MOV     SI,0                       ;Initialize pointer
           MOV     CH,0                       ;Clear upper CX register
           MOV     CL,BUFFLN                  ;Loop count for ASCII char
           MOV     AX,0                       ;Register used to zero ASC
```

Figure 6.8b The program DECASC which reads a number from the keyboard,
converts it to internal decimal, converts it back to ASCII, and prints the number on
the display.

```
DO3:
              MOV      ASC[SI],AL           ;Zero ASC buffer area
              INC      SI
          LOOP DO3
                                           ;
          DECASC    BINV,ASC               ;Convert back to ASCII.  MACRO
                                           ;
          MOV       AX,CCOUNT              ;Reload output
          MOV       DI,AX                  ;Set DI = character total
          MOV       SI,0                   ;Initialize pointer
DO5:
              MOV      AL,ASC[SI]          ;Move characters to output
              MOV      MESO3[SI],AL
              INC      SI
              CMP      SI,DI               ;Check for last character
          JNAE DO5
                                           ;
          MESSG     2                      ;Indicate start output.  MACRO
          MOV       AL,BYTE PTR CCOUNT     ;Get length character buffer
          MOV       BUFFLN,AL              ;Reset character buffer
                                           ;
          MESSG     3                      ;Output message.  MACRO
                                           ;
          RET
CDA       ENDP
CSEG      ENDS
          END       CDA
```

Figure 6.8b (*Continued*)

zero. Finally, the third dump illustrates the values for ASC after BINV has been converted back to ASCII.

6.3.3 Timer Program

This discussion deals with the program TIMER.ASM illustrated in Figure 6.12. The program contains further examples of pseudo-ops. From a mechanical viewpoint the program asks for a timer interval (both minutes and seconds must be specified) and displays the elapsed time until the timed interval ends. The timer can be used to time events up to one hour.

Figure 6.12 concentrates on two simple structures; the IF and the DO structures. The emphasis here is on the natural way that these structures can be nested and intermingled to control the decision-making in the code without interrupting the flow of activity downward through the program. Clearly, the DO structures result in looping but they appear in such an orderly fashion that the organization of the program from top-to-bottom is easily interpreted.

In TIMER.ASM one of the DO structures employs a conditional test (the DO UNTIL trailing test) which is very convenient for loop structures. This is used in cases where the number of iterations cannot be specified at the start of the loop. In the timer program the first DO structure is used to read in the minutes and seconds in the timed interval. A small nested DO is used to transfer the input ASCII characters to the variable array ASC, which is used by the routine ASCDEC for conversion from ASCII to internal decimal format. The resulting input is stored in either MINUT, for minutes, or SECOND, for seconds.

TABLE 6.8 ASCII CHARACTER SET (FIRST 128 CHARACTERS)

Character	HEX	Character	HEX	Character	HEX	Character	HEX
NULL	00	#	23	F	46	i	69
OPEN FACE	01	$	24	G	47	j	6A
CLOSED FACE	02	%	25	H	48	k	6B
HEART	03	&	26	I	49	l	6C
DIAMOND	04	'	27	J	4A	m	6D
CLUB	05	(	28	K	4B	n	6E
SPADE	06	)	29	L	4C	o	6F
BEEP	07	*	2A	M	4D		
WHITE DOT	08	+	2B	N	4E	p	70
BLACK CIRCLE	09	,	2C	O	4F	q	71
WHITE CIRCLE	0A	-	2D			r	72
MALE	0B	.	2E	P	50	s	73
FEMALE	0C	/	2F	Q	51	t	74
NOTE	0D			R	52	u	75
NOTE	0E						
SUN	0F	0	30	S	53	v	76
		1	31	T	54	w	77
R. ARROW	10	2	32	U	55	x	78
L. ARROW	11	3	33	V	56	y	79
V. ARROW	12	4	34	W	57	z	7A
DOUBLE EXCL.	13	5	35	X	58	L. BRACK.	7B
PARAGRAPH	14	6	36	Y	59	BOLD COLON	7C
CIRCLE "S"	15	7	37	Z	5A	R. BRACK.	7D
FULL BAR	16	8	38	L. BRACK.	5B	APPROXIMATE	7E
V. ARROW/LINE	17	9	39	L. SLASH	5C	OPN TRIANG.	7F
UP ARROW	18	:	3A	R. BRACK.	5D		
DN ARROW	19	;	3B	"UP" SIGN	5E		
R. ARROW	1A	L.T.	3C	—	5F		
L. ARROW	1B	=	3D				
BRACKET	1C	G.T.	3E	APOSTROPHE	60		
HOR. ARROW	1D	?	3F	a	61		
				b	62		
UP TRIANGLE	1E	@	40	c	63		
DN TRIANGLE	1F	A	41	d	64		
		B	42	e	65		
BLANK	20	C	43	f	66		
EXCLAM.	21	D	44	g	67		
QUOTE	22	E	45	h	68		

At this point the clock is set to zero using the interrupt 1AH. This is accomplished using the macro TIMCL with AH = 3. CH contains hours, CL contains minutes, DH contains seconds, and DL contains an optional Daylight Savings indicator. The contents of these registers are Binary Coded Decimal (BCD) in which each byte can hold a number between 0 and 99. Each nibble represents a single digit between 0 and 9. Calling the same interrupt with AH = 2 reads the clock. Once read, both the seconds and minutes returned by the clock must be converted to internal decimal from BCD. This is accomplished using a procedure BCDDEC.

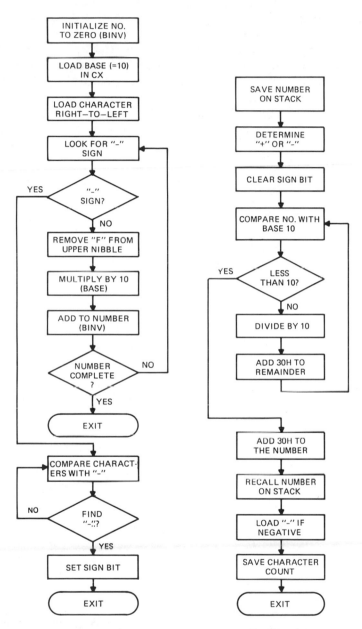

Figure 6.9a   The functional flow chart for the macro ASCDEC which converts ASCII numbers to decimal.

Figure 6.9b   The functional flow chart for the macro DECASC.

The second set of DO structures (bounded by the DO UNTIL trailing test) contain the code that reads the clock all but the first time, and checks to see when the specified time interval has elapsed. The variable TT is used to hold the clock minutes and seconds, while CX is redefined for the inner DO structure loop count. These minute and second values are converted to ASCII for output to the screen. A new set of clock values is read and converted to internal decimal, and the seconds are compared with the previous iteration's second value (SEC1). If these two second values are the same, it indicates one second has not elapsed and nothing is displayed. When they differ, the next second has occurred and the second count on the display is incremented. The final decision is whether or not the timer interval has been reached. To check this BX is loaded with the minutes (BH) and seconds (BL)

```
;        MAC2LIB - MACRO LIBRARY NO. 2 (MAC2LIB.LIB)
;
;                          This macro library has the ASCII/Decimal
;                          conversion routines: ASCDEC and DECASC.
;
DECASC   MACRO    BINV,ASC
         LOCAL EXIT1,DO1,IF1
;
;                          Input in BINV, output 6-bytes starting
;                          with ASC.  Negative numbers have bit
;                          15 set. The variable CCOUNT keeps track of
;                          the number of ASCII characters generated.
;
                                    ;
         MOV AX,0
         MOV AX,BINV                ;Load AX number (-32765,32765)
         PUSH AX
         MOV SI, OFFSET ASC[5]      ;Initialize with ASCII char. max
         MOV CX,10                  ;Divide base factor
                                    ;
         OR AX,AX                   ;Set or clear sign flag
         JNS START
         SHL AX,1                   ;Clear sign bit
         SHR AX,1                   ;Move number back to normal form
DO1:
         CMP AX,10                  ;Compare with base value
         JB EXIT1
         MOV DX,0                   ;Clear upper numerator register
         DIV CX
         ADD DL,30H                 ;Convert to ASCII character
         MOV [SI],DL                ;Save at ASC pointer value
         DEC SI
         JMP DO1
EXIT1:
         ADD AL,30H                 ;Convert last ASCII char
         MOV [SI],AL                ;load zero in last ASCII char.
                                    ;
         POP AX                     ;Recall initial number/sign check
         OR AX,AX                   ;Set sign flag if negative number
         JNS IF1
         DEC SI
         MOV BL,2DH                 ;Load "minus" sign
         MOV [SI],BL                ;Store "minus" sign in output char.
IF1:     MOV AX,6                   ;Save fixed ASCII char. count
         MOV CCOUNT,AX              ;Keep ASCII count at 6 characters
         ENDM
                                    ;
```

Figure 6.9c   The macro library, MAC2LIB.LIB, which contains the two macros for converting ASCII to decimal numbers and decimal to ASCII.

```
ASCDEC   MACRO    BINV,ACS
         LOCAL DO2,DO3,IF2,IF3,OUT1
;
;                        This macro assumes ASCII character loaded
;                        and length = BUFFLN.
;
         MOV DINV,0              ;Initialize output
         MOV BL,BUFFLN          ;Load buffer length
         MOV BH,0               ;Clear upper BX register
         MOV CX,10              ;Decimal base multiplier
         LEA SI,ASC-1           ;Load SI with characters - 1
         MOV DI,0               ;Clear upper multiplicand register
         MOV AX,1               ;Initialize base 1st decimal place
         MOV BASE,AX            ;Load base
DO2:
         MOV AL,[SI+BX]         ;Load right-to-left char.
         CMP AL,2DH             ;Compare with "minus" sign
         JE IF2                 ;Middle exit
         AND AX,000FH           ;Truncates the ASCII to nibble
         MUL BASE               ;Multiply by base
         ADD BINV,AX            ;Add result to decimal subtotal
         MOV AX,BASE            ;Add decimal values
         MUL CX                 ;Multiply base by 10 to get next digit
         MOV BASE,AX            ;Store result
         DEC BX
         JNZ DO2
         JMP OUT1               ;Not negative number
IF2:
         MOV BL,BUFFLN          ;Check negative character
         MOV BH,0               ;Clear upper BX register
         MOV SI,0               ;Initialize pointer
DO3:
         MOV AL,ASC[SI]         ;Load character
         MOV AH,0               ;Clear upper register
         CMP AL,2DH             ;Compare char. with "minus" sign
         JE IF3                 ;Middle exit
         INC SI
         CMP SI,BX              ;Check end of characters
         JB  DO3
         JMP OUT1
IF3:
         OR BINV,8000H          ;Number is negative
OUT1:    NOP
         ENDM
```

Figure 6.9c (*Continued*)

and compared to AX which contains MINUT and SECOND in the same order. Once BX becomes greater than or equal to AX, the loop is terminated and an end-time-interval message displayed.

Many of the programs in this chapter have been run on the IBM Personal Computer AT using DOS version 3.3. The programs for Chapters 2 and 4 were developed using an IBM PC. Basically, all the code developed in Chapters 2, 4, 5, and 6 can be used interchangeably on either machine and can be run on an IBM Personal Computer XT or a PS/2 computer. When the 8087 and 80287 coprocessor chips are discussed, differences in programming will become apparent.

Figure 6.13 contains the BCD to internal decimal conversion procedure. This procedure only converts to a two digit BCD number contained in one byte. Both the high- and low-byte values are masked with the high-byte value (the 10's position) multiplied by 10 and then added to the low-byte value. The result of this operation

```
Input number (-32765,32765).

-23456
The number is equal to:


-23456


Input number (-32765,32765).

0
The number is equal to:


    0


Input number (-32765,32765).

23456
The number is equal to:


  23456


Input number (-32765,32765).

-4444
The number is equal to:


 -4444


Input number (-32765,32765).

4444
The number is equal to:


  4444
```

Figure 6.10   This figure illustrates the interactive session for four cases where DECASC.ASM reads a number, converts it, and displays the outcome.

yields an internal decimal equivalent. Since no decision logic is needed for this conversion, no structures appear in this procedure.

Finally, Figure 6.14 represents a typical time run intended to illustrate the format of the screen display. The interval selected, three seconds, allows the entire display to be presented. Normally the screen continues to scroll upward as each time interval of one second is displayed until the appearance of the end-time-interval message. This program has illustrated the use of the 1AH interrupt and the conversion of BCD numbers to internal decimal in addition to providing another example of the usage of the structured programming concept.

The advantages of structured programming and macros are probably becoming clear. Long groups of assembler statements are avoided by using the structure statements to break the program logic into smaller segments that are frequently dominated by CALL instructions (which further reduce the difficulty in following the flow of executions) or macros. Macros are used for shorter functional groups of instructions. Basically the CALL instruction references a sequence of instructions contained in a procedure which performs a specific known function. Thus, a single

```
DEBUG DA1.EXE
-G CS:0009

AX=134C  BX=0000  CX=0550  DX=0000  SP=031C  BP=0000  SI=0000  DI=0000
DS=134C  ES=1322  SS=1355  CS=1332  IP=0009   NV UP EI PL ZR NA PE NC
1332:0009 B406           MOV       AH,06
-D DS:003B
134C:0030                                         20 20 20 20 20
134C:0040  20 24 1F 00 20 20 20 20-20 20 20 20 20 20 20 20    $..
134C:0050  20 20 20 20 20 20 20 20-20 20 20 20 20 20 20 20
134C:0060  20 20 20 24 00 00 20 20-20 20 20 20 20 20 20 20     $..
134C:0070  20 20 20 20 20 20 20 20-20 20 20 20 20 20 20 20
134C:0080  20 20 20 20 20 24 20 00-00 00 00 00 00 00 00 00      $ ........
134C:0090  53 54 41 43 4B 20 20 20-53 54 41 43 4B 20 20 20    STACK   STACK
134C:00A0  53 54 41 43 4B 20 20 20-53 54 41 43 4B 20 20 20    STACK   STACK
134C:00B0  53 54 41 43 4B 20 20 20-53 54 41               STACK   STA
-G CS:00D2
Input number (-32765,32765).    23456
AX=86A0  BX=0000  CX=000A  DX=0001  SP=031C  BP=0000  SI=0065  DI=0000
DS=134C  ES=1322  SS=1355  CS=1332  IP=00D2   NV UP EI PL ZR NA PE CY
1332:00D2 BE0000           MOV       SI,0000
-D DS:003B
134C:0030                                         20 20 20 20 20
134C:0040  20 24 1F 05 32 33 34 35-36 20 20 20 20 20 20 20    $ 23456
134C:0050  20 20 20 20 00 00 00 20-20 20 20 20 20 20 20 20
134C:0060  20 20 20 24 A0 5B 32 33-34 35 36 20 20 20 20 20     $.[23456
134C:0070  20 20 20 20 20 20 20 20-20 20 20 20 20 20 20 20
134C:0080  20 20 20 20 20 24 20 A0-86 00 00 00 00 00 00 00      $ ........
134C:0090  53 54 41 43 4B 20 20 20-53 54 41 43 4B 20 20 20    STACK   STACK
134C:00A0  53 54 41 43 4B 20 20 20-53 54 41 43 4B 20 20 20    STACK   STACK
134C:00B0  53 54 41 43 4B 20 20 20-53 54 41               STACK   STA
-G CS:00E5

AX=0000  BX=0000  CX=0000  DX=0001  SP=031C  BP=0000  SI=0005  DI=0000
DS=134C  ES=1322  SS=1355  CS=1332  IP=00E5   NV UP EI PL NZ NA PE CY
1332:00E5 B80000           MOV       AX,0000
-D DS:003B
134C:0030                                         20 20 20 20 20
134C:0040  20 24 1F 05 32 33 34 35-36 20 20 20 20 20 20 20    $..23456
134C:0050  20 20 20 20 20 20 20 20-20 20 20 20 20 20 20 20
134C:0060  20 20 20 24 A0 5B 00 00-00 00 00 20 20 20 20 20     $.[.....
134C:0070  20 20 20 20 20 20 20 20-20 20 20 20 20 20 20 20
134C:0080  20 20 20 20 20 24 20 A0-86 00 00 00 00 00 00 00      $ ........
134C:0090  53 54 41 43 4B 20 20 20-53 54 41 43 4B 20 20 20    STACK   STACK
134C:00A0  53 54 41 43 4B 20 20 20-53 54 41 43 4B 20 20 20    STACK   STACK
134C:00B0  53 54 41 43 4B 20 20 20-53 54 41               STACK   STA
-G CS:0120

AX=0006  BX=0000  CX=000A  DX=0033  SP=031C  BP=0000  SI=0067  DI=0000
DS=134C  ES=1322  SS=1355  CS=1332  IP=0120   NV UP EI PL NZ NA PE NC
1332:0120 A18900           MOV       AX,[0089]              DS:0089=0006
-D DS:003B
134C:0030                                         20 20 20 20 20
134C:0040  20 24 1F 05 32 33 34 35-36 20 20 20 20 20 20 20    $..23456
134C:0050  20 20 20 20 20 20 20 20-20 20 20 20 20 20 20 20
134C:0060  20 20 20 24 A0 5B 00 20-00 01 00 00 20 20 20 20     $.[.23456
134C:0070  20 20 20 20 20 20 20 20-20 20 20 20 20 20 20 20
134C:0080  20 20 20 20 20 24 20 A0-86 06 00 00 00 00 00 00      $ ........
134C:0090  53 54 41 43 4B 20 20 20-53 54 41 43 4B 20 20 20    STACK   STACK
134C:00A0  53 54 41 43 4B 20 20 20-53 54 41 43 4B 20 20 20    STACK   STACK
134C:00B0  53 54 41 43 4B 20 20 20-53 54 41               STACK   STA
-G
The number is equal to:    23456
Program terminated normally
-Q
```

Figure 6.11 This is a sample DEBUG session with DA1.ASM illustrating how memory changes during execution.

```
PAGE      55,132
TITLE     TIMER    - DETERMINES TIMER INTERVAL (TIMER.SAL)
;
;         DESCRIPTION: This program allows the user to set a
;         time interval (up to 1 hour) and then continuously
;         update the time on the screen until the time interval
;         has transpired.
;
EXTRN     CLSCREN:FAR,MESSAGE:FAR,KEYBD:FAR,ASCDEC:FAR,DECASC:FAR
EXTRN     BCDDEC:FAR
;
TIMECL    MACRO
          MOV      AH,3                ;Set time option
          MOV      CH,0                ;Clear hours
          MOV      CL,0                ;Clear minutes
          MOV      DH,0                ;Clear seconds
          MOV      DL,0                ;Clear optional Daylight Savings
          INT      1AH
                                       ;
ENDM
;
STACK     SEGMENT PARA STACK 'STACK'
          DB       64 DUP(' ')
STACK     ENDS
;
DATA      SEGMENT PARA PUBLIC 'DATA'
          PUBLIC   BINV,BUFFLN,BUFFMX,CHAR,ASC,BASE,BLANK,CCOUNT
          PUBLIC   X
;
MESO2     DB       'Input timer interval (minutes)','$'
MESO3     DB       'Input timer interval (seconds)','$'
MESO4     DB       'End timer interval','$'
MESO5     DB       80 DUP(' '),'$'
;
BUFFMX    DB       80
BUFFLN    DB       ?
CHAR      DB       80 DUP(' '),'$'     ;End keyboard buffer
;
SEC1      DB       ?                   ;Contains sec. for suppress out
HOUR      DB       ?
MINUT     DB       ?
SECOND    DB       ?
;
ASC       DB       80 DUP(' '),'$'
TT        DB       ?,?,?               ;Dummy variable
BINV      DW       ?                   ;ASCII/Int. Decimal transfer
CCOUNT    DW       ?
BASE      DW       ?
BLANK     DB       ' '
X         DB       ?                   ;Dummy variable for passing BCD
;
DATA      ENDS
;
CSEG      SEGMENT PARA PUBLIC 'CODE'
TIMER     PROC     FAR
          ASSUME   CS:CSEG,SS:STACK,DS:DATA
                                       ;
          PUSH     DS
          SUB      AX,AX
          PUSH     AX
                                       ;
          MOV      AX,SEG DATA
          MOV      DS,AX
```

Figure 6.12 The program TIMER.ASM which calculates a timed interval and indicates elapsed time on the screen.

```
            CALL      CLSCREN                 ;Clear screen
            MOV       CX,2                    ;Loop count
                                              ;
DO1:
            CMP     CX,1
            JNE ELSE2
                      MOV       DX,OFFSET MESO2 ;Message timer (minutes)
            JMP SHORT OUT2
ELSE2:
                      MOV       DX,OFFSET MESO3 ;Message timer (seconds)
OUT2:
            CALL      MESSAGE                 ;Output message
            CALL      KEYBD                   ;Read response
            MOV       AL,BUFFLN               ;No. characters read
            MOV       AH,0
            MOV       SI,0                    ;Init. index count
            PUSH      CX                      ;Reuse count index
            MOV       CX,AX                   ;Load new count
                                              ;
DO5:
                      MOV       AL,CHAR[SI]   ;Transfer input to ASC
                      MOV       ASC[SI],AL
                      INC       SI
            LOOP DO5

            POP       CX                      ;Recall outer loop index
            CALL      ASCDEC                  ;Convert ASCII to int. decimal
            MOV       AX,BINV                 ;Load result in AX
            MOV       AH,0                    ;Clear AH, result less 256
                                              ;
            CMP     CX,1
            JNE ELSE7
                      MOV       MINUT,AL      ;Save minute setting
            JMP SHORT OUT7
ELSE7:
                      MOV       SECOND,AL     ;Save seconds settind
OUT7:
            LOOP DO1
                                              ;
            TIMECL                            ;Zero out time.   MACRO
                                              ;
            MOV       AL,3AH                  ;" : "
            MOV       MESO5[5],AL             ;Colon in output message
            MOV       AH,2                    ;Read timer
            INT       1AH
                                              ;
            MOV       X,CL                    ;Convert BCD min. to decimal
            CALL      BCDDEC
            MOV       CL,X
            MOV       X,DH                    ;Convert BCD sec. to decimal
            CALL      BCDDEC
            MOV       DH,X
            MOV       SEC1,DH
                                              ;
DO11:
                                              ;
            MOV       TT,DH                   ;Load seconds
            MOV       TT[1],CL                ;Load minutes
            MOV       CX,2                    ;Loop count
            MOV       SI,0                    ;Start with seconds
            MOV       DI,7                    ;Output message byte position
```

Figure 6.12 (*Continued*)

```
      DO12:
                    MOV       DH,0              ;Clear upper input to DECASC
                    MOV       DL,TT[SI]         ;Lower input to DECASC
                    MOV       BINV,DX           ;Load DECASC input
                    CALL      DECASC
                    MOV       AL,ASC[5]         ;ASCII conversion
                    MOV       MESO5[DI],AL      ;Output message
                    MOV       AL,ASC[4]         ;Second ASCII digit
                    MOV       MESO5[DI-1],AL    ;Second digit in output
                    INC       SI
                    SUB       DI,3
                  LOOP DO12
                                                ;
                                                ;
                    MOV       AH,2              ;Read timer
                    INT       1AH
                                                ;
                    MOV       X,CL              ;Convert BCD min. to decimal
                    CALL      BCDDEC
                    MOV       CL,X
                    MOV       X,DH              ;Convert BCD sec. to decimal
                    CALL      BCDDEC
                    MOV       DH,X
                    CMP       DH,SEC1
                    JE IF14
                    PUSH      AX
                    PUSH      BX
                    PUSH      CX
                    PUSH      DX
                    MOV       DX,OFFSET MESO5   ;Timer output
                    CALL      MESSAGE
                    POP       DX
                    POP       CX
                    POP       BX
                    POP       AX
      IF14:
                                                ;
                    MOV       SEC1,DH
                                                ;
                    MOV       BH,CL             ;Load minutes in upper BX
                    MOV       BL,DH             ;Load seconds in lower BX
                    MOV       AH,MINUT          ;Load timed minutes in upper AX
                    MOV       AL,SECOND         ;Load times seconds in lower AX
                    CMP       BX,AX
                  JNGE DO11
                  PUSH      CX
                  PUSH      DX
                  MOV       DX,OFFSET MESO4     ;End timer operation
                  CALL      MESSAGE
                  POP       DX
                  POP       CX
                                                ;
                                                ;
                  RET
      TIMER       ENDP
      CSEG        ENDS
                  END       TIMER
```

Figure 6.12 (*Continued*)

glance at the CALL instructions tells the user what function is to be accomplished. Macros, on the other hand, replace a macro call with expanded code during assembly. All in all, the goal of reducing code complexity and increasing code modularity can be achieved reasonably, using macros. The ASCII to decimal (ASCDEC) and decimal to ASCII (DECASC) routines are procedure equivalents for the corresponding macros. Message output (MESSAGE), keyboard read (KEYBD),

```
PAGE       55,132
TITLE      BCDDEC  - BCD TO DECIMAL CONVERSION (BCDDEC.ASM)
;
;          DESCRIPTION: This procedure takes a 2 digit BCD
;          number in X and returns its decimal value in X.
;
EXTRN      X:BYTE
;
CSEG       SEGMENT PARA PUBLIC 'CODE'
           PUBLIC  BCDDEC
BCDDEC     PROC    FAR
           ASSUME  CS:CSEG
                                              ;
           PUSH    DS
                                              ;
           PUSH    CX                         ;Preserve reg.
           PUSH    AX
           PUSH    BX
           PUSH    DX
           MOV     BL,X                       ;Load BCD value
           MOV     BH,X                       ;Load BCD value
           AND     BL,00001111B               ;Mask 1's digit
           AND     BH,11110000B               ;Mask 10's digit
           MOV     CL,4                       ;Shift bit count
           SHR     BH,CL                      ;BH contains shifted 10's digit
           MOV     AX,0                       ;Clear multiplicand
           MOV     AL,BH                      ;Load lower reg.
           MOV     CX,10                      ;Multiplier for 10's digit
           MUL     CX                         ;Multiply by 10 (10's digit)
           ADD     BL,AL                      ;Calc. decimal equivalent
           MOV     X,BL
           POP     DX
           POP     BX
           POP     AX
           POP     CX
                                              ;
           POP     DS
                                              ;
           RET
BCDDEC     ENDP
CSEG       ENDS
           END
```

Figure 6.13   The procedure BCDDEC for converting two-digit BCD to internal decimal.

```
Input timer interval (seconds)

3
Input timer interval (minutes)

0
    0: 0



    0: 1



    0: 2


End timer interval
```

Figure 6.14   Typical interactive session with TIMER.EXE that illustrates screen features for three-second time interval.

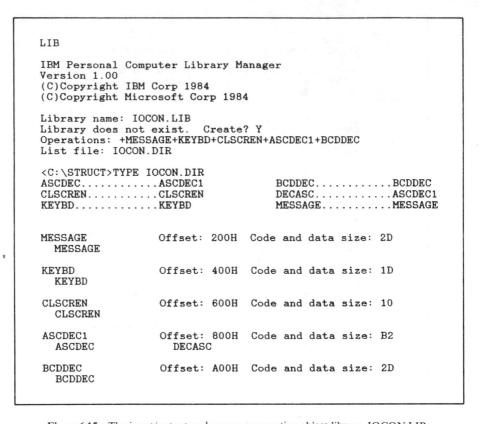

```
LIB

IBM Personal Computer Library Manager
Version 1.00
(C)Copyright IBM Corp 1984
(C)Copyright Microsoft Corp 1984

Library name: IOCON.LIB
Library does not exist.   Create? Y
Operations: +MESSAGE+KEYBD+CLSCREN+ASCDEC1+BCDDEC
List file: IOCON.DIR

<C:\STRUCT>TYPE IOCON.DIR
ASCDEC...........ASCDEC1              BCDDEC...........BCDDEC
CLSCREN..........CLSCREN              DECASC...........ASCDEC1
KEYBD............KEYBD                MESSAGE..........MESSAGE


MESSAGE              Offset: 200H  Code and data size: 2D
   MESSAGE

KEYBD               Offset: 400H  Code and data size: 1D
   KEYBD

CLSCREN             Offset: 600H  Code and data size: 10
   CLSCREN

ASCDEC1             Offset: 800H  Code and data size: B2
   ASCDEC                  DECASC

BCDDEC              Offset: A00H  Code and data size: 2D
   BCDDEC
```

Figure 6.15   The input/output and conversion routine object library, IOCON.LIB.

and screen clear (CLSCREN) procedures have all been discussed earlier. These procedures have been included with BCDDEC in a new object library called IOCON.LIB, for I/O and conversion. Figure 6.15 illustrates the contents of this library.

6.3.4 Waveform Analysis

This program presents an additional example of structures and macros. The basic program reads a signal-to-noise (SNR) ratio value and a signal frequency and generates a waveform consisting of signal plus additive Gaussian noise. This is then plotted. Figure 6.16 presents the .ASM file for the waveform analysis. The module is called RTWAVE.

The data segment contains several variable definitions which bear explanation. The array SNR1 is a look-up table which translates an input signal-to-noise ratio (SNR) into a multiplier. The input SNR must be specified as an integer value between 0 and 20dB. The value contained in SNR1 is the voltage equivalent of this

```
      PAGE      55,132
      TITLE     RTWAVE  - REAL TIME WAVEFORM (RTWAVE.ASM)
      ;
      ;         DESCRIPTION: This program reads in the SNR and frequency
      ;         of a waveform and plots a representative output
      ;         based on corruption with random Gaussian noise.
      ;
      IF1
                INCLUDE MAC4LIB.LIB
      ENDIF
      ;
      EXTRN     SIG:FAR,MESSAGE:FAR,KEYBD:FAR,TICK11:FAR,BOX11:FAR
      EXTRN     LABEL1:FAR,WFPLT:FAR,CLSCREN:FAR,GRAND:FAR,ASCDEC:FAR
      ;
      STACK     SEGMENT PARA STACK 'STACK'
                DB      64 DUP('STACK    ')
      STACK     ENDS
      ;
      DATA      SEGMENT PARA PUBLIC 'DATA'
                PUBLIC  SY,SNR1,SNR,FREQ,FT,XN,NN,SN,BUFFMX,BUFFLN,CHAR
                PUBLIC  ASC,BINV,CCOUNT,COUNT,COUNT1,COUNT2,COUNT3,BASE
                PUBLIC  BLANK,XBEG,XEND,YBEG,YEND,XB,XE,YB,YE,XT,YT,XMAX
                PUBLIC  XMIN,YMAX,YMIN,X,Y,TABLE1,TABLE2,STARTX,STARTY
                PUBLIC  YPOS,XPOS,DDIVIS,XINC,SIGN
      ;
      SY        DW      ?                       ;Graph scale factor
      SNR1      DB      10,11,13,14,16,18,20,22,25,28
                DB      32,35,40,45,50,56,63,71,79,89,100 ;0-20dB factor
      SIGN      DB      ?                       ;Sign of cosine used by SIGNAL
      SNR       DB      ?
      FREQ      DW      ?
      XN        DW      129 DUP(' ')            ;Signal values - word quantity
      NN        DW      129 DUP(' ')            ;Noise values - word quantities
      SN        DW      129 DUP(' ')            ;Waveform values
      FT        DW      ?                       ;Frequency x time
      XINC      DW      ?                       ;X-axis increment
                                                ;
      MESO1     DB      'Input frequency 0-5 kHz. ','$'
      MESO2     DB      'Input SNR in integer dB (0-20dB max).','$'
      MESO3     DB      'Input title (30 char.)','$'
                                                ;
      SCALE     DW      37,41,48,52,60,67,74,82,93,104
                DW      119,130,148,167,185,208,233,263,293,330,370
                                                ;
      BUFFMX    DB      80
      BUFFLN    DB      ?
      CHAR      DB      80 DUP(' '),'$'
                                                ;
      ASC       DB      80 DUP(' '),'$'
      BINV      DW      ?
      CCOUNT    DW      ?
      BASE      DW      ?
      BLANK     DB      ' '
                                                ;Corners box
      XBEG      DW      75
      XEND      DW      285
      YBEG      DW      25
      YEND      DW      175
```

Figure 6.16 The main calling program RTWAVE.ASM, which reads signal-to-noise and frequency and plots the resulting waveform, corrupted by Gaussian noise.

```
XB        DW        ?                                    ;XBEG parameter for box & ticks
XE        DW        ?                                    ;XEND parameter for box & ticks
YB        DW        ?                                    ;YBEG parameter for box & ticks
YE        DW        ?                                    ;YEND parameter for box & ticks
XT        DW        145,215                              ;X-axis ticks
YT        DW        100                                  ;Y-axis ticks
XMAX      DW        77                                   ;Y-axis tick limit (max)
XMIN      DW        73                                   ;Y-axis tick limit (min)
YMAX      DW        177                                  ;X-axis tick limit (max)
YMIN      DW        173                                  ;X-axis tick limit (min)
X         DW        0                                    ;Dummy
Y         DW        0                                    ;Dummy
COUNT     DW        2                                    ;Number X-axis ticks
TABLE1    DB        31 DUP(' ')                          ;Title
COUNT1    DW        ?                                    ;Count title characters
STARTX    DW        ?                                    ;Start X-axis title
STARTY    DW        0
XPOS      DB        3,3,3,8,17,26,35
YPOS      DB        3,13,22,24,24,24,24
                                                         ;
TABLE2    DB        ' ','1','.','0'
          DB        ' ','0','.','0'
          DB        '-','1','.','0'
          DB        ' ','0','.','0'
          DB        ' ','3','.','5'
          DB        ' ','7','.','0'
          DB        '1','0','.','5'
                                                 ;
COUNT2    DW        4                            ;Number characters in numeral
COUNT3    DW        6                            ;Number characters in plot
DDIVIS    DW        105                          ;Number X-intervals
                                                 ;
DATA      ENDS
                                                 ;
CSEG      SEGMENT PARA PUBLIC 'CODE'
WAVE      PROC      FAR
          ASSUME    CS:CSEG,DS:DATA,SS:STACK
          PUSH      DS
          SUB       AX,AX
          PUSH      AX
                                                 ;
          MOV       AX,SEG DATA
          MOV       DS,AX
                                                 ;
          CALL      CLSCREN                      ;Clear screen
          MOV       CX,2                         ;Count for reads
DO1:
          CMP       CX,1
          JNE ELSE1
          MOV       DX,OFFSET MESO2 ;Read SNR
          JMP SHORT IF1
ELSE1:
          MOV       DX,OFFSET MESO1 ;Read frequency
IF1:
          CALL      MESSAGE                      ;Output message
          CALL      KEYBD                        ;Read keyboard
          MOV       AL,BUFFLN                    ;Number characters read
          MOV       AH,0                         ;Clear upper register
          MOV       SI,0                         ;Initialize index
          PUSH      CX
          MOV       CX,AX                        ;Load inner loop count
```

Figure 6.16 (*Continued*)

```
DO5:
                MOV     AL,CHAR[SI]         ;Transfer input to ASC
                MOV     ASC[SI],AL
                INC     SI
        LOOP DO5
        POP     CX                          ;Recall outer loop index
        MOV     AX,0                        ;Clear AX
        CALL    ASCDEC                      ;ASCII to int. decimal
        MOV     AX,BINV                     ;Load result in AX
        CMP     CX,1
        JNE ELSE2
                MOV     SI,AX               ;Pointer to SNR array
                MOV     AL,SNR1[SI]         ;SNR byte quantity
                MOV     SNR,AL              ;Save SNR
                MOV     AX,SI               ;Convert to word index
                MOV     BX,2
                MOV     DX,0                ;Clear upper register
                MUL     BX
                MOV     SI,AX               ;SI now word index
                MOV     AX,SCALE[SI]
                MOV     SY,AX               ;Graph scale factor
        JMP SHORT IF2
ELSE2:
                MOV     FREQ,AX             ;Save frequency (0-10kHz)
IF2:
        LOOP DO1                            ;Generate 129 cosines
        MOV     DX,0
        MOV     BX,10                       ;Scale frequency - low freq.
                                            ;end loses significance
        MOV     AX,FREQ                     ;Load frequency
        DIV     BX                          ;Sacle by 10
        MOV     BX,36                       ;scaled by 360 degrees
        MOV     DX,0                        ;Clear upper register
        MUL     BX                          ;Multiply by degree factor
        MOV     DX,0                        ;Clear upper register
        MOV     BX,100                      ;Scale factor:10(-4) seconds
        DIV     BX                          ;Get proper scaling
        MOV     FT,AX                       ;Save frequency x time
        MOV     CX,129                      ;Loop count
        MOV     SI,0                        ;Initialize index
        MOV     DI,0
DO11:
                INC     DI
                CALL    SIG                 ;Generate signal
                ADD     SI,2                ;Increment word index
        LOOP DO11
        MOV     SI,0                        ;Init. index
        MOV     CX,129                      ;Loop count
        MOV     AX,4096                     ;Load random number seed
DO13:
                PUSH    CX                  ;Save loop count
                CALL    GRAND               ;Gaussian random number
                MOV     NN[SI],CX           ;Save noise
                ADD     SI,2                ;Increment word index
                POP     CX                  ;Recall loop count
        LOOP DO13
                                            ;Add XN and NN taking into
                                            ;account sign bit
        MOV     CX,128                      ;Loop count
        MOV     SI,0                        ;Initialize index
;       (DO     LONG)                       ;Difficult to reduce (LONG)
```

Figure 6.16 (*Continued*)

```
DO15:
                PUSH    CX                      ;Save loop count
                MOV     CL,15                   ;Shift count
                MOV     AX,XN[SI]               ;Load signal AX
                SHR     AX,CL                   ;Clear all but sign bit
                CMP     AX,1                    ;Look for sign bit set
           JNE ELSE3
                MOV     AX,NN[SI]               ;Load noise
                SHR     AX,CL                   ;Clear all but sign bit
                CMP     AX,1                    ;Look for sign bit set
                JNE ELSE4
                    SHL     XN[SI],1            ;Clear sign
                    SHR     XN[SI],1
                    SHL     NN[SI],1            ;Clear sign
                    SHR     NN[SI],1
                    MOV     AX,XN[SI]
                    MOV     BX,NN[SI]
                    ADD     AX,BX               ;Add signal and noise
                    OR      AX,8000H            ;Result negative
                JMP SHORT IF4
ELSE4:
                    MOV     AX,XN[SI]
                    SHL     AX,1                ;Clear sign
                    SHR     AX,1
                    CMP     AX,NN[SI]
                    JNGE ELSE5
                        SUB     AX,NN[SI]
                        OR      AX,8000H ;Negative result
                    JMP SHORT IF5
ELSE5:
                        SUB     NN[SI],AX
                        MOV     AX,NN[SI]
IF5:
IF4:
           JMP SHORT IF3
ELSE3:
                                                ;Positive signal
                MOV     AX,NN[SI]
                SHR     AX,CL                   ;Clear all but sign bit
                CMP     AX,1
                JNE ELSE6
                    MOV     AX,NN[SI]
                    SHL     AX,1                ;Clear sign bit
                    SHR     AX,1
                    CMP     AX,XN[SI]
                    JNGE ELSE7
                        SUB     AX,XN[SI]
                        OR      AX,8000H ;Negative result
                    JMP SHORT IF7
ELSE7:
                        SUB     XN[SI],AX
                        MOV     AX,XN[SI]
IF7:
                JMP SHORT IF6
ELSE6:
                    MOV     AX,XN[SI]
                    ADD     AX,NN[SI]
```

Figure 6.16 (*Continued*)

```
IF6:
IF3:
            MOV     DX,AX           ;Save value
            MOV     CL,15           ;Shift-check negative number
            SHR     AX,CL
            CMP     AX,1            ;Negative if equal
            JNE ELSE8
                MOV     AX,DX       ;Reload AX
                SHL     AX,1        ;Clear sign bit
                SHR     AX,1
                MOV     BX,SY       ;Scale result
                MOV     DX,0        ;Clear upper register
                DIV     BX
                MOV     SN[SI],AX   ;Save signal
                OR      SN[SI],8000H ;Set sign bit
            JMP SHORT IF8
ELSE8:
                MOV     AX,DX       ;Reload AX
                MOV     BX,SY       ;Scale result
                MOV     DX,0        ;Clear upper register
                DIV     BX
                MOV     SN[SI],AX
IF8:
                                    ;
            MOV     AX,SN[SI]       ;Reduce by 3dB because summed
            MOV     CL,15           ;Shift count
            SHR     AX,CL           ;Clear all but sign bit
            CMP     AX,1            ;Check for negative number
            JNE ELSE9
                MOV     AX,SN[SI]   ;Negative waveform
                SHL     AX,1        ;Clear sign bit
                SHR     AX,1
                MOV     DX,0        ;Clear upper register
                MOV     BX,2        ;Divisor
                DIV     BX
                MOV     SN[SI],AX   ;Save adjusted waveform
                OR      SN[SI],8000H ;Set sign bit
            JMP SHORT IF9
ELSE9:
                MOV     AX,SN[SI]   ;Reduce by 3dB because summed
                MOV     DX,0        ;Clear upper register
                MOV     BX,2        ;Divisor
                DIV     BX
                MOV     SN[SI],AX   ;Save reduced value
IF9:
            POP     CX
            DEC     CX              ;Decrement loop count
            ADD     SI,2            ;Increment word index
            CMP     CX,0            ;Compare with zero
;           (ENDDO   E,LONG)
            JE OUT1
            JMP DO15
OUT1:
            MOV     DX,OFFSET MESO3 ;Read title
            CALL    MESSAGE         ;Output request
            CALL    KEYRD           ;Read input
            MOV     AX,WORD PTR BUFFLN ;Save title length
            MOV     AH,0            ;Clear upper register
            MOV     COUNT1,AX       ;COUNT1 used by LABEL1
            MOV     DL,BUFFLN       ;Load title character count
```

Figure 6.16 (*Continued*)

```
                MOV     DH,0                    ;Clear DH
                MOV     SI,DX                   ;Length input string
                LEA     BX,CHAR                 ;Load effective address buffer
                MOV     AH,BLANK                ;Put  blank  in AH
                MOV     BYTE PTR [BX+SI],AH     ;Replace carriage return
                MOV     SI,0                    ;Initialize index
        DO38:
                    MOV     AL,CHAR[SI]
                    MOV     TABLE1[SI],AL       ;Save title
                    INC     SI
                    CMP     SI,DX               ;Compare index with count
                JNGE DO38
                                                ;
                CALL    CLSCREN                 ;Clear screen
                                                ;Load box corner parameters
                MOV     AX,XBEG
                MOV     XB,AX
                MOV     AX,XEND
                MOV     XE,AX
                MOV     AX,YBEG
                MOV     YB,AX
                MOV     AX,YEND
                MOV     YE,AX
                                                ;
                CALL    BOX11                   ;Draw box on screen
                                                ;
                                                ;Reload corner parameters
                MOV     AX,XBEG
                MOV     XB,AX
                MOV     AX,XEND
                MOV     XE,AX
                MOV     AX,YBEG
                MOV     YB,AX
                MOV     AX,YEND
                MOV     YE,AX
                                                ;
                CALL    TICK11                  ;Tick marks
                                                ;
                TITLEL  COUNT1                  ;Plot title. MACRO
                CALL    LABEL1                  ;Plot labels
                MOV     CX,105                  ;Load loop count
                MOV     SI,0
                CALL    WFPLT                   ;Plot waveforms
                SCDEL                           ;MACRO to delay screen
                RT80M                           ;MACRO return to 80 x 25
                                                ;
                RET
        WAVE    ENDP
        CSEG    ENDS
                END     WAVE
```

Figure 6.16 (*Continued*)

SNR scaled by 10. The scaling by 10 insures that two significant digits will be retained. The relationship between signal power and voltage amplitude is

$$S = 20 \log_{10}(V)$$

where S is in dBV and V is the voltage amplitude. Since we plan to use a noise power value from GRAND (see in Chapter 4) which has unity variance, the signal-to-noise ratio will be

$$\text{SNR} = 20 \log_{10}[(V)/(\sigma_{\text{noise}} = 1)]$$

$$= 20 \log_{10}(V)$$

For SNR = 3dB, for example, $V - 1.413$ and multiplying by 10 and rounding yields SNR1 = 14 for this case.

A second look-up table presented in the data segment is the plotter scaling. For all graphics, the output is normalized so that each SNR input yields similar processes on the graph. Given the noise alone, the output from GRAND spans the integer range −2,752 to 2,752. Graphically this translates to a point range of −75 to 75; hence, a scale factor of 37 joins these two scales. If noise were plotted by itself the output of GRAND would need to be divided by 37 to match the screen range of −75 to 75. In actuality, the signal power effectively doubles this value so a division by 2 is made. For SNR = 20dB, the unnormalized plot range is −27,520 × 2 to 27,520 × 2; hence the waveform value must be divided further by 370 (37 × 10) to obtain a normalized value. The array SCALE contains all these normalized values.

The signal to be corrupted by noise is a sinusoid and satisfies

$$x_n = S \cos(2\pi f t_0 n)$$

where t_0 is the time base; f, the frequency; and n, the iteration number. The frequency is to be read during the interactive session ($t_0 = 0.10$ milliseconds). The factor "two pi" does not appear in the program because we use the look-up table from COSSIN (Chapter 4) which takes values directly in degrees rather than radians. This signal value is saved in the array XN. Similarly, the noise values are saved in the array NN.

Also defined in the data segment are the I/O buffer for message input and the associated output messages. Finally, the last portion of the data segment is devoted to variables used in defining the plot output (box corners, tick marks, title and label positions, and so on).

The first procedure call is to clear the screen (CLSCREEN). This is followed by a loop structure. The loop count (CX) is set to two which serves to read in the two needed parameters, SNR and frequency. This outer DO structure contains an inner DO and several IF structures. Its function is to read in parameters from the keyboard and load two variables, SNR and SY, from the look-up tables. When CX = 1, the SNR is read and when CX = 2 the frequency is input. Following this initial setup of input parameters, the arrays XN and NN are loaded.

In order to load the signal array, the phase (frequency times time) in degrees is set up and the procedure SIG called. SIG, in turn, calls COSSIN which returns a cosine value. This is multiplied by an appropriate signal level to define XN. The sign of XN and NN is determined by whether bit 15 is set or not. Suitable bookkeeping is provided to handle this sign bit and insure that signed arithmetic is carried out correctly. The program is set up to generate 129 values of signal, noise, and waveform. Once the signal values are generated using SIG, the noise values are generated using GRAND. All the needed routines for producing the Gaussian random output are contained in MATHLIB.LIB, as is the sine and cosine generator, COSSIN, which is also used by GRAND.

The code which adds XN and NN for 128 of the values is contained within another DO structure. This structure uses an unconditional jump to achieve a LONG return to the start label. We considered placing this addition in a special purpose procedure; however, it is just as easily grasped as part of the main program code. Essentially, the code must consider a negative or positive signal added to negative or positive noise. This naturally breaks down into four blocks of code where each possibility is considered. In the program, negative signal is added to negative noise first. Next, negative signal and positive noise are considered. Third, positive signal and negative noise are added, and the last portion of the code adds positive signal to positive noise. In two of the additions, the result can be positive or negative depending on which quantity is greater. The logic considers all these possibilities based on the setting of the sign bit and appropriate IF structures. Finally, the resulting summed waveform is reduced by 3dB for normalization.

```
PAGE      55,132
TITLE     SIGNAL   - THIS PROCEDURE CALCULATES SIGNAL (SIGNAL.ASM)
;
;         DESCRIPTION: Procedure accepts a frequency x time (x360)
;         in AX (degrees) and calculates a signal which is
;         returned in the array XN.
;
EXTRN     SNR:BYTE,FT:WORD,XN:WORD,COSSIN:FAR,SIGN:BYTE
;
CSEG      SEGMENT PARA PUBLIC 'CODE'
          PUBLIC  SIG
SIG       PROC    FAR
          ASSUME  CS:CSEG
                                                  ;
          PUSH    DS
          PUSH    CX
          MOV     AX,FT
          MOV     DX,0
          MUL     DI                      ;Calculate phasor
          PUSH    DI
          PUSH    SI
          CMP     AX,360                  ;Determine quadrant
          JLE IF1
                  MOV     CX,AX           ;Save input
                  MOV     BX,360          ;Divisor
                  MOV     DX,0            ;Clear upper register
                  DIV     BX              ;Truncated multiplier
                  MOV     BX,AX           ;Get multiplier
                  MOV     DX,0            ;Clear upper register
                  MOV     AX,360
                  MUL     BX              ;Integer x 360
                  SUB     CX,AX           ;One of 4 quadrants
                  XCHG    AX,CX           ;Swap
IF1:
          CALL    COSSIN                  ;Get cosine
                                          ;
          MOV     DX,CX                   ;Save cosine
          MOV     AX,CX                   ;Work variable for cosine
          MOV     CL,15                   ;Shift 15 bits
          SHR     AX,CL                   ;Clear all but sign bit
          CMP     AX,1
          JE ELSE1
                  MOV     AL,0            ;Set SIGN = 0 for positive
                  MOV     SIGN,AL
          JMP SHORT IF2
```

Figure 6.17 The procedure SIG which generates a sinusoidal signal based on frequency × time (FT).

```
    ELSE1:
                    MOV       AL,1                     ;Set SIGN = 1 for negative
                    MOV       SIGN,AL
    IF2:
                    MOV       CX,DX                    ;Recall cosine
                    SHL       CX,1                     ;Clear sign bit
                    SHR       CX,1
                    MOV       AX,CX
                    MOV       BX,100                   ;Scale O(100)
                    MOV       DX,0                     ;Clear upper register
                    DIV       BX
                    MOV       BX,275                   ;Scale by 275
                    MOV       DX,0
                    MUL       BX                       ;O(27500)
                    MOV       BX,100
                    MOV       DX,0
                    DIV       BX                       ;O(275)
                    MOV       BL,SNR                   ;Load SNR
                    MOV       BH,0                     ;Clear upper register
                    MOV       DX,0
                    MUL       BX                       ;O(27500 max)
                                                       ;
                    POP       SI
                    CMP       SIGN,1                   ;Check for negative number
                    MOV       XN[SI],AX                ;Save signal
                    JNE IF3
                        OR    XN[SI],8000H             ;If negative set sign bit
    IF3:
                    POP       DI
                    POP       CX
                    POP       DS
                                                       ;
                    RET
    SIG             ENDP
    CSEG            ENDS
                    END
```

Figure 6.17 (*Continued*)

Following generation of the waveform SN, the program sets up the screen for plotting and graphs the result. First, the graph title is read from the keyboard. Next the screen is cleared and a box drawn with tick marks using BOX11 and TICK11 from GRAPHLIB.LIB. Initially, a macro library MAC4LIB.LIB was loaded. This library contains only the macros TITLEL, SCDEL, and RT80M from MAC1LIB.LIB. These macros are rather short, and since they are now expanded outside any structures, they do not affect the length of code between conditional branches.

Following the generating of the box and tick marks, the title is displayed using TITLEL. Then the graph labels are displayed using the procedure LABEL1 which must be linked separately. This procedure has not been included as part of GRAPHLIB.LIB. Once the labels are generated, the procedure WFPLT is called to plot the waveform. In this program 105 values are plotted for a total displayed time of 10.5 milliseconds. Finally, the screen delay macro SCDEL and return to 80 × 25 mode macro, RT80M, are used before returning to DOS.

Figure 6.17 illustrates the procedure SIG which generates the signal values. This procedure initially takes the phasor input and reduces it to one of the four possible quadrants between 0 and 360 degrees. An IF structure is used to accomplish this. Note the use of the XCHG instructions. Following the call to COSSIN, the resulting cosine value must be appropriately scaled. This value is too large by 10,000. For 0dB the output value should scale to $-2,750$ to 2,750 and for 20dB (the maximum SNR considered) the scaled value will be from $-27,500$ to 27,500 (remember the cosine falls in the range -1 to 1).

Figure 6.18 presents the procedure WFPLT. This procedure uses a number of IF structures to set up and graph the points contained in SN. The routine does not call CONNL1 but simply connects each positive and negative point with a vertical line using the procedure LINEVV. LINEVV (and LINEHH) is an added procedure

```
PAGE      55,132
TITLE     WFPLT   - WAVEFORM PLOT ROUTINE (WFPLT.ASM)
;
;         DESCRIPTION: This procedure uses LINEV to graph
;         the waveform.  It notes whether the points are
;         positive or negative.
;
EXTRN     DDIVIS:WORD,XEND:WORD,XBEG:WORD,YBEG:WORD,YEND:WORD
EXTRN     XB:WORD,XE:WORD,YB:WORD,YE:WORD,X:WORD,SN:WORD
EXTRN     XINC:WORD,LINEVV:FAR
;
CSEG      SEGMENT PARA PUBLIC 'CODE'
          PUBLIC  WFPLT
WFPLT     PROC    FAR
          ASSUME  CS:CSEG
                                                  ;
          PUSH    DS
                                                  ;
          MOV     AX,XEND                 ;Load interval end point
          SUB     AX,XBEG                 ;Calc. X-interval
          MOV     DX,0
          MOV     BX,DDIVIS               ;Load no. X-intervals
          DIV     BX
          MOV     XINC,AX                 ;Save X-increment
                                                  ;
          MOV     AX,XBEG
          MOV     X,AX
          MOV     SI,0
DO1:
          PUSH    CX
          MOV     AX,SN[SI]
          MOV     CL,15
          SHR     AX,CL                   ;Clear all but sign bit
          CMP     AX,0
          JNE ELSE2
              MOV     AX,SN[SI]           ;Positive number
              MOV     BX,100              ;100=center graph coords.
              SUB     BX,AX
              CMP     BX,100              ;Check for zero signal
              JE ELSE1
                  MOV     YB,BX
                  MOV     BX,100
                  MOV     YE,BX
                  CALL    LINEVV
              JMP· SHORT IF2
```

Figure 6.18   The procedure WFPLT which plots points between 0 and some positive or negative amplitude. This routine uses LINEVV to connect the points.

```
ELSE1:
                        MOV       CX,X              ;Write dot
                        MOV       DX,100            ;Dot corresponds to "zero"
                        MOV       AH,12
                        MOV       AL,1              ;Attribute 1
                        INT       10H
        IF2:
                JMP SHORT IF3
        ELSE2:
                        MOV       AX,SN[SI]         ;Negative number
                        SHL       AX,1
                        SHR       AX,1              ;Clear sign bit
                        MOV       BX,100
                        ADD       AX,BX
                        CMP       AX,100            ;Check for negative "zero"
                        JE ELSE3
                        MOV       YB,BX
                        MOV       YE,AX
                        CALL      LINEVV
                JMP SHORT IF4
        ELSE3:
                        MOV       CX,X              ;Write dot
                        MOV       DX,100            ;Dot corresponds to "zero"
                        MOV       AH,12
                        MOV       AL,1              ;Attribute 1
                        INT       10H
        IF4:
        IF3:
                ADD       SI,2                      ;Increment SI word count
                MOV       AX,X
                ADD       AX,XINC
                MOV       X,AX
                POP       CX
            LOOP DO1
                                                    ;
                POP       DS
                RET
WFPLT       ENDP
CSEG        ENDS
            END
```

Figure 6.18 (*Continued*)

appearing in GRAPHLIB.LIB. It is a FAR procedure. The procedure LINEV (and LINEH) is a NEAR procedure and cannot be called from a different code segment module. The procedure LINEVV (along with LINEHH) is illustrated in Figure 6.19. The following procedure generates the linking for RTWAVE.

LINK RTWAVE+WFPLT+SIGNAL+LABEL11

IBM Personal Computer Linker
Version 2.10 (C)Copyright IBM Corp 1981, 1982, 1983

Run File [RTWAVE.EXE]:
List File [NUL.MAP]:
Libraries [.LIB]: GRAPHLIB+MATHLIB+IOCON

```
PAGE 55,132
TITLE LINEVV - FAR PROCEDURE TO DRAW VERT/HOR LINE (LINEVV.ASM)
                                 ;
                                 ;Uses data segment DATA
                                 ;
        EXTRN XBEG:WORD,XEND:WORD,YBEG:WORD,YEND:WORD
        EXTRN X:WORD,Y:WORD
        EXTRN XB:WORD,XE:WORD,YB:WORD,YE:WORD
                                 ;
CSEG    SEGMENT PARA PUBLIC 'CODE'
        PUBLIC LINEVV,LINEHH
LINEHH  PROC    FAR
        ASSUME CS:CSEG
                                 ;This proc generates a hor. line
        MOV DX,Y
        MOV CX,XB                ;Load begin X-value
DO1:    MOV AH,12                ;Write dot
        MOV AL,1                 ;Attribute 1
        INT 10H
        ADD CX,1                 ;Increment X-value
        MOV BX,CX
        SUB BX,XE                ;Check X-value end point
        JNE DO1
        RET
LINEHH  ENDP

                                 ;
LINEVV  PROC    FAR
                                 ;This proc generates a vertical line
        MOV CX,X
        MOV DX,YB                ;Load begin Y-value
DO2:    MOV AH,12                ;Write dot
        MOV AL,1                 ;Attribute 1
        INT 10H
        ADD DX,1                 ;Increment Y-value
        MOV BX,DX
        SUB BX,YE                ;Check Y-value end point
        JNE DO2
        RET
LINEVV  ENDP
                                 ;
CSEG    ENDS
        END
```

Figure 6.19   The FAR procedures LINEVV and LINEHH, used to generate vertical and horizontal lines, respectively.

Graphical output from RTWAVE is illustrated in Figures 6.20, 6.21, and 6.22. These figures present the normalized waveform output for signal-to-noise ratios of 0dB and 20dB at frequencies of 200Hz, 800Hz, and 1600Hz, respectively. As is to be expected, the high signal-to-noise ratio (20dB) demonstrates very little corruption of the sinusoidal signal by the additive noise. At 0dB SNR, however, if the signal and noise power are comparable, a considerable corruption of the signal is evident.

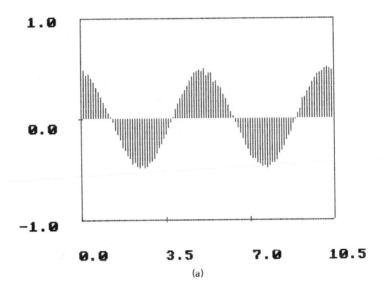

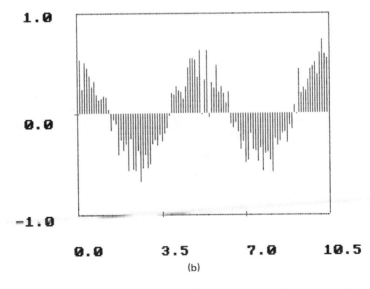

Figure 6.20 Output from RTWAVE.EXE illustrating waveform for signal-to-noise ratios (a) 20dB and (b) 0dB. Time interval plotted is 10.5 milliseconds for 200 Hz.

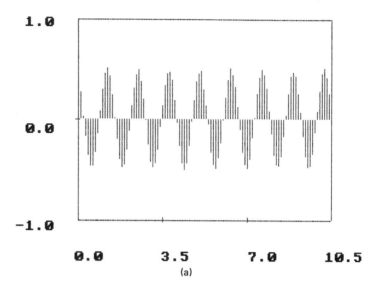

(a)

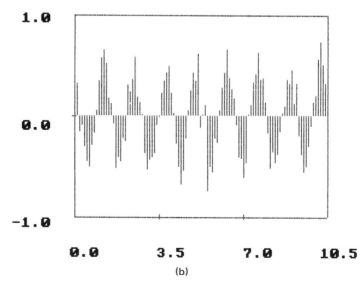

(b)

Figure 6.21   Output from RTWAVE.EXE illustrating waveform for signal-to-noise ratios (a) 20dB and (b) 0dB. Time interval plotted is 10.5 milliseconds for 800 Hz.

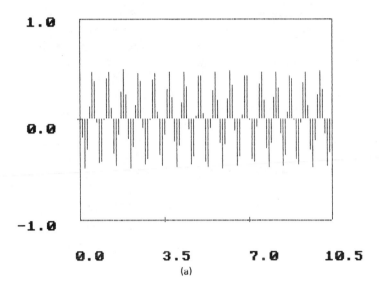

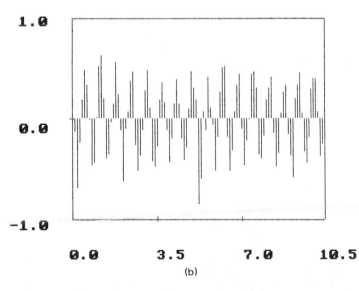

Figure 6.22 Output from RTWAVE.EXE illustrating waveform for signal-to-noise ratios (a) 20dB and (b) 0dB. Time interval plotted is 10.5 milliseconds for 1600 Hz.

6.4 SUMMARY

This chapter has presented the Macro Assembler operators and pseudo-ops. Particular attention was devoted to the macro construction that allows special purpose and repetitive code to be inserted in a source program at assembly time. The disadvantage of macros is that they can expand source code beyond 128 bytes between a conditional jump instruction and the target label. The LOCAL pseudo-op allows the generation of macro labels which are not duplicated during pass 1.

Following the discussion of operators and pseudo-ops, several program examples are presented. These examples are intended to illustrate some of the pseudo-ops, macro libraries, and use of structure constructs. As indicated, this chapter completes the basic description of the Macro Assembler. In Chapter 7 the topic of extended file management, which allows the programmer to perform disk or diskette I/O, is explored. This aspect of assembler programming is essential for establishing a capability to store and access data files. Although not part of the basic 8088 instruction set, coprocessor instructions are provided in the Macro Assembler version 2.0. This is the subject of Chapter 8. Finally, Chapters 9 and 10 address the BIOS and the system hardware.

REFERENCES

1. *Macro Assembler, Version 1.0.* IBM Personal Computer-Computer Language Series. IBM Corp. P.O. Box 1328, Boca Raton, FL 33432 (1981).
2. *Macro Assembler Version 2.00.* IBM Personal Computer Software. IBM Corp. P.O. Box 1328, Boca Raton, FL 33432 (1984).
3. *Macro Assembler Version 2.00 Reference.* IBM Personal Computer Software. IBM Corp. P.O. Box 1328, Boca Raton, FL 33421 (1984).
4. *The Value Line Investment Summary.* Value Line, Inc., 711 Third Ave., New York, NY 10017 (1986).

PROBLEMS

6.1. Write a macro that beeps the speaker.

6.2. Write a macro that clears the screen, prints an error message, and exits the program.

6.3. Write a macro that checks a character and generates an error message when this character is not an ASCII number or minus sign.

6.4. Write a macro to initialize the printer, read status, and output a single character.

6.5. Write a macro that cubes a number.

6.6. Write a macro that calculates a number to the 3/2 power. Note: The number must be less than 65535 when cubed.

6.7. Write a macro that draws a horizontal line from XBEG to XEND; which draws a vertical line from YBEG to YEND. Assume the program is in graphics mode.

6.8. Write a macro that puts the screen in 320 × 200 graphics mode (X = 1) or 640 × 200 graphics model (X = 2).

6.9. Write a macro that generates a line feed to the screen; a carriage return; a line feed and carriage return.

6.10. Write a macro that generates the sine of an angle; the cosine of an angle (for all angles less than or equal to 32768 degrees).

6.11. Write two FAR procedures: DECASC and ASCDEC, that perform decimal-to-ASCII and ASCII-to-decimal conversion. They should reflect the processing indicated in the macros with similar name. These procedures can be called by the linker when generating TIMER.EXE.

7

Extended File Management

Up to now we have had no method for permanently saving and accessing data files under program control. The stock and index data in the previous chapter, for example, were entered into variables in the program data segment. Each new program using this data requires similar entries. It is clearly desirable to be able to generate data files, store them on disk or diskette, and access these files directly from a program during execution. To do this it is necessary to understand extended file management, and that is the purpose of this chapter.

7.1 AN INTRODUCTION TO DISK I/O

The generation of and access to data files or databases have been treated extensively as a topic in database management literature (for example [1–3]). In this section numerical databases are used with simplified approaches to generation and access. The goal of the section is to provide an understanding of disk file management and allow the user to expand on these techniques for particular applications. There are basically two types of file handling that may be employed with the IBM PC, XT, and AT: sequential file handling and random access. Section 7.2 describes the use of sequential file handling. Since the files used in this chapter are numerical data and are relatively short, sequential file handling will be the focus of the discussion. Random access techniques become important when the basic record appearing in the database has more than one field. Also, it is usually necessary to introduce the notion of an index when using random access, because some realization of the database order is required. At the conclusion of this chapter the reader will have an understanding of extended file management and be able to access files sequentially on disk under program control. In keeping with the modular approach to program design, this will greatly expand the programmer's capability to develop complex tasks by breaking them down into smaller tasks and using disk I/O for intermediate storage.

The primary vehicle for accomplishing disk I/O is through the INT 21H function calls. The first approach taken is to use functions 16H (create file), 1AH (fix Disk Transfer Address) 15H (write from Disk Transfer Address), 10H (close file), 14H (read file), and 0FH (open file). The use of these function calls will become clear in the next section. A broader set of function calls employs the notion of a file handle. These calls are not restricted to files in the current directory, and they allow the application program to define the type of access permitted on concurrent files. We shall discuss these function calls as an alternative means for achieving disk I/O.

7.2 SEQUENTIAL DISK FILE MANAGEMENT

Sequential file management implies that all data items in the file are read consecutively one after another. This is exactly what happens. Figure 7.1 illustrates the layout for a typical diskette. There are single-sided and double-sided diskettes. Each side contains forty concentric rings called tracks. These tracks are numbered 0 through 39 with the innermost track being 39. Each track is, in turn, divided into eight sectors numbered 1 though 8, and each sector contains 512 bytes. For some versions of DOS, nine sectors comprise a track. For single-sided diskettes, a total storage capacity of roughly 160K bytes (163,840) is achieved; for double-sided

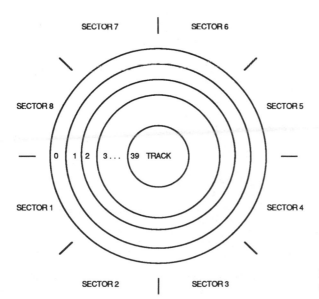

Figure 7.1 Layout for a typical 8 sector diskette showing track numbering.

diskettes, this is roughly 320K bytes; and for diskettes with nine-sector tracks, the storage is roughly 360K bytes.

During formatting, DOS generates directory information and file allocation tables (FAT). The FAT areas and directories allow DOS to keep track of file entries. These entries are, in turn, used by the INT 21H function calls in transparent fashion so that the programmer need only understand the function call to achieve disk or diskette I/O.

The data area is where all user information resides. As indicated above, the function calls avoid any need for actually addressing FATs and directories at the byte level. These functions automatically initiate any FAT or directory entries. This is not to say that the user cannot access the FAT and directories. Some of the more primitive memory accesses do provide for direct user control; however, the usefulness of the INT 21H functions generally does not require such detailed programming.

How then does the programmer set up parameters for disk or diskette I/O? Using the first approach alluded to earlier, two areas must be defined in the data segment called by the routines that accomplish disk I/O. These areas are the File Control Block (FCB) and the Disk Transfer Address (DTA) area. Figure 7.2 presents the structure of the FCB. Both a standard FCB and an extended FCB can be used. In this chapter we will always use the standard FCB. The reader is referred to the *DOS Technical Reference* [4] manual for extended FCB usage. When using the extended FCB, additional registers come into use during the function call.

The first byte of the FCB contains the drive number: 0-default, 1-A, 2-B, and so forth. The next eight bytes contain the file name, and the following three bytes contain the extension. Each write to the disk I/O buffer consists of one record. This

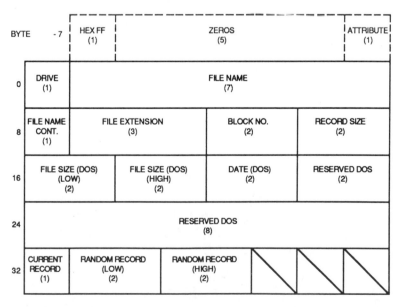

Figure 7.2 File Control Block contiguous byte allocation illustrating placement of file and disk information.

record should be sized large enough to contain all the information associated with a data item. For example, if an individual name requires three bytes and a social security number requires 4 bytes, the record containing both should be at least seven bytes long. A block consists of 128 records. The two bytes following the file extension must contain the block number. This should be initialized to 0 and will be changed by DOS as needed. The two bytes following block number are record size. This is usually set after the file is opened. Both block number and record size are word quantities. (All FCB parameters are defined as byte quantities unless otherwise specified.) The next four bytes are the file size defined by DOS and represent a double word quantity. Following file size is a word quantity for the date, defined by DOS. Next is a ten byte reserved area for use by DOS. The last two areas are associated with record bookkeeping. The first byte in these areas is the current record and should be initialized to zero. This record number is relative within the block. The last double word quantity is used for random access and specifies the relative record number in relation to the beginning of the file. This completes the specification of the FCB area as it must appear in the data segment.

DOS uses the FCB for disk I/O bookkeeping. Some of the parameters appearing in this block are subject to change by DOS during I/O and should be initialized after the file is opened. The program to be presented shortly illustrates this aspect of the FCB. Since the user will probably want to write a general purpose routine that reads a file name and extension, loads these into the FCB, and accomplishes the disk I/O, it is generally useful to load this area initially with blanks.

The Data Transfer Address area is simply an area reserved in memory for transferring data to and from the disk. This area is special and must be allocated with a function call AH = 1AH (using INT 21H). The allocation is done after the file is opened in the following way.

```
      ...
      MOV AH,1AH        ; DTA function call
      LEA DX, DDTA      ; Load DX
      INT 21H
      ...
```

Here the DTA starting address has been chosen to be DDTA, a variable in memory. The DX register must contain the starting address for the DTA when the function call is made. The DTA area in memory must be at least as long as the record length and good programming practice is to make them equivalent.

So far we have said little about the form of the function calls. To see how they are implemented, assume an FCB is defined with the label FCBLB. To create a file the sequence is

```
      ...
      MOV AH,16H        ; Attempt to create file
      LEA DX,FCBLB      ; FCB label
      INT 21H
      ...
```

To write from the DTA the sequence is

```
        ...
        MOV AH,15H          ; Write from DTA
        LEA DX,FCBLB        ; FCB label
        INT 21H
        ...
```

To close the file the sequence is

```
        ...
        MOV AH,10H          ; Close file
        LEA DX,FCBLB        ; FCB label
        INT 21H
        ...
```

To open a file already created the sequence is

```
        ...
        MOV AH,0FH          ; Open file
        LEA DX,FCBLB        ; FCB label
        INT 21H
        ...
```

To read the file the sequence is

```
        ...
        MOV AH,14H          ; Read file
        LEA DX,FCBLB        ; FCB label
        INT 21H
        ...
```

Once the above operations are executed, the programmer may need to act on the outcome. For example, he needs to know if a disk file was opened or written and he needs to know when the end-of-file (EOF) is reached on a disk write. This information is provided through the return values appearing in the registers following the interrupt. Table 7.1 presents the parameter values returned for each of the above disk I/O function calls. In some cases these results will not be checked; however, for such terminators as EOF these are the only way to know a sequential read is complete.

Having sketched the general requirements for sequential disk I/O, it will now be useful to consider some program examples that address the use of extended file management. The first two examples are general programs that create and read files, respectively.

TABLE 7.1 RETURN VALUES FOR
DISK I/O FUNCTION CALLS

Function	Return
0FH	AL = 00H if file opened
	AL = FFH if file not opened
10H	AL = 00H if file is found
	AL = FFH if file is not found
14H	AL = 00H if read successful
	AL = 01H if EOF
	AL = 02H if DTA overflow
	AL = 03H if partial read
15H	AL = 00H if write successful
	AL = 01H if diskette full
	AL = 02H if DTA too small
16H	AL = 00H if file created
	AL = FFH if file not created

7.2.1 How to Create a Disk File

In order to generate a database it is necessary to have a program that reads in values and writes them to disk under a particular filename. If the input value is a number it must, of course, be converted to internal binary before it can be used in a program. If the value is an alphabetic quantity it should be retained in convenient ASCII format. The data that we will input to files are going to be largely numerical and, consequently, the program developed in this subsection reads in numbers, converts them to internal binary, and writes them to a disk under the requested disk filename.

Figure 7.3 presents the main calling program FILOPCR.ASM, which calls three procedures (FILECR, FILEW, CLOSEF) that create the file, write the input data to disk, and close the file, respectively. Figure 7.4 illustrates these three routines and the associated data segment DATACR, which contains the FCB and DTA. These routines were linked with the command

LINK FILOPCR + FILECR

The DTA area begins with the variable DDTA and occupies 4 bytes specified by LLEN. For a record consisting of 1 data word (2 bytes) this allows a margin of 2 bytes per record. As indicated earlier, it will be convenient to also initialize each record to 4 bytes, the DTA size. Assuming, for example, we write 36 data words in a given stock table or index to a file, each stock table or index will occupy 144 bytes on disk with this record size. The LABEL pseudo-op is used to define the beginning of the FCB area, appropriately labeled FCBLB. Next the drive is specified to be drive B (number 2) and both the filename, denoted by NNAME, and extension, denoted by EEXT, are filled with blank characters. These will later be changed when a file name and extension are input to the program. The block designator is initialized to 0, and

```
PAGE 55,132
TITLE FILOPCK - CHECKS DISK FILE I/O ROUTINES (FILOPCK.ASM)
;
;                    DESCRIPTION: This program checks the disk
;                    file routines: FILEOP,FILEW,CLOSEF, and
;                    READF.
;
           EXTRN FILEOP:FAR,FILEW:FAR,CLOSEF:FAR,READF:FAR
           EXTRN FILECR:FAR
                              ;
STACK      SEGMENT PARA STACK 'STACK'
           DB       64 DUP('STACK    ')
STACK      ENDS
                              ;
CSEG       SEGMENT PARA PUBLIC 'CODE'
CFIO       PROC    FAR
           ASSUME   CS:CSEG,SS:STACK
                              ;
           PUSH DS
           SUB AX,AX
           PUSH AX
                              ;
           CALL FILECR        ;Creates disk file
           CALL FILEW         ;Writes disk file
           CALL CLOSEF        ;Closes the disk file
                              ;
           CALL FILEOP        ;Open disk file
           CALL READF         ;Read disk file
           CALL CLOSEF        ;Close disk file
                              ;
           RET
CFIO       ENDP
CSEG       ENDS
           END     CFIO
```

Figure 7.3 The main calling program FILOPCK.ASM, which creates a disk file using a File Control Block.

the first 128 records and the remaining FCB parameters are uninitialized except for the current record number, FECDE1, which is set to 0.

The first procedure illustrated, FILECR, is the procedure that creates the file. This procedure queries the user for a filename and extension, reads these values from the keyboard, and sets NNAME and EEXT, respectively. Having defined the filename and extension, function call 16H is made to create the file. The normal return for this function is to set AL = 0, indicating the file was created. After checking for a normal return, the procedure initializes the record size to four bytes and calls function 1AH to fix the DTA area. Once this is accomplished, DOS knows that the DTA area DDTA will be used to transfer data to disk.

The procedure FILEW accomplishes the actual data write to the disk. This procedure is set up to read numbers from the keyboard and output them to a disk. In this fashion a database can be created from the keyboard. The first action of the procedure, after initializing DS, is to request a number between −32765 and 32765 and read the input. Next the procedure looks for a termination character which has been chosen to be the backslash, (\). If the backslash is found, processing terminates. If a number has been input, it is converted to internal binary with the macro

```
PAGE 55,132
TITLE FILECR - THIS PROCEDURE CREATES DISK FILE(FILECR.ASM)
;                DESCRIPTION: The procedure creates a disk file
;                after querying for the appropriate FCB parameters.
;
IF1
        INCLUDE MAC1LIB.LIB
        INCLUDE MAC2LIB.LIB
ENDIF
                                        ;
DATACR  SEGMENT PARA PUBLIC 'DATA'
LLEN    EQU     4
DDTA    DB      LLEN DUP(' ')                   ;DTA
                                        ;This portion devoted to FCB
FCBLB   LABEL   BYTE
DRIVE   DB      2                       ;Drive B
NNAME   DB      8 DUP(' ')              ;File name definition
EEXT    DB      3 DUP(' ')              ;File extension
BBLOCK  DW      0                       ;Initialize block to 0
RECSZ   DW      ?                       ;Logical record size, initialize after open
FILESZ  DD      ?                       ;DOS File Size (DOS)
DDATE   DW      ?                       ;DOS will get date (DOS)
RESERV  DT      ?                       ;DOS Reserved (DOS)
RECDE1  DB      0                       ;Current record number
RECDE2  DD      ?                       ;Relative record number
                                        ;
                                        ;
MESO1   DB      'Input Disk File Name (8 char. max).   ','$'
MESO2   DB      'Input Disk File Extension (3 char. max).   ','$'
MESO3   DB      'Error on open disk file.   ','$'
MESO4   DB      'Input number (-32765,32765) - "\" terminates.  ','$'
MESO5   DB      6 DUP(' '),'$'
MESO6   DB      'Error on write attempt.  ','$'
                                        ;
BUFFMX  DB      80                      ;Maximum buffer size
BUFFLN  DB      ?
CHAR    DB      80 DUP(' '),'$'
                                        ;
BLANK   DB      ' '
DDATA   DW      128 DUP(' ')
CCOUNT  DW      0
ASC     DB      80 DUP(' ')
BINV    DW      0
BASE    DW      0                       ;Needed for macro
                                        ;
DATACR  ENDS
                                        ;
CFCR    SEGMENT PARA PUBLIC 'CODE'
        PUBLIC FILECR,FILEW,CLOSEF
FILECR  PROC    FAR
        ASSUME CS:CFCR,DS:DATACR
                                        ;
        PUSH DS
                                        ;
        MOV AX,SEG DATACR
        MOV DS,AX
                                        ;
        MESSG 1                         ;Read in filename message (MACRO)
        KEYBD                           ;Actual read from keyboard (MACRO)
        MOV SI,0                        ;Initialize character counter
        MOV CH,0                        ;Clear upper half CX.
        MOV CL,BUFFLN                   ;Character buffer length
```

Figure 7.4   The routines FILCR, FILEW, and CLOSEF that create, write, and close
a file. All routines access the associated data segment DATACR.

```
DO1:
                MOV AL,CHAR[SI]
                MOV NNAME[SI],AL   ;Load character in filename
                INC SI             ;Increment counter
                CMP SI,CX          ;Compare with total characters
        JB DO1
                                   ;
        MESSG 2                    ;Read filename extension (MACRO)
        KEYBD                      ;Actual read (MACRO)
        MOV SI,0                   ;Initialize character count
        MOV CH,0                   ;Clear upper half CX
        MOV CL,BUFFLN              ;Character buffer length
DO2:
                MOV AL,CHAR[SI]    ;Move character to AX
                MOV EEXT[SI],AL    ;Load character in extension
                INC SI
                CMP SI,CX          ;Compare with total character
        JB DO2                     ;Jump if below
                                   ;
        MOV AH,16H                 ;Attempt to create file
        LEA DX,FCBLB               ;FCB label start
        INT 21H
        CMP AL,0
        JNZ ELSE1                  ;Jump on error
                                   ;
                MOV AX,LLEN        ;Initialize record size
                MOV RECSZ,AX       ;FCB size parameter loaded
                LEA DX,DDTA        ;Address of DTA
                MOV AH,1AH         ;Fix DTA address
                INT 21H
        JMP IF1                    ;Jump to continue
                                   ;
ELSE1:
                MESSG 3            ;Error message (MACRO)
                POP DS
                RET
                                   ;
IF1:
        POP DS
        RET
FILECR  ENDP
                                   ;
FILEW   PROC    FAR
;
;               DESCRIPTION: This routine reads and writes numbers
;               to the disk file.
;
        PUSH DS
                                   ;
        MOV AX,SEG DATACR
        MOV DS,AX
                                   ;
DO3:
                MESSG 4            ;Message request input (MACRO)
                KEYBD              ;Actual input (MACRO)
                MOV SI,0           ;Load input pointer
                MOV CH,0
                MOV CL,BUFFLN      ;Buffer length
DO4:
                MOV AL,CHAR[SI]    ;Transfer character from input
                MOV AH,5CH         ;Terminator
                CMP AL,AH          ;Check for terminator: \
```

Figure 7.4 (*Continued*)

```
                    JNE IF2          ;If no terminator continue
                    POP DS
                    RET
       IF2:
                    MOV ASC[SI],AL   ;Load intermediate buffer
                    INC SI
                    CMP SI,CX        ;Compare pointer maximum character
             JB DO4                  ;Jump if more to go
                                     ;
                    ASCDEC BINV,ASC  ;Convert number (MACRO)
                                     ;
                    MOV SI,0         ;Initialize DTA pointer
                    MOV AX,BINV      ;Load decimal number
                    MOV DDTA[SI],AL
                    MOV DDTA[SI+1],AH
                                     ;
                                     ;
                    MOV AH,15H       ;Write from DTA
                    LEA DX,FCBLB
                    INT 21H
                                     ;
                    CMP AL,0         ;Check for error on write
             JNZ OUT1                ;Jump on error
             JMP DO3                 ;Unconditional jump start
       OUT1:
             MESSG 6                 ;Error message
                                     ;
             POP DS
             RET
       FILEW ENDP
                                     ;
       CLOSEF PROC    FAR
       ;
       ;              DESCRIPTION: This procedure closes the file.
       ;
             PUSH DS
                                     ;
             MOV AX,SEG DATACR
             MOV DS,AX
                                     ;
             MOV AH,10H
             LEA DX,FCBLB
             INT 21H
                                     ;
             POP DS
             RET
       CLOSEF ENDP
                                     ;
       CFCR  ENDS
             END     FILECR
```

Figure 7.4 (*Continued*)

ASCDEC. The DTA area is then loaded with the output internal binary value in BINV. Following the loading of the DTA area, function call 15H is made to write the record to disk. At this point DOS writes the record into a disk buffer which is allowed to fill before either the file is closed or the buffer is filled to sector size. When either of these conditions occurs the buffer is written to disk. After the disk write, AL = 0 is returned for a successful write.

Finally, the procedure CLOSEF is called to close the file. This procedure merely calls function 10H and returns to DOS. Using the program FILOPCK, the stock tables and index are created on diskette. Figure 7.5 illustrates a listing of the

```
DIR A:

Volume in drive A has no label
Directory of  A:\

COMMAND   COM   17792  10-20-83   12:00p
TBLDJA    DAT     144   1-01-80   12:03a
TBLIBM    DAT     144   1-01-80   12:06a
TBLDEC    DAT     144   1-01-80   12:09a
TBLHPC    DAT     144   1-01-80   12:11a
TBLSPC    DAT     144   1-01-80   12:14a
TBLSTC    DAT     144   1-01-80   12:16a
TBLDAT    DAT      80   1-01-80   12:02a
        8 File(s)      314368 bytes free
```

Figure 7.5 The data diskette listing illustrating stock and index tables created using FILOPCK.ASM.

data diskette containing these files. The time and date were based on DOS default values and each file consists of 144 bytes of data (36 stock or index values times 4 bytes per record). Now it will be useful to consider a program which reads a general disk file.

7.2.2 How to Read a Disk File

Figure 7.6 contains the main calling program FILOPRD.ASM that reads a disk file and loads the calling program data segment variable array DDATA1 with these data values. The procedure FILEOP opens the file, READF reads the file, and CLOSE1 closes the file. At this point, the data is stored in an array associated with the read procedures and must be transferred to the main calling program data segment. The small procedure DISKCT goes into this data segment associated with the read procedure and gets the data count for the number of data values stored there. This count value is returned to the calling program using the CX register for parameter passing. Next the procedure DISKTF transfers these data values using the AX register for the transfer. The SI register is used to pass the pointer index to the data table containing the input data variables (located in the external module containing the read procedures and associated data segment).

Figure 7.7 illustrates the module containing the read procedures and associated data segment DATARD. The programs were linked with the command

LINK FILOPRD+FILERD

The first portion of this data segment is devoted to defining the DTA and FCB in a fashion identical to the approach used to create the file. The third procedure appearing in the listing is FILEOP, the file open procedure. This procedure begins by asking for the file name and extension, initializing the block, record size, and current record, and calling function 0FH to open the file. If AL = 0 on return from the function call, the file was opened successfully. Next the record size is initialized and the DTA fixed with function call 1AH.

The actual read of the disk file is accomplished by the procedure READF, the second procedure appearing in the module. The read takes place within an iterative loop with exit condition when EOF is encountered. Within this loop, function call 14H is made to read the current file record. After each read. DOS increments the

```
PAGE      55,132
TITLE     FILOPRD - CHECKS DISK FILE READ (FILOPRD.ASM)
;
;                     DESCRIPTION: This program checks the disk
;                     file routines: FILERD,CLOSE1, and READF.
;
          EXTRN     FILEOP:FAR,CLOSE1:FAR,READF:FAR
          EXTRN     DISKTF:FAR,DISKCT:FAR
                                                    ;
STACK     SEGMENT PARA STACK 'STACK'
          DB        64 DUP('STACK   ')
STACK     ENDS
                                                    ;
DATA      SEGMENT PARA PUBLIC 'DATA'
                                                    ;
DDATA1    DW        128 DUP(' ')          ;Data area to contain disk words
                                                    ;
DATA      ENDS
CSEG      SEGMENT PARA PUBLIC 'CODE'
CFIO      PROC      FAR
          ASSUME    CS:CSEG,SS:STACK,DS:DATA
                                                    ;
          PUSH      DS
          SUB       AX,AX
          PUSH      AX
                                                    ;
          MOV       AX,SEG DATA
          MOV       DS,AX
                                                    ;
          CALL      FILEOP                ;Open disk file
          CALL      READF                 ;Read disk file
          CALL      CLOSE1                ;Close disk file
                                                    ;
          CALL      DISKCT                ;Returns disk read count
          MOV       SI,0                  ;Pointer to data area
DO1:
              CALL      DISKTF            ;Transfer disk read
              MOV       DDATA1[SI],AX
              ADD       SI,2
          LOOP DO1
                                                    ;
          RET
CFIO      ENDP
CSEG      ENDS
          END       CFIO
```

Figure 7.6 The main calling program, FILOPRD.ASM, which opens, reads, and closes a disk file. The data read in is transferred to DDATA1 in the data segment.

current record number. Following the read the first two bytes of the DTA area are transferred to the variable array DDATA. These two bytes contain the value for the data word generated earlier with the creation routine, and the remaining two bytes, left in the record for possible future use, simply fill it out. This process is repeated until an EOF is encountered. At this point, the variable COUNT is set equal to the number of data values read from the disk and the printer is initialized. Next the macro DECASC, defined in Chapter 6, is used to convert the internal binary number to ASCII format, and the number is printed on the line printer using function call 05H. After a line feed and carriage return, each data value read from disk is printed on the line printer for verification. The user may want to disable this function for large databases.

```
PAGE 55,132
TITLE FILERD - THIS PROCEDURE READS DISK FILE(FILERD.ASM)
;                      DESCRIPTION: The procedure reads a diskette file
;                      after querying for the appropriate FCB parameters.
;
IF1
        INCLUDE MAC1LIB.LIB
        INCLUDE MAC2LIB.LIB
ENDIF
                                         ;
DATARD  SEGMENT PARA PUBLIC 'DATA'
LLEN1   EQU     4
DDTA1   DB      LLEN1 DUP(' ')                 ;DTA
                                         ;This portion devoted to FCB
FCBLB1  LABEL   BYTE
DRIVE1  DB      2                        ;Drive B
NNAME1  DB      8 DUP(' ')               ;File name definition
EEXT1   db      3 DUP(' ')               ;File extension
BBLOCK1 DW      0                        ;Initialize block to 0
RECSZ1  DW      ?                        ;Logical record size, init. after open
FILESZ1 DD      ?                        ;DOS File Size (DOS)
DDATE1  DW      ?                        ;DOS will get date (DOS)
RESERV1 DT      ?                        ;DOS Reserved (DOS)
RECDE11 DB      0                        ;Current record number
RECDE21 DD      ?                        ;Relative record number
                                         ;
MESO1   DB      'Input Disk File Name (8 char. max).    ','$'
MESO2   DB      'Input Disk File Extension (3 char. max).    ','$'
MESO3   DB      'Error on open disk file.   ','$'
MESO5   DB      6 DUP(' '),'$'
MESO7   DB      'Error on opening old file.  ','$'
MESO8   DB      'Error no data read - EOF.  ','$'
MESO9   DB      'Error DTA too small.  ','$'
                                         ;
BUFFMX  DB      80                       ;Max buffer size
BUFFLN  DB      ?
CHAR    DB      80 DUP(' '),'$'
                                         ;
BLANK   DB      ' '
DDATA   DW      128 DUP(' ')
CCOUNT  DW      0
ASC     DB      80 DUP(' ')
BINV    DW      0
BASE    DW      0                        ;Needed for macro.
COUNT   DW      0                        ;Counter for disk read - words
                                         ;
DATARD  ENDS
                                         ;
CFRD    SEGMENT PARA PUBLIC 'CODE'
        PUBLIC FILEOP,READF,CLOSE1,DISKTF,DISKCT
                                         ;
CLOSE1  PROC    FAR
        ASSUME CS:CFRD,DS:DATARD
;
;                      DESCRIPTION: This procedure closes the file.
;
        PUSH DS
                                         ;
        MOV AX,SEG DATARD
        MOV DS,AX
                                         ;
        MOV AH,10H
```

Figure 7.7   The routines FILEOP, READF, CLOSE1, DISKTF, and DISKCT used for opening, reading, closing, and transferring the contents of a disk file to the calling program.

```
        LEA DX,FCBLB1
        INT 21H
                                    ;
        POP DS
        RET
CLOSE1  ENDP
                                    ;
READF   PROC    FAR
;
;               DESCRIPTION: This routine reads the file on
;               disk.
;
        PUSH DS
                                    ;
        MOV AX,SEG DATARD
        MOV DS,AX
        MOV DI,0              ;Initialize index
                             ;Read file
DO1:
        MOV SI,0             ;Initialize pointer
        MOV AH,14H           ;Start read
        LEA DX,FCBLB1
        INT 21H
                             ;
        CMP AL,0             ;Check for successful read
        JE IF1
            CMP AL,3         ;Check for partial read
            JE IF1
                             ;
                CMP AL,1     ;EOF
                JE OUT1      ;Jump to process disk input
                             ;
                MESSG 9      ;DTA too small
                POP DS
                RET
                             ;
                             ;
IF1:
        MOV AL,DDTA1[SI]  ;Load 1st byte DTA area
        MOV AH,DDTA1[SI+1] ;Load 2nd byte DTA area
        MOV DDATA[DI],AX  ;Transfer DTA word memory
        ADD DI,2          ;Increment index word length
        JMP DO1
                             ;
OUT1:
        MOV COUNT,DI         ;Save count
        MOV DX,0             ;Printer 0
        MOV AH,1             ;Initialize printer
        INT 17H
                             ;
        MOV DI,0             ;Pointer to disk data
DO2:
        MOV AX,DDATA[DI]  ;Load decimal to ASCII variable
        MOV BINV,AX
                             ;
        MOV SI,0          ;Fill ASC buffer with blanks
        MOV CX,6          ;Length buffer
DO3:
            MOV AL,20H    ;Load blank character
            MOV ASC[SI],AL
            INC SI
        LOOP DO3
```

Figure 7.7 (*Continued*)

```
                    DECASC BINV,ASC ;Dec-to-ASC conversion (MACRO)
                                    ;
                    ADD DI,2
                                    ;
                    MOV CX,CCOUNT   ;Print output
                    MOV SI,0        ;Character count index
DO4:
                        MOV AL,ASC[SI]
                        MOV DL,AL       ;Print character
                        MOV AH,5
                        INT 21H
                        INC SI
                LOOP DO4
                                    ;
                    MOV AH,5        ;Line feed
                    MOV DL,0AH
                    INT 21H
                                    ;
                    MOV AH,5        ;Carriage return
                    MOV DL,0DH
                    INT 21H
                                    ;
                    MOV AX,COUNT    ;Compare word limit
                    CMP DI,AX
            JAE OUT2                ;Terminate output if at end
            JMP DO2                 ;Continue output
OUT2:
            POP DS
            RET
                                    ;
READF   ENDP
FILEOP  PROC    FAR
;
;                   DESCRIPTION:This procedure opens file.
;
            PUSH DS
                                    ;
            MOV AX,SEG DATARD
            MOV DS,AX
                                    ;
            MESSG 1                 ;Read in filename message  (MACRO)
            KEYBD                   ;Actual read   (MACRO)
            MOV SI,0
            MOV CH,0                ;Clear upper half CX
            MOV CL,BUFFLN           ;Character buffer length
DO5:
                        MOV AL,CHAR[SI]
                        MOV NNAME1[SI],AL ;Ld char in filename
                        INC SI
                        CMP SI,CX       ;Compare with total characters
                JB DO5
                                    ;
            MESSG 2                 ;Ask for filename extension  (MACRO)
            KEYBD                   ;Actual read  (MACRO)
            MOV SI,0                ;Initialize character count
            MOV CH,0                ;Clear upper CX
            MOV CL,BUFFLN           ;Load buffer count
DO6:
                        MOV AL,CHAR[SI] ;Move into AX
                        MOV EEXT1[SI],AL ;Load extension into FCB
                        INC SI
                        CMP SI,CX
                JB DO6
```

Figure 7.7 (*Continued*)

```
            MOV AX,0
            MOV BBLOCK1,AX            ;Reinitialize block
            MOV RECSZ1,AX            ;Reinitialize record size
            MOV RECDE11,AL           ;Reinitialize current record
                                     ;
            MOV AH,0FH               ;Open file
            LEA DX,FCBLB1
            INT 21H
                                     ;
            CMP AL,0                 ;If 0 no error
            JNZ ELSE1
                                     ;
                MOV AX,LLEN1         ;Initialize record size
                MOV RECSZ1,AX        ;FCB size parameter loaded
                LEA DX,DDTA1         ;Address of DTA
                MOV AH,1AH           ;Fix DTA address
                INT 21H
            JMP IF2
                                     ;
ELSE1:
                MESSG 7              ;Error message. MACRO
                RET
                                     ;
IF2:
        POP DS
        RET
FILEOP  ENDP
                                     ;
DISKTF  PROC    FAR
;
;                   DESCRIPTION:This procedure transfers the words read
;                   from disk to the calling program data area.  The
;                   transfer uses AX and COUNT is transferred using
;                   CX in the procedure DISKCT.  This sets up a loop
;                   counter.  SI is the table pointer defined in the
;                   calling program.
;
        PUSH DS
                                     ;
        MOV AX,SEG DATARD
        MOV DS,AX
                                     ;
        MOV AX,DDATA[SI]
                                     ;
        POP DS
        RET
DISKTF  ENDP
                                     ;
DISKCT  PROC    FAR
;
;                   DESCRIPTION: This procedure gets the disk read word
;                   count number for transfer to the calling program.
;                   The count is returned in CX.
;
        PUSH DS
                                     ;
        MOV AX,SEG DATARD
        MOV DS,AX
                                     ;
        MOV CX,COUNT                 ;Count value to be returned
                                     ;
        POP DS
        RET
DISKCT  ENDP
                                     ;
CFRD    ENDS
        END     READF
```

Figure 7.7 (*Continued*)

The first procedure appearing in this listing is CLOSE1, which closes the file. This procedure is identical to CLOSEF. We have renamed it to avoid conflict when the create file and read file modules are stored in an object library. The fifth file in the listing is DISKCT, which transfers COUNT, the number of data values read, to the calling program via CX. Finally, the fourth procedure in the listing, DISKTF, transfers the data values from data segment DATARD, contained in the variable array DDATA, to the calling program. This transfer is accomplished using the AX register, with SI passed as a pointer to the array value.

Several cautions should be mentioned about the programming techniques employed in these routines. First, as has been mentioned, when using macros to expand the program code, such as MESSG X and KEYBD, the length of the intervening code can exceed 128 bytes between jump statements and jump labels in the .ASM file. This means that short-range jumps are out of range. Second, macros can change the values of registers from their value prior to entry into the macro. For example, if an index pointer is initialized prior to the macro expansion, its value may change upon exit from the macro. To avoid problems, the user should push the register onto the stack prior to the macro call and then pop it off the stack following the call. This can, of course, be done as part of the macro call.

The program FILDPRD (Figure 7.6) was executed using DEBUG in order to see what was loaded in the variable area DDATA1. During execution, the stock index for the Dow Jones Average, TBLDJA.DAT, was loaded. Figure 7.8 illustrates the values loaded in DDATA1, appearing at data segment address 1313:0000. All addresses were obtained from the list file. These data values are, of course, in the Dow Jones format and represent the 36 values for the Dow Jones Average presented earlier.

7.2.3 Example: Stock Variation and Moving Average

As an additional example of disk I/O use, access the stock and index tables, now on disk, and examine the variation in performance history. A slight smoothing of the data can be accomplished by performing a forward moving average (an average over the current monthly value and later points). The reader can, no doubt, think of other programs of interest; however, this example is intended to provide a comparison of two stock history variations using smoothing. The comparison will be achieved through visual inspection of each stock's performance variation (or index), which will be presented graphically. An application for this program would be to observe how

```
Program terminated normally
-D DS:0000
1313:0000   51 04 6F 04 88 04 C9 04-CE 04 F1 04 EC 04 BA 04   Q.o............
1313:0010   F6 04 0A 05 14 05 F6 04-0A 05 B0 04 A1 04 A6 04   ................
1313:0020   A6 04 6A 04 6A 04 BF 04-C4 04 BF 04 D8 04 B5 04   ..j.j...........
1313:0030   05 05 0F 05 14 05 00 05-19 05 1E 05 46 05 3C 05   ............F.<.
1313:0040   2D 05 69 05 C8 05 CB 05-20 00 20 00 20 00 20 00   -.i..... ....
1313:0050   20 00 20 00 20 00 20 00-20 00 20 00 20 00 20 00    . . . . . . . .
1313:0060   20 00 20 00 20 00 20 00-20 00 20 00 20 00 20 00    . . . . . . . .
1313:0070   20 00 20 00 20 00 20 00-20 00 20 00 20 00 20 00    . . . . . . . .
-Q
```

Figure 7.8 Results of running FILOPRD using DEBUG. The array DDATA1 is illustrated with the Dow Jones Average values loaded.

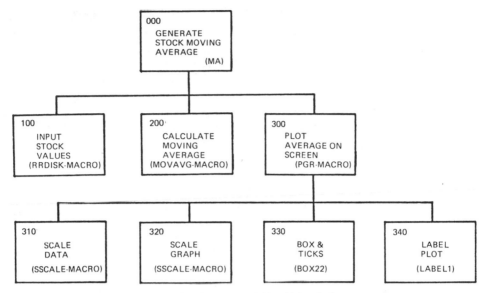

Figure 7.9   Structure chart for the program MA, which calculates a moving average of stock values.

closely the smoothed highs and lows of each stock or index follow each other. For example, does IBM stock follow the overall market fluctuations as represented by the Dow Jones Average?

Figure 7.9 contains the Structure Chart for a program that calculates this moving average. Figure 7.10a illustrates the flow chart for the program MA.ASM which reads two stock files from disk, calculates a moving average, determines the maximum and minimum values, sets up the graphics scale and plots the result. Figure 7.10b presents this program. In this program a third macro library, MAC3LIB.LIB, is used to contain new macros associated with disk read, scaling for the plot, and calculating the moving averages.

The question of whether a particular function is best performed as a procedure call or a macro has a number of qualifying aspects. In some respects macros are easier to use than procedures because they do not require external definitions. Structurally, however, macros do not have clear lines of demarcation and one must be careful when using them to expand the code to avoid having registers inadvertently redefined in an unexpected fashion. Also such conveniences as short-range jumps can become out of range when an intervening macro expands the code beyond 128 bytes. As is seen in the program MA.ASM, a mix of macros and procedures is needed to insure modular development of code. The primary guiding factors should be the efficiency of the resulting program and, equally important, the ease with which the program logic can be understood by both the programmer and others likely to use this code.

The program MA.ASM begins with the loading of two macro libraries: MAC1LIB.LIB, which contains the keyboard and display routines, and MAC3LIB-.LIB, which contains the disk I/O calling macros and the stock-averaging-plus-display scaling. The data segment is quite extensive since it contains all the keyboard and display variables, the scaling variables, and the variables needed to pass coordinate parameters and labels for the plotting routines. The reader will find all variables referenced in the program and macros, as well as the labeling procedure and CONNL1, defined in this segment. The word variables, ARRAY1 and ARRAY2, contain the data locations that correspond to the information to be loaded from disk. The variable N denotes the number of points to be included in the moving average, and M corresponds to the number of data intervals (each of N points in sliding scale fashion) to be considered for the moving average. $M - 1$ points are actually replaced in the moving average.

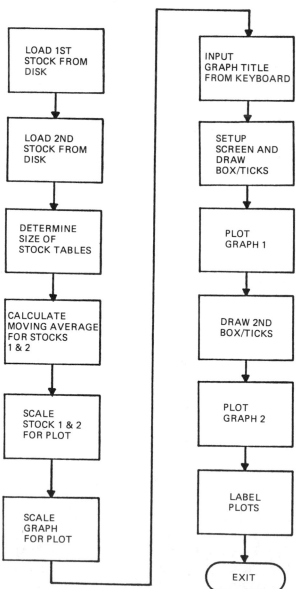

Figure 7.10a The flow chart for the program MA.

```
PAGE      55,132
TITLE     MA       - CALCULATES MOVING AVERAGE (MA.ASM)
;
;                  DESCRIPTION: This program reads two disk files,
;                  calculates their moving average, and plots
;                  the result. 30 points are plotted.
;
                                                        ;
          EXTRN    BOX22:FAR,TICK11:FAR,LABEL1:FAR
          EXTRN    DISKCT:FAR,DISKTF:FAR
          EXTRN    FILEOP:FAR,READF:FAR,CLOSE1:FAR,CONNL1:FAR
                                                        ;
IF1
          INCLUDE MAC1LIB.LIB
          INCLUDE MAC3LIB.LIB
          PURGE   MXMN,PLOTGR,SCALE
ENDIF
                                                        ;
STACK     SEGMENT PARA STACK 'STACK'
          DB      64 DUP('STACK    ')
STACK     ENDS
                                                        ;
DATA      SEGMENT PARA PUBLIC 'DATA'
          PUBLIC  XBEG,XEND,YBEG,YEND,XT,YT,XMAX,XMIN,YMAX,YMIN,X,Y,COUNT
          PUBLIC  TABLE1,TABLE2,TABLE3,COUNT1,COUNT2,COUNT3,STARTX,STARTY
          PUBLIC  XPOS,YPOS,SSMUL,XB,XE,YB,YE
MESO1     DB      'Input title (max 30 characters).   ','$'
MESO10    DB      'Error: plot range exceeded.   ','$'
                                                        ;
SUM       DW      0                   ;Partial sum
COUNT11   DW      0                   ;Array count variable
N         DW      5                   ;Moving average (MA) interval length
M         DW      30                  ;Number data intervals (M - 1)
M2        DW      60                  ;Byte equivalent of M
NT        DW      36                  ;Number of array points

MAX1      DW      ?                   ;Max array1
MAX2      DW      ?                   ;Max array2
MIN1      DW      ?                   ;Min array1
MIN2      DW      ?                   ;Min array2
N1        DW      ?
                                                        ;
ARRAY1    DW      128 DUP(' ')
ARRAY2    DW      128 DUP(' ')
BLANK     DB      ' '
                                                        ;
                                                        ;
BUFFMX    DB      31                  ;Start keyboard buffer
BUFFLN    DB      ?
CHAR      DB      31 DUP(' '),'$'     ;End keyboard buffer
                                                        ;
                                                        ;Plot parameters start here
XBEG      DW      75                  ;Corners box
XEND      DW      225
YBEG      DW      25
YEND      DW      75
XB        DW      ?                   ;XBEG parameter for box & ticks
XE        DW      ?                   ;XEND parameter for box & ticks
YB        DW      ?                   ;YBEG parameter for box & ticks
YE        DW      ?                   ;YEND parameter for box & ticks
XT        DW      125,175             ;X-axis tick points
YT        DW      50                  ;Y-axis tick point
XMAX      DW      77                  ;Y-axis tick limit (max)
XMIN      DW      73                  ;Y-axis tick limit (min)
YMAX      DW      77                  ;X-axis tick limit (max)
YMIN      DW      73                  ;X-axis tick limit (min)
X         DW      0                   ;Dummy
```

Figure 7.10b The program MA.ASM which compares the smoothed variation in two stocks (or an index) and graphs the output.

```
Y          DW       0                              ;Dummy
COUNT      DW       2                              ;Count number X ticks
GPMAX      DW       ?                              ;Maximum point on graph (screen coord.)
                                                   ;End plot parameters
                                                   ;
                                                   ;Start title & label parameters
TABLE1     DB       31 DUP(' ')                    ;This table contains title
COUNT1     DW       ?                              ;Count title characters
STARTX     DW       ?                              ;Start X-axis title
STARTY     DW       0                              ;Y-axis title on row 0
XPOS       DB       3,3,3,3,7,13,19,25
YPOS       DB       3,10,15,22,24,24,24,24
TABLE2     DB       7 DUP(' '),'0',7 DUP(' '),'0'
           DB       ' ',' ',' ','8','3'
           DB       ' ',' ',' ','8','4'
           DB       ' ',' ',' ','8','5'
           DB       ' ',' ',' ','8','6'            ;Title & label table
                                                   ;
TABLE3     DB       ' ','1','0','0'
           DB       ' ','2','0','0'
           DB       ' ','3','0','0'
           DB       ' ','4','0','0'                ;Scale label options
                                                   ;
MMMAX      DW       100,200,300,400
NSCALE     DW       4                              ;Number scale options
COUNT2     DW       4                              ;Characters in scale labels
COUNT3     DW       7                              ;Total number labels in plot(+1)
SSMUL      DW       ?                              ;Scale factor for graph
XINC       DW       ?                              ;X-axis increment length
Y00        DB       ?                              ;Interval end points
Y11        DB       ?
COUNT4     DW       ?                              ;Used to determine plot limit
MIN        DW       0                              ;MIN plot value
MAX        DW       ?                              ;MAX plot value
NERR       DW       ?                              ;Error indicator
                                                   ;
DATA       ENDS
                                                   ;
CSEG       SEGMENT PARA PUBLIC 'CODE'
                                                   ;
MAPP       PROC     FAR                            ;Moving Average Plot Procedure
           ASSUME   CS:CSEG,DS:DATA,SS:STACK
                                                   ;
           PUSH     DS
           SUB      AX,AX
           PUSH     AX
                                                   ;
           MOV      AX,SEG DATA
           MOV      DS,AX
                                                   ;
           CLS                                     ;Clear screen. MACRO
                                                   ;
           RRDISK   1                              ;Load ARRAY1 from disk (MACRO)
           RRDISK   2                              ;Load ARRAY2 from disk (MACRO)
           CALL     DISKCT                         ;Get array length
           SHR      CX,1                           ;Divide array length by 2
           MOV      COUNT11,CX                     ;Save word count
                                                   ;
           MOVAVG   1                              ;Calculate MA for ARRAY1 (MACRO)
           MOVAVG   2                              ;Calculate MA for ARRAY2 (MACRO)
                                                   ;
           SSCALE   1                              ;Scale ARRAY1 (MACRO)
           SSCALE   2                              ;Scale ARRAY2 (MACRO)
                                                   ;These 2 macro calls generated
                                                   ;MAX1,MAX2,MIN1, & MIN2.
                                                   ;
           MOV      AX,MAX1
           CMP      MAX2,AX                        ;Compare MAX1 & MAX2
```

Figure 7.10b (*Continued*)

```
        JNAE IF1
            MOV     AX,MAX2                 ;Replace if greater
IF1:
        MOV     MAX,AX                      ;Load maximum
                                            ;
        SSCALE1 MAX                         ;Scale graph for plot (MACRO)
        MOV     AX,0
        CMP     NERR,AX                     ;Check scale option error
        JE IF2
            RET
IF2:
        MESSG   1                           ;Macro
        KEYBD                               ;Read title. MACRO
        MOV     AX,WORD PTR BUFFLN          ;Save title length
        MOV     AH,0
        MOV     COUNT1,AX                   ;Save length for LABEL1
        MOV     DL,BUFFLN                   ;Load title char count
        MOV     DH,0
        SUB     DX,1                        ;Eliminate carriage return
        MOV     SI,0                        ;Initialize index
DO1:
            MOV     AL,CHAR[SI]
            MOV     TABLE1[SI],AL           ;Save title
            INC     SI                      ;Increment title character index
            CMP     SI,DX                   ;Compare with total title character
        JNA DO1
                                            ;
        SCDEL                               ;Screen delay (MACRO)
                                            ;
        CLS                                 ;Clear screen
        CLS1                                ;Set 320 x 200 graphics mode
                                            ;Load box corner parameters
        MOV     AX,XBEG
        MOV     XB,AX
        MOV     AX,XEND
        MOV     XE,AX
        MOV     AX,YBEG
        MOV     YB,AX
        MOV     AX,YEND
        MOV     YE,AX
                                            ;
        CALL    BOX22                       ;Call box procedure
                                            ;Reload box corner parameters
        MOV     AX,XBEG
        MOV     XB,AX
        MOV     AX,XEND
        MOV     XE,AX
        MOV     AX,YBEG
        MOV     YB,AX
        MOV     AX,YEND
        MOV     YE,AX
                                            ;
        CALL    TICK11                      ;Call tick mark procedure
                                            ;
        MOV     AX,75
        MOV     GPMAX,AX                    ;Maximum point on graph
        PGR     1                           ;Plot upper graph
                                            ;
        MOV     AX,125                      ;Load 2nd graph parameters
        MOV     YBEG,AX
        MOV     AX,175
        MOV     YEND,AX
        MOV     AX,150
        MOV     YT,AX
        MOV     AX,177
        MOV     YMAX,AX
        MOV     AX,173
        MOV     YMIN,AX
```

Figure 7.10b (*Continued*)

```
         MOV     AX,XBEG
         MOV     XB,AX
         MOV     AX,XEND
         MOV     XE,AX
         MOV     AX,YBEG
         MOV     YB,AX
         MOV     AX,YEND
         MOV     YE,AX
                                       ;
         CALL    BOX22
                                       ;
         MOV     AX,XBEG               ;Reload graph parameters
         MOV     XB,AX
         MOV     AX,XEND
         MOV     XE,AX
         MOV     AX,YBEG
         MOV     YB,AX
         MOV     AX,YEND
         MOV     YE,AX
                                       ;
         CALL    TICK11
                                       ;
         MOV     AX,175
         MOV     GPMAX,AX              ;Max screen coord. 2nd plot
         PGR     2                    ;Plot array2 (MACRO)
                                       ;
                                       ;
         CALL    LABEL1               ;Procedure to label graph
         SCDEL                        ;Delay screen. MACRO
         RT80M                        ;Return to 80 x 25 (MACRO)
                                       ;
         RET
MAPP     ENDP
                                       ;
CSEG     ENDS
         END     MAPP
```

Figure 7.10b (*Continued*)

The macro RRDISK X is used to read in the data from disk. (This and other macros are illustrated in Figure 7.14 and will be discussed later.) Following the input of two data sequences from disk, a moving average is calculated for each array of data. The variable COUNT11 is used to specify the array length for each data sequence read from disk. Both disk readings must input data history of the same length if a proper comparison of these data sequences is to be done. The macro SSCALE X calculates a minimum and maximum for the portions of the array to be averaged and plotted. Next, this macro subtracts the minimum array value from all other points in the moving average. This yields a variation between 0 and the maximum of ARRAY&X minus the minimum. This variation effectively removes any scale differences between data sequences. It allows a comparison of the two sequences based only on the relative differences of one point to another within the sequence. The largest range of array variations is next determined, and this serves as the basis for scaling the subsequent graphics. The macro SSCALE X sets up the graph scaling. Following the input of a suitable title for the graph, the screen is cleared and the 320×200 graphics mode is initiated.

A new box procedure, BOX22, is called. This procedure differs from BOX11 in that it does not automatically clear the screen and set the 320×200 graphics mode since these functions have already been performed. In other respects, the BOX22 procedure is identical to BOX11, except it has the additional feature that horizontal and vertical lines are drawn at each tick mark. It was necessary to remove the clear screen function and 320×200 graphics mode set up from the box procedure because two graphs will be plotted on the screen for comparison. The macro PGR X actually performs the plotting function, and once graphs are plotted the procedure LABEL1 is used to label the graph.

A typical interactive session with the program MA.EXE is illustrated in Figure 7.11. Here the Dow Jones Average is compared to the stock history variation for IBM. In both cases the variation with a five-point moving average is compared. Figure 7.12(a) illustrates the resulting graphic output. The plot cuts off at the twenty-ninth point ($M - 1$, where $M = 30$), and since a forward moving average of five points is used, it is clear that points beyond number 31 (out of 36) could not be calculated because of insufficient data. From the figure it is clear that IBM stock only compares with the Dow Jones variation in an overall sense. The local minimums appearing in both curves do not track one-to-one; however, the major increases and decreases do tend to follow one another. In 1985 the IBM stock appears to level off while the Dow Jones Average increases. A second comparison between the Dow Jones variation and the variation in Digital Equipment Corporation stock is presented in Figure 7.12(b). This figure shows a steady overall decline for the DEC variation, except for a minimum in late 1983 and an upward surge in the late 1984-early 1985 time frame. Again, when taken on an individual basis it would appear that for this class of stocks the Dow Jones Average is not a good indicator. It should be remembered that the function being graphed is the averaged variation in stock price, not the actual price of the stock. Figures 7.12(c) and 7.12(d) illustrate comparisons of the variation for Hewlett-Packard and Storage Technology and for IBM and Sperry. In Figure 7.12(c) the Hewlett-Packard variation is quite uniform across the months graphed, indicating very little change in performance. The graph for Storage Technology, however, demonstrates the steady decline in price of this stock. Even though the price of Hewlett-Packard stock is greater than that for Storage Technology, the latter displays a much wider variation in performance. The IBM and Sperry Corporation comparison comes the closest to actually yielding a one-to-one agreement in performance.

Figure 7.13 contains the BOX22 procedure used for generating the box and internal graph marker lines. This procedure is a modification of the BOX11 procedure, as previously indicated. The NEAR procedures LINEH1 and LINEV1 have been included as part of this portion of the code segment. This routine was added to

```
Input Disk File Name (8 char. max).

TBLDJA
Input Disk File Extension (3 char. max).

DAT
Input Disk File Name (8 char. max).

TBLIBM
Input Disk File Extension (3 char. max).

DAT
Input title (max 30 characters).

DJA/IBM Variation (5 Pt Ave)
```

Figure 7.11 Sample input session for MA.ASM with Dow Jones Average compared to IBM stock history.

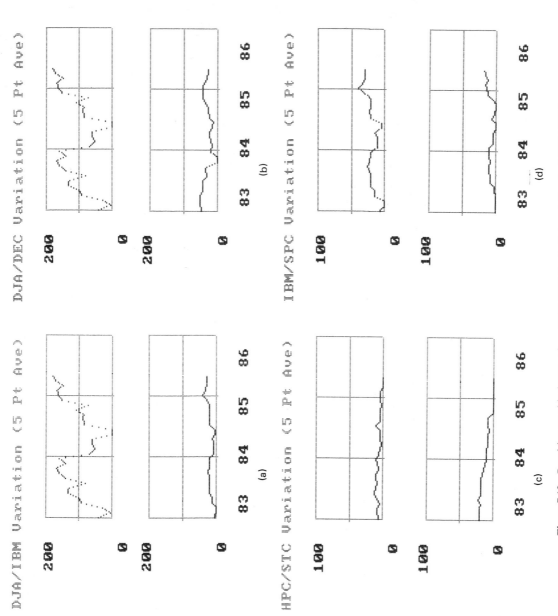

Figure 7.12 Resulting graphical output from MAS.ASM illustrating variation for (a) DJA/IBM, (b) DJA/DEC, (c) HPC/STC, and (d) IBM/SPC.

258

```
edlin bo
PAGE 55,132
TITLE BOX - DRAWS BOX/TICK MARKS 100 X 200 BOX(BOX.ASM)
                                  ;
                                  ;Uses data segment DATA
                                  ;
        EXTRN XBEG:WORD,XEND:WORD,YBEG:WORD,YEND:WORD,XT:WORD,YT:WORD
        EXTRN XMAX:WORD,XMIN:WORD,YMAX:WORD,YMIN:WORD,X:WORD,Y:WORD
        EXTRN COUNT:WORD
        EXTRN XB:WORD,XE:WORD,YB:WORD,YE:WORD
                                  ;
CSEG    SEGMENT PARA PUBLIC 'CODE'
        PUBLIC BOX22
BOX22   PROC    FAR
        ASSUME CS:CSEG
        PUSH DS
                                  ;
                                  ;
                                  ;Procedure to draw a box
                                  ;
        MOV AX,YB                 ;Start Y point horizontal line
        MOV Y,AX
        CALL LINEH1               ;Draw line
        MOV AX,YE                 ;Start Y-axis point for 2nd line
        MOV Y,AX
        CALL LINEH1               ;Draw horizontal line
                                  ;
        MOV AX,XB                 ;Start X point vertical line
        MOV X,AX
        CALL LINEV1               ;Draw vertical line
        MOV AX,XE                 ;Start X-axis point 2nd line
        MOV X,AX
        CALL LINEV1               ;Draw 2nd vertical line
                                  ;
        MOV AX,YT                 ;Draw line at Y-axis ticks
        MOV Y,AX
        CALL LINEH1
                                  ;
        MOV BX,COUNT              ;Vertical lines at X-axis ticks
        MOV DI,0                  ;Counter
        MOV SI,0                  ;Initialize pointer X tick variable
DO1:
            MOV AX,XT[SI]         ;Load X tick position
            PUSH BX              ;Save BX for reuse in line procedures
            MOV X,AX
            PUSH DI               ;Preserve DI from INT 10H change
            PUSH SI               ;Preserve SI from INT 10H change
            CALL LINEV1
            POP SI                ;Recall SI
            POP DI                ;Recall DI
            ADD SI,2              ;Increment word amount
            INC DI                ;Increment counter by 1
            POP BX                ;Recall BX value = COUNT
            CMP DI,BX             ;Check to see end of tick marks
        JB  DO1
                                  ;
        POP DS
        RET
BOX22   ENDP
                                  ;
```

Figure 7.13 The general purpose box and tick mark routines that require a screen clear and 320 × 200 mode to be set externally.

```
LINEH1   PROC     NEAR
                                    ;Procedure for horizontal line
         MOV DX,Y
         MOV CX,XB                  ;Load begin X-value
DO2:
                  MOV AH,12         ;Write dot
                  MOV AL,1          ;Attribute 1
                  INT 10H
                  ADD CX,1          ;Increment X-value
                  MOV BX,CX
                  SUB BX,XE         ;Check X-value end point
         JNE DO2
         RET
LINEH1   ENDP
                                    ;
LINEV1   PROC     NEAR
                                    ;Procedure for vertical line
         MOV CX,X
         MOV DX,YB                  ;Load begin Y-value
DO3:
                  MOV AH,12         ;Write dot
                  MOV AL,1          ;Attribute 1
                  INT 10H
                  ADD DX,1          ;Increment Y-value
                  MOV BX,DX
                  SUB BX,YE         ;Check Y-value end point
         JNE DO3
         RET
LINEV1   ENDP
                                    ;
CSEG     ENDS
         END      BOX22
```

Figure 7.13 (*Continued*)

GRAPHLIB.LIB as part of the object modules called by MA.ASM. The RRDISK macro, previously mentioned, calls three procedures that were externally defined in the module FILERD.OBJ. This module was used earlier in this chapter. The linking sequence for MA.ASM is

```
LINK

IBM Personal Computer Linker
Version 2.10(c) Copyright IBM Corp. 1981, 1982, 1983

Object Modules (.OBJ): MA + FILERD
Run File (MA.EXE):
List File (NUL.MAP):
Libraries (.LIB): GRAPHLIB
```

Figure 7.14 presents the macros that are contained as part of MAC3LIB.LIB, used to obtain the disk files and create the graphics output for MA.ASM. The first macro, RRDISK, opens the file, reads it, and closes it. Next, the procedure DISKCT is called to obtain a variable count and DISKTF is called to transfer the input data sequence to the main calling program segment. All these procedures are contained in the object module FILERD.OBJ. The second macro, MXMN1 X, calculates a

```
;         MAC3LIB.LIB - MACRO LIBRARY NO. 3 (MAC3LIB.LIB)
;
;                         This MACRO library is used with the
;                         disk input/output routines and
;                         moving average routines.
;
RRDISK    MACRO    X
          LOCAL DO11
;
;                         This macro does the disk read and loads
;                         the variable data array ARRAY&X.
;
          CALL FILEOP              ;Open file
          CALL READF              ;Read file into associated data seg.
          CALL CLOSE1             ;Close file
                                  ;
          CALL DISKCT             ;Obtain variable count
          MOV SI,0                ;Init. array pointer
DO11:
              CALL DISKTF         ;Transfer 1 word
              MOV ARRAY&X[SI],AX  ;Word transferred
              ADD SI,2            ;Increment word pointer
          LOOP DO11
                                  ;
          ENDM
                                  ;
MXMN1     MACRO    X
          LOCAL DO1,IF1,DO2,IF2
;
;         This macro calculates the min/max for ARRAY&X which is
;         located in DATA.  The length of the array in words is N1.
;
          MOV SI,2                ;2nd word
          MOV CX,N1               ;Loop counter
          SUB CX,1                ;Total increments in array
          MOV DX,ARRAY&X[0]       ;Load first array value
DO1:
              CLC
              CMP DX,ARRAY&X[SI]   ;Cmp with next value
              JBE IF1             ;Jump if DX less
              MOV DX,ARRAY&X[SI]  ;Replace with smaller
IF1:
              ADD SI,2            ;Inc to next word
          LOOP DO1
          MOV MIN&X,DX            ;Save minmium
                                  ;
          MOV SI,2
          MOV CX,N1               ;Loop counter
          SUB CX,1                ;Total increments in array
          MOV DX,ARRAY&X[0]       ;Load first array value
DO2:
              CLC
              CMP DX,ARRAY&X[SI]   ;Cmp with next value
              JAE IF2             ;Jmp if DX >
              MOV DX,ARRAY&X[SI]  ;Replace larger
IF2:
              ADD SI,2            ;Inc next word
          LOOP DO2
          MOV MAX&X,DX            ;Save maximum
                                  ;
          ENDM
                                  ;
```

Figure 7.14 The macro library MAC3LIB.LIB, which contains the disk read macro, associated-moving average macro and the scaling macro.

```
MOVAVG  MACRO    X
        LOCAL    DO3,DO4
;
;       This macro calculates a general moving average for an
;       array: ARRAY&X, across N points per interval and M
;       intervals.
;
;
        MOV BP,0                  ;Init. interval pointer
DO3:
            MOV SI,0              ;Init. ptr
            MOV AX,0
            MOV SUM,AX            ;Clear partial sum
            MOV CX,N             ;Load MA interval length
DO4:
                MOV AX,ARRAY&X[BP][SI]
                ADD SUM,AX       ;Increase partial sum
                ADD SI,2         ;Inc ptr
            LOOP DO4
                                 ;
            MOV AX,SUM           ;Divide by interval length
            MOV DX,0             ;Clear upper reg.
            MOV BX,N
            DIV BX
            MOV ARRAY&X[BP],AX   ;Reload array
            CMP DI,M2            ;M2 = 2 x M
            ADD BP,2
        JB DO3
                                 ;
        ENDM
                                 ;
SSCALE  MACRO    X
        LOCAL DO5
;
;       This macro determines a new scale netween 0 and
;       MAX - MIN for ARRAY&X.
;
        MOV AX,M                 ;Get array size in words
        MOV N1,AX
                                 ;
        MXMN1   X                ;MIN/MAX routine.  MACRO
                                 ;
        MOV SI,0                 ;Clear index pointer
        MOV BX,MIN&X             ;Setup minimum value
        MOV CX,COUNT11           ;Initialize loop count
DO5:
            MOV AX,ARRAY&X[SI]
            SUB AX,BX
            MOV ARRAY&X[SI],AX   ;Save array=data-(min)
            ADD SI,2             ;Increment word count
        LOOP DO5
                                 ;
        MXMN1   X                ;MIN/MAX routine. MACRO
                                 ;
        ENDM
                                 ;
SSCALE1 MACRO    MAX
        LOCAL DO6,OUT1,DO7
;
```

Figure 7.14 (*Continued*)

```
;            This macro computes the scale values (from NSCALE options)
;            and loads them into TABLE2 (from TABLE3).
;
             MOV AX,0
             MOV NERR,AX              ;Init. NERR to no error condition
             MOV DI,0                 ;Table pointer multiplier
             MOV CX,NSCALE            ;Init. no. scale values
             MOV SI,0                 ;SI pointer to max values
DO6:
                  MOV AX,MMMAX[SI]
                  MOV BX,MMMAX[SI] ;Save scale max
                  CMP MAX,AX        ;Compare MAX with scale options
                  JBE OUT1          ;Jmp out loop
                  ADD SI,2
                  INC DI
             LOOP DO6
                                ;
             MESSG 10           ;Error - scale options exceeded
             MOV AX,1
             MOV NERR,AX        ;Set error parameter
             RET
                                ;
OUT1:
             MOV AX,COUNT2           ;Load TABLE2
             MOV DX,0                 ;Clear upper reg.
             MUL DI
             MOV SI,AX                ;Pointer to TABLE3
             MOV DI,0                 ;Pointer to TABLE2
DO7:
                  MOV AL,TABLE3[SI] ;Ld TABLE2 with label
                  MOV TABLE2[DI],AL
                  MOV TABLE2[DI+8],AL ;2nd box label
                  INC SI
                  INC DI
                  CMP DI,COUNT2     ;Cmp with label char cnt.
             JBE DO7
                                   ;Calculate scale multiplier
             MOV AX,5000           ;Scale factor numerator x 100
             MOV DX,0              ;Clear upper reg.
             DIV BX               ;5000/MAX - Recall BX with MMMAX
             MOV SSMUL,AX          ;Scale factor
                                   ;
             ENDM
                                   ;
PGR     MACRO   X
             LOCAL DO8
;
;            This general macro plots graph for ARRAY&X, M= no.
;            X-intervals.
;
             MOV AX,XEND             ;Start XINC calculation
             SUB AX,XBEG             ;AX = (XEND - XBEG)
             MOV DX,0                ;Clear upper reg.
             MOV BX,NT               ;Load total number array pts.
             DIV BX                  ;Calculate X-increment length
             MOV XINC,AX
                                     |
             MOV SI,0                ;Pointer to array table
             MOV AX,M
             SUB AX,1                ;M - 1 points averaged
             MOV COUNT4,AX           ;Load graph point limit to be plotted
             MOV DI,0                ;Load counter
                                     ;
```

Figure 7.14 (*Continued*)

```
DO8:
                    MOV CX,100          ;Ld scale divisor
                    MOV AX,ARRAY&X[SI]
                    MUL SSMUL           ;Multiply by scale
                    MOV DX,0            ;Clear upper register
                    DIV CX              ;Remove scaling factor of 100
                    MOV BX,AX           ;Invert points on graph
                    MOV AX,GPMAX        ;Maximum point on graph
                    SUB AX,BX           ;Inverted point
                    MOV Y00,AL          ;Save first point
                                        ;
                    MOV AX,ARRAY&X[SI+2] ;2nd pt on graph
                    MUL SSMUL
                    MOV DX,0
                    DIV CX
                    MOV BX,AX
                    MOV AX,GPMAX
                    SUB AX,BX
                    MOV Y11,AL          ;Save second point
                                        ;End loading Y-values
                                        ;
                    MOV AX,XINC         ;Calculate XSTART
                    MOV DX,0
                    MUL DI              ;Multiply XINC by connection pt. no.
                    ADD AX,XBEG         ;Add starting value
                    MOV BX,AX           ;Save XSTART parameter
                    ADD AX,XINC         ;Increment next plot point by XINC
                    MOV CX,AX           ;Save XEND parameter
                    MOV DH,Y00
                    MOV DL,Y11
                                        ;
                    CALL CONNL1         ;Plot points
                    ADD SI,2
                    INC DI
                    CMP DI,COUNT4       ;Check for plot limit
              JB   DO8
                                        ;
              ENDM
CLS1          MACRO
   ;
   ;          This macro sets the 320 x 200 graphics
   ;          mode.
   ;
              MOV AH,0                  ;Set mode
              MOV AL,5                  ;320 x 200 graphics
              INT 10H
                                        ;
              ENDM
```

Figure 7.14 (*Continued*)

general maximum and minimum for ARRAY&X. These values are loaded in
MAX&X and MIN&X, respectively. When X = 1 the values correspond to MAX1
and MIN1 of ARRAY1 (once the operators assign X). The maximum-minimum
macro is very similar to earlier routines we have used, except that is has been
generalized to the variable ARRAY and not to an array in the extra segment.

The third macro, MOVAVG X, calculates the moving average for ARRAY&X.
This average is over N forward points, with the first point reloaded with the
average. The averaging process continues sliding forward one point at a time until
M − 1 points have been averaged. The SSCALE macro simply calculates the

variation between 0 and the maximum variation point for the intervals considered. This macro calls MXMN1 twice: first, to generate the overall maximum and minimum and subtract out the minimum, and second, to generate the new maximum and minimum (0) for the variation.

SSCALE1 scales the data for graphics output. In this situation each graph is 50 screen units high. SSCALE1 obtains a scale multiplier based on this height and the overall scale maximum determined from the array MMMAX. The scale multiplier SSMUL is used by PGR X to plot the graph points. The macro PGR X sets up the graph increments and calls the procedure CONNL1 to generate the connecting points. The data is assumed to exist in ARRAY&X. All the macros contained in MAC3LIB.LIB assume that the data to be operated on lies in ARRAY&X, where X must be defined at assembly. The last macro, CLS1, simply sets the 320×200 graphics mode.

7.2.4 Disk I/O Using File Handles

File handles have been previously mentioned as an alternative technique for performing extended file management. According to IBM, function calls involving file handles are the preferred approach to implementing disk and diskette input and output. Although the techniques are similar to those employed when specifying an FCB and DTA, there are some rather subtle differences. The purpose of this subsection is to describe the use of the file-handle function calls in the context of the previously defined disk I/O programs, which are based on the use of FCBs and DTAs. Also, while the file-handle functions no longer specifically use a Data Transfer Address, they do require an address in memory for the ASCII character string record which is to be transferred to and from the disk; and it will be useful to retain the DTA nomenclature when referring to this address space.

The file-handle function calls are 3CH (create file), 40H (write file), 3EH (close file handle), 3DH (open file handle), 3FH (read file), and 44H (I/O status). The following assembler code corresponds to typical sequences for implementing each of the above file handle operations.

Create file:

```
        ...
        CLC                    ; Clear carry flag
        MOV AH,3CH             ; Create file
        LEA DX,NNAME          ; Load ASCII string pointer
        MOV CX,0              ; File attribute
        INT 21H
        MOV HHANDLE,AX        ; Same file handle
        JNC XX1              ; Jump if create OK
        MESSG 11            ; Error message 11
        POP DS             ; Recall data segment pointer
        RET               ; Return
XX1:    ...
```

Write file:

```
          ...
          CLC                    ; Clear carry flag
          MOV AH,40H             ; Write file
          MOV BX,HHANDLE         ; Load file handle
          LEA DX,DTA             ; Address string to write from
          MOV CX,RECSZB          ; Number of bytes per record
          INT 21H

                                 ;
          MOV EERROR,AX          ; Save possible error condition
          JNC XXZ                ; Jump if write successful
          MESSG 12               ; Error message 12
          POP DS                 ; Recall data segment pointer
          RET                    ; Return
XX2:      ...
```

Close file:

```
          ...
          CLC                    ; Clear carry flag
          MOV AH,3EH             ; Close file handle function
          MOV BX,HHANDLE         ; Load file handle
          INT 21H

                                 ;
          MOV EERROR,AX          ; Save possible error condition
          JNC XX3                ; Jump if close successful
          MESSG 13               ; Error message 13
          POP DS                 ; Recall data segment pointer
          RET                    ; Return
XX3:      ...
```

Open file:

```
          ...
          CLC                    ; Clear carry flag
          MOV AH,3DH             ; Open file function
          LEA DX,NNAME           ; Load address file path name
          MOV AL,2               ; Access: 0 = read, 1 = write, 2 = both
          INT 21H

                                 ;
          MOV HHANDLE,AX         ;
          JNC XX4                ; Jump if open successful
          MESSG 14               ; Error message 14
          POP DS                 ; Recall data segment pointer
          RET                    ; Return
          ...
```

```
PAGE 55,132
TITLE FILECR1 - THIS PROCEDURE CREATES DISK FILE(FILECR1.ASM)
;               DESCRIPTION: The procedure creates a disk file
;               using file handles.
;
IF1
        INCLUDE MAC1LIB.LIB
        INCLUDE MAC2LIB.LIB
ENDIF
                                            ;
DATACR  SEGMENT PARA PUBLIC 'DATA'
LLEN    EQU     4
DDTA    DB      LLEN DUP(' ')               ;DTA
                                    ;This section devoted to file handle
NNAME   DB      80 DUP(' ')         ;File name definition
RECSZB  DW      ?                   ;Logical record size, initialize later
HHANDLE DW      ?                   ;File Handle
EERROR  DW      ?                   ;Error return parameter
                                    ;
                                    ;
MESO1   DB      'Input ASCII string identifying file.  ','$'
MESO3   DB      'Error on open disk file.  ','$'
MESO4   DB      'Input number (-32765,32765) - "\" terminates.  ','$'
MESO5   DB      6 DUP(' '),'$'
MESO11  DB      'Create File error.  ','$'
MESO12  DB      'Write File error.  ','$'
MESO13  DB      'Close File error.  ','$'
                                    ;
BUFFMX  DB      80                  ;Maximum buffer size
BUFFLN  DB      ?
CHAR    DB      80 DUP(' '),'$'
                                    ;
BLANK   DB      ' '
DDATA   DW      128 DUP(' ')
CCOUNT  DW      0
ASC     DB      80 DUP(' ')
BINV    DW      0
BASE    DW      0                   ;Needed for macro
                                    ;
DATACR  ENDS
                                    ;
CFCR    SEGMENT PARA PUBLIC 'CODE'
        PUBLIC FILECR1,FILEW1,CLOSEF1
FILECR1 PROC    FAR
        ASSUME CS:CFCR,DS:DATACR
                                    ;
        PUSH DS
                                    ;
        MOV AX,SEG DATACR
        MOV DS,AX
                                    ;
        MESSG 1                     ;Read filename message (MACRO)
        KEYBD                       ;Actual read from keyboard (MACRO)
        MOV SI,0                    ;Initialize character counter
        MOV CH,0                    ;Clear upper half of CX
        MOV CL,BUFFLN               ;Character buffer length
```

Figure 7.15   Program FILECR1.ASM which creates a disk file using file handles.

```
DO1:
              MOV  AL,CHAR[SI]
              MOV  NNAME[SI],AL  ;Load character in filename
              INC  SI            ;Increment counter
              CMP  SI,CX         ;Compare with total character
        JB DO1
                                 ;
        MOV  AL,0                ;Load 0 for last byte
        MOV  NNAME[SI],AL
                                 ;
        CLC                      ;Clear carry flag
        MOV  AH,3CH              ;Create file
        LEA  DX,NNAME            ;Load pointer to ASCII string
        MOV  CX,0                ;File attribute
        INT  21H
                                 ;
        MOV  HHANDLE,AX          ;Save returned File Handle
        AND  AX,0001H            ;Setup to check for error
        CMP  AX,0                ;Compare for error
        JE IF1
              MESSG  11          ;Create file error
              POP  DS
              RET
IF1:
        MOV  AX,LLEN             ;Initialize record size
        MOV  RECSZB,AX           ;Load record size byte count
                                 ;
        POP  DS
        RET
                                 ;
FILECR1 ENDP
                                 ;
FILEW1  PROC    FAR
;
;             DESCRIPTION: This routine reads and writes numbers
;             to the disk file.
;
        PUSH DS
                                 ;
        MOV  AX,SEG DATACR
        MOV  DS,AX
                                 ;
DO3:
              MESSG 4            ;Message request input (MACRO)
              KEYBD              ;Actual input (MACRO)
              MOV  SI,0          ;Load input pointer
              MOV  CH,0
              MOV  CL,BUFFLN     ;Buffer length
DO2:
              MOV  AL,CHAR[SI] ;Transfer character
              MOV  AH,5CH      ;Terminator
              CMP  AL,AH       ;Check for terminator
        JNE IF2
                      POP  DS
                      RET
IF2:
              MOV  ASC[SI],AL   ;Load buffer
              INC  SI
              CMP  SI,CX        ;Compare pointer
```

Figure 7.15 (*Continued*)

```
           JB  DO2                      ;Jump if more to go
                                        ;
                   ASCDEC BINV,ASC      ;Convert number (MACRO)
                                        ;
                   MOV  SI,0            ;Initialize DTA pointer
                   MOV  AX,BINV         ;Load decimal number
                   MOV  DDTA[SI],AL
                   MOV  DDTA[SI+1],AH
                                        ;
                                        ;
                   CLC                  ;Clear carry flag
                   MOV  AH,40H          ;Write file
                   MOV  BX,HHANDLE      ;Load File Handle
                   LEA  DX,DDTA         ;Address string to write
                   MOV  CX,RECSZB       ;Number bytes to write
                   INT  21H
                                        ;
                   MOV  EERROR,AX       ;Load possible error condition
                   AND  AX,0001H        ;Set up check for error
                   CMP  AX,0            ;Compare for error
           JE  IF3
                       MESSG 12         ;Output write file error
                       POP  DS
                       RET
                                        ;
IF3:
           JMP  DO3
                                        ;
FILEW1     ENDP
                                        ;
CLOSEF1 PROC     FAR
;
;                   DESCRIPTION: This procedure closes the file.
;
           PUSH DS
                                        ;
           MOV  AX,SEG DATACR
           MOV  DS,AX
                                        ;
           CLC                          ;Clear carry flag
           MOV  AH,3EH                  ;Close File Handle
           MOV  BX,HHANDLE              ;Load Handle
           INT  21H
                                        ;
           MOV  EERROR,AX               ;Load possible error condition
           AND  AX,0001H                ;Setup to check for error
           CMP  AX,0                    ;Compare for error
           JE  IF4
                   MESSG 13             ;Output close file error
IF4:
           POP  DS
                                        ;
           RET
CLOSEF1 ENDP
                                        ;
CFCR    ENDS
        END      FILECR1
```

Figure 7.15 (*Continued*)

```
PAGE 55,132
TITLE FILERD1 - THIS PROCEDURE READS DISK FILE(FILERD1.ASM)
;                  DESCRIPTION: The procedure reads a diskette file
;                  using the File Handle to access the disk.
;
IF1
        INCLUDE MAC1LIB.LIB
        INCLUDE MAC2LIB.LIB
ENDIF
                                    ;
DATARD   SEGMENT PARA PUBLIC 'DATA'
LLEN1    EQU     4
DDTA1    DB      LLEN1 DUP(' ')              ;DTA
                                    ;This portion devoted to File Handle
NNAME1   DB      80 DUP(' ')        ;File name definition
RECSZB1  DW      ?                  ;Logical record initialize after open
HHANDLE  DW      ?                  ;File Handle
EERROR   DW      ?                  ;Error parameter return
                                    ;
                                    ;
MESO1    DB      'Input ASCII string identifying file.  ','$'
MESO5    DB      6 DUP(' '),'$'
MESO11   DB      'Open file error.  ','$'
MESO12   DB      'Read file error.  ','$'
MESO13   DB      'Close file error.  ','$'
                                    ;
BUFFMX   DB      80                 ;Maximum buffer size
BUFFLN   DB      ?
CHAR     DB      80 DUP(' '),'$'
                                    ;
BLANK    DB      ' '
DDATA    DW      128 DUP(' ')
CCOUNT   DW      0
ASC      DB      80 DUP(' ')
BINV     DW      0
BASE     DW      0                  ;Needed for macro.
COUNT    DW      0                  ;Counter for disk read - words
                                    ;
DATARD   ENDS
                                    ;
CFRD     SEGMENT PARA PUBLIC 'CODE'
         PUBLIC FILEOP1,READF1,CLOSE11,DISKTF1,DISKCT1
                                    ;
CLOSE11  PROC    FAR
         ASSUME CS:CFRD,DS:DATARD
;
;                  DESCRIPTION: This procedure closes the file.
;
         PUSH DS
                                    ;
         MOV AX,SEG DATARD
         MOV DS,AX
                                    ;
         CLC                        ;Clear carry flag
         MOV AH,3EH                 ;Close File Handle
         MOV BX,HHANDLE             ;Load Handle
         INT 21H
                                    ;
         MOV EERROR,AX              ;Dummy storage error condition
         JNC XX3
         MESSG    13                ;Output close file error
```

Figure 7.16 Program FILERD1.ASM which reads a diskette file using file handles.

```
                                        ;
XX3:      POP DS
          RET
CLOSE11 ENDP
                                        ;
READF1    PROC    FAR
;
;                 DESCRIPTION: This routine reads the file on
;                 disk.
;
          PUSH DS
                                        ;
          MOV AX,SEG DATARD
          MOV DS,AX
          MOV DI,0                ;Initialize index
                                 ;Read file
DO1:
                MOV SI,0         ;Initialize pointer
                                        ;
                MOV AH,3FH       ;Read file
                MOV BX,HHANDLE   ;Load File Handle
                LEA DX,DDTA1     ;Load read string address
                MOV CX,RECSZB1   ;Initialize record size
                INT 21H
                                        ;
                MOV AH,44H       ;Check for EOF
                MOV AL,06H       ;Input status
                INT 21H
                                        ;
                CMP AL,00H       ;If equal EOF
          JNE ELSE1
          JMP OUT1                      ;Jump EOF to finish processing
                                        ;
                                        ;
                                        ;
ELSE1:
                MOV AL,DDTA1[SI] ;Load 1st byte DTA area
                MOV AH,DDTA1[SI+1]  ;Load 2nd byte DTA area
                MOV DDATA[DI],AX   ;Transfer DTA word to memory
                ADD DI,2         ;Increment index word length
          JMP DO1
                                        ;
OUT1:
          MOV COUNT,DI                 ;Save count
          MOV DX,0                     ;Printer 0
          MOV AH,1          ·          ;Initialize printer
          INT 17H
                                        ;
          MOV DI,0                     ;Pointer to disk data
DO4:
                MOV AX,DDATA[DI] ;Load decimal to ASCII data
                MOV BINV,AX
                                        ;
                MOV SI,0         ;Clear ASC buffer with blanks
                MOV CX,6         ;Length buffer
DO2:
                    MOV AL,20H   ;Load blank character
                    MOV ASC[SI],AL
                    INC SI
          LOOP DO2
                                        ;
```

Figure 7.16 (*Continued*)

```
                    DECASC BINV,ASC  ;Decimal-to-ASCII conversion (MACRO)
                                     ;
                    ADD DI,2
                                     ;
                    MOV CX,CCOUNT    ;Print output
                    MOV SI,0         ;Character count index
DO3:
                       MOV AL,ASC[SI]
                       MOV DL,AL     ;Print character
                       MOV AH,5
                       INT 21H
                       INC SI
             LOOP DO3
                                     ;
                       MOV AH,5      ;Line feed
                       MOV DL,0AH
                       INT 21H

                       MOV AH,5      ;Carriage return
                       MOV DL,0DH
                       INT 21H
                                     ;
                       MOV AX,COUNT  ;Compare word limit
                       CMP DI,AX
          JAE OUT2                   ;Terminate output if at end
          JMP DO4                    ;Continue output
OUT2:
          POP DS
          RET
                                     ;
READF1    ENDP
FILEOP1 PROC    FAR
;
;                   DESCRIPTION:This procedure opens file.
;
          PUSH DS
                                     ;
          MOV AX,SEG DATARD
          MOV DS,AX
                                     ;
          MESSG 1                    ;Read in filename message   (MACRO)
          KEYBD                      ;Actual read   (MACRO)
          MOV SI,0
          MOV CH,0                   ;Clear upper half CX
          MOV CL,BUFFLN              ;Character buffer length
DO5:
             MOV AL,CHAR[SI]
             MOV NNAME1[SI],AL ;Load character in filename
             INC SI
             CMP SI,CX             ;Compare with total characters
          JB DO5
                                     ;
          MOV AL,0                   ;Load 0 for last byte
          MOV NNAME1[SI],AL          ;Last byte in string set
                                     ;
          CLC                        ;Clear carry flag
          MOV AH,3DH                 ;Open File Handle
          LEA DX,NNAME1              ;Load effective address - file
          MOV AL,2                   ;Access: 0 = read, 1 = write, 2 = both
          INT 21H
```

Figure 7.16 (*Continued*)

```
                    ;
         MOV HHANDLE,AX              ;Save File Handle
         JNC IF1
               MESSG 13              ;Error message on open
               POP DS
               RET
                    ;
IF1:
         MOV AX,LLEN1                ;Load record byte count
         MOV RECSZB1,AX
                    ;
         POP DS
         RET
                    ;
FILEOP1 ENDP
                    ;
DISKTF1 PROC    FAR
;
;               DESCRIPTION:This procedure transfers the words read
;               from disk to the calling program data area.  The
;               transfer uses AX and COUNT is transferred using
;               CX in the procedure DISKCT1. This sets up a loop
;               counter.  SI is the table pointer defined in the
;               calling program.
;
         PUSH DS
                    ;
         MOV AX,SEG DATARD
         MOV DS,AX
                    ;
         MOV AX,DDATA[SI]
                    ;
         POP DS
         RET
DISKTF1 ENDP
                    ;
DISKCT1 PROC    FAR
;
;               DESCRIPTION: This procedure gets the disk read word
;               count number for transfer to the calling program.
;               The count is returned in CX.
;
         PUSH DS
                    ;
         MOV AX,SEG DATARD
         MOV DS,AX
                    ;
         MOV CX,COUNT               ;Count value to be returned
                    ;
         POP DS
         RET
DISKCT1 ENDP
                    ;
CFRD     ENDS
         END     READF1
```

Figure 7.16 (*Continued*)

Read file:

```
        LL3:  ···
              CLC                    ; Clear carry flag
              MOV AM,3FH             ; Read file function
              MOV BX,HHANDLE         ; Load file handle
              LEA DX,DTA             ; Load read string address
              MOV CX,RECSB1          ; Load record size
              INT 21H
                                     ;
              MOV AH,44H             ; I/O function call
              MOV AL,07H             ; Output EOF check
              INT 21H
                                     ;
              CMP AL,OOH             ; AL = FFH no EOF
              JE LL1                 ; AL = OOH if EOF
              JMP LL3
        LL1:  ···
```

These function calls have been incorporated in the programs FILCR and FILERD, which formerly were used to create and read files using FCBs and DTAs. Figure 7.15 illustrates the procedures for FILECR1 that employ the techniques for creating files using file handles. Similarly, Figure 7.16 illustrates the procedures for FILERD1 that use file handles to open and read an existing file. As the reader can see, the approaches are very similar. The major difference being that DOS uses the file handle for all subsequent reference to the disk file. Also, the ASCII string used to transfer the file record (in this case with starting address DDTA) has been kept in the same form. The file identifier, NNAME, must contain the drive, path, filename and extension; and consequently, is more general than the earlier FCB definition which did not allow for path specification.

7.3 SUMMARY

This chapter completes our study of the basic Macro Assembler features using disk and diskette I/O. The utility of macros for expanding code where repeated operations take place was highly visible in the routines that read from the keyboard and output to the display. The stock market example of this chapter illustrates the need for a permanent yet portable storage medium. Clearly one would not like to have to enter large data tables any more than necessary. The issue of extended file management greatly enhances the user's ability to write flexible, modular, general-purpose programs that are capable of handling large databases under program control. The problem of making data bases portable and accessible through a user program represents the last major hurdle to generating large-scale software packages using the Macro Assembler.

The discussion of this chapter concludes the general refinements of the version 1.0 Macro Assembler plus some version 2.0 features. In the next chapter, the coprocessor will be examined and this constitutes a significant step forward in the discussion of the IBM Macro Assembler capabilities. The major version 2.0 enhancement has been the addition of a set of instructions for the 8087 or 80287 coprocessor chip. This enhancement will occupy a significant amount of discussion time. It provides the Macro Assembler with full "number crunching" capabilities.

REFERENCES

1. Foard, R. M. "A Data Manager Using Entity-Relationships." *PC Tech Journal.* 3, 10 (1985): 96. P.O. Box 2968, Boulder, CO 80321.
2. Roberts, J. "A Data Manager for the Self-Reliant User." *PC Tech Journal.* 4, 10 (1986): 146. P.O. Box 2968, Boulder, CO 80321.
3. Ketabchi, M. A., Berzius, V. "Modeling and Managing CAD Databases." *Computer*, 20, 2 (1987). 10662 Los Vaqueros Circle, Los Alamitos, CA 90720.
4. *Disk Operating System Technical Reference.* IBM Personal Computer Software. IBM Corp. P.O. Box 1328, Boca Raton, FL 33432 (1985).

PROBLEMS

7.1. Write a macro to (a) allocate a DTA; (b) create a file; (c) close a file; (d) open a file; (e) write to a file; and (f) read from a file using File Control Blocks.

7.2. Write a procedure that generates 4096 Gaussian random numbers and writes them to disk.

7.3. Develop a procedure that creates a file and writes a string to this file looking for a delimiter $.

7.4. Write a macro to (a) create a file; (b) write a file; (c) close a file; (d) open a file; and (e) read a file using file handles.

7.5. Write a procedure that outputs 1024 word-size integers to disk using file handles. Assume a create file macro

```
CRFH NNAME,HHANDLE
```

(NNAME = path name, HHANDLE = handle); a write file macro

```
WRFH DTA,RECSZB,HHANDLE
```

(DTA = start of string to write. RECSZB = record size); and a close file macro

```
CLFH HHANDLE
```

7.6. Using the random numbers from problem 7.2, average these numbers. What is the trend in the result? Assume an open file macro

```
OPFH NNAME,HHANDLE
```

(NNAME = path, HHANDLE = handle); a read file macro

                          RDFH HHANDLE,RECSB1,DTA

(RECSB1 = record size in bytes and DTA = string read); and a close file macro

                               CLFH HHANDLE

7.7. Do problem 7.6 with File Control Blocks. Assume an open file macro

                                OPNFL FCBLB

(FCBLB = FCB label); a read file macro

                                 RDFL FCBLB

a close file macro

                                CLOFL FCBLB

and a DTA allocation macro

                               DTAALLC DDTA

7.8. What modification to the module FILECR.ASM and FILERD.ASM is needed if the stock library is to use minimum space on disk?

7.9. Explain how different variable areas are used for disk I/O when two or more disk storage areas are accessed from the same program using RRDISK X.

8

The Coprocessor

Version 2.0 of the Macro Assembler contains significant enhancements on the capabilities of version 1.0. This assembler contains support for the AT's 80286 microprocessor, with several special instructions for this chip; also, both the 8087 and 80287 coprocessors are supported in version 2.0. The coprocessor support takes the form of a complete set of additional instructions devoted exclusively to both the 8087 and 80287 [1,2]. Programming these instructions is identical for the 8087 and 80287; except that the 80287 incorporates some of the needed wait states directly into its instructions. Prior to the development of version 2.0, the programmer was forced to rely on the ESC instruction to access the 8087.

As part of version 2.0, IBM has added the object library manager that was described earlier. We have seen how useful it is to create object libraries of procedures that perform general purpose functions. Object libraries enhance the programming objectives of this book, to provide clear and readable software and to modularize the code whenever possible, during development.

8.1 INTRODUCTION TO THE 8087 AND 80287

This subsection describes the Intel 8087 and 80287 coprocessor or Numeric Processor Extension (NPX), as it is referred to by Intel. Table 8.1 illustrates the relative speed increase of the 8087 over the 8086 (the 8088's big brother) based on numbers supplied by Intel for typical instructions. Table 8.1 represents only part of the story as to the

TABLE 8.1 RELATIVE SPEED INCREASE OF 8087
COPROCESSOR [3]

Instruction type	Relative increase in speed over 8086
Single Precision Multiply	84
Double Precision Multiply	78
Add	94
Single Precision Divide	82
Compare	144
Single Precision Load	189
Single Precision Store	67
Square Root*	544
Tangent*	144
Exponentiation*	171

* Based on simulated code

8087's attractiveness. We have seen instances in earlier discussions in this book where integer scaling was necessary and, in some cases, significance was eventually lost in the output of final calculations because the overall dynamic range of the computation exceeded 65,535 at some point. The coprocessor avoids this problem because it uses internal registers which are 80-bits wide and, consequently, maintains an internal dynamic range of 10^{4932} (contrast this, for example, with the Control Data Corporation 6400 general purpose computer that has a 60-bit word.)

Figure 8.1 illustrates the 8087 and 80287 coprocessor architecture. The processor consists of a control unit (CU) and a numeric execution unit (NEU). The CU maintains synchronization with the IBM PC's 8088. This control unit monitors the 8088 status signals to determine when an 8087 instruction has been fetched by the central processor unit (CPU). The CPU maintains an instruction queue which is

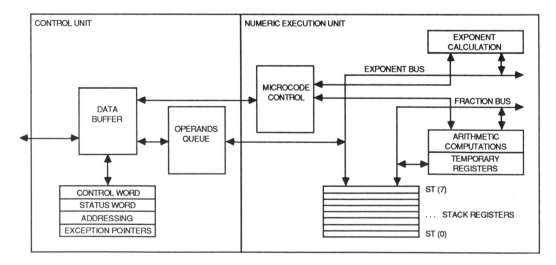

Figure 8.1 The 8087 and 80287 Functional Block Diagram (Courtesy of Intel).

identical to the 8088; however, the NEU microcode control unit processes these instructions following decoding. All operand information is passed to the NEU via the CU, which provides the interface to the outside world. Each of the eight registers in the 8087 register stack is 80-bits wide; these are designated as ST(0), ST(1), ... ST(7). The format for register storage is temporary-real, which will be described in the next subsection. Since all computations are to be accomplished using these eight registers, debugging the 8087 becomes difficult because DEBUG does not automatically display the content of these registers. During the debug process, the appropriate registers must be off loaded into memory and examined in order to observe changes in their content.

In addition to the eight register stack used by the coprocessor to effect internal computation, the 8087 also has a status word register, a control word register, a tag word register and room for exception pointers. The status word, as defined by Intel, subdivides as follows.

15								7						
B	C3	ST		C2	C1	C0	1R		PE	UE	OE	ZE	DE	IE

B = Busy
C3 = Condition code (also C2, C1, and C0)
ST = Stack top pointer (000 = ST[0], ... 111 = ST[7])
IR = Interrupt Request
PE = Precision
UE = Underflow
OE = Overflow
ZE = Zero Divide
DE = Denormalized Operand
IE = Invalid Operation

The 8087 compare instruction, for example, posts its results to C3, C2, C1 and C0 of the status word. Since this is used for conditional branching, the status word must be stored in memory and then examined by an 8088 instruction to ascertain the proper condition for subsequent 8088 operation. Most of the important control word operations are included in the status word format; hence, we will only occasionally examine the control word. Similarly the tag word and exception pointers will not be of particular interest in this book.

Table 8.2 illustrates the various instruction types available for the 8087. The goal of this section is to delineate the use of most of these instructions. Many of these 8087 instructions will be used in programming the examples that follow. Prior to examining the actual mechanics for programming the 8087, it is necessary to describe the handling of data to be input to and internal to the coprocessor. The data representation used by the coprocessor is the topic for the next subsection. Following this discussion we will examine the implementation of coprocessor instructions in

TABLE 8.2 8087 COPROCESSOR INSTRUCTION TYPES

Type	8087 instruction	Comments
Data Transfer	FLD,FST,FSTP,FXCH,FILD,FIST, FISTP,FBLD,FBSTP	These instructions affect real number, integer, and binary coded decimal storage and loading from memory.
Addition	FADD,FADDP,FIADD	These instructions affect real and integer add as well as add and pop.
Subtraction	FSUB,FSUBP,FISUB,FSUBR,FSUBRP, FISUBR	These instructions affect integer and real subtraction as well as subtract and pop and reverse subtraction.
Multiplication	FMUL,FMULP,FIMUL	These instructions affect real and integer multiplication as well as multiply and pop.
Division	FDIV,FDIVP,FIDIV,FDIVR,FDIVRP, FIDIVR	These instructions affect real and integer division and divide and pop as well as reverse division.
Miscellaneous	FSQRT,FSCALE,FPREM,FRNDINT, FXTRACT,FABS,FCHS	These instructions affect various mathematical operations such as the square root and absolute value.
Comparison	FCOM,FCOMP,FCOMPP,FICOM, FICOMP,FTST,FXAM	These instructions affect real and integer comparison and test.
Transcendental	FPTAN,FPATAN,F2XM1,FYL2X, FYL2XP1	These instructions are used to generate special trigonometric, power, and logarithmic functions.
Constant	FLDZ,FLD1,FLDP1,FLDL2T,FLDL2E, FLDLG2,FLDLN2	These instructions load various constants.
Control	FINIT/FNINIT,FDISI/FNDISI, FENI/FNENI,FLDCW, FSTCW/FNSTCW,FSTSW/FNSTSW, FCLEX/FNCLEX, FSTENV/FNSTENV,FLDENV, FSAVE/FNSAVE,FRSTOR,FINCSTP, FFREE,FDECSTP,FNOP,FWAIT	These instructions are used to control the processor.

various programming examples. Also, we will consider each instruction type in some detail, as we did for the 8088.

8.1.1 Data Representations and Numerical Conversion

In the coding for previous portions of this book, the handling of numerical data has always involved integer arithmetic. In order to achieve significance without introducing rounding errors it was necessary, in most cases, to scale calculations at intermediate points. All discussion was predicted on maintaining word accuracy in calculations, which implies that any arithmetic operation loses significance when the resulting scaled outcome exceeds 65,535. It is, of course, possible to develop special purpose routines to handle 32-bit arithmetic operations in software, as well as 64-bit and larger. We have not pursued this avenue of development until now because the introduction of the 8087 and 80287 capabilities essentially circumvent the need for such routines. In order to load the coprocessor, however, such routines will now be used. Intel has designed these coprocessors so that they handle arithmetic operations with a temporary real integer format that is 80-bits wide and has a numerical dynamic range of 10^{-4932} to 10^{4932}. The major difficulty in using these coprocessors becomes one of setting up numerical data for proper acceptance by the coprocessor. Similarly, converting the data back to usable form once the coprocessor has finished operating on the data is equally important. The purpose of this subsection is to consider in some detail the various data formats for both the 8088 and 80286 and the two coprocessors, 8087 and 80287.

Figure 8.2 illustrates a small program that simply defines some variables and loads registers. The purpose of this program is to demonstrate the way in which data is formatted and to introduce the scientific decimal notation used to define numbers

```
IBM Personal Computer MACRO Assembler   Version 2.00   Page  1-1
NUMCK   - NUMERICAL CK (NUMCK.SAL)                      05-22-87


                        PAGE    55,132
                        TITLE   NUMCK   - NUMERICAL CK (NUMCK.SAL)
                        ;
                        ;       DESCRIPTION: This routine is intended to serve
                        ;       as a DEBUG tool for displaying internal numerical
                        ;       format.
                        ;
0000                    STACK   SEGMENT PARA STACK 'STACK'
0000      40 [                  DB      64 DUP('STACK    ')
          53 54 41 43
          4B 20 20 20
                        ]

0200                    STACK   ENDS
                        ;
0000                    DATA    SEGMENT PARA PUBLIC 'DATA'
                        ;
0000  7F                VAR1    DB      127             ;Integer byte
0001  007F              VAR2    DW      127             ;Integer word
0003  7F 00 00 00       VAR3    DD      127             ;Integer double word
0007  A0 86 01 00       VAR4    DD      100000          ;Integer double word
000B  00 50 43 91       VAR5    DD      1.E5            ;Real double word
000F  00 00 2F 88       VAR6    DD      1.75E2          ;Real double word
0013  00 00 00 00 00 24 VAR7    DQ      1.0E6           ;Long real
      74 94
                        ;
001B                    DATA    ENDS
0000                    CSEG    SEGMENT PARA PUBLIC 'CODE'
0000                    NUMCK   PROC    FAR
                                ASSUME  CS:CSEG,SS:STACK,DS:DATA
                                                        ;
0000  1E                        PUSH    DS
0001  2B C0                     SUB     AX,AX
0003  50                        PUSH    AX
                                                        ;
0004  B8 ---- R                 MOV     AX,SEG DATA
0007  8E D8                     MOV     DS,AX
                                                        ;
0009  A0 0000 R                 MOV     AL,VAR1
                                                        ;
000C  CB                        RET
000D                    NUMCK   ENDP
000D                    CSEG    ENDS
                                END     NUMCK
```

Figure 8.2 The assembler listing for NUMCK.LST, a program intended to illustrate the format of various numerical types used by the Macro Assembler.

with exponents. These formats all apply to the basic Macro Assembler conventions for the 8088 and 80286. In the figure, assembled code is displayed next to the memory offset, and it is this representation that we will examine to see how the assembler loads variables of different types in memory.

The first variable appearing in the data segment has been initialized to 127 and is a byte variable. This has the hexadecimal notation 7F. The second variable, VAR2, is a word variable which has also been initialized to the integer value 127. This is stored as 007F, where the byte distinction is not made. VAR3 is a double word quantity (4 bytes) and is loaded with 127 which stores in hexadecimal as

$$7F \ 00 \ 00 \ 00$$

Since bytes are stored in reverse order, this double word actually is defined as follows.

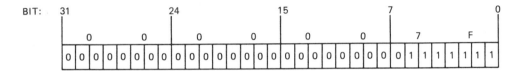

The next variable, VAR4, has been initialized to the integer value 100,000. This loads as hexadecimal

$$A0 \ 86 \ 01 \ 00$$

and is defined as

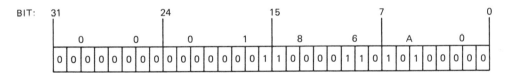

It should be pointed out that for integers, each bit position is defined as a positive power of two. For example, bit 0 represents $2^0 = 1$. The above number satisfies

$$2^5 + 2^7 + 2^9 + 2^{10} + 2^{15} + 2^{16} = 100,000$$

For these double word definitions, the range of values that may be represented is 0 to 4×10^9 or approximately -2×10^9 to 2×10^9. This is ample for most real-world applications.

Continuing on, we consider VAR5, a real double-word variable. IBM refers to this as a single-precision real-number format or single-precision Microsoft Binary real format. How does the assembler load such a number? Essentially, the single-precision real format takes the form

where E7, E6,... E0 are the exponent bits, S is the sign bit, and f1, f2,... f23 are the significand bits. Further explanation is needed, however, because the single-precision real format is stored in normalized form. The significand is assumed to have the form

$$1.x_1x_2x_3x_4x_5...$$

where only $x_1x_2x_3x_4x_5...$ are represented by the binary equivalents f1, f2,... f23. The decimal point is assumed to be to the left of f1 and the leading one is suppressed. The exponent has an additive bias of 129; thus, this quantity must be subtracted to obtain the true exponent.

To see an example of this representation, consider VAR5 which stores as

$$00\ 50\ 43\ 91$$

and loads as

$$91\ 43\ 50\ 00$$

In bit representation, this becomes

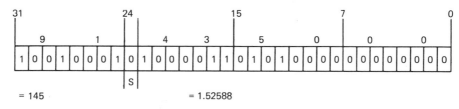

where $2^{-1} + 2^{-6} + 2^{-7} + 2^{-9} + 2^{-11} + 1.0 = 1.52588$. Removing the exponential bias, $145 - 129 = 16$, the number becomes

$$1.52588 \times 2^{16} = 100,000$$

Similarly, VAR6 is stored as

$$00\ 00\ 2F\ 88$$

and loaded as

$$88\ 2F\ 00\ 00$$

This has a single-precision representation of

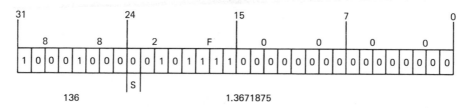

where $2^{-2} + 2^{-4} + 2^{-5} + 2^{-6} + 2^{-7} + 1.0 = 1.3671875$. Removing the exponential bias, $136 - 129 = 7$, the number becomes

$$1.3671875 \times 2^7 = 175$$

Finally, consider the quadword VAR7. This is a long real and is stored as

$$00 \ 00 \ 00 \ 00 \ 00 \ 24 \ 74 \ 94$$

and loads as

$$94 \ 74 \ 24 \ 00 \ 00 \ 00 \ 00 \ 00$$

This has a double precision representation as

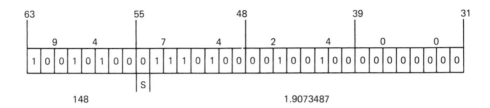

where $2^{-1} + 2^{-2} + 2^{-3} + 2^{-5} + 2^{-10} + 2^{-13} + 1.0 = 1.9073487$. Removing the exponent bias, $148 - 129 = 19$, the number becomes

$$1.9073487 \times 2^{19} = 1{,}000{,}000$$

These formats apply to the 8088 and 80286 internal representations. Now it is useful to consider the 8087 and 80287 representations. Table 8.3 illustrates the coprocessor formats. It is clear that the integer types are identical with the Microsoft integer definitions using DW, DD, and DQ, respectively, to correspond to word, short and long 8087 integer types. The reals have the sign bit repositioned and, except for the short real, the number of significand and exponent digits is slightly different when comparing the coprocessor and Microsoft formats. Finally, the packed decimal is, of course, new. Table 8.4 presents the range of each of the integer and real formats. It is important to recognize that the sign bit for the coprocessor real numbers is always the most significant bit, while for the Microsoft format it is buried in the number at bits 23 and 55, respectively, for the single- and double-precision results. In the coprocessor format the exponent bias is 127 (shortened), 1023 (long real), and 16383 (temporary real). The double-precision Microsoft format is

E7	...	E0	S	f1 f2	...	f55
63		56	54			0

where the nomenclature is the same as for the single-precision result. The 80-bit temporary real format used by the coprocessor conforms to the ten-byte (DT) memory storage allocation.

A major point of interest is how one goes about loading numbers into the coprocessor format. Essentially the 8088 and 80286 are most conveniently pro-

TABLE 8.3 THE COPROCESSOR NUMERICAL REPRESENTATIONS

Type	Representation

Word Integer
```
| s |        MAG        |
 15                     0
```

Short Integer
```
| s |         MAG          |
 31                        0
```

Long Integer
```
| s |              MAG              |
 63                                0
```

Short Real
```
| s | EXP |      SIG      |
 31     23                0
```

Long Real
```
| s | EXP |         SIG         |
 63      52                      0
```

Temporary Real
```
| s |  EXP  |           SIG           |
 79       64                           0
```

Packed Decimal
```
| s | X |      18 BCD DIGIT PAIRS      |
 79    72                              0
```

grammed as integer-based processors. Any calculation that is based on internally generated values can, of course, assume the integer or Microsoft real formats prior to input to the coprocessor and undergo suitable conversion to the coprocessor format. Once conversion has taken place, the coprocessor handles all numbers in the temporary real format; hence, integer and real arithmetic can be mixed. The 8088 and

TABLE 8.4 NUMERICAL RANGE

Type	Coprocessor EXP	Coprocessor MAG/SIG	Microsoft EXP	Microsoft MAG/SIG
Word Integer	—	$-32{,}768, 32{,}768$	—	$-32{,}768, 32{,}768$
Short Integer	—	$-2 \times 10^9, 2 \times 10^9$*	—	$-2 \times 10^9, 2 \times 10^9$*
Long Integer	—	$-9 \times 10^{18}, 9 \times 10^{18}$*	—	$-9 \times 10^{18}, 9 \times 10^{18}$*
Short Real	$-127, 127$	$-2.0, +2.0$	$-127, 127$	$-2.0, +2.0$
Long Real	$-1{,}023, 1{,}023$	$-2.0, +2.0$	$-127, 127$	$-2.0, +2.0$
Temporary Real	$-16{,}383, 16{,}383$	$-2.0, +2.0$	—	—

* approximate

80286 processor instructions operate on 16-bit word quantities or 8-bit byte quantities. This is not to say, as has been mentioned, that routines extending the significance of memory operands could not be developed for multiplication and division, for example, the most troublesome operations because of underflow and overflow. Where this discussion is leading is to the problem faced by the programmer who wants to input a number from the keyboard to be used by the coprocessor. The number consists of ASCII characters that must first be converted to internal binary format and then to coprocessor format. As long as the number is an integer and less than 65,535 it can be treated as a single-precision word, and the normal ASCDEC routine can be used for the conversion.

Since we would like to be able to input numbers from the keyboard that exceed 65,535, it is necessary to develop a set of routines for this purpose. The strategy to be employed is to use DX and AX for the upper and lower portions of the integer, respectively. All input/output will use single-precision integer arithmetic, thereby allowing integers within the range of -2×10^9 to 2×10^9. This will greatly expand our numerical significance and begin to allow the power of the coprocessor to be explored. Figure 8.3 illustrates the HASCDEC procedure, which converts ASCII to internal binary integers. This procedure is similar to ASCDEC, appearing in Chapter 6 in macro form, except it considers a double-word output, BBINV, and calls a multiplication routine, MUL3216, which multiplies a 32-bit number by a 16-bit number and returns a 32-bit number. Figure 8.4 illustrates this 32-bit multiplication. Basically, the lower multiplicand in AX is multiplied by BX and a set of partial products generated: HP1 (from DX) and LP1 (from AX). LP1 is the lower portion of the product. Then, the high multiplicand is loaded in AX (DX = 0) and a high partial product generated: HP2 (from DX) and LP2 (from AX). HP2 cannot be other than zero for these calculations since the result is assumed a priori to fit in 32 bits. Next the quantities LP2 and HP1 are needed, and this output constitutes the high 32-bit output. Schematically, with AX = LM1 and DX = HM1 to start the calculation

$$
\begin{array}{r}
\text{HM1} \quad \text{LM1} \\
\times \qquad\qquad \text{BX} \\
\hline
\text{HP1} \quad \text{LP1} \\
+(\text{HP2}) \qquad \text{LP2} \qquad\qquad \\
\hline
(\text{HP2}) \quad \text{HP1} + \text{LP2} \quad \text{LP1}
\end{array}
$$

These outputs are returned in AX (lower) and BX (upper) as well as the double word MULD.

The approach taken in this discussion and future programming of the 8087 and 80287 is to take all inputs from the keyboard as 32-bit single-precision integers, which has already been mentioned. Appropriate scaling will be implemented intermediately where needed to allow for decimal fractions. The use of this format for keyboard input means that any numbers input from the keyboard will be immediately in the 8087 and 80287 short integer format. Thus, we have achieved a technique for generating input to the coprocessor directly from the keyboard. Similarly, a method

```
PAGE      55,132
TITLE     HASCDEC - 32 BIT ASCDEC CONVERSION
;
;         DESCRIPTION: This routine reads in an ASCII no. less
;         than 4 x 10(9) and converts it to a 32-bit internal
;         decimal number.
;
.8087
EXTRN     BUFFLN:BYTE,ASC:BYTE,MUL3216:FAR,BASE:DWORD,MULD:DWORD
EXTRN     BBINV:DWORD,BBH:WORD,BBL:WORD
;
CSEG      SEGMENT PARA PUBLIC 'CODE'
          PUBLIC  HASCDEC
HASCDEC PROC      FAR
          ASSUME  CS:CSEG                            ;

          PUSH    DS
                                                     ;
          MOV     BL,BUFFLN                 ;Load buffer length
          MOV     BH,0                      ;Clear upper BX
          LEA     SI,ASC-1                  ;Load SI with char.-1
          MOV     DI,BX                     ;Count index for no. char.
          MOV     AX,1                      ;Lower base start
          MOV     DX,0                      ;Upper base start
          LEA     BX,BASE                   ;Base start address
          MOV     DS:[BX],AX                ;Lower base
          MOV     DS:[BX+2],DX              ;Upper base
          LEA     BX,BBINV                  ;Address output
          MOV     DS:[BX],DX                ;Clear lower output
          MOV     DS:[BX+2],DX              ;Clear upper output
                                                     ;
          ADD     SI,DI                     ;Generate char. address
          MOV     AL,[SI]                   ;Load first character
DO1:
              CMP     AL,2DH                ;Compare with "-"
              JE ELSE1
                  AND     AX,000FH          ;Truncate AX to nibble
                  MOV     BX,AX             ;Load multiplier
                  PUSH    BX                ;Save multiplier
                  LEA     BX,BASE           ;Base address
                  MOV     AX,DS:[BX]        ;Load lower base
                  MOV     DX,DS:[BX+2]      ;Load upper base
                  POP     BX                ;Recall multiplier
                  CALL    MUL3216           ;32-bit multiply
                  MOV     BBL,AX            ;Low product
                  MOV     BBH,BX            ;High product
                  LEA     BX,BBINV          ;Address output
                  MOV     AX,DS:[BX]        ;Lower output
                  MOV     DX,DS:[BX+2]      ;Upper output
                  ADD     AX,BBL            ;Add lower
                  ADC     DX,BBH            ;Add/carry upper
                  MOV     DS:[BX],AX        ;Save lower BBINV
                  MOV     DS:[BX+2],DX      ;Save upper BBINV
                  LEA     BX,BASE           ;Base address
                  MOV     AX,DS:[BX]        ;Load lower base
                  MOV     DX,DS:[BX+2]      ;Load upper base
                  MOV     BX,10             ;Base multiplier
                  CALL    MUL3216           ;32-bit multiply
                  MOV     CX,BX             ;Translate BX to CX
                  LEA     BX,BASE           ;Base address
                  MOV     DS:[BX],AX        ;Save lower base
```

Figure 8.3 The procedure HASCDEC for converting 32-bit ASCII numbers to internal decimal format. This is the .ASM file.

```
                    MOV      DS:[BX+2],CX      ;Save upper base
                    DEC      SI                ;Decrement pointer
                    DEC      DI                ;Decrement counter
                    MOV      AL,[SI]           ;Load next character
              JMP SHORT IF2
       ELSE1:
                    LEA      BX,BBINV          ;Address output
                    MOV      DX,DS:[BX+2]      ;Load upper output
                    OR       DX,8000H          ;Negative sign
                    MOV      DS:[BX+2],DX      ;Save negative no.
                    DEC      SI                ;Decrement pointer
                    DEC      DI                ;Decrement counter
                    MOV      AL,[SI]           ;Error if this is used
       IF2:
              CMP        DI,0                  ;Compare count
         JNE DO1
                                                 ;
         POP        DS
         RET
HASCDEC  ENDP
CSEG     ENDS
         END
```

Figure 8.3 (*Continued*)

for generating 32-bit output (short integer format) to the display is needed. Figure 8.5 illustrates the procedure HDECASC, which converts a 32-bit internal binary number (BBINV) to ASCII output loaded in the array ASC. This routine is similar to DECASC, a macro discussed in Chapter 6. The division by 10 is based on a 32-bit dividend. The routine DIV3216, which appears in Figure 8.6, essentially accomplishes the division of a 32-bit number by a 16-bit number and is used by HDECASC for the decimal to ASCII conversion.

In order to check the adequacy of these conversion routines, the program HASCCK.ASM was developed, and this program appears in Figure 8.7. HASCCK reads in a 32-bit number, converts it to internal binary in BBINV, converts the number back to ASCII, and outputs the number to the display. Figure 8.8 illustrates a composite set of test numbers, run using HASCCK, and their interactive response. The program HASCCK.EXE was generated with the following link sequence.

LINK HASCCK + HASCDEC + HDECASC + DIV3216 + MUL3216

Also, the library IOCON.LIB was loaded. For future reference, all the above routines will be loaded into IOCON.LIB, as part of the input/output conversion library, except, of course, HASCCK.OBJ.

8.1.2 A Simple Coprocessor Example

This subsection uses a simple example to address the issue of programming the coprocessor. The goal of the subsection is to illustrate a representative set of coprocessor instructions and show how they interact to accomplish a simple task. To do this, it is necessary to introduce several specific instructions and describe how they should be programmed. The next rather lengthy subsection discusses each processor instruction in some depth; and it is intended to serve as a formal description for these

```
PAGE      55,132
TITLE     MUL3216 - MULTIPLY 32-BIT BY 16-BIT (MUL3216.ASM)
;
;         DESCRIPTION: This procedure multiplies a 32-bit input
;         in AX(lower) and DX(higher) by a 16-bit multiplier (BX).
;         The input values are selected,however, not to exceed
;         32-bit significance so that only a double word return
;         is made in MULD (which must be specified as double
;         word).
;
.8087
EXTRN     MULD:DWORD,HM1:WORD,LM1:WORD,HP1:WORD,LP1:WORD
EXTRN     HP2:WORD,LP2:WORD
;
CSEG      SEGMENT PARA PUBLIC 'CODE'
          PUBLIC  MUL3216
MUL3216 PROC      FAR
          ASSUME  CS:CSEG                            ;
                                                     ;
          PUSH    DS                                 ;
                                                     ;
          MOV     HM1,DX          ;Load upper multiplicand in HM1
          MOV     LM1,AX          ;Load lower multiplicand in LM1
          MUL     BX              ;Multiply LM1 by 16-bit BX
          MOV     HP1,DX          ;High-order partial product 1
          MOV     LP1,AX          ;Low-order partial product 1
          MOV     AX,HM1          ;Load upper multiplicand
          MOV     DX,0            ;Clear DX
          MUL     BX              ;Multiply HM1 by 16-bit BX
          MOV     HP2,DX          ;High-order partial product 2
          MOV     LP2,AX          ;Low-order partial product 2
                                  ;
                                  ;Perform addition
                                  ;
          MOV     AX,LP1          ;Load lower 16-bit product
          MOV     BX,HP1          ;Upper 16-bit partial product
          ADD     BX,LP2          ;Add partial product 2 (lower)
                                  ;
                                  ;The resulting multiply has
                                  ;been chosen to be less than
                                  ;4 x 10(9), hence generate DD
          LEA     BP,MULD
          MOV     DS:[BP],AX
          MOV     DS:[BP+2],BX
                                                     ;
          POP     DS
                                                     ;
          RET
MUL3216 ENDP
CSEG      ENDS
          END
```

Figure 8.4   The procedure MUL3216 which multiplies a 32-bit number by a 16-bit number. This is the .ASM file.

instructions. This subsection, however, will provide a starting point from which to view coprocessor programming.

Figure 8.9 illustrates an assembler listing for the program COPROC.ASM. Aside from the usual loading of the data segment register, only 8087 and 80287 instructions are used in the program. Four double-word variables, HM1, HM2, HM3, and HM4, are defined in the data segment. HM1 is initialized to 100,000 and HM2 to 10. The instruction FINIT initializes the 8087 coprocessor and is equivalent to a hardware reset with all ST registers set to 0. Next the integer multiplier, 10, contained in HM2 is loaded into the ST register using FILD HM2. The integer multiplication instruction, FIMUL, is used to multiply ST times the integer memory reference HM1. The form of this multiplication

FIMUL HM1

is such that explicit reference to the stack register, ST(0), is not needed. This is the integer memory form for an instruction, and it is implicitly understood that ST(0) is used in the multiplication with the product returned to ST: ST = ST(0). Here ST is considered the destination operand and HM1 the source operand. The integer store

```
PAGE      55,132
TITLE     HDECASC - 32 BIT DECASC CONVERSION (HDECASC.ASM)
;
;
;         DESCRIPTION: This routine reads an internal decimal
;         number in DX (upper) and AX (lower) and converts it
;         to ASCII.
;
.8087
EXTRN     BBINV:DWORD,ASC:BYTE,CCOUNT:WORD,REM:WORD,DIV3216:FAR
;
CSEG      SEGMENT PARA PUBLIC 'CODE'
          PUBLIC  HDECASC
HDECASC PROC      FAR
          ASSUME  CS:CSEG

          PUSH    DS                          ;
                                              ;
          LEA     BX,BBINV                    ;Address input double word
          MOV     DX,DS:[BX+2]                ;Load DX
          MOV     AX,DS:[BX]                  ;Load AX
          MOV     SI,OFFSET ASC[10]           ;ASCII character maximum
          CMP     DX,0                        ;Check upper loaded
          JE ELSE1
              PUSH    DX                      ;Save DX while sign check
              SHL     DX,1                    ;Clear any sign flag
              SHR     DX,1
DO2:
                  MOV     BX,10               ;Divisor
                  CALL    DIV3216
                  MOV     CX,REM              ;Save remainder
                  ADD     CL,30H              ;Convert to ASCII number
                  MOV     [SI],CL             ;Load ASCII string
                  DEC     SI
                  PUSH    AX
                  SHL     AX,1                ;Clear sign bit if needed
                  SHR     AX,1
                  CMP     AX,10               ;Check last digit
                  POP     AX                  ;Recall old AX
              JNL DO2
              ADD     AL,30H                  ;Convert last ASCII character
              MOV     [SI],AL                 ;Load string
              POP     DX                      ;Recall DX to check sign
              MOV     CL,15
              SHR     DX,CL                   ;Clear all but sign bit
              CMP     DX,0                    ;Check for 0 sign bit
              JE IF4
                  DEC     SI                  .
                  MOV     BL,2DH              ;Load minus sign
                  MOV     [SI],BL
IF4:
          JMP SHORT IF1
ELSE1:
              PUSH    AX
```

Figure 8.5 The procedure HDECASC which converts a 32-bit internal decimal number to ASCII. This is the .ASM file.

```
DO3:
                MOV     BX,10           ;Divisor
                MOV     DX,0            ;Clear upper register
                DIV     BX
                ADD     DL,30H          ;Convert to ASCII character
                MOV     [SI],DL         ;Load string
                DEC     SI
                CMP     AX,10           ;Check last digit
         JNL DO3
         ADD        AL,30H             ;Convert last ASCII character
         MOV        [SI],AL
         POP        AX                 ;Recall AX for sign check
IF1:
         MOV     AX,11
         MOV     CCOUNT,AX              ;Save count ASCII character maximum
                                        ;
         POP     DS
                                        ;
         RET
HDECASC  ENDP
CSEG     ENDS
         END
```

Figure 8.5 (*Continued*)

instruction, FIST, takes the stack top, in this case ST(0), and loads it in the destination HM3. Similarly, since the numbers on the stack are in temporary real format, the product could be returned as a real number using FST. The store real instruction, FST, is also used to store the product in HM4. The instructions make implicit use of the ST stack registers in some cases. It is necessary to examine each instruction type to determine how a particular instruction uses the stack. This implicit use of the stack by various instructions will become apparent in the next subsection.

Figure 8.10 represents a typical DEBUG session for COPROC.EXE on the IBM AT with the 80287 coprocessor. Comparison of this figure with Figure 8.9 demonstrates the operation of the coprocessor. Note that none of the 80286 registers change while the coprocessor instructions are executing; thus, it is difficult to follow the coprocessor execution. Each coprocessor instruction execution is immediately preceded by a WAIT instruction. This is an 80286 CPU instruction that halts the CPU until its TEST pin is driven LOW by the 80287. DEBUG explicitly demonstrates the coprocessor instructions as we step through the program. Following the FAR return instruction, a dump of the data segment starting with offset 0000H is made. Examination of Figure 8.9 indicates that HM3 is located at address 0008H. Bytes 8, 9, 10, and 11 of the double word HM3 store as

$$40\ 42\ 0F\ 00$$

and load as

$$00\ 0F\ 42\ 40$$

This latter value is 1,000,000, which is simply the product of HM1 and HM2; thus, the integer multiplication was performed correctly. The variable HM4 is stored at bytes 12, 13, 14, and 15 (000C through 000F) and has the following values

$$00\ 24\ 74\ 49$$

```
PAGE      55,132
TITLE     DIV3216 - 32-BIT DIVISION
;
;
;         DESCRIPTION: This routine divides a 32-bit number by
;         a 16-bit divisor.  The input is DX (upper) and AX (lower)
;         dividend and BX divisor.  The output is QUO a doubleword
;         or DX and AX with the remainder in REM.
;
.8087
EXTRN     QUO:DWORD,REM:WORD,BBB:WORD
;
CSEG      SEGMENT PARA PUBLIC 'CODE'
          PUBLIC  DIV3216
DIV3216 PROC      FAR
          ASSUME  CS:CSEG

          PUSH    DS                          ;

          CMP     DX,0                        ;
          JE ELSE1                            ;Check for upper value
              PUSH    AX                      ;Save lower
              MOV     AX,DX                   ;Load higher in AX
              MOV     DX,0                    ;Clear DX
              DIV     BX
              POP     CX                      ;Recall lower
              MOV     BBB,AX                  ;Save quotient
              MOV     AX,CX                   ;Load AX with lower
                                              ;Do not clear DX
              DIV     BX
              MOV     REM,DX                  ;Save remainder
              MOV     DX,BBB                  ;Upper quotient in DX
                                              ;Lower quotient in AX
          JMP SHORT IF1
ELSE1:
              DIV     BX                      ;Divide by BX
              MOV     REM,DX                  ;Save remainder
              MOV     DX,0                    ;Clear DX
IF1:
          LEA     BX,QUO                      ;Load DD
          MOV     DS:[BX+2],DX
          MOV     DS:[BX],AX

          POP     DS                          ;
          RET
DIV3216 ENDP
CSEG      ENDS
          END
```

Figure 8.6   The procedure DIV3216 which divides a 32-bit integer by a 16-bit word. This is the .ASM file.

This loads as

$$49 \ 74 \ 24 \ 00$$

which appears as the short real

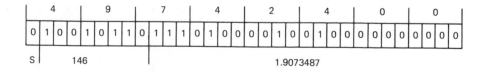

```
PAGE      55,132
TITLE     HASCCK  - CHECK 32-BIT ARITHMETIC (HASCCK.ASM)
;
EXTRN     MESSAGE:FAR,KEYBD:FAR,CLSCREN:FAR,HASCDEC:FAR
EXTRN     HDECASC:FAR
;
STACK     SEGMENT PARA STACK 'STACK'
          DB      64 DUP('STACK   ')
STACK     ENDS
;
DATA      SEGMENT PARA PUBLIC 'DATA'
          PUBLIC  BUFFMX,BUFFLN,CHAR,ASC,BBINV,BASE,BLANK,MULD
          PUBLIC  BBH,BBL,HM1,LM1,HP1,LP1,HP2,LP2
          PUBLIC  QUO,BBB,REM,CCOUNT
;
MESO1     DB      'Input test number.','$'
MESO2     DB      80 DUP(' '),'$'
                                            ;
BUFFMX    DB      80
BUFFLN    DB      ?
CHAR      DB      80 DUP(' '),'$'
                                            ;
ASC       DB      80 DUP(' '),'$'
BBINV     DD      ?
BBL       DW      ?
BBH       DW      ?
MULD      DD      ?
HM1       DW      ?
LM1       DW      ?
HP1       DW      ?
LP1       DW      ?
HP2       DW      ?
LP2       DW      ?
BASE      DW      ?
BLANK     DB      ' '
QUO       DD      ?
BBB       DW      ?
REM       DW      ?
CCOUNT    DW      ?
                                            ;Corners box
                                            ;
DATA      ENDS
                                            ;
CSEG      SEGMENT PARA PUBLIC 'CODE'
HASC      PROC    FAR
          ASSUME  CS:CSEG,DS:DATA,SS:STACK
          PUSH    DS
          SUB     AX,AX
          PUSH    AX
                                            ;
          MOV     AX,SEG DATA
          MOV     DS,AX
                                            ;
          CALL    CLSCREN             ;Clear screen
          MOV     DX,OFFSET MESO1     ;Read TEST
          CALL    MESSAGE             ;Output message
          CALL    KEYBD               ;Read keyboard
```

Figure 8.7   The main calling program HASCCK.ASM, which reads a number from the keyboard, converts it to internal decimal, converts it back to ASCII, and displays it. This is the .ASM file.

```
           MOV      AL,BUFFLN              ;Number characters read
           MOV      AH,0                   ;Clear upper register
           MOV      SI,0                   ;Initialize index
           MOV      CX,AX                  ;Load inner loop count
DO1:
               MOV      AL,CHAR[SI]         ;Transfer input to ASC
               MOV      ASC[SI],AL
               INC      SI
           LOOP DO1
           MOV      AX,0                   ;Clear AX
           CALL     HASCDEC                ;ASCII to 32-bit
           MOV      CX,11                  ;Load output character maximum
           MOV      SI,0
DO3:
               MOV      AL,20H              ;Clear ASC
               MOV      ASC[SI],AL
               INC      SI
           LOOP DO3
           CALL     HDECASC                ;Convert to ASCII
           MOV      CX,11
           MOV      SI,0
DO5:
               MOV      AL,ASC[SI]          ;Load converted values output
               MOV      MESO2[SI],AL
               INC      SI
           LOOP DO5
           MOV      DX,OFFSET MESO2
           CALL     MESSAGE                ;Output string
           RET
HASC       ENDP
CSEG       ENDS
           END      HASC
```

Figure 8.7 (*Continued*)

```
Input test number.          Input test number.

1000000                     5000
      1000000                     5000


Input test number.          Input test number.

-1000000                    -5000
      -1000000                    -5000


Input test number.          Input test number.

500000                      50000
      500000                      50000


Input test number.          Input test number.

-500000                     -50000
      -500000                     -50000
```

Figure 8.8 Representative interactive sessions using HASCCK to demonstrate the ASCII-to-decimal and decimal-to-ASCII conversion process for 32-bit integers.

```
IBM Personal Computer MACRO Assembler   Version 2.00   Page   1-1
COPROC  - FIRST COPROCESSOR PROGRAM (COPROC.SAL)                05-22-87


                        PAGE    55,132
                        TITLE   COPROC  - FIRST COPROCESSOR PROGRAM (COPROC.SAL)
                        ;
                        ;       DESCRIPTION: This program uses the coprocessor to
                        ;       multiply 100,000 by 10 and shift the values, as well
                        ;       as the result, in and out of the ST registers.
                        ;
                        .8087                               ;Coprocessor
                        ;
0000            STACK   SEGMENT PARA    STACK 'STACK'
0000    40 [            DB      64 DUP('STACK    ')

        53 54 41 43
        4B 20 20 20
                ]

0200            STACK   ENDS
                        ;
0000            DATA    SEGMENT PARA PUBLIC 'DATA'
                        ;
0000 A0 B6 01 00  HM1   DD      100000                      ;Integer multiplicand
0004 0A 00 00 00  HM2   DD      10                          ;Integer multiplier
0008 ????????     HM3   DD      ?                           ;Integer result
000C ????????     HM4   DD      ?                           ;Real result
                        ;
0010            DATA    ENDS
                        ;
0000            CSEG    SEGMENT PARA PUBLIC 'CODE'
0000            COPROC  PROC    FAR
                        ASSUME  CS:CSEG,DS:DATA,SS:STACK
                                                            ;
0000 1E                 PUSH    DS
0001 2B C0              SUB     AX,AX
0003 50                 PUSH    AX
                                                            ;
0004 BB ---- R          MOV     AX,SEG DATA
0007 8E D8              MOV     DS,AX
                                                            ;
0009 9B DB E3           FINIT                               ;Initialize coprocessor
000C 9B DB 06 0004 R    FILD    HM2                         ;Load 10 nn stack (ST)
0011 9B DA 0E 0000 R    FIMUL   HM1                         ;Multiply-result returned in ST
0016 9B DB 16 0008 R    FIST    HM3                         ;Result loaded in HM3 - integer
001B 9B D9 16 000C R    FST     HM4                         ;Result loaded in HM4 - real
                                                            ;
0020 CB                 RET
0021            COPROC  ENDP
0021            CSEG    ENDS
                        END     COPROC
```

Figure 8.9   Assembler listing for the program COPROC.ASM. This program illustrates the use of the numerical coprocessor.

The significand evaluates as $2^{-1} + 2^{-2} + 2^{-3} + 2^{-5} + 2^{-10} + 2^{-13} + 1.0 = 1.9073487$. Removing the exponential bias, $146 - 127 = 19$, the number becomes

$$1.9073487 \times 2^{19} = 1,000,000$$

This number has been stored in 80287 or 8087 short real format.

Figure 8.11 illustrates a typical DEBUG session for COPROC.EXE on the IBM PC with the 8087 coprocessor. Observe that the processor does not halt at the coprocessor instructions. Only the 8088 WAIT instructions result in a single step halt. How do these instructions impact the processing? The WAIT instructions act on the 8088. Each WAIT encountered allows the 8088 to suspend processing while the 8087 executes. At the completion of an instruction, the 8087 sets the TEST line LOW and the 8088 can fetch another 8087 or 8088 instruction. In Figure 8.11, DEBUG simply displays a sequence of WAITs and the 8087 instructions are never indicated, but they are executed.

```
DEBUG COPROC.EXE
-T

AX=0000  BX=0000  CX=0240  DX=0000  SP=01FE  BP=0000  SI=0000  DI=0000
DS=12DD  ES=12DD  SS=12F1  CS=12ED  IP=0001  NV UP EI PL NZ NA PO NC
12ED:0001 2BC0          SUB     AX,AX
-T

AX=0000  BX=0000  CX=0240  DX=0000  SP=01FE  BP=0000  SI=0000  DI=0000
DS=12DD  ES=12DD  SS=12F1  CS=12ED  IP=0003  NV UP EI PL ZR NA PE NC
12ED:0003 50            PUSH    AX
-T

AX=0000  BX=0000  CX=0240  DX=0000  SP=01FC  BP=0000  SI=0000  DI=0000
DS=12DD  ES=12DD  SS=12F1  CS=12ED  IP=0004  NV UP EI PL ZR NA PE NC
12ED:0004 B8F012        MOV     AX,12F0
-T

AX=12F0  BX=0000  CX=0240  DX=0000  SP=01FC  BP=0000  SI=0000  DI=0000
DS=12DD  ES=12DD  SS=12F1  CS=12ED  IP=0007  NV UP EI PL ZR NA PE NC
12ED:0007 8ED8          MOV     DS,AX
-T

AX=12F0  BX=0000  CX=0240  DX=0000  SP=01FC  BP=0000  SI=0000  DI=0000
DS=12F0  ES=12DD  SS=12F1  CS=12ED  IP=0009  NV UP EI PL ZR NA PE NC
12ED:0009 9B            WAIT
-T

AX=12F0  BX=0000  CX=0240  DX=0000  SP=01FC  BP=0000  SI=0000  DI=0000
DS=12F0  ES=12DD  SS=12F1  CS=12ED  IP=000A  NV UP EI PL ZR NA PE NC
12ED:000A DBE3              FINIT
-T

AX=12F0  BX=0000  CX=0240  DX=0000  SP=01FC  BP=0000  SI=0000  DI=0000
DS=12F0  ES=12DD  SS=12F1  CS=12ED  IP=000C  NV UP EI PL ZR NA PE NC
12ED:000C 9B            WAIT
-T

AX=12F0  BX=0000  CX=0240  DX=0000  SP=01FC  BP=0000  SI=0000  DI=0000
DS=12F0  ES=12DD  SS=12F1  CS=12ED  IP=000D  NV UP EI PL ZR NA PE NC
12ED:000D DB060400          FILD    DWORD PTR [0004]           DS:0004=00
0A
-T

AX=12F0  BX=0000  CX=0240  DX=0000  SP=01FC  BP=0000  SI=0000  DI=0000
DS=12F0  ES=12DD  SS=12F1  CS=12ED  IP=0011  NV UP EI PL ZR NA PE NC
12ED:0011 9B            WAIT
-T

AX=12F0  BX=0000  CX=0240  DX=0000  SP=01FC  BP=0000  SI=0000  DI=0000
DS=12F0  ES=12DD  SS=12F1  CS=12ED  IP=0012  NV UP EI PL ZR NA PE NC
12ED:0012 DA0E0000          FIMUL   DWORD PTR [0000]           DS:0000=A0
-T

AX=12F0  BX=0000  CX=0240  DX=0000  SP=01FC  BP=0000  SI=0000  DI=0000
DS=12F0  ES=12DD  SS=12F1  CS=12ED  IP=0016  NV UP EI PL ZR NA PE NC
12ED:0016 9B            WAIT
-T

AX=12F0  BX=0000  CX=0240  DX=0000  SP=01FC  BP=0000  SI=0000  DI=0000
DS=12F0  ES=12DD  SS=12F1  CS=12ED  IP=0017  NV UP EI PL ZR NA PE NC
12ED:0017 DB160800          FIST    DWORD PTR [0008]           DS:0008=00
00
-T
```

Figure 8.10 Typical DEBUG session with COPROC.EXE using the 80287 coprocessor (IBM AT). Underlined results demonstrate the product 1,000,000 in real and integer format.

```
AX=12F0  BX=0000  CX=0240  DX=0000  SP=01FC  BP=0000  SI=0000  DI=0000
DS=12F0  ES=12DD  SS=12F1  CS=12ED  IP=001B    NV UP EI PL ZR NA PE NC
12ED:001B 9B              WAIT
-T

AX=12F0  BX=0000  CX=0240  DX=0000  SP=01FC  BP=0000  SI=0000  DI=0000
DS=12F0  ES=12DD  SS=12F1  CS=12ED  IP=001C    NV UP EI PL ZR NA PE NC
12ED:001C D9160C00        FST      DWORD PTR [000C]              DS:000C=0
000
-T

AX=12F0  BX=0000  CX=0240  DX=0000  SP=01FC  BP=0000  SI=0000  DI=0000
DS=12F0  ES=12DD  SS=12F1  CS=12ED  IP=0020    NV UP EI PL ZR NA PE NC
12ED:0020 CB              RETF
-D DS:0000
12F0:0000  A0 86 01 00 0A 00 00 00-40 42 0F 00 00 24 74 49   ........@B...$tI
12F0:0010  53 54 41 43 4B 20 20 20-53 54 41 43 4B 20 20 20   STACK   STACK
12F0:0020  53 54 41 43 4B 20 20 20-53 54 41 43 4B 20 20 20   STACK   STACK
12F0:0030  53 54 41 43 4B 20 20 20-53 54 41 43 4B 20 20 20   STACK   STACK
12F0:0040  53 54 41 43 4B 20 20 20-53 54 41 43 4B 20 20 20   STACK   STACK
12F0:0050  53 54 41 43 4B 20 20 20-53 54 41 43 4B 20 20 20   STACK   STACK
12F0:0060  53 54 41 43 4B 20 20 20-53 54 41 43 4B 20 20 20   STACK   STACK
12F0:0070  53 54 41 43 4B 20 20 20-53 54 41 43 4B 20 20 20   STACK   STACK
-G

Program terminated normally
-Q
```

Figure 8.10 (*Continued*)

The output presented in Figure 8.10 halts at each 80287 coprocessor instruction, such as FIST. In practice the 80286 checks the 80287 hardware to see if it is complete and no WAIT state is needed. The version 2.0 Macro Assembler, however, automatically puts in the WAIT to insure compatibility with the 8087 systems which need these instructions for synchronization.

8.1.3 The 8087 and 80287 Instruction Set

The purpose of this subsection is to present the 8087 and 80287 instruction set with an emphasis on how to manipulate the register stack and how to generate special purpose functions. The 8087 is an efficient processor and makes special use of the register stack to handle operands and improve performance. Table 8.5 illustrates the five approaches to formatting operands for the arithmetic instructions. Normally, when two operands are specified, the first operand is the destination, which eventually contains the result, and the second operand is the source. Frequently, however, one or more operands are implicit and in this case the operand in question is the stack top, ST(0), or ST(1). Here the stack register has the usual designation ST, ST(0) for the top, ST(1) next, and so forth through ST(7), the stack bottom. The abbreviated designation ST always refers to the top location, ST(0), as has been indicated. In Table 8.5, the classical stack refers to ST(0) as the source and ST(1) as the destination, with both operands implicit. Since they are implicit, any instruction using this operand format would have no operands specified. The register format is explicit and ST must be specified as well as one of the remaining registers. Either may be source or destination. The register pop format contains ST as source and ST(i) as destination ($i = 1, \ldots 7$). Finally, real-memory and integer-memory formats use ST as the destination. With these thoughts regarding operand format in mind, it is useful to consider the instruction classes of Table 8.2.

```
b:debug b:coproc.exe
-t

AX=0000  BX=0000  CX=0240  DX=0000  SP=01FE  BP=0000  SI=0000  DI=0000
DS=0CE8  ES=0CE8  SS=0CFC  CS=0CF8  IP=0001    NV UP EI PL NZ NA PO NC
0CF8:0001 2BC0           SUB     AX,AX
-t

AX=0000  BX=0000  CX=0240  DX=0000  SP=01FE  BP=0000  SI=0000  DI=0000
DS=0CE8  ES=0CE8  SS=0CFC  CS=0CF8  IP=0003    NV UP EI PL ZR NA PE NC
0CF8:0003 50            PUSH    AX
-t

AX=0000  BX=0000  CX=0240  DX=0000  SP=01FC  BP=0000  SI=0000  DI=0000
DS=0CE8  ES=0CE8  SS=0CFC  CS=0CF8  IP=0004    NV UP EI PL ZR NA PE NC
0CF8:0004 B8FB0C        MOV     AX,0CFB
-t

AX=0CFB  BX=0000  CX=0240  DX=0000  SP=01FC  BP=0000  SI=0000  DI=0000
DS=0CE8  ES=0CE8  SS=0CFC  CS=0CF8  IP=0007    NV UP EI PL ZR NA PE NC
0CF8:0007 8ED8          MOV     DS,AX
-t

AX=0CFB  BX=0000  CX=0240  DX=0000  SP=01FC  BP=0000  SI=0000  DI=0000
DS=0CFB  ES=0CE8  SS=0CFC  CS=0CF8  IP=0009    NV UP EI PL ZR NA PE NC
0CF8:0009 9B            WAIT
-t

AX=0CFB  BX=0000  CX=0240  DX=0000  SP=01FC  BP=0000  SI=0000  DI=0000
DS=0CFB  ES=0CE8  SS=0CFC  CS=0CF8  IP=000C    NV UP EI PL ZR NA PE NC
0CF8:000C 9B            WAIT
-t

AX=0CFB  BX=0000  CX=0240  DX=0000  SP=01FC  BP=0000  SI=0000  DI=0000
DS=0CFB  ES=0CE8  SS=0CFC  CS=0CF8  IP=0011    NV UP EI PL ZR NA PE NC
0CF8:0011 9B            WAIT
-t

AX=0CFB  BX=0000  CX=0240  DX=0000  SP=01FC  BP=0000  SI=0000  DI=0000
DS=0CFB  ES=0CE8  SS=0CFC  CS=0CF8  IP=0016    NV UP EI PL ZR NA PE NC
0CF8:0016 9B            WAIT
-t

AX=0CFB  BX=0000  CX=0240  DX=0000  SP=01FC  BP=0000  SI=0000  DI=0000
DS=0CFB  ES=0CE8  SS=0CFC  CS=0CF8  IP=001B    NV UP EI PL ZR NA PE NC
0CF8:001B 9B            WAIT
-t

AX=0CFB  BX=0000  CX=0240  DX=0000  SP=01FC  BP=0000  SI=0000  DI=0000
DS=0CFB  ES=0CE8  SS=0CFC  CS=0CF8  IP=0020    NV UP EI PL ZR NA PE NC
0CF8:0020 CB            RETF
-t

AX=0CFB  BX=0000  CX=0240  DX=0000  SP=0200  BP=0000  SI=0000  DI=0000
DS=0CFB  ES=0CE8  SS=0CFC  CS=0CE8  IP=0000    NV UP EI PL ZR NA PE NC
0CE8:0000 CD20          INT     20
-d ds:0000
0CFB:0000   A0 86 01 00 0A 00 00 00-40 42 0F 00 00 24 74 49   ........@B...$tI
0CFB:0010   53 54 41 43 4B 20 20 20-53 54 41 43 4B 20 20 20   STACK   STACK
0CFB:0020   53 54 41 43 4B 20 20 20-53 54 41 43 4B 20 20 20   STACK   STACK
0CFB:0030   53 54 41 43 4B 20 20 20-53 54 41 43 4B 20 20 20   STACK   STACK
0CFB:0040   53 54 41 43 4B 20 20 20-53 54 41 43 4B 20 20 20   STACK   STACK
0CFB:0050   53 54 41 43 4B 20 20 20-53 54 41 43 4B 20 20 20   STACK   STACK
0CFB:0060   53 54 41 43 4B 20 20 20-53 54 41 43 4B 20 20 20   STACK   STACK
0CFB:0070   53 54 41 43 4B 20 20 20-53 54 41 43 4B 20 20 20   STACK   STACK
-g

Program terminated normally
-q
```

Figure 8.11 Typical DEBUG session with COPROC.EXE using the 8087 coprocessor (IBM PC). Underlined results demonstrate the product 1,000,000 in real and integer format.

TABLE 8.5 THE COPROCESSOR ARITHMETIC OPERAND FORMATS

Type	Format	Comments
Classical Stack	ST(1), ST(0)	The destination is ST(1) and the source is ST(0) or (ST). Both operands are implicit.
Register	ST(i), ST or ST, ST(i)	The destination is ST(i) and the source is ST or vice versa.
Register Pop	ST(i), ST(0)	The destination is ST(i) and the source is ST. The source is popped off the stack following execution of this instruction.
Real Memory	ST, real memory	The destination is ST(0), which is implicit, and the source is a real-memory operand.
Integer Memory	ST, integer memory	The destination is ST(0), which is implicit, and the source is an integer-memory operand.

Table 8.6 presents the instruction for transferring data to and from the internal registers of the 8087. Basically these instructions take data in one of the 8087 specified formats and convert it to 80-bit temporary real format. FLD loads the specified real source data in ST. FST executes the converse and takes ST and stores it in the specified real memory or register operand. If the destination is a memory operand, its type (DD, DQ or DT) will determine the form of the stored output. FSTP simply stores ST, as does FST, but it also pops ST off the stack. FXCH exchanges ST with

TABLE 8.6 THE COPROCESSOR DATA TRANSFER INSTRUCTIONS

Instruction	Purpose	Comments
FLD source	Load Real	This instruction pushes the source data onto the top of the register stack, ST(0).
FST destination	Store Real	This instruction copies ST(0) into the indicated destination (real) which can be a memory operand or register.
FSTP destination	Store Real and Pop	This instruction copies ST(0) into the indicated destination and then pops ST(0) off the stack.
FXCH destination	Exchange ST	This instruction exchanges ST(0) with the indicated destination.
FILD source	Load Integer	This instruction pushes the source data (integer) onto the top of the stack, ST(0)
FIST destination	Store Integer	This instruction stores ST(0), the stack top, in the indicated destination which must be an integer memory operand.
FISTP destination	Store Integer and Pop	This instruction stores ST(0), the stack top, in the indicated destination which must be an integer memory operand and then pops ST(0) off the stack.
FBLD source	Load BCD	This instruction pushes the source, which must be a BCD number, onto the stack at ST(0).
FBSTP destination	Store BCD and Pop	This instruction stores ST(0) as a BCD number at the destination and pops ST(0) off the stack.

TABLE 8.7 THE COPROCESSOR ADDITION INSTRUCTIONS

Instruction	Purpose	Comments
FADD	Real Addition	This instruction can be used without operands. It assumes ST(1) is added to ST(0) with the result in ST(0), with a real-memory operand added to ST(0), or with explicit reference to ST(0) added to another register.
FADDP destination, source	Real Add and Pop	The source is ST(0) and the destination must be another stack register. The result is left in the alternate stack register used as the destination.
FIADD integer memory	Integer Addition	The destination, ST(0), is added to the source, integer memory, and the sum returned in ST(0).

the destination. FILD, FIST, and FISTP perform the same functions as FLD, FST, and FSTP except that they operate on integers instead of real numbers. FBLD loads a binary coded decimal (BCD) number onto the stack top. FBSTP stores a BCD number at the specified destination, from ST, and pops ST. These instructions, then, are used to get numbers into and out of the 8087 stack registers. This is the mechanism by which data is moved into a position where it may be processed by the 8087.

There are three addition instructions for the 8087 and these are illustrated in Table 8.7. The first, FADD, performs real addition and can take the form

```
FADD
FADD real-memory
FADD ST(0), ST(i) or FADD ST(i), ST(0)
```

In the first case, ST(0) is added to ST(1) and the result stored in ST(1). In the second case, the destination is ST(0) and is implicit. The third case is self-explanatory. A second instruction is the add and pop, FADDP, which must have as a destination an alternate stack register, ST(i) and as the source, ST(0). Finally, the third instruction is FIADD for integer addition. The destination is implicit: ST(0).

Table 8.8 contains the subtraction instructions. These instructions are similar to the division instructions and unlike those for addition and multiplication in that they are unsymmetrical. In addition for example, either the source can be added to the destination or vice versa with no change in the sum. For subtraction, however, the result of subtracting the source from the destination is the negative of that for subtracting the destination from the source. Hence, the subtraction instructions include reversal instructions that change the order of the subtraction. The instruction FSUB can take the following forms.

```
FSUB
FSUB real-memory
FSUB ST, ST(i) or FSUB ST(i), ST
```

TABLE 8.8 THE COPROCESSOR SUBTRACTION INSTRUCTIONS

Instruction	Purpose	Comments
FSUB	Real Subtraction	This instruction can be used without operands. It assumes ST(1) is the destination and ST(0) is subtracted from it with the result in ST(1), with a real-memory operand subtracted from ST(0) and the result in ST(0), or with explicit reference to ST(0) and another register (the destination containing the result).
FSUBP destination, source	Real Subtract and Pop	The source, ST(0), is subtracted from the destination, another stack register, and the result stored in the destination.
FISUB source	Integer Subtraction	The destination, ST(0), has the source operand, an integer-memory operand, subtracted from it and the result is stored in ST(0).
FSUBR	Real Reversed Subtract	The destination is subtracted from the source and the result left in the destination. The operand configuration is the same as for FSUB.
FSUBRP	Real Reversed Subtract and Pop	This instruction is the same as FSUBP except the destination is subtracted from the source. ST(0) still serves as the source operand.
FISUBR source	Integer Reversed Subtract	This instruction is the same as FISUB except the destination is subtracted from the source. The source is still an integer-memory operand.

In the first of these, the destination, ST(1), has the source, ST(0), subtracted from it, and both operands are implicit. In the second, the destination is ST and this is implicit. Finally, the third form is self-explanatory. A second instruction FSUBP has ST as the source and another register, ST(i), as the destination. ST is popped following the subtraction. FISUB has ST as the implicit destination with an integer-memory operand as the source. The three instructions FSUBP, FSUBRP, and FISUBR act exactly like FSUB, FSUBP, and FISUB, except that the destination is subtracted from the source.

Multiplication instructions are indicated in Table 8.9. FMUL can take one of three forms:

```
FMUL
FMUL real-memory
FMUL ST, ST(i)  or  FMUL ST(i), ST
```

In the first form above, ST is the source and ST(1), the destination (both implicit), with the product left in ST(1). The second form simply multiplies the real-memory source times the implicit destination, ST. Finally, the third form multiplies ST times the register ST(i) where either can be the destination. The FMULP instruction requires that ST be specified as the source and another register, ST(i) as the destination. The product is returned in ST(i) and the stack is popped. Next, FIMUL

TABLE 8.9 THE COPROCESSOR MULTIPLICATION INSTRUCTIONS

Instruction	Purpose	Comments
FMUL	Real Multiply	This instruction multiplies the destination operand by the source and returns the product in the destination. The instruction can be executed with no operands, ST(0) is the implied source and ST(1) the destination, with the source specified as a real-memory operand and ST(0) the destination, and with both destination register and source register, one of which is ST(0), specified.
FMULP destination, source	Real Multiply and Pop	This instruction uses ST(0) as the source operand and another register as the destination. The product is returned in the destination register and the stack top popped.
FIMUL source	Integer Multiply	This instruction multiplies the destination by the source and returns the product in the destination. The destination is ST(0) and source is an integer-memory operand.

generates integer multiplication. The source is an integer-memory operand and the destination is ST, which is implicit. The product returns in the ST register.

Divide instructions are, as indicated, asymmetric. These instructions appear in Table 8.10. FDIV, which produces real division, has the following forms.

```
FDIV
FDIV real-memory
FDIV ST, ST(i) or FDIV ST(i), ST
```

Again, the first form has ST as the implicit source operand and ST(1) as the implicit destination. The destination is the dividend and the source is the divisor. The second form has ST as the destination (dividend) and this is implicit. Finally, the third form is self-explanatory. The instruction FDIVP uses ST as a source operand and another register, ST(i), as the destination. The source is the divisor and the destination is the dividend and, as is true for all divide instructions, the quotient is returned in the destination operand. FDIVP pops the stack following execution of the division. FIDIV performs integer division with the source being an integer-memory operand and acting as the divisor. ST is the destination and this is the implicit dividend. The three instructions FDIVR, FDIVRP, and FIDIVR operate like FDIV, FDIVP, and FIDIV, respectively, except the source and destination have reversed roles. That is to say, the source acts as the dividend and the destination as the divisor. The destination, however, still contains the result at the completion of the instruction execution.

The 8087 has several special purpose instructions that fall in a miscellaneous category. Table 8.11 illustrates these instructions. None of these instructions have

TABLE 8.10 THE COPROCESSOR DIVISION INSTRUCTIONS

Instruction	Purpose	Comments
FDIV	Real Divide	This instruction divides the destination by the source and returns the quotient to the destination. The instruction can be executed with no operands, ST(0) is the implied source and ST(1) the implied destination, with a source specified and ST(0) the implied destination, and with a source, ST(0), and destination (another register) specified.
FDIVP destination, source	Real Divide and Pop	This instruction divides the destination by the source and returns the quotient to the destination. It then pops the top of the 8087 stack. The source is the ST(0) register and the destination operand is another stack register.
FIDIV source	Integer Divide	This instruction divides the destination by the source and returns the quotient to the destination. The destination is ST(0) and the source is an integer-memory operand.
FDIVR	Real Reversed Divide	This instruction is identical with FDIV except the source is divided by the destination. The quotient is still returned in the destination.
FDIVRP destination, source	Real Reversed Divide and Pop	This instruction is identical to FDIVP except the source is divided by the destination. The quotient is still returned in the destination.
FIDIVR source	Integer Divide Reversed	This instruction is identical to FIDIV except the source is divided by the destination. The quotient is still returned in the destination.

operands specified; all are implicit. The first calculates the square root of the number contained in the stack top, ST (FSQRT). FSCALE adds the integer equivalent of ST(1) to the exponent of ST. This is equivalent to multiplying ST by 2 raised to the integer power of ST(1). FPREM is the 8087 modulo instruction. It takes the modulo of ST relative to the number in ST(1) as base. The remainder is returned in ST. The instruction FRNDINT rounds the stack top to an integer value. The rules for this rounding are based on the contents of the RC field in the control word

RC

00 round to nearest integer
01 round downward
10 round upward
11 round toward 0

FXTRACT factors the number in ST into a significand and exponent expressed in real numbers. The exponent becomes ST(1) and the significand ST(0). FABS yields the absolute value of ST and FCHS reverses the sign of ST.

execution. The angular variable, z, must lie in the range 0 to 90°. The following identities are based on y and x as returned.

$$SIN(z) = y/SQRT(y^2 + x^2)$$
$$COS(z) = x/SQRT(y^2 + x^2)$$
$$COT(z) = 1/TAN(z)$$
$$SEC(z) = 1/COS(z)$$
$$CSC(z) = 1/SIN(z)$$

The instruction FPATAN calculates $z = ARCTAN(y/x)$ where x is ST and y is ST(1), with z returned in ST and lying in the range of 0 to 90° (in radians). F2XM2 generates

$$2^x - 1$$

where x is the value of ST which must be in the range (0,0.5). The result is returned in ST. To obtain a number 2^x add one to the result. Consider the following term.

$$2^{x\log_2 M}$$

If $M = 2^N$, then $\log_2 M = N$ and

$$2^{x\log_2 M} = (2^x)^N$$
$$= (2^N)^x$$
$$= M^x$$

Thus, any base can be raised to the power x using the identity

$$M^x = 2^{x\log_2 M}$$

The instruction FYLZX calculates

$$y \log_2 x$$

where y is ST(1) and x is ST. Clearly, the result is suitable for calculating M^x using the previous instruction provided that

$$y \log_2 x$$

falls in the range 0 to 0.5. The last instruction FYL2X1 returns

$$y \log_2 (x + 1)$$

Here x is ST and must lie in the range 0 to $1 - 1/SQRT(2)$; y is ST(1); and the result is returned in ST following a pop. A useful sequence of identities is

$$x = M^{\log_M x}$$
$$= 2^{\log_2 x}$$

From this follows

$$\log_2 x = \log_2(M^{\log_M x})$$
$$= \log_M x \log_2 M$$

and

$$\log_M x = \log_2 x / \log_2 M$$

We have already seen this result used when $M = 10$.

The instruction FYLZX calculates $y \log_2 x$. If we set $ST(1) = 1$ this yields

$$\log_2 x$$

Table 8.14 contains the constant instructions, and two of these load $\log_2 10$ (FLDL2T) and $\log_2 e$ (FLDL2E) into ST. It is clear that the above identity indicates that a simple division yields $\log_{10} x$ and $\log_e x$, respectively. Similarly, FLDLG2 and FLDLN2 load $\log_{10} 2$ and $\log_2 x$ from base 10 and e. The other three instructions in Table 8.14 load ST with $+0.0$(FLDZ), $+1.0$(FLD1), and pi (FLDPI).

The last set of coprocessor instructions are the control instructions contained in Table 8.15. The instructions FINIT and FNINIT are functionally equivalent and serve to initialize the processor. This condition sets the control word to 03FFH and zeros all stack elements and the status word; condition codes become undefined. The FNINIT instruction does not issue an 8088 wait state prior to execution. FDISI and FNDISI set the interrupt enable mask in the control word and, consequently, disable 8087 interrupts. FNDISI is, of course, the no-wait form of the instruction. FENI and FNENI are the opposite of FDISI and FNDISI in that they clear the interrupt enable mask and enable 8087 interrupts. FLDCW replaces the current 8087 control word with one defined by the source. FSTCW and FNSTCW write the current control word to the memory location specified by the destination. FSTSW and FNSTSW write the current status word to the memory location specified by the destination. FCLEX and FNCLEX clear all exception flags, the interrupt request flag, and the busy flag. FSTENV and FNSTENV write the status, control, and tag words to the memory location starting at destination. FLDENV loads the status, control, and tag words from the memory location starting at source. FSAVE and FNSAVE write the status, control, and tag words and the register stack to the memory location specified

TABLE 8.14 THE COPROCESSOR CONSTANT INSTRUCTIONS

Instruction	Purpose	Comments
FLDZ	Load Zero	This instruction loads $+0.0$ in ST(0).
FLD1	Load $+1.0$	This instruction loads $+1.0$ in ST(0).
FLDP1	Load Pi	This instruction loads pi into ST(0).
FLDL2T	Load $\log_2 10$	This instruction loads $\log_2 10$ into the stack top, ST(0).
FLDL2E	Load $\log_2 e$	This instruction loads $\log_2 e$ into ST(0).
FLDLG2	Load $\log_{10} 2$	This instruction loads $\log_{10} 2$ into ST(0).
FLDLN2	Load $\log_e 2$	This instruction loads $\log_e 2$ into ST(0).

where

M_P = Principal portion of monthly payment
M_I = Interest portion of monthly payment
P_R = Principal loan amount remaining

Everything in these equations is straightforward except the principal loan amount remaining. This can be calculated iteratively. Initially, P_R is equal to the full loan amount, L, times the interest rate, R, subtracted from L.

$$P_R(\text{1st payment}) = L - LR$$

$$= L(1 - R).$$

Here P_R(1st payment) constitutes the remaining principal. It stands to reason that the second payment should only contain an interest amount equivalent to the interest on this remaining principal. Hence

$$P_R(\text{2nd payment}) = P_R(\text{1st payment})(1 - R).$$

Clearly, the principal portion of the monthly payment, M_P, must also be calculated iteratively since it too is based on P_R.

Figure 8.12 illustrates the Structure Chart for a program that calculates a monthly mortgage payment and then plots the associated principal and interest with the loan's duration. Figure 8.13a illustrates the flow chart for MORTPLT.ASM, the calling program, and Figure 8.13b presents the source code for this module. MORTPLT calls the procedures MPAY1, for calculation of the monthly payment, and PRIN, for generating and plotting the principal and interest. These calls result in several levels of additional procedure calls, and all variables used by these calling routines are defined in the data segment DATA, contained in the main calling

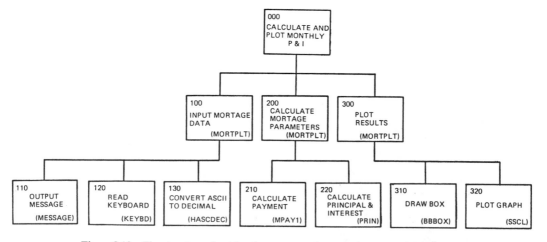

Figure 8.12   The structure chart for the program that calculates monthly mortgage payments and associated principal and interest.

program. Consequently, as part of the data segment definition, a great many variables are defined as PUBLIC. Most of the variables are identified using comments. The second block, however, needs some explanation. The variable M is a double word and is used throughout the code as either a dummy or as the base variable which is raised to some power. This variable is used extensively with the 8087 in these programs. MM1, MM2, and MM3 are used in the procedure MX as temporary storage, that is, as variables containing control and status words for the

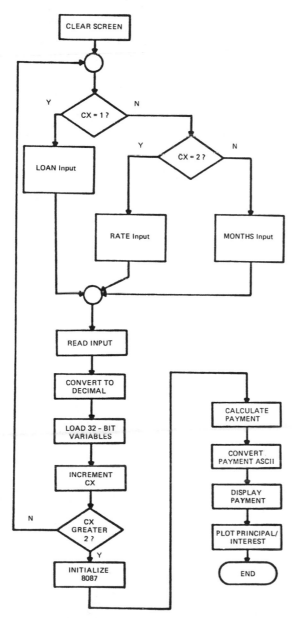

Figure 8.13a Functional flow chart for the program MORTPLT.ASM.

```
COUNT2   DW      4                       ;Characters in each label
COUNT3   DW      5                       ;Number labels in plot - 1
XINC     DW      ?                       ;X-axis increment
COUNT4   DW      0                       ;Index for plot points
                                         ;
DATA     ENDS
                                         ;
CSEG     SEGMENT PARA PUBLIC 'CODE'
MORT     PROC    FAR
         ASSUME  CS:CSEG,SS:STACK,DS:DATA
                                         ;
         PUSH    DS
         SUB     AX,AX
         PUSH    AX
                                         ;
         MOV     AX,SEG DATA
         MOV     DS,AX
                                         ;
         CALL    CLSCREN                 ;Clear screen
         MOV     CX,3                    ;Loop count
DO1:
             CMP     CX,1
             JNE ELSE1
                 MOV     DX,OFFSET MESO1 ;Load input message for LOAN
             JMP SHORT IF2
ELSE1:
             CMP     CX,2
             JNE ELSE2
                 MOV     DX,OFFSET MESO2 ;Load annual rate message
             JMP SHORT IF3
ELSE2:
                 MOV     DX,OFFSET MESO3 ;Ld months financed msg
IF3:
IF2:
                                         ;
         PUSH    CX
         CALL    MESSAGE                 ;Output message
         CALL    KEYBD                   ;Read response
         POP     CX
                                         ;
         MOV     AL,BUFFLN
         MOV     AH,0
         MOV     SI,0                    ;Init. character counter
         PUSH    CX                      ;Save outside loop counter
         MOV     CX,AX                   ;Load inner loop counter
DO2:
             MOV     AL,CHAR[SI]
             MOV     ASC[SI],AL          ;Transfer message to ASC
             INC     SI
         LOOP DO2
         POP     CX                      ;Recall outer loop counter
         MOV     AX,0                    ;Clear AX
                                         ;
         PUSH    CX
         CALL    HASCDEC                 ;Convert ASCII to decimal
         POP     CX
                                         ;
         CMP     CX,1
         LEA     BX,BBINV[0]             ;Address internal decimal
         MOV     DX,DS:[BX+2]            ;Upper word
         MOV     AX,DS:[BX]              ;Lower word
         JNE ELSE3
             LEA     BX,LOAN[0]          ;Address LOAN
```

Figure 8.13b (*Continued*)

```
                    MOV        DS:[BX+2],DX        ;Upper
                    MOV        DS:[BX],AX          ;Lower
               JMP SHORT IF4
ELSE3:
                    CMP        CX,2
                    JNE ELSE4
                         LEA        BX,RATE[0]    ;Address RATE
                         MOV        DS:[BX+2],DX ;Upper
                         MOV        DS:[BX],AX   ;Lower
               JMP SHORT IF5
ELSE4:
                         LEA        BX,MONTHS     ;Address MONTHS
                         MOV        DS:[BX],AX    ;Lower
IF5:
IF4:
          LOOP DO1

          FINIT                                  ;
                                                 ;Initialize 8087
                                                 ;
          CALL       MPAY1                       ;Procedure to calculate payment
                                                 ;
          FWAIT
                                                 ;
          LEA        BX,MPAY                      ;Load address payment
          MOV        AX,DS:[BX]                   ;Lower
          MOV        DX,DS:[BX+2]                 ;Upper
          LEA        BX,BBINV                     ;Input 32-bit decimal
          MOV        DS:[BX],AX                   ;Lower
          MOV        DS:[BX+2],DX                 ;Upper
                                                 ;
          MOV        AL,0                         ;Clear AL
          MOV        SI,0                         ;Initialize index
DO3:                                             ;
               MOV        ASC[SI],AL              ;Clear ASCII output
               INC        SI                      ;Increment index
               CMP        SI,0AH                  ;Compare with 11 count
          JNG DO3

          CALL       HDECASC                      ;Convert payment to ASCII
                                                 ;
          MOV        CX,CCOUNT                    ;Loop count for output char.
          MOV        SI,0                         ;Index for char.
DO4:                                             ;
               MOV        AL,ASC[SI]              ;Move characters to output
               MOV        MESO5[SI],AL
               INC        SI                      ;Increment index
          LOOP DO4
                                                 ;
          MOV        DX,OFFSET MESO4              ;Payment message
          CALL       MESSAGE
                                                 ;
          MOV        DX,OFFSET MESO5              ;Output payment
          CALL       MESSAGE
                                                 ;
          CALL       PRIN                         ;Plot principal/interest
                                                 ;
          RET
MORT      ENDP
CSEG      ENDS
          END        MORT
```

Figure 8.13b (*Continued*)

```
              FLD1                              ;Push 1.0 onto stack
              FSUB      ST,ST(1)                ;1-1/(1+RATE)**MONTHS
              FLD1                              ;Push 1.0 onto stack
              FDIV      ST,ST(1)                ;1/(1-1/(1+RATE)**MONTHS)
              FILD      LOAN                    ;Push LOAN onto stack
              FMUL      ST,ST(1)                ;Product in ST
              FLD       RATE1                   ;Push RATE! onto stack
              FMUL      ST,ST(1)                ;Mortgage payment in ST
              FIST      MPAY                    ;Store result
                                                ;
              POP       DX
              POP       CX
              POP       BX
              POP       AX
              POP       DS
                                                ;
              RET
MPAY1         ENDP
CSEG          ENDS
              END
```

Figure 8.14b (*Continued*)

FILD could have been preceded by an FWAIT; however, no error results because the last statement prior to the load placed a zero in the upper double word address. Had this entry been non-zero an error would have resulted in subsequent processing due to loss of synchronization.

The routine MX is called by MPAY1 to generate $(1 + rate)^{MONTHS}$. The flow chart for this routine is illustrated in Figure 8.15a and the source code is in Figure 8.15b. Bascially M is loaded with $1 + RATE1$ and XX with MONTHS. MX then calculates the power based on techniques discussed earlier. Since FYL2X can be applied only to arguments in the range $0 \leq x \leq 0.5$, OHALF is used to generate a fraction within this range for values in the range $0.5 < x \leq 1.0$. FSQRT is used to obtain the square root of 2 to complete this calculation. For those cases when the fraction is initially in the range $0 \leq x \leq 0.5$, only FYLZX is needed to determine the fractional power. FSCALE is, of course, used to generate the integer power of 2. A very important instruction is the reset at the end of this routine. This FINIT instruction returns the control word to its normal state. Without this change, incorrect rounding will occur and erroneous results will be obtained.

The flow chart for the procedure PRIN is illustrated in Figure 8.16a and the source code in Figure 8.16b. This routine uses the coprocessor to initially calculate the monthly principal and interest paid. For these calculations, the FWAIT instruction is needed to achieve 8088 synchronization with the 8087. Running this procedure without the FWAIT instructions will lead to errors. These instructions are needed to delay 8088 execution whenever the memory operand is used by the 8088 and then by the 8087 (or vice versa). The array VAR1 is loaded, based on a pointer to PRINC (remember INTER follows PRINC(0) by 720 bytes exactly), for both plots. The routine BBBOX draws a box and tick marks, SSCL scales and plots the graph, and LABEL1 labels the plot.

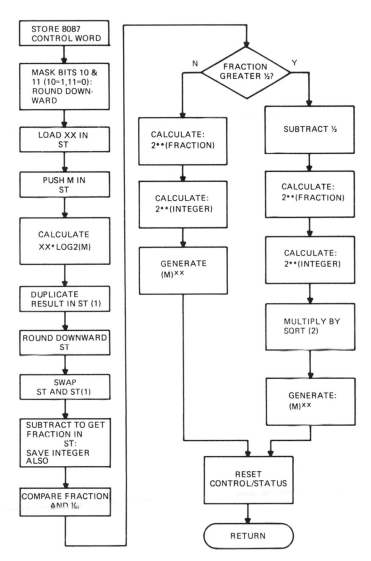

Figure 8.15a   The functional flow chart for the procedure MX.

Here M is the pointer to TABLE4 and N is a value depending on the loan length: 10 years ($N = 1$), 15 years ($N = 2$), and 30 years ($N = 3$). The reader should examine TABLE4 to validate this pointer. The familiar routine CONNL1 is used to connect the plot points. Figure 8.19 presents the linker entries for linking MORTPLT. This routine requires the six files previously illustrated plus the libraries IOCON and GRAPHLIB.

Figure 8.20 demonstrates the interactive output from MORTPLOT.EXE, prior to the graphics. The program reads in the number of months financed for 10, 15 or 30 years, the annual interest times 10,000 in round integer format, and the loan amount. All values must be integer. The monthly mortgage is calculated to the nearest dollar and output. Figure 8.20 illustrates a screen copy of the output from MORTPLT.EXE for three cases, 360, 180, and 120 months at 12.88% with $98,000 financed. The monthly payments are $1,075, $1,232, and $1,456, respectively. We

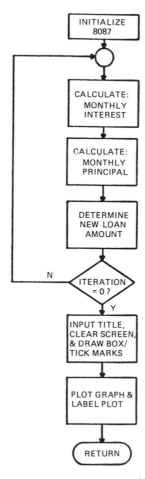

Figure 8.16a The functional flow chart for the procedure PRIN.

```
PAGE    55,132
TITLE   PI      - PRINCIPAL AND INTEREST (PI.ASM)
;
;       DESCRIPTION:This routine determines the principal and
;       interest and calls a graphics procedure.
;
.8087
IF1
        INCLUDE MAC4LIB.LIB
ENDIF
;
EXTRN   MONTHS:WORD,MPAY:DWORD,RATE1:DWORD,LOAN:DWORD,M:DWORD
EXTRN   PRINC:WORD,INTER:WORD,LIMIT:WORD,VAR1:WORD,BUFFLN:BYTE
EXTRN   CHAR:BYTE,TABLE1:BYTE,COUNT1:WORD,MESO6:BYTE
EXTRN   CLSCREN:FAR,BBBOX:FAR,SSCL:FAR
EXTRN   XX:DWORD,MESSAGE:FAR,KEYBD:FAR,LABEL1:FAR
;
CSEG    SEGMENT PARA PUBLIC 'CODE'
        PUBLIC  PRIN
PRIN    PROC    FAR
        ASSUME  CS:CSEG
                                                ;
        PUSH    DS
                                                ;
        FINIT                                   ;Initialize 8087
                                                ;
        MOV     CX,MONTHS               ;Loop count
        MOV     LIMIT,CX                ;Load alternate month variable
        MOV     SI,0                    ;Clear index
        FLD     RATE1                   ;Monthly rate in ST
        FILD    LOAN                    ;LOAN in ST,RATE1 in ST(1)
DO1:
        FMUL    ST,ST(1)                ;Product in ST
        FISTP   M                       ;Interest in M, pop ST
        FWAIT
        LEA     BX,M                    ;Address interest
        MOV     AX,DS:[BX]              ;Interest in AX
        LEA     BX,MPAY                 ;Address payment
        MOV     DX,DS:[BX]              ;Payment in DX
        MOV     INTER[SI],AX            ;Save interest
        SUB     DX,AX                   ;DX=Payment-Interest
        MOV     PRINC[SI],DX            ;Save principal
        ADD     SI,2                    ;Increment word index
        FILD    LOAN                    ;Load loan
        LEA     BX,XX                   ;Dummy variable
        MOV     DS:[BX],DX              ;Principal in XX
        MOV     AX,0                    ;Clear AX
        MOV     DS:[BX+2],AX            ;Clear upper
        FWAIT
        FILD    XX                      ;Load principal in ST-integer
        FSUBP   ST(1),ST                ;New loan in ST
        FIST    LOAN                    ;Reload loan
        LOOP DO1
                                                ;
```

Figure 8.16b The procedure PRIN, which computes the monthly principal and interest portions of the payment and calls a graphics interface. This is a .ASM file and 8087 instructions are used.

in relation to the month of the loan. Similarly, Figures 8.22 and 8.23 present the same results for 15-year and 10-year loans. In each case, the annual interest is 12.88 % and the loan amount, $98,000. These graphs correspond to the monthly payments shown in Figure 8.20. The area under these curves constitutes the total principal paid (loan amount) and total interest paid. Clearly, the interest is much larger than the loan value. Also, a comparison of the last three figures demonstrates that the shorter the loan payment period, the greater the initial principal portion of the payment.

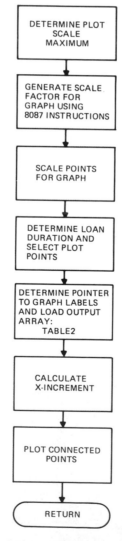

Figure 8.18a The functional flow chart for the procedure SSCL.

```
PAGE      55,132
TITLE     SSCL     SCALING ROUTINE FOR GRAPHICS(SSCL.ASM)
;
;         DESCRIPTION: This routine scales the plot variables
;         and sets up the graphics and plots the output.
;
.8087
;
EXTRN     LIMIT:WORD,VAR1:WORD,MAX:WORD,COUNT2:WORD,TABLE3:BYTE
EXTRN     TABLE2:BYTE,SSMUL:WORD,M:DWORD,MONTHS:WORD,MMULT:WORD
EXTRN     XEND:WORD,XBEG:WORD,XINC:WORD,CONNL1:FAR,TABLE4:BYTE
;
CSEG      SEGMENT PARA PUBLIC 'CODE'
          PUBLIC  SSCL
SSCL      PROC    FAR
          ASSUME  CS:CSEG

          PUSH    DS                        ;

          MOV     AX,0                      ;Initialize MAX comparison
          MOV     SI,0                      ;Init. index
          MOV     CX,MONTHS                 ;Count limit
DO1:
          CMP     VAR1[SI],AX               ;Compare for MAX
          JNG IF1
          MOV     AX,VAR1[SI]               ;Replace AX-running max
IF1:
          ADD     SI,2                      ;Increment word pointer
          LOOP DO1
          MOV     MAX,AX                    ;Load MAX,assume MIN > 0
          CMP     AX,500                    ;Check MAX vs 500
          JNLE ELSE1
          MOV     DI,0                      ;1st pointer
          JMP SHORT IF2
ELSE1:
          CMP     AX,1000                   ;Check MAX vs 1000
          JNLE ELSE2
          MOV     DI,1                      ;2nd pointer
          JMP SHORT IF3
ELSE2:
          CMP     AX,1500                   ;Check MAX vs 1500
          JNLE ELSE3
          MOV     DI,2                      ;3rd pointer
          JMP SHORT IF4
ELSE3:
          MOV     DI,3                      ;4th pointer
IF4:
IF3:
IF2:
          MOV     AX,4                      ;Multiplier TABLE3 word
          MUL     DI                        ;Point to TABLE3 entry
          MOV     BX,AX                     ;Save in BX
          MOV     CX,COUNT2                 ;Characters in each label
          MOV     SI,0                      ;Initialize index
DO2:
          MOV     AL,TABLE3[BX]             ;Load from Y-axis limits
          MOV     TABLE2[SI],AL             ;Y-axis upper limit
          INC     BX                        ;Increment TABLE3 pointer
          INC     SI                        ;Increment TABLE2 index
          LOOP DO2
                                            ;Scale points
```

Figure 8.18b   The procedure SSCL, which scales the plot variables and sets up the graph labels. This is a .ASM file and 8087 instructions are used.

```
LINK

IBM Personal Computer Linker
Version 2.10 (C)Copyright IBM Corp 1981, 1982, 1983

Object Modules [.OBJ]: MORTPLT+MORPAY+MX+PI+BBBOX+SSCL
Run File [MORTPLT.EXE]:
List File [NUL.MAP]:
Libraries [.LIB]: IOCON+GRAPHLIB
```

Figure 8.19   The link sequence for generating MORTPLT.EXE.

```
Input months financed (10,15, or 30 years).


360
Input annual interest x 10000 - round integer.


1288
Input loan amount .


98000
Monthly mortgage is (dollars):


       1075


Input months financed (10,15, or 30 years).


180
Input annual interest x 10000 - round integer.


1288
Input loan amount .


98000
Monthly mortgage is (dollars):


        1232


Input months financed (10,15, or 30 years).


120
Input annual interest x 10000 - round integer.


1288
Input loan amount .


98000
Monthly mortgage is (dollars):


     1456
```

Figure 8.20   Representative interactive sessions with the program MORTPLT, which calculates mortgage payments. The cases indicated are for 360, 180, and 120 months at 12.88% with $98,000 financed. The monthly payment is returned.

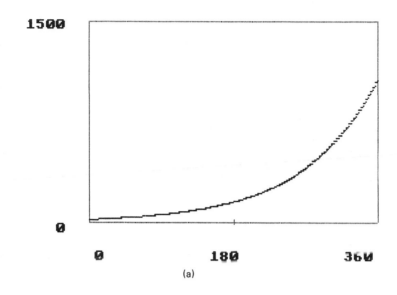

(a)

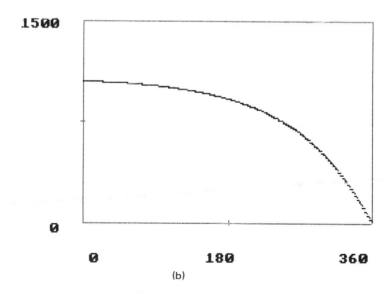

(b)

Figure 8.21 Plots of the monthly (a) principal and (b) interest portions of the payment in relation to the payment month. The case illustrated is for 12.88% interest rate, $98,000 financed, and a loan duration of 30 years.

8.3 SUMMARY

The purpose of this chapter was to provide an introduction to the IBM Macro Assembler version 2.0 coprocessor instructions. The added coprocessor instructions allow, for the first time, easy access to the 8087 and 80287 numerical processor chips. We have assumed that by now the reader is reasonably familiar with the 8088 architecture and its associated stack. Programming the coprocessor is very similar, with the 8087 internal registers in stack form, ST(0) to ST(7). The coprocessor instruction set is delineated along with a fairly comprehensive discussion of number format (integer, real, and BCD). This latter discussion is essential for an understanding of how to program the 8087. Once number format and conversion has been developed, an example (rather lengthy) of programming the coprocessor is presented. This example is intended to serve as a basis for understanding how the coprocessor works. Many of the pitfalls associated with coprocessor programming become apparent through this example.

This feature, the addition of a coprocessor instruction set, greatly improves the Macro Assembler and makes it comparable to higher-level languages for ease and accuracy of "number crunching." Coupling this feature with the speed of execution afforded by the assembler and with access to the system peripherals leads to a rather formidable language capability, particularly when the intended program will be computation intensive. Another feature of the language is its facility for accessing the system at the chip level. Essentially, an understanding of the system at the chip level must rely heavily on a concurrent understanding of the associated microprocessor (8088 and 80286) assembler. The next chapter addresses these issues in more detail. It must be remembered that screen graphics, for example, is generally not available through higher-level language instructions and the programmer must either write his own graphics routines in assembler (subsequently to be interfaced to the higher-level language program) or use a commercially supplied package.

With these thoughts in mind regarding the version 2.0 enhancements, we now proceed to a discussion of the system hardware mentioned above. Chapter 9 investigates the Basic Input/Output System (BIOS) interrupt service routines (hardware drivers) in the context of programming the individual chips. An understanding of Chapter 9 (on the BIOS) and Chapter 10 (on the system board) is required for those programmers interested in a full system-level description of the Macro Assembler interface to the IBM PC, XT, and AT. Also, those programmers interested in writing their own drivers for special purpose I/O devices should become familiar with these chapters.

REFERENCES

1. *Macro Assembler Version 2.00*. IBM Personal Computer Software. IBM Corp. P.O. Box 1328. Boca Raton, FL 33432 (1984).
2. *Macro Assembler Version 2.00 Reference*. IBM Personal Computer Software. IBM Corp. P.O. Box 1328. Boca Raton, FL 33432 (1984).

3. *iAPX 86/88, 186/188 User's Manual: Programmer's Reference.* Intel Corporation, Literature Sales. P.O. Box 58130, Santa Clara, CA 95052-8130 (1985). (21091-003)

4. Burington, R. S. *Handbook of Mathematical Tables and Formulas.* McGraw-Hill Book Co., New York, NY (1962), p. 269.

PROBLEMS

8.1. Illustrate the byte storage for the following numbers: (a) 1,500,000; (b) 250,000; (c) 7.4E4; (d) −2.5E5; and (e) 75,000.

8.2. Define the numbers appearing in problem 8.1 in the coprocessor format.

8.3. Write the coprocessor instruction sequence that obtains a real-memory operand, X, squares that operand, and returns the squared value to the memory location.

8.4. Write the coprocessor instruction sequence that obtains two real-memory operands (X and Y), divides Y by X, and returns the quotient in Y.

8.5. Write coprocessor code to calculate the sine-term corresponding to a Gaussian random number. Assume that X1 and X2 are double word variables containing random numbers between 0 and 1 and D2 is −2.0E0 with D1 = 2.0E0. Assume the result is to be returned in a double word variable S1. (See procedure GRAND.)

8.6. Using the procedure MX (in Figure 8.15b), write a routine that accepts a double word quantity, Y1, and a double word quantity, X1, and calculates Y1 raised to the power X1. Assume Y1 and X1 are integers.

8.7. Given an angle, Z, in radians, define the steps needed to return the tangent of this angle in Z.

8.8. Write the code needed to calculate X mod Y where both X and Y are assumed to be real.

8.9. Write code to calculate the area of a circle, assuming the radius is initially in a real variable, A.

8.10. Write code to calculate the volume of a cylinder of radius A and height D. Return the answer in V.

8.11. Write code to calculate the power dissipated in a one-ohm resistor when a voltage drop of V is measured across this resistor. Return the power in decibels relative to one volt (dBV). Assume 20 is loaded in TWENTY.

9

BIOS Service Routines

The subject of this chapter is the ROM Basic Input/Output System programming that is used for hardware device interfacing for the IBM microcomputers. IBM has intended that these BIOS service routines serve as the link between the system and associated peripherals such as the printer, keyboard, and display. The goal of separating this code from the system was to relieve the programmer of the burden for handling peripheral interfaces. The DOS code is proprietary as is the BASIC language processor in the system ROM. The BIOS service routines, however, are available in the Technical References for each system and serve as the basis for understanding system I/O. These hardware drivers are written in assembler and constitute the interface with the chips. In this chapter, we will examine some of this BIOS code and see first hand how IBM uses assembler to implement hardware drivers. *It is recommended that the reader obtain a copy of the Technical Reference for the appropriate IBM system.* The PC BIOS service code is slightly different than IBM's Macro Assembler because it was written using an Intel Development System. The actual instructions, however, are identical. A comparison among IBM micro-computer BIOS routines demonstrates that the AT version is much more modular than the other versions. Of course, this AT code is also much more extensive. The modularity for the AT code is similar to that employed in this book.

Table 9.1 illustrates the I/O port addresses for the allowed devices on the IBM microcomputers. These addresses must appear on the address bus in order to access the device in question. We include this table because it reflects the chip selection process and represents the exact address (port) that must be used with the IN and

TABLE 9.1 THE INPUT/OUTPUT PORT ADDRESSING FOR THE PC, XT, AND AT.

PC		XT		AT	
Port # (HEX)	Device	Port # (HEX)	Device	Port # (HEX)	Device
00–0F	DMA Controller 8237	00–0F	DMA Controller 8237	00–0F	DMA Controller 1, 8237
20–21	Programmable Interrupt Controller 8259A	20–21	Programmable Interrupt Controller 8259A	20–3F	PIC 1, 8259A, Master
40–43	Timer 8253	40–43	Timer 8253	40–5F	Timer 8254
60–63	Programmable Peripheral Interface 3255	60–63	Programmable Peripheral Interface 8255	60–6F	Keyboard 8042
80–83	DMA Page Registers	80–33	DMA Page Registers	80–9F	DMA Page Registers
3F8–3FF	RS-232-C Adapter	200–20F	Game I/O Adapter	200–207	Game I/O Adapter
3F0–3F7	Floppy Disk Drive Adapter	210–217	Expansion Unit		
2F8–2FF	Reserved	2F8–2FF	RS-232-C Adapter (Secondary)		
378–37F	Parallel Printer Port	320–32F	Fixed Disk		
300–30F	Color/Graphics Adapter	378–37F	Printer	378–37F	Printer 1
278–27F	Reserved				
200–20F	Game I/O Adapter				

(Continued)

TABLE 9.1 (*Continued*)

PC		XT		AT	
Port #(HEX)	Device	Port #(HEX)	Device	Port #(HEX)	Device
380–38F	Monochrome/Printer Adapter	390–393	Cluster	3A0–3AF	Binary Synchronous Communications 1
		3A0–3A9	Binary Synchronous Communications (Primary)		
				380–38F	Monochrome/Printer Adapter
		380–38F	Monochrome/Printer Adapter	300–30F	Color Graphics Adapter
		300–30F	Color Graphics Adapter	3F0–3F7	Diskette Controller
		3F0–3F7	Floppy Disk Drive Adapter	3F8–3FF	Serial Port 1
		3F8–3FF	RS-232-C Adapter (Primary)	70–7F	Real Time Clock
				A0–8F	PIC 2, 8259A, Slave
				C0–0F	DMA Controller 2, 8237
				F0	Clear Coprocessor Busy 80287
				F1	Reset 80287
				F8–FF	80287 Coprocessor
				1F0–1F8	Fixed Disk
				278–27F	Parallel Printer Port 2
				2F8–2FF	Serial Port 2
				360–36F	Reserved
				3C0–3CF	Reserved

Reprinted by permission from the *Technical Reference* copyright 1981 by International Business Machines Corporation.

OUT instructions. This I/O port address is determined by the hardware configuration.

We cannot consider every device appearing in Table 9.1. This chapter is intended to demonstrate the hardware-software interface for a representative set of devices and illustrate the use of assembler for achieving this interface. Since the assembler incorporates the Intel 8088, 80286, and 80386 instructions, it is the language for programming this interface. Once the reader understands these BIOS service routines, it will be possible to address the remainder of the I/O service programming. Further, the reader will be in a position to add hardware peripherals based on appropriate hardware port addressing logic and additional service routines in memory. Logically, these routines will reside near BIOS locations and be accessed using vectors in a way similar to normal interrupt processing.

Access of the peripherals is through the IN and OUT instructions. These instructions have the form (byte transfer)

```
IN AL,DX
OUT DX,AL
```

where the data byte is held in AL and DX contains the port address. (A word can also be transferred using AX.) These instructions are key to understanding the BIOS service routines because all I/O transfers are accomplished using IN and OUT.

Finally, some disclaimer should be specified concerning the representations of actual BIOS code. In the examples, selected portions of the code are used for illustrative purposes. In the case of the IBM PC this code has matching offsets and line numbers based on what appears in the *IBM Technical Reference* [1]. The following sections contain illustrations of how the actual BIOS code functions. References to the hardware use the IBM nomenclature; the presence of an asterisk, for example, means the particular signal in question is active when it is LOW (LOW being -5 volts, usually). Also, the occurrence of a bar over the signal name denotes a similar meaning. Usually the asterisk will be used in the text and the bar in figures.

9.1 PARALLEL PRINTER I/O

The parallel printer input/output is a reasonable place to start discussing the ROM BIOS service routines because of its simplicity. Basically, IBM controls parallel printer I/O from the monochrome printer adapter card or another parallel I/O card, and we will be able to see how this port works, based on diagrams from the *IBM Technical Reference* and the ROM BIOS code. The process of exploring this service routine naturally subdivides into chip selection and the service function.

9.1.1 The Printer Selection Process

The printer selection process is based on correctly sending an appropriate port address, via the address bus, which can be decoded and used to generate the chip select or equivalent signals. This is needed to turn on the chips responsible for

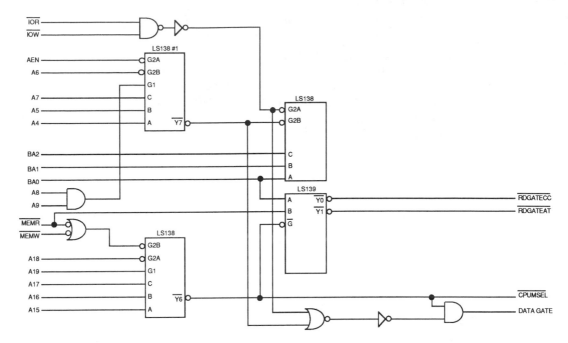

Figure 9.1   Generation of the DATAGATE signal. Reprinted by permission from the *Technical Reference* copyright 1981 by International Business Machines Corporation.

handling the printer processing. These port addresses are fixed, based on the hardware configuration; and as shown in Table 9.1 they occupy the range from 3B0H to 3BFH for the IBM PC. It is useful to consider how this range of port addresses selects the parallel printer I/O.

Consider Figure 9.1: This is the high-order chip selection logic. The upper LS138 demultiplexer is used to select the port based on address lines A4 − A7 and A8 − A9. To see how this works note that an output Y7* is indicated. This output eventually makes its way to the signal DATAGATE. For the time being, assume DATAGATE must be LOW to enable the printer as we will see shortly: If this condition is true, Y7* must go LOW to select the printer. (The NOR output must be HIGH followed by a LOW inverter output.) Based on the truth table for the LS138, which is presented in Table 9.2, the bits (A0 − A9) in the address word in the figure must be as follows in order to set Y7* LOW.

A9	A8	A7	A6	A5	A4	A3	A2	A1	A0
1	1	1	0	1	1	x	x	x	x

3	B	x

Thus, the hardware selection (using the LS138) is wired to accept port addresses (3BXH) for the parallel printer. The logic appearing in Figure 9.1 is for the IBM PC

TABLE 9.2 LS138 TRUTH TABLE

Inputs						Outputs							
A	B	C	G2B	G2A	G1	Y0	Y1	Y2	Y3	Y4	Y5	Y6	Y7
x	x	x	1	x	x	1	1	1	1	1	1	1	1
x	x	x	x	1	x	1	1	1	1	1	1	1	1
x	x	x	x	x	0	1	1	1	1	1	1	1	1
0	0	0	0	0	1	0							
1	0	0	0	0	1		0						
0	1	0	0	0	1			0			All 1s		
1	1	0	0	0	1				0				
0	0	1	0	0	1					0			
1	0	1	0	0	1						0		
0	1	1	0	0	1			All 1s				0	
1	1	1	0	0	1								0

and based on the *IBM Technical Reference* logic for the printer portion of the monochrome display and parallel printer adapter. This address, 3BXH, is in agreement with Table 9.1.

The lower LS138 uses bits A15 through A19 of the address and sets Y6* LOW when the following address is on the address bus.

A19	A18	A17	A16	A15	A14	A13	A12	A11	A10
1	0	1	1	0	x	x	x	x	x

B   –   –   hexadecimal

Both Y6* and Y7* are input to the AND logic leading to DATAGATE as output signal. If Y7* is LOW, DATAGATE is LOW. We have seen for addresses 3BXH (X = 0, ... F) that Y7* is LOW. Similarly, for addresses in the range BxxxxH, Y6* will be LOW and DATAGATE will be set. This range of addresses encompasses the monochrome display adapter refresh screen memory map (B0000H–B0F9FH) which is a 4K region corresponding to the monochrome screen pixel locations: $80 \times 25 = 2000$ locations (with a location and attribute expressed for each). Thus, DATAGATE also becomes LOW if the address is in the monochrome video buffer region.

Returning to the parallel printer, what is accomplished when DATAGATE goes LOW? Figure 9.2 illustrates the printer pin out signals and associated logic. DATAGATE is input to the LS245 Chip Enable (CE) line. When LOW, this line selects the data bus signals going to the printer and monochrome video: Direction is specified by whether or not a memory or I/O read is called for. If IOR* or MEMR* are LOW, information is to be output to the printer or screen.

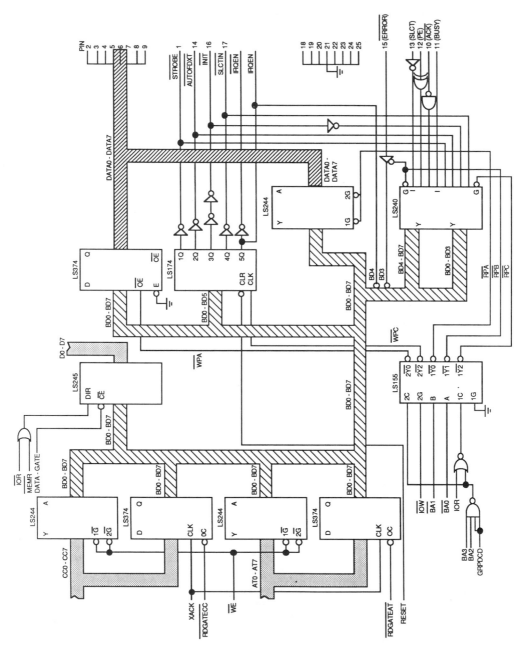

Figure 9.2 The matrix printer (adapter) environment. Reprinted by permission from the *Technical Reference* copyright 1981 by International Business Machines Corporation.

There are four more address lines to consider, BA0 to BA3. These are input to the LS155 decoder in Figure 9.2. This decoder has the following truth table.

TABLE 9.3 THE LS155 DECODER TRUTH TABLE

Address		Enable A		Output A				Enable B		Output B			
A	B	1C	1G	1Y0	1Y1	1Y2	1Y3	2C	2G	2Y0	2Y1	2Y2	2Y3
x	x	0	x	1	1	1	1	1	x	1	1	1	1
x	x	x	1	1	1	1	1	x	1	1	1	1	1
0	0	1	0	0	1	1	1	0	0	0	1	1	1
1	0	1	0	1	0	1	1	0	0	1	0	1	1
0	1	1	0	1	1	0	1	0	0	1	1	0	1
1	1	1	0	1	1	1	0	0	0	1	1	1	0

The output values marked in the boxes are of interest and will be highlighted. In a situation where BA2 and BA3 are HIGH, we have the possible ports

BA3   BA0   PORT

| 1 | 1 | 0 | 0 |

3B [C] H

BA3   BA0

| 1 | 1 | 0 | 1 |

3B [D] H

BA3   BA0

| 1 | 1 | 1 | 0 |

3B [E] H

BA3   BA0

| 1 | 1 | 1 | 1 |

3B [F] H

These are all allowed parallel printer ports. What signals are output from the LS155 when these ports are set? Figure 9.2 illustrates that the following signals are output from the LS155.

TABLE 9.4 THE OUTPUT FROM LS155

Address (Port)	Signals (Pin)	Signals (Chip)
3BCH	$1\overline{Y0}$(LOW) & $2\overline{Y0}$(LOW)	$\overline{RPA}$(LOW & $\overline{WPA}$(LOW)
3BDH	$1\overline{Y1}$(LOW)	$\overline{RPB}$(LOW)
3BEH	$1\overline{Y2}$(LOW) & $2\overline{Y2}$(LOW)	$\overline{RPC}$(LOW) & $\overline{WPC}$(LOW)
3BFH	—	

Consider port 3BCH. When this port is selected, RPA* and WPA* go LOW. The WPA* line is attached to the Latch Enable Line of the LS374, and when LOW, this line forces the latch to hold its data inputs (BD0-BD7). A latch is a storage device that can be switched to place the stored signals onto a bus. When WPA* goes HIGH, the latch becomes transparent and data (BD0-BD7) is transferred out (DATA0-DATA7). Thus, addressing port 3BCH simply latches the data and prepares it for output to the printer using pins 2 through 9 of the 25-pin D-type connector.

When 3BDH is the port selected, RPB* goes LOW. This enables the upper four outputs from the LS240 buffer. A buffer is a simple storage device. The input from pin 11 (appearing on pin 8 of the LS240 in Figure 9.2 and *IBM Technical Reference*) of the D-type parallel printer connector is buffered to BD7, the bit seven position of the data coming from the printer. This bit can thus be monitored so that a HIGH indicates a BUSY condition.

Finally, when 3BEH is addressed, RPC* and WPC* go LOW. Examination of WPC* indicates that it effectively enables the LS174 flip-flops. This means that whatever appears on data lines BD0 through BD4 (BD5 results in no output) is transferred to LS174 pin signals 1Q, 2Q, 3Q, 4Q and 5Q, respectively. Thus, if the printer is looking for a LOW STROBE* signal, bit 0 must be set HIGH (output is inverted between chip and printer D-type connector), which results in the STROBE* signal being set LOW.

To completely understand the usage of the port addresses discussed here, we must go to the ROM BIOS code and see dynamically how these addresses are called. This is the subject of the next subsection.

9.1.2 Printer ROM BIOS Code

In the previous subsection we have seen the effect of placing various I/O port addresses on the address bus. This presentation did not, however, attempt to sequence the placement of these addresses and associated data in time. Consider a timing diagram for the parallel printer interface appearing in Figure 9.3. First data is sent to the printer using port 3BCH. This data is latched and held as previously described. Next, the BUSY line is polled or examined repeatedly until it goes HIGH. This tells the IBM PC that the printer is free to accept a new data character. The printer controls this BUSY signal. Finally, when BUSY goes HIGH,

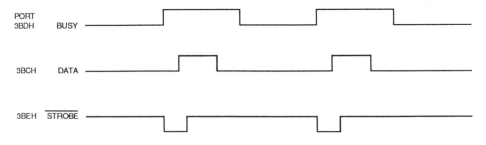

Figure 9.3   The printer control signals.

the STROBE* line is set LOW, telling the printer that a new data character is ready to be output. The BUSY line is checked through port 3BDH and the STROBE* sent through port 3BEH, as discussed in the previous sections.

How does the ROM BIOS code function? Examining that and seeing how code of this type is used for control with the IBM PC is the goal of this chapter. Figure 9.4a illustrates the loading of the port addresses in the ROM BIOS code for the IBM PC. Indicated are the addresses in ROM and the line number, as well as the actual code and comment. Note that in line 61, the base addresses are initialized (PRINTER_BASE). Room is provided for four printer base addresses. These would be the addresses used in the port I/O instructions. We must wait until the code segment is defined for these to actually be specified. At line number 986 the first printer address is specified. Since this will always be the monochrome display parallel printer adapter card address, we expect 3BCH, and indeed it is there. The remaining

```
Address      Line #                                                    Comment

0040         59          DATA    SEGMENT AT 40H

                         . . .

0008         61          PRINTER_BASE   DW     4 DUP(?)        ;ADDRESSES OF PRINTERS

                         . . .

             173         DATA ENDS

                         . . .

F000         193         CODE    SEGMENT AT 0F000H
0000         194                         DB     57344 DUP(?)   ;FILL LOWEST 56K

                         . . .

F4B1         985         F4      LABEL   WORD                  ;PRINTER SOURCE TABLE
E4B1         986                         DW     3BCH
E4B3         987                         DW     378H
E4B5         988                         DW     278H
E4B7         989         F4E     LABEL   WORD

                         . . .

E5B2         1146        MOV     BP,OFFSET F4                  ;PRT_SRC_TBL
E5B5         1147        MOV     SI,0
E5B8         1148  F16:
E5B8         1149        MOV     DX,CS:[BP]                    ;GET PRINTER BASE ADDR

                                                   }  code to check to see if
                                                      printer present

E5C4         1155        JNE     F17                          ;NO    CHECK NEXT PRT CD
E5C6         1156        MOV     PRINTER_BASE [SI] ,DX        ;YES - STORE PRT BASE ADDR
E5CA         1157        INC     SI                           :INCREMENT TO NEXT WORD
E5CB         1158        INC     SI
E5CC         1159  F17:
E5CC         1160        INC     BP                           ;POINT TO NEXT BASE ADDR
E5CD         1161        INC     BP
E5CE         1162        CMP     BP,OFFSET F4E                ;ALL POSSIBLE ADDR CHECKED?
E5D2         1163        JNE     F16                          ;PRT_BASE

                         . . .
```

Figure 9.4a ROM BIOS code that accomplishes loading of the printer port base addresses. Reprinted by permission from the *Technical Reference* copyright 1981 by International Business Machines Corporation.

```
Address      Line #                                              Comment

            3008      ;PRINTER_IO
            3009      ;        THIS ROUTINE PROVIDES COMMUNICATION WITH THE PRINTER
            3010      ;        (AH)=0 PRINT THE CHARACTER IN (AL)
            3011      ;        ON RETURN,AH=1 IF CHARACTER COULD NOT BE PRINTED (TIME OUT)
            3012      ;        OTHER BITS SET AS ON NORMAL STATUS CALL

                  ...

            3025      ;        (DX) = PRINTER TO BE USED (0,1,2)...

                  ...

EFD2        3033      PRINTER_IO        PROC       FAR
EFD2        3034          STI                                     ;INTERRUPTS BACK ON

                  ...

EFDD        3042          MOV    SI,DX                            ;GET PRINTER PARM
EFDF        3043          SHL    SI,1                             ;WORD OFFSET INTO TABLE
EFE1        3044          MOV    DX,PRINTER_BASE [SI]             ;GET BASE ADDR FOR PRINTER CARD
EFE5        3045          OR     DX,DX                            ;TEST DX FOR 0, INDICATING NO PRT
EFE7        3046          JZ     B1                               ;RETURN
EFE9        3047          OR     AH,AH                            ;TEST FOR AH=0
EFEB        3048          JZ     B2                               ;PRINT AL

                  ...

EFFB        3063      B2:
EFFB        3064          PUSH   AX
EFFC        3065          MOV    BL,10                            ;TIME OUT VALUE
EFFE        3066          XOR    CX,CX                            ;ESTABLISH SHIFT COUNT
F000        3067          OUT    DX,AL                            ;OUTPUT CHAR TO PORT
F001        3068          INC    DX                               ;POINT TO STATUS PORT
F002        3069      B3:                                         ;WAIT BUSY
F002        3070          IN     AL,DX                            ;GET STATUS
F003        3071          MOV    AH,AL                            ;STATUS TO AH ALSO
F005        3072          TEST   AL,80H                           ;IS THE PRINTER CURRENTLY BUSY
F007        3073          JNZ    B4                               ;OUT_STROBE

                  ...

F017        3080      B4:                                         ;OUT_STROBE
F017        3081          MOV    AL,0DH                           ;SET THE STROBE HIGH
F019        3082          INC    DX                               ;STROBE IS BIT 0
F01A        3083          OUT    DX,AL
F01B        3084          MOV    AL,0CH                           ;SET THE STROBE LOW
F01D        3085          OUT    DX,AL
F01E        3086          POP    AX                               ;RECOVER THE OUTPUT CHAR

                                                          }
                                                          }  code gets printer status
                                                          }
                  ...
EFFA        3059          IRET
```

Figure 9.4b The ROM BIOS code that handles parallel printer I/O. Reprinted by permission from the *Technical Reference* copyright 1981 by International Business Machines Corporation.

code simply counts and checks the printers to be sure that the PRINTER_BASE addresses are loaded properly. Notice how the code jumps around.

Now we consider the actual printer I/O service routine in Figure 9.4b. Again this figure is based on an abbreviated code description taken from the *IBM Technical Reference*, Appendix A. The routine PRINTER_IO actually handles printer input/output in the BIOS code. First the base address for the appropriate printer is loaded into DX. For the monochrome printer adapter card, this address is pointed to with SI = 0. This is the address 3BCH contained in PRINTER_BASE(0). Next the register AH is checked: if it is zero the character in AL will print. This is the case we

have considered in Figure 9.4b; hence the code illustrated reflects branching based on
AH = 0. Following the branch to B2, the character in AL is output to port 3BCH
through the OUT DX,AL command in line 3067. At this point, the BUSY signal
must be checked. To do this, the system must examine port 3BDH. In line 3068, DX
is incremented to yield 3BDH and bit 7 is checked to see if it is LOW. This check is
accomplished by first inputting the byte in 3BDH through the IN AL,DX instruction
in 3070. Next a test is performed using TEST AL,80H in line 3072. This test
effectively generates an AND function between bit 7 of AL (the BUSY signal on pin 22
of the D-type connector) and the set bit in 80H. The output of this test is zero if bit 7
of AL is 0 (BUSY signal LOW), and it is one if bit 7 of AL is 1 (BUSY signal
HIGH). Essentially the printer sets its BUSY line LOW when it is busy and sets it
HIGH when it is available to accept data. When this BUSY signal goes HIGH the
JNZ B4 instruction causes a branch to B4. As long as the BUSY signal is LOW this
conditional jump does not execute, and the processing eventually jumps back to label
B3.

Following receipt of the HIGH on bit seven and the jump to B4, the STROBE*
is output. The STROBE* signal, as indicated in Figure 9.2, is contained on pin 1 of
the 25-pin D-type connector. This corresponds to bit 0 of the output byte. Observe
that the data output in Figure 9.2 passes through an inverter; hence to obtain a LOW
output on the STROBE* line, a HIGH data bit must be present for bit 0 of the output
byte. In line 3082 the port number is incremented to yield 3BEH as the selected
port. This activates the LS174 flip-flop and the OUT AL,DX in 3083 outputs AL to
this port. Bit zero of this port, of course, is the STROBE* line. Since AL = 0DH, bit
0 is HIGH and the STROBE* line is driven LOW. Immediately following this
output, AL is loaded with 0CH (setting bit 0 LOW) and the output in line 3085
returns the STROBE* to a HIGH condition.

This discussion briefly illustrates how the BIOS I/O instructions are translated
into signals within the IBM PC. The relationship between chip selection based on
port addressing and the actual operation of the code has been illustrated. It is, of
course, the dynamic nature of the code that accomplishes the machine operation, and
this has been demonstrated for printer I/O, based on the signal behavior illustrated in
Figure 9.3. In other words, the handshaking between the IBM PC and the printer, as
evidenced in Figure 9.3, is necessary to achieve printer operation, and this handshaking has been accomplished by the BIOS code as described above.

9.1.3 IBM PC, XT, and AT Printer Port Differences

The IBM XT BIOS code which accomplishes parallel printer I/O is virtually identical
to that for the IBM PC. This code is contained in lines 3078–3200 of the *IBM
Technical Reference Personal Computer XT and Portable Personal Computer* manual
(Section 5 of reference 2). The portion of the code that handles the time-out while
waiting for the BUSY signal to go HIGH is slightly different. The PRINTER_BASE
port addresses for the parallel printer I/O (in the XT) are identical to those for the
IBM PC and are defined in lines 5337–5341 of the IBM XT ROM BIOS code.

The printer I/O processing for the IBM AT has the same port addressing as for
the PC and XT (see AT ROM BIOS code page 5-167 of the *IBM Technical Reference*

Personal Computer AT: PRINTER_TABLE). Here the three addresses are 3BCH, 378H, and 278H for the PRINTER_BASE area. The basic AT parallel printer I/O processing (INT 17H) is again very similar to that for the PC and XT (page 5-123 of the above reference [3]).

9.2 THE PIC, PPI AND DMA CONTROLLER

This section is devoted to a discussion of the Programmable Interrupt Controller (8259A), the 8255A Programmable Peripheral Interface, and the 8237A Direct Memory Access Controller. We will look at the chip selection process and chip initialization. Again, we can expect the port addressing for each chip to reflect the hardware layout.

9.2.1 The Chip Selection Process, 8259A, 8255A and 8237A

For the IBM PC, the data areas are defined in lines 1 through 198 of the ROM BIOS listing (see *IBM Technical Reference*). Figure 9.5 presents the equates section from this data area. How are these equates defined? Consider lines 9 and 10, the 8259A port address assignments. These values are addresses 20H and 21H and are symbolically represented by INTA00 and INTA01, respectively. When the IN and OUT

Address	Line #				Comments
		. . .			
0060	5	PORT_A	EQU	60H	;8255 PORT A ADDR
0061	6	PORT_B	EQU	61H	;8255 PORT B ADDR
0062	7	PORT_C	EQU	62H	;8255 PORT C ADDR
0063	8	CMD_PORT	EQU	63H	
0020	9	INTA00	EQU	20H	;8259 PORT
0021	10	INTA01	EQU	21H	;8259 PORT
0020	11	EOI	EQU	20H	
0040	12	TIMER	EQU	40H	
0043	13	TIM_CTL	EQU	43H	;8253 TIMER CONTROL PORT ADDR
0040	14	TIMER0	EQU	40H	;8253 TIMER/CNTER 0 PORT ADDR
0001	15	TMINT	EQU	01H	
0008	16	DMA08	EQU	08H	;DMA STATUS REG PORT
0000	17	DMA	EQU	00	;DMA CHANNEL 0 ADDR REG PORT
0540	18	MAX_PERIOD	EQU	540H	
0410	19	MIN_PERIOD	EQU	410H	
0060	20	KBD_IN	EQU	60H	;KEYBOARD DATA IN ADDR PORT
0002	21	KBDINT	EQU	02	;KEYBOARD INTR MASK
0060	22	KB_DATA	EQU	60H	;KEYBOARD SCAN CODE PORT
0061	23	KB_CTL	EQU	61H	;CONTROL BITS FOR KB SENSE
		. . .			

Figure 9.5 ROM BIOS code for the data area equates. Reprinted by permission from the *Technical Reference* copyright 1981 by International Business Machines Corporation.

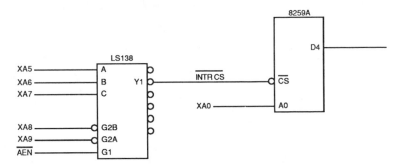

Figure 9.6   Selection logic for the 8259A. Reprinted by permission from the *Technical Reference* copyright 1981 by International Business Machines Corporation.

instructions are used with addresses 20H and 21H, the 8259A must somehow be selected. The key word here is select. Remember many chips have a chip select signal that effectively activates the chip for processing.

The CS* pin is used in conjunction with A0 (among others) to decipher various 8088 commands. Figure 9.6 presents the 8259A selection logic based on the truth table appearing in Table 9.2. This logic includes an LS138 decoder and the 8259A. In order for the chip select line, CS* of the 8259A, to be selected, Y1 of the LS138 must go LOW. Clearly, for this line to go LOW, some combination of addresses XA5 to XA9 must be satisfied. Table 9.5 illustrates what these address lines produce on Y1 as output from the LS138. (For Y1 = 0 above XA5 = 1, XA6 = XA7 = XA8 = XA9 = 0. This corresponds to address 2XH.) Examination of this table demonstrates that only one combination of XA5 and XA9 yields a LOW on Y1: the address 2XH, where X simply indicates that the first four bits are unspecified in the address. This result is in agreement with Table 9.1, where ports 20H and 21H have been indicated as appropriate for the 8259A. Now we need to understand how the first character (0 or 1 in 20H and 21H, respectively) is obtained. As might be expected, the A0 line comes

TABLE 9.5   THE Y1 OUTPUT AND ADDRESS FROM THE LS138 SELECTING THE PIC

A	B	C	G2A	G2B	G1	Y1	Address
X	X	X	1	X	x	1	—
x	x	x	x	1	x	1	—
X	X	X	x	X	0	1	—
0	0	0	0	0	1	1	0XH
1	0	0	0	0	1	0	2XH
0	1	0	0	0	1	1	4XH
1	1	0	0	0	1	1	6XH
0	0	1	0	0	1	1	8XH
1	0	1	0	0	1	1	AXH
0	1	1	0	0	1	1	CXH
1	1	1	0	0	1	1	EXH

x = don't care; X = indeterminate address value

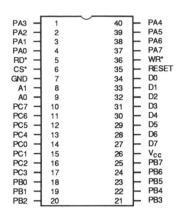

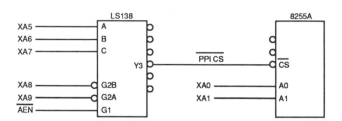

Figure 9.7 The 8255A pin allocation (Courtesy of Intel).

Figure 9.8 The 8255A PPI chip select logic. Reprinted by permission from the *Technical Reference* copyright 1981 by International
Business Machines Corporation.

into play. Obviously this line can select only 2 ports. Since it corresponds to the XA0 input, 20H and 21H must be selected. That is, address line XA0 goes HIGH or LOW as the first character in the address is a 1 or 0, respectively.

Let us consider a second set of equates: the Programmable Peripheral Interface (8255A) appearing in Table 9.1. Figure 9.7 illustrates the pin out for the 8255A. Figure 9.8 presents the chip select logic used in the IBM PC. Table 9.6 illustrates the LS138 Y3 output for the 8255A in a manner similar to that for Y1 used with the 8259A. As this table indicates, only addresses 6XH produce a LOW Y3 and select the 8255A. (Here XA5 = A = 1, XA6 = B = 1, XA7 = C = 0, XA8 = G2A = 0, and XA0 = G2B = 0.)

Returning to Table 9.1, we see that ports numbered 60H through 63H are to be accessed using the 8255A. Again, address lines A0 and A1 come into play. Also, the read and write capability of the chip must be considered. Basically the 8255A PPI is intended to interface peripheral equipment and the system data bus. This implies a bidirectional transfer of data through one of three sets of port lines, PA0-PA7, PB0-PB7, and PC0-PC7 (see Figure 9.7). This data, in turn, must transfer to the data bus lines D0-D7 as the port in question is selected.

Table 9.7 illustrates the internal selection of ports for read and write operations based on Intel descriptions for the signals for the 8255A. In this table it is assumed the

TABLE 9.6 THE Y3 OUTPUT AND ADDRESS FROM
THE LS138 SELECTING THE PPI

A	B	C	G2A	G2B	G1	Y3	Address
	· · ·			· · ·		(all 1s)	· · ·
1	1	0	0	0	1	0	6XH
	· · ·			· · ·		(all 1s)	· · ·

TABLE 9.7 8255A PORT READ-WRITE SELECTION
(COURTESY OF INTEL CORPORATION)

A0	A1	RD*	WR*	CS*	Operation
0	0	0	1	0	PORT A to Data Bus (Input Read)
1	0	0	1	0	PORT B to Data Bus (Input Read)
0	1	0	1	0	PORT C to Data Bus (Input Read)
0	0	1	0	0	Data Bus to PORT A (Output Write)
1	0	1	0	0	Data Bus to PORT B (Output Write)
0	1	1	0	0	Data Bus to PORT C (Output Write)

chip has been selected (CS* = 0 with addresses 6XH). Address lines A0 and A1 combine to yield 0, 1, or 2 as indicated in the table with the selection being

$$\text{PORT A} - 60\text{H}$$
$$\text{PORT B} - 61\text{H}$$
$$\text{PORT C} - 62\text{H}$$

This is in agreement with Table 9.1. These three ports have the following characteristics:

1. PORT A is an 8-bit data output latch and buffer with an additional 8-bit data input latch.
2. PORT B is an 8-bit data input/output latch and buffer with an 8-bit data input buffer.
3. PORT C is an 8-bit data output latch and buffer and an 8-bit data input buffer.

The determination of which port mode is used depends on programming as evidenced by Table 9.7. The PORT C can also be used as two 4-bit ports, with each 4-bit port containing a 4-bit latch, and used for control signal output and status signal input in conjunction with PORT A and PORT B. This mode of operation is used in the IBM PC, along with the normal 8-bit mode, and corresponds to the following signal conditions: A0 = A1 = 1, RD* = 1, WR* = 0 and CS* = 0. This is an output write operation in the 8088 nomenclature or Data Bus to Control transfer. The port address for this mode is 63H (A0 = A1 = 1) and this agrees with Table 9.1.

In this second example of port addressing, derived using the data area equates, the 8255A ports have been defined with reference to the port address appearing on the address bus. As pointed out, these addresses or port numbers appear in the IN and OUT instructions and are specific to the IBM PC system configuration determined by the chip selection logic in conjunction with other signals.

Another example is the 8237A DMA Controller. How are the port addresses 00 through 0FH on Table 9.1 used to select this chip? Again the LS138 is the key. This decoder-demultiplexer has the Y0 output (the output tied to the 8237A CS*) LOW only for XA5 = XA6 = XA7 = XA8 = XA9 = 0. This corresponds to the address

TABLE 9.8 THE 8237A REGISTER OPERATIONS
(PARTIAL; COURTESY OF INTEL CORPORATION).

A0	A1	A2	A3	IOR*	IOW*	Register	Port #
0	0	0	0	1	0	Channel 0 Base/Address	00
0	0	0	0	0	1	Channel 0 Current Addr.	00
1	0	0	0	1	0	Channel 0 Base/Count	01
1	0	0	0	0	1	Channel 0 Current Count	01
0	1	0	0	1	0	Channel 1 Base/Address	02
0	1	0	0	0	1	Channel 1 Current Addr.	02
1	1	0	0	1	0	Channel 1 Base/Count	03
1	1	0	0	0	1	Channel 1 Current Count	03
0	0	1	0	1	0	Channel 2 Base/Addr.	04
0	0	1	0	0	1	Channel 2 Current Addr.	04
1	0	1	0	1	0	Channel 2 Base/Count	05
1	0	1	0	0	1	Channel 2 Current Count	05
0	1	1	0	1	0	Channel 3 Base/Addr.	06
0	1	1	0	0	1	Channel 3 Current Addr.	06
1	1	1	0	1	0	Channel 3 Base/Count	07
1	1	1	0	0	1	Channel 3 Current Count	07
0	0	0	1	1	0	Command-Write	08
1	1	0	1	1	0	Mode-Write	0B
1	0	0	1	1	0	Request Write	09
0	1	0	1	1	0	Mask Set/Reset	0A
1	1	1	1	1	0	Mask Write	0F
1	0	1	1	0	1	Temp. Read	0D
0	0	0	1	0	1	Status Read	08

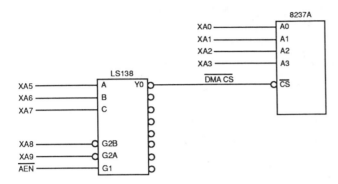

Figure 9.9   The 8237A DMA Controller chip select function. Reprinted by permission from the *Technical Reference* copyright 1981 by International Business Machines Corporation.

range specified by 0XH. What about the X digit in this hexadecimal address? This value depends on how A0, A1, A2, and A3 are defined, as well as IOR* and IOW*. Table 9.8 presents the register operations for the 8237A as a function of these bits.

In Table 9.8, only a partial set of register operations has been defined. We have not listed the software command codes used in the Program Condition, for example. Nevertheless, Table 9.8 demonstrates port addressing using the lower nibble, and we expect port addresses in the range 00 through 0FH in order to select the DMA Controller. This is in agreement with Figure 9.9.

9.2.2 The 8259A and 8237A Initialization

The PIC has a fairly elaborate procedure for initialization based on the fact that it has a number of allowable modes of operation. The initialization process is based on a possible four word input denoted Initialization Command Words 1 through 4, ICW1, ICW2, ICW3, and ICW4. These words are sent from the 8088 in the IBM PC to the 8259A by the chip Data Bus (D0–D7). For the IBM PC, only words ICW1, ICW2, and ICW4 are required because the PC has only one PIC and this operates as the Master. The following format applies to ICW1 and is based on the Intel reference *Microsystem Components Handbook: Microprocessors Volume I* [4].

	A0		D7	D6	D5	D4	D3	D2	D1	D0
ICW1:	0		A7	A6	A5	1	LTIM	ADI	SNGL	IC4

where

IC4:	ICW4 needed (1) or not needed (0)
SNGL:	Single 8259A (1) or cascade mode (0)
ADI:	Call Address Interval of 4 (1) or 8 (0)
LTIM:	Level (1) or Edge (0) Triggered Mode
A5–A7:	Not used
A0:	Zero Bit of Port Address

Similarly, Initialization Command Words 2 and 4 are defined as follows:

A0		D7	D6	D5	D4	D3	D2	D1	D0
ICW2: 1		T7	T6	T5	T4	T3	A10	A9	A8

A10–A8: Ignored in the iAPX 86 system mode
T7–T3: Bits 7–3 of the interrupt vector address (byte)
A0: Zero bit of port address

		D7	D6	D5	D4	D3	D2	D1	D0
ICW4: 1		0	0	0	SFNM	BUF	M/S	AE01	MPM

MPM: 8086/8088 Mode (1) or MCS-80/85 Mode (0)
AEOI: Auto (1) or Normal (0) EDI
M/S: Buffered Mode Master (1) or Slave (0)
BUF: Buffered Mode (1) or Non-Buffered Mode (0)
SFNM: Special Fully Nested Mode (1) or Non-Nested (0).

It is worthwhile to briefly discuss the form of these initialization words as they relate to the IBM PC and XT. The 8259A issues a byte during the second interrupt cycle that points to the interrupt vector table. This byte specifies the position of the desired interrupt in the vector table. How is all this accomplished using the setup from these Initialization Command Words?

ICW1 is identified by the 8259A because (aside from the 8259A chip select) the port address has bit zero set to 0(A0). Additionally, 8259A looks for bit D4 to be equal to a one. This starts the initialization cycle. Bits D7 through D5 are not used by the IBM PC and XT because it is designed to operate in the iAPX 86 mode (MPM bit set in ICW4). The LTIM bit indicates whether the 8259A will use level or edge detection logic on the interrupt inputs. (For the IBM PC and XT, ITIM = 0.) ADI only applies to the MCS-80, 85 system operation (MPM = 0) and is used to designate which address decoding field is to be used for vectoring (4 or 8 interval). SNGL = 1 corresponds to a single 8259A, as in the IBM PC or XT. Finally, IC4 = 1 indicates that the IBM PC and XT will need ICW4 to be interpreted. For the IBM PC and XT ICW1 will load as follows.

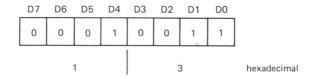

D7	D6	D5	D4	D3	D2	D1	D0
0	0	0	1	0	0	1	1

1   3   hexadecimal

The second initialization word is derived based on Table 9.9.

TABLE 9.9 THE 8259A INTERRUPT LINES (COURTESY OF INTEL).

Interrupt Input	D7–D3	D2	D1	D0
IR7	T7–T3	1	1	1
IR6	T7–T3	1	1	0
IR5	T7–T3	1	0	1
IR4	T7–T3	1	0	0
IR3	T7–T3	0	1	1
IR2	T7–T3	0	1	0
IR1	T7–T3	0	0	1
IR0	T7–T3	0	0	0

The IBM PC and XT have the following interrupt lines set on the 8259A.

IR0   Timer Interrupt

IR1   Keyboard Interrupt

IR2-IR7   I/O Channel Interrupts

The interrupt vector byte for the timer will be of the form

	D7	D6	D5	D4	D3	D2	D1	D0
ICW2:	T7	T6	T5	T4	T3	0	0	0

Remember in Chapter 5 when interrupts were discussed, the timer interrupt was set at 8. This corresponds to an ICW2 of the form

D7	D6	D5	D4	D3	D2	D1	D0
0	0	0	0	1	0	0	0

0   8   hexadecimal

The vector address is F000:FEA5 from Figure 5.1 (4 × 8).

If the keyboard interrupt had been selected, we would have had

	D7	D6	D5	D4	D3	D2	D1	D0
ICW2:	T7	T6	T5	T4	T3	0	0	1

From Chapter 5, the keyboard interrupt was set at 9. This corresponds to an ICW2 of the form

D7	D6	D5	D4	D3	D2	D1	D0
0	0	0	0	1	0	0	1

0   9   hexadecimal

The vector address is F000:E987 from Figure 5.1 (4 × 9). The setting of bits D7 through D3 in ICW2 is determined by the programmer, based on interrupt vector number. In the IBM PC and XT, the 8259A interrupts assume that bits D7 through D4 are equal to zero. IBM could have selected alternate settings for these bits if desired. The present configuration forces the 8259A interrupts to be defined as interrupts 08, 09, 0AH, 0BH, 0CH, 0EH, and 0FH. This is because only bit D3 of ICW2 is set among bits D7 through D3 and the remaining bits (D2-D0) are set according to the table indicated above.

Next, how is ICW4 set for the IBM PC and XT? The IBM PC and XT systems run in iAPX 86 mode (MPM = 1), normal end of interrupt (AEI0 = 0), M/S = 0 since we have a single 8259A (SNGL = 1 in ICW1), BUF = 2 for buffered mode, and SFNM = 0 for non-nested mode. This results in an ICW4 of the form

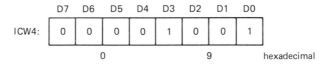

Figure 9.10 illustrates the initialization sequence for the IBM PC (from the early *IBM Technical Reference*). Note that this initialization sets up the type 8 interrupt vector. Also note that ICW1 is output to port 20H while ICW2 and ICW4 are output to port 21H as indicated in Figure 9.5. This is in keeping with the requirement that the port address bit A0 be 0 for ICW1 and 1 for ICW2 and ICW4.

The above discussion briefly outlines the initialization procedure for the PIC used in the IBM PC and XT. This initialization is based on the Intel procedure for using the 8259A, as configured in the IBM PC and XT.

Figure 9.11 illustrates the BIOS IBM PC code for checking the 8237A count and address registers. These are ports 00, 01, 02, 03, 04, 05, 06 and 07 appearing in Table 9.8. The figure begins with an excerpt from the data segment equates, which loads the base DMA port addresses. Next a pattern of all ones is loaded with AL and each byte

```
Address     Line #                              Comments


                      . . .
            480     ;------------------------------------------------------
            481     ;          INITIALIZE THE 8259 INTERRUPT CONTROLLER CHIP
            482     ;------------------------------------------------------
E199        483     C21:
E199        484           MOV   AL,13H              ;ICW1-EDGE,SNGL,ICW4
E19B        485           OUT   INTA00,AL
E19D        486           MOV   AL,8                ;SETUP ICW2-INT TYPE 8(8-F)
E19F        487           OUT   INTA01,AL
E1A1        488           MOV   AL,9                ;SETUP ICW4-BUFFERED,8086 MODE
E1A3        489           OUT   INTA01,AL

                      . . .
```

Figure 9.10 The initialization sequence for the 8259A. Reprinted by permission from the *Technical Reference* copyright 1981 by International Business Machines Corporation.

```
Address      Line #                                              Comment

0008         16            DMA08   EQU     08      ;DMA STATUS REG PORT ADDR
0000         17            DMA     EQU     00      ;DMA CHANNEL 0 ADDR REG PORT ADDR

                 . . .

             396      ;   WRAP DMA CHANNELS ADDRESS AND COUNT REGISTERS

                 . . .

E119 B0FF    398           MOV     AL,0FFH         ;WRITE PATTERN 0FFH TO ALL REG
E11B 8AD8    399    C16:    MOV     BL,AL           ;SAVE PATTERN FOR COMPARE
E11D 8AF8    400           MOV     BH,AL
E11F B90800  401           MOV     CX,8            ;SETUP LOOP COUNT
E122 BA0000  402           MOV     DX,DMA          ;SETUP IO PORT ADDR OF REG
E125 EE      403    C17:    OUT     DX,AL           ;WRITE PATTERN TO REG,LSB
E126 EE      404           OUT     DX,AL           ;MSB OF 16 BIT REG
E127 B80101  405           MOV     AX,0101H        ;AX TO ANOTHER PAT BEFORE READ
E12A EC      406           IN      AL,DX           ;READ 16-BIT DMA CH REG,LSB
E12B 8AE0    407           MOV     AH,AL           ;SAVE LSB OF 16-BIT REG
E12D EC      408           IN      AL,DX           ;READ MSB OF DMA CH REG
E12E 3BD8    409           CMP     BX,AX           ;PATTERN READ AS WRITTEN?
E130 7403    410           JE      C18             ;YES - CHECK NEXT REG
E132 E97AFF  411           JMP     ERR01           ;NO - HALT THE SYSTEM
E135         412    C18:                            ;NXT_DMA_CH
E135 42      413           INC     DX              ;SET IO PORT TO NEXT CH REG
E136 E2ED    414           LOOP    C17             ;WRITE PATTERN TO NEXT REG

                 . . .
```

Figure 9.11   The code that checks the 8237A address and count registers. Reprinted by permission from the *Technical Reference* copyright 1981 by International Business Machines Corporation.

```
Address      Line #                                              Comments

                 . . .

             418      ;   INITIALIZE AND START DMA FOR MEMORY REFRESH
             419
E13C B0FF    420           MOV     AL,0FFH         ;SET CNT OF 64K FOR RAM REFRESH
E13E E601    421           OUT     DMA+1,AL
E140 E601    422           OUT     DMA+1,AL
E142 B058    423           MOV     AL,058H         ;SET DMA MODE,CH 0,READ,AUTOINT
E144 E60B    424           OUT     DMA+0BH,AL      ;WRITE DMA MODE REG
E146 B000    425           MOV     AL,0            ;ENABLE DMA CONTROLLER
E148 E608    426           OUT     DMA+8,AL        ;SETUP DMA COMMAND REG
E14A E60A    427           OUT     DMA+10,AL       ;ENABLE CH 0 FOR REFRESH
E14C B041    428           MOV     AL,41H          ;SET MODE FOR CH 1
E14E E60B    429           OUT     DMA+0BH,AL
E150 B042    430           MOV     AL,42H          ;SET MODE FOR CH 2
E152 E60B    431           OUT     DMA+0BH,AL
E154 B043    432           MOV     AL,43H          ;SET MODE FOR CH 3
E156 E60B    433           OUT     DMA+0BH,AL

                 . . .
```

Figure 9.12   The ROM BIOS code which initializes the 8237A. Reprinted by permission from the *Technical Reference* copyright 1981 by International Business Machines Corporation.

of BX, in turn, is loaded with 0FFH. The loop count for loading eight registers is set to 8. The first loop iteration uses port address 00, and once the above pattern is output, the accumulator is reloaded with a discriminating pattern (0101H). Following this, AX is loaded with the contents of register 00, which should be 0FFFFH. The resulting pattern is next compared to BX and any errors are noted. The port address is then incremented and the next DMA count-address port checked.

Figure 9.12 presents the code for initializing the DMA controller for memory refresh. First, the bytes containing 0FFH are loaded into port 01, the channel 0 current count register: This is a write operation. It loads the 16-bit count register with 0FFFFH, which is one less than 64K. Next port 0BH, the mode-write register control (see Table 9.8), is loaded with 058H. What does this value signify? To answer this we must examine the Intel format for this register.

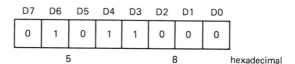

A: 00 (channel 0), 01 (channel 1), 10 (channel 2), or 11 (channel 3)

B: 00 (verify transfer), 01 (write transfer), 10 (read transfer), 11 (illegal) or don't care if bits D4 and D5 set

C: Autoinitialization (0) disable or (1) enable

D: Address (0) increment or (1) decrement

E: 00 (demand mode), 01 (single mode), 10 (block mode), or 11 (cascade mode)

Since we have

D7	D6	D5	D4	D3	D2	D1	D0
0	1	0	1	1	0	0	0

5   8   hexadecimal

it is clear that channel 0 is selected, read transfer is to occur, autoinitialization is enabled, and address increment mode and a single controller chip are to be used. Once this is output, port 8 is selected and the IOR* condition set (remember we just selected read transfer). Port 8 with IOR* set selects the command-write control and this sets the command register. This register, according to Intel, is defined as follows:

D0: Memory-to-memory enable (1) or disable (0)

D1: Channel 0 address hold enable (1), disable (0), or don't care if D0 = 0

D2: Controller disable (1) or enable (0)

D3: Compressed timing (1) or normal (0)

D4: Rotating priority (1) or fixed (0)

D5: Extended write selection (1), late (0), or don't care if D2 = 1

D6:   DREQ sense active HIGH (0) or LOW (1)

D7:   DACK sense active HIGH (0) or LOW (1)

As the coding in Figure 9.12 illustrates, the command register is loaded with 00H. This disables memory-to-memory transfer, enables the controller, sets normal timing and fixed priority, and sets DREQ and DACK to sense on HIGH. Next port 0AH, the Mask Set/Reset port, is sent 00H which enables channel 0. The mask register can be set and reset two ways. These are essentially equivalent and the second technique (courtesy of Intel) is based on the following interpretation of this register.

D0:   Channel 0 mask bit set (1) or clear (0)

D1:   Channel 1 mask bit set (1) or clear (0)

D2:   Channel 2 mask bit set (1) or clear (0)

D3:   Channel 3 mask bit set (1) or clear (0)

D4–D7:   Don't care

Obviously the output (0000H) to port 0AH resets the port.

The remaining sets of instructions output a 41H and 43H to port 0BH. This is the mode-write register control. With the instructions, autoinitialization is disabled and channels 1, 2, and 3 are set to the single mode.

By now the reader has begun to perceive the pattern for programming the IBM PC and XT system board chips. Once the chip selection is accomplished by appropriate port addressing, the output register (usually the accumulator) reads or writes to the chip with the necessary byte or word format. This format is dictated by Intel in the case of many of the IBM PC, XT, or AT chips that are manufactured by Intel. The actual programming and debugging of driver software is a time-consuming activity. We only looked at some of the final debugged code and avoided the tedious process by which this code was obtained. In the next subsection we will examine additional IBM PC BIOS code and look at the run-time implications for some of this processing.

9.3 THE VIDEO DISPLAY PROCESSING

The BIOS programming contains many examples of software interfaces between the microprocessor and associated peripherals. So far, we have examined printer I/O and some chips in the system (chip select and initialization). This section considers a more extended example, video display input/output processing. It is first necessary to understand how the display operates. The display consists of both analog and digital circuitry and the digital circuitry effectively controls the analog operation. In the following discussion we first examine the display characteristics. Then the digital interface is presented. Finally, portions of the actual BIOS code appropriate for controlling the cathode ray tube (CRT) are considered. IBM has two types of displays, a monochrome and a color-graphics display. In this discussion, the monochrome display is considered. The digital interface addresses both the chips used and the IBM PC circuits.

9.3.1 CRT Operation

The CRT is an evacuated glass tube with fluorescent coating on one end and an electron gun at the other end. In between are magnetic deflection coils or electrostatic deflection plates internal to the tube. These change the position of the electron beam used to illuminate the coating (phosphor) on the screen end. By electrically varying the magnetic or electric field, the electron beam can be made to trace a pattern on the screen. The coils used to achieve deflection correspond to two independent signals for most CRTs used with the IBM microcomputers, a horizontal deflection signal and a vertical deflection signal. In the case of the IBM PC, XT, and AT displays, the beam is scanned horizontally across the CRT and moved vertically downward to each successive line during the retrace until the entire CRT has been scanned. This is referred to as raster scanning, and the electron beam is blanked during retrace for each horizontal and vertical line and when the beam is returned to the top of the screen.

Figures are generated by turning the electron gun on and off to create dots on the screen which, when closely spaced together, give the appearance of a connected line. We have already seen the effects of such raster scanning in Chapter 5. The monochrome display can only be used for generating text-oriented characters. For this display, each character is generated from a matrix that is 9 dots high and 7 dots wide. In order to separate one character from another, this 7×9 dot matrix is imbedded in a larger 9×14 dot matrix. On each side of the character is a blank vertical column, above the character are two horizontal blank rows, and below the character are three blank rows. These blank regions serve to provide row and column separations for each character on the monochrome screen.

The monochrome screen has 720 dots in each horizontal raster row and 350 raster rows across the screen. It also has a longer persistence phosphor than most displays, so that a slower vertical scan rate can be used. For the IBM monochrome display a 50 Hz vertical scan rate is used, as opposed to a 60 Hz vertical scan rate used by most displays. The vertical scan rate means that the entire screen is scanned 50 times per second. If each scan consists of 350 lines, then a single line is scanned at the following rate.

$$f_{HOR.SCAN} = 350 \text{ (lines/screen)} \times 50 \text{ (screen/second)}$$

$$= 17.5 \times 10^3 \text{ lines/second}$$

Thus the horizontal scan rate is 17.5 KHz which is slightly higher than the normal television rate (15.75 KHz). From the *IBM Technical Reference* we see that the dot clock frequency is 16.257 MHz. Thus, it is possible to determine approximately the total characters per line.

$$17.5 \times 10^3 \text{ (line/second)} \times 9 \text{ (dot width/character)} \times X\text{(character/line)}$$

$$= 16.257 \times 10^6 \text{ (dot/second)}$$

Solving this gives roughly 103 characters/line. Since some of the time involved in writing a line consists of retrace, only about 80% of the horizontal scan time can be used for character generation. This accounts for the 80-character line used in the IBM monochrome display. The other 23 characters are absorbed by the retrace interval when the electron beam is blanked.

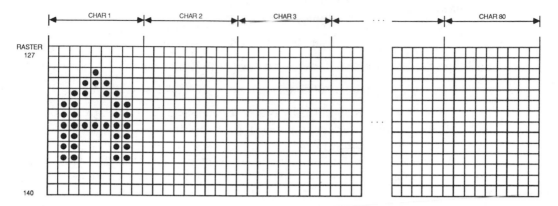

Figure 9.13 A typical IBM monochrome display line format illustrating the character placement and raster scanning. The letter A is shown as it appears in line 10 of the IBM monochrome display.

So far, we have described the performance of the CRT monitor's analog circuits. These circuits are typically driven by three signals from the associated digital controller: Horizontal Synchronization (HSYNC), Vertical Synchronization (VSYNC), and the VIDEO signal. This latter signal can have multiple outputs in the case of color monitors. Since the horizontal and vertical scanning is continuous, the synchronization signals merely control the width and height, respectively, of this scanning. This is the form of CRT control used in the IBM monochrome adapter. In this adapter, the HSYNC, VSYNC, and VIDEO signals are generated from a Motorola 6845 CRT Controller chip. This chip must synchronize the dot pattern generated with the VIDEO signal and the horizontal-vertical scan rate to yield characters on the display. Figure 9.13 illustrates the display behavior for the 10th character line on the IBM monochrome display. Clearly, the CRT controller must have the capability of synchronizing HSYNC, VSYNC, and VIDEO to properly generate these signals.

The IBM monochrome adapter character set consists of 256 characters in the ASCII format. Chapter 6 presented the first 128 of these characters. It takes 8 bits to specify 256 characters and if these 8 bits are specified from a parallel bit stream, some device must convert the character selected into a serial output to the VIDEO signal. Also, since each character is formed from a set of 9 raster scans (14 including blanks), the device in question must consider what raster line is being considered and generate the appropriate dots for that line. Finally, as Figure 9.13 indicates, the raster scan within a given line must encompass all 80 characters on the line. Thus, the device must know ahead of time all the characters on a given line so that each of the 14 raster scans for that line can present the proper dot pattern for the characters on that raster.

The above discussion implies a need for two more components in addition to the CRT controller, which turns the dots on and off.

1. Screen Buffer to store the character pattern for an entire screen
2. Character Generator to generate the dot pattern for a character based on the screen buffer input

For the IBM monochrome display there are 25 lines per screen or frame.

$$350(\text{rasters/frame})/14(\text{rasters/line}) = 25 \text{ lines/frame}.$$

Each line has 80 characters; thus a screen buffer must have the following memory:

$$25(\text{lines/frame}) \times 80(\text{characters/line}) = 2000(\text{characters/frame}).$$

In ASCII, a character is specified by one byte; hence this translates to a 2000 byte buffer. Since memory comes in multiples of powers of two, a 2048 byte buffer would be required (16K dot memory).

The buffer consists of memory and addressing logic and is conceptually simple; the character generator is more complex. Consider a single character, the A in Figure 9.13. This can be stored in matrix of 9×14 (126) elements. The actual character occupies 7×9 (63) elements. If each row of the character is selected in turn and all bits in that row are shifted simultaneously into a shift register in parallel; the shift register can then be used to serially load the VIDEO signal.

What signal lines are needed? First, we need four raster signals to specify up to 14 rasters per character line; a maximum total of 16 is allowed. Next we must have eight address signals in order to select 1 of 256 characters. Finally, since each character raster is seven dots wide, we need a minimum of seven register positions in the shift register. Shift registers are typically multiples of powers of two; hence we assume an 8-bit wide shift register. This means that the logic must translate the nine-element width per character (7 character elements/raster and 2 blanks) into an 8-bit parallel shift register output. The storage capacity for such a generator would have to be 16K: 256 characters $\times$ (7 horizontal dots $\times$ 9 vertical dots)/character = 16,128 dots.

Figure 9.14a presents a representative character generator functional block diagram. Figure 9.14b illustrates the IBM monochrome adapter character generator based on the *IBM Technical Reference*. Not all signals are indicated. Basically, each character from screen memory is buffered as data through the LS273 buffer, into the character generator designated MK 36000. This character data (CC0-CC7) also serves as the character address for the character generator PROM input (A3–A10). The raster address is specified by lines RA0, RA1, RA2, and ROMAII; the last line is really RA3 when writing to the screen. Finally, the shift register LS166 loads the parallel outputs into eight register positions on the LOAD* strobe

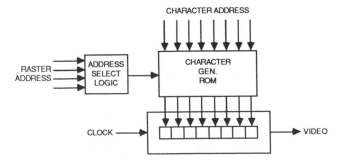

Figure 9.14a A functional block diagram of a representative character generator.

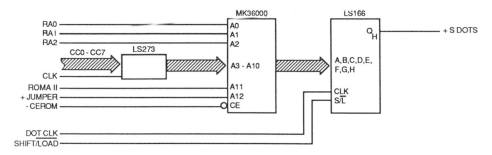

Figure 9.14b The IBM monochrome adapter character generator. Reprinted by permission from the *Technical Reference* copyright 1981 by International Business Machines Corporation.

(positions A, B, C, D, E, F, G, H) and shifts them out at the DOTCLK rate. The character generator PROM is a special purpose IBM PROM that contains the IBM character set. In the author's PC system this is a Motorola XE3201 chip built to IBM's specification. The raster addressing and timing are provided by the 6845, which we consider in the next section.

Figure 9.15 illustrates the screen buffer memory for the IBM monochrome adapter. This figure only illustrates that portion of the screen buffer memory that is used by the monochrome adapter (outputs CC0-CC7). (We have ignored memory that is devoted to dot attributes.) Also illustrated in the figure is the multiplexing for reading and writing to this screen buffer memory and the 6845 controller, which actually regulates the screen buffer I/O and provides other signals such as HSYNC, VSYNC and raster selection (RA0-RA3). We will return to the 6845. For now, however, consider the screen buffer memory. This memory is comprised of four National Semiconductor MM2114L 4096-Bit (1024 × 4) static RAMs. Hence, the total complement of 16K screen buffer memory is achieved. The 2114L static RAM is constructed so that it may be easily ganged to yield multiple banks of storage.

Consider a situation where the 8088 is writing characters to the screen buffer. Then signals on BA1, BA2, BA3, and A4–A10 are output from the LS157s as RMA0 through RMA9 (1024 address locations). Line A11 and BA0, however, are used to select which member of the 2114L pair is to be written. Here, line BA0 must be LOW to write to the screen buffer. Line A11 simply toggles between one 2114L or another in a given bank as this bit is set or unset. Since each 2114L has provision for 4 I/O lines, it can at most contain memory for one-half of the data byte (lines CC0-CC3 or CC4-CC7). The entire data byte requires two banks of 2114Ls with each 2114L having the same address but different data bits on input/output.

Not shown in the figure is a second pair of 2114L banks. This set of RAM is activated when BA0 goes HIGH and contains the attribute for the corresponding dot. The reader is referred to the *IBM Technical Reference* for a description of this processing. We will only address the display dot generation itself and not discuss the attribute aspect of the monochrome adapter processing.

So far in this subsection, we have seen the way in which characters are generated and the way that the screen is mapped for the IBM monochrome adapter. Also, the

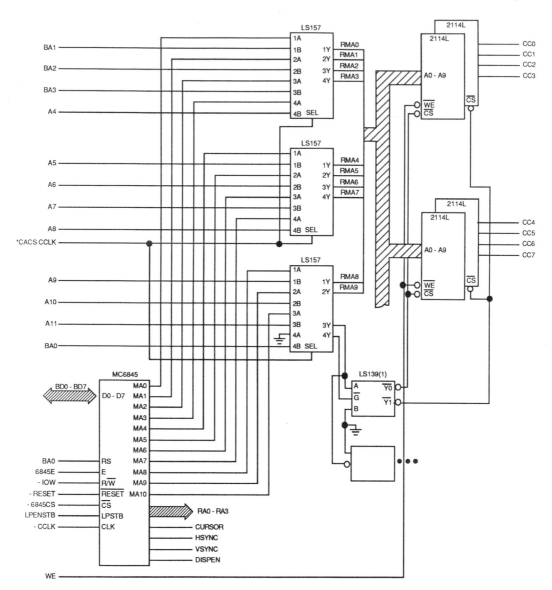

Figure 9.15 The IBM monochrome adapter screen buffer environment. Reprinted by permission from the *Technical Reference* copyright 1981 by International Business Machines Corporation.

performance of the CRT in response to HSYNC, VSYNC, and VIDEO has been addressed. The regulation of the dot pattern in the VIDEO signal is based on digital signals. It is this processing that can be affected and controlled by the 8088. In the next subsection we focus on the 6845 CRT controller. This discussion examines the way in which the 6845 generates CRT control signals appropriate for character display.

9.3.2 The Display Digital Interface

This subsection describes the digital interface between the CRT signals HSYNC, VSYNC, and VIDEO and the 8088 microprocessor. The video signal corresponds to S DOTS in Figure 9.14b. An overall functional block diagram for the IBM monochrome adapter is presented in Figure 9.16. The major control element for the CRT is the Motorola 6845 and we now consider this chip. Figure 9.17 illustrates the pin designations for the 6845.

Pin 1 is ground and pin 2, the reset line. Pin 3 is a light pen strobe. We only briefly mention this pin; the light pen is used to pick up signals from the CRT screen when a dot is illuminated and store them in memory for later use. Pins 4 through 17 are the screen memory address. On the IBM monochrome adapter only pins 4 through 14 are used since this is sufficient to address 1024 elements. Pin 18 enables the display output (S DOTS) and Pin 19 enables the cursor. Pins 20, 21, 22, and 23 supply +5 volts, clock, read-write selection and chip enable, respectively. Pins 24 and 25 supply the internal register select and chip select, respectively. The 6845 has 19 internal registers that control various actions. These registers consist of 1 address register and 18 control registers. All control registers are accessed via the address register; hence only one register port is needed. The chip select must be set LOW to access the chip. If RS is LOW, then data information input on the data ports is sent to the address register. If RS is HIGH the data information is assumed to go to the selected internal register. Information sent to the address register (CS*, RS = 0,0) is assumed to be an address, and information sent to an internal register (RS = 0,1) is assumed to be a parameter.

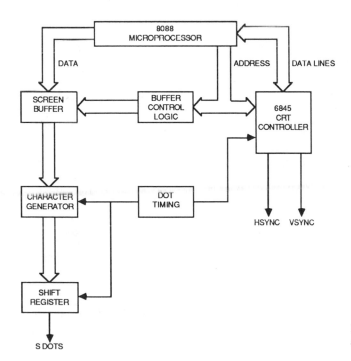

Figure 9.16 The IBM monochrome adapter video processing environment.

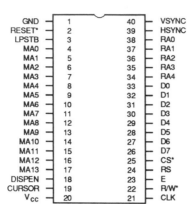

GND —	1	40 — VSYNC
RESET* —	2	39 — HSYNC
LPSTB —	3	38 — RA0
MA0 —	4	37 — RA1
MA1 —	5	36 — RA2
MA2 —	6	35 — RA3
MA3 —	7	34 — RA4
MA4 —	8	33 — D0
MA5 —	9	32 — D1
MA6 —	10	31 — D2
MA7 —	11	30 — D3
MA8 —	12	29 — D4
MA9 —	13	28 — D5
MA10 —	14	27 — D6
MA11 —	15	26 — D7
MA12 —	16	25 — CS*
MA13 —	17	24 — RS
DISPEN —	18	23 — E
CURSOR —	19	22 — R/W*
V_{cc} —	20	21 — CLK

Figure 9.17 The 6845 CRT controller pin description. Copyright 1987 by Motorola, Inc.

Pins 26 through 33 contain the parameter information to be exchanged between the 8088 and the 6845. These lines are bidirectional so that the CPU can query the CRT controller as well as supply control information. The four lines from pins 34 through 38 contain the raster number. These lines are used by the character generator to determine the dot row of a character as previously discussed. Finally, pins 39 and 40 contain the HSYNC and VSYNC signals. Table 9.10 describes the 6845 internal registers.

Based on Table 9.1, the following bits must be set to select the 6845 (x indicates a don't-care situation).

A9	A8		A7	A6	A5	A4	A3	A2	A1	A0
1	1		1	0	1	1	x	x	x	x

Figure 9.18 illustrates the chip selection logic for the IBM monochrome adapter. Examination of Table 9.2 demonstrates that Y7 of the LS138 appearing in Figure 9.18 goes LOW when the above bits are set as indicated. In addition to these address bits being set as above, the AEN line must go LOW. This address enable line goes LOW as a preface to an address being placed on the address bus by the 8088. The RS pin is attached to the A0 line (as recommended by Motorola) and, consequently, the address

TABLE 9.10   THE 6845 INTERNAL REGISTERS. COPYRIGHT 1987 BY MOTOROLA, INC.

Register	Name	Register Number	Comments
AR	Address Register	—	This is a 5-bit register used to select 18 internal control registers (R0–R17). When RS and CW* are LOW this register is selected. (RS = 1 for all other 6845 registers.)
R0	Horizontal Total	0	This register is to define the total number of horizontal characters per line including retrace. It contains a number N for N + 1 total characters.
R1	Horizontal Displayed	1	This register contains the total number of horizontal characters displayed.

R2	Horizontal Sync Position	2	This register contains the horizontal sync position as a multiple of the character clock. This signal "fine tunes" the location or spacing of each character along the horizontal raster line.
R3	Sync Width	3	This register sets the horizontal and vertical sync pulse widths. The horizontal width is set by the lower nibble as a multiple of the character clock. The vertical width is set by the upper nibble as a multiple of the raster period.
R4	Vertical Total	4	This register contains the total number of lines per frame. When N = total lines, the register contains $N - 1$.
R5	Vertical Total Adjust	5	This register contains a number representing the number of rasters per frame to adjust for optimum performance.
R6	Vertical Displayed	6	This register contains the number of displayed rows.
R7	Vertical Sync Position	7	This register contains the vertical sync position as a multiple, in time, of the horizontal character clock. It cannot exceed the total horizontal character period.
R8	Interface and Skew	8	This register programs interface and skew. In the noninterface mode the even number and odd number fields have their rasters scanned in duplicate fashion. In the interface sync mode the rasters of odd number fields are scanned between the even number fields. In the combined mode the scanning is the same as interface sync but the odd frame pattern is different from the even frame pattern. Bits 7 and 6 determine the cursor skew and bits 5 and 4 the DISPTMG skew. Typically, 0, 1, or 2 character skew is possible plus blanking.
R9	Maximum Raster Address	9	Defines the total number of rasters per character including space. It is a 5-bit register.
R10	Cursor Start Raster	10	Determines the cursor position in the character raster. This register contains the start position.
R11	Cursor End Raster	11	This register contains the cursor end raster address.
R12,R13	Start Address	12,13	These 8-bit registers (total 16 bits of address) are used to program the first refresh memory address. Bits 6 and 7 of R12 are not used.
R14,R15	Cursor	14,15	These two 8-bit registers contain the cursor address. Bits 6 and 7 of R14 are not used.
R16,R17	Light Pen	16,17	These two 8-bit registers contain the light pen position. Bits 6 and 7 of R16 are not used.

register of the 6845 is selected when A0 = 0, while one of the remaining internal registers is selected when A0 = 1.

It should be pointed out that DISPEN (display enable signal), HSYNC, VSYNC, and the CURSOR signal are all related to the character clock (CCLK). This clock is used to drive the 6845 CLK pin. Remember that the characters are output at some multiple of the horizontal scan rate (we estimated 103). In the next subsection,

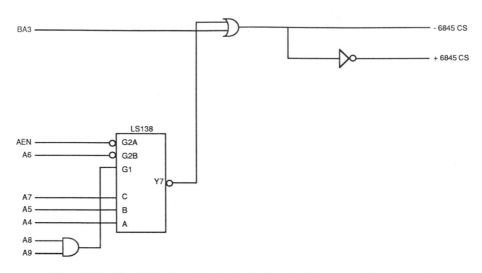

Figure 9.18   The 6845 chip selection logic. Reprinted by permission from the *Technical Reference* copyright 1981 by International Business Machines Corporation.

we will see that the 6845 is programmed for 98 characters per line. This calls for a character clock rate of

$$17.5\mathrm{KHz}(\text{line/second}) \times 98(\text{characters/line}) = 1.715\mathrm{MHz}(\text{characters/second}).$$

This rate is slightly more than ten times the dot clock frequency (which is 16.257MHz). Since this dot clock frequency is divided to give the character clock, a division by ten is needed. Figure 9.19 illustrates the logic used to divide the clock. The 16.257MHz clock is input to a multiplexer (LS153) where it is selected and sent to the divider chain. The clock is divided five times by two clock periods each. Hence, the character clock is 1.6257MHz. How, then, do we scan the CRT properly? Basically, a region at the bottom of the scan is allocated for vertical scan adjustment. If in actuality we have 350 raster lines, solving the following equation for X tells the number of raster scan lines needed at this character clock rate:

$$1.715 \times 10^6(\text{characters/second}) \times 350 \text{ lines}$$

$$= 1.6257 \times 10^6(\text{characters/second}) \times X \text{ lines}$$

Here $X = 369.2$. Assuming an added blank character line (14 rasters allowed for retrace) and a vertical adjustment of 6 raster lines, it follows that 370 raster lines will result. In the next subsection we see that this is what IBM has done.

This completes the discussion of the digital interface. Basically, only the 6845 has been considered. In the next section the BIOS code is presented. Here the emphasis will be on 6845 set up and writing dots to the screen. All other submodes will be left to the reader.

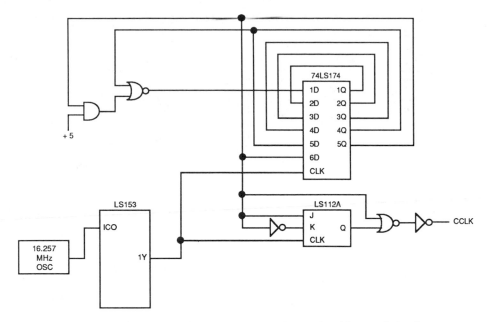

Figure 9.19   The character clock dividing network. Reprinted by permission from the *Technical Reference* copyright 1981 by International Business Machines Corporation.

9.3.3 INT 10H: A Hardware Perspective

Interrupt 10H of the BIOS code (starting at address F000:F065 in the IBM PC version) is the service routine that handles the display processing. This routine begins with a definition of a pointer, M1, that has each successive word location pointing to a video routine. The form of this pointer is

```
M1 LABEL WORD
       DW     OFFSET SET_MODE
       DW     OFFSET SET_CTYPE
       DW     OFFSET SET_CPOS
       ...
       DW     OFFSET WRITE_DOT
       DW     OFFSET READ_DOT
   MIL EQU    $_M1
```

From examining the INT 10H options table in Chapter 5, it becomes clear that, based on the AH value upon entry to INT 10H, a pointer can be developed that points to the word offset from M1 that contains the procedure associated with the AH function. For example, AH = 0 points to M1, which is the address of the offset for procedure

```
Address    Line #                                      Comments
                    . . .
F065       3262    VIDEO_IO        PROC     NEAR
F065       3263       STI                              ;INTERRUPTS BACK ON
F066       3264       CLD                              ;SET DIRECTION FORWARD
F067       3265       PUSH    ES
F068       3266       PUSH    DS                        ;SAVE SEGMENT REGISTERS
F069       3267       PUSH    DX
F06A       3268       PUSH    CX
F06B       3269       PUSH    BX
F06C       3270       PUSH    SI
F06D       3271       PUSH    DI
F06E       3272       PUSH    AX                        ;SAVE AX VALUE
F06F       3273       MOV     AL,AH                     ;GET INTO LOW BYTE
F071       3274       XOR     AH,AH                     ;ZERO TO HIGH BYTE
F073       3275       SAL     AX,1                      ;*2 FOR TABLE LOOKUP
F075       3276       MOV     SI,AX                     ;PUT INTO SI FOR BRANCH
F077       3277       CMP     AX,MIL                    ;TEST FOR WITHIN RANGE
F07A       3278       JB      M2                        ;BRANCH AROUND BRANCH
F07C       3279       POP     AX                        ;THROW AWAY THE PARAMETER
F07D       3280       JMP     VIDEO_RETURN              ;DO NOTHING IF NOT IN RANGE
F080       3281    M2:   MOV     AX,DATA
F083       3282       MOV     DS,AX
F085       3283       MOV     AX,0B800H                 ;SEGMENT FOR COLOR CARD
F088       3284       MOV     DI,EQUIP_FLAG             ;GET EQUIPMENT SETTING
F08C       3285       AND     DI,39H                    ;ISOLATE CRT SWITCHES
F090       3286       CMP     DI,30H                    ;IS SETTING FOR BW CARD?
F093       3287       JNE     M3
F095       3288       MOV     AX,0B000H                 ;SEGMENT FOR BW CARD
F098       3289    M3:   MOV     ES,AX                   ;SETUP TO POINT AT VIDEO RAM AREAS
F09A       3290       POP     AX                        ;RECOVER VALUE
F09B       3291       MOV     AH,CRT_MODE               ;GET CURRENT MODE INTO AH
F09F       3292       JMP     WORD PTR CS:[SI+OFFSET M1]
           3293    VIDEO_IO        ENDP
                    . . .
```

Figure 9.20 The video routine that sets up the INT 10H processing. Reprinted by permission from the *Technical Reference* copyright 1981 by International Business Machines Corporation.

SET_MODE. Similarly, AH = 2 points to the second word after M1, which is the address of the offset for procedure SET_CPOS, the Set Cursor Position routine.

The first video routine, VIDEO_IO, sets up the INT 10H processing based on AH. Figure 9.20 illustrates the code which accomplishes this processing. Upon entry, AX is saved on the stack and then examined to determine which of the service procedures should be processed. If AH is out of range, a jump to VIDEO_RETURN takes place and the stack is popped prior to return to the calling routine. MIL is defined as the range of byte values AH can assume to correctly point to a video service routine. In the IBM PC, MIL is equal to 30. This corresponds to a word pointer range of 15 for AH. If AH is in range, the data segment DATA is loaded starting at label M2. Next the equipment setting is examined to determine whether a monochrome or color card is in the system. The equipment flag register looks like

A15   ...   A2 A1 A0
| | |x| | | | |x| | | | | | | | |

where A13 and A8 are unused. The above flag register has the following definition:

A0:   Diskettes (1) or no diskettes (0)

A1:   8087 (2) or no 8087 (0)

A2–A3:   Early IBM PC 32K RAM (01), 48K RAM (10), and
            64K RAM (11) on system board

A4–A5:   Unused video (00), 40 × 25 color card (01), 80 × 25
            color card (10), 80 × 25 monochrome (11)

A6–A7:   Number of disk drives; 1 (00), 2 (01), 3 (10), and 4 (11)

A9–A11:   Number of RS-232 cards attached

A12:   Game Card (1) or No Game Card (0)

A14–A15   Number of printers attached

Clearly, if EQUIP_FLAG is ANDed with 0030H and then compared to this value, the result will be true for the monochrome adapter present. Otherwise, it will be assumed that the display is color. Finally, this routine loads the extra segment address for color card processing (B800H) or monochrome processing (B000H) and jumps to the correct service procedure. This latter jump is based on the statement

JMP WORD PTR CS:[SI+OFFSET M1]

```
Address     Line #                                          Comments

                  . . .
FOFC        3339    SET_MODE      PROC    NEAR
FOFC        3340            MOV   DX,03D4H           ;ADDRESS OF COLOR CARD
FOFF        3341            MOV   BL,0               ;MODE SET FOR COLOR CARD
F101        3342            CMP   DI,30H             ;IS BW CARD INSTALLED?
F104        3343            JNE   M8                 ;OK WITH COLOR
F106        3344            MOV   AL,7               ;INDICATE BW CARD MODE
F108        3345            MOV   DX,03B4H           ;ADDRESS OF BW CARD
F10B        3346            INC   BL                 ;MODE SET FOR BW CARD
F10D        3347    M8:     MOV   AH,AL              ;SAVE MODE IN AH
F10F        3348            MOV   CRT_MODE,AL        ;SAVE IN GLOBAL VARIABLE
F112        3349            MOV   ADDR_6845,DX       ;SAVE ADDRESS OF BASE
F116        3350            PUSH  DS                 ;SAVE POINTER TO DATA SEGMENT
F117        3351            PUSH  AX                 ;SAVE MODE
F118        3352            PUSH  DX                 ;SAVE OUTPUT PORT VALUE
F119        3353            ADD   DX,4               ;POINT TO CONTROL REGISTER
F11C        3354            MOV   AL,BL              ;GET MODE SET FOR CARD
F11E        3355            OUT   DX,AL              ;RESET VIDEO
F11F        3356            POP   DX                 ;BACK TO BASE REGISTER
F120        3357            SUB   AX,AX              ;SET UP FOR ABSO SEGMENT
F122        3358            MOV   DS,AX              ;ESTABLISH VECTOR TABLE ADDRESSING
            3359            ASSUME DS:ABSO
                  . . .
```

Figure 9.21   The SET_MODE procedure used to prepare for output of parameters to the 6845. Reprinted by permission from the *Technical Reference* copyright 1981 by International Business Machines Corporation.

Here SI contains the offset of the procedure, such as SET_MODE, from M1. CRT_MODE is initialized in the data segment and reset in the service procedure SET_MODE. It is typically 7 for the 80 × 25 BW mode.

In this subsection we will consider portions of the SET_MODE video I/O routine. This represents a good example of the hardware interface. Figure 9.21 illustrates the setup for loading the 6845 registers with parameters. Initially, the check for the monochrome adapter yields a jump to M8 if the color card is present. Address 03B4H is loaded into DX for the monochrome card. Also BL is set equal to 1. Next the value that was loaded internally into AL(7) is loaded into CRT_MODE. The value 03B4H is saved as the address for the 6845, ADDR_6845. Input BA0 to RS on the 6845 must be set LOW for an address 03B4H (bit zero of this address). Thus this base address selects the address register in the 6845. Note that 03B8H and 03B6H also select this register.

```
Address      Line #                                    Comments

               . . .
F124         3360        LDS     BX,PARM_PTR       ;GET POINTER TO VIDEO PARMS
F128         3361        POP     AX                ;RECOVER PARMS
               . . .
F129         3363        MOV     CX,M4             ;LENGTH OF EACH ROW OF TABLE
F12C         3364        CMP     AH,2              ;DETERMINE WHICH ONE TO USE
F12F         3365        JC      M9                ;MODE IS 0 OR 1
F131         3366   .    ADD     BX,CX             ;MOVE TO NEXT ROW OF INIT TABLE
F133         3367        CMP     AH,4
F136         3368        JC      M9                ;MODE IS 2 OR 3
F138         3369        ADD     BX,CX             ;MOVE TO GRAPHICS ROW OF INIT_TABLE
F13A         3370        CMP     AH,7
F13D         3371        JC      M9                ;MODE IS 4,5,6
F13F         3372        ADD     BX,CX             :MOVE TO BW ROW OF TABLE
             3373
             3374   ;----------BX POINTS TO CORRECT ROW OF INITIALIZATION TABLE
             3375
F141         3376   M9:                            ;OUT_INIT
F141         3377        PUSH    AX                ;SAVE MODE IN AH
F142         3378        XOR     AH,AH             ;AH WILL SERVE AS REG NUMBER
             3379
             3380   ;----------LOOP THROUGH TABLE,OUTPUTTING REG ADDR,THEN VALUE
             3381
F144         3382   M10:                           ;INIT LOOP
F144         3383        MOV     AL,AH             ;GET 6845 REGISTER NUMBER
F146         3384        OUT     DX,AL
F147         3385        INC     DX                ;POINT TO DATA PORT
F148         3386        INC     AH                ;NEXT REGISTER VALUE
F14A         3387        MOV     AL, BX            ;GET TABLE VALUE
F14C         3388        OUT     DX,AL             :OUT TO CHIP
F14D         3389        INC     BX                ;NEXT IN TABLE
F14E         3390        DEC     DX                ;BACK TO POINTER REGISTER
F14F         3391        LOOP    M10               ;DO THE WHOLE TABLE

               . . .
```

Figure 9.22 The SET_MODE code that outputs the 6845 register parameters. Reprinted by permission from the *Technical Reference* copyright 1981 by International Business Machines Corporation.

Figure 9.22 illustrates the code that loads the various registers of the 6845. For the monochrome card this parameter table, pointed to by PARM_PTR, consists of the following values:

```
    ...
    DB   61H, 50H, 52H, 0FH, 19H, 6, 19H
    DB   19H, 2, 0DH, 0BH, 0CH
    DB   0, 0, 0, 0
    ...
```

What do these values represent? Returning to Table 9.10, it is clear that for the monochrome display the parameter values appearing in Table 9.11 are appropriate. We have already used some of these values to demonstrate how IBM compensates for scanning the CRT using division by ten of the dot clock.

In the code appearing in Figure 9.22, DX contains the control register address at the start of the loop. As each parameter value is accessed by

```
MOV AL,BX
```

where BX contains the parameter address, DX is incremented to access the next internal register. Only 5 bits of the address are used by the 6845's address register to access the other internal registers.

This completes the INT 10H BIOS code to be examined. While it represents but a small portion of the INT 10H service routine, it is a very important portion. Essentially, we have seen how the CRT controller is set up and initialized for the monochrome display. The setup for the color-graphics adapter is similar, except each character is on an 8 × 8 field. Most of the remaining INT 10H routines deal with ways screen memory is modified to output dots (in graphics mode), to change the cursor position, to scroll, and other functions that require modification to screen memory.

TABLE 9.11 PARAMETER VALUES FOR IBM MONOCHROME VIDEO DISPLAY: 6845 DATA VALUES

Parameter	Value	Comments
Horizontal Total	98	Number horizontal characters including retrace.
Horizontal Displayed	80	Number horizontal characters displayed
Horizontal Sync Position	82	Position of sync (horizontal) pulse
Snyc Width	15	Width of horizontal sync pulse (this leaves one character position for retrace)
Vertical Total	26	25 lines per frame plus one line for retrace
Vertical Total Adjust	6	This is the number of adjustable rasters per frame
Vertical Displayed	25	25 lines displayed
Vertical Sync Position	25	Sync at 25th line
Interlace and Skew	2	Non-interlace mode
Maximum Raster Address	13	Fourteen lines of raster per character
Cursor Start Raster	11	Cursor starts on 11th raster
Cursor End Raster	12	Cursor continues to 12th raster
Start Address	(0, 0)	First refresh memory address
Cursor	(0, 0)	Cursor address

9.4 THE RS-232C COMMUNICATIONS ADAPTER

In this subsection we examine the BIOS programming for the asynchronous communication adapter used in the IBM PC. This adapter is based on the National Semiconductor INS 8250 Asynchronous Communications Element (ACE) which is the chip used to achieve communications [5]. The ACE is a form of Universal Asynchronous Receiver-Transmitter; UART is the generic nomenclature for such a device [6]. In order to adequately understand the 8250, RS-232C communications, and the BIOS code associated with this processing, it is useful to begin with a brief discussion of communications protocol. Then the hardware and software can be addressed.

9.4.1 The RS-232C Interface

In the early days of data communications, the American Telephone and Telegraph Company possessed the primary means for providing data communications service. Consequently, AT&T in large measure defined the modems and interfaces for achieving such communications. Since many manufacturers needed information about these interfaces, the Electrical Industry Association (EIA) developed a standard interface between Data Terminal Equipment (DTE) and Data Communication Equipment (DCE) that was based on serial transmission of information. This interface standard is the RS-232C interface and constitutes the standard used by IBM in its Asynchronous Communications Adapter. The RS-232C standard encompasses both an electrical characteristic and a signal identification. In many cases an interface is defined which uses a subset of the full RS-232C specification; yet this interface is referred to as RS-232C compatible. Care must be exercised when interfacing to peripheral equipment to make sure it is compatible with the RS-232C interface as implemented by IBM. Table 9.12 illustrates the standard RS-232C interface as implemented by IBM.

The pins indicated in Table 9.12 are normally those found on the standard DB-25 type connector which has 25 pins. If two RS-232C interfaces are to be connected, the usual technique is to construct a cable that accomplishes a null-modem

TABLE 9.12 STANDARD RS-232C PIN SELECTION AND SIGNAL IDENTIFICATION

Pin	Signal name	Comments
1	Chassis Ground	Grounds connected units
2	Transmitted Data (TD)	Output data from the interface
3	Received Data (RD)	Input data to the interface
4	Request to Send (RTS)	Defines ready to send data condition
5	Clear to Send (CTS)	Input signal permitting transmission
6	Data Set Ready (DSR)	Input notifying ready status
7	Signal Ground	Common signal-only ground
8	Data Carrier Detect (CD)	Indicates carrier present
20	Data Terminal Ready (DTR)	Output signal indicating ready to transmit
21	Ring Indicator (RI)	Carry over from ringing phones

configuration. This configuration crosses pins 2 and 3, 4 and 5, and 6 and 20 so that the transmit line of one, for example, is input on the receive line of the other. Generally, pin 8 is used to light an LED indicating carrier present when interfacing using modems. Pins 7 and 1 are coupled directly through to 7 and 1, respectively.

The RS-232C standard interface can be thought of as existing at two levels, a unit interface level and a modem interface level. The modem interface is used for communications over longer distances, while the unit interface level generally has stand-alone cabling. In the modem interface, the TD signal is converted to tonal data and transmitted as a frequency division (FD) signal with a 0 or 1 corresponding to one of two alternative tones.

9.4.2 The 8250 ACE

Figure 9.23 illustrates the pin description and associated signal identifiers for the 8250 ACE. This UART converts incoming parallel data from the microprocessor system to serial data (through a clocked counter-shift register) for output over a data communications circuit. Similarly, it converts incoming serial data from another unit to parallel data to be output to its associated microprocessor system. The 8250 is fully programmable and has ten internal registers for establishing the communications protocol. Table 9.13 describes these registers. In Table 9.13 the state of A0, A1, and A2 (the register select signals) is indicated in order to access each of the 8250 internal registers.

The pins 1 through 8 contain the input/output signals to be loaded into or read from each internal register. Pin 9 is the 16-times-baud-rate receiver clock frequency. This signal may be tied to the BAUDOUT* (pin 15) signal to generate a receiver clock. Pins 10 and 11 are the serial communications link output signals. These are tied to pins 3 and 2, respectively, of the RS-232C connector following line driver adjustment. Pins 12 through 14 are the 8250 chip select signals. When CS0 and CS1 are HIGH and CS2* is LOW the chip is selected. Pin 15 is the 16-times-transmit clock. Pins 16 and 17 are the reference oscillator input. Pins 18 and 19 are the data output strobe pins: When DOSTR is HIGH, for example, while the chip is selected, the 8088 is allowed to write data or control words into a selected 8250 internal register. Pin 20 is GROUND. Pins 21 and 22 are the data input strobe pins: When

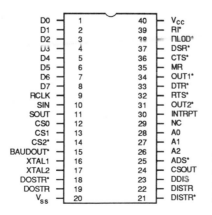

Figure 9.23 The 8250 asynchronous communication element pin description. Reprinted with permission National Semiconductor Corp.

TABLE 9.13 THE 8250 INTERNAL REGISTERS.

Register	Register select			Comments
	A2	A1	A0	
Receiver Buffer Register (RBR)	0	0	0	This is a read-only register with data input. (DLAB = 0)
Transmitter Holding Register (THR)	0	0	0	This is a write-only register with data output. (DLAB = 0)
Interrupt Enable Register (IER)	0	0	1	The first four bits enable received data available, transmitter holding register empty, receiver line status enable, and modem status enable.
Interrupt Identification Register (IIR)	0	1	0	Bit 0 indicates interrupt and bits 1 and 2 the bit set in the IE register.
Line Control Register (LCR)	0	1	1	This register contains the communications protocol: bits 0 and 1 = word length select, bit 2 = # stop bits, bit 3 = parity enable, bit 4 = even parity select, bit 5 = stick parity, bit 6 = spacing output and bit 7 = access to divisor latches of baud rate generator.
MODEM Control Register (MCR)	1	0	0	Sets DTR, RTS, and two user-designated output lines which act like ancillary DTR lines.
Line Status Register (LSR)	1	0	1	Errors: Data Ready (DR), Overrun Error (OE), Parity Error (PE), Framing Error (FE), Break Interrupt (BI), THR Empty, Transmit Shift Register Empty.
MODEM Status Register (MSR)	1	1	0	CTS, DSR, RI, Signal Detect, DSR state change, CTS state change, RI state change, Received Line Signal Detect State change.
Divisor Latch (LS) (DLL)	0	0	0	Least significant baud rate generator divisor value. Yields output baud frequency 16 times desired value (DLAB = 1).
Divisor Latch (MS) (DLM)	0	0	1	Most significant baud rate generator divisor value. (DLAB = 1)

Reprinted with permission National Semiconductor Corp.

DISTR is HIGH, for example, while the chip is selected, the 8088 is allowed to read status information from a selected 8250 internal register. Pin 23 goes LOW whenever the 8088 is reading an 8250 internal register. Pin 24 goes HIGH when the chip is selected. Pin 25 can be used to latch the register select lines, when LOW. Pins 26 through 28 are the register select lines used to select the internal register in question. Pin 30 goes HIGH when a fault occurs. Pins 31 and 34 are ancillary DSR* signals. Pin 32 is the request-to-send line. Pin 33 is the data-terminal-ready line. Pin 35 is a master reset. Pin 36 is the clear-to-send line. Pin 37 is the data-set-ready line. Pin 38 is the receive line signal detect (carrier detect signal). Pin 39 is the ring indicator signal, and pin 40 is the +5 volt supply input.

Many of these pins retain the nomenclature of the old telephone convention. Typically, CTS, RTS, DSR, DTR, and RI are derived from early telephone usage and

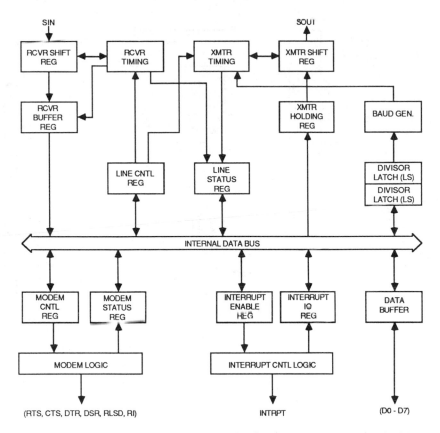

Figure 9.24 The functional block diagram for the INS8250 ACE. Reprinted with permission National Semiconductor Corp.

directly translate in terms of the RS-232C equivalent. In Table 9.13 part of the register select process considers the Division Latch Access Bit (DLAB) from the Line Control Register. This is the most significant bit of that register. Figure 9.24 illustrates a functional block diagram of the 8250 with its internal register structure indicated.

9.4.3 The Asynchronous Communications Adapter

Before considering the BIOS code used to achieve asynchronous communications, it is useful to examine the asynchronous communications card itself. Figure 9.25 illustrates the card layout. In the figure, the DB-25 connector specifies the RS-232C pins used as indicated in Table 9.12. In addition to these pins, IBM also provides the capability for a transmit clock (pins 9 and 11) and a receive clock (pins 18 and 25).

Examining the 8250 appearing in Figure 9.25 demonstrates that data is input bidirectionally through a transceiver. The NAND gate with output to CS2* has

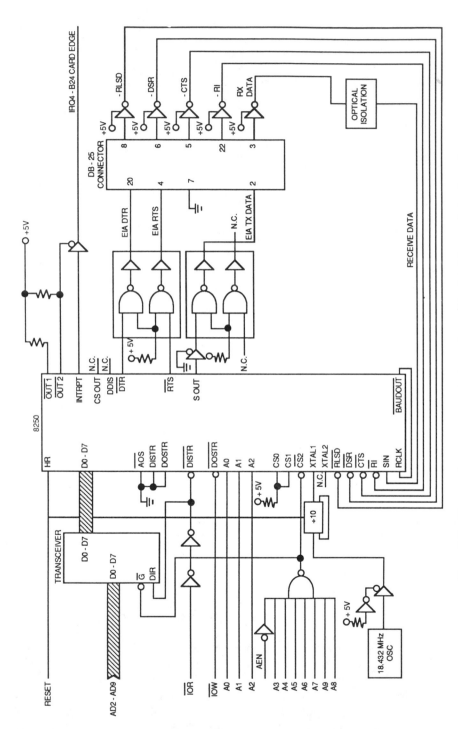

Figure 9.25 The asynchronous communications adapter. Reprinted by permission from the *Technical Reference* copyright 1981 by International Business Machines Corporation.

inputs A3 through A9 (address lines). Thus, the CS2* chip select goes LOW when the following address is specified:

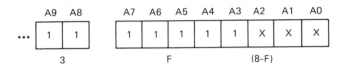

This address range is 3F8H-3FFH and agrees with Table 9.1. The Xs are set to select internal registers. The bidirectional data input with D0-D7 can use data to be passed between the 8088 and the 8250 internal registers when CS2* selects the chip (CS0 and CS1 are always HIGH). The IOR* signal controls the transceiver data direction: For an LS245, for example, when the DIR pin is set LOW the transceiver will receive data from the 8250. When IOR* is LOW, data is read from the 8250 registers into the 8088. Similarly, when DOSTR* is LOW (IOW* goes LOW), data is written from the 8088 into a selected 8250 register.

For the IBM Asynchronous Communications Adapter, the receive clock rate is set equal to the transmit rate (BAUDOUT* = RCLK). Each of the modem controls is appropriately connected to the proper pin (RLSD*, DSR*, CRS*, DTR*, RTS*, or RI*). The transmit data (SOUT) and receive data (SIN) lines are appropriately coupled to the proper pins of the 8250. The 8250 converts serial data appearing on the SIN line to parallel data and outputs it using the D0-D7 bidirectional data lines, when in a read data condition. Similarly, the 8250 converts parallel data appearing on the D0-D7 bidirectional data lines to serial data and outputs it using SOUT, when in an output data condition.

A0, A1, and A2 are set to select an internal register as indicated in Table 9.13. Since these bits can set between (000) and (111), the address range specified above is appropriate.

9.4.4 Programming the 8250

The asynchronous communications BIOS service routine, INT 14H, has four functions.

  1. Initialize the command port (AH = 0)
  2. Send a character (in AL) out the port (AH = 1)
  3. Receive a character (placed in AL) from the port (AH = 2)
  4. Return port status in AL (AH = 3)

During the initialization process, several parameters must be set to define the communications line. These parameters include the data word length (7 or 8 bits), the number of stop bits indicating end of a data word (0 or 1 bits), odd or even parity as indicated by the parity bit (odd parity indicates the parity bit is always adjusted to give a total number of set bits, including the data word and parity, odd), and the baud rate or data rate. Here baud approximately translates as bits per second. Table 9.14 illustrates the AL bit settings for initialization (AH = 0).

Figure 9.26 illustrates the INT 14H code that selects the appropriate service routine function. SI is loaded with 0 or 2 (after the shift) to set up the correct RS-232C card as specified by DX at the call to INT 14H. The RS-232C addresses are loaded into RS232_BASE in the BIOS initialization routines, lines 1169 and 1176 of the BIOS code in the early *IBM Technical Reference*. These addresses are 3F8H and 2F8H, for card 1 and 2, respectively. We shall ignore the 2F8H address (second card) and focus on 3F8H. This address is as specified in Table 9.1 for the base address of the 8250 registers. (The 2F8H address is accessed once appropriate Dual In Line Package (DIP) switches are set on the system board.) Next, AH is examined and a jump made to the appropriate portion of the code which processes the selected function.

The first function is the initialization routine (AH = 0). This code appears in Figure 9.27, based on the *IBM Technical Reference*. The first execution is to set up the line control register at address 3F8H + 3 or 3FBH. The line control register is

BIT:	7	6	5	4	3	2	1	0
	DLAB	SET BREAK	STICK PARITY	EVEN PARITY SELECT	PARITY ENABLE	NO.STOP BITS	WORD LENGTH 1	WORD LENGTH 0

Here DLAB = Divisor Latch Access Bit. By outputting DX = 3FBH with AL = 80H, the only bit set is DLAB. At this point AH contains the parameter values initially appearing in AL at the call for INT 14H. These parameters are transferred to DL using MOV DL,AH. Next the baud rate is put in the low order DL bits by rotating left four times (see Table 9.14). The last rotation effectively shifts the baud rate bits to lie on a word boundary. ANDing DX with 0EH clears all bits except 1, 2, and 3, the bits containing the baud rate selection. DI is loaded with the offset of the following table (offset A1).

A1	Label	Word		
		DW	1047	; 110 BAUD
		DW	768	; 150
		DW	384	; 300
		DW	192	; 600
		DW	96	; 1200
		DW	48	; 2400
		DW	24	; 4800
		DW	12	; 9600

TABLE 9.14 AL BIT SETTINGS VICE PARAMETERS (AH = 0)

Baud rate	Bit 7	6	5	Parity	Bit 4	3	Stop bit	Bit 2	Word length	Bit 1	0
110	0	0	0	NONE	X	0	1	0	7	1	0
150	0	0	1	ODD	0	1	2	1	8	1	1
300	0	1	0	EVEN	1	1					
600	0	1	1								
1200	1	0	0								
2400	1	0	1								
4800	1	1	0								
9600	1	1	1								

```
Line #                                    Comment
      . . .
1481   RS232_IO                 PROC     FAR
1482
1483   ;------ VECTOR TO APPROPRIATE ROUTINE
1484
1485           STI              ;INTERRUPTS BACK ON
1486           PUSH   DS        ;SAVE SEGMENT
1487           PUSH   DX
1488           PUSH   SI
1489           PUSH   DI
1490           PUSH   CX
1491           MOV    SI,DX     ;RS232 VALUE TO SI
1492           SHL    SI,1      ;WORD OFFSET
1493           MOV    DX,DATA
1494           MOV    DS,DX     ;SET UP OUR SEGMENT
1495           MOV    DX,RS232_BASE [SI]     ;GET BASE ADDRESS
1496           OR     DX,DX     ;TEST FOR 0 BASE ADDRESS
1497           JZ     A3        ;RETURN
1498           OR     AH,AH     ;TEST FOR AH =0
1499           JZ     A4        ;COMM INIT
1500           DEC    AH        ;TEST FOR AH = 1
1501           JNZ    A5
1502           DEC    AH        ;TEST FOR AH = 2
1503           JNZ    A2
1504           JMP    A12       :RECEIVE INTO AL
1505   A2:
1506           DEC    AH        ;TEST FOR AH = 3
1507           JNZ    A3
1508           JMP    A18       ;COMM STATUS
1509   A3:
1510           POP    CX
      . . .
```

Figure 9.26 The RS232 I/O processing for initialization, selection of a transmit or receive character, and port status. Reprinted by permission from the *Technical Reference* copyright 1981 by International Business Machines Corporation.

```
    Line #                                    Comment


                        ...
    1519    A4:
    1520            MOV     AH,AL                ;SAVE INIT PARMS IN AH
    1521            ADD     DX,3                 ;POINT TO 8250 CONTROL REG
    1522            MOV     AL,80H
    1523            OUT     DX,AL                ;SET DLAB=1
    1524
    1525    ;------DETERMINE BAUD RATE DIVISOR
    1526
    1527            MOV     DL,AH                ;GET PARMS TO DL
    1528            ROL     DL,1
    1529            ROL     DL,1                 ;GET BAUD RATE TERM TO LOW BITS
    1530            ROL     DL,1
    1531            ROL     DL,1                 ;*2 FOR WORD TABLE ACCESS
    1532            AND     DX,0EH               ;ISOLATE THEM
    1533            MOV     DI,OFFSET A1         ;BASE OF TABLE
    1534            ADD     DI,DX                :PUT INTO INDEX REGISTER
    1535            MOV     DX,RS232_BASE [SI]    ;POINT TO HIGH ORDER OF DIVISION
    1536            INC     DX
    1537            MOV     AL,CS: [DI+1]        ;GET HIGH ORDER
    1538            OUT     DX,AL                ;SET MS OF DIV TO 0
    1539            DEC     DX
    1540            MOV     AL,CS: [DI]          ;GET LOW ORDER OF DIV
    1541            OUT     DX,AL                ;SET LOW OF DIV
    1542            ADD     DX,3
    1543            MOV     AL,AH                ;GET PARMS BACK
    1544            AND     AL,01FH              ;STRIP OFF BAUD BITS
    1545            OUT     DX,AL                ;LINE CONTROL TO 8 BITS
    1546            SUB     DX,2
    1547            MOV     AL,0
    1548            OUT     DX,AL                ;INTERRUPT ENABLES OFF
                        ...
```

Figure 9.27 The 8250 initialization. Reprinted by permission from the *Technical Reference* copyright 1981 by International Business Machines Corporation.

This table appears in the INT 14H code. The values appearing in this table are the 8250 divisor used to generate the 16-times clock for the indicated baud rate. Using

```
        MOV  DI,OFFSET A1
        ADD  DI,DX
             ...
        MOV  AL,CS:[DI+I]
        OUT  DX,AL
        DEC  DX
        MOV  AL,CS:[DI]
        OUT  DX,AL
             ...
```

IBM sets up the Divisor Latch most significant and least significant bits. Remember DLAB = 1 (see Table 9.13) and DX is first set back to 3F7H and then decremented to 3F8H for the Divisor Latches.

Figure 9.28 contains the BIOS code used to send a character in AL over the communications lines. This portion of the service routine does extensive checking of

```
Line #                                                    Comment


                      . . .
1553    A5:
1554            PUSH    AX              ;SAVE CHAR TO SEND
1555            ADD     DX,4            ;MODEM CONTROL REG
1556            MOV     AL,3            ;DTR AND RTS
1557            OUT     DX,AL           ;DTR,RTS
1558            XOR     CX,CX           ;INIT TIME OUT COUNT
1559            ADD     DX,2            ;MODEM STAT REG
1560    A6:                             ;WAIT DSR
1561            IN      AL,DX           ;GET MODEM STAT
1562            TEST    AL,20H          ;DSR
1563            JNZ     A7              ;TEST CTS
1564            LOOP    A6              ;WAIT DSR
1565            POP     AX
1566            OR      AH,80           ;INDICATE TIME OUT
1567            JMP     A3              ;RETURN
1568    A7:
1569            SUB     CX,CX
1570    A8:
1571            IN      AL,DX           ;GET MODEM STAT
1572            TEST    AL,10H          ;TEST CTS
1573            JNZ     A9              ;CTS
1574            LOOP    A8              ;WAIT CTS
1575            POP     AX              ;TIME OUT
1576            OR      AH,80H
1577            JMP     A3
1578    A9:
1579            DEC     DX              ;LINE STATUS REG
1580    SUB     CX,CX                   ;INIT WAIT COUNT
1581    A10:
1582            IN      AL,DX           ;GET STAT
1583            TEST    AL,20H          ;XMIT READY?
1584            JNZ     A11             ;OUTPUT CHAR.
1585            LOOP    A10             ;GO BACK/TEST TIME OUT
1586            POP     AX
1587            OR      AH,80H          ;SET TIME OUT BIT
1588            JMP     A3
1589    A11:                            ;OUTPUT CHAR.
1590            SUB     DX,5            ;DATA PORT
1591            POP     CX
1592            MOV     AL,CL           ;GET CHAR. TO AL
1593            OUT     DX,AL           ;OUTPUT CHAR.
                      . . .
```

Figure 9.28 The 8250 processing for sending a character. Reprinted by permission from the *Technical Reference* copyright 1981 by International Business Machines Corporation.

DSR and CTS before sending out the character. First the modem control register is selected at 3FCH (3F8H + 4 = 3FCH). Both Data Terminal Ready and Request-to-Send are set up. The modem control register is specified as follows.

BIT:	7	6	5	4	3	2	1	0
	0	0	0	LOOP	OUT 2	OUT 1	RTS	DTR

Outputting a 03H to this register sets DTR and RTS. The time out count is set (FFFFH) and the modem status register selected (3FCH + 2 = 3FEH). This register looks like

BIT:	7	6	5	4	3	2	1	0
	RLSD	RI	DSR	CTS	Delta RLSD	Trailing Edge Ring. Ind.	Delta Data Set Ready	Delta Clear to Send

By TESTing with 20H, the DSR signal (bit 5) is checked. Once this bit is set, the modem status register contents are TESTed with 10H to check to see when CTS is set. Following the setting of CTS by the receiving computer, the register select (DX) is decremented to address 3FDH and the line status register is selected. Next the transmitter status is checked. The line status register is as follows.

BIT:	7	6	5	4	3	2	1	0
	0	Xmit Shift Reg. Empty	Xmit Hold. Reg. Empty	Break Interrupt	Framing Error	Parity Error	Overrun Error	Data Ready

By TESTing the contents of this register with 20H, the Xmit Holding Register can be checked to see if it is empty. When bit 5 of this register is set a character has been transferred to the Xmit Shift Register. Finally, the next character is loaded and sent. To do this the register select (DX) is decremented to 3F8H and the transmitter holding register loaded with the character stored on the stack.

Figure 9.29 illustrates the service code for receiving a character from the communications line. First the modem control register is selected at address 3FCH. Next the register is loaded with 01H to set DTR. Following this, the modem status register at 3FEH is checked using 20H to see if DSR is set. The line status register at 3FDH is then checked and TESTed with 01H to see if bit 0 is set (Data Ready). Then the character is input using port 3F8H (see Table 9.13). Observe from Figure 9.24 that both the receiver buffer and transmitter holding register access the rest of the system through the 8250 data buffer which is bidirectional. Thus, the internal registers must be checked to see whether this buffer has a receive or transmit character.

This discussion has considered the operation of the IBM Asynchronous Communications Adapter. The RS-232C protocol was examined and the National Semiconductor 8250 ACE described. Finally, the IBM BIOS code appropriate for this processing was highlighted.

9.5 THE IBM AT BIOS ROUTINES

The IBM AT has an architecture that is conceptually similar to the PC and XT. Table 9.15 briefly discusses the differences among the BIOS interrupt service routines for the PC, XT, and AT. In many cases, the function of the code is the same but slight variations have been introduced. The proprietary DOS system programming would, of course, reflect differences also.

```
line #                                    Comment


    . . .
1598    A12:
1599            AND     BIOS_BREAK,07FH      ;TURN OFF BREAK BIT
1600            ADD     DX,4                 ;MODEM CONTROL REG
1601            MOV     AL,1                 ;DTR
1602            OUT     DX,AL
1603            ADD     DX,2                 ;MODEM STAT REG
1604            SUB     CX,CX                ;TIME OUT COUNT
1605    A13:                                 ;WAIT DSR
1606            IN      AL,DX                ;MODEM STAT
1607            TEST    AL,20H               ;DSR
1608            JNZ     A15                  ;DSR READY?
1609            LOOP    A13                  ;WAIT DSR
1610    A14:
1611            MOV     AH,80H               ;SET TIME OUT ERROR
1612            JMP     A3                   ;RETURN WITH ERROR
1613    A15:
1614            DEC     DX                   ;LINE STAT REG
1615    A16:
1616            IN      AL,DX                ;GET STATUS
1617            TEST    AL,1                 ;RECEIVE BUFFER FULL?
1618            JNZ     A17                  ;GET CHAR.
1619            TEST    BIOS_BREAK,80H       ;TEST BREAK
1620            JZ      A16                  ;LOOP OTHERWISE
1621            JMP     A14                  ;SET TIME OUT ERROR
1622    A17:
1623            AND     AL,1EH               ;TEST FOR ERROR COND
1624            MOV     AH,AL                ;SAVE PART STAT
1625            MOV     DX,RS232_BASE [SI]   ;DATA PORT
1626            IN      AL,DX                ;GET CHAR FROM COMM LINE
    . . .
```

Figure 9.29 The 8250 processing for receiving a character. Reprinted by permission from the *Technical Reference* copyright 1981 by International Business Machines Corporation.

TABLE 9.15 IBM PC, XT, AT BIOS INTERRUPT DIFFERENCES

Interrupt	Description	Comments
0	Divide by Zero	IMR test same. Timer check out similar in concept but different in form. AT much more extensive.
1	Single Step	See INT 0H comments.
2	Nonmaskable	The AT uses ports 70H (CMOS port) and 80H (8042 status port) while the PC and XT use 20H and 21H (the two 8259A ports). Significantly different code.
3	Breakpoint	See INT 0H above.
4	Overflow	See INT 0H above.
5	Print Screen	Identical among PC, XT, and AT.
6–7	Reserved	—
8	Timer	Substantially the same yielding 18.2 interrupts/second.

(Continued)

TABLE 9.15 (*Continued*)

Interrupt	Description	Comments
9	Keyboard	Essentially equivalent among PC, XT, and AT.
A	Reserved	—
B	Communications	This interrupt exists for the AT, not for the PC or XT.
C	Communications	This interrupt exists for the AT, not for the PC or XT.
D	Alternate Printer	This interrupt exists for the AT, not for the PC or XT.
E	Diskette	The AT processing includes provision for 1.2M floppy diskette processing. This interrupt has the same functions for the AT as found in the PC and XT, except the AT version is significantly expanded.
F	Printer	Exists for the AT, not for the PC or XT.
10	Video I/O	The AT version is similar to the PC and XT version except a capability to write a string to the screen has been added.
11	Equipment Check	This reflects each system's capabilities.
12	Memory	This reflects each system's capabilities.
13	Diskette/Disk	This routine reflects diskette control for the PC and disk control for the AT and XT.
14	Communications	The AT routine is very similar to the PC and XT routine, except the communications port status is checked a number of times for the AT processing, with an added procedure.
15	Cassette	—
16	Keyboard	Functionally the same but logically different because the AT keyboard is different from the PC or XT keyboard. Quite a bit of similarity, however, among routines. (LED on AT keyboard.)
17	Printer	Substantially the same from both functional and logical viewpoint.
18	BASIC	Cassette BASIC for PC.
19	Bootstrap	Reflects each system's capabilities.
1A	Time of Day	This interrupt is significantly expanded in the AT BIOS code. The addition of a battery keeps a 24-hour clock. Provides for an alarm (AT).
1B	Keyboard Break	Similar.
1C	Timer Tick	Similar.
1D	Video initialization	Identical set up for 6845.
1E	Diskette Parameters	Reflects each system's capabilities.
1F	Video Graphics Char.	Identical.

9.6 SUMMARY

This chapter has attempted to expose the reader to examples of assembler driver programming by using portions of the IBM BIOS coding as examples. Many features of this programming have been left to the reader to explore. The overall BIOS architecture, for example, is structured so that it can be conveniently burned into PROM, since this BIOS code is located in the system board PROM. Subtle changes were necessary to accomplish this. All variables, for example, that do not change can be initialized as part of the code segment, but variables that change must be located in a data segment area that can be specified with a RAM address at link and locate time. Thus, unlike the applications code in this book where all data variables are located in the data segment, the BIOS data segment contains only those variables that change during execution.

We have looked at a number of devices in this chapter and have seen how they are programmed. Much of this programming is dependent on the nature of the chips used in the processing. The reader should contact the chip manufacturers for data sheets on these chips in order to acquire a greater understanding of their operation. Finally, the BIOS code examples have been extracted from the *IBM Technical Reference*. The early version of this code has been used by way of illustration. The BIOS code for the XT and AT has been briefly compared. The reader should obtain a reference manual for the appropriate system.

REFERENCES

1. *Technical Reference Personal Computer*. Personal Computer Hardware Reference Library. IBM Corp. P.O. Box 1328. Boca Raton, FL 33432 (1981).
2. *Technical Reference Personal Computer XT and Portable Personal Computer*. Personal Computer Hardware Reference Library. IBM Corp. P.O. Box 1328. Boca Raton, FL 33432 (1983).
3. *Technical Reference Personal Computer AT*. Personal Computer Hardware Reference Library. IBM Corp. P.O. Box 1328. Boca Raton, FL 33432 (1984).
4. *Microsystem Components Handbook: Microprocessors Volume I*. Intel Literature Distribution, Mail Stop SC6-714. 3065 Bowers Avenue, Santa Clara, CA 95061 (1987).
5. "NS16450/INS8250A/NS16C450/INS82C50A Asynchronous Communications Element." National Semiconductor Corp. 2900 Semiconductor Drive, Santa Clara, CA 95052-8090 (1985).
6. McNamara, J. E. *Technical Aspects of Data Communication*. Digital Press, Educational Services. Digital Equipment Corp. Bedford, MA (1982), p. 283.

PROBLEMS

9.1. When the printer is being selected, what happens if bit 6 of the port address is set? How does this affect the output of the LS138 appearing in Figure 6.1 (which has A6 input through G2B)?

9.2. In selecting the 8259A, what happens if the address enable (AEN*) line goes LOW?

9.3. What happens if an address 64H is used in selecting the PPI port? 63H selects what port?

9.4. During initialization of the 8259A PIC, why is ICW3 omitted from the setup coding in the IBM PC BIOS programming?

9.5. Can ICW1 ever be an even number for the PIC initialization of the IBM PC? Where does ICW2 get bits 7 through 3 assigned? Can these bits be specified without a knowledge of the hardware configuration? In the IBM AT, will ICW4 ever have bit 2 set?

9.6. Why are all variables appearing in the data segment initialized? What would happen during a PROM burn to any variables that must be initialized and are located in the data segment? Variables that must be initialized at run-time are normally located where in memory?

9.7. When initializing the 8237A DMA Controller, what is the significance of placing the chip in the block transfer mode? (Remember the way in which the 8237A moves data around.) How is this accomplished?

9.8. Why does the initial estimate of 103 characters/line for the IBM monochrome screen appear to be in error with the actual number of characters/line (including retrace) set at 98? How can the extra characters be absorbed into the overall raster scanning when a dot clock frequency of 16.257MHz is used?

9.9. How does one arrive at a requirement for 16K of screen buffer memory for the IBM monochrome display?

9.10. How large must the dot attribute memory be for the IBM color display adapter? When BA0 is HIGH, what happens to attempts to write to the IBM monochrome adapter card?

9.11. How many address lines of the 6845 are used and how does this map to the 8088 address word? When A0 = 0, which internal 6845 register is selected?

9.12. For the IBM PC, the table PARM_PTR appearing in the INT 10H BIOS code indicates 6 raster lines for vertical adjust, 26 lines for the vertical total and 25 lines displayed. How are these totals reconciled in lieu of the IBM monochrome display adapter dot clock frequency?

9.13. The internal register R8 has the following fields,

D7	D6	D5	D4	D3	D2	D1	D0
C1	C0	D1	D0	X	X	V	S

where

	Non-Interlace	Interlace Sync	Interlace Sync/Video
V =	0	1	0	1
S =	0	0	1	1

	Non-Skew	1-Char Skew	2-Char Skew	No Output
D0	0	1	0	1
D1	0	0	1	1
C0	0	1	0	1
C1	0	0	1	1

What is the 6845 interface and skew configuration for the IBM PC?

9.14. Construct a baud rate table illustrating the baud rate divisor values for 50, 75, 110, 150, 300, 600, 1200, 2400, 4800, 9600, and 19,200 baud rate values. Assume the baud rate clock is generated using a 1.8432 MHz crystal and the divisor is used to correspond with a 16-times clock.

9.15. During initialization of the 8250 ACE parameters, with AL = AAH, what are the communications parameters and what is AH?

9.16.* How are DTR, DSR, CTS, RTS, and RI to be connected in a typical null-modem configuration which would permit communications, for example, between an IBM PC, XT, or AT and the Hewlett-Packard 7470A plotter?

10

Systems Programming Considerations

The third major programming area to be considered in this book is systems programming. Since most system programming involves machine-dependent code, we must further consider the hardware associated with the IBM family of microcomputers [1]. In this book we have differentiated between applications programming, hardware driver programming, and systems software. The latter two functions overlap when the hardware drivers are written for subsystems that are technically considered as part of the overall system (a diskette drive, for example, versus a special-purpose hardware device such as an analog-to-digital converter). Systems software provided with the IBM microcomputers includes both DOS and the BIOS service routines. We shall, however, continue to refer to the BIOS routines as hardware drivers and classify them as a subset of the overall systems software. In order to clarify these issues we first consider the question of how an operating system is defined. DOS, being the IBM microcomputer operating system, is the dominant systems software layer associated with these microcomputers. Next the system board is examined for the IBM PC, as well as the XT and AT. This latter discussion provides the basis for understanding many of the BIOS and DOS systems control functions. Finally, systems programming techniques are defined, with particular emphasis on the software employed in the IBM microcomputers. The setting of hardware address values using software is the key to understanding systems hardware programming.

In the previous chapter, several of the BIOS service functions were examined in detail. We will further reexamine the BIOS code in section 10.3 when system issues are addressed. At that time the focus will be on control of program operation instead of device manipulation, and routines associated with booting and memory management will be considered. The systems programming emphasized in this text is the operating system (vice compilers, debuggers, etc.).

10.1 WHAT IS SYSTEMS PROGRAMMING?

We have already seen several different types of programming emphasized. Both hardware driver and systems programming can be efficiently implemented using the Macro Assembler with the IBM PC, XT, AT, and PS/2 microcomputers. If the 8087 or 80287 coprocessor is included, many application examples can be optimally developed using assembler. We have devoted considerable effort to understanding how to program applications code and hardware drivers in assembler. What about systems programming? First, we need to consider the nature of programs that fall under the systems category: Having done this, we will be able to understand how such programs are developed. The goal of this chapter is to provide the reader with a sufficient awareness of systems programming concepts that these concepts can be readily applied to the IBM microcomputer systems. In this regard, we should emphasize that IBM has provided DOS as a proprietary software package and, consequently, no source code is available. The reader will need to consider DOS in a general context and the *DOS Technical Reference* [2] is very helpful in understanding this program. Associated with this examination of DOS will be ancillary information related to the general systems programming field.

A modern computer, such as the IBM PC, XT, or AT, consists of a central processor unit (CPU), associated memory and interface chips, and other devices for storage and input/output. The goal of the systems program is to properly keep track of all subsystems and integrate them so that users will be able to access peripherals through the system software and accomplish tasks [3–5]. Clearly, most users should be insulated from these peripheral control functions; hence, the system program is designed to provide such a user-friendly environment. The first layer of the systems program environment is the operating system. DOS is this layer and it calls BIOS to accomplish a subset of the I/O functions. Thus, the hardware drivers defined in the BIOS perform as part of the overall system programming I/O.

As indicated above, we consider the system board hardware first because this is the basis upon which the system programming resides. To understand how the bootstrap function occurs, for example, it is valuable to have a knowledge of the system board. Also, an understanding of hardware is essential to a knowledge of how various commands cause the chips to interact. In the following section we briefly consider the IBM PC system board. The focus of this book is the Macro Assembler language; however, to program in the Macro Assembler environment the reader must understand port addressing and handshaking, as well as how to load the various registers of peripheral chips such as the 8259A. This is true if the reader intends to access the system resources. Some system resources can be directly accessed using system programming service functions: the DOS and BIOS interrupts and function calls.

10.2 THE IBM MICROCOMPUTER SYSTEM BOARD: PC, XT, AT

The Macro Assembler language is the language of choice for developing an understanding of the IBM microcomputer hardware and its internal interfacing. There are many levels with which this discussion could begin. The approach taken in this book is to bypass a physical description, which relies heavily on circuit logic considerations, and proceed directly to a system level discussion. This approach is possible because in practice the system is conceptually integrated using the assembler language, the topic of the book. The subject of how IBM microcomputer hardware is integrated from a systems viewpoint is quite complex. In this chapter we touch on the system board configuration [6]. Figure 10.1 illustrates the functional block diagram for the IBM PC system board.

10.2.1 The 8088 Central Processor Unit

Figure 10.2a illustrates the Intel 8088 microprocessor. This is a 40-pin integrated circuit that is designed to work in a multiplexed environment; that is, some of the pins are shared in time. (A bar over a signal in some figures indicates it is active in a LOW condition. Similarly an asterisk by a signal name in the text indicates the signal is active LOW). The reader probably wonders over what time frame and how this sharing occurs to achieve multiplexing. Basically the 8088 operates over a time interval referred to as a bus cycle. In general, the exact length of this bus cycle is undefined, however, it is divided into four phases (T_1, T_2, T_3 and T_4) which are clearly defined by the characteristics of the signals on the pins. For example, the clock pin (CLK) goes LOW at the beginning of each phase. In addition, during a Read cycle, when data is read into the 8088, the pin DT/R* goes LOW just after the start of T_1 and goes HIGH just after T_4. Figure 10.2b illustrates timing for a typical Read cycle. The status of the various pins during the T_1, T_2, T_3, and T_4 time periods determines the nature of the bus cycle in question. Sometimes, it is necessary to add one or more wait states, T_w, and these are inserted between T_3 and T_4. These occur, for example, during instruction execution for long instructions, synchronization, and coprocessor interfacing.

Several of the multiplexed pins are those marked Address/Data 0 to 7 (AD0, AD1,... AD7). The actual multiplexing is described in the Intel literature, *iAPX 86/88, 186/188 User's Manual-Hardware Reference* [7]. The main advantage of multiplexing is that fewer pins are needed. In principal, a chip of any complexity could be constructed; however, limitations on the design have to be imposed at some point and this is one Intel chose to apply to the 8088. Table 10.1 illustrates the associated pin signals for the 8088. A very important pin is number 33, the minimum-maximum (MN/MX*) control pin. When grounded, this pin serves to put the 8088 in the maximum mode. When HIGH, this pin forces the 8088 into the minimum mode. Each of these modes has a number of pins that are redefined depending on which mode the 8088 is in. For the IBM Personal Computer systems, the 8088 is operated in maximum mode (pin 33 is grounded).

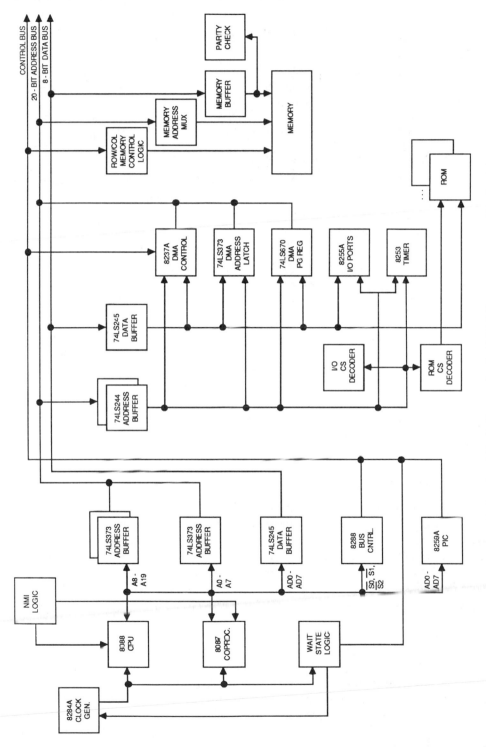

Figure 10.1 The functional block diagram for the IBM PC computer system. Reprinted by permission from the *Technical Reference* copyright 1981 by International Business Machines Corporation.

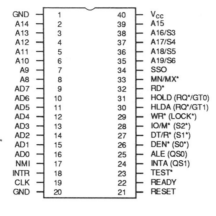

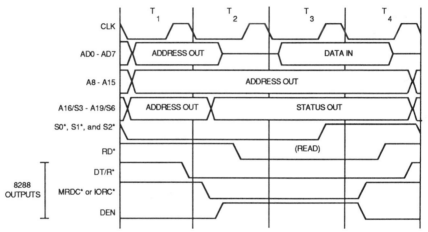

GND	1	40	Vcc
A14	2	39	A15
A13	3	38	A16/S3
A12	4	37	A17/S4
A11	5	36	A18/S5
A10	6	35	A19/S6
A9	7	34	SSO
A8	8	33	MN/MX*
AD7	9	32	RD*
AD6	10	31	HOLD (RQ*/GT0)
AD5	11	30	HLDA (RQ*/GT1)
AD4	12	29	WR* (LOCK*)
AD3	13	28	IO/M* (S2*)
AD2	14	27	DT/R* (S1*)
AD1	15	26	DEN* (S0*)
AD0	16	25	ALE (QS0)
NMI	17	24	INTA (QS1)
INTR	18	23	TEST*
CLK	19	22	READY
GND	20	21	RESET

Figure 10.2a The pin identifiers for the 8088 microprocessor. Courtesy of Intel Corporation.

Figure 10.2b Typical 8088 Read cycle. Courtesy of Intel Corporation.

The maximum mode is intended for operation with a more extended chip set. Typically, the Intel 8288 Bus Controller (to be discussed later) might serve as the source for Data Enable signals based on status signals from the 8088: Status 0, Status 1, and Status 2 (S0*, S1*, & S2*). (In the minimum mode this signal would be derived from pin 26 of the 8088). The maximum mode allows the hardware designer to have more flexibility in board layout and hardware functionalism because more pins (and consequently, more signals) are available through additional chips, which are integrated with the CPU.

Pins 17 and 18 refer to interrupt signals. The 8088 can have interrupts that are initiated either by software or hardware. Software interrupts occur in program execution where branches in the logic divert the program flow to alternate code. Hardware interrupts, however, originate from logic that is external to the 8088 processor. Both these interrupt functions cause the program execution to branch to a new location. In the Intel processor design the use of vector interrupt instructions facilitates the occurrence of an interrupt. Basically, memory locations 0 through 3FFH are reserved as a vector table. Each entry in the table is represented by 2 16-bit

TABLE 10.1   8088 PIN DESCRIPTORS

Pin	Name	Description
1	Ground (GND)	This pin is held at ground potential.
2	Address 14 (A14)	Address pin number 14
3	Address 13 (A13)	Address pin number 13
4	Address 12 (A12)	Address pin number 12
5	Address 11 (A11)	Address pin number 11
6	Address 10 (A10)	Address pin number 10
7	Address 9 (A9)	Address pin number 9
8	Address 8 (A8)	Address pin number 8
9	Address/Data 7 (AD7)	Multiplexed address and data pin number 7
10	Address/Data 6 (AD6)	Multiplexed address and data pin number 6
11	Address/Data 5 (AD5)	Multiplexed address and data pin number 5
12	Address/Data 4 (AD4)	Multiplexed address and data pin number 4
13	Address/Data 3 (AD3)	Multiplexed address and data pin number 3
14	Address/Data 2 (AD2)	Multiplexcd address and data pin number 2
15	Address/Data 1 (AD1)	Multiplexcd address and data pin number 1
16	Address/Data 0 (AD0)	Multiplexed address and data pin number 0
17	Non-Maskable Interrupt (NMI)	When set HIGH, this pin causes an interrupt of type 2 (equivalent to INT2H) to occur with the corresponding vector to the entry point determined by the address at 0000:0004.
18	Interrupt Request (INTR)	This signal is sampled during T_4 of each instruction to check for an interrupt (it is active HIGH).
19	Clock (CLK)	This input to the 8088 provides the basis for all timing information during operation.
20	Ground (GND)	This pin is held at ground potential.
21	Reset (RESET)	This signal terminates processing when held active HIGH for 4 clock cycles.
22	Ready (READY)	This signal is the acknowledgement from an input/output device or memory that data will be passed (it is active HIGH).
23	Test (TEST*)	This input signal is checked during a WAIT instruction to see if it is LOW. If LOW, execution continues. The 8087 uses this input for synchronization.
24	Queue Status 1 (QS1)	See pin 25.
25	Queue Status 2 (QS2)	These signals determine the condition of 8088 instruction queue:

QS1	QS2	Condition
0	0	NOP
0	1	1st byte of Op code to EU
1	0	Empty
1	1	Subsequent byte of Op code to EU

Pin	Name	Description
26	Status 0 (S0*)	See pin 28.
27	Status 1 (S1*)	Scc pin 28.

(Continued)

TABLE 10.1 (*Continued*)

Pin	Name	Description
28	Status 2 (S2*)	These signals are used by the Bus Controller (8288) to generate access control signals:

S2*	S1*	S0*	Condition
0	0	0	Interrupt Acknowledge
0	0	1	Read I/O Port
0	1	0	Write I/O Port
0	1	1	Halt
1	0	0	Code Access
1	0	1	Read Memory
1	1	0	WriteMemory
1	1	1	Passive

Pin	Name	Description
29	Lock (LOCK*)	This prevents other system control functions from gaining control of the system bus while LOCK* is LOW.
30	Request/Grant 0 (RQ/GT0)	See pin 31.
31	Request/Grant 1 (RQ/GT1)	These pins force the 8088 to give up control of the local bus at the end of the current bus cycle.
32	Read (RD*)	When LOW, this pin indicates that the 8088 is reading from memory or an I/O device.
33	Minimum/Maximum (MN/MX)	When LOW this is the maximum mode.
34	Status Line	This line, when held LOW, indicates status information is available during T_2, T_3, and T_4.
35	Address 19/Status 6 (A19/S6)	See pin 38.
36	Address 18/Status 5 (A18/S5)	See pin 38.
37	Address 17/Status 4 (A17/S4)	See pin 38.
38	Address 16/Status 3 (A16/S3)	During address operations these are the four most significant bits. S5 is the interrupt enable flag bit and other status information is passed in register:

S4	S3	Condition
0	0	Alternate Data (ES)
0	1	Stack (SS)
1	0	Code (CS)
1	1	Data (DS)

Pin	Name	Description
39	Address 15 (A15)	Address pin number 15.
40	+5 Volts (VCC)	This is the high voltage pin.

(Courtesy of Intel Corporation).

addresses (segment and offset). These addresses point to a memory location where the "vectored" instruction to be processed next resides. When an interrupt occurs, the 8088 calculates the vector table location for the address of the "vectored" instruction. For software interrupts the processor merely multiplies the interrupt number by 4 and goes to this location. Consider the video processing interrupt, INT 10H. This instruction causes location 40H to be processed (0000:0040).

The above discussion points out how software vectoring takes place. What about pin 18? Here we have a single pin. How can vectoring be achieved from a signal on this pin? This hardware interrupt requires an additional chip, the 8259A Programmable Interrupt Controller. These user defined hardware interrupts occur as follows: The INTR bit goes HIGH, the interrupt flag (a bit in the 8088 flag register) is set to enable interrupts, and the 8088 executes an interrupt acknowledgement sequence. This sequence consists of two INTA bus cycles (T_1, T_2, T_3 and T_4 sequences). The first cycle starts with INTA* LOW and allows the system to get ready to present the interrupt type number on the second cycle. During the second cycle, INTA* goes LOW and the 8259A places a byte on the data bus which is the same as the software interrupt vector number (the value 10H in the video processing example). This byte points to the vector table in memory which in turn vectors the processing to the interrupt service routine.

10.2.2 The 8288 Bus Controller and Buffers

Figure 10.3a illustrates the 8288 bus controller pin allocation. Figure 10.3b is a functional block diagram for the 8288. We have seen how the 8088 generates S0*, S1* and S2* which are used as input to the STATUS DECODER in the maximum

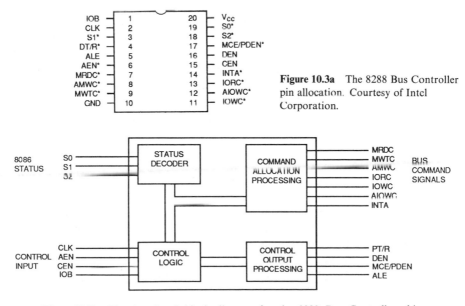

Figure 10.3a   The 8288 Bus Controller pin allocation. Courtesy of Intel Corporation.

Figure 10.3b   The functional block diagram for the 8288 Bus Controller chip. Courtesy of Intel Corporation.

mode. Where do the remaining control signals come from? They must come from associated hardware. The 8288 is primarily intended as a device for use by the 8088 in accessing the bus. Figure 10.4 presents the 8288 environment for the IBM PC from the *IBM Technical Reference* manual. Table 10.2 illustrates the signals for the 8288. The 8288 is used to control the latching of address and data information onto the address and data buses, respectively.

Latching is a term applied to a specific type of circuit behavior whereby output lines are held in a particular state (HIGH or LOW) to reflect the input conditions. Hence, latching of address information amounts to holding a line HIGH on the address bus if that particular bit is set for a positive logic condition. The devices which latch address data in the IBM PC are LS373 integrated circuits.

The 8288 must tell the LS373s when to latch out address data. Examination of Figure 10.4 demonstrates that the 20-bit address, characteristic of the 8088, is output to the system bus through these LS373s. Each LS373 consists of 8 input lines, 8 output lines, power connections, a Latch Enable (E), and an Output Enable (OE*). The address on the inputs is transferred to the latch outputs when E is HIGH. This occurs when the 8288 drives its Address Latch Enable (ALE) line HIGH. The latch outputs, in turn, are able to place the signals on the system address bus when OE* is LOW. This occurs when AEN BRD is LOW. Note that all the signals that are active LOW have their pins denoted with a small circle.

In summary, the 8288 must drive ALE HIGH at the same time AEN BRD is LOW for the LS373s to output the 8088 address to the system address bus. The ALE signal occurs once during each bus cycle and serves to strobe the latch inputs to the latch outputs. How does AEN BRD get set LOW? Figure 10.5 illustrates the logic associated with this signal. The far left side of this figure shows S0*, S1*, and S2* input to an 8-input NAND circuit. This circuit has a truth table as indicated in Table 10.3. In this table, A, B,... H denote inputs, and the AND function is also indicated. Here all outputs for the NAND are HIGH except when all inputs are HIGH. Normally in the passive state S0*, S1*, and S2* are HIGH and the bus is not locked (LOCK* = HIGH). Then the NAND output is LOW. For all other status conditions, an address will usually be of interest (for example, memory or I/O read-write) and at least one of the status bits (S0*, SI*, or S2*) will be LOW. Thus, the NAND output will be HIGH. This output, in turn, will feed an inverter which changes the HIGH back to LOW. Consequently, in a read-write state a LOW is passed to D3 of the LS175 while in the passive state a HIGH is passed to D3 of the LS175.

The LS175 chip is a flip-flop (four per chip) and it effectively transfers the output to Q3. This output is again clocked through a second flip-flop (LS74) and back to D0 of the LS175. AEN BRD is then the output that will be LOW for active S0*, S1*, and S2* and HIGH for the passive state. The complementary output is returned from Q0* and is AEN*. Clearly, when a read-write operation takes place it is necessary to output an address. Then S0*, S1* and S2* may go LOW which causes AEN BRD to go LOW; and OE* is set LOW on each LS373. Thus, when E goes HIGH, because the 8288 sets ALE HIGH, an address is clocked out onto the system address bus.

In Figure 10.4 a second bus control function is indicated: The 8288 controls transfer of data to and from the system data bus through the LS245 transceiver. The

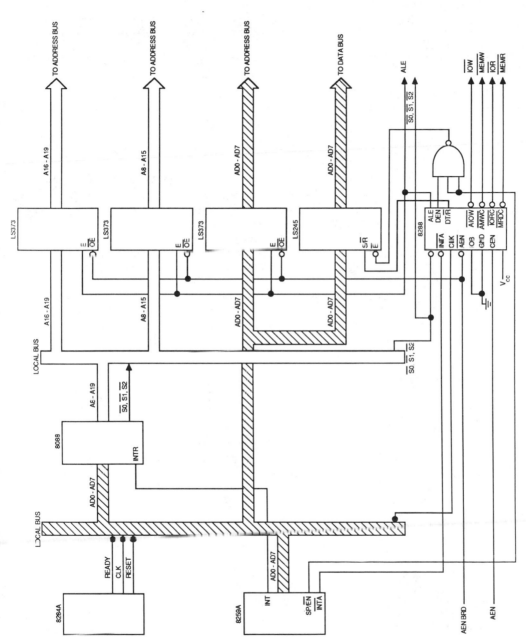

Figure 10.4 The 8288 Bus Controller environment in the IBM PC computer system. Reprinted by permission from the *Technical Reference* copyright 1981 by International Business Machines Corporation.

TABLE 10.2 8288 PIN DESCRIPTIONS

Pin	Name	Description
1	Input/Output Bus Mode (IOB)	When HIGH the 8088 is in the I/O Bus mode, when LOW it is in the System Bus mode. The LOW condition exists in the IBM PC.
2	Clock (CLK)	This input to the 8288 provides the basis for all timing information during operation.
3	Status Input Pin (SI*)	See pin 19.
4	Data Transmit/Receive (DTR*)	When HIGH the condition corresponds to a Transmit through the transceivers. A LOW indicates a read condition.
5	Address Latch Enable (ALE)	This signal is used to strobe an address into the address latches.
6	Address Enable (AEN*)	When LOW, this signal enables the 8288 command outputs.
7	Memory Read Command (MRDC*)	This is an 8288 command line. When LOW this line causes memory to load data onto the data bus.
8	Advanced Memory Write Command (AMWC*)	This is an 8288 command line. When LOW this line gives an early indication of a memory write.
9	Memory Write Command (MWTC*)	This is an 8288 command line. When LOW this line causes memory to read data from the data bus.
10	Ground (GND)	This pin is held at ground potential.
11	I/O Write Command (IOWC*)	This is an 8288 command line. When LOW this line causes an I/O device to read data on the data bus.
12	Advanced I/O Write Command (AIOWC*)	This is an 8288 command line. When LOW this line causes an I/O write command to be issued (earlier in the machine cycle).
13	I/O Read Command (IORC*)	This is an 8288 command line. When LOW this line causes an I/O device to load data onto the data bus.
14	Interrupt Acknowledge (INTA*)	This line acknowledges an interrupt to a device and indicates that vectoring information should be placed on the data bus.
15	Command Enable (CEN)	When HIGH all command lines are enabled.
16	Data Enable (DEN)	When HIGH this signal enables data transceivers.
17	Master Cascade Enable/Peripheral Data Enable (MCE/PDEN*)	For the IBM PC this is the MCE option that reads an address from a PIC onto the data bus during an interrupt sequence.
18	Status Input Pin 2 (S2*)	See pin 19.
19	Status Input Pin 0 (S0*)	These three pins are input from the 8088. They are decoded according to their meaning (see 8088 pin description) and used to generate control signals via the 8288 command lines (MRDC*, AMWC*, MWTC*, 10WC*, A10WC*, and 10RC*).
20	+5 Volts (VCC)	This is the high voltage pin.

(Courtesy of Intel Corporation).

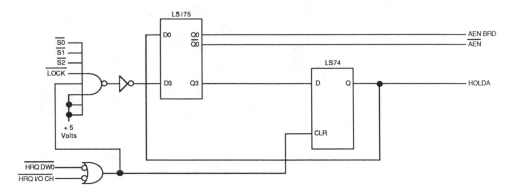

Figure 10.5   The discrete logic associated with the AEN BRD signal used by the 8288 to transfer addresses between the 8088 and the system bus. Reprinted by permission from the *Technical Reference* copyright 1981 by International Business Machines Corporation.

LS245 also buffers information; however, it is two-way and must have a signal indicating direction. This signal is the send-receive (S/R*) pin. The 8288 has a DT/R* signal which goes HIGH to indicate Transmit (write condition) and LOW to indicate Receive (read condition). These conditions are based on the S0*, S1*, and S2* input levels from the 8088. The S/R* setting on the LS245 is determined by the 8288 when data is to be read or written. The LS245 has the following lines: 8 input, 8 output (for which the direction can be reversed), power, a direction line (S/R*), and an Enable line (E*). The Enable Line must be set LOW to allow the LS245 to transfer data.

In the IBM PC, the data buffer (LS245) enable line is driven by a three-input NAND gate. In Figure 10.4, two of these inputs are tied together and are tied, in turn, to the EN* output of the 8259A Programmable Interrupt Controller (PIC). The 8259A normally keeps EN* HIGH so the 8288 can access the data bus. The 8288 has a second input to the above-mentioned NAND: the Data Enable (DEN) signal. This signal goes HIGH when AEN* is HIGH (or CEN on the 8288 input). When both of these NAND inputs are HIGH the LS245 enable line goes LOW and data can be passed in the specified direction.

It should be pointed out that the passing of data vice addresses using the 8288 occurs at different points in the bus cycle. Figure 10.6 illustrates the timing for this situation. Both data passing and address passing require that AEN* be HIGH (and consequently AEN BRD be LOW and DEN HIGH). Similarly, both the data and

TABLE 10.3 8-INPUT NAND OPERATION

A	B	C	D	E	F	G	H	AND	NAND
1	1	1	1	1	1	1	1	1	0
0	1	1	1	1	1	1	1	0	1
1	0	1	1	1	1	1	1	0	1
			...					...	...
0	0	0	0	0	0	0	0	0	1

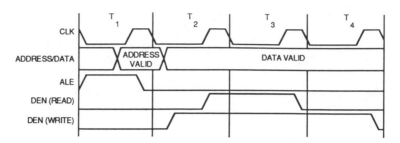

Figure 10.6 Timing for data vice address read/write using the 8288. Courtesy of Intel Corporation.

address transmission on the bus must have the buffer chips enabled as discussed. The NAND function for input to the LS245 E* line is in Table 10.4.

Since the LS245 can pass data between the 8088 local bus and the IBM PC system data bus, how does the 8259A put data on the 8088 local bus without a conflict? Remember the 8259A outputs an interrupt pointer to the vector table when subject to a hardware interrupt. These pointers are loaded into the 8259A during system initialization. The sequence to be followed is initiated with an interrupt. The 8259A has eight interrupt lines (IR0-IR7) which are set through hardware by raising a line HIGH. The 8259A assesses the priority of the interrupt request and raises INT HIGH, if appropriate. The 8088 responds with S0*, S1* and S2* all set LOW to 8288. The 8288, in turn, generates an INTA* back to the 8259A to acknowledge the interrupt. The 8088 initiates a second response and the 8288 sends a second INTA* to the 8259A. This second response causes the 8259A to release the 8-bit pointer on the data bus. The 8259A keeps EN* LOW so that the NAND output to the LS245 is HIGH and there is no contention for the data bus. Figure 10.7 illustrates this timing.

Returning to Figure 10.3b, we see a number of lines as yet unspecified. For the IBM PC, the IOB control input is strapped LOW. This puts the 8288 in the System Bus mode where there is always a delay between AEN* going LOW and a command output (Bus Command Signals). In this mode only one system bus is used. When IOB is LOW the MCE/PDEN* output acts in the MCE mode (Master Cascade Enable). For the IBM PC this output is not connected. The remaining signals are 8288 control bus output signals. These signals are as specified in Table 10.5.

Table 10.5 completes the specification of the 8288 Bus Controller in the IBM PC environment. We have seen how this chip is used to define and control the IBM PC system buses: system address, system data, and system control buses.

TABLE 10.4 NAND FUNCTION FOR INPUT TO THE LS245

EN*(8259A)	DEN(8288)	E*(LS245)
1	1	0 (Transceiver enabled)
0	1	1
1	0	1
0	0	1

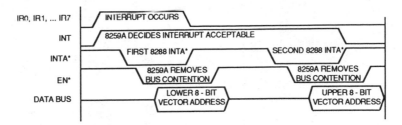

Figure 10.7   8259A Interrupt Timing. Courtesy of Intel Corporation.

10.2.3 The 8259A Programmable Interrupt Controller

Returning to Figure 10.1, the system functional block diagram, we see that the Programmable Interrupt Controller (PIC) responds to interrupts generated on one of its eight IR lines (IR0–IR7). Figure 10.8 illustrates the 8259A pin allocations. Table 10.6 presents the signals. The CS* pin is the Chip Select and when set LOW this enables RD* and WR* to communicate between the 8088 and the 8259A. RD* enables the 8259A to release status onto the data bus when this pin is LOW. When WR* is LOW the 8259A can accept command words from the 8088. The three pins CAS0, CAS1 and CAS2 are not used in the IBM PC. A0 is used in conjunction with CS*, RD*, and WR* to decipher various 8088 commands. It is usually tied to the A0 address line for the 8088.

10.2.4 The System ROM

Figure 10.1 shows that addresses are buffered to the Read Only Memory (ROM) and the external address bus using LS244 (74LS244) address buffers. Similarly, data is buffered to the external data bus using the now familiar LS245 (74LS245) data buffers. It is useful to see how this transfer of information takes place. Figure 10.9 illustrates the associated logic for achieving the ROM and bus interface. The two LS244 buffers have address lines A0 through A7 and A8 through A12, respectively, as inputs. This provides an address capability to 8192 (8K) bytes of ROM memory. Add to this the six chip select signals (CS2* to CS7*) and the full ROM complement can be addressed (six chips with 8K bytes per chip). Notice also that the address

TABLE 10.5   REMAINING 8288 BUS CONTROLLER COMMANDS

Command	Function
AIOWC*	*Advanced I/O Write Command* gives I/O devices an indication of a write.
IOWC*	Not used on IBM PC.
IORC*	*I/O Read Command* instructs an I/O device to put its data on the data bus.
AMWC*	*Advanced Memory Write Command* gives memory an early indication of a memory write.
MWTC*	Not used on IBM PC.
MRDC*	*Memory Read Command* instructs memory to put its data on the data bus.

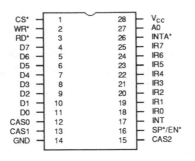

Figure 10.8 The 8259A Programmable Interrupt Controller pin allocation. Courtesy of Intel Corporation.

output of the LS244 serves to generate an external address bus (XA0–XA9); the address lines XA10, XA11, and XA12 are not used. Addresses A0 through A7 are enabled when AEN BRD goes LOW. This occurs for active S0*, S1*, or S2* and is only HIGH in the passive state. The second LS244 has both OE* pins tied to ground so A8 through A12 are always enabled.

What about the external data bus? A single LS245 transceiver is used to set up this bus. When AEN BRD is LOW this transceiver is enabled. The eight data lines either transfer data to the system bus or to the external data bus depending on the direction pin. (Data transferred into the system bus can also come from the ROM chips.)

The direction logic has two possible input conditions which depend on the status of 8288 command lines. Basically, the S/R* line must go LOW to indicate a read condition. This can only take place if one of the inputs to the NOR circuit (shown in Figure 10.9) is HIGH. Since two AND circuits (with inverting inputs) feed this NOR, both inputs to one of the ANDs must be LOW if a read condition is to be obtained. The lower AND circuit has the Memory Read line (MEMR*) and the ROM Address Selection line (ROM ADDR SEL*) as inputs. When these are LOW, ROM is read. The upper AND has the I/O Read line (IOR*) and address line A9 (XA9) as inputs. When these are LOW, system board read I/O is permitted. Note that expansion board I/O cannot use addresses with XA9 LOW because these addresses correspond to system board addresses (port addresses 0–1FFH).

In summary, the ROM and bus driver logic uses two LS244 buffers for handling external and ROM addressing and two LS245 transceivers for handling data (plus associated logic). Figure 10.9 illustrates the overall signal characteristics. The chip select lines enable individual ROM chips that are accessed with the 8K address range provided by lines A0 through A12.

Before considering the random access memory (RAM) processing, it is useful to examine the behavior of the I/O CS Decode (input/output chip select decode) and ROM CS Decode (read only memory chip select decode) logic. In order for many chips to become active in a circuit they must be enabled through the chip select signal. Earlier we saw that ROM chips must be activated using a LOW on the chip select line. The logic to be considered here deals with setting these chip select lines in the I/O and ROM processing. Figure 10.10 illustrates the associated circuitry. Figure 10.10 is based on a similar figure in the *IBM Technical Reference* manual that also includes the logic for dynamic random access memory (RAM) refresh and access. Central to this figure is the LS138 (74LS138) decoder discussed in Chapter 9.

TABLE 10.6 8259A PIN DESCRIPTION

Pin	Name	Description
1	Chip Select (CS*)	When LOW, this pin enables read and write conditions between the 8088 and the 8259A.
2	Write (WR*)	When LOW, this enables the 8259A to accept commands from the 8088.
3	Read (RD*)	When LOW, this enables the 8259A to load status onto the data bus.
4	Bidirectional Data 7 (D7)	Control, status, & interrupt-vector data.
5	Bidirectional Data 6 (D6)	Control, status, & interrupt-vector data.
6	Bidirectional Data 5 (D5)	Control, status, & interrupt-vector data.
7	Bidirectional Data 4 (D4)	Control, status, & interrupt-vector data.
8	Bidirectional Data 3 (D3)	Control, status, & interrupt-vector data.
9	Bidirectional Data 2 (D2)	Control, status, & interrupt-vector data.
10	Bidirectional Data 1 (D1)	Control, status, & interrupt-vector data.
11	Bidirectional Data 0 (D0)	Control, status, & interrupt-vector data.
12	Cascade 0 (CAS0)	See pin 15.
13	Cascade 1 (CAS1)	See pin 15.
14	Ground (GND)	This pin is held at ground potential.
15	Cascade 2 (CAS2)	These pins allow one 8259A to serve as a master and control a second (slave).
16	Slave Program/Enable Buffer (SP*/EN*)	This pin must be used in conjunction with IR0–IR7 to determine its function. In the "buffer" mode it can be used to control transceivers. When not in this mode it can be used to designate a master.
17	Interrupt (INT)	When HIGH this pin indicates a valid interrupt request.
18	Interrupt Request 0 (IR0)	Interrupt Request Line 0.
19	Interrupt Request 1 (IR1)	Interrupt Request Line 1.
20	Interrupt Request 2 (IR2)	Interrupt Request Line 2.
21	Interrupt Request 3 (IR3)	Interrupt Request Line 3.
22	Interrupt Request 4 (IR4)	Interrupt Request Line 4.
23	Interrupt Request 5 (IR5)	Interrupt Request Line 5.
24	Interrupt Request 6 (IR6)	Interrupt Request Line 6.
25	Interrupt Request 7 (IR7)	Interrupt Request Line 7.
26	Interrupt Acknowledge (INTA*)	This pin is set by the 8088 and when set LOW in the proper sequence enables the 8259A to place interrupt-vector data onto the data bus.
27	A0 Address Line (A0)	This pin is used by the 8259A in conjunction with other pins to define the status of various command words.
28	+5 Volts (VCC)	This is the high voltage pin.

(Courtesy of Intel Corporation).

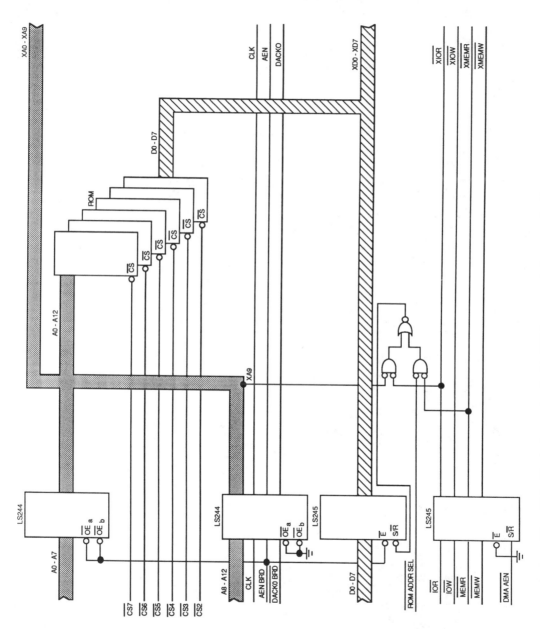

Figure 10.9 The logic associated with ROM usage and the external address and data bus interface. Reprinted by permission from the *Technical Reference* copyright 1981 by International Business Machines Corporation.

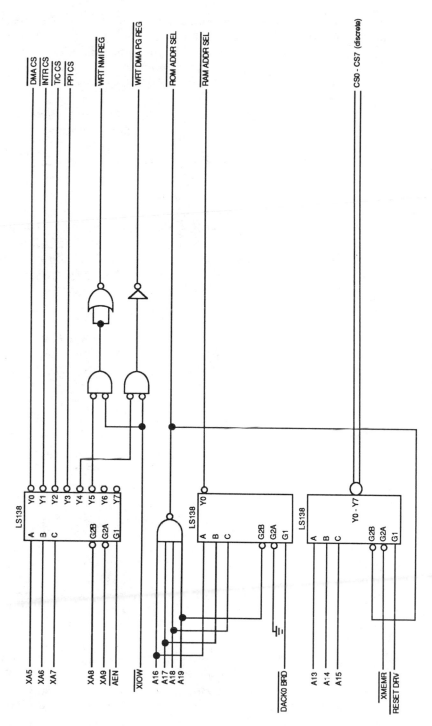

Figure 10.10 I/O and chip selection logic. Reprinted by permission from the *Technical Reference* copyright 1981 by International Business Machines Corporation.

Figure 10.10 effectively demonstrates when various signals can be expected to initiate particular chip selects. The upper LS138 in the figure has the external address lines XA5 through XA9 as inputs. Since the setting of these lines causes various chip selects, it is clear that lines XA0 through XA4 do not matter to these chips as far as selection is concerned. This means that 32 low bit positions can be used as needed to specify ports within one of the selected chips.

Consider when all address values (XA5–XA9) are LOW and AEN* is HIGH. Then Y0 is set LOW and the 8237A DMA Controller is selected (see Figure 10.1). This results from DMA CS*, out of the upper LS138, going LOW. Remember that when AEN* is HIGH, the 8288 Bus Controller is specifying that data is to be transferred. (The 8237A is a Direct Memory Access (DMA) controller which is designed to improve system performance by allowing external devices to directly transfer data from the system memory.) As indicated in the truth table, when address line XA5 goes HIGH, Y1 is set LOW and the 8259A PIC is selected. When line B is set HIGH, Y2 is set LOW and the 8253 Programmable Interval Timer selected. (The 8253 is a timer-counter and can be an event counter, elapsed time indicator, or delay device, to name only a few uses.) When addresses XA5 and XA6 are HIGH, Y3 is set LOW and the 8255A Programmable Peripheral Interface selected. The function of the 8255A is that of a general purpose I/O component to interface principal equipment to the system bus.

The next two output chip select signals, WRT NMI REG* and WRT DMA PG REG*, require that the I/O write command line (XIOW*) be LOW from the 8288. If XA7 is HIGH, then the DMA page register is selected through WRT DMA PG REG* going LOW. If XA5 and XA7 go HIGH then WRT NMI REG* is selected.

Located below the first LS138 appearing in Figure 10.10 is a four-input NAND gate. This gate yields a LOW output only when all four inputs are HIGH. These inputs are address lines A16, A17, A18 and A19, corresponding to the upper four address bits in the 20-bit 8088 address. In Chapter 3 a memory map was presented for the IBM PC. The upper four bits being set would correspond to hexadecimal addresses given by

$$\text{Fxxxx}$$

where x can be some hexadecimal value. This address range specifies upper memory where the system board ROM area exists. Thus, it is not too surprising that a LOW on the output of this NAND gate would correspond to the ROM ADDR SEL* signal, a signal that selects addresses used by the ROM chips. Similarly when these addresses (A16, A17, A18 and A19) are all LOW and the DACKO BRD is HIGH, RAM addresses are selected, and Y0 of the second LS138 is LOW and RAM ADDR SEL* is LOW.

Finally, the individual ROM chip select signals must be defined and are set through the third LS138 shown in Figure 10.10. Treating bit A12 as LOW, it is possible to map the addresses for each chip select (ROM) as indicated in Table 10.7. How is this table to be interpreted? Basically for all system board ROM the most significant bits are set to yield an F for the hexadecimal position of these four bits. Table 10.7 illustrates the low end values for the next four bits. The IBM PC does not start using ROM until encountering addresses of F4000 or greater; thus, based on

TABLE 10.7   THE CHIP SELECT ADDRESSING FOR ROM.

Select	Address lines				20-bit address
	A15	A14	A13	A12	
CS0*	0	0	0	0	F0xxx
CS1*	0	0	1	0	F2xxx
CS2*	0	1	0	0	F4xxx
CS3*	0	1	1	0	F6xxx
CS4*	1	0	0	0	F8xxx
CS5*	1	0	1	0	FAxxx
CS6*	1	1	0	0	FCxxx
CS7*	1	1	1	0	FExxx

Table 10.7, CS0* and CS1* are not used. Table 10.7 illustrates the mapping of ROM memory with the ROM chip select signals (CS0–CS7*). The Basic Input/Output System (BIOS), occupies memory locations FE000 and greater. Thus, BIOS must be resident in the ROM chip selected by CS7*.

10.2.5 Dynamic RAM

This subsection deals with the use of dynamic RAM in the IBM PC. Dynamic RAM is a special type of RAM device. Basically, RAM can be designed to retain its setting, once this setting is determined by an input singal, as long as power is applied to the chip. This is called static RAM and requires that each address cell or bit have a number of transistors to support static retention of signals (memory). A simpler memory cell is based on the dynamic RAM concept in which a single memory cell consists of only one transistor. This transistor is either set or not and must be periodically refreshed to maintain its state. This dynamic RAM lends itself to large arrays of memory on a chip. In the early IBM PC, four banks of $16K \times 1$ bit dynamic RAM chips are used to achieve the 64K byte memory. Each bank consists of nine of the $16K \times 1$ bit chips (8 bits per byte plus 1 extra bit for parity). The logic associated with selecting a given bank and refreshing the RAM is illustrated in Figure 10.11.

Again, the bank selection logic (similar to chip selection) is based on two LS138 decoders. The CAS* output signal from the time delay line of the 8253 is reset every 120 microseconds (the output of the NAND circuit appears below the time delay element in Figure 10.11). During this period, each of the bits in the RAM storage for each column must have been refreshed. The CAS* (Column Address Strobe) signal is reset every 120 microseconds. Thus, each memory cell is refreshed so that a new row is read every 15 microseconds (120/8).

The uppermost LS138 sets up the column address strobe for each bank. Table 10.8 illustrates how this maps onto memory. Here both RAM ADDR SEL* and CAS* are assumed LOW. Note that RAM ADDR SEL* is only LOW when RAM memory addresses are selected, as discussed earlier. Table 10.8 thus illustrates how the bank select CAS* signals are selected, based on upper address line setting (A14 and A15).

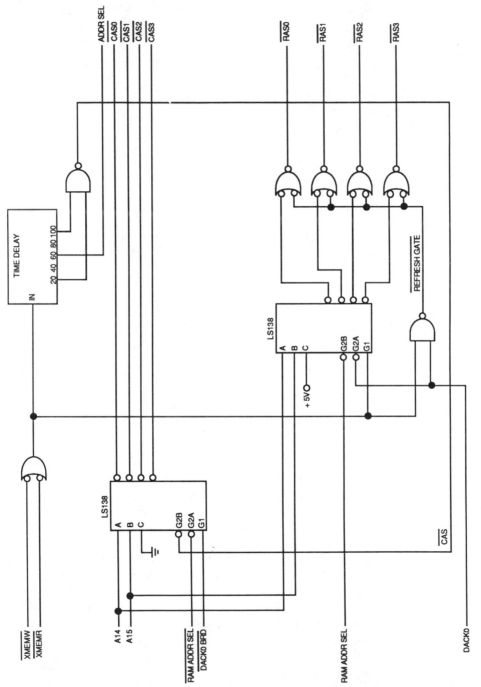

Figure 10.11 Dynamic RAM selection logic (for a single bank) and refresh circuitry. Reprinted by permission from the *Technical Reference* copyright 1981 by International Business Machines Corporation.

410

TABLE 10.8 CAS* SELECT IN RELATION TO A14 AND A15.

A14	A15	CAS0*	CAS1*	CAS2*	CAS3*	20-bit memory
0	0	0	1	1	1	00000
1	0	1	0	1	1	04000
0	1	1	1	0	1	08000
1	1	1	1	1	0	0C000

What about the RAS* (Row Address Strobe) signals that are also required by memory chips? Each bank of chips in the IBM PC memory is simultaneously activated by CAS* and RAS* signals. Note that the dynamic RAM used in the early IBM PCs is being considered here. This basically consists of the 16K × 1 bit chips. Each chip has seven address lines and the column address and row address are multiplexed over these lines. (Think of the 16K × 1 bit memory as a large matrix.) Thus, RAS* signals are also used to help select banks. It is clear that since 14 address bits are used in addressing each RAM chip (7 bits per multiplexing interval) a total number of 16K dynamic RAM cells can be accessed.

The time delay output at 60 microseconds (Figure 10.11) causes ADDR SEL to go HIGH. This selects whether a row or column address is being used. The row addresses come first, then the column addresses. The second LS138 appearing in Figure 10.11 determines the RAS* signal status. Table 10.9 illustrates the RAS* status in relation to A14 and A15. Remember, the row address strobe is selected when RAS* values are LOW. It is interesting to note that the RAS* lines are also LOW when a refresh signal is present (Figure 10.11, note output of the NOR gates with inverting inputs). This provides for refresh but no memory read or write. Note that RAM ADDR SEL must be LOW for the row address strobe to execute properly.

Figure 10.12 illustrates the actual RAM logic. We have an LS245 transceiver which puts data (D0–D7) on the RAM bus (MD0–MD7) when XMEMR* is HIGH. Also, the memory address selection, MEM ADDR SEL, must be HIGH. On the right hand side of this figure are the first two banks of 16K and 1 bit dynamic RAM. (Here there are nine chips per bank: 8 bits per byte plus 1 parity bit.) The data is clocked into the eight chips comprising a byte whenever the CAS* and RAS* signals are simultaneously LOW, and an appropriate address sequence is presented to the chip. The address sequence is generated by the LS158 (74LS158) multiplexers. These multiplexers take in 14 bits of address and multiplex out 2 seven-bit row and column addresses. These are sent to the bank which is active through the memory address bus lines. The LS280 (74LS280) is simply used to provide parity checking. Note that the

TABLE 10.9 RAS* STATUS IN RELATION TO A14 AND A15.

A14	A15	RAS0*	RAS1*	RAS2	RAS3
0	0	0	1	1	1
1	0	1	0	1	1
0	1	1	1	0	1
1	1	1	1	1	0

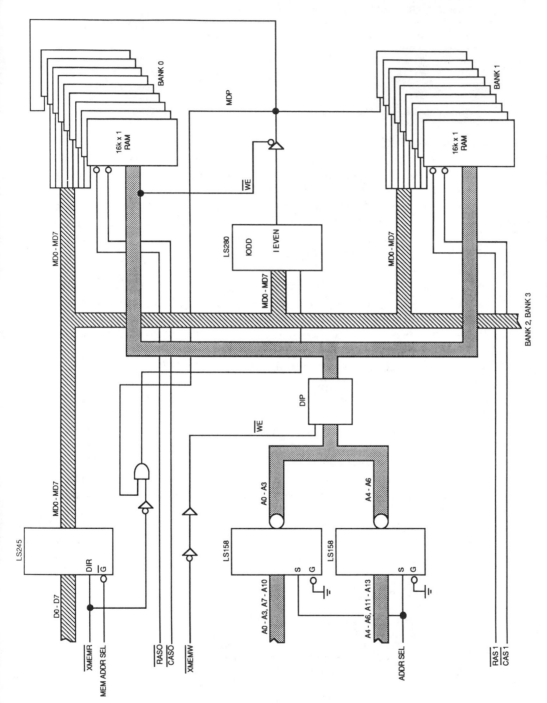

Figure 10.12 The logic associated with RAM address and data transfers. Two of the four banks are illustrated. Reprinted by permission from the *Technical Reference* copyright 1981 by International Business Machines Corporation.

address selection, ADDR SEL, line must be HIGH to select synchronized input and the Enable line (G) must be LOW to enable the LS158s. Figure 10.12 illustrates two of the four banks of dynamic RAM and the CAS* and RAS* signals do the selection among these banks based on previous logic considerations.

10.2.6 The DMA Function

In general, memory transfers are slow, and Intel has developed the 8237A Programmable DMA Controller chip to help speed up the transfer process. This direct memory access processor is designed to facilitate three types of data transfers:

1. I/O-to-memory
2. Memory-to-I/O
3. Memory-to-memory

The 8237A has pin designations as specified in Figure 10.13a. Table 10.10 illustrates the signals. As can be seen, the complexity of this chip approaches that of a microprocessor. The advantage of using a DMA controller is that when a number of data items are to be transferred, the 8088 can simply provide the 8237A with a starting address and a word count. The 8237A will then automatically transfer all the data independent of the 8088.

Examination of the pins appearing in Figure 10.13a indicates the usual signals associated with I/O and memory (IOR*, IOW*, MEMR*, and MEMW*). The CLK, CS*, RESET, and READY signals are all similar to those previously discussed. HLDA is a signal which when held HIGH by the processor (8088) indicates that the processor has relinquished the system buses. The four DMA request lines (DREQ0–DREQ3) are used by peripherals to obtain DMA service. These very important lines are used by the selected I/O devices to notify the 8237A that an I/O-to-memory transfer is about to be initiated. The DRE0 signals can also be manipulated internally as, for example, during memory-to-memory transfers. Signals DB0 through DB7 are the eight bidirectional data bus lines. The processor can obtain information about the 8237A over these lines. The 8237A has 12 register groups and the 8088 can obtain the contents of an Address register, a Status register, the

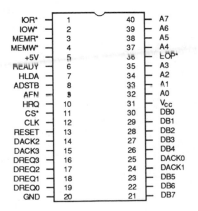

Figure 10.13a   The 8237A DMA Controller pin allocation. Courtesy of Intel Corporation.

TABLE 10.10 8237A PIN DESCRIPTIONS

Pin	Name	Description
1	I/O Read (IOR*)	This is a bidirectional control line. In the Idle cycle it accepts an input (LOW) from the 8088 to cause the control register data to be output. In the Active cycle it outputs a LOW to a peripheral to indicate a data access from the peripheral (DMA write transfer).
2	I/O Write (IOW*)	This is a bidirectional control line. In the Idle cycle it accepts an input (LOW) from the 8088 to cause control data register to be input to the 8237A. In the Active cycle it outputs a LOW to a peripheral to indicate data access to the peripheral (DMA Read transfer).
3	Memory Read (MEMR*)	This control signal is used to access data from a memory location (DMA Read or memory-to-memory).
4	Memory Write (MEMW*)	This control signal is used to write data to a memory location.
5	Logic HIGH	Logic HIGH
6	Ready (READY)	This pin causes the read and write pins to remain LOW for an extended time during these operations to accommodate slow memory.
7	Hold Acknowledge (HLDA)	When LOW this signal indicates that the 8088 retains control of the system bus.
8	Address Strobe (ADSTB)	When HIGH this signal is used to load a latch with the *upper* address byte.
9	Address Enable (AEN)	This signal enables the 8-bit latch containing the *upper* address byte onto the address bus.
10	Hold Request (HRQ)	This request to the 8088 asks for control of the system bus when HIGH.
11	Chip Select (CS*)	When LOW this allows the 8237A to communicate via the data bus.
12	Clock Input (CLK)	This input to the 8237A provides the basis for all timing information during operation.
13	Reset (RESET)	An active HIGH clears the Command, Status, Request, and Temporary registers.
14	DMA Acknowledge 2 (DACK2)	See pin 25.
15	DMA Acknowledge 3 (DACK3)	See pin 25.
16	DMA Request 3 (DREQ3)	See pin 19.
17	DMA Request 2 (DREQ2)	See pin 19.
18	DMA Request 1 (DREQ1)	See pin 19.
19	DMA Request 0 (DREQ0)	These lines go to individual peripheral circuits and are used to request DMA service. When a HIGH is received by the 8237A, that channel is generating a request input.
20	Ground (GND)	This pin is held at ground potential.
21	Data Bus 7 (DB7)	Bidirectional line for Data Bus pin 7
22	Data Bus 6 (DB6)	Bidirectional line for Data Bus pin 6

23	Data Bus 5 (DB5)	Bidirectional line for Data Bus pin 5
24	DMA Acknowledge 1 (DACK1)	See pin 25.
25	DMA Acknowledge 0 (DACK0)	These lines are used to notify the DREQn pin that it has been granted a DMA cycle.
26	Data Bus 4 (DB4)	Bidirectional line for Data Bus pin 4
27	Data Bus 3 (DB3)	Bidirectional line for Data Bus pin 3
28	Data Bus 2 (DB2)	Bidirectional line for Data Bus pin 2
29	Data Bus 1 (DB1)	Bidirectional line for Data Bus pin 1
30	Data Bus 0 (DB0)	Bidirectional line for Data Bus pin 0
31	+5 Volts (VCC)	This is the high voltage pin.
32	Address 0 (A0)	Bidirectional address line pin 0
33	Address 1 (A1)	Bidirectional address line pin 1
34	Address 2 (A2)	Bidirectional address line pin 2
35	Address 3 (A3)	Bidirectional address line pin 3
36	End of Process (EOP*)	Bidirectional signal: an external LOW from the 8237A occurs when the terminal count is reached.
37	Address 4 (A4)	Output address line pin 4
38	Address 5 (A5)	Output address line pin 5
39	Address 6 (A6)	Output address line pin 6
40	Address 7 (A7)	Output address line pin 7

(Courtesy of Intel Corporation).

Temporary register or a Word Count register via these lines. We will return to these registers in a moment. The processor can also program the 8237A registers through these data bus lines. Finally, during active DMA service the 8237A outputs the most significant eight bits of the DMA address onto these data bus lines, where they are in turn strobed into an external latch using the ADSTB signal. It is very important to recognize that these data bus lines are multiplexed, and during a DMA cycle the address bits A8 through A15 are strobed into a latch during one portion of the cycle.

Before continuing to describe the 8237A signals, we need to examine the Controller's register structure which has been mentioned above. Basically, there are six 16-bit register types: four base address registers, four base word count registers, four current address registers, four current word count registers, one temporary address register, and one temporary word count register. The base address register holds the start address for the DMA service channel. The word count register holds the number of words to be transferred for the DMA service channel. The current address and word count registers hold the updated information during the DMA service for the channel in question. The temporary address and word count registers are used in the automatic decrement or increment process following a single DMA transfer. In addition to these 16-bit registers are three 8-bit registers (the status, command, and temporary registers), four 6-bit mode registers, and two 4-bit (Mask and Request) registers.

Now we return to the 8237A pin signals. The EOP* signal goes LOW when a transfer has been completed. The address lines A0 to A3 are bidirectional and in the idle cycle (no DMA service) are used by the 8088 to address the 8237A register to be read. In an active cycle (full DMA service) these address lines are outputs for the four

least significant address bits. Address lines A4 through A7 are simply output lines for
the upper four bits of the first address byte. The lines DACK0 to DACK3 notify the
individual peripherals when one has been granted a DMA cycle. Finally, AEN is the
Address Enable line.

Briefly, then, how is a DMA transfer accomplished? Consider first an I/O-to-
memory transfer. The I/O device requesting the transfer sets the DREQ line it is
attached to, HIGH. The 8237A in turn raises HRQ to the 8088. The 8088 responds
with HLDA HIGH, indicating it has given up control of the system buses. The
Address Enable (AEN) line goes HIGH which prevents other chips from attempting
to respond to bus signals. Next the memory address is loaded on the address
bus. This is accomplished by ADSTB going HIGH to strobe out A8 to A15 from the
8237A's Current Address register. Similarly lines A0 through A7 output the lower
byte of this current address. Note that this address is obtained from the current
address register which, in turn, started with the base address register value loaded by
the 8088. The final portion of the transfer takes place when DACK, MEMW* and
IOR* all become set (MEMW* and IOR* LOW and DACK HIGH) and the I/O
device outputs data through the data bus which is then loaded into memory at the
specified address. This timing is illustrated in Figure 10.13b.

Figure 10.14 illustrates the signal and data connections for DMA processing. The lower eight bits of the address are buffered through an LS244 and the upper
eight bits (A8–A15) are latched through the LS373. The LS670 is a four word by four
bit register file that can be used to locate the 64K DMA page within the one megabyte
memory.

A memory-to-I/O transfer is identical to the I/O-to-memory transfer except
during the final portion of the transfer DACK MEMR* and IOW* are set (MEMR*
and IOW* LOW and DACK HIGH). The memory-to-memory transfer is slightly
different from transfers involving I/O. Figure 10.15 illustrates this timing. The

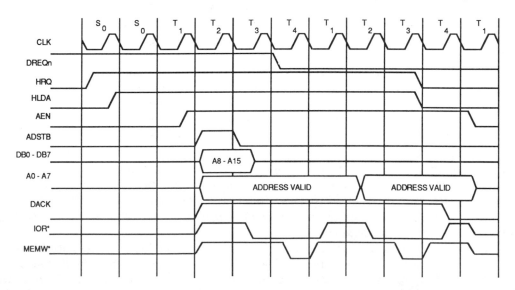

Figure 10.13b   Typical DMA timing. Courtesy of Intel Corporation.

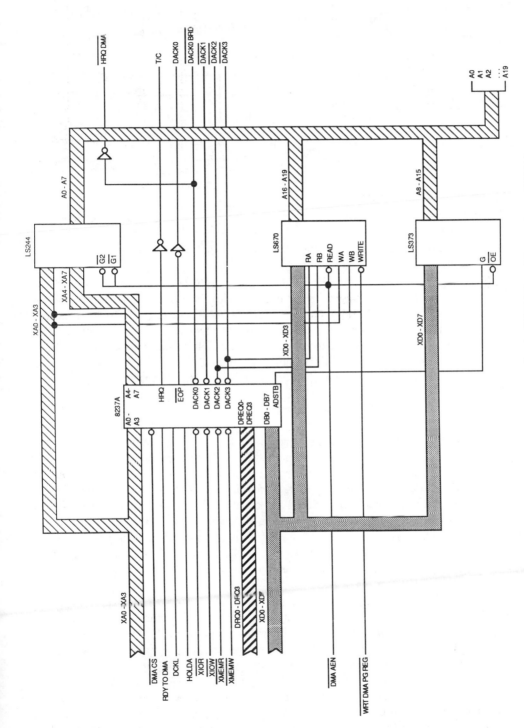

Figure 10.14 The signal and data environment for the 8237A Direct Memory Access (DMA) Controller in the IBM PC. Reprinted by permission from the *Technical Reference* copyright 1981 by International Business Machines Corporation.

417

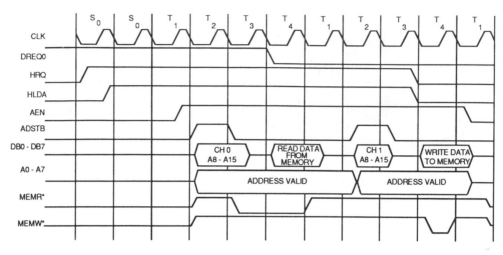

Figure 10.15   Memory-to-Memory DMA timing. Courtesy of Intel Corporation.

transfer requires two channels. First, DREQ0 is set HIGH. Then HRQ is raised and the 8088 raises HLDA. The channel 0 current address register value is used as the address for reading data from memory. This byte is stored in the 8237A temporary register and channel 1 performs a transfer of this temporary register byte to the memory location corresponding to the channel 1 current address register value. In all cases, the transfers continue (I/O or memory) until the base word count value has been achieved, indicating that all the desired data has been transferred.

10.2.7 PC, XT, and AT Differences

This section has briefly outlined the operation of most of the major components on the IBM PC system board. We have not addressed the speaker, keyboard and I/O channels (expansion boards). The discussion is based on the system layout as illustrated in the *IBM Technical Reference* manual. The figures included in the preceding discussion were abbreviated for clarity. The goal of this section is now probably clear: It is to provide a working description of IBM PC, XT, and AT hardware at a level that can serve as a basis for an understanding of how the system is programmed. That is, to provide a hardware background that will allow the reader to understand how the actual Macro Assembler instructions are used to program the chips in the system.

      The reader should recognize, of course, that we can only touch on the topic of programming the chips in the IBM PC system. Chips such as the 8259A require a set of Initialization Command Words and Operation Command Words (as illustrated in Chapter 9). These are words that should be programmed in assembler and addressed to the 8259A during initialization. This is but a sample of the sort of processing that the system programmer must accomplish to get the IBM PC to function.

      The *IBM Technical Reference, Personal Computer XT and Portable Personal Computer* [8] details the signal flow for the XT computer. In the previous discussion we focused on the IBM PC system board configuration, and it will be useful to continue to talk about the system board. For the XT there are notably several major differences between the XT and PC systems. Specifically, the XT system board has four banks of dynamic RAM which consists of 64K × 1 bit RAM chips instead of 16K × 1 bit chips. Thus, the system board RAM can occupy up to 256K bytes of memory. Signals associated with memory decoding and memory chip selection must behave slightly differently in the XT. Basically, however, the system board has a very similar layout to that for the IBM PC. Table 10.11 lists the major differences by subsystem. There are other differences between the two systems, of course. For example the IBM XT comes with a ten megabyte hard disk and disk controller, plus a single 360K floppy. The IBM PC is only configured for 360K floppy drives and controllers. The XT has room for eight expansion boards off the system board, whereas, the PC has provision for only using five I/O channels for the expansion boards.

Perhaps the easiest place to start discussing the AT is from the perspective of the system overview. This is true because we have already seen an overview of the PC and XT and are now able to examine the AT processing in light of such a framework, while using the system similarities as a basis for common understanding. Figure 10.16 illustrates the AT system board functional block diagram. Again, this figure has been simplified, based on the functional block diagram for the AT appearing in the *IBM Technical Reference, Personal Computer AT* [9].

The architecture of the AT is conceptually similar to that of the PC and XT. On the left side of Figure 10.16 we see that the AT system microprocessor is an 80286 and the coprocessor is an 80287. The 80286 is packaged in a 68-pin leadless chip carrier, which means that the user potentially has access to more signals. It is clear from Figure 10.16 that the AT has 24 address lines and 18 data lines for their respective buses. Unlike the PC, these address and data lines are not multiplexed and each is handled separately by the 80286. Only 16 data lines are used by the 80286. These lines are latched onto the system data bus via an LS646 (D0–D7) and an LS245 (D8–D15). The latching is controlled by an 82288 Bus Controller. In Figure 10.16

TABLE 10.11   MAJOR DIFFERENCES BETWEEN IBM PC AND XT BY SUBSYSTEM.

Subsystem	Discussion
1. Processor	Redistribution of address line latching with LS244 used for A8–A19. Some discrete logic reconfiguration.
2. Decoding	Minor changes
3. Chip Select Decoding	Faster refresh signal. Use of a 24S10 in place of a LS138 for RAM address selection logic.
4. DMA	Minor changes
5. ROM and Drivers	The XT is set up for 32K × 8 bit ROM chips versus the 8K × 8 bit ROM chips in the PC. The PC uses only lines A0 to A12 for addressing ROM while the XT uses lines A0 to A14 to achieve the 32K address range. This extra 2 address lines necessitates another LS244 buffer with an overall reconfiguration of signals.
6. RAM	The memory is allocated in 64K × 1 bit chips and this requires that the input address lines to the LS158 multiplexers have addresses A0 to A15 for the XT.

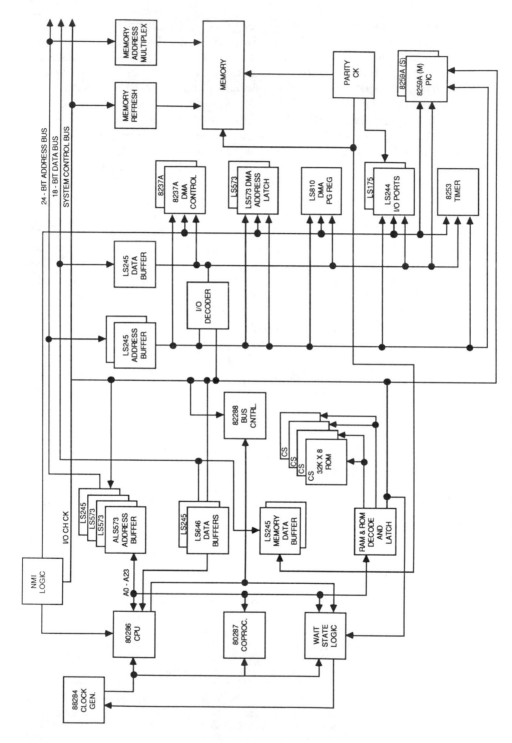

Figure 10.16 The functional block diagram for the IBM AT computer system. Reprinted by permission from the *Technical Reference* copyright 1981 by International Business Machines Corporation.

this latching enable is indicated by the control bus and the 82288 provides both a direction signal (DT/R*), plus an enable signal. The latter is generated from the 82288 Data Enable (DEN) using a pair of NAND gates that are set when the latch chip select (NPCS) and the Bus High Enable (BHE) signal are also set. Basically, this latching function is very similar to that depicted for the PC in Figure 10.1.

Addresses are buffered onto the 24-bit address bus by three LS573 and one LS245 buffer. Two of the LS573s buffer the address lines A1 to A8 and A9 to A16. The LS245 buffers lines A17 through A23, and line A0 is output through discrete logic. The remaining LS573 is cross buffered with lines A17 to A19 and with the BHE signal, which it latches out to the address bus and control bus, as needed.

The RAM and ROM decoding logic uses LS245s for ROM address latching. One LS245 latches A1 to A8 and the second latches A9 to A16. A 28542 and LS573 are used for input RAM, RAS and CAS decoding. The 80286 addresses memory in two halves. Data lines MD0 through MD7 are selected based on CAS0L or CAS1L, while data lines MD8 through MD15 are selected based on column signals CAS0H or CAS1H. The row address strobes for these banks are RAS0 and RAS1 for banks 0 and 1, and RAS2 and RAS3 for banks 2 and 3.

The ROM used in the AT (actually Erasable Programmable Read Only Memory or EPROM) uses 15 address lines per chip. This provides for an address space of 32K (roughly, 2 raised to the 15th power). Each EPROM also has 8 data lines that provide for a 32K × 8 bit ROM chip. Remember in the PC each ROM had only a single data bit per address cell. It required 8 chips to use the full complement of data lines, which constituted a byte.

As in the PC, the address bus feeds two LS245 address buffers that set up the external address bus. This bus, in turn, is used to drive the I/O decoding logic, the DMA function, I/O ports and timer, and the two 8259A PICs. The LS245 simply latches the addresses from the system address bus into this external bus area.

The 8237A DMA controllers provide for an I/O space which has eight request lines (DREQ0–DREQ8). Each 8237A services four lines. Address lines A0 through A7 are input to the 8237A directly and lines A8 through A15 are latched by an LS573 using the ADSTB output. The two 8259A PICs are used in a Master (M) and Slave (S) configuration. Interrupt lines IRQ0 through IRQ7 are used by the Master and IRQ2 is the Slave input. The slave services interrupt lines IRQ8 through IRQ15.

The RAM on the far right side of Figure 10.16 is conceptually similar to that used by the PC. The row and column allocation is as previously discussed in Table 10.10. Each RAM chip has eight address lines plus two RAS lines. Since the row and column data is multiplexed onto the chip, the eight row by eight column (by one RAS) yield an address space of 64K × 1 bit. The second RAS line yields an additional 64K × 1 bit address space for a total of 128K × 1 bit per chip. Each bank then has eight chips to form a byte plus an additional chip for parity checking. This completes the description for the AT system board, based on Figure 10.16.

As we have seen, the AT is conceptually similar to the PC. It has an expanded bus structure and runs at a faster clock rate. The 88284 clock generator typically runs about twice as fast as the 8284A appearing in the PC and has the potential to run substantially faster than this. The increase in address and data capability, however, greatly expands the AT potential. Couple this with an expanded I/O space and the increase in speed, and one obtains a significantly more powerful computer. These considerations have, of course, only examined the system board characteristics. The addition of an expanded hard disk, for example, increases the capacity of the AT for many storage intensive operations such as an improved data base management capability.

The 80286 has 24 physical address pins which provides for a 16-megabyte address space. This can be mapped to one gigabyte of virtual address space using the memory management capabilities. There are two modes of operation; iAPX 86 Real Address Mode and Protected Virtual Address Mode. In the Real Address Mode the 80286 is object code compatible with the 8086 and 8088 and can address up to one megabyte of memory. Initially, only Real Address Mode software was developed for the AT.

10.3 SYSTEMS PROGRAMMING TECHNIQUES

In an abstract sense, this section serves as a definition of operating system software. We saw in section 10.2 how the hardware operates to accomplish such actions as chip selection (also considered in Chapter 9), based on software addresses. Now it is time to take a step back and examine the overall system environment. The essential components needed for system programming in general and operating systems in particular are processes, input/output, memory management, and file systems. Figure 10.17 presents a high-level block structure for the IBM microcomputer software system environment. Clearly illustrated are the four components delineated above. Each of these components is discussed in the following subsections.

10.3.1 Processes

To paraphrase Tanenbaum [3], a process is a block of code executing in a program environment. It includes the linked object code, data and stack areas, all CPU registers, and any additional hardware and software needed to execute the program. DOS, through version 3.3, is a single-task operating system. Hence, DOS can only service one process at a time. The familiar roll-out that occurs on multitasking systems is not applicable in the DOS environment. Figure 10.17 has no provision for multitasking (no process table or preserved core image). The function of process management, however, does take place. Once executing, each process continues to completion under DOS. The category of operations falling under the Command Processor constitutes process management in DOS. There are three process categories that can be implemented individually under the command processor shell: resident processor actions (including selected interrupt service and external command execution for tasks like formatting disks), internal command processes (such as locating a file on disk under program control or assigning a time to a file creation by maintaining a count with the system timer), and the initialization processes (implemented when the system boots).

It does not take a great deal of imagination to envision how disk I/O processes might be handled in the DOS environment. A rather interesting example of a process,

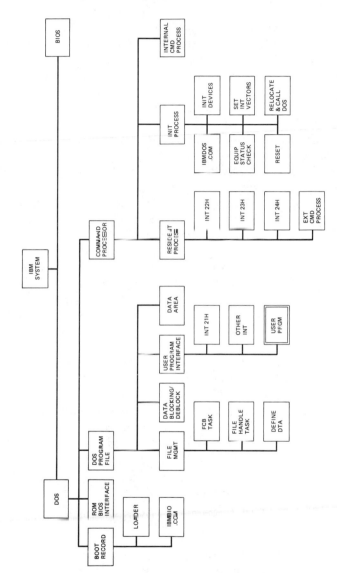

Figure 10.17 IBM DOS Operating System Architecture.

424   Systems Programming Considerations   Chap. 10

however, is the initialization process that takes place upon power-up. It will be instructive to consider this process in some detail, and the "child" activities illustrated in Figure 10.17 will then become clearer. Also, the system hardware discussed in section 10.2 will now appear in a more integrated fashion. Figure 10.18 illustrates schematically the initialization process for the IBM PC. How does initialization work? Obviously the processor must jump to a known address at some point in the initialization process. Intel has designed the 8088 and the 8086 to initialize the CS register FFFFH and IP to 0. The code that resides at this location must then begin the rest of the initialization process. In the IBM PC the power-on reset starts the 8088 or 8086 at the above address; the instruction residing at FFFF:0000 is input to the CPU for execution. This instruction, in the case of the IBM PC, is a jump to the entry point RESET which resides at address F0000:E05B in the BIOS code. Following the jump, the code checks for error conditions: It checks reading and writing registers, performs checksum error checks on the ROM code, tests the 8237A DMA initialization, initializes the 8259A (with interrupts enabled), performs an 8259A interrupt controller test, checks the timer, and installs a temporary interrupt service routine. Then at address F0000:E2EC, code to load the interrupt vector table is executed.

Following loading of the vector table, some additional "housekeeping" functions are performed and the system prepares to initialize the system boot. At address F000:E620, a jump to BOOT_STRAP takes place and the bootstrap process begins. At this point the equipment status check, initialization of devices, interrupt vector table load, and reset have all executed. The process, BOOT_STRAP, prepares to perform an Initial Program Load (IPL) from the diskette in drive A or the fixed disk. A single section (512 bytes) is read using interrupt 13H. If the read is unsuccessful, INT 18H is used to load BASIC. If the read is successful a jump to BOOT_LOCN takes place.

The INT 13H call essentially starts the process for loading IBMDOS.COM and the boot record with IBMBIO.COM. The routine pointed to by BOOT_LOCN has been loaded as part of DOS and the code is unavailable for comment. We can, however, make several remarks about this code based on general inferences about how such code functions. First, as the tasks appearing in Figure 10.17 indicate, DOS is eventually called as the final initialization process. The core of this process is a loop which could have the form

```
DOSCALL:
        NOP
        JMP DOSCALL
```

This infinite loop insures that the processor continues to function at all times and does not hang. How, then, do we enter the system? The only way to do so is through hardware interrupts using the resident process. Typically, the user might type in

```
PRGM.EXE
```

at the keyboard and, when the ENTER key is struck, an interrupt would be generated to the 8259A (INT 9) to cause the loop to stop executing. Control then would transfer

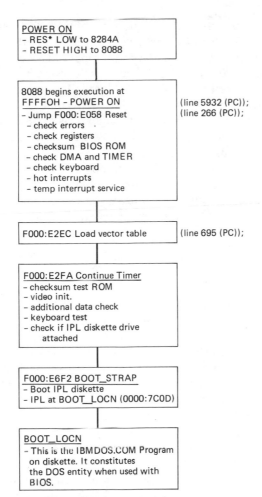

POWER ON
- RES* LOW to 8284A
- RESET HIGH to 8088

8088 begins execution at
FFFFOH – POWER ON
- Jump F000:E058 Reset
  - check errors ·
  - check registers
  - checksum BIOS ROM
  - check DMA and TIMER
  - check keyboard
  - hot interrupts
  - temp interrupt service

(line 5932 (PC));
(line 266 (PC));

F000:E2EC Load vector table

(line 695 (PC));

F000:E2FA Continue Timer
- checksum test ROM
- video init.
- additional data check
- keyboard test
- check if IPL diskette drive
    attached

F000:E6F2 BOOT_STRAP
- Boot IPL diskette
- IPL at BOOT_LOCN (0000:7C0D)

BOOT_LOCN
- This is the IBMDOS.COM Program
  on diskette. It constitutes
  the DOS entity when used with
  BIOS.

Figure 10.18   The IBM PC Initialization
Process.

to a DOS entry point in the DOS Program File. The transfer would be based on the execution of an External Command Process that determined that the input was a run-time file and not some special reserved-word that denoted another DOS command.

As part of the relocation and call to DOS during initialization, working tables and the Program Segment Prefix (PSP) area are set up. Once the DOS Program File begins execution a User Program Interface is defined for the example above. Also, File Management begins to occur with the File Management subfunction. This latter activity includes setting up the appropriate data area for file handles or the FCB to access the executable file (in this case PRGM.EXE which resides on the default drive). Following completion of the program, the DOS Program File returns control to DOS, thus executing the above-mentioned loop, and DOS waits for another hardware interrupt to signal entry to another task.

It is probably clear that a substantial amount of operating system activity involves input/output. We have seen how initialization takes place. The only ambiguous portion of this process is the actual relocation and call to DOS. The first two

PSP bytes are a call to INT 20H, the DOS program terminate. The remaining PSP areas are delineated in the *DOS Technical Reference* and illustrate the needed DOS parameters for setting up the DOS Program File and Resident Process. When a .EXE program is defined by the Linker DS and ES are set to point to the PSP start address. CS, IP, SS, and SP are set to values passed by the Linker. Hence, the DOS Program File receives executable instructions and data that resides at known addresses. Thus, the entire system process can be thought of as a continuous program moving from module to module with an infinite loop at the core of DOS that can be interrupted by a hardware action.

Obviously, we do not know exactly how DOS operates because IBM has not released the code. The above procedure is exact until the entry to DOS. At this point it becomes facsimile, but is reasonable. The functions described above have a core NOP loop that DOS can be expected to implement. It is the recommended approach in the Intel literature.

10.3.2 I/O

As we have seen, there are two considerations to be applied to I/O; the interpretation of how the hardware operates and the structure of the software drivers. Both are essential to an understanding of how to handle I/O. There are two categories of I/O devices in DOS, block devices, which pass and store data in groups of bytes, and character devices, which accept input from or output to a stream of characters (single byte entities). Each I/O device consists of a mechanical peripheral hardware (a disk drive, for example) and an electronic controller or adapter that interfaces to the remaining system. The controller has intelligent integrated circuits that receive and return data through an internal I/O bus. The processing of this data in response to more global instructions is the function of the service routine, and this service is usually initiated by an interrupt call.

In the IBM microprocessor software, most of the I/O service routines reside in the ROM BIOS code. DOS provides the interface to this code through a ROM BIOS interface routine. Under the User Program Interface, the INT 21H function calls (many of which accomplish I/O operations), and remaining interrupt processing jump using the vector table addresses to the appropriate service functions. The INT 21H routines, however, are resident in DOS and these service functions, in turn, call BIOS routines as needed. The later versions of DOS provide for a device-independent format to access peripherals. This format sets up and calls function 44H; however, a device-handler is still needed to service the peripheral. This handler must be in the device-independent format required by function 44H. Chapter 9 has considered I/O drivers for the IBM PC in some detail and the reader is referred to this discussion for an example of how I/O is implemented in the microcomputer environment.

10.3.3 Memory Management

The idea of memory management with the IBM microcomputers has evolved considerably with the PS/2 models. Basically, the 8088 and 8086 had a limited capability for implementing sophisticated memory management schemes. When programs were linked, enough overhead code (pipes) was defined to allow the PSP area to connect to the user code, which in turn had access to the ROM service routines. This linking was defined by the linker based on segment and offset addresses. The offset addresses are determined by the assembler (or compiler) and passed to the linker by known locations. The linker generates the appropriate relocated address with correct segment allocation. The 8088 and 8086 CPU processes these addresses in program fashion to fetch the correct instruction sequence. To do this it must, of course, generate a correct 20-bit address. Clearly, the linker must be aware of the memory limitations of the system when generating run-time code. Thus, DOS has a minimal memory management function and this is reflected in Figure 10.17.

The 80286 (AT, XT286, and PS/2 Models 50 and 60) have a substantial capability for multitasking and virtual memory use. DOS 3.3 does not provide for these capabilities, however, and it is only with the advent of OS/2 that the Protected Mode software takes advantage of this memory management feature. We saw in Chapter 2 that the Protected Mode architecture for the 80286 and 80386 provides descriptions used in the definition of global and local program areas. These areas can be used as the basis for multitasking, with memory management at the core of this activity. The Global Descriptor Table (GDT) contains global descriptions that correspond to virtual segment addresses (24-bit) for "housekeeping" and protection information. This table must be set up at link-time and accessed by DOS at run-time. Similarly, the Local Descriptor Table(s) (LDT) contains local segment address information. There is a single GDT but possibly more than one LDT because of multitasking.

In Protected Mode, as in conventional 8088 or 8086 addressing, there is a 32-bit address consisting of a 16-bit offset and a segment selector (also, 16-bit). The upper 13-bits of the selector correspond to an INDEX which, when multiplied by 8 and added to the base address of the descriptor table, points to the correct segment descriptor entry. The segment descriptor contains the 24-bit segment base (physical base address) which, when added to the 16-bit offset, generates a 24-bit physical address, corresponding to a possible 16-megabyte memory access (2^{24}). The 32-bit 80386 has a similar scheme which is outlined in Chapter 2. Before concluding this section, we shall consider the final systems programming area; file systems.

10.3.4 File Systems

We have seen how files are created, stored, and retrieved (from disk or diskette, for example) in the IBM microcomputer environment. Naming convention includes a file name and extension. DOS is not particularly device-independent because, except for the default drive, the drive location must be specified. DOS has data files, directories, and block-character files. The latter are used to model I/O-type devices. Since files are stored on disk or diskette, the management of disk space is a major DOS concern. We saw in Chapter 7 that files are stored in blocks with appropriate headers to chain the blocks together. Access of files is through the DOS function calls which, in turn, call the disk I/O service routines.

The DOS file management scheme uses the FAT as previously discussed in Chapter 7. This approach is suboptimal because the file pointers in the FAT are randomly located and, hence, the entire FAT must be used for every file access, up to the sequential location of the file pointer desired. Clearly, as disk space increases, as it has in the PS/2 Models 60 and 80, the FATs get larger and more difficult to access.

The DOS directory contains entries of the following form.

8	3	1	10	2	2	2	4
File Name	Ext	Attributes		Time	Date	First Block	Size

Each directory entry is used to chain to the next entry. A block is nominally 512 bytes. We will not consider the implications of multitasking because DOS does not support this feature. Under OS/2, however, shared files can require special management. The protection mechanisms intrinsic to the 80286 and 80386 allow the sharing of files during run-time. In section 10.4 we will consider an additional feature provided for the 80386 CPU, a cache memory that allows faster access for such things as data items.

Within the IBM microcomputer environment, the normal file system, provided as part of DOS, functions in a straightforward fashion because it is single-threaded, serving only one user. As OS/2 becomes more well-known, concurrency and multitasking will be dominant themes, and system design techniques like atomic updates, concurrency control, serializability, and locking will become major considerations [3, pp. 274–277]. Protection and security are readily implemented in the PS/2 computers (80286 and 80386) and even the Model 30 has a password checking feature.

10.4 SYSTEMS PROGRAMMING FOR 80386-BASED COMPUTERS

When programming microprocessors in an implementation such as the IBM microcomputer family, a major systems programming consideration is the flexibility of the microprocessor instruction set. We saw in Chapter 2 that both the Intel 80286 and 80386 possess substantial systems capability through special registers and instructions. These instructions are not part of the normal IBM Macro Assembler instruction set. System designers intending to develop operating system code, for example, must resort to Intel assemblers to program the instructions. This is not to say that IBM will not provide such a capability: We merely point out that for application-oriented assemblers, the system instructions are unnecessary.

For the 80286- and 80386-based microcomputers, memory management and file protection are accomplished using the registers and selectors discussed in Chapter 2. One aspect of the 80386 which is new and interesting is the notion of a cache subsystem. The 80386 can operate at 16MHz and has a 32-bit word and a bus cycle of 125 nanoseconds. This yields a maximum bandwidth of 32 megabytes per second. (125 nanoseconds correspond to an 8MHz rate for bus cycles and there are four bytes per word: $4 \times 8 \times 10^6 = 32$ megabyte per second.) Clearly, memory access rates must match these speeds if the processor is not to slow down. Because most memory is of the slower dynamic RAM (DRAM) type, a technique for matching the processor to this DRAM must be developed. Since static RAM (SRAM) is capable of high-speed access, it becomes reasonable to think about using small amounts of SRAM as an intermediate buffer between the 80386 and DRAM. SRAM is too costly to be considered for large-scale memory applications. This intermediate buffer is called a cache, and it requires an additional controller to manage the cache. Some of the data in DRAM is duplicated in the cache with the hope that it will contain sequentially called code sequences; thereby, allowing blocks of executable code or data to be moved into high speed memory. The success with which these blocks are chosen to contain the needed code sequences is referred to as the hit rate, and the hit rate is a measure of how efficiently the cache has been designed.

While the cache is not intrinsic to the 80386, this particular microprocessor can make efficient use of such a subsystem because of its high speed. As SRAM costs drop and DRAM speeds increase the notion of cache memory management can be expected to evolve.

The PS/2 Model 80 is IBM's 80386 contribution to the personal computer family. From a process viewpoint the initial OS/2 software serves primarily to support the 80286 systems capabilities; hence, it will continue to run as a subset of the Model 80 potential. I/O can be mapped into either a 64K address space, with the usual port mapping, or a full 4 gigabyte physical memory address space. In the latter case, devices are treated as though they are normal memory locations, while in the former case, I/O-mapped devices can be accessed only through IN, OUT, INS, and OUTS instructions. The address bus consists of 30 address lines (A2–A31) and four byte-enable lines (BE0# –BE3#). The address pins identify a 4-byte location (one of the 32-bit 80386) words and each byte-enable pin selects a different byte within this word. For I/O purposes address decoding can be simplified by staggering the addresses of I/O devices so that, for example, these devices are assigned values at every fourth address. Then the byte-enable outputs can be ignored for I/O accesses.

Memory management for the 80386-based computers can emulate the 16-bit members of this family or can use the newer 32-bit management scheme. As we have indicated, OS/2 uses the earlier scheme. Both the normal 80286 and 8088-8086 schemes are presented in Chapter 2, as well as the 80386 scheme.

10.5 SUMMARY

This chapter has attempted to provide a brief glimpse into the world of systems programming with an emphasis on topics of interest to the assembly language programmer. The purpose of the section on system board circuitry is to provide an understanding of how system addresses are defined. This is essential for memory management and development of such systems software as the linker.

The principal aspect of system board operation from the software perspective is the correct generation of address sequences and chip selection. Many of the system functions appear in transparent fashion to the systems programmer; however, addresses are particularly important entities that reflect the manner in which the hardware is wired together. This correlation, hardware circuits and software addressing, is the method by which the chips are activated to receive commands through other input lines from the data bus. Clearly, it is easiest (although not absolutely essential if languages like C are used and appropriate files included) to achieve these hardware-software interfaces using assembly language.

We next considered a more abstract treatment of operating system software and its implications (primarily) for DOS. Finally, several aspects of 80386 systems programming were examined.

REFERENCES

1. Beck, L. L. *System Software*: *An Introduction to Systems Programming*. Addison-Wesley Publ. Co., Inc. Reading, MA (1985), p. 3.
2. *Disk Operating System Technical Reference*. IBM Corp. P.O. Box 1328. Boca Raton, FL 33432 (1985).
3. Tanenbaum, A. S. *Operating Systems*: *Design and Implementation*. Prentice Hall,. Englewood Cliffs, NJ (1987), p. 2.
4. Katzan, H. *Operating Systems*: *A Pragmatic Approach*. Van Nostrand Reinhold Co. New York, NY (1986), p. 5.
5. Furht, B., and Miltutinovic, V. "A Survey of Microprocessor Architectures for Memory Management." *Computer* (IEEE Computer Society), 20, 3 (1987): 48.
6. Morse, S. *The 8086/8088 Primer*: *An Introduction to Their Architecture System Design and Programming*. Hayden Book Co., Inc. Hasbrouck Heights, NJ (1982).

PROBLEMS

10.1. What will the value of S1* be when the 8288 has its DT/R* line set LOW? What will the value of S0* be when the 8288 has its DT/R line set HIGH?

10.2. When the 8088 queue status lines are set with QS1 HIGH and QS2 LOW, what is being processed by the arithmetic logical unit?

10.3. Why can address lines AD0 through AD7 be latched using a simple 74LS373 buffer, but these same lines, in data mode, must be buffered using a 74LS245 transceiver?

10.4. If the 8288 Command Enable (CEN) line is HIGH, does address information or data information latch onto the system bus?

10.5. In Figure 10.5, what is the status of the signal out of Q (on the LS74) when all inputs to the NAND circuit appearing on the left side are HIGH (the 8088 passive state)?

10.6. When the 8088 desires to latch data onto the system data bus, at what level does the 8259A set the Enable signal EN*, and to what does the 8288 set its DT/R* line?

10.7. If the system read-only-memory (ROM) consisted of 64K × 8 bit chips, how many address lines would be required to address each ROM chip?

10.8. I/O can be achieved externally from ports equal to or greater than 200H, but system board port addresses exist below 200H. Therefore, the data latching function must be inhibited from external sources for ports below 200H. How does the IBM PC insure that no data from external peripherals can access the 8088 for port addresses below 200H?

10.9. In the I/O and ROM chip selection logic, when address lines A16, A17, A18 and A19 are all LOW, is ROM or RAM selected? If these address lines are all HIGH, is ROM or RAM selected? How does this coincide with the fact that IBM has placed all ROM addresses above F0000H for ROM on the system board?

10.10. If a ROM chip starts with address F4000H and, in the case of the IBM PC, has chip select signal CS2*, what is the starting address of the ROM chip selected by CS5*?

10.11. In Figure 10.11, the RAM selection logic is illustrated. When address lines A14 and A15 are both HIGH, what portion of RAM is being selected? What column address strobe and row address strobe is active?

10.12. During a DMA transfer, what 8237A signal is used to strobe the upper address bits onto the system address bus? If the DMA address enable line is HIGH, can the DMA process take place?

10.13. Why does the IBM XT require 15 address lines for accessing ROM?

10.14. If the IBM PC can access one megabyte of memory using 20-bit address lines, what can the IBM AT access, assuming no virtual memory addressing takes place?

A

Program Routines
Used in This Book

The following table summarizes the programs (procedures) developed in this book. Page numbers are indicated along with the description. Table 2 contains the object libraries.

TABLE 1 LISTING OF PROGRAMS DEVELOPED IN THIS BOOK

Name	Discussion	Page
FIRASM.ASM	This is an initial sample program to illustrate assembler.	30
ADDEM.ASM	This program illustrates 5 of the 7 addressing modes.	37
MINMAX.ASM	This program determines the minimum value and maximum value from the array TABLE1.	63
BRACKET.ASM	This program searches a list of numbers and determines how many values fall within a range of limits.	72
ROOTPG.ASM	This routine calculates the square root of a list of word quantities in TABLE1. It calls WORDSR.	100
WORDSR.ASM	This procedure receives a number in AX, calculates its square root, and returns the value in AX.	102
SORT.ASM	This program performs an exchange sort on the numbers in TABLE1.	106
CKLN.ASM	This is the main calling program for computing natural logarithm. It calls LNLOG.	108
LNLOG.ASM	This procedure calculates natural logarithms of numbers between 0 and 1.	109

(Continued)

TABLE 1 (*Continued*)

Name	Discussion	Page
CSCK.ASM	This is the main calling program involved in calculating sine and cosine. It calls COSSIN.	111
COSSIN.ASM	This procedure calculates the sine and cosine of the input value in AX.	113
RAND1.ASM	This procedure generates a random number between 0 and 1 based on a previous random number or a seed number.	117
CKGRAN.ASM	This is the main calling program that generates two Gaussian random numbers.	118
GRAND.ASM	This procedure generates two Gaussian random numbers. It calls RAND1, LNLOG, WORDSR and COSSIN.	120
BOX320.ASM	This routine contains the BOX1 and TICK1 procedures for generating a box and tick marks in 320×200. It also contains LINEH and LINEV for drawing horizontal and vertical lines, respectively.	141
CONNL1.ASM	This general purpose plotting procedure connects two points with raster dots.	144
CLINE1.ASM	This is the calling program for generating raster examples. It calls CONNL1, BOX1, and TICK1.	147
PLOTRN.ASM	This is the main calling program for generating a plot of Gaussian random numbers. It calls GRAND, BOX1, TICK1 and LLABEL.	149
LLABEL.ASM	This procedure labels the Gaussian random number graph.	152
CPRINT.ASM	This program reads characters from the keyboard, writes them to the screen, and prints them.	160
STKPLT1.ASM	This program graphs stock performance for selected stock histories: IBM, DEC, HP, Sperry, STC and the Dow Jones.	188
MACILIB.LIB	This macro library contains MESSG, KEYBD, CLS, MXMN, SCALE, TITLEL, SCDEL, RT80M, PLOTGR.	196
BOX1.ASM	This routine contains BOX11 and TICK11 which allow box and tick variables to be set externally.	200
LABEL1.ASM	This general purpose label routine allows variables to be set in calling program.	202
DA.ASM	This routine contains procedures for converting ASCII to decimal.	204
MAC2LIB.LIB	This macro library contains DECASC, ASCDEC.	208
FILOPCK.ASM	This main calling program creates a disk file using a FCB. It calls FILECR, FILEW, and CLOSEF.	240
FILECR.ASM	This routine contains the procedures FILECR, FILEW, and CLOSEF.	241
FILOPRD.ASM	This main calling program reads a disk file using FILEOP, READF, and CLOSE1.	245
FILERD.ASM	This routine contains the procedures FILEOP, READF, CLOSE1, DISKTF, and DISKCT. It uses FCB.	246
MA.ASM	This program calculates the moving average for the stock program. It reads stocks from disk, calculates moving average, and plots.	253
BOX22.ASM	This program contains BOX22 (BOX11 with CLS and mode set removed), LINEH1, and LINEV1.	259

MAC3LIB.LIB	This macro library contains MXMN1, MOVAVG, SSCALE, SSCALE1, PGR, CLS1.	261
FILECR1.ASM	This procedure creates a disk file using the file handles. It contains FILEW1, CLOSEF1, and FILECR1.	267
STRU1.ASM	This is a structure program. It reads and qualifies a password. It calls MESSAGE.	164
MESSAGE.ASM	This simple procedure reads a message from screen buffer and displays the message. This may be used in place of macro.	167
KEYBD.ASM	This simple procedure reads the keyboard. It may be used in place of macro.	168
TIMER.ASM	This structure program illustrates the timer function based on INT 1AH.	212
BCDDEC.ASM	This procedure converts two digit BCD numbers to internal decimals.	215
RTWAVE.ASM	This is the main calling program for plotting waveforms.	217
SIGNAL.ASM	This contains the procedure SIG that generates a sinusoidal signal based on frequency and time.	224
WFPLT.ASM	This procedure uses LINEVV to graph the waveform in RTWAVE.	226
LINEVV.ASM	This contains the FAR procedures LINEVV and LINEHH.	228
NUMCK.LST	This listing output for NUMCK.ASM illustrates the various Macro Assembler number formats.	281
HASCDEC.ASM	This procedure converts 32-bit ASCII numbers to internal decimal format.	287
MUL3216.ASM	This procedure multiplies a 32-bit number by a 16-bit number.	289
HDECASC.ASM	This procedure converts a 32-bit internal decimal number to ASCII.	290
DIV3216.ASM	This procedure divides a 32-bit integer by a 16-bit word.	292
HASCCK.ASM	This main calling program reads a number (32-bit) from the keyboard, converts it to internal decimal, converts it back to ASCII, and displays it.	293
COPROC.LST	This listing output is for COPROC.ASM that illustrates a use of the coprocessor.	295
MORTPLT.ASM	This is the main calling program for mortgage payment calculation using 8087.	312
MORPAY.ASM	This procedure contains the routine MPAY1 that computes monthly mortgage payment using 8087.	317
PI.ASM	This program computes monthly principal and interest and calls graphics. It uses the 8087.	323
BBBOX.ASM	This procedure calls routines from GRAPHLIB and plots.	325
SSCL.ASM	This procedure scales plot variables and sets up graph labels.	327

TABLE 2 LIBRARIES USED IN THIS BOOK

Name	Discussion
MATHLIB	Contains callable routines GRAND, WORDSR, RAND1, COSSIN, LNLOG.
GRAPHLIB	Contains callable routines BOX1, TICK1, CONNL1, LABEL1, BOX11, TICK11, LINEVV.
IOCON	Contains callable routines MESSAGE, KEYBD, CLSCREN, ASCDEC1, BCDDEC.

B

A Structured Assembly Language Utility (SALUT)

The purpose of this appendix is to illustrate a structured assembler technique for optimizing generation of assembler code. In the following sections, we describe the IBM utility SALUT and include programming examples.

B.1 THE SALUT UTILITY

One goal throughout the development of programming languages has been a search for uniformity in the resulting code and a flow of control that allows ease in understanding. IBM has generated such a package with their version 2.0 Macro Assembler enhancements. This utility program is called SALUT and it has three optional functions.

1. To convert special purpose structure statements appearing in the assembler program into assembler source code
2. To provide formatting and indenting of assembler source code to improve readability
3. To replace tab characters with blanks

SALUT's primary function is the first option, above, the conversion of special purpose structure statements into assembler source code. This is where the real power of the SALUT utility becomes apparent. To begin programming in the context of SALUT will appear awkward at first because of its implicit heavy reliance on conditional-like structures. The elimination of such features as conditional and unconditional jump statements from the source code implies a totally new approach to assembler programming philosophy.

Table B.1 illustrates the 13 special purpose structure statements available through SALUT. Each statement corresponds to either a starting structure, an intermediate branching structure, an intermediate entry point, or a termination structure. The user can begin to see the rigor needed to program using these statements because

TABLE B.1   SPECIAL PURPOSE STRUCTURE STATEMENTS USED WITH SALUT

Statement	Parameters	Comments
$1F	condition (,AND/OR)(,LONG)	This structure statement results in a conditional jump with the AND/OR parameters allowing multiple statements to be joined. The LONG option provides for jumps beyond 128 bytes although it should only be used in exceptional cases.
$ELSE	(LONG)	This structure performs an optional branch within an IF structure. The syntax is familiar as the IF...THEN...ELSE structure, now a common part of BASIC programming. Again, the LONG option allows jumps beyond 128 bytes.
$ENDIF		Termination label for the IF structure.
$DO	(COMPLEX,(LONG))	This defines a repetitive structure similar to the FORTRAN DO loop. The subsequent instructions are executed repeatedly until a condition arises that allows branching out of the DO structure. Again, the LONG option allows jumps beyond 128 bytes within the DO structure. The COMPLEX option usually denotes a branching path from the interior to the DO source code. All DO structures are terminated by $ENDDO.
$ENDDO	(condition/LOOPxx(,AND/OR)) (,LONG)	Condition corresponds to a comparison which precedes the statement, and if this comparison satisfies the condition the DO iteration terminates. LOOPxx serves the same function as a condition. AND/OR allows multiple statements to be joined and LONG has its usual meaning.
$SEARCH	(COMPLEX(,LONG))	This structure is an alternate form of the DO structure and implements a loop architecture. The $SEARCH statement must appear as the first structure statement and defines the starting label for the iterative loop. If COMPLEX is used as an option, branching from the middle of intervening code takes place. LONG has its usual meaning.

(Continued)

TABLE B.1 (*Continued*)

Statement	Parameters	Comments
$EXITIF	condition(,AND/OR)(,LONG) (,NUL)	This structure allows exit conditions from an IF conditional structure, depending on the result of the previous comparison, if in agreement with the $EXITIF condition. AND/OR allows the connecting of multiple statements. Again, LONG allows a jump beyond 128 bytes. The NUL option means there is no success process and no $ORELSE. In this case the exit is to the ending label.
$ORELSE	(LONG)	This structure follows an $EXITIF and determines the failure path. LONG has its usual meaning.
$ENDLOOP	(condition/LOOPxx(,AND/OR)) (,LONG)	This structure is used with $SEARCH and marks the return to the starting label if the condition is true or the LOOPxx satisfies the previous comparison. AND/OR is used to connect multiple statements and LONG has its usual meaning.
$LEAVE	condition(,AND/OR)(,LONG)	If the corresponding condition is true, this structure exits the $DO, $SEARCH, or $ORELSE structure. AND/OR and LONG have their usual meanings.
$ENDSRCH		This structure defines the end label for the $SEARCH structure.
$STRTDO		Used with the $DO structure, this structure provides for a middle entry to the DO. It is essentially an alternate "start DO" entry point. Also used wit!. $LEAVE.
$STRTSRCH		Used with $SEARCH, $ORELSE, or $LEAVE, this structure provides an alternate start entry point.

the flow of the resulting program is downward, except for any branching back to the starting label using $DO or $SEARCH. Such branching, however, actually constitutes an iterative loop construct (not a true conditional construct) and all intervening code can be read from top-to-bottom.

Consider the $IF structure statement. Normally this statement will appear as

$IF M

Here M is a condition like those illustrated in Table B.2. The flags associated with this condition must have been previously set using a comparison-type instruction. Each time a structure statement is used that requires a condition, the programmer must precede the statement with a comparison in order to test the program logic

TABLE B.2 CONDITIONS FOR STRUCTURE STATEMENTS

Condition	Meaning	Flags	Comments
A	Above	CF = 0 and ZF = 0	Comparison greater
AE	Above/Equal	CF = 0	Comparison greater or equal
B	Below	CF = 1	Comparison less
BE	Below/Equal	CF = 1 or ZF = 1	Comparison less or equal
C	Carry	CF = 1	Carry took place
CXZ	CX is zero	CF or ZF = 0	Count index set to zero
E	Equal	ZF = 1	Comparison shows no difference
G	Greater	ZF = 0 and SF = OF	Signed number comparison greater
GE	Greater/Equal	SF = OF	Signed number comparison greater or equal
L	Less	SF xor OF = 1	Signed number comparison less
LE	Less/Equal	SF xor OF(or ZF) = 1	Signed number comparison less or equal
NA	Not Above	CF = 1 or ZF = 1	Comparison is less or equal
NAE	Not Above/Equal	CF = 1	Comparison is less
NB	Not Below	CF = 0	Comparison is greater or equal
NBE	Not Below/Equal	CF = 0 and ZF = 0	Comparison is greater
NC	Not Carry	CF = 0	No carry
NE	Not Equal	ZF = 0	Comparison unequal
NG	Not Greater	SF xor OF(or ZF) = 1	Signed number comparison less or equal
NGE	Not Greater/Equal	SF xor OF = 1	Signed number comparison less
NL	Not Less	SF = OF	Signed number comparison greater or equal
NLE	Not Less/Equal	ZF = 0 and SF = OF	Signed number comparison greater
NO	Not Overflow	OF = 0	No overflow occurred
NP	Not Parity	PF = 0	Parity flag not set
NS	Not Sign	SF = 0	No underflow
NZ	Not Zero	ZF = 0	Comparison not equal
O	Overflow	OF = 1	Overflow occurred
P	Parity	PF = 1	Parity flag set
PE	Parity Even	PF = 1	Communications
PO	Parity Odd	PF = 0	Communications
S	Sign	SF = 1	Sign flag set
Z	Zero	ZF = 0	Comparison equal

properly prior to execution of the structure. The $ELSE structure provides an alternate process path through the IF, should the IF test fail. As has been illustrated, all IF structures must terminate with an $ENDIF statement which is converted to a termination label for the IF construct by SALUT. Figures B.1 and B.2 present flow charts for the complete IF structures. Also presented is the assembler code. The labels indicated in the assembler portion of these tables are not the literal labels

STRUCTURE	STATEMENTS	ASSEMBLER	COMMENTS
	$IF M	JNM $$A01	-- Jump if M is false
	A1	A1	-- Executable "success" code
	$ENDIF	$$A01:	-- Jump label

Figure B.1   The simple IF structure (no ELSE).

generated by SALUT. The convention used in the tables is to indicate a similar label convention for each label point ($$A01, $$A02, ...) in order to make the assembler easily readable. SALUT actually defines label mnemonics associated with the generating structure. At this point in the discussion, however, it is useful to use similar label syntax when describing the resulting assembler, the output from SALUT. In the programming example to follow, the SALUT syntax will become clear. The branching structures appearing in Figures B.1 and B.2 constitute the simplest possible conditionals which can be defined using the Macro Assembler. SALUT allows these structures to be nested within each other, thereby providing for successively higher order branching. Also, these structures may be chained together at any level of nesting.

Figure B.3 illustrates the DO WHILE structure with a leading test that takes place prior to any process execution. The execution of this structure results in an initial comparison that terminates the DO loop when a "success" occurs, followed by execution of the single process and iteration of the loop. Typically, a count index can be set prior to entering the test and decremented during each iteration until a comparison demonstrates that the index has reached some value, at which time the

STRUCTURE	STATEMENTS	ASSEMBLER	COMMENTS
	$IF M	JNM $$A01	-- Jump if M is false
	A1	A1	--Executable "success" code
	$ELSE	JMP $$A02	-- Jump unconditional
		$$A01:	--Conditional jump label
	A2	A2	--Executable "failure" code
	$ENDIF	$$A02:	--Unconditional jump label

Figure B.2   The IF structure with ELSE option.

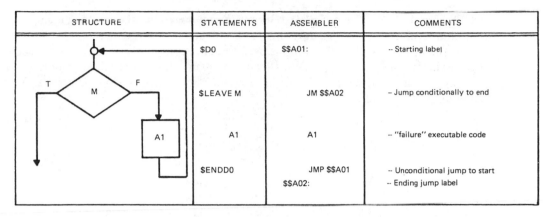

STRUCTURE	STATEMENTS	ASSEMBLER	COMMENTS
	$DO	$$A01:	-- Starting label
	$LEAVE M	JM $$A02	-- Jump conditionally to end
	A1	A1	-- "failure" executable code
	$ENDDO	JMP $$A01 $$A02:	-- Unconditional jump to start -- Ending jump label

Figure B.3 The DO WHILE structure with a leading test.

execution leaves the loop. This very useful structure can be employed whenever repetitive execution of a process is called for with the increment of a pointer or counter, for example.

Figure B.4 presents a similar structure except the test takes place after execution of the process DO UNTIL. This structure has one less statement than the DO WHILE and effectively accomplishes the same function. The exception to this occurs during the first iteration where the process code must be executed prior to testing. Again, the process code, A1, is executed only under "failure" conditions. A "success" results in termination of the loop. All the DO structures end with an $ENDDO statement. This statement can have a loop option such as

$ENDDO LOOP

which automatically decrements the count register, CX. Another possible loop option would be

$ENDDO LOOPE

STRUCTURE	STATEMENTS	ASSEMBLER	COMMENTS
	$DO	$$A01:	-- Starting label
	A1	A1	-- "failure" executable code
	$ENDDO M	JNM $$A01	-- Conditional jump to start

Figure B.4 The DO WHILE structure with a trailing test.

which branches to the "success" path when CX is not zero but the zero flag is set. The CX count value is, of course, decremented each time through the loop.

    The options AND or OR can be used to connect multiple structure statements. For example, consider a DO structure from which an exit is desired if the numbers 1, 2 or 3 are input to the keyboard, such as a menu for selecting various functions. The code might look like the following:

```
    ...
    $DO
    ...
    CALL MESSAGE 1      ; Message asking for input
    CALL KEYBD          ; Input to keyboard buffer
    MOV AX, CHAR        ; CHAR contains character read
    CMP AX, 1
    $ENDDO E, OR
    CMP AX, 2
    $ENDDO E, OR
    CMP AX, 3
    $ENDDO E
    ...
```

Figure B.5 represents the DO COMPLEX structure with a middle exit. This structure allows for the execution of two processes, one for "failure" and one for "success". It has the disadvantage that the "failure" process is executed upon entry

STRUCTURE	STATEMENTS	ASSEMBLER	COMMENTS
	$DO COMPLEX	$$A01:	-- Starting label
A1	A1	A1	-- First executable code
M	$LEAVE M	JM $$A02	-- Conditional jump out of DO
A2	A2	A2	-- "failure" process
	$ENDDO	JMP $$A01	-- Unconditional jump to start
		$$A02:	

Figure B.5 The DO COMPLEX structure with a middle exit.

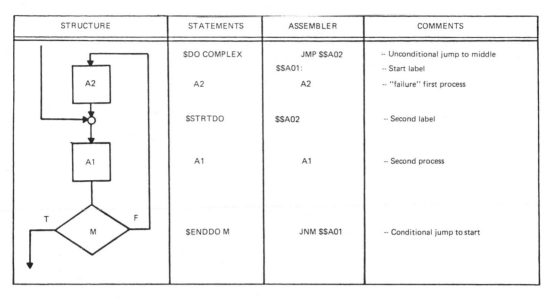

STRUCTURE	STATEMENTS	ASSEMBLER	COMMENTS
	$DO COMPLEX	JMP $$A02	-- Unconditional jump to middle
		$$A01:	-- Start label
A2	A2	A2	-- "failure" first process
	$STRTDO	$$A02	-- Second label
A1	A1	A1	-- Second process
M	$ENDDO M	JNM $$A01	-- Conditional jump to start

Figure B.6   The DO COMPLEX structure with the alternate form middle exit.

and prior to the first test. Figure B.6 is an alternate form for this structure in which both processes are executed each time through the loop except the first iteration. In this latter situation only the A1 process executes.

Figure B.7 shows the first of four SEARCH structures. These statements complete the possible structure representations available under SALUT. The first structure is the SEARCH UNTIL with trailing test. All SEARCH structures execute four or five processes and, hence, can be used for more complex testing relationships. In Figure B.7 the process A1 is executed prior to the first test and following entry into the structure. All returns to the start label following a failure to exit from the loop will include the execution of this process. The first test takes place after execution of A1 and constitutes an exit from the "success" process if the condition results in a false comparison. If the test yields a true comparison the "success" process executes followed by an exit from the structure. When the exit from the "success" process occurs, A3 executes and the loop reaches the second test. If the second test yields a true result the structure repeats; however, a false comparison branches to the "failure" process and exits from the structure.

Figure B.8 is the SEARCH WHILE structure with leading test. Again, this structure includes two tests. The first executable code is the $LEAVE test which branches to the "failure" process when a true test result occurs. The A1 process is executed following a false test result. After A1 the $EXITIF branch takes place and a true result for this test results in execution of the "success" process. Once the "success" process is executed the structure exits the SEARCH mode. If the $EXITIF comparison yields a false result, the program branches to process A3, executes it, and then returns to the start of the SEARCH structure. In general either Figure B.7 or B.8 can be applied to virtually all dual test processes.

STRUCTURE	STATEMENTS	ASSEMBLER	COMMENTS
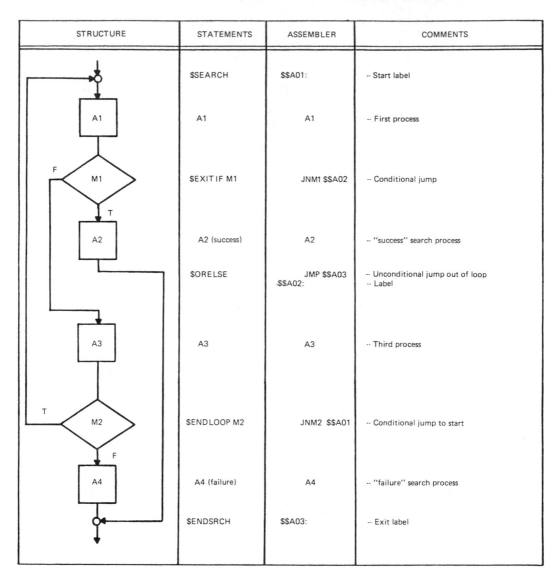	$SEARCH	$$A01:	-- Start label
	A1	A1	-- First process
	$EXITIF M1	JNM1 $$A02	-- Conditional jump
	A2 (success)	A2	-- "success" search process
	$ORELSE	JMP $$A03 $$A02:	-- Unconditional jump out of loop -- Label
	A3	A3	-- Third process
	$ENDLOOP M2	JNM2 $$A01	-- Conditional jump to start
	A4 (failure)	A4	-- "failure" search process
	$ENDSRCH	$$A03:	-- Exit label

Figure B.7   The SEARCH UNTIL structure with a trailing test.

Figures B.9 and B.10 illustrate two alternative configurations for the SEARCH COMPLEX structure with middle exit test. In the first structure (Figure B.9), process A1 always executes prior to the first structure, the $EXITIF branch. This latter structure branches to the "success" process, A2, if the test is true. Following execution of the "success" process the program exits the SEARCH structure. If the $EXITIF test is false the execution branches to process A3, executes, and tests for the "failure" process using $LEAVE. A true result for this second test yields the "failure"

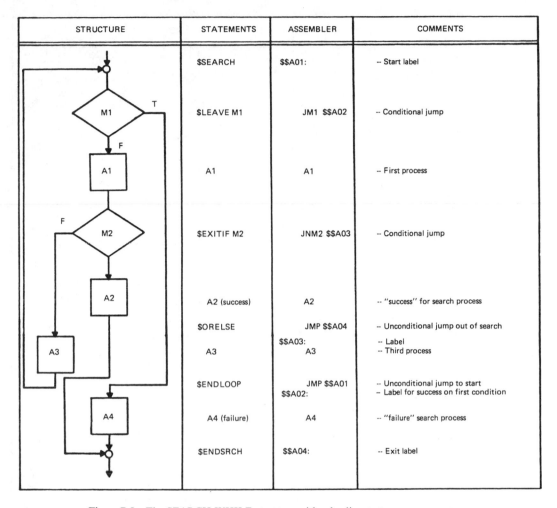

STRUCTURE	STATEMENTS	ASSEMBLER	COMMENTS
	$SEARCH	$$A01:	-- Start label
M1	$LEAVE M1	JM1 $$A02	-- Conditional jump
A1	A1	A1	-- First process
M2	$EXITIF M2	JNM2 $$A03	-- Conditional jump
A2	A2 (success)	A2	-- "success" for search process
	$ORELSE	JMP $$A04	-- Unconditional jump out of search
A3	A3	$$A03: A3	-- Label -- Third process
	$ENDLOOP	JMP $$A01 $$A02:	-- Unconditional jump to start -- Label for success on first condition
A4	A4 (failure)	A4	-- "failure" search process
	$ENDSRCH	$$A04:	-- Exit label

Figure B.8   The SEARCH WHILE structure with a leading test.

process while a false result causes process A4 to execute followed by a return to the beginning of the SEARCH.

Figure B.10 illustrates the second SEARCH structure with five processes. Entry to this structure occurs at the $STRTSRCH statement, which follows process A4. Again, process A1 executes followed by the $EXITIF test. Passing this test causes the "success" process to execute followed by an exit from the SEARCH structure. If this test fails, process A3 executes followed by the second test, $ENDLOOP. Failure of this second test causes the "failure" process to execute and then exit from the SEARCH structure. If the test fails, the execution returns to the beginning of the SEARCH process and process A4 executes.

STRUCTURE	STATEMENTS	ASSEMBLER	COMMENTS

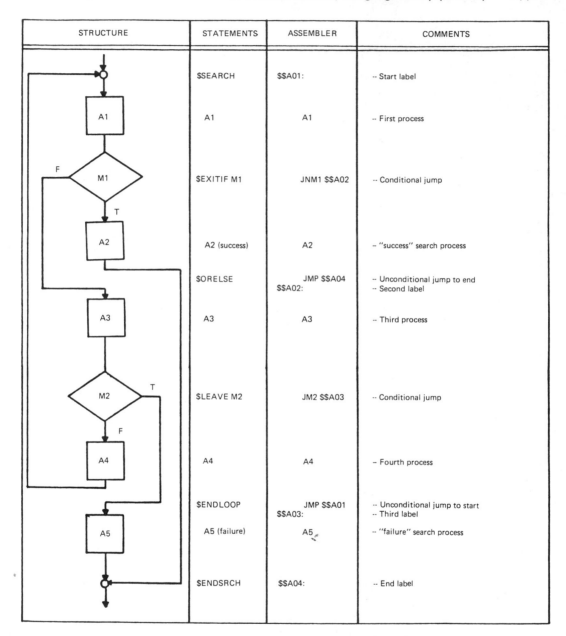

$SEARCH	$$A01:	-- Start label
A1	A1	-- First process
$EXITIF M1	JNM1 $$A02	-- Conditional jump
A2 (success)	A2	– "success" search process
$ORELSE	JMP $$A04 $$A02:	-- Unconditional jump to end -- Second label
A3	A3	-- Third process
$LEAVE M2	JM2 $$A03	-- Conditional jump
A4	A4	– Fourth process
$ENDLOOP	JMP $$A01 $$A03:	-- Unconditional jump to start -- Third label
A5 (failure)	A5	-- "failure" search process
$ENDSRCH	$$A04:	-- End label

Figure B.9   The SEARCH COMPLEX structure with a middle exit.

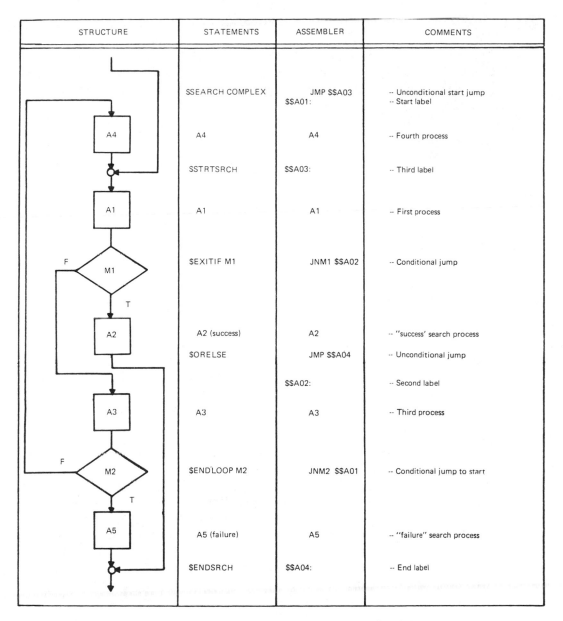

STRUCTURE	STATEMENTS	ASSEMBLER	COMMENTS
	$SEARCH COMPLEX	JMP $$A03	-- Unconditional start jump
		$$A01:	-- Start label
A4	A4	A4	-- Fourth process
	$STRTSRCH	$$A03:	-- Third label
A1	A1	A1	-- First process
M1	$EXITIF M1	JNM1 $$A02	-- Conditional jump
A2	A2 (success)	A2	-- "success' search process
	$ORELSE	JMP $$A04	-- Unconditional jump
		$$A02:	-- Second label
A3	A3	A3	-- Third process
M2	$END LOOP M2	JNM2 $$A01	-- Conditional jump to start
A5	A5 (failure)	A5	-- "failure" search process
	$ENDSRCH	$$A04:	-- End label

Figure B.10   The SEARCH COMPLEX structure with a middle exit loop.

While it is useful to describe the functional characteristics of the various SALUT structures, there is no substitute for actually casting a program in the framework of one or more of these artifacts. Only through repeated use of each of the SALUT structures can the programmer hope to develop a feel for this philosophy of programming. To repeat what was presented earlier, the goal of this book is to describe Macro Assembler and build on each stage of the preceding discussion.

B.2 A STRUCTURED PROGRAMMING EXAMPLE

The BRACKET.ASM program appearing in Figure 3.5a is a good candidate for simple modification to the structured format. This program has two loop structures and two conditional branching structures, with the outer loop structure implemented as a conditional branch. Since the loop structure has the form

```
         ...

     MOV CX,NUMBER

         ...

     LABEL:

         ...

     LOOP LABEL

         ...
```

it follows that only one loop can be nested using the LOOP instruction without PUSHing and POPing the CX register. Hence, the use of a conditional branch in the BRACKET program avoids the need for a PUSH and POP of CX for the outer loop.

Figure B.11 presents the modified BRACKET.ASM program as a .SAL program, BRACKET.SAL. This program (actually BRACKET2.SAL) has been run through the SALUT utility once to obtain the format modifications (indentation) available through SALUT. The reader should note that no jump statements appear in this .SAL program. Also, the absence of labels is rather pronounced and the downward flow of the program is easily read. Figure B.12 illustrates the SALUT session that was used to reformat the BRACKET.SAL program and generate a corresponding BRACKET.ASM program. This .ASM program is illustrated in Figure B.13. It should be noted that the .ASM program is different from the program in Figure 3.5a. In Figure B.13 the structure statements have been commented out with semicolons, and the utility replaced them with conditional jump statements: These instructions are the ones that must be interpreted by the assembler.

Several remarks are in order about the format of the programs that are input to SALUT. First

> All structure statements input to the SALUT utility must begin in column two or higher.

```
PAGE     40,132
TITLE    BRACKET - CALCULATES BRACKETED QUANTITIES(BRACKET.ASM)
;
;        DESCRIPTION: This routine calculates
;        the bracket values of the list TABLE1
;        contained in the data segment.
;
STACK    SEGMENT PARA STACK 'STACK'
                                             ;
         DB      64 DUP('STACK    ')
                                             ;
STACK    ENDS
                                             ;
DATA     SEGMENT PARA PUBLIC 'DATA'
                                             ;
TABLE1   DB      254,223,187,54,135,23,77,44,218,199
         DB      162,209,85,24,107,233,151,36,92,100
RANGEL   DB      0,51,101,151,201
RANGEU   DB      50,100,150,200,255
NUMB     DW      20
NUMR     DW      5
NUMTAB   DB      0,0,0,0,0
                                             ;
DATA     ENDS
                                             ;
CSEG     SEGMENT PARA PUBLIC 'CODE'
                                             ;
BRACKET PROC    FAR
         ASSUME  CS:CSEG,DS:DATA,SS:STACK
         PUSH    DS
         SUB     AX,AX
         PUSH    AX
                                             ;
         MOV     AX, SEG DATA                ;Load AX with DATA segment address
         MOV     DS,AX                       ;Load DS with address in AX
                                             ;
         MOV     SI,0                        ;Beginning list index
         MOV     BX,OFFSET TABLE1            ;Offset for list
         $DO
             MOV     DI,0                    ;Beginning bracket index
             MOV     CX,NUMR                 ;Load CX with bracket count
             MOV     DH,TABLE1[BX][SI]       ;Load DH with list value
             $DO
                 CMP     DH,RANGEL[DI]       ;Compare lower bracket edge
                 $IF     AE
                     CMP     DH,RANGEU[DI]
                     $IF     BE
                         INC     NUMTAB[DI] ;Increment bracket count
                     $ENDIF
                 $ENDIF
                 INC     DI                  ;Increment bracket index
             $ENDDO LOOP
             INC     SI                      ;Increment list index
             CMP     SI,NUMB
         $ENDDO AE
                                             ;
         RET
BRACKET ENDP
CSEG     ENDS
         END     BRACKET
```

Figure B.11   The SALUT Version of BRACKET (BRACKET.SAL).

```
      SALUT

      <C:\STRUCT>
      IBM Personal Computer SALUT Version 1.00
       Structured Assembly Language Utilities
            (C) Copyright IBM Corp, 1984

      F = Format Assembler Source
      P = Preprocess Structured Macros
      Q = Quit the program
      R = Replace tabs with blanks
      (a,b,c,d) = Set indent and tabs where:
        a=Structure indent  c=Operand column
        b=Opcode column      d=Remark column

      Enter your options: F,P

      Input filespec [C:\STRUCT\?????????.SAL]: BRACKET2

      Output filespec [C:\STRUCT\BRACKET2.SAL]:

      Prep filespec [C:\STRUCT\BRACKET2.ASM]:


      Input file will be renamed C:\STRUCT\BRACKET2.BAK


      F = Format Assembler Source
      P = Preprocess Structured Macros
      Q = Quit the program
      R = Replace tabs with blanks
      (a,b,c,d) = Set indent and tabs where:
        a=Structure indent  c=Operand column
        b=Opcode column      d=Remark column

      Enter your options: Q

      SALUT completed
```

Figure B.12   The SALUT session used to process BRACKET.SAL.

The importance of this caveat is that should a structure statement inadvertently begin in column 1, the utility will ignore the statement, treating it as a label. In all programs used with SALUT the comments are set off by semicolons as recommended. IBM does not recommend the use of the COMMENT pseudo-op with SALUT.

The MACRO pseudo-op causes the assembler source code to expand during pass 1. The figures presented in this appendix demonstrate that the assembler source code output from SALUT makes use of conditional jump statements to achieve branching. Since these jump statements are short-range the intervening source code cannot exceed 128 bytes unless the LONG option is used if permitted. It is very easy to expand source code beyond this range with macros and, consequently, caution must be employed when designing program code using SALUT if such expansion is to occur.

```
PAGE      40,132
TITLE     BRACKET - CALCULATES BRACKETED QUANTITIES(BRACKET.ASM)
;
;         DESCRIPTION: This routine calculates
;         the bracket values of the list TABLE1
;         contained in the data segment.
;
STACK     SEGMENT PARA STACK 'STACK'
                                               ;
          DB      64 DUP('STACK    ')
                                               ;
STACK     ENDS
                                               ;
DATA      SEGMENT PARA PUBLIC 'DATA'
                                               ;
TABLE1    DB      254,223,187,54,135,23,77,44,218,199
          DB      162,209,85,24,107,233,151,36,92,100
RANGEL    DB      0,51,101,151,201
RANGEU    DB      50,100,150,200,255
NUMB      DW      20
NUMR      DW      5
NUMTAB    DB      0,0,0,0,0
                                               ;
DATA      ENDS
                                               ;
CSEG      SEGMENT PARA PUBLIC 'CODE'
                                               ;
BRACKET PROC      FAR
        ASSUME    CS:CSEG,DS:DATA,SS:STACK
        PUSH      DS
        SUB       AX,AX
        PUSH      AX
                                               ;
        MOV       AX, SEG DATA          ;Load AX with DATA segment address
        MOV       DS,AX                 ;Load DS with address in AX
                                               ;
        MOV       SI,0                  ;Beginning list index
        MOV       BX,OFFSET TABLE1      ;Offset for list
;          $DO
$$DO1:
          MOV       DI,0                ;Beginning bracket index
          MOV       CX,NUMR             ;Load CX with bracket count
          MOV       DH,TABLE1[BX][SI]   ;Load DH with list value
          $DO
$$DO2:
              CMP     DH,RANGEL[DI]     ;Compare lower bracket edge
;             $IF     AE
              JNAE $$IF3
                  CMP     DH,RANGEU[DI]
;                 $IF     BE
                  JNBE $$IF4
                      INC     NUMTAB[DI] ;Increment bracket count
                  $ENDIF
$$IF4:
;                 $ENDIF
$$IF3:
                  INC     DI            ;Increment bracket index
;             $ENDDO  LOOP
              LOOP $$DO2
              INC     SI                ;Increment list index
              CMP     SI,NUMB
;          $ENDDO  AE
           JNAE $$DO1
                                               ;
          RET
BRACKET ENDP
CSEG    ENDS
        END       BRACKET
```

Figure B.13   The BRACKET.ASM file output from SALUT.

C
Interfacing Assembler and the C Language

C is a versatile and portable language that has great appeal in the microcomputer community because of its modular implementation and structured nature. This appendix illustrates how assembly language routines are used in conjunction with C programs. Since C is a higher-level language, it is plausible that the calling sequence would normally exist with C programs constituting the major software implementation, and assembly language routines serving to complement such programming where speed or special purpose hardware access is needed.

The version of C used in the example of this appendix is version 4.0 of the Microsoft C language. C programs are machine portable with the hardware interface contained in associated files included in the program that represent the standard C library for the machine in question. In the Microsoft version for the IBM microcomputers, there is a special-purpose include file, dos.h. This file contains many of the required hardware interface assembly language routines needed to interface to the BIOS code. Hence, a good understanding of the BIOS will allow the IBM microcomputer C programmer to accomplish a great deal of interfacing normally done with assembly language. The user, however, does not achieve a fully adequate understanding without some knowledge of the assembler.

For applications requiring optimized execution, assembly language is, of course, the preferred and only technique. A typical example would be the use of a Fast Fourier Transform (FFT) for performing spectral arithmetic in a real-time environment. Here the requisite throughput would dictate that assembly language be used for the FFT and the special purpose device driver which implements the analog-to-digital conversion (ADC). In database development, assembly language routines are still the preferred approach for rapid sorting and accessing of information.

The following discussion presents a C program which generates Gaussian random numbers and plots them on the display. This is a familiar problem that we dealt with in Chapter 5. The example differs in that the C program calls several assembly language routines to accomplish screen and keyboard interface. Finally, program code is presented which illustrates how this same assembly language code would be implemented in C as used on the IBM microcomputers. Central to this latter implementation is the inclusion of the dos.h file, which is written in assembly language by the compiler designers. As might be expected, the assembly language routines simply call the needed interrupts for display processing and the compiled code generated by the C program sequence is very similar. This example was selected for its familiarity and simplicity. While it does not necessarily show assembly language routines to have a distinct advantage over C code, which is actually easier to follow once the library files are assumed, it very clearly demonstrates the interface techniques.

Throughout this discussion it is assumed that the reader possesses some knowledge of the C language. Figure C.1 illustrates the major calling program with the function main(). This program calls four functions: box(), which generates the box and calls a tick mark function and sets up the 320×200 graphics mode; grand(), which generates the Gaussian random numbers; plotpoint(), which plots the points; and plotterm, which terminates the plot. In this plot 50 points are graphed.

```
/*Gaussian random number calling plot program*/

#include <stdio.h>
int xvalue[4] = {75,125,175,225};
int yvalue[1] = {100};
float xx[51];
float yy[51];
int n;
float num1,num2;

main()
        {
        box();
        for (n = 0; n <= 50; n++)
                {
              . xx[n] = (n*5.)+25.;
                grand();
                yy[n] = 100. - (num1*75./10.0);
                }
        for (n = 0; n <= 49; n++)
                plotpoint(xx[n],xx[n+1],yy[n],yy[n+1]);
        plotterm();
        }
```

Figure C.1   The main calling program for generating Gaussian random numbers, GAUSSCK.C (C language).

Figures C.2a and b illustrate the box and tick generators. These functions call three assembly language routines: SCRCL(), SC320(), and WRDOT(). All these routines were compiled or assembled separately, hence the "extern" declarations. They are linked in an identical fashion to the linking accomplished with assembly routines alone. Basically, the object code generated by the assembler MASM is identical in structure to that generated by the C compiler. Hence, the linker cannot distinguish between how the code was initially developed. In Figures C.2a and b, two of the procedures written in assembly language do not receive or return parameters to the calling function. The third procedure, WRDOT(), however, does pass parameters. Also, remember that in assembly language various segments must be defined. We must be sure that the form of the assembly language routines to be interfaced properly designates correct segment names. It is this linking of parameters and memory locations that must be correctly accomplished in order to allow the interface of assembly language to C compiled code.

```
/*
**      #include    <stdio.h>
**      int xvalue[4] = {75,125,175,225};
**      int yvalue[1] = {100};                          */
box()                                   /* This routine draws box*/
        {
        int row;
        int col;

        int xbeg = 25;
        int xend = 275;
        int ybeg = 25;
        int yend = 175;

        row = ybeg;             /*Initialize row*/
        col = xbeg;             /*Initialize col*/

        SCRCL();                /* Screen clear */
        SC320();                /* 320 x 200 mode */
                                /*Draw left vertical line*/
        for (row = ybeg; row <= yend; row++)
                WRDOT(row,col);
        row = row - 1;
                                /*Draw bottom horizontal line*/
        for (col = xbeg; col <= xend; col++)
                WRDOT(row,col);
        col = col - 1;
                                /*Draw right vertical line*/
        for (row = yend; row >= ybeg; row--)
                WRDOT(row,col);
        row = row + 1;
                                /*Draw top horizontal line*/
        for (col = xend; col >= xbeg; col--)
                WRDOT(row,col);
        col = col + 1;
                                /*Draw ticks*/
        tick();


        }
```

Figure C.2a   The C function box() used to generate a box and tick marks on the display.

```
tick()
        {
        int sxtick = 173;
        int extick = 177;
        int sytick = 23;
        int eytick = 27;
        int n,row,col;

        extern int xvalue[],yvalue[];

        for (n = 0; n <= 3; n++)
                {
                col = xvalue[n];
                for (row = sxtick; row <= extick; row++)
                        WRDOT(row,col);
                }

        row = yvalue[0];
        for (col = sytick; col <= eytick; col++)
                WRDOT(row,col);
        }
```

Figure C.2b   The C function tick() called by box() and used for the actual tick mark creation.

The first of the two needed conventions, indicated above, is the technique for passing parameters when calling an assembly language routine from a C procedure. These parameters are passed using a stack frame located in high memory and set up by the compiler. When an assembly language routine that is set up as a C function receives control through a C function call, the routine must preserve BP, SI, and DI; set BP = SP; and save any other registers whose contents are modified by the assembly language code.

Parameters passed to the assembly language routine are positive offsets from the stack-frame pointer. This pointer locates the beginning of the stack frame for the called routine. Each C function has an associated stack frame that contains the location of all parameters. When entering a called routine, the new code must first preserve the old stack frame pointer because at exit this must be restored. Hence, upon entry a PUSH BP must be implemented. Next the new stack frame pointer must be placed in BP. Since this is located in SP, a simple MOV BP, SP accomplishes this task. Finally, local variables are at negative offsets from SP, and SP must be reallocated to allow for these variables (plus SI and DI in version 4.0). Knowledge of the byte size for local variables allows this allocation to be performed. For example, if four-word-size local variables are used, eight bytes must be preserved as well as two bytes each for SI and DI. Hence, the instruction SUB SP,12 is needed.

Located on the stack frame (which is now pointed to by BP) are two bytes for the calling routine's BP register, bytes BP and BP + 1. Also, the offset (NEAR call) or offset plus segment (FAR call) are loaded at BP + 2 and BP + 3 (offset) and PB + 4 and BP + 5 (segment). Thus, parameters cannot begin loading until BP + 4 (NEAR call) or BP + 6 (FAR call) is loaded. Parameters are then loaded in the order that they are encountered in the calling program. This is very important because it is the only knowledge provided for understanding parameter order. Upon exit, all registers must be restored and any values returned use the AX and DX registers.

In Microsoft C, any C variable can be accessed by the assembler if the name is preceded by an underscore. For example, the function WRDOT, called in a C program, has an assembler representation _WRDOT. This is how the second needed convention is implemented. In the event that the assembly language routine modifies SS, CS, or DS, these registers must be saved. (SS and DS are usually equal in C programs.) When the Microsoft C compiler generates object code, an assembler equivalency can be developed. This equivalency illustrates that the C code for SMALL memory model uses _TEXT as the code segment label and _DATA as the data segment label. These labels can then be preserved to insure that called assembly language routines access the proper segments. Once in assembly language, changes in various segment addresses can then be properly controlled.

```
PAGE 40,132
TITLE SCRCL - SCREEN CLEAR FOR CALL FROM "C"
;
;          DESCRIPTION: This routine clears the screen when called
;          from a C program.  The stack is preserved.
;
_TEXT    SEGMENT BYTE PUBLIC 'CODE'
         ASSUME CS:_TEXT
         PUBLIC _SCRCL
_SCRCL   PROC    NEAR
                                          ;
BEGIN1:  PUSH BP                          ;save caller's frame pointer
         MOV BP,SP                        ;frame pointer to old BP
         SUB SP,8                         ;allocate local variable on stack
         PUSH DI
         PUSH SI
         PUSH AX
         PUSH BX
         PUSH CX
         PUSH DX
                                          ;
         MOV AH,6                         ;Scroll active page up
         MOV AL,0                         ;Blanks entire page
         MOV CX,0                         ;(CH,CL)=(row,column) up left
         MOV DH,23                        ;Row lower right
         MOV DL,79                        ;Column lower right
         MOV BH,7                         ;Blank attribute
         INT 10H
                                          ;
         POP DX
         POP CX
         POP BX
         POP AX
         POP SI
         POP DI
         MOV SP,BP
         POP BP
                                          ;
         RET
                                          ;
_SCRCL   ENDP
_TEXT    ENDS
         END
```

Figure C.3   The assembly language routine, SCRCL, used to clear the screen.

Figures C.3, C.4, and C.5 are the assembly language routines needed by box(). Note that only a code segment is indicated. In C.5, the row and column values are at $BP+4$ and $BP+6$, respectively. Figure C.6 contains the C code for generating the Gaussian random number, plotting the points (again, using WRDOT), and terminating the plot with a return to the normal 80×25 mode. Note that the code in each of these C functions is greatly simplified over the assembler code developed in the examples in this book. This is as it should be with the emphasis on assembly language for driver programming and high-speed application requirements. Figures C.7 and C.8 illustrate the last two assembly language routines needed by the function plotterm(). Finally, Figure C.9 presents the C code equivalent to each of the assembly language functions described previously. It is clear that the library function, int86(), is the key to this code. This routine resides in the library file dos.h and is, of course, written in assembler. Also, the union REGS is needed. Figure C.10 illustrates the graphic output for these programs, which is identical whether the assembly language or C programs are used.

```
PAGE 40,132
TITLE SC320 - ROUTINE TO SET 320 X 200 GRAPHICS MODE
;
;         DESCRIPTION: Sets the 320 x 200 graphics mode
;
_TEXT     SEGMENT BYTE PUBLIC 'CODE'
          ASSUME CS:_TEXT
          PUBLIC _SC320
_SC320    PROC    NEAR
                                              ;
          PUSH BP                             ;save caller's frame pointer
          MOV BP,SP                           ;frame pointer to old BP
          SUB SP,8                            ;allocate local variable space
          PUSH DI
          PUSH SI
          PUSH AX
          PUSH BX
          PUSH CX
          PUSH DX
                                              ;
          MOV AH,0                            ;Set mode
          MOV AL,5                            ;320 x 200 graphics mode
          INT 10H                             ;Interrupt
                                              ;
          POP DX
          POP CX
          POP BX
          POP AX
          POP SI
          POP DI
          MOV SP,BP
          POP BP
                                              ;
          RET
_SC320    ENDP
_TEXT     ENDS
          END
```

Figure C.4 The assembly language routine, SC320, used to set up the 320×200 graphics mode.

```
PAGE 40,132
TITLE WRDOT - ROUTINE TO WRITE DOT
;
;        DESCRIPTION: This routine writes a dot at the row = [BP+4] and
;        column = [BP+6] since the function call is NEAR.
;
_TEXT    SEGMENT BYTE PUBLIC 'CODE'
         ASSUME CS:_TEXT
         PUBLIC   _WRDOT
_WRDOT   PROC     NEAR
                                                 ;
         PUSH BP                                 ;save caller's frame pointer
         MOV BP,SP                               ;frame pointer to old BP
         SUB SP,8                                ;allocate local variable space
         PUSH DI
         PUSH SI
         PUSH AX
         PUSH BX
         PUSH CX
         PUSH DX
                                                 ;
         MOV DX,[BP+4]                           ;Row value
         MOV CX,[BP+6]                           ;Column value
         MOV AL,1                                ;Attribute 1
         MOV AH,12                               ;Write dot
         INT 10H                                 ;Interrupt
                                                 ;
         POP DX
         POP CX
         POP BX
         POP AX
         POP SI
         POP DI
         MOV SP,BP
         POP BP
                                                 ;
         RET
                                                 ;
_WRDOT   ENDP
_TEXT    ENDS
         END
```

Figure C.5   The assembly language routine, WRDOT, used to write a dot on the screen.

```
/*Gaussian random number pair*/

#include <stdlib.h>
#include <math.h>

grand()
        {
        extern float num1,num2;
        double x1,x2,pi = 3.141592654,arg1,arg2,x,y;
        double z,w;

        x1 = rand();
        x2 = rand();
        x1 = x1/32767.;
        x2 = x2/32767.;

        y = x1;
        x = -2.*log(y);
        arg1 = sqrt(x);
        z = 2.*pi*x2;
        arg2 = sin(z);
        num1 = arg1*arg2;
        w = z;
        arg2 = cos(w);
        num2 = arg1*arg2;

        }
/* This routine plots a connecting line*/

plotpoint (x1,x2,y1,y2)
        float x1,x2,y1,y2;

        {
        float m;
        int row;
        int col;

        if (x1 == x2)
                m = 1000;                       /*Upper limit on slope*/

        else
                m = (y2 - y1)/(x2 - x1);

        for (col = x1; col <= x2; col++)
                {
                row = y1 + m*(col - x1);
                WRDOT(row,col);
                }
        }
/*Assembler calls to return to 80 x 25 mode with delay*/

plotterm()
        {
        KEYDEL();
        SC80();
        }
```

Figure C.6   The C language functions grand(), plotpoint(), and plotterm().

```
PAGE 40,132
TITLE KEYDEL - KEYBOARD DELAY
;
;       DESCRIPTION: This routine waits for a keyboard interrupt
;       to continue the processing.
;
_TEXT   SEGMENT BYTE PUBLIC 'CODE'
        ASSUME CS:_TEXT
        PUBLIC _KEYDEL
_KEYDEL PROC    NEAR
                                        ;
        PUSH BP                         ;Save caller's frame pointer
        MOV BP,SP                       ;Frame pointer to old BP
        SUB SP,8                        ;Allocate local variable space
        PUSH DI
        PUSH SI
        PUSH AX
        PUSH BX
        PUSH CX
        PUSH DX

        MOV AH,0                        ;
        INT 16H                         ;Keyboard interrupt
                                        ;Wait for keystroke to continue
        POP DX                          ;
        POP CX
        POP BX
        POP AX
        POP SI
        POP DI
        MOV SP,BP
        POP BP
                                        ;
        RET
_KEYDEL ENDP
_TEXT   ENDS
        END
```

Figure C.7 The assembly language routine, KEYDEL, used to generate a screen delay.

```
PAGE 40,132
TITLE SC80 - ROUTINE TO SET 80 X 25 ALPHA MODE
;
;        DESCRIPTION: Calls interrupt to set 80 x 25 alpha mode
;
_TEXT    SEGMENT BYTE PUBLIC 'CODE'
         ASSUME CS:_TEXT
         PUBLIC _SC80
_SC80    PROC    NEAR

                                        ;
         PUSH BP                        ;Save caller's frame pointer
         MOV BP,SP                      ;Frame pointer to old BP
         SUB SP,8                       ;Allocate local variable space
         PUSH DI
         PUSH SI
         PUSH AX
         PUSH BX
         PUSH CX
         PUSH DX

                                        ;
         MOV AH,0                       ;Set mode
         MOV AL,2                       ;80 x 24 alpha B/W mode
         INT 10H                        ;Interrupt
                                        ;
         POP DX
         POP CX
         POP BX
         POP AX
         POP SI
         POP DI
         MOV SP,BP
         POP BP

                                        ;
         RET
_SC80    ENDP
_TEXT    ENDS
         END
```

Figure C.8   The assembly language routine, SC80, used to return to 80 × 25 alpha
mode.

```
/* This file, CPLOT.C, contains plot routines written in C */

#include <dos.h>

SCRCL()                                  /* Function to clear screen */
        {
        union REGS regs;

        regs.h.ah = 6;                   /* Scroll active page up */
        regs.h.al = 0;                   /* Blanks entire page */
        regs.h.ch = 0;                   /* row = 0 upper left */
        regs.h.cl = 0;                   /* column = 0 upper left */
        regs.h.dh = 23;                  /* row lower right */
        regs.h.dl = 79;                  /* col lower right */
        regs.h.bh = 7;                   /* Blank attribute */

        int86(0x10,&regs,&regs);
        }

WRDOT(row,col)                           /* Function to write dot-graphics */
        int row,col;

        {
        union REGS regs;

        regs.x.dx = row;                 /* Row value */
        regs.x.cx = col;                 /* Column value */
        regs.h.al = 1;                   /* Attribute 1 */
        regs.h.ah = 12;                  /* Write dot */

        int86(0x10,&regs,&regs);
        }

SC320()                                  /* Function to set graphics mode */
        {
        union REGS regs;

        regs.h.ah = 0;                   /* Set mode */
        regs.h.al = 5;                   /* 320 x 200 graphics mode */

        int86(0x10,&regs,&regs);
        }

SC80()                                   /* Function to set alpha mode */
        {
        union REGS regs;

        regs.h.ah = 0;                   /* Set mode */
        regs.h.al = 2;                   /* 80 x 25 BW alpha mode */

        int86(0x10,&regs,&regs);
        }

KEYDEL()                                 /* Function set delay */
        {
        union REGS regs;

        regs.h.ah = 0;                   /* Keyboard interrupt */

        int86(0x16,&regs,&regs);         /* Wait for keystroke */
        }
```

Figure C.9 The C language function equivalents for SCRCL, WRDOT, SC320, SC80, and KEYDEL.

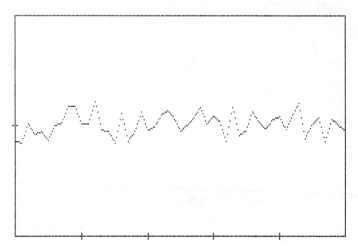

Figure C.10 The output graph from GAUSSCK.EXE illustrating the plot of 50 Gaussian random numbers.

Answers to Selected
Odd-Numbered Problems

CHAPTER 1

1.1. In general, compilers tend to have structured methods for interpreting sequences of instructions. Frequently syntax can be rigid and cumbersome because of the flexibility needed to interpret code from among many program options. Hence, the equivalent assembler generated in conjunction with compiler object code is usually not optimized. As languages become more structured and organized, the compiled code will more closely approximate assembly language code designed to perform the same function.

1.3. The 8259A outputs an interrupt vector to the CPU on the data bus. This vector is a number between 0 and 255. The vector is multiplied by 4 to point to an address in memory at which is located an interrupt service routine. Similarly, when a software interrupt takes place, such as INT 10H, the vector is 10H, and this is multiplied by 4 to yield the address at which a second address for the service routine corresponding to the Video I/O processing is located. The vector 10H, when multiplied by 4, yields an address, 0040H, as offset, and these are located at segment 0000H.

1.5. In this instruction the contents of a 16-bit register, BX, are being subtracted from an 8-bit register, AL.

1.7. (a) 5387 is

$$0001\ 0101\ 0000\ 1011 \quad \text{(binary)}$$
$$150B \quad \text{(hexadecimal)}$$

(b) 254 is

$$0000\ 0000\ 1111\ 1110 \quad \text{(binary)}$$
$$00FE \quad \text{(hexadecimal)}$$

(c) 1024 is

$$0000\ 0100\ 0000\ 0000\ \text{(binary)}$$
$$0400\ \text{(hexadecimal)}$$

(d) 512 is

$$0000\ 0010\ 0000\ 0000\ \text{(binary)}$$
$$0200\ \text{(hexadecimal)}$$

(e) 32768 is

$$1000\ 0000\ 0000\ 0000\ \text{(binary)}$$
$$8000\ \text{(hexadecimal)}$$

1.9. (a) F3F2
     (b) E0E0
     (c) 1F20
     (d) 201
     (e) 8002

1.11. The maximum value that a 32-bit register can hold is approximately

$$4.2949673 \times 10^9\ \text{(unsigned maximum)}.$$

Signed arithmetic allows values between (approximately)

$$-2.1474836 \times 10^9 \quad \text{and} \quad +2.1474836 \times 10^9$$

(signed range).

1.13. Two hexadecimal digits are needed to specify a byte: FF (hexadecimal) is equal to 255. Four hexadecimal digits are needed to specify a word: FFFF (hexadecimal) is 65535.

CHAPTER 2

2.1. The 8088 has an 8-bit data bus; hence, it is intended to interface with chips having 8-bit registers. The instruction

OUT DX,AX

moves the contents of AX (a 16-bit register) onto the data bus at address DX = ADDRESS_IO. Clearly, output of a 16-bit data variable is not allowed with a single move. The 16-bit register is allowed with 8086 machines.

2.3. Using the segment-offset notation, the following addresses are allowed for the IBM PC and XT or any 8086-family computer: (a) allowed (FF221H), (b) not allowed, (c) not allowed, (d) allowed (FF100H), and (e) allowed (FEFF0H).

2.5. The Flag register settings must reflect the Carry Flag being set and the Auxiliary Carry Flag being set. Flag register values: (a) allowed, (b) not allowed, and (c) not allowed.

2.7. Using two's complement arithmetic yields (a) F000H, (b) 9B8AH, and (c) F200H.

2.9. The instructions are incorrect as follows:
     (a) MOV 18D,AX A variable cannot be moved into an immediate location.
     (b) SUB BX,AL An 8-bit quantity cannot be subtracted from a 16-bit value.
     (c) MOV CX,BH An 8-bit value cannot move into a 16-bit location (register).
     (d) SUB 21D,17D An immediate value cannot be subtracted from an immediate value.
     (e) MOV AX,70000D 70000D is larger than a 16-bit value (max 65535).

2.11. The CS register changes under DOS when the program initially begins with a FAR jump from the Program Segment Prefix area. Similarly, it returns to this area with a FAR return at the conclusion of the program. Both these changes are controlled by DOS. The assigned segment register values are determined by the linker during linking. Actually two functions take place during the link process: All needed routines are linked together and they are located relative to each other with known addresses.

2.13. (a) F060H, (b) 1C20H, (c) 0, and (d) 1900H.

2.15. Using segment override.

```
            ...
DATAES    SEGMENT PARA PUBLIC 'DATA'
          D1D DW 2400
DATAES    ENDS
            ...
CSEG      SEGMENT PARA PUBLIC 'CODE'
START     PROC FAR
          ASSUME CS:CSEG, DS:DATA, SS:STACK, ES:DATAES
            ...
          MOV AX,SEG DATAES
          MOV ES,AX
            ...
          MOV BX,00H
          MOV AX,ES:[BX]
            ...
```

CHAPTER 3

3.1. 70–100 lines of code.

3.3. When a separately assembled module has its own data or extra segment, these segment variables are only accessible while the segment address is loaded in the correct segment register. Hence a module can be expected to have its own data or extra segment *only* when the variables associated with that segment are not required by other modules, which use variables from other segments. The usual approach would be to specify, for example, a single data segment and use this segment throughout the program. Variables in a data segment, which changes during program execution, remain fixed as the segment changes from one module to another. This is because these variables reside at unique memory locations that can always be found upon entry of the proper segment address into the corresponding segment register. The extra segment solves many of the problems alluded to above because it provides an area for local module storage. Essentially, the programmer can fix the data segment address and change the extra segment address to accommodate variables associated only with a given module. Aside from the data segment, some parameters passing between modules can be accomplished via the CPU registers.

3.5. Changing modules can involve using the stack to hold parameter values. Using this approach, attention must be paid to the nature of the module call. If the module is located in a NEAR code segment, only the offset address is pushed on the stack. If the module call was to a FAR segment, both the segment and offset addresses are pushed on the stack. All changes in module execution must preserve the first two bytes (NEAR call) or first four bytes (FAR call) upon entry into the new module. Only at addresses below these locations can parameter data be accessed.

3.7. In the situation where a module at the next lower level is subordinated to two modules at the level being considered, in a structure chart, some method must be defined for handling cases where the lower level module exists as a single subordinate module. Normally this might occur for only one of the higher modules but the function still must be illustrated in the corresponding structure chart. Several approaches are possible. One could avoid repeating the common module and could cross-connect from each higher level. The preferred approach is to darken the upper right-hand corner of the common module

and carry it forward under each higher level module. In some cases this can result in an occurrence of a single lower level module.

3.9. The GO TO construct allows virtually unlimited movement within a program. If programming is undisciplined, the development can lead to jumps in logic back and forth in the code with no clear progression towards the end. Readers familiar with patching are used to seeing these quick fixes with unconditional branching around intervening code. Such a style makes following the logic of a program very difficult. As programming theory developed, the need to avoid such unrestrained motion was seen as paramount. Structured concepts favored the elimination of the GO TO. It was found that motion forward and backward was needed but in a formal sense. Backward motion implied the execution of the same code in repeated fashion. Loops were defined for this task. Similarly, forward motion, other than normal execution, required a branching or decision capability. The CASE-type structure developed for this task.

3.11. A set of guidelines could be as follows:
1. Use BEGIN and END to delineate the beginning and end of the program and indent intervening code.
2. Mark all loops by beginning LOOP... and end ENDLOOP, and indent each loop in a structured manner.
3. All flow of execution must be downward except for loops.
4. Each execution line must contain a single action.
5. Conditional branching must be accomplished using single tests or comparisons and must branch downward to end with an ENDIF. These conditionals should have the construct

$$(IF)...(THEN)...(ELSE)...ENDIF$$

6. Conditional code should be structurally indented.
7. Pseudo code should reflect one task.
8. Pseudo code should start with a basic idea and then be filled out with complete task descriptions. At completion, the pseudo code should be close to one-to-one with assembler code. The pseudo code will be suitable for comments.

3.13. (See Figure for 3.13)

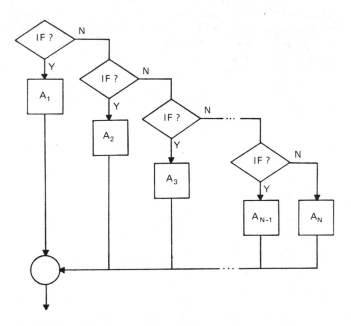

Figure for CASE-type structure (problem 3.13).

CHAPTER 4

4.1.   (a) 1234H
     (b) NEG AX = EDCCH
        NEG BX = undefined
     (c) FFFFH
     (d) EDCBH

4.3.

```
        ...
            MOV CX,ALE                ; ALEN = word variable
DO1:
            MOV SI,OFFSET ARRAY       ; ARRAY = string buffer
REP         MOV AL,DS:[SI]
            XOR AL,46H                ; IF1-compare with F
            JNZ IF1
                MOV AH,1              ; THEN1-set if F
IF1:                                  ; End IF
        LOOP DO1                      ; End DO
        ...
```

4.5.

```
        ...
        MOV CX,NUM1
DO1:
            PUSH CX
            MOV CX,NUM2
DO2:
                ...
        LOOP DO2
        POP CX
        LOOP DO1
        ...
```

4.7. Since the procedure PROC1 can change the status of CX, as well as other registers, these registers should be preserved on the stack. This can be accomplished in either the calling program or the procedure itself. The latter method is preferred because the procedure keeps track of what registers it uses and "knows" to PUSH and POP those registers upon entry and exit, respectively. Modifying the calling program in this example yields

```
        ...
        MOV CX,NUM1
DO1:
            ...
            PUSH CX
            CALL PROC1
            POP CX
            ...
        LOOP DO1
        ...
```

4.9. The fact that a second data segment address is loaded into DS upon entry to CHECK destroys the default offset for AA1. This variable cannot be accessed via the call to CHECK.

4.11.

```
...
MOV AX,LN[BX]
MOV BX,10000
SUB BX,AX
OR  BX,8000H
MOV AX,BX
...
```

4.13. The procedure for doing this would be identical to LNLOG except the look-up table would change to reflect the new range of numbers with appropriate input scaling. You cannot use LNLOG because

$$\log_{10} x = \log_e x / \log_e 10$$

and it is impossible to scale the LNLOG output so that significance can be kept in the division. In a later chapter, routines with greater than 16-bit accuracy will be considered.

CHAPTER 5

5.1.

```
                    ...
        EXTERN      LINEV:FAR,LINEH:FAR

                                                ;
                                                ; Assume YBEG,YEND,XBEG,
                                                ; and XEND initially loaded
                                                ; Add XSTART,XWIDTH,HEIGHT
                    ...
        CBOX        SEGMENT PARA PUBLIC 'CODE'
        BAR         PROC FAR
                    ASSUME CS:CBOX,DS:DATABOX
                    MOV XSTART,AX               ; X-origin
                    MOV XWIDTH,DX               ; X-width
                    MOV HEIGHT,BX               ; Bar height
                    MOV X,AX                    ; Fix X-axis position
                    MOV XBEG,AX                 ; Reload XBEG
                    MOV AX,YBEG                 ; Y-axis beginning
                    ADD AX,HEIGHT               ; Height bar
                    MOV YEND,AX                 ; Define and
                    CALL LINEV
                    MOV AX,X                    ; Fix beginning x-axis
                    ADD AX,XWIDTH               ; Add width
                    MOV X,AX                    ; Fix X-axis position and
                    MOV XEND,AX                 ;
                    CALL LINEV                  ; Draw 2nd line
                    MOV AX.YEND                 ;
                    MOV Y,AX
                    CALL LINEH                  ; Draw horizontal line
                    RET
        BAR         ENDP
                    ...
```

5.3.

```
                    ...
        MESOUT      DB 'Input Y-terminate or N-continue'
                    DB '$'
        BUFFMX      DB 80
        BUFFLN      DB ?
        CHAR        DB 80 DUP(' ')
                    DB '$'
                    ...
        CHECK       PROC FAR
                    ASSUME CS:CSEG, DS:DATA, SS:STACK
        DO1:                                    ;
                    LEA DX,MESOUT               ; Write prompt
                    MOV AH,9                    ; Function 9
                    INT 21H
                                                ;
```

```
                MOV AH,6              ; Line feed
                MOV DL,0AH
                INT 21H
                                     ; Carriage return

                MOV AH,6
                MOV DL,0DH
                INT 21H
                                     ;
                LEA DX,BUFFMX        ; Read keyboard
                MOV AH,10
                INT 21H
                MOV AH,6             ; Line feed
                MOV DL,0AH
                INT 21H
                                     ;
                MOV AH,6             ; Carriage return
                MOV DL, 0DH
                INT 21H

                MOV AL,CHAR[0]       ; Load character
                CMP AL,59H           ; Compare Y
                JZ IF1
                CMP AL,4EH           ; Compare N
                JNZ DO1
                ...                  ; N result
IF1:            ...                  ; Y result
                ...
```

5.5.

```
        ...
        MOV CH,HOURS
        MOV CL,MIN
        MOV DH,SEC
        MOV DL,HSEC
        MOV AH,2DH
        INT 21H
        ...
```

5.7.

```
        ...
        MOV AH, 2AH
        INT 21H
        MOV DAYW,AL     ; Day of week
        MOV YEAR,CX     ; Year
        MOV MON,DH      ; Month
        MOV DAYM,DL     ; Day of month
        ...
```

5.9. Using DOS function calls.

```
...
MOV DL,CHAR      ; Load character
MOV AH,4
INT 21H
...
```

Using INT 14H.

```
...
MOV AL,CHAR      ; Load character
MOV AH,1
INT 14H
...
```

5.11. Using DOS Function calls.

```
...
MOV AH,7
INT 21H
MOV CHAR,AL
...
```

Using INT 16H.

```
...
MOV AH,0
INT 14H
MOV CHAR,AL
...
```

CHAPTER 6

6.1. Based on the BIOS Beep procedure.

```
BEEP       MACRO
           LOCAL G7
           PUSH AX
           PUSH BX
           PUSH CX
           PUSH DX
           MOV BL,6
           MOV AL,C8H
           OUT 43H,AL          ; Timer-Mode Register
           MOV AX,533H         ; Divisor for 1000Hz
           OUT 42H,AL          ; Timer 2CNT-LSB
           MOV AL,AH
```

```
                OUT 42H,AL              ; Timer 2 CNT-MSB
                IN  AL,61H              ; Setting of Port
                MOV AH,AL
                OR  AL,03               ; Turn speaker on
                OUT 61H,AL
                SUB CX,CX
        G7      LOOP G7
                DEC BL                  ; Delay CNT Expired
                JNZ G7
                MOV AL,AH
                OUT 61H,AL
                POP DX
                POP CX
                POP BX
                POP AX
        BEEP    ENDM
6.3.


        CKNUM   MACRO
                LOCAL IF1
        ;
        ;       Byte is assumed in AL
        ;
                MOV AH,2DH              ; Check minus sign
                CMP AL,AH
                JZ  IF1
                MOV AH,30H              ; Check 0
                CMP AL,AH
                JZ  IF1
                MOV AH,31H              ; Check 1
                CMP AL,AH
                JZ  IF1
                MOV AH,32H              ; Check 2
                CMP AL,AH
                JZ  IF1
                MOV AH,33H              ; Check 3
                CMP AL,AH
                JZ  IF1
                MOV AH,34H              ; Check 4
                CMP AL,AH
                JZ  IF1
                MOV AH,35H              ; Check 5
                CMP AL,AH
                JZ  IF1
                MOV AH,36H              ; Check 6
                CMP AL,AH
                JZ  IF1
                MOV AH,37H              ; Check 7
                CMP AL,AH
                JZ  IF1
```

```
                MOV AH,38H          ; Check 8
                CMP AL,AH
                JZ IF1
                MOV AH,39H          ; Check 9
                CMP AL,AH
                JZ IF1
                JMP CONT
IF1:
                LEA DX,MESOER       ; Error message
                MOV AH,9
                INT 21H
                RET
CONT:
CKNUM   ENDM
```

6.5.

```
CUBE    MACRO X
;
;       The number to be cubed is X
;
                PUSH AX
                PUSH BX
                PUSH DX
                MOV AX,X            ; Number in X
                MOV BX,X
                MUL BX
                MUL BX
                MOV X,AX            ; Return cube in X
                POP DX
                POP BX
                POP AX
CUBE    ENDM
```

6.7. Horizontal Line.

```
HLINE       MACRO XBEG, XEND, Y
            LOCAL DO1
;
;           Horizontal line...assumes 320 × 200 graphics
;           Y = y-axis position
;
                PUSH DX
                PUSH BX
                PUSH AX
                PUSH CX
                MOV DX,Y
                MOV DX,XBEG
DO1:
                MOV AH,12           ; DO1
                MOV AL,1
```

```
                         INT 10H
                         ADD  CX,1
                         MOV   BX,CX
                         SUB  BX,XEND
                         JNE  DO1
                      POP CX
                      POP AX
                      POP BX
                      POP DX
HLINE            ENDM
```

Vertical Line.

```
VLINE            MACRO YBEG,YEND,X
                 LOCAL DO1
;
;                Vertical Line...assumes 320 × 200 graphics
;                X = x-axis position
;
                 PUSH DX
                 PUSH BX
                 PUSH AX
                 PUSH CX
                 MOV CX,X
                 MOV DX,YBEG
DO1:
                    MOV AH,12
                    MOV AL,1
                    INT 10H
                    ADD DX,1
                    MOV BX,DX
                    SUB BX,YEND
                    JNE DO1
                 POP CX
                 POP AX
                 POP BX
                 POP DX
VLINE            ENDM
```

6.9. Line Feed.

```
LF    MACRO
      MOV AH,6
      MOV DL,0AH
      INT 21H
LF    ENDM
```

```
PAGE      55,132
TITLE     ASCDEC1 - ASCII TO DECIMAL AND REVERSE
;
;         DESCRIPTION: These procedures convert ASCII to decimal
;         and vice versa.
;
EXTRN     ASC:BYTE,BINV:WORD,CCOUNT:WORD,BUFFLN:BYTE,BASE:WORD
;
CSEG      SEGMENT PARA PUBLIC 'CODE'
          PUBLIC  ASCDEC,DECASC
;
;         This procedure converts decimal to ASCII. BINV is
;         the internal decimal number and ASC is the output
;         ASCII array.
;
DECASC    PROC    FAR
          ASSUME  CS:CSEG

          PUSH    DS                       ;
          PUSH    AX
          PUSH    BX
          PUSH    CX
          PUSH    DX
          PUSH    SI

          MOV     AX,0                     ;
          MOV     AX,BINV                  ;Load AX number (-32765,32765)
          PUSH    AX
          MOV     SI, OFFSET ASC[5]        ;Initialize with ASCII char. max
          MOV     CX,10                    ;Divide base factor
                                           ;
          OR      AX,AX                    ;Set or clear sign flag
          JNS     DO1
          SHL     AX,1                     ;Clear sign bit
          SHR     AX,1                     ;Move number back to normal
DO1:
          CMP         AX,10                ;Cmp with base value
          JB          OUT1
          MOV         DX,0                 ;Clear upper num reg
          DIV         CX
          ADD         DL,30H               ;Convert to ASCII
          MOV         [SI],DL              ;Save at ASC ptr value
          DEC         SI
          JMP         DO1
OUT1:
          ADD     AL,30H                   ;Convert last ASCII character
          MOV     [SI],AL                  ;load zero in last ASCII char.

          POP     AX                       ;
          OR      AX,AX                    ;Recall initial number/sign check
          JNS     IF1                      ;Set sign flag if negative number
                  DEC         SI
                  MOV         BL,2DH       ;Load "minus"
                  MOV         [SI],BL      ;Store "minus" in out char.
IF1:
          MOV     AX,6                     ;Save fixed ASCII char. count
          MOV     CCOUNT,AX                ;Keep ASCII count at 6 characters
                                           ;
          POP     SI
          POP     DX
          POP     CX
          POP     BX
          POP     AX
          POP     DS
                                           ;
          RET
DECASC    ENDP
                                           ;
```

Routine corresponding to Problem 6.11.

```
ASCDEC  PROC    FAR
;
;       This procedure converts ASCII to internal decimal. ASC
;       is the input ASCII array and BINV is the output internal
;       decimal number.
;
        PUSH    DS
        PUSH    AX
        PUSH    BX
        PUSH    CX
        PUSH    DX
        PUSH    SI
                                                ;
        MOV     BINV,0                          ;Initialize output
        MOV     BL,BUFFLN                       ;Load buffer length
        MOV     BH,0                            ;Clear upper BX register
        MOV     CX,10                           ;Decimal base multiplier
        LEA     SI,ASC-1                        ;Load SI with characters - 1
        MOV     DI,0                            ;Clear upper multiplicand register
        MOV     AX,1                            ;Initialize base 1st decimal place
        MOV     BASE,AX                         ;Load base
DO11:
                MOV     AL,[SI+BX]              ;Ld right-to-left char
                CMP     AL,2DH                  ;Cmp with "minus"
                JE      OUT11
                AND     AX,000FH                ;Truncate ASCII to nibble
                MUL     BASE                    ;Mul by base
                ADD     BINV,AX                 ;Add result to decimal sub
                MOV     AX,BASE                 ;Add decimal values
                MUL     CX                      ;Base times 10
                MOV     BASE,AX
                DEC     BX
                JNZ     DO11
        JMP     END11                           ;Not neg. no.
OUT11:
        MOV     BL,BUFFLN                       ;Check negative character
        MOV     BH,0                            ;Clear upper BX register
        MOV     SI,0                            ;Initialize pointer
DO12:
                MOV     AL,ASC[SI]              ;Ld char
                MOV     AH,0                    ;Clear upper reg
                CMP     AL,2DH                  ;Cmp char with "minus"
                JE      OUT12
                INC     SI
                CMP     SI,BX                   ;Ck end char
                JB      DO12
        JMP     END11
OUT12:
        OR      BINV,8000H                      ;Number is negative
END11:
        NOP
                                                ;
        POP     SI
        POP     DX
        POP     CX
        POP     BX
        POP     AX
        POP     DS
                                                ;
        RET
ASCDEC  ENDP
CSEG    ENDS
        END

<C:\AFINAL>
```

(Continued)

Carriage Return.

```
CR    MACRO
      MOV AH,6
      MOV DL,0DH
      INT 21H
CR    ENDM
```

Both Line Feed and Carriage Return.

```
NLINE    MACRO
         MOV AH,6
         MOV DL,0AH
         INT 21H
         MOV AH,6
         MOV DL,0DH
         INT 21H
NLINE    ENDM
```

6.11. See the corresponding figure illustrating DECASC and ASCDEC.

CHAPTER 7

7.1. (a) Allocate DTA.

```
DTAALLC    MACRO DDTA
           MOV AH,1AH
           LEA DX, DDTA        ; Assumes DDTA defined
           INT 21H
DTAALLC    ENDM
```

(b) Create a File.

```
CREFL    MACRO FCBLB
         MOV AH,16H
         LEA DX,FCBLB        ; FCB label
         INT 21H
CREFL    ENDM
```

(c) Close a File.

```
CLOFL    MACRO FCBLR
         MOV AH,10H
         LEA DX,FCBLB        ; FCB label
         INT 21H
CLOFL    ENDM
```

(d) Open a File

```
OPNFL      MACRO FCBLB
           MOV AH,0FH
           LEA DX,FCBLB        ; FCB label
           INT 21H
OPNFL      ENDM
```

(e) Write to a File.

```
WRTFL      MACRO FCBLB
           MOV AH,15H
           LEA DX,FCBLB        ; FCB label
           INT 21H
WRTFL      ENDM
```

(f) Read a File.

```
RDFL       MACRO FCBLB
           MOV AH,14H
           LEA DX,FCBLB        ; FCB label
           INT 21H
RDFL       ENDM
```

7.3.

```
STR1NW     PROC FAR
           ASSUME CS:CSEG, DS:DATA, SS:STACK
           PUSH DS
           SUB AX,AX
           PUSH AX

                                      ;
           MOV AX,SEG DATA
           MOV DS,AX

                                      ;
           CALL FILECR              ; Create file
           MOV SI,0
DO1:
           MOV DI,0
           MOV AL,CHAR[SI]          ; Load next character
           CMP AL,24H               ; Check for $
           JZ ELSE1
              MOV DDTA[DI],AL        ; Assumes byte record size
              MOV AH,15H             ; Write file
              LEA DX,FCBLB
              INT 21H
           INC SI
           JMP DO1
ELSE1:
           CALL CLOSEF              ; Close file
           RET
STR1NW     ENDP
```

7.5.

```
      OUTPT     PROC
          ;
          ;          This procedure outputs the 1024 integers in ARRAY
          ;          Assume the file path is stored in NNAME.
          ;
                     MOV SI,0
                     MOV CX,1024                      ; Load count
                     MOV AX,2
                     MOV RECSZB,AX
                     CRFH NNAME,HHANDLE               ; Handle returned (problem 7.4)
      DO1:
                         PUSH CX
                         MOV AH,ARRAY[SI]
                         MOV DTA,AH
                         MOV AH,ARRAY[SI+1]
                         MOV DTA[1],AH
                         WRFH DTA.RECSZB,HHANDL       ; Write MACRO (problem 7.4)
                                                      ;
                         ADD SI,2                     ; Word increment
                         POP CX
                         LOOP DO1
                     CLFH HHANDLE                     ; Close MACRO (problem 7.4)
                     RET
      OUTPT     ENDP
```

7.7.

```
      AVGRN     PROC
          ;
          ;          File control Blocks used.        NNAME=path.
          ;
          ;
                     MOV SI,0
                     MOV CX,4096
                     MOV AX,2
                                                      ; Initialize
                     MOV AX,0
                     MOV BBLOCK1,AX                   ; Block
                     MOV RECSZ1,AX                    ; Record site
                     MOV RECDE11,AX                   ; Current record
                     OPNFL FCBLB                      ; Open MACRO (problem 7.1)
                                                      ;
                     MOV AX,1                         ; Record size
                     MOV RECSZ1,AX
                                                      ;
                     DTAALLC DDTA                     ; Allocate DTA to DDTA.MACRO
                                                      ;
      DO1:
                         PUSH CX
                         RDFL FCBLB
                         MOV AX,DDTA
```

```
              MOV ARRAY[SI],AX
              ADD SI,2
              POP CX
              LOOP DO1
                                      ;
              CLOFL FCBLB             ; Close MACRO (problem 7.1)
              CALL AVERAGE            ; Do the averaging here
              RET
   AVGRN   ENDP
```

7.9. The parameter passed to this macro has a variable X which is appended to an array variable ARRAY&X. Calling

RRDISK 10

uses an array, ARRAY10, which must be defined in the data segment. Similarly, a call

RRDISK 11

would access ARRAY11 for disk I/O in the same program. Of course, all ARRAY&X variables referenced this way must be defined in the data segment.

CHAPTER 8

8.1. (a) 60 E3 16 00   (double word)
      (b) 90 D0 03 00   (double word)
      (c) 00 11 10 91   (double word)
      (d) 00 24 F4 92   (double word)
      (e) F8 24 01 00   (double word)

8.3.

```
   ...
   FLD X
   FMUL X
   FST X
   ...
```

8.5.

```
          ...
   DATA   SEGMENT PARA PUBLIC 'DATA'
     X1   DD        ?
     X2   DD        ?
     Y1   DD        ?
     Y2   DD        ?
     Y3   DD        ?
     D2   DD       -2.E0
     D3   DD        2.E0
     S1   DD        ?
     C1   DD        ?
```

```
DATA      SEGMENT PARA PUBLIC 'DATA'
          ...
          FLD1                          ; Load +1.0 into ST
          FLD X1                        ; Load X2 into ST,1 in ST(1)
          FYL2X                         ; Log 2(X1) in ST(0)
          FLDLZE                        ; Log 2(e) in ST
          FDIV                          ; Result in ST(1)
          FSTP Y3                       ; Result in ST
          FLD D2
          FMUL                          ; Result in ST(1)
          FXCH ST(1)                    ; Result in ST
          FSQRT
          FST Y1                        ; Square root term in Y1
          FLD D3                        ;
          FLDPI
          FMUL                          ; 2 PI in ST(1)
          FSTP Y3
          FLD X2
          FMUL                          ; Angle argument in ST(1)
          FSTP Y3                       ; Angle argument in ST
          FPTAN                         ; Y or X returned for term
          FSTP S1                       ; Y value stored or popped
          FST C1                        ; X value stored, not popped
          FLD C1                        ; Load X value ST
          FMUL                          ; X**2 in ST(1)
          FSTP Y3                       ; Now in ST
          FLD S1                        ; Load Y value
          FLD S1                        ; Again
          FMUL                          ; Y**2 ST(1),X**2 ST(2)
          FSTP Y3                       ; Y**2 ST,X**2 ST(1)
          FADD                          ; Result in ST(1)
          FSTP Y3                       ; Result in ST
          FSQRT                         ; Sine-cosine divisor
          FLD C1                        ; Load X value ST
          FXCH ST(1)                    ; Swap stack top
          FDIV                          ; (Cosine) in ST(1)
          FSTP Y4                       ; Save divisor
          FSTP C1                       ; Save cosine
          FLD S1                        ; Load Y value
          FLD Y4                        ; Load divisor
          FDIV                          ; (Sine) in ST(1)
          FSTP Y3                       ; Dummy POP sine ST
          FLD Y1                        ; Random number root term
          FMUL
          FXCH ST(1)                    ; R.N.root ST(1),Gaussian#1ST
          FSTP C1                       ; Gaussian cosine-term
          FLD S1
          FMUL
          FXCH ST(1)
          FSTP S1                       ; Save Gaussian sine-term
          ...
```

8.7.

   ...

```
FLD Z                ; Z in ST
FPTAN                ; Y in ST(1),X in ST
FDIVP ST(1),ST       ; Calculate Y/X, POP
FST Z                ; Store in Z
```

   ...

8.9.

   ...

```
FLD A                ; Load radius
FLD A                ; Radius in ST,ST(1)
FMULP ST(1),ST       ; Radius square in ST
FLDPI                ; PI in ST
FMULP ST(1)ST        ; Answer in ST
FST A                ; Area in A
```

   ...

8.11.

   ...

```
FLD1                 ; 1 in ST
FLD V                ; Voltage in ST, 1 in ST(1)
FYL2X
FLDL2T               ; Log(2)(10) in ST
FDIVP ST(1),ST       ; Log (10)(V) in ST
FLD TWENTY
FMULP ST(1),ST
FST V                ; Decibel value in V
```

   ...

CHAPTER 9

9.1. The address selected is 3FXH which is not a monochrome-printer adapter port. Hence the matrix printer will not be addressed. The output of the LS138 can never have a LOW on pins Y0,...Y7 because G2B is set to 1.

9.3. 64H yields

A7	A6	A5	A4	A3	A2	A1	A0
0	1	1	0	0	1	0	0

       6   4

This means that Y3 from the LS138 (Figure 9.8) can go LOW and PORT A is selected for an Input Read (RD*) = 0 and WR* = 1) or an Output Write (RD* = 1 and WR* = 0). 63H selects no port!

9.5. ICW1 is always odd for the IBM PC. This is true since bit 0 is always set (IC4 = 1 corresponds to the need for ICW4). ICW2 gets bits T_7 to T_3 from the interrupt vector to be associated with a given interrupt line. The low order bits, T_2, T_1, and T_0 are representative of the interrupt line. For example, IR7 has bits 0 to 2 set HIGH and bits 7 to 3 contain the remaining address as input via ICW2. These bits require that interrupt line numbers be associated with a vector. To this extent the hardware must be known. In the IBM AT bit 2 of ICW4 will be set for the master PIC.

9.7. In Block Transfer mode the 8237A is activated by DREQn. It continues to make a transfer until a Terminal Count is reached or an End of Process is encountered. To enter the Block Transfer mode, bits 7 and 6 of the mode register must be set to 1 and 0, respectively.

9.9. The screen buffer must hold 80 characters/line × 25 lines/frame = 2000 characters/frame. Essentially the buffer has a single frame. Each character consists of 8 bits; hence 16K bit memory is needed for the screen buffer.

9.11. The monochrome adapter has a refresh memory address output (from the 6845) consisting of pins MA0 to MA10. This corresponds to eleven lines or 2048 possible address locations. The screen buffer requires 2000 bytes of storage for the buffer (and 2000 bytes for the attribute on the color monitor); hence the eleven lines indicated are sufficient. When A0 = 0, RS is LOW and the 6845 address register is selected.

9.13. The register is loaded with 2. Thus, only bit D1 is set and this corresponds to the non-skew and non-interlace mode.

9.15. From Table 9.14 we have
   (a) 2400 baud
   (b) odd parity
   (c) 1-stop bit
   (d) 7 bit word

CHAPTER 10

10.1   When the 8288 has its DT/R* line set LOW, it places the bidirectional transceiver (LS245) in a read state. This corresponds to data input to the 8088 and S1* is LOW. When DT/R* is HIGH, S0* will be LOW.

10.3.   The lines AD0 through AD7 pass buffered addresses in one direction only when coupled to the address bus. Hence, a simple latch suffices and no bidirectional transceiver is needed.

10.5.   Q is HIGH

10.7.   In Figure 10.9, 13 address lines are used to address 8K of ROM per chip. To address 64K would require an increase of 8 or a total of 16 address lines.

10.9.   When A16, A17, A18, and A19 are all LOW, RAM is selected. When all HIGH, ROM is selected. When A16, A17, A18, and A19 are HIGH (ROM selected), the address on the address bus is FxxxxH.

10.11.   When A14 and A15 are both HIGH, Bank 3 is being selected. The column and row address strobes active are CAS3* and RAS3*.

10.13.   The XT has four times the ROM on its system board as the early PC. Hence, since the PC uses 13 address lines to access ROM, the XT would need 15.

Index

B

C

D